ALTERNATIVE PRAYER BOOK
1984

ALTERNATIVE PRAYER BOOK 1984

according to the use of
THE CHURCH OF IRELAND

BY AUTHORITY OF THE GENERAL SYNOD
OF THE CHURCH OF IRELAND

COLLINS

Collins Liturgical Publications
distributed in Ireland by
Educational Company of Ireland
21 Talbot Street, Dublin 1

Collins Liturgical Publications
187 Piccadilly, London W1V 9DA

ISBN
Pew edition: 0 00 599775 5
Desk edition: 0 00 599776 3

First published 1984

Typographical design by Colin Reed
Data capture by Morton Word Processing, Scarborough
Made and printed by William Collins Sons & Co, Glasgow

CONTENTS

PREFACE

The Church of Ireland has inherited a long tradition of liturgical worship going back to Celtic times. When the Normans came to Ireland in the twelfth century the Sarum Use, that of the church of Salisbury, became the standard form of worship, and this continued until the Reformation. The Book of Common Prayer in English first appeared in 1549, and revisions were made in 1552, 1559 and 1662. When the Church of Ireland was disestablished in 1871 steps were at once taken to make changes in the 1662 Book of Common Prayer, and a revised book was published in 1878. Since then it has been accepted that revision is a continuing process. The General Synod of 1909 initiated a further revision to adapt the services of the church 'to the requirements of the present time' without making any modification in doctrine. This revision was published in 1926, and two alternative forms of Evening Prayer were added in 1933.

The General Synod of 1962 set up a Liturgical Advisory Committee to bring forward proposals for a further revision. Again the guiding principle was laid down that there should be no change in the essential doctrines of the church as they are set out in the Book of Common Prayer.

Provision was made to allow the use of revised services for a trial period. When the House of Bishops had approved their content these services were introduced on an experimental basis so that the members of the worshipping community could be involved in the process of revision. As the services were used deficiencies came to light and improvements were suggested. The culmination of this process came when the Liturgical Advisory Committee prepared each service for the General Synod which gave detailed consideration to the text and finally gave the two-thirds majority required by the law of the church.

In the work of revision one of the factors which demanded attention was the language of worship. The historic link between the Prayer Book and the Bible set a precedent. The English Bible of 1535 and the 1549 Book of Common Prayer were in the idiom of the time. The publication of the Authorized Version of 1611 had close links with the Prayer Book of 1662. The New English Bible New Testament was first published in 1961, the year before the present prayer book revision began. It is one of many versions in modern English, and these are now so widely used that the church has had to take seriously the need

7

to have similar language in worship. Other considerations
included the need for variety and greater flexibility in services,
and the desirability of more congregational participation.

Revision of forms of worship has been a feature of church life
in many parts of the world and in most branches of the christian
church in recent years. All the churches of the Anglican Communion have been involved, and the bishops gave a lead at the
Lambeth Conferences of 1968 and 1978. A Liturgical Consultation was called after the 1968 Conference to draw up an agreed
framework for the Holy Communion service and this has
proved to be effective in providing a pattern for Anglican
worship throughout the world. The traditional form of Morning
and Evening Prayer remains.

A prayer book provides a structure and a form of words which
enable the members of the church to share more fully in
common prayer. This liturgy becomes worship when the people
of God make the prayers their own prayers, and turn in faith to
God, Father, Son, and Holy Spirit. Words used in worship have
power to shape faith and kindle devotion without claiming to be
fully adequate to that task. Only the grace of God can make up
what is lacking in the faltering words of men.

This book does not replace the Book of Common Prayer but provides authorized alternative services for use in public worship.

CALENDAR AND RULES TO ORDER THE SERVICE

THE CALENDAR

PRINCIPAL HOLY DAYS

Easter Day,   Ascension Day,   Pentecost (Whitsunday)
Christmas Day,   The Epiphany
Maundy Thursday,   Good Friday
Every Sunday in the year

HOLY DAYS

1 Jan	The Naming of Jesus, or The Circumcision of Christ
25	The Conversion of St Paul
1 Feb	St Brigid
2	The Presentation of Christ in the Temple
17 Mar	St Patrick
25	The Annunciation of our Lord to the Blessed Virgin Mary
25 April	St Mark the Evangelist
1 May	St Philip and St James, Apostles
14	St Matthias the Apostle
31	The Visit of the Blessed Virgin Mary to Elizabeth
9 June	St Columba
11	St Barnabas the Apostle
24	The Birth of St John the Baptist
29	St Peter the Apostle
3 July	St Thomas the Apostle
22	St Mary Magdalene
25	St James the Apostle
6 Aug	The Transfiguration of our Lord
24	St Bartholomew the Apostle
8 Sept	The Birth of the Blessed Virgin Mary
21	St Matthew the Apostle
29	St Michael and All Angels
18 Oct	St Luke the Evangelist
28	St Simon and St Jude, Apostles
1 Nov	All Saints
30	St Andrew the Apostle
26 Dec	St Stephen the first Martyr
27	St John the Evangelist
28	The Holy Innocents

DAYS OF SPECIAL OBSERVANCE

Ash Wednesday, the first day of Lent

Monday, Tuesday and Wednesday in Holy Week

Easter Eve

Christmas Eve

Ember Days, days of prayer for those ordained or preparing for
   ordination: the Wednesday, Friday and Saturday after the first
   Sunday in Lent, the Feast of Pentecost, 14 September, 13
   December
   The Ember Collect is also to be said in each parish on the Sunday
   before a bishop is to be consecrated, and in each church in a
   diocese on the Sunday before a priest or deacon is to be ordained
   to serve in that diocese

Rogation Days, days of prayer for God's blessing on the fruits of the
   earth and the labours of men: the Monday, Tuesday and Wednesday after the Fifth Sunday after Easter

Thanksgiving for Harvest

Intercession and Thanksgiving are offered for the Missionary Work
   of the Church at St Andrew's-tide, and Prayer for Christian Unity
   from 18 to 25 January

DAYS OF DISCIPLINE AND SELF-DENIAL

Ash Wednesday, Good Friday

The other weekdays in Lent

All the Fridays in the year except Christmas Day, the Epiphany, the
Fridays after Christmas Day and Easter Day, Holy Days falling
outside Lent

THE DATE OF EASTER
unless other provision is made

1985 April 7	1999 April 4	2013
1986 March 30	2000 April 23	2014 Apri.
1987 April 19	2001 April 15	2015 April 5
1988 April 3	2002 March 31	2016 March 27
1989 March 26	2003 April 20	2017 April 16
1990 April 15	2004 April 11	2018 April 1
1991 March 31	2005 March 27	2019 April 21
1992 April 19	2006 April 16	2020 April 12
1993 April 11	2007 April 8	2021 April 4
1994 April 3	2008 March 23	2022 April 17
1995 April 16	2009 April 12	2023 April 9
1996 April 7	2010 April 4	2024 March 31
1997 March 30	2011 April 24	2025 April 20
1998 April 12	2012 April 8	

A TABLE OF MOVEABLE FEASTS
ACCORDING TO THE DATE OF EASTER

Sundays after Christmas (/leap year)	Sundays after Epiphany (/leap year)	Sunday 9 before Easter (/leap year)	Ash Wednesday (/leap year)	Easter Day
2	1	18/19 Jan	4/5 Feb	22 Mar
2/1	1	19/20	5/6	23
1	1/2	20/21	6/7	24
1	2	21/22	7/8	25
1/2	2	22/23	8/9	26
2	2	23/24	9/10	27
2	2	24/25	10/11	28
2	2	25/26	11/12	29
2/1	2	26/27	12/13	30
1	2/3	27/28	13/14	31
1	3	28/29	14/15	1 Apr
1/2	3	29/30	15/16	2
2	3	30/31	16/17	3
2	3	31/1 Feb	17/18	4
2	3	1/2 Feb	18/19	5
2/1	3	2/3	19/20	6
1	3/4	3/4	20/21	7
1	4	4/5	21/22	8
1/2	4	5/6	22/23	9
2	4	6/7	23/24	10
2	4	7/8	24/25	11
2	4	8/9	25/26	12
2/1	4	9/10	26/27	13
1	4/5	10/11	27/28	14
1	5	11/12	28/29	15
1/2	5	12/13	1 Mar	16
2	5	13/14	2	17
2	5	14/15	3	18
2	5	15/16	4	19
2/1	5	16/17	5	20
1	5/6	17/18	6	21
1	6	18/19	7	22
1/2	6	19/20	8	23
2	6	20/21	9	24
2	6	21/22	10	25

Ascension Day	Pentecost (Whit-sunday)	Sundays after Pentecost	Sunday 9 before Christmas	Advent Sunday
30 Apr	10 May	23	25 Oct	29 Nov
1 May	11	23	26	30
2	12	23	27	1 Dec
3	13	23	28	2
4	14	23	29	3
5	15	22	23 Oct	27 Nov
6	16	22	24	28
7	17	22	25	29
8	18	22	26	30
9	19	22	27	1 Dec
10	20	22	28	2
11	21	22	29	3
12	22	21	23 Oct	27 Nov
13	23	21	24	28
14	24	21	25	29
15	25	21	26	30
16	26	21	27	1 Dec
17	27	21	28	2
18	28	21	29	3
19	29	20	23 Oct	27 Nov
20	30	20	24	28
21	31	20	25	29
22	1 June	20	26	30
23	2	20	27	1 Dec
24	3	20	28	2
25	4	20	29	3
26	5	19	23 Oct	27 Nov
27	6	19	24	28
28	7	19	25	29
29	8	19	26	30
30	9	19	27	1 Dec
31	10	19	28	2
1 June	11	19	29	3
2	12	18	23 Oct	27 Nov
3	13	18	24	28

RULES TO ORDER THE SERVICE

1 The readings and all else which is proper to the service of the Sundays in Advent, Christmas Day, the First and Second Sundays after Christmas, the Epiphany, the Presentation of Christ, Ash Wednesday, the Sundays in Lent, the days of Holy Week and Easter Week, the Sundays after Easter, Ascension Day, the Sunday after Ascension Day, Pentecost, Trinity Sunday, All Saints' Day and St Patrick's Day are said on the appointed days and are not replaced by the services of any other days.

2 When a Holy Day falls on one of the days to which reference is made in Rule 1, it is transferred to the first available day.

3 When a Holy Day falls on a Sunday other than those to which reference is made in Rule 1, it may be observed on the Sunday or it may be transferred to the following day.

4 The service of Evening Prayer appointed for a Holy Day may be used on the evening of the Holy Day or on the evening before the Holy Day.

5 The collect, psalms and readings appointed for the Thanksgiving for Harvest may replace those appointed for the day.

6 On weekdays the collect of the previous Sunday is said unless other provision is made.

7 Readings at Holy Communion on weekdays may be taken from the principal Sunday set of either year unless other provision is made.

A TABLE OF TRANSFERENCES
required by the Rules

Annunciation	falling on a Sunday in Lent or on any day between Palm Sunday and the First Sunday after Easter, both inclusive	must be transferred
St Mark	falling on Easter Day or any day to the First Sunday after Easter inclusive or on any Sunday in Eastertide	must be transferred
St Philip and St James or St Matthias	falling on Ascension Day or a Sunday	must be transferred
St Barnabas or St Columba	falling on Pentecost or Trinity Sunday	must be transferred
St Andrew	falling on a Sunday	must be transferred
St Stephen St John Holy Innocents or the Naming of Jesus	falling on the Sunday after Christmas Day	must be transferred

CONCERNING THE SERVICES OF THE CHURCH

1 **The Holy Communion** as the central act of worship, and Morning and Evening Prayer, are the regular services of public worship in the Church of Ireland.

   It is the duty and privilege of members of the Church to join in public worship on the Lord's Day as the weekly commemoration of the Resurrection, and on other major festivals; to communicate regularly and frequently after careful preparation; and to contribute generously to the maintenance of the Church, to the spread of the Gospel and to works of charity.

2 **Rubrics.** The rubrics in this book have been deliberately kept to a minimum. When a certain posture is particularly appropriate it is indicated thus – *Stand* or *Kneel*. Where a rubric states that a section is to be 'said', this is to be understood to include 'or sung' and vice versa.

3 **Bible Versions.** Any version sanctioned for use in public worship by the House of Bishops may be used for the Sentences, the Psalms and the Readings.

   The Table of Lessons and the Collects, Epistles and Gospels in the Book of Common Prayer (1926) may be used as alternatives to the provisions in this book.

4 **Pointing.** The Canticles and Psalms are pointed for singing to Anglican chants. When they are read, the pointing is to be regarded as the punctuation. (See the detailed note on pointing on page 105).

5 **Hymns.** Hymns may be sung in these services otherwise than where provision is made for them. In the selection of hymns careful attention should be given to see that they are appropriate to the theme of the Bible readings and sermon.

6 **Sermon.** A sermon should be preached on Sundays and on the major festivals.

7 **Silence.** A short period of silence may be kept at any point in the service at the discretion of the minister.

8 **Use of Versions of Prescribed Forms of Divine Service.**
This matter shall be dealt with in accordance with the
provisions of Canon 5.

9 **Holy Communion**
  a The priest who presides at Holy Communion must be
    episcopally ordained. The minister who reads the
    Gospel may be a priest or a deacon or a licensed reader.
    The bishop of the diocese may permit lay persons
    approved by him to assist the priest in the administra-
    tion of the Holy Communion.
  b Holy Communion shall not be celebrated unless there
    is at least one person present to communicate together
    with the priest.
  c The Ten Commandments should be read at least four
    times a year. They are appropriate in Advent and Lent.
  d At the time of the Communion the holy table is to have
    a white cloth on it.
  e Any of the consecrated bread and wine remaining after
    communion is to be reverently consumed.

10 **Morning or Evening Prayer and Holy Communion** may
be used together. In which case
  a Sections 1 – 13 and 16 – 17 of Morning or Evening
    Prayer are used.
  b The Gospel is read at section 12 and is followed by the
    sermon.
  c In addition to the Collects there are to be prayers for
    the Church and for the world.
  d The prayer 'We do not presume . . .' (Holy Com-
    munion section 19) may be said, and Holy Communion
    begins with The Peace (section 20).

11 **Holy Baptism.** When Baptism is used with Holy Communion it follows section 4 of the Holy Communion
service, and the Holy Communion resumes with the
Intercession (section 13). When it is used with Morning or
Evening Prayer it follows the Old Testament reading or
the Collects. The readings may be either those of the
Baptism service or those of the day. On a major festival
the readings of the day are used.

12 **Morning and Evening Prayer on Weekdays** may begin at section 5, The Ministry of the Word.

13 **Banns of Marriage** are read after the Nicene Creed at Holy Communion or after the second lesson at Morning or Evening Prayer.

14 **Collect Endings.** In the case of any collect ending with the words 'Christ our Lord', the minister may add, 'who lives and reigns with you and the Holy Spirit, one God, now and for ever.'

SENTENCES
OF SCRIPTURE

SENTENCES OF SCRIPTURE

GENERAL

God is spirit, and those who worship him
must worship in spirit and in truth.   *John 4.24*

Worship the Lord in the beauty of holiness:
let the whole earth stand in awe of him.   *Psalm 96.9*

Seek the Lord while he may be found;
call upon him while he is near.   *Isaiah 55.6*

Jesus said: Come to me, all whose work is hard,
whose load is heavy, and I will refresh you.   *Matt. 11.28*

They who wait for the Lord shall renew their strength,
they shall mount up with wings like eagles,
they shall run and not be weary,
they shall walk and not faint.   *Isaiah 40.31*

Other sentences from Holy Scripture may be used.

SEASONAL

Advent

The glory of the Lord shall be revealed,
and all mankind shall see it.   *Isaiah 40.5*

Christmas

Unto us a child is born,
unto us a son is given,
and his name shall be called
Wonderful, Counsellor,
the mighty God,
the everlasting Father,
the Prince of Peace.   *Isaiah 9.6*

Epiphany

The grace of God has appeared
for the salvation of all men.   *Titus 2.11*

Lent

The Lord our God is merciful and forgiving,
even though we have rebelled against him.
We have not obeyed the Lord our God
nor kept the laws he gave us.   *Daniel 9.9*

Passiontide and Holy Week

God shows his love for us,
in that while we were yet sinners
Christ died for us.   *Rom.5.8*

Christ himself bore our sins
in his body on the tree,
that we might die to sin
and live to righteousness.   *1 Peter 2.24*

Easter

Praise be to the God and Father
of our Lord Jesus Christ.
In his great mercy
we have been born anew into a living hope
by the resurrection of Jesus Christ from the dead.   *1 Peter 1.3*

Ascension

We have a great high priest
who has passed through the heavens,
Jesus the Son of God.
Let us then with confidence
draw near to the throne of grace,
that we may receive mercy,
and find grace to help in time of need.   *Heb.4.14,16*

Pentecost

You shall receive power
when the Holy Spirit has come upon you;
and you shall be my witnesses.   *Acts 1.8*

Trinity Sunday

Holy, holy, holy is the Lord Almighty,
who was and is and is to come.   *Revelation 4.8*

Rogation and Harvest

The earth is the Lord's and all that is in it:
let the heavens rejoice and let the earth be glad.
Psalms 24.1; 96.11

Time of Trouble

God is our refuge and strength,
an ever present help in trouble.   *Psalm 46.1*

Unity

Christ is our peace, who has made us one,
and has broken down the barrier which divided us.
Eph. 2.14

MORNING
AND EVENING
PRAYER

MORNING AND EVENING PRAYER
Daily throughout the year

Stand

1 The appropriate greeting and/or Sentence of Scripture is said.

Grace to you and peace from God our Father
and the Lord Jesus Christ.   *Phil. 1.2*
Thanks be to God.   *2 Cor. 9.15*

Christmas and Epiphany

Behold, I bring you good tidings of great joy,
which shall be to all people:
for unto you is born in the city of David,
a Saviour who is Christ the Lord.   *Luke 2.10,11*
Thanks be to God.

Easter

Christ is risen.
The Lord is risen indeed. Alleluia.   *Luke 24.34*

Ascension

God exalted Jesus at his right hand
as Lord and Saviour,
to give repentance to Israel
and forgiveness of sins.   *Acts 5.31*
Thanks be to God.

Pentecost

God's love has been shed abroad in our hearts
through the Holy Spirit he has given us.   *Rom. 5.5*
Thanks be to God.

The Sentences of Scripture are on pp.23–25.

29

2 The minister may say

Beloved in Christ,
we are come together to offer to Almighty God
our worship and praise and thanksgiving,
to confess our sins and to be forgiven,
to hear and receive his holy word,
to bring before him our needs
and the needs of the world,
and to pray that in the power of his Spirit
we may serve him and know the greatness of his love.

He may speak briefly on the theme of the service.
He may read one of these penitential Sentences:

If we say we have no sin we deceive ourselves,
and the truth is not in us.
If we confess our sins, God is faithful and just
and will forgive our sins and cleanse us
from all unrighteousness. *1 John 1.8,9*

I will arise and go to my father,
and I will say to him,
Father, I have sinned against heaven and before you;
I am no longer worthy to be called your son. *Luke 15.18,19*

Blessed is he whose sin is forgiven:
whose iniquity is put away. *Psalm 32.1*

3 The minister says

Let us confess our sins to God our Father.
Kneel
After a short pause for self-examination all say

Almighty God, our heavenly Father,
we have sinned against you
and against our fellow-men
in thought and word and deed,
through negligence, through weakness,
through our own deliberate fault.
We are truly sorry
and repent of all our sins.
For the sake of your Son Jesus Christ
who died for us,
forgive us all that is past;
and grant that we may serve you in newness of life
to the glory of your name.   Amen.

4 The priest pronounces the absolution:

Almighty God, who forgives all who truly repent,
have mercy on you,
pardon and deliver you from all your sins,
confirm and strengthen you in all goodness,
and keep you in eternal life;
through Jesus Christ our Lord. **Amen.**

If no priest is present the absolution is omitted and the following
prayer may be said:
Merciful Lord,
grant to your faithful people pardon and peace,
that we may be cleansed from all our sins,
and serve you with a quiet mind;
through Jesus Christ our Lord. **Amen.**

THE MINISTRY OF THE WORD

Stand

5 Minister   O Lord, open our lips:
   People   **and our mouth will proclaim your praise.**

   Minister   O God, make speed to save us:
   People   **O Lord, make haste to help us.**

   Minister   Glory to the Father, and to the Son,
           and to the Holy Spirit:
   People   **as it was in the beginning, is now,**
           and shall be for ever.   Amen.

   Minister   Praise the Lord:
   People   **the Lord's name be praised.**

6 FIRST CANTICLE

At Morning Prayer

1 VENITE Psalm 95.1–7 or 1–11 (p.106).
or
2 JUBILATE Psalm 100 (p.108), may be sung.

In Eastertide
3 THE EASTER ANTHEMS (p.110) are sung.

At Evening Prayer

9 HAIL, GLADDENING LIGHT (p.125) may be sung.

In Eastertide
3 THE EASTER ANTHEMS (p.110) are sung.

7 PSALM

One or more of the appointed PSALMS is sung, ending with

Glory to the Father and | to the | Son:
   and | to the | Holy Spirit;

as it was in the be|ginning is | now:
   and shall be for | ever | A-|men.

8 FIRST READING

The first reading, from the OLD TESTAMENT

The reader says

The Old Testament reading is from . . . chapter . . .
beginning at verse . . .

After the reading silence may be kept.

9 SECOND CANTICLE

At Morning Prayer

4 BENEDICTUS The Song of Zechariah (p.112).
or
10 GREAT AND WONDERFUL (p.125).
or
11 URBS FORTITUDINIS (p.126).
or
5 BENEDICITE (p.114).

At Evening Prayer

7 MAGNIFICAT The Song of the Blessed Virgin Mary (p.122).
or
14 BLESS THE LORD (p.129).

When appropriate a morning canticle may be sung in the
evening, and vice versa.

10 SECOND READING

The second reading, from the NEW TESTAMENT

The reader says

The New Testament reading is from . . . chapter . . .
beginning at verse . . .

After the reading silence may be kept.

1 ## THIRD CANTICLE

At Morning Prayer

6 TE DEUM in full, or part 1, or part 2, or both these parts (p.118).

or

12 GLORIA IN EXCELSIS (p.127).

or

13 SAVIOUR OF THE WORLD (p.128).

At Evening Prayer

8 NUNC DIMITTIS The Song of Simeon (p.124).

or

15 GLORY AND HONOUR (p.130).

or

16 THE SONG OF CHRIST'S GLORY (p.130).

2 When there are two New Testament readings THE GOSPEL reading follows here. (See Concerning the Services of the Church 10b.)

3 ## THE APOSTLES' CREED

I believe in God, the Father almighty,
  creator of heaven and earth.

I believe in Jesus Christ, his only Son, our Lord.
  He was conceived by the power of the Holy Spirit
    and born of the Virgin Mary.
  He suffered under Pontius Pilate,
    was crucified, died and was buried.
  He descended to the dead.
  On the third day he rose again.
  He ascended into heaven,
    and is seated at the right hand of the Father.
  He will come again to judge the living and the dead.

I believe in the Holy Spirit,
  the holy catholic Church,
  the communion of saints,
  the forgiveness of sins,
  the resurrection of the body,
  and the life everlasting. Amen.

THE PRAYERS

14   Minister The Lord be with you.
                    And also with you.

Kneel

Let us pray.

Lord, have mercy.
Christ, have mercy.
Lord, have mercy.

15 **Our Father in heaven,**
     hallowed be your name,
     your kingdom come,
     your will be done,
       on earth as in heaven.
  Give us today our daily bread.
  Forgive us our sins
     as we forgive those who sin against us.
  Lead us not into temptation
     but deliver us from evil.

  For the kingdom, the power, and the glory are yours
     now and for ever.   Amen.

or

Our Father, who art in heaven,
  hallowed be thy name,
  thy kingdom come,
  thy will be done,
    on earth as it is in heaven.
Give us this day our daily bread.
And forgive us our trespasses
  as we forgive those who trespass against us.
And lead us not into temptation
  but deliver us from evil.

For thine is the kingdom the power and the glory
  for ever and ever.   Amen.

6   The versicles and responses may be said.

Show us your mercy, O Lord:
and grant us your salvation.

(N.I.) O Lord, save the Queen:
and grant her government wisdom.

(R.I.) O Lord, save the President:
and grant our government wisdom.

Let your ministers be clothed with righteousness:
and let your servants shout for joy.

O Lord, save your people:
and bless those whom you have chosen.

Give peace in our time, O Lord:
and let your glory be over all the earth.

O God, make clean our hearts within us:
and renew us by your Holy Spirit.

or

O Lord, show thy mercy upon us:
and grant us thy salvation.

(N.I.) O Lord, save the Queen:
and mercifully hear us when we call upon thee.

(R.I.) O Lord, save the President:
and mercifully hear us when we call upon thee.

Endue thy ministers with righteousness:
and make thy chosen people joyful.

O Lord, save thy people:
and bless thine inheritance.

Give peace in our time, O Lord:
for it is thou Lord only that makest us dwell in safety.

O God, make clean our hearts within us:
and take not thy Holy Spirit from us.

7   THE COLLECT of the day.

18 **At Morning Prayer** one or more of these collects:

O God, the author of peace and lover of concord,
to know you is eternal life,
and to serve you is perfect freedom:
Defend us in all assaults of our enemies,
that we, surely trusting in your protection,
may not fear the power of any adversaries;
through Jesus Christ our Lord.   **Amen.**

O Lord, our heavenly Father,
almighty and everliving God,
we give you thanks for bringing us safely to this day:
Keep us from falling into sin
or running into danger,
and in all things guide us to know and do your will;
through Jesus Christ our Lord.   **Amen.**

Direct us, Lord, in all our doings,
with your most gracious favour,
and further us with your continual help;
that in all our works begun, continued and ended in you,
we may glorify your holy name,
and finally by your mercy attain everlasting life;
through Jesus Christ our Lord.   **Amen.**

Heavenly Father,
in whom we live and move and have our being:
We pray you that your Holy Spirit
may guide and govern us
in all the cares and occupations of our daily life,
and give us grace to do your will;
through Jesus Christ our Lord.   **Amen.**

At Evening Prayer one or more of these collects:

O God
from whom all holy desires
all good judgments
and all just works proceed:
Give to your servants
that peace which the world cannot give,
that our hearts may be set to obey your commandments,
and that we, being defended from the fear of our enemies,
may pass our time in rest and quietness;
through Jesus Christ your Son our Lord.   **Amen.**

Lighten our darkness, we beseech you, O Lord,
and in your great mercy defend us
from all perils and dangers of this night;
for the love of your only Son, our Saviour Jesus Christ.
Amen.

Grant, O Lord,
that the word which we hear this day
may so take root in our hearts,
that we, living in accordance with your holy will,
may ever praise and magnify your glorious name;
through Jesus Christ our Lord.   **Amen.**

9   A hymn or anthem may be sung.

A sermon may be preached.

Prayers and thanksgivings, or the Litany, may be said.

The order in which these occur is at the discretion of the minister.

0   **THE ENDING**

The service ends with one or more of the following:

Minister   The Lord be with you.
And also with you.

Let us bless the Lord.
Thanks be to God.

The grace of our Lord Jesus Christ,
and the love of God,
and the fellowship of the Holy Spirit,
be with us all evermore.   **Amen.**   *2 Cor. 13.14*

Almighty and merciful God,
the Father, the Son, and the Holy Spirit,
bless and preserve us.   **Amen.**

To God, who by the power at work within us,
is able to do far more abundantly
than all we ask or think,
to him be glory in the Church and in Christ Jesus
to all generations for ever and ever.   **Amen.**   *Eph. 3.20*

To the King of Ages, immortal, invisible, the only God,
be honour and glory for ever and ever.   **Amen.**   *1 Tim. 1.17*

May the God of hope
fill you with all joy and peace in believing,
so that by the Holy Spirit
you may abound in hope. **Amen.**   *Rom 15.13*

The Lord bless us and keep us:
The Lord make his face to shine upon us
and be gracious to us:
The Lord lift up his countenance upon us
and give us peace. **Amen.**   *Numbers 6.24–26*

MORNING PRAYER
Shorter Form

This form may be used on weekdays, and is also suitable for family prayers in the home.

1　Sentence of Scripture (pp.23–25).

2　O Lord, open our lips. Section 5.

3　Psalm. Section 7.

4　One or two readings, the second from the New Testament.

5　Canticle

Monday	6	Te Deum (p.118).
Tuesday	5	Benedicite (p.114).
Wednesday	4	Benedictus (p.112).
Thursday	11	Urbs Fortitudinis, (p.126).
or	12	Gloria in Excelsis (p.127).
Friday	13	Saviour of the World (p.128).
Saturday	10	Great and Wonderful (p.125).

6　The Creed may be said. Section 13.

7　Lesser Litany and Lord's Prayer. Sections 14, 15.

8　The Collect of the day and one or more collects. Sections 17, 18.

9　Weekday intercessions and thanksgivings (pp.97 ff.).

10　The ending. Section 20.

EVENING PRAYER
Shorter Form

This form may be used on weekdays, and is also suitable for family prayers in the home.

1   Sentence of Scripture (pp.23–25).

2   Penitence. Section 4.

3   O Lord, open our lips. Section 5.

4   Psalm. Section 7.

5   Reading from the New Testament.

6   Canticle

Monday	7	Magnificat (p.122).
Tuesday	14	Bless the Lord (p.129).
Wednesday	8	Nunc Dimittis (p.124).
Thursday	16	The Song of Christ's Glory (p.130).
Friday	15	Glory and Honour (p.130).
Saturday	3	The Easter Anthems (p.110).

7   Lesser Litany and Lord's Prayer. Section 14, 15.

8   The Collect of the day may be said. Section 17.

9   One of the collects. Section 18.

10   Weekday intercessions and thanksgivings (pp.97ff.).

11   The ending. Section 20.

AN ORDER
FOR THE CELEBRATION
OF THE
HOLY COMMUNION

also called

THE LORD'S SUPPER

or

THE EUCHARIST

AN ORDER FOR
THE CELEBRATION OF
THE HOLY COMMUNION
also called The Lord's Supper or The Eucharist

Stand

1 The appropriate greeting shall be used and a sentence of Scripture may be said.

Priest

The Lord be with you.
And also with you.

or

Grace to you and peace from God our Father
and the Lord Jesus Christ.   *Phil. 1.2*
Thanks be to God.

Christmas and Epiphany

Behold, I bring you good tidings of great joy,
which shall be to all people:
for unto you is born (this day) in the City of David,
a Saviour who is Christ our Lord.   *Luke 2.10,11*
Thanks be to God.

Easter

Christ is risen.
The Lord is risen indeed. Alleluia.   *Luke 24.34*

Ascension

God exalted Jesus at his right hand as Lord and Saviour,
to give repentance to Israel
and forgiveness of sins.   *Acts 5.31*
Thanks be to God.

Pentecost

God's love has been shed abroad in our hearts
through the Holy Spirit he has given us.   *Rom. 5.5*
Thanks be to God.

The Sentences of Scripture are on pp.23–25.

2   All say

**Almighty God
to whom all hearts are open,
all desires known,
and from whom no secrets are hidden:
Cleanse the thoughts of our hearts
by the inspiration of your Holy Spirit,
that we may perfectly love you,
and worthily magnify your holy name:
through Christ our Lord.   Amen.**

3   This canticle may be omitted in Advent and Lent and on weekdays which are not holy days.

**Glory to God in the highest,
and peace to his people on earth.**

**Lord God, heavenly King,
almighty God and Father,
we worship you, we give you thanks,
we praise you for your glory.**

**Lord Jesus Christ, only Son of the Father,
Lord God, Lamb of God,
you take away the sin of the world:
have mercy on us;
you are seated at the right hand of the Father:
receive our prayer.**

**For you alone are the Holy One,
you alone are the Lord,
you alone are the Most High,
Jesus Christ,
with the Holy Spirit,
in the glory of God the Father.   Amen.**

4   The priest says THE COLLECT of the day.

THE MINISTRY OF THE WORD

Sit

5 THE OLD TESTAMENT READING

The reader says

The Old Testament reading is from . . . chapter . . .
beginning at verse. . . .

At the end of the reading he may say

This is the word of the Lord.
Thanks be to God.

Silence may be kept.

6 THE PSALM

After the reading, one of the appointed Psalms, or a part of it, may
be said or sung.

7 THE EPISTLE

The reader says

The Epistle is from . . . chapter . . . beginning at verse. . . .

At the end of the reading he may say

This is the word of the Lord.
Thanks be to God.

8 A canticle, psalm, hymn or anthem may be sung.

Stand

9 THE GOSPEL

The minister who reads the Gospel says

The Holy Gospel is written in the Gospel according to . . .
in the . . . chapter beginning at verse . . .
Glory to Christ our Saviour.

At the end of the reading the minister says

This is the Gospel of Christ.
Praise to Christ our Lord.

10 THE SERMON may be preached here or after the Creed.

11 THE NICENE CREED is said at least on Sundays and the greater festivals.

We believe in one God,
   the Father, the Almighty,
   maker of heaven and earth,
   of all that is
   seen and unseen.

We believe in one Lord, Jesus Christ,
   the only Son of God,
   eternally begotten of the Father,
   God from God, Light from Light,
   true God from true God,
   begotten, not made,
   of one Being with the Father.
   Through him all things were made.
For us men and for our salvation
   he came down from heaven;
by the power of the Holy Spirit
   he became incarnate of the Virgin Mary,
      and was made man.
For our sake he was crucified under Pontius Pilate;
   he suffered death and was buried.
   On the third day he rose again
      in accordance with the Scriptures;
   he ascended into heaven
      and is seated at the right hand of the Father.
He will come again in glory
   to judge the living and the dead,
   and his kingdom will have no end.

We believe in the Holy Spirit,
   the Lord, the giver of life,
   who proceeds from the Father and the Son.
   With the Father and the Son he is worshipped
      and glorified.
   He has spoken through the Prophets.
   We believe in one holy catholic and apostolic Church.
   We acknowledge one baptism for the forgiveness of
      sins.
   We look for the resurrection of the dead,
      and the life of the world to come.   Amen.

2 Banns of Marriage are read here.

A hymn may be sung.

THE INTERCESSIONS

3 The Intercessions and Thanksgivings are led by the priest or by
others appointed by him, using either of the following forms:

THE FIRST FORM

Let us pray.

Almighty and everliving God
hear the prayers which we offer in faith:

For peace, and for the salvation of all men,
 Lord, in your mercy
 hear our prayer.

For the one holy catholic and apostolic Church,
and for the unity of all Christian people,
 Lord, in your mercy
 hear our prayer.

For all who minister in the Church,
for bishops, priests and deacons,
 Lord, in your mercy
 hear our prayer.

For those who learn and those who teach the Christian faith,
 Lord, in your mercy
 hear our prayer.

For all who live and work in this parish,
 Lord, in your mercy
 hear our prayer.

For families, and for those who live alone,
 Lord, in your mercy
 hear our prayer.

For the sick and afflicted, and for those who care for them,
 Lord, in your mercy
 hear our prayer.

For all in authority, and especially for
(N.I.) Elizabeth our Queen,
(R.I.) our President,
 Lord, in your mercy
 hear our prayer.

For those who work for peace, justice and righteousness
throughout the world,

Lord, in your mercy
hear our prayer.

For . . .

Lord, in your mercy
hear our prayer.

Rejoicing in the fellowship of your holy apostles and
martyrs, and of all your servants departed this life in your
faith and fear, we commend ourselves and one another and
our whole life to you, Lord God; through Jesus Christ our
Saviour. **Amen.**

THE SECOND FORM

Let us pray.

Almighty God, our heavenly Father,
you promised through your Son Jesus Christ
to hear the prayers of those who ask in faith:

We pray for your Church in all the world . . .
for this diocese and for . . . our bishop
for . . .

Grant that we, and all who confess your name,
may be united in your truth,
live together in your love,
and reveal your glory in the world.

Lord, in your mercy
hear our prayer.

We pray for the nations of the world . . .
for this country and for
(N.I.) Elizabeth our Queen,
(R.I.) our President,
for all in authority
and for the communities in which we live and work . . .

Guide the people of this land and of all the nations
in the ways of justice and of peace,
that we may honour one another
and serve the common good.

Lord, in your mercy
hear our prayer.

We pray for the sick . . . the poor . . .
and those in trouble . . . (and for . . .)

> Save and comfort all who suffer,
> that they may hold to you through good and ill,
> and trust in your unfailing love.

> Lord, in your mercy
> **hear our prayer.**

We bless your holy name for all your servants
who have died in faith, (for . . .)

> We rejoice in the faithful witness of your people
> in every age, and pray that we may share with them
> the joys of your eternal kingdom.

> **Merciful Father,**
> **accept these our prayers**
> **for the sake of your Son**
> **our Saviour Jesus Christ.   Amen.**

PENITENCE

14 The priest says

Hear what our Lord Jesus Christ says:

You shall love the Lord your God with all your heart
and with all your soul and with all your mind.
This is the first and great commandment.
And the second is like it.
You shall love your neighbour as yourself.
On these two commandments depend all the law
and the prophets.   *Matt. 22.37–39*

Lord, have mercy on us,
and write these your laws in our hearts.

or

Hear these commandments which God has given to his
people, and take them to heart.

> 1 I AM THE LORD YOUR GOD; YOU SHALL HAVE NO OTHER GODS
> BUT ME.
> You shall love the Lord your God with all your heart,
> with all your soul, and with all your mind and with all
> your strength.   *Matt. 22.37*

2 YOU SHALL NOT MAKE FOR YOURSELF ANY IDOL.
God is Spirit, and those who worship him must worship
in spirit and in truth.   *John 4.24*

3 YOU SHALL NOT DISHONOUR THE NAME OF THE LORD YOUR
GOD.
You shall worship him with awe and reverence.
Heb. 12.28

4 REMEMBER THE LORD'S DAY AND KEEP IT HOLY.
Christ is risen from the dead: set your minds on things
that are above, not on things that are on the earth.
Col. 3.1,2

**Lord, have mercy on us,
and write these your laws in our hearts.**

5 HONOUR YOUR FATHER AND MOTHER.
Live as servants of God, honour all men, love the
brotherhood.   *1 Peter 2.16,17*

6 YOU SHALL NOT COMMIT MURDER.
Be reconciled to your brother; overcome evil with
good.   *Matt. 5.24; Rom. 13.21*

7 YOU SHALL NOT COMMIT ADULTERY.
Know that your body is a temple of the Holy Spirit.
1 Cor. 6.19

8 YOU SHALL NOT STEAL.
Be honest in all that you do and care for those in
need.   *Eph. 4.28*

9 YOU SHALL NOT BE A FALSE WITNESS.
Let everyone speak the truth.   *Eph. 4.25*

10 YOU SHALL NOT COVET ANYTHING WHICH BELONGS TO YOUR
NEIGHBOUR.
Remember the words of the Lord Jesus: It is more blessed
to give than to receive. Love your neighbour as yourself,
for love is the fulfilling of the law.   *Acts 20.35; Rom. 13.9,10*

**Lord, have mercy on us,
and write all these your laws in our hearts.**

or

The Ten Commandments may be read in the shorter form as
printed in capitals above, or in full (p.69).

15 The priest, or one of the ministers, says
God so loved the world that he gave his only Son Jesus
Christ to save us from our sins, to intercede for us in heaven,
and to bring us to eternal life.

or

He may say one or more of the following sentences:
Jesus says, Come to me, all that labour and are heavy laden,
and I will refresh you.   *Matt. 11.28*

God so loved the world that he gave his only Son, that all
who believe in him should not perish but have eternal
life.   *John 3.16*

This is a true saying, and worthy by all men to be received,
that Christ Jesus came into the world to save sinners.
1 Tim. 1.15

If any man sin, we have an advocate with the Father, Jesus
Christ the righteous: and he is the propitiation for our
sins.   *1 John 2.1,2*

16 Then he says
Let us therefore confess our sins in penitence and faith,
firmly resolved to keep God's commandments, and to live in
love and peace with all men.

17 After a short pause for self examination, all say
Almighty God, our heavenly Father,
we have sinned in thought and word and deed,
and in what we have left undone.
We are truly sorry, and we humbly repent.
For the sake of your Son, Jesus Christ,
have mercy on us and forgive us,
that we may walk in newness of life
to the glory of your name.   Amen.

18 The priest, or the bishop if he is present, pronounces the
absolution:
Almighty God,
who forgives all who truly repent,
have mercy on you,
pardon and deliver you from all your sins,
confirm and strengthen you in all goodness,
and keep you in eternal life;
through Jesus Christ our Lord.   **Amen.**

19 All then say together

**We do not presume
to come to this your table, merciful Lord,
trusting in our own righteousness
but in your manifold and great mercies.
We are not worthy
so much as to gather up the crumbs under your table.
But you are the same Lord
whose nature is always to have mercy.
Grant us therefore, gracious Lord,
so to eat the flesh of your dear Son Jesus Christ
and to drink his blood,
that our sinful bodies may be made clean by his body,
and our souls washed through his most precious blood,
and that we may evermore dwell in him
   and he in us.   Amen.**

THE PEACE

Stand

20 The priest says

Christ is our peace.
He has reconciled us to God
in one body by the cross.
We meet in his name and share his peace.

or

Jesus said, A new commandment I give to you,
that you love one another:
even as I have loved you,
that you also love one another. *John 13.34*

21 He then says

The peace of the Lord be always with you.
And also with you.

Those present may give one another a sign of peace.

THE OFFERTORY

22 The priest may say one or more sentences of Scripture, p.70.

A hymn may be sung.

The alms of the people may be brought to the Lord's Table.

The bread and wine for communion are placed on the Lord's Table if this has not already been done.

All may say together

**Lord, yours is the greatness
and the power and the glory
and the victory and the majesty;
for all things come from you
and of your own we give you.**   *1 Chron. 29.11,14*

THE MINISTRY OF THE SACRAMENT

The Taking of the Bread and Wine and the Giving of Thanks

Stand

23 The priest takes the bread and wine into his hands. He may say

Christ our passover has been sacrificed for us;
therefore let us celebrate the feast.   *1 Cor. 5.7,8*

24 The priest says

The Lord be with you.
And also with you.
or
The Lord is here.
His Spirit is with us.

Lift up your hearts.
We lift them up to the Lord.

Let us give thanks to the Lord our God.
It is right to give him thanks and praise.

Father, almighty and everliving God,
at all times and in all places
it is right for us to give you thanks and praise:

When there is a proper preface it follows here (pp.65 ff.)

And so with all your people,
with angels and archangels,
and with all the company of heaven,
we proclaim your great and glorious name,
for ever praising you and saying:

Holy, holy, holy Lord,
God of power and might,
heaven and earth are full of your glory.
Hosanna in the highest.

The congregation may kneel

Blessed are you, Father,
the creator and sustainer of all things;
you made man in your own image,
and more wonderfully restored him
when you freed him from the slavery of sin;
for in your love and mercy
you gave your only Son Jesus Christ to become man
and suffer death on the cross to redeem us;
he made there the one complete and all-sufficient sacrifice
for the sins of the whole world:
he instituted,
and in his holy Gospel commanded us to continue,
a perpetual memory of his precious death
until he comes again:

On the night that he was betrayed he took bread;
and when he had given thanks to you, he broke it,
and gave it to his disciples, saying, Take, eat,

The priest lays his hand on the bread

this is my body which is given for you.
Do this in remembrance of me.

In the same way, after supper he took the cup;
and when he had given thanks to you,
he gave it to them, saying, Drink this, all of you,

The priest lays his hand on the cup

for this is my blood of the new covenant
which is shed for you and for many
for the forgiveness of sins.
Do this, as often as you drink it,
in remembrance of me.

Therefore, Father, with this bread and this cup
we do as Christ your Son commanded:
we remember his passion and death,
we celebrate his resurrection and ascension,
and we look for the coming of his kingdom.

Accept through him this our sacrifice
of praise and thanksgiving;
and as we eat and drink these holy gifts,
grant by the power of the life-giving Spirit
that we may be made one in your holy Church
and partakers of the body and blood of your Son,
that he may dwell in us and we in him:

Through the same Jesus Christ our Lord,
by whom, and with whom, in the unity of the Holy Spirit,
all honour and glory are yours, Almighty Father,
for ever and ever. **Amen.**

25 The priest says

As our Saviour Christ has taught us, so we pray

**Our Father in heaven,
    hallowed be your name,
    your kingdom come,
    your will be done,
        on earth as in heaven.
Give us today our daily bread.
Forgive us our sins
    as we forgive those who sin against us.
Lead us not into temptation
    but deliver us from evil.**

**For the kingdom, the power, and the glory are yours
    now and for ever. Amen.**

or

The Lord's Prayer may be said in the old form.

The Breaking of the Bread
and the Giving of the Bread and Wine

26 As the priest breaks the bread he says

The bread which we break
is a sharing in the body of Christ.
**We, being many, are one body
for we all share in the one bread.** *1 Cor. 10.16,17*

27 The priest receives communion.

Communicants are given the consecrated bread and wine with
the words

The body of our Lord Jesus Christ, which was given for you,
preserve your body and soul to eternal life. Take and eat this
in remembrance that Christ died for you and feed on him in
your heart by faith with thanksgiving.

The blood of our Lord Jesus Christ, which was shed for you,
preserve your body and soul to eternal life. Drink this in
remembrance that Christ's blood was shed for you, and be
thankful.

or

The priest says

Draw near and receive the body of our Lord Jesus Christ
which he gave for you, and his blood which he shed for you.
Remember that he died for you, and feed on him in your
hearts by faith with thanksgiving.

Communicants are given the consecrated bread and wine with
the words

The body of Christ keep you in eternal life.
The blood of Christ keep you in eternal life.

After receiving the communicant says
Amen.

28 The following may be sung during the Communion:

Blessed is he who comes in the name of the Lord.
Hosanna in the highest.

Jesus, Lamb of God, have mercy on us.
Jesus, bearer of our sins, have mercy on us.
Jesus, Redeemer of the world, give us your peace.

or

Lamb of God, you take away the sins of the world;
have mercy on us.

Lamb of God, you take away the sins of the world;
have mercy on us.

Lamb of God, you take away the sins of the world;
grant us peace.

Other hymns or anthems may be sung.

AFTER COMMUNION

29 A period of silence may be kept.

30 The priest may say

Father of all, we give you thanks and praise, that when we
were still far off you met us in your Son and brought us
home. Dying and living he declared your love, gave us
grace, and opened the gate of glory.

May we who share Christ's body live his risen life;
we who drink his cup bring life to others;
we whom the Spirit lights give light to the world.
Keep us firm in the hope you have set before us,
so that we and all your children shall be free,
and the whole earth live to praise your name;
through Christ our Lord.   **Amen.**

31 The priest says

Let us pray.

Almighty God,
we thank you for feeding us
with the spiritual food
of the body and blood of your Son Jesus Christ.
Through him we offer you our souls and bodies
to be a living sacrifice.
Send us out in the power of your Spirit
to live and work to your praise and glory.   Amen.

32 The priest, or the bishop if he is present, says

The peace of God, which passes all understanding,
keep your hearts and minds
in the knowledge and love of God,
and of his Son Jesus Christ our Lord.

On the occasions for which a seasonal blessing is provided it is
used in place of The peace of God . . .

And the blessing of God Almighty,
the Father, the Son, and the Holy Spirit,
be with you and remain with you always. **Amen.**

33 The following dismissal may be used:

Go in peace to love and serve the Lord.
In the name of Christ. Amen.

THE MINISTRY OF THE SACRAMENT
AN ALTERNATIVE ORDER

The Taking of the Bread and Wine and the Giving of Thanks

Stand

23a The priest takes the bread and wine into his hands. He may say

Christ our passover has been sacrificed for us;
therefore let us celebrate the feast. *1 Cor.5.7,8*

24a The priest says

The Lord be with you.
And also with you.
or
The Lord is here.
His Spirit is with us.

Lift up your hearts.
We lift them up to the Lord.

Let us give thanks to the Lord our God.
It is right to give him thanks and praise.

All glory and honour, thanks and praise
be given to you at all times and in all places,
Lord, holy Father, true and living God,
through Jesus Christ our Lord.
For he is your eternal Word
through whom you have created all things
from the beginning
and formed us in your own image.

In your great love you gave him
to be made man for us and to share our common life.

In obedience to your will
your Son our Saviour offered himself as a perfect sacrifice,
and died on the cross for our redemption.
Through him you have freed us from the slavery of sin
and reconciled us to yourself,
our God and Father.

He is our great high priest
whom you raised from death
and exalted to your right hand on high
where he ever lives to intercede for us.

Through him you have sent upon us
your holy and life-giving Spirit
and made us a royal priesthood
called to serve you for ever.

Therefore with angels and archangels
and with all the company of heaven
we proclaim your great and glorious name,
for ever praising you and saying:

Holy, holy, holy Lord,
God of power and might,
heaven and earth are full of your glory.
Hosanna in the highest.

Merciful Father, we thank you
for these gifts of your creation, this bread and this wine,
and we pray that we who eat and drink them
in the fellowship of the Holy Spirit
in obedience to our Saviour Christ
in remembrance of his death and passion
may be partakers of his body and his blood,

He takes the bread into his hands and says

who on the night he was betrayed took bread;
and when he had given you thanks
he broke it, and gave it to his disciples, saying,
'Take, eat. This is my body which is given for you;
Do this in remembrance of me.'

He takes the cup into his hands and says

After supper, he took the cup,
and again giving you thanks
he gave it to his disciples, saying,
'Drink from this, all of you.
This is my blood of the new covenant
which is shed for you and for many
for the forgiveness of sins.
Do this, as often as you drink it, in remembrance of me.'

Christ has died;
Christ is risen;
Christ will come again.

Father, with this bread and this cup,
we do as our Saviour has commanded;
we celebrate the redemption he has won for us;
we proclaim his perfect sacrifice
made once for all upon the cross,
his mighty resurrection and glorious ascension;
and we look for his coming
to fulfil all things according to your will.

Renew us by your Holy Spirit,
unite us in the body of your Son,
and bring us with all your people
into the joy of your eternal kingdom;
through Jesus Christ our Lord,
with whom and in whom,
by the power of the Holy Spirit,
we worship you, Father almighty,
in songs of never-ending praise:

Blessing and honour and glory and power
are yours for ever and ever.   Amen.

25a The priest says here or at 29a

As our Saviour Christ has taught us, so we pray

Our Father in heaven,
hallowed be your name,
your kingdom come,
your will be done,
on earth as in heaven.
Give us today our daily bread.
Forgive us our sins
as we forgive those who sin against us.
Lead us not into temptation
but deliver us from evil.

For the kingdom, the power, and the glory are yours
now and for ever.   Amen.

or

The Lord's Prayer may be said in the old form.

The Breaking of the Bread
and the Giving of the Bread and Wine

26a As the priest breaks the bread he says

The bread which we break
is a sharing in the body of Christ.
We, being many, are one body
for we all share in the one bread.   *1 Cor. 10.16,17*

27a The priest receives communion.

Communicants are given the consecrated bread and wine with the words

The body of our Lord Jesus Christ, which was given for you, preserve your body and soul to eternal life. Take and eat this in remembrance that Christ died for you, and feed on him in your heart by faith with thanksgiving.

The blood of our Lord Jesus Christ, which was shed for you, preserve your body and soul to eternal life. Drink this in remembrance that Christ's blood was shed for you, and be thankful.

or

The priest says

Draw near and receive the body of our Lord Jesus Christ which he gave for you, and his blood which he shed for you. Remember that he died for you, and feed on him in your hearts by faith with thanksgiving.

Communicants are given the consecrated bread and wine with the words

The body of Christ keep you in eternal life.
The blood of Christ keep you in eternal life.

After receiving the communicant says
Amen.

28a The following may be sung during the Communion.

Blessed is he who comes in the name of the Lord.
Hosanna in the highest.

Jesus, Lamb of God, have mercy on us.
Jesus, bearer of our sins, have mercy on us.
Jesus, Redeemer of the world, give us your peace.

or

Lamb of God, you take away the sins of the world;
have mercy on us.

Lamb of God, you take away the sins of the world;
have mercy on us.

Lamb of God, you take away the sins of the world;
grant us peace.

Other hymns or anthems may be sung.

AFTER COMMUNION

29a If the Lord's Prayer has not already been said, it is said here.
A period of silence may be kept.

30a The priest says

Father, we thank you
that you feed us who have received these holy mysteries
with the spiritual food of the body and blood of our Saviour
Jesus Christ.
We thank you for this assurance
of your goodness and love,
and that we are living members of his body
and heirs of his eternal kingdom.
Accept this our sacrifice of praise and thanksgiving,
and help us to grow in love and obedience,
that with all your saints we may worship you for ever.
Amen.

31a All say together

**Father, we offer ourselves to you
as a living sacrifice
through Jesus Christ our Lord.
Send us out in the power of your Spirit
to live and work to your praise and glory.   Amen.**

32a The priest, or the bishop if he is present, says

The peace of God, which passes all understanding,
keep your hearts and minds
in the knowledge and love of God,
and of his Son Jesus Christ our Lord.

On the occasions for which a seasonal blessing is provided it is
used in place of **The peace of God . . .**

And the blessing of God Almighty,
the Father, the Son, and the Holy Spirit,
be with you and remain with you always.   **Amen.**

33a The following dismissal may be used:

Go in peace to love and serve the Lord.
In the name of Christ.   Amen.

THE PROPER PREFACES AND BLESSINGS

Note: Proper prefaces are not used in *The Ministry of the Sacrament, An Alternative Order*.

Advent

Preface
You have given salvation to man
through the coming of your Son
our Saviour Jesus Christ,
and by him you will make all things new
when he returns in glory to judge the world:

Blessing
Christ the sun of righteousness shine upon you,
gladden your hearts
and scatter the darkness from before you:

Christmas

Preface
You have given Jesus Christ your only Son
to be born of the Virgin Mary,
and through him you have given us power
to become the sons of God:

Blessing
Christ, who by his incarnation gathered into one
all things earthly and heavenly,
fill you with his joy and peace:

Epiphany

Preface
For Jesus Christ our Lord
who in the likeness of man revealed your glory,
to bring us out of darkness
into the splendour of his light:

Blessing
Christ the Son be manifest to you,
that your lives may be a light to the world:

Lent

Preface

Through Jesus Christ our Lord,
who was in every way tempted as we are
yet did not sin;
by whose grace we are able to overcome all our temptations:

Blessing

Christ give you grace to grow in holiness,
to deny yourselves,
and to take up your cross and follow him:

Passiontide and Holy Week

Preface

Through Jesus Christ our Saviour,
who, for the redemption of the world,
humbled himself to death on the cross;
that, being lifted up from the earth,
he might draw all men to himself:

Blessing

Christ draw you to himself
and grant that you find in his cross
a sure ground for faith,
a firm support for hope,
and the assurance of sins forgiven:

Easter

Preface

And above all we praise you
for the glorious resurrection of your Son
Jesus Christ our Lord,
the true paschal Lamb who was sacrificed for us;
by dying he destroyed our death;
by rising he restored our life:

Blessing

The God of peace,
who brought again from the dead our Lord Jesus,
that great shepherd of the sheep,
through the blood of the eternal covenant,
make you perfect in every good work to do his will,
working in you that which is well-pleasing in his sight:

or

The God of peace,
who brought again from the dead our Lord Jesus,
that great shepherd of the sheep,
make you perfect in every good work to do his will:

Ascension

Preface
Through Jesus Christ our Lord,
who after he had risen from the dead
ascended into heaven,
where he is seated at your right hand
to intercede for us
and to prepare a place for us in glory:

Blessing
Christ make you faithful and strong to do his will,
that you may reign with him in glory:

Pentecost

Preface
Through Jesus Christ our Lord,
according to whose promise
the Holy Spirit came to dwell in us,
making us your children,
and giving us power to proclaim the gospel throughout the
world:

Blessing
The Spirit of truth lead you into all truth,
give you grace to confess that Jesus Christ is Lord,
and to proclaim the wonderful works of God:

Trinity Sunday

Preface
You have revealed your glory
as the glory of your Son and of the Holy Spirit:
three persons equal in majesty,
undivided in splendour,
yet one Lord, one God,
ever to be worshipped and adored:

Blessing
God the Holy Trinity
make you strong in faith and love,
defend you,
and guide you in truth and peace:

Annunciation

Preface
You chose the Blessed Virgin Mary
to be the mother of your Son
and so exalted the humble and meek;
your angel hailed her as most highly favoured,
and with all generations we call her blessed:

Blessing
Christ the Son of God, born of Mary,
fill you with his grace
to trust his promises and obey his will:

Transfiguration

Preface
Through Jesus Christ our Lord,
whose divine glory shone forth upon the holy mountain
before the chosen witnesses of his majesty;
when your own voice from heaven
proclaimed him your beloved Son.

Blessing
The God of all grace,
who called you to his eternal glory in Christ Jesus,
establish, strengthen and settle you in the faith:

Saints' Days

Preface
In the saints
you have given us an example of godly living,
that, rejoicing in their fellowship,
we may run with perseverance the race that is set before us,
and with them receive the unfading crown of glory:

Blessing
God give you grace
to share the inheritance of his saints in glory:

Note: A proper preface is not required for St Michael and All
Angels.

Baptism and Confirmation

The preface and blessing of Pentecost may be used.

Funerals

The preface and blessing of Easter are used.

THE TEN COMMANDMENTS: FULL FORM

Exodus 20.1–17

See also pp. 49 ff.

1 God spoke all these words, saying, I am the Lord your God who brought you out of the land of Egypt, out of the house of bondage. You shall have no other gods before me.

2 You shall not make for yourself a graven image, or any likeness of anything that is in heaven above, or that is in the earth beneath, or that is in the water under the earth; you shall not bow down to them or serve them; for I the Lord your God am a jealous God, visiting the iniquity of the fathers upon the children to the third and fourth generation of those who hate me, but showing steadfast love to thousands of those who love me and keep my commandments.

3 You shall not take the name of the Lord your God in vain, for the Lord will not hold him guiltless who takes his name in vain.

4 Remember the sabbath day, to keep it holy. Six days you shall labour, and do all your work; but the seventh day is a sabbath to the Lord your God; in it you shall not do any work, you, or your son, or your daughter, your man-servant, or maidservant, or your cattle, or the sojourner who is within your gates, for in six days the Lord made heaven and earth, the sea, and all that is in them, and rested the seventh day; therefore the Lord blessed the sabbath day and hallowed it.

Lord, have mercy on us,
and write these your laws in our hearts.

5 Honour your father and your mother that your days may be long in the land which the Lord your God gives you.

6 You shall not kill.

7 You shall not commit adultery.

8 You shall not steal.

9 You shall not bear false witness against your neighbour.

10 You shall not covet your neighbour's house, you shall not covet your neighbour's wife, or his manservant, or his maidservant, or his ox, or his ass, or anything that is your neighbour's.

Lord, have mercy on us,
and write all these your laws in our hearts.

SENTENCES WHICH MAY BE USED AT THE OFFERTORY

22 Remember the words of the Lord Jesus who himself said, It is more blessèd to give than to receive. *Acts. 20.35*

Not everyone who calls me, Lord, Lord, will enter the kingdom of heaven, but only those who do the will of my Father in heaven. *Matt. 7.21*

No one shall come into the presence of the Lord empty-handed. Let every man give what he can. *Deut. 16.16,17*

Remember to show kindness and to share what you have with others, for such are the sacrifices of which God approves. *Heb. 13.16*

Let thanksgiving be your sacrifice to God, and fulfil the vows you make to the most high. *Psalm 50.14*

Give the Lord the glory due to his name; enter his courts with an offering. *Psalm 96.8*

Other sentences may be said.

WHEN THE CONSECRATED ELEMENTS ARE INSUFFICIENT

If either or both of the consecrated elements are insufficient, the priest returns to the holy table and adds more, saying these words and laying his hand on the bread and/or cup:

Father,
giving thanks over the bread and the cup
according to the institution of your Son Jesus Christ,
who said, Take, eat, this is my body.

and/or

Drink this, this is my blood.

We pray that this bread/wine also may be to us
    his body/blood,
to be received in remembrance of him.

A LATE
EVENING OFFICE

A LATE EVENING OFFICE

1   Minister   Blessed be our God for all time,
now and for evermore.
Amen.

Glory to you, our God, glory be to you.
Holy Spirit, Comforter,
treasure of all goodness and giver of life,
come and dwell in us,
cleanse us from all sin,
and in your love bring us to salvation.

**Holy God, holy and strong,
holy and immortal,
have mercy on us.**

2   PSALM 134

Come bless the Lord all you servants of the Lord:
you that by night stand in the house of the Lord.

Lift up your hands toward the holy place:
and bless the Lord.

May the Lord bless you from Zion:
the Lord who made heaven and earth.

Glory to the Father, and to the Son,
  and to the Holy Spirit:
**as it was in the beginning, is now,
  and shall be for ever.   Amen.**

3   NEW TESTAMENT READING

4   MEDITATION

5   THE SONG OF SIMEON (Canticle 8 p.124) *and/or* a HYMN

6   PRAYER

Let us pray to the Lord
with all our heart and with all our soul.
Lord, have mercy.

Let us pray for all Christian people,
that they may live in love and truth.
Lord, have mercy.

Let us pray for all ministers of the Church,
and for our brothers and sisters in Christ.
Lord, have mercy.

Let us pray for peace throughout the world,
and for all governments.
Lord, have mercy.

Let us pray for our neighbours
and for all our friends.
Lord, have mercy.

Let us pray for those who hate us
as we pray for those who love us.
Lord, have mercy.

Let us pray for refugees and prisoners,
and for all who are exposed to the dangers of travel.
Lord, have mercy.

Let us pray for all sick people,
for the sorrowful and the dying.
Lord, have mercy.

Let us pray for the abundance of the fruits of the earth,
and that the poor and hungry may receive a just share.
Lord, have mercy.

Let us remember our brothers and sisters
who have entered into eternal rest.
Blessed are the dead who die in the Lord.

7   COLLECT OF THE WEEK OR OF THE DAY

The Lord be with you.
And also with you.
Let us pray:

Silence. Collect.
Amen.

8   OPEN OR SILENT PRAYER

Our Father in heaven
   hallowed be your name,
   your kingdom come,
   your will be done,
      on earth as in heaven.
Give us today our daily bread.
Forgive us our sins
   as we forgive those who sin against us.
Lead us not into temptation
   but deliver us from evil.   Amen.

or

Our Father, who art in heaven,
   hallowed be thy name,
   thy kingdom come,
   thy will be done,
      on earth as it is in heaven.
Give us this day our daily bread.
And forgive us our trespasses
   as we forgive those who trespass against us.
And lead us not into temptation
   but deliver us from evil.   Amen.

COMMON COLLECT

Lord Almighty,
come and scatter the darkness of our hearts
by the light of your presence;
that we may know you,
the Light of the world
and the one true God,
blessed this night and for evermore.   Amen.

BLESSING

Let us bless the Lord.
Thanks be to God.

May the Almighty and merciful God,
the Father, the Son, and the Holy Spirit,
bless us and keep us.
Amen.

Our Father in heaven,
hallowed be your name,
your kingdom come,
your will be done,
on earth as in heaven.
Give us today our daily bread.
Forgive us our sins
as we forgive those who sin against us.
Lead us not into temptation
but deliver us from evil. Amen

Our Father, who art in heaven,
hallowed be thy name,
thy kingdom come,
thy will be done,
on earth as it is in heaven.
Give us this day our daily bread.
And forgive us our trespasses
as we forgive those who trespass against us.
And lead us not into temptation
but deliver us from evil. Amen

born a virgin,
come that in the darkness of our hearts
by the radiant of thy presency
that we may know you
in Light of the world
and for the living God
bless this night and our evening. Amen

... wakes be for God
Thanks be to God

May the Lord bless and his children
the Father, the Son, and the Holy Spirit
bless us and keep us
Amen

THE LITANY

THE LITANY

The Litany is recommended for use on Sundays, Wednesdays and Fridays and on Rogation Days.

When it is used as a separate service it may be preceded by a Psalm, canticle or hymn and one of the readings of the day.

It may be said in whole or in part. Sections 1 and 5 should always be said. The minister may introduce particular intercessions in any of the suffrages.

1 God the Father, creator of heaven and earth,
   have mercy on us.

   God the Son, redeemer of the world,
   have mercy on us.

   God the Holy Spirit, giver of life,
   have mercy on us.

   Holy, blessed and glorious Trinity,
   three Persons in one God,
   have mercy on us.

2 Save us, good Lord,
   from all sin and wickedness,
   from pride, hypocrisy and conceit,
   from envy, hatred and malice, and all uncharitableness,
   save us, good Lord.

   From sins of thought, word and deed,
   from the lusts of the flesh,
   from the deceits of the world and the snares of the devil,
   save us, good Lord.

   From fire, storm and flood,
   from disease, pestilence and want,
   from war and murder, and from dying unprepared,
   save us, good Lord.

   From all false doctrine,
   from hardness of heart,
   and from contempt of your word and commandment,
   save us, good Lord.

In times of sorrow and in times of joy,
in the hour of death,
and in the day of judgment,
save us, good Lord.

3 Save us, Lord Christ,
by the mystery of your holy incarnation,
by your birth, childhood and obedience,
by your baptism, fasting and temptation,
save us, Lord Christ.

By your ministry in word and work,
by your mighty acts of power,
and by your preaching of the kingdom,
save us, Lord Christ.

By your agony and trial,
by your cross and passion,
and by your precious death and burial,
save us, Lord Christ.

By your mighty resurrection,
by your glorious ascension,
and by your sending of the Holy Spirit,
save us, Lord Christ.

4 FOR THE CHURCH

Hear us, good Lord:
govern and direct your holy Church,
fill it with love and truth,
and grant it that unity which is your will,
hear us, good Lord.

Give your Church courage to preach the gospel
and to make disciples of all the nations,
hear us, good Lord.

Give knowledge and understanding
to bishops, priests and deacons,
that by their life and teaching
they may proclaim your word,
hear us, good Lord.

Give all people grace to receive your word
and to bring forth the fruit of the Spirit,
hear us, good Lord.

Bring all who have erred and are deceived
into the way of truth,
hear us, good Lord.

FOR THE STATE

Guard and bless our rulers, especially . . .
and grant that they may trust in you,
and seek your honour and glory,
hear us, good Lord.

Bless our country, and give grace,
wisdom and understanding to all in authority,
hear us, good Lord.

Bless those who administer the law,
that they may uphold justice in honesty and truth,
hear us, good Lord.

Bless and keep all who maintain peace and safety,
hear us, good Lord.

Give to all nations unity, peace and concord,
hear us, good Lord.

FOR ALL PEOPLE ACCORDING TO THEIR NEEDS

Strengthen the faithful,
comfort and help the faint-hearted,
raise up those who fall, and drive out all evil,
hear us, good Lord.

Support and encourage all who are in poverty,
unemployment or distress,
protect those whose work is dangerous,
and keep in safety all who travel,
hear us, good Lord.

Keep fathers, mothers and children
united in their family life,
and give them wisdom and strength in times of stress,
hear us, good Lord.

Heal the sick, care for the old and lonely,
and comfort the bereaved,
hear us, good Lord.

Show your pity on victims of strife,
on the homeless and the hungry,
on prisoners, and on all who live in fear,
hear us, good Lord.

Forgive our enemies, persecutors and slanderers,
and turn their hearts,
hear us, good Lord.

Guide and direct all who influence others
through the written or the spoken word,
and inspire all who serve mankind
in science, industry and art,
hear us, good Lord.

Bless and keep all your people,
hear us, good Lord.

Teach us to use the resources of the earth to your glory,
that all may share in your goodness
and praise you for your loving kindness,
hear us, good Lord.

5 Saviour of the world,
forgive our sins, known and unknown,
things done, and left undone;
grant us the grace of your Holy Spirit
that we may amend our lives according to your holy word,
and share with all your people
the joys of your eternal kingdom.

Jesus, Lamb of God,
have mercy on us.

Jesus, bearer of our sins,
have mercy on us.

Jesus, Redeemer of the world,
give us your peace.

The end of the Litany.
When the Litany is used as a separate service it is followed by the
Lord's Prayer.

Our Father in heaven
   hallowed be your name,
   your kingdom come,
   your will be done,
     on earth as in heaven.
Give us today our daily bread.
Forgive us our sins
   as we forgive those who sin against us.
Lead us not into temptation
   but deliver us from evil.   Amen.

or

Our Father, who art in heaven,
** hallowed be thy name,**
** thy kingdom come,**
** thy will be done,**
**   on earth as it is in heaven.**
Give us this day our daily bread.
And forgive us our trespasses
** as we forgive those who trespass against us.**
And lead us not into temptation
** but deliver us from evil.   Amen.**

COLLECTS
AND PRAYERS FOR
VARIOUS
OCCASIONS

COLLECTS AND PRAYERS FOR VARIOUS OCCASIONS

THE RENEWAL OF THE CHURCH

1 God the Holy Spirit,
    come in power and bring new life to the Church;
    renew us in love and service,
    and enable us to be faithful
    to our Lord and Saviour Jesus Christ.   **Amen.**

ALL MANKIND

2 O God, creator and preserver of all mankind,
    bless the people of all nations,
    reconcile those who are divided,
    relieve the hungry and oppressed,
    bring joy to the sorrowing, and peace and hope to all;
    through Jesus Christ our Lord.   **Amen.**

COMMUNITY AND WORLD PEACE

3 Almighty God,
    from whom all thoughts of truth and peace proceed;
    Kindle in the hearts of all men the true love of peace,
    and guide with your pure and peaceable wisdom
    those who take counsel for the nations of the world;
    that in tranquillity your kingdom may go forward
    till the earth is filled with the knowledge of your love;
    through Jesus Christ our Lord.   **Amen.**

4 Almighty God,
    whose will is to restore all things in your beloved Son,
    the king of all;
    Govern the hearts and minds of those in authority,
    and bring the families of the nations,
    divided and rent asunder by the ravages of sin,
    to be subject to his just and gentle rule;
    who lives and reigns with you and the Holy Spirit,
    one God, now and for ever.   **Amen.**

IRELAND

5 Almighty God,
   we commend the people of this land
      to your care and protection.
   Give our rulers (especially . . .), the government
      and all in authority,
   wisdom and strength
   to work for the welfare of all in the community,
   so that we may live in security and peace;
   through Jesus Christ our Lord.   **Amen.**

FOR USE IN NORTHERN IRELAND

6 Almighty God,
   we pray you to bless our sovereign lady,
      Queen Elizabeth,
   the parliaments in the Commonwealth,
      and all in authority;
   that they may order all things
      in wisdom, righteousness and peace
   to the honour of your name
   and the good of your Church and people;
   through Jesus Christ our Lord.   **Amen.**

THE EUROPEAN COMMUNITY

7 O Lord our heavenly Father,
   we pray you to guide and direct
      the members of the European Community.
   Draw us closer to one another,
   and help us to attain justice and freedom,
   and to use our resources for the good of all mankind;
   through Jesus Christ our Lord.   **Amen.**

THE SICK AND SUFFERING

8 Heavenly Father,
   we pray for the sick and suffering.
   Help them to know your love
   that they may seek strength from you,
   and find peace and healing in your presence;
   through Jesus Christ our Lord.   **Amen.**

THE BEREAVED

9 Give faith and comfort, O Lord,
   to all who are bereaved (especially to . . .)
   Strengthen them to meet the days to come
   with steadfastness and patience,
   not sorrowing as those without hope,
   but in thankful remembrance of your mercy in the past,
   and waiting for a joyful reunion in heaven;
   through Jesus Christ our Lord.   **Amen.**

PRAYERS OF THANKSGIVING AND DEDICATION

10 **Almighty God and merciful Father,**
   we give you hearty thanks
   for all your goodness and loving kindness to us
   and to all people.
   We bless you for our creation and preservation
   and for all the blessings of this life;
   but above all for your love
   in redeeming the world by our Lord Jesus Christ;
   for the means of grace and for the hope of glory.
   Give us a due sense of your mercy
   that our hearts may be thankful,
   and that we may praise you
   not only with our lips but in our lives,
   by giving up ourselves to your service,
   and by walking before you
   in holiness and righteousness all our days;
   through Jesus Christ our Lord.   Amen.

11 **Almighty God, we praise you for the blessings**
   brought to mankind through your Church.
   We bless you for the grace of the sacraments,
   for our fellowship in Christ
   with you and with each other,
   for the teaching of the Scriptures,
   and for the preaching of your word.
   We thank you for the holy example of your saints,
   for your faithful servants departed this life,
   and for the memory and example
   of all that has been true and good in their lives.
   Number us with them
   in the company of the redeemed in heaven;
   through Jesus Christ our Lord.   Amen.

12 **Almighty God,**
we thank you for the gift of your holy word.
May it be a lantern to our feet,
a light to our paths,
and a strength in our lives.
Take us and use us
to love and serve all men
in the power of the Holy Spirit
and in the name of your Son,
Jesus Christ our Lord.   Amen.

CONCLUDING PRAYERS

13 Almighty God,
you have given us grace
at this time with one accord
to make our common supplications to you;
and you have promised that when two or three
are gathered together in your name
you will grant their requests.
Fulfil now, O Lord,
the desires and petitions of your servants,
as may be most expedient for them,
granting us in this world knowledge of your truth,
and in the world to come, life everlasting.   **Amen.**

14 Heavenly Father,
you have promised through your Son Jesus Christ,
that when we meet in his name,
and pray according to his mind,
he will be among us and hear our prayer.
In love and wisdom fulfil our desires,
and give us your greatest gift,
which is to know you, the only true God,
and Jesus Christ our Lord, who lives and reigns
with you and the Holy Spirit,
one God, now and for ever.   **Amen.**

15 Be with us, Lord, in all our prayers,
and direct our way toward the attainment of salvation;
that in the changes and chances of this mortal life
we may always be defended by your gracious help;
through Jesus Christ our Lord.   **Amen.**

16 Almighty and eternal God,
   sanctify our hearts and bodies
   in the ways of your laws
   and in the works of your commandments;
   that under your protection we may be preserved
   in body and soul;
   through Jesus Christ our Lord.   **Amen.**

17 Direct us, O Lord, in all our doings
   with your most gracious favour,
   and further us with your continual help;
   that in all our works begun, continued and ended in you,
   we may glorify your holy name,
   and finally by your mercy attain everlasting life;
   through Jesus Christ our Lord.   **Amen.**

18 **Almighty God,**
   the fountain of all wisdom,
   you know our needs before we ask,
   and our ignorance in asking;
   have compassion on our weakness,
   and give us those things
   which for our unworthiness we dare not,
   and for our blindness we cannot ask;
   for the sake of your Son, Jesus Christ our Lord.   Amen.

19 Almighty God,
   you have promised to hear the prayers
   of those who ask in your Son's name;
   we pray that what we have asked faithfully
   we may obtain effectually;
   through Jesus Christ our Lord.   **Amen.**

WEEKDAY
INTERCESSIONS
AND
THANKSGIVINGS

WEEKDAY INTERCESSIONS AND THANKSGIVINGS

MONDAY

Creation in Christ: Creation and Providence

Almighty God,
maker of all good things and Father of all men;
you have shown us in Christ the purpose of your creation
and call us to be responsible in the world.

Intercession

We pray for THE WORLD
    all the nations . . .
    our own country . . . .
    those in authority . . .
    the peace of the world . . .
    racial harmony . . .
    those who maintain order . . .

Thanksgiving

Almighty God, we give you thanks

for the order of created things
    the resources of the earth
    and the gift of human life . . .

for the continuing work of creation,
    man's share in it,
    and for creative vision and inventive skill . . .

for your faithfulness to man in patience and in love,
    and for every human response of obedience
    and humble achievement . . .

Concluding prayer

May we delight in your purpose
and work to bring all things to their true end;
through Jesus Christ our Lord.   Amen.

TUESDAY

The Incarnate Life of Christ: Revelation and Human Knowledge

God our Father,
you gave your Son, Jesus Christ
to share our life on earth,
to grow in wisdom,
to toil with his hands,
and to make known the ways of your kingdom.

Intercession

We pray for THE COMMUNITY
    those who work . . .
    the unemployed . . .
    those in education . . .
    those in research . . .
    those in communications . . .
    those who maintain the life of the community . . .

Thanksgiving

God our Father, we give you thanks

for Christ's revelation of yourself,
    his care for people,
    and his joy in obedience . . .

for the value he gave to human labour,
    the strength he promised us for service,
    the call to follow in his way . . .

for all opportunities of work and of leisure,
    all truth that we have learned,
    and all discoveries that man has made . . .

Concluding prayer

**Give us growing reverence for the truth,
and such wisdom in the use of knowledge
that your kingdom may be advanced
and your name glorified;
through Jesus Christ our Lord.   Amen.**

WEDNESDAY

The Cross of Christ: Reconciliation and Human Relationships

Holy Father,
you have reconciled us to yourself in Christ;
by your Spirit
you enable us to live as your children.

Intercession

We pray for PERSONAL RELATIONSHIPS
 the home, and family life . . .
 children deprived of home . . .
 friends, relations and neighbours . . .
 relationships in daily life and work . . .
 those who are estranged . . .
 ministries of care and healing . . .

Thanksgiving

Holy Father, we give you thanks

for the obedience of Christ fulfilled in the cross,
 his bearing of the sin of the world,
 his mercy for the world, which never fails . . .

for the joy of human love and friendship,
 the lives to which our own are bound,
 the gift of peace with you and each other . . .

for the communities in whose life we share
 and all relationships
 in which reconciliation may be known . . .

Concluding prayer

**Help us to share in Christ's ministry
and to love and serve one another in peace;
through the same Jesus Christ our Lord,
who in the unity of the Spirit
is one with you for ever.   Amen.**

THURSDAY

The Resurrection of Christ: The Divine Society, the Church

Eternal God,
you have raised Jesus Christ from the dead
and exalted him to your right hand in glory,
and through him called your Church into being,
that your people might know you,
and that they might make your name known.

Intercession

We pray for THE CHURCH
    the Church universal, and local . . .
    the unity of the Church . . .
    the ministries of the Church . . .
    the mission of the Church . . .
    the renewal of the Church . . .
    all Christians in this place . . .

Thanksgiving

Eternal God, we give you thanks

for the apostolic gospel committed to your Church,
    the continuing presence and power of your Spirit,
    the ministry of Word, Sacrament and Prayer . . .

for the divine mission in which we are called to share,
    the will to unity and its fruit in common action,
    the faithful witness of those who are true to Christ . . .

for all works of compassion
    and every service that proclaims your love.

Concluding prayer

**In peace and unity
may your people offer the unfailing sacrifice of praise,
and make your glory known;
through Jesus Christ our Lord.   Amen.**

FRIDAY

The Priestly Ministry of Christ: All that meets Human Need

Gracious God and Father,
you have given your Son for us all,
that his death might be our life
and his affliction our peace.

Intercession

We pray for THE SUFFERING
   the hungry . . .
   the refugees . . .
   the prisoners . . .
   the persecuted . . .
   all who bring sin and suffering to others . . .
   ministries of care and relief . . .

Thanksgiving

Gracious God and Father, we give you thanks

for the cross of Christ at the heart of creation,
   the presence of Christ in our weakness and strength,
   the power of Christ to transform our suffering . . .

for all ministries of healing,
   all agencies of relief,
   all that sets men free from pain, fear and distress . . .

for the assurance that your mercy knows no limit,
   and for the privilege of sharing
   your work of renewal through prayer.

Concluding prayer

**In darkness and in light,
in trouble and in joy,
help us to trust your love, to serve your purpose
and to praise your name;
through Jesus Christ our Lord.   Amen.**

SATURDAY

Consummation in Christ: The Fulfilment of the Divine Purpose

Eternal God,
you have declared in Christ
the completion of all your purpose of love.

Intercession

We pray for THOSE IN NEED
    the tempted and despairing . . . .
    the sick and handicapped . . .
    the aged . . . and the dying . . .
    the ministries of care and healing . . .
    those who mourn . . .

Thanksgiving

Eternal God, we give thanks
for the triumphs of the gospel that herald your salvation
    the signs of renewal that declare
        the coming of your kingdom,
    the human lives that reveal your work of grace . . .

for all those who have died in faith . . .

for the unceasing praise of the company of heaven,
    the promise to those who mourn
        that all tears shall be wiped away,
    the pledge of death destroyed and victory won . . .

for our foretaste of eternal life
        through baptism and eucharist,
    our hope in the Spirit,
    and the communion of saints . . .

Concluding prayer

**May we live by faith, walk in hope and be renewed in love,
until the world reflects your glory
and you are all in all.
Even so, come Lord Jesus.   Amen.**

THE CANTICLES

A NOTE ON CHANTING THE CANTICLES AND PSALMS

The psalms and canticles are pointed for singing to Anglican chants. In good chanting the rhythm and sense of the words are of paramount importance and should be similar to good deliberate speaking, with a natural flexible flow free from monotony and exaggeration.

⏐ in the text corresponds with a bar line in the chant.

· between two words or syllables shows the division of notes within the bar.

* shows where a breath should be taken. A shorter break, or mental comma, made without taking a breath, is indicated by an extra space between words. Breath is to be taken at the end of lines except when the pointing clearly forbids it, or when ‿ is used to indicate a carry-over to the following line.

† indicates the use of the second half of a double chant.

Verses between square brackets may be omitted.

A double space between verses indicates a change of mood in the psalm.

The Jewish doxologies which conclude Books 1 to 4 of the Psalter (see Psalms 41, 72, 89, 106) are enclosed within round brackets. When 'Glory to the Father . . .' is used, they may be omitted.

The following notes, for congregations and choirs alike, may assist towards good chanting:

From time to time it is good practice to read aloud together in a deliberate manner to establish the natural flow of the phrases. Then some of the singers should chant softly while the others continue to read.

The recitation portion in each verse (before the first bar line) should not be hurried. Particular care should be taken not to distort the two syllables before the first bar line.

A final unstressed syllable of a verse should be sung lightly. Prepositions and conjunctions should generally be sung lightly.

Single syllable words vary in length and importance, unimportant ones should be sung lightly. Long words should be given due spaciousness and rhythm. In good chanting the words always sound fluent and natural.

THE CANTICLES

1   VENITE   *Psalm 95 verses 1 – 7 or 1 – 11*

1 O come let us sing | out · to the | Lord:
   let us shout in triumph to the | rock of | our sal|vation.

2 Let us come before his | face with | thanksgiving:
   and cry | out · to him | joyfully · in | psalms.

3 For the Lord is a | great | God:
   and a great | king a·bove | all | gods.

4 In his hand are the | depths · of the | earth:
   and the peaks of the | mountains · are | his | also.

†5 The sea is his and | he | made it:
   his hands | moulded | dry | land.

6 Come let us worship and | bow | down:
   and kneel be|fore the | Lord our | maker.

7 For he is the | Lord our | God:
   we are his | people · and the | sheep of · his | pasture.

[8 Today if only you would | hear his | voice:
   do not harden your | hearts · as you | did · in the |
   wilderness.

9 When your | fathers | tested me:
   put me to the proof though | they had | seen my |
   works.

10 Forty years long I loathed that gener|ation · and | said:
   It is a people who err in their hearts
     for they | do not | know my | ways.

11 Of whom I | swore · in my | wrath:
   They | shall not | enter · my | rest.]

Glory to the Father and | to the | Son:
   and | to the | Holy | Spirit;

as it was in the be|ginning · is | now:
   and shall be for | ever | A-|men.

VENITE   *(Old form)*

1 O come let us | sing un·to the | Lord:
      let us heartily rejoice in the | strength of |
            our sal|vation.

2 Let us come before his | presence · with | thanksgiving:
      and shew ourselves | glad in | him with | psalms.

3 For the Lord is a | great | God:
      and a great | King a·bove | all | gods.

4 In his hand are all the corners | of the | earth:
      and the strength of the | hills is | his | also.

†5 The sea is his and | he | made it:
      and his | hands pre|pared the · dry | land.

6 O come let us worship and | fall | down:
      and kneel be|fore the | Lord our | Maker.

7 For he is the | Lord our | God:
      and we are the people of his pasture |
            and the | sheep of · his | hand.

[8 Today if ye will | hear his | voice:
      harden not your hearts * as in the provocation
            and as in the day of temp|tation | in the | wilderness;

9 When your | fathers | tempted me:
      prov-ed | me and | saw my | works.

10 Forty years long was I grieved with this gener|ation ·
            and | said:
      It is a people that do err in their hearts
            for they | have not | known my | ways.

11 Unto whom I sware | in my | wrath:
      that they should not | enter | into · my | rest.]

   Glory to the Father and | to the | Son:
      and | to the | Holy | Spirit;

   as it was in the be|ginning · is | now:
      and shall be for | ever | A-|men.

2 JUBILATE

Psalm 100

1 O shout to the Lord in triumph | all the | earth:
   serve the Lord with gladness
       and come before his | face with | songs of | joy.

2 Know that the Lord | he is | God:
   it is he who has made us and we are his
       we are his | people · and the | sheep of · his | pasture.

3 Come into his gates with thanksgiving
       and into his | courts with | praise:
   give thanks to him and | bless his | holy | name.

4 For the Lord is good * his loving mercy | is for | ever:
   his faithfulness through|out all | gener|ations.

   Glory to the Father and | to the | Son:
       and to | the | Holy | Spirit;

   as it was in the be|ginning · is | now:
       and shall be for | ever | A-|men.

JUBILATE   *(Old form)*

1 O be joyful in the Lord I all ye I lands:
    serve the Lord with gladness
        and come before his I presence I with a I song.

2 Be ye sure that the Lord I he is I God:
    it is he that hath made us and not we ourselves
        we are his people I and the I sheep of · his I pasture.

3 O go your way into his gates with thanksgiving
        and into his I courts with I praise:
    be thankful unto him and speak I good of I his I name.

4 For the Lord is gracious   his mercy is I everllasting:
    and his truth endureth from generlation · to I
        generlation.

  Glory to the Father and I to the I Son:
    and I to the I Holy I Spirit;

  as it was in the belginning · is I now:
    and shall be for I ever I A-lmen.

3 THE EASTER ANTHEMS

1 Cor.5.7,8   Rom.6.9-11   1 Cor.15.20-22

1 Christ our passover has been | sacri·ficed | for us:
   therefore let us | cele|brate the | feast.

2 Not with the old leaven of cor|ruption · and | wickedness:
   but with the unleavened | bread of · sin|cerity · and |
   truth.

3 Christ   once raised from the dead | dies no | more:
   death has no | more do|minion | over him.

4 In dying   he died to sin | once for | all:
   in | living · he | lives to | God.

5 See yourselves therefore as | dead to | sin:
   and alive to God in | Jesus | Christ our | Lord.

6 Christ has been | raised · from the | dead:
   the | firstfruits · of | those who | sleep.

7 For as by | man came | death:
   by man has come also the resur|rection | of the | dead.

8 For as in | Adam · all | die:
   even so in Christ shall | all be | made a|live.

Glory to the Father and | to the | Son:
   and | to the | Holy | Spirit;

as it was in the be|ginning · is | now:
   and shall be for | ever | A-|men.

THE EASTER ANTHEMS *(Old form)*

1 Christ our passover is | sacri·ficed | for us:
      therefore let | us | keep the | feast,

2 Not with the old leaven
            nor with the leaven of | malice · and | wickedness:
      but with the unleavened bread | of sin|cerity · and |
            truth.

3 Christ being raised from the dead | dieth · no | more:
      death hath no | more do|minion | over him.

4 For in that he died   he died unto | sin | once:
      but in that he liveth   he | liveth | unto | God.

5 Likewise reckon ye also yourselves to be dead indeed |
            unto | sin:
      but alive unto God through | Jesus | Christ our | Lord.

6 Christ is | risen · from the | dead:
      and become the first|fruits of | them that | slept.

7 For since by | man came | death:
      by man came also the resur|rection | of the | dead.

8 For as in Adam | all | die:
      even so in Christ shall | all be | made a|live.

Glory to the Father and | to the | Son:
      and | to the | Holy | Spirit;

as it was in the be|ginning · is | now:
      and shall be for | ever | A-|men.

4 BENEDICTUS   The Song of Zechariah

Luke 1.68-79

1 Blessèd be the Lord the | God of | Israel:
   he has come to his | people · and | set them | free.

2 He has raised up for us a | mighty | saviour:
   born of the | house · of his | servant | David.

3 Through his holy prophets he | promised · of | old:
   that he would save us from our enemies
      from the | hands of | those who | hate us.

4 He promised to show | mercy · to our | fathers:
   and to re|member his | holy | covenant.

5 This was the oath he swore to our | father | Abraham:
   to set us | free · from the | hand of · our | enemies.

6 Free to worship him with|out | fear:
   holy and righteous in his sight | all the | days · of our |
      life.

7 You my child shall be called the prophet of the | Most |
      High:
   for you will go before the | Lord · to pre|pare his | way.

8 To give his people knowledge | of sal|vation:
   by the for|giveness · of | all their | sins.

9 In the tender compassion | of our | God:
   the dawn from on | high shall | break up|on us.

10 To shine on those who dwell in darkness ⌣
      and the | shadow · of | death:
   and to guide our feet | into · the | way of | peace.

   Glory to the Father and | to the | Son:
      and | to the | Holy | Spirit;

   as it was in the be|ginning · is | now:
      and shall be for | ever | A-|men.

BENEDICTUS   *(Old form)*

1 Bless-ed be the Lord | God of | Israel:
    for he hath visited | and re|deemed his | people,

2 And hath raised up a mighty sal|vation | for us:
    in the | house of · his | servant | David;

3 As he spake by the mouth of his | holy | Prophets:
    which have been | since the | world be|gan;

4 That we should be | saved · from our | enemies:
    and from the | hands of | all that | hate us,

5 To perform the mercy | promised · to our | forefathers:
    and to re|member · his | holy | covenant;

6 To perform the oath which he sware⌣
        to our | fore·father | Abraham:
    that | he would | give | us,

7 That we being delivered out of the | hand of · our |
        enemies:
    might serve | him with|out | fear,

8 In holiness and | righteous·ness be|fore him:
    all the | days | of our | life.

9 And thou child shalt be called the | Prophet · of the |
        Highest:
    for thou shalt go before the face of the | Lord ·
        to pre|pare his | ways;

10 To give knowledge of salvation | unto · his | people:
    for the re|mission | of their | sins,

11 Through the tender mercy | of our | God:
    whereby the day-spring from on | high hath | visit·ed |
        us,

12 To give light to them that sit in darkness
        and in the | shadow · of | death:
    and to guide our feet | into · the | way of | peace.

Glory to the Father and | to the | Son:
    and | to the | Holy | Spirit;

as it was in the be|ginning · is | now:
    and shall be for | ever | A-|men.

5 BENEDICITE

The Song of the Three 35-65

1 Bless the Lord | all cre|ated things:
   sing his | praise · and ex|alt him · for | ever.
2 Bless the | Lord you | heavens:
   sing his | praise · and ex|alt him · for | ever.

3 Bless the Lord you | angels · of the | Lord:
   bless the | Lord all | you his | hosts.
4 Bless the Lord you waters a|bove the | heavens:
   sing his | praise · and ex|alt him · for | ever.

5 Bless the Lord | sun and | moon:
   bless the | Lord you | stars of | heaven.
6 Bless the Lord all | rain and | dew:
   sing his | praise · and ex|alt him · for | ever.

7 Bless the Lord all | winds that | blow:
   bless the | Lord you | fire and | heat.
8 Bless the Lord scorching wind and | bitter | cold:
   sing his | praise · and ex|alt him · for | ever.

9 Bless the Lord dews and | falling | snows:
   bless the | Lord you | nights and | days.
10 Bless the Lord | light and | darkness:
   sing his | praise · and ex|alt him · for | ever.

11 Bless the Lord | frost and | cold:
   bless the | Lord you | ice and | snow.
12 Bless the Lord | lightnings · and | clouds:
   sing his | praise · and ex|alt him · for | ever.

13 O let the earth | bless the | Lord:
   bless the | Lord you | mountains · and | hills.
14 Bless the Lord all that | grows · in the | ground:
   sing his | praise · and ex|alt him · for | ever.

15 Bless the | Lord you | springs:
   bless the | Lord you | seas and | rivers.
16 Bless the Lord you whales and all that | swim · in the |
   waters:
   sing his | praise · and ex|alt him · for | ever.

17 Bless the Lord all ǀ birds · of the ǀ air:
    bless the ǀ Lord you ǀ beasts and ǀ cattle.
18 Bless the Lord all ǀ men · on the ǀ earth:
    sing his ǀ praise · and exǀalt him · for ǀ ever.

19 O people of God ǀ bless the ǀ Lord:
    bless the ǀ Lord you ǀ priests · of the ǀ Lord.
20 Bless the Lord you ǀ servants · of the ǀ Lord:
    sing his ǀ praise · and exǀalt him · for ǀ ever.

21 Bless the Lord all men of ǀ upright ǀ spirit:
    bless the Lord you that are ǀ holy · and ǀ humble · in ǀ
        heart.
22 Bless the Father the Son and the ǀ Holy ǀ Spirit:
    sing his ǀ praise · and exǀalt him · for ǀ ever.

Old form overleaf

BENEDICITE   *(Old form)*

1 O all ye works of the Lord ı bless · ye the ı Lord:
  praise him and ı magni·fy ı him for ı ever.

2 O ye Angels of the Lord ı bless · ye the ı Lord:
  O ye ı Heavens ı bless · ye the ı Lord.

3 O ye Waters that be above the Firmament ı ⌣
      bless · ye the ı Lord:
  O all ye Powers of the ı Lord ı bless · ye the ı Lord.

4 O ye Sun and Moon ı bless · ye the ı Lord:
  O ye Stars of ı Heaven ı bless · ye the ı Lord.

5 O ye Showers and Dew ı bless · ye the ı Lord:
  O ye Winds of ı God ı bless · ye the ı Lord.

6 O ye Fire and Heat ı bless · ye the ı Lord:
  O ye Winter and ı Summer ı bless · ye the ı Lord.

7 O ye Dews and Frosts ı bless · ye the ı Lord:
  O ye Frost and ı Cold ı bless · ye the ı Lord.

8 O ye Ice and Snow ı bless · ye the ı Lord:
  O ye Nights and ı Days ı bless · ye the ı Lord.

†9 O ye Light and Darkness ı bless · ye the ı Lord:
  O ye Lightnings and ı Clouds ı bless · ye the ı Lord.

10 O let the Earth ı bless the ı Lord:
  yea let it praise him and ı magni·fy ı him for ı ever.

11 O ye Mountains and Hills ı bless · ye the ı Lord:
  O all ye Green Things upon the ı Earth ı ⌣
      bless · ye the ı Lord.

12 O ye Wells ı bless · ye the ı Lord:
  O ye Seas and ı Floods ı bless · ye the ı Lord.

13 O ye Whales and all that move in the Waters ı ⌣
      bless · ye the ı Lord:
  O all ye Fowls of the ı Air ı bless · ye the ı Lord.

†14 O all ye Beasts and Cattle ı bless · ye the ı Lord:
  O ye Children of ı Men ı bless · ye the ı Lord.

15 O let Israel | bless the | Lord:
    praise him and | magni·fy | him for | ever.

16 O ye Priests of the Lord | bless · ye the | Lord:
    O ye Servants of the | Lord | bless · ye the | Lord.

17 O ye Spirits and Souls of the Righteous | bless · ye the |
    Lord:
    O ye holy and humble Men of | heart | bless · ye the |
    Lord.

18 O Ananias Azarias and Misael | bless · ye the | Lord:
    praise him and | magni·fy him for | ever.

†19 Bless the Father the Son and the | Holy | Spirit:
    sing his | praise · and ex|alt him · for | ever.

6 TE DEUM

Part 1

1 You are I God   we I praise you:
   you are the I Lord and I we ac|claim you;

2 You are the e|ternal I Father:
   all cre|ation I worships I you.

3 To you all angels * all the I powers of I heaven:
   cherubim and seraphim I sing in I endless I praise,

4 Holy holy holy Lord * God of I power and I might:
   heaven and I earth are I full of · your I glory.

5 The glorious company of a|postles I praise you:
   the noble fellowship of prophets praise you
      the white-robed I army of I martyrs I praise you.

6 Throughout the world the holy I Church ac|claims you:
   Father   of I majes|ty un|bounded;

†7 Your true and only Son I worthy of I worship:
   and the Holy I Spirit I advocate · and I guide.

Part 2

8 You Christ are the I King of I glory:
   the e|ternal I Son · of the I Father.

9 When you became man to I set us I free:
   you did not ab|hor the I Virgin's I womb.

10 You overcame the I sting of I death:
   and opened the kingdom of I heaven to I all be|lievers.

11 You are seated at God's right I hand in I glory:
   we believe that you will I come   and I be our I judge.

12 Come then Lord to the I help of · your I people:
   bought with the I price of I your own I blood.

13 And bring us I with your I saints:
   to I ever|lasting I glory.

Part 3

14 Save your people Lord and | bless · your in|heritance:
  govern them and up|hold them | now and | always.

15 Day by | day we | bless you:
  we | praise your | name for | ever.

16 Today Lord keep us from | all | sin:
  have | mercy · on us | Lord have | mercy.

17 Lord show us your | love and | mercy:
  for we | put our |trust in | you.

†18 In you Lord | is our | hope:
  may we | never | be con|founded.

Old form overleaf

TE DEUM *(Old form)*

Part 1

1 We praise I thee O I God:
  we acknowledge I thee to I be the I Lord.

2 All the earth doth I worship I thee:
  the I Father I ever I lasting.

3 To thee all angels cry aloud
    the heavens and all the I Powers there I in:
  to thee Cherubim and Seraphim con I tin·ual I ly do I cry,

4 Holy Holy Holy * Lord I God · of Sa I baoth:
  heaven and earth are full of the I Majes·ty I of thy I
    glory.

5 The glorious company of the Apostles I praise I thee:
  the goodly fellowship of the I Prophets I praise I thee.

6 The I noble I army: ⌣
  of I Martyrs I praise I thee.

7 The I holy I Church:
  throughout all the world I doth ac I knowledge I thee;

8 The Father of an I infin·ite I Majesty:
  thine honourable true and only Son
    also the I Holy I Ghost the I Comforter.

Part 2

9 Thou I art the I King: ⌣
  of I glory I O I Christ.

10 Thou art the ever I lasting I Son: ⌣
  of I – the I Fa I ther.

11 When thou tookest upon thee to de I liver I man:
  thou didst not ab I hor the I Virgin's I womb.

12 When thou hadst overcome the I sharpness · of I death:
  thou didst open the kingdom of I heaven · to I
    all be I lievers.

13 Thou sittest at the right I hand of I God:
  in the I glory I of the I Father.

14 We be I lieve that I thou: ⌣
  shalt I come to I be our I judge.

15 We therefore pray thee | help thy | servants:
whom thou hast redeem-ed | with thy | precious |
blood.

16 Make them to be numbered | with thy | Saints:
in | glory | ever|lasting.

Part 3

17 O Lord save thy people   and | bless thine | heritage:
govern them and | lift them | up for | ever.

18 Day by day we | magni·fy | thee:
and we worship thy Name ever | world with|out |
end.

19 Vouch|safe O | Lord:
to | keep us · this | day with·out | sin.

20 O Lord have | mercy · up|on us:
have | mercy · up|on | us.

21 O Lord let thy mercy | lighten · up|on us:
as our | trust | is in | thee.

22 O Lord in thee | have I | trusted:
let me | never | be con|founded.

7 MAGNIFICAT   The Song of the Blessed Virgin Mary

Luke 1.46-55

1 My soul proclaims the | greatness · of the | Lord:
  my spirit re|joices in | God my | Saviour.

2 For he has looked with favour on his | lowly | servant:
  and from this day all gener|ations · will | call me |
  blessèd.

†3 The Almighty has done | great things | for me:
  and | holy | is his | name.

4 He has mercy on | those who | fear him:
  in | every | gener|ation.

5 He has shown the | strength · of his | arm:
  he has scattered the | proud in | their con|ceit.

6 He has cast down the mighty | from their | thrones:
  and has | lifted | up the | lowly.

7 He has filled the hungry with | good | things:
  and sent the | rich · empty|handed a|way.

8 He has come to the help of his | servant | Israel:
  for he has re|membered · his | promise of | mercy.

9 The promise he | made · to our | fathers:
  to Abraham | and his | children · for | ever.

  Glory to the Father and | to the | Son:
  and | to the | Holy | Spirit;

  as it was in the be|ginning · is | now:
  and shall be for | ever | A-|men.

MAGNIFICAT   *(Old form)*

1 My soul doth | magni·fy the | Lord:
   and my spirit hath re|joiced in | God my | Saviour.

2 For | he · hath re|garded: ‿
   the lowliness | of his | hand|maiden.

3 For | – be|hold:
   from henceforth all gener|ations · shall | call me |
      blessèd.

4 For he that is mighty hath | magni·fied | me:
   and | holy | is his | Name.

†5 And his mercy is on | them that | fear him:
   through|out all | gener|ations.

6 He hath shew-ed | strength · with his | arm:
   he hath scattered the proud‿
      in the imagin|ation | of their | hearts.

7 He hath put down the mighty | from their | seat:
   and hath ex|alted · the | humble · and | meek.

8 He hath filled the hungry with | good | things:
   and the rich | he hath · sent | empty · a|way.

9 He remembering his mercy hath holpen his | servant |
      Israel:
   as he promised to our forefathers
      Abraham | and his | seed for | ever.

   Glory to the Father and | to the | Son:
   and | to the | Holy | Spirit;

   as it was in the be|ginning · is | now:
   and shall be for | ever | A-|men.

8 NUNC DIMITTIS   The Song of Simeon

Luke 2.29-32

1 Lord now you let your servant I go in I peace:
  your I word has I been ful|filled.

2 My own eyes have I seen the · sal|vation:
  which you have prepared in the I sight of I every I
    people.

3 A light to re|veal you · to the I nations:
  and the I glory · of your I people I Israel.

  Glory to the Father and I to the I Son:
    and I to the I Holy I Spirit;

  as it was in the be|ginning · is I now:
    and shall be for I ever I   A-|men.

NUNC DIMITTIS *(Old form)*

1 Lord   now lettest thou thy servant de|part in I peace:
  ac|cording I to thy I word.

2 For mine eyes have seen I thy sal|vation:
  which thou hast prepared be|fore the I face of · all I
    people;

3 To be a light to I lighten · the I Gentiles:
  and to be the glory of thy I people I Isra|el.

  Glory to the Father and I to the I Son:
    and I to the I Holy I Spirit;

  as it was in the be|ginning · is I now:
    and shall be for I ever I   A-|men.

HAIL, GLADDENING LIGHT

1 Hail, gladdening light, of his pure glory poured,
   Who is the immortal Father, heavenly, blest,
   Holiest of holies, Jesus Christ our Lord.

2 Now we are come to the sun's hour of rest.
   The lights of evening round us shine:
   We hymn the Father, Son, and Holy Spirit divine.

3 Worthiest art thou at all times to be sung
   With undefiled tongue.
   Son of our God, giver of life, alone:
   Therefore in all the world thy glories, Lord, they own.

GREAT AND WONDERFUL

Revelation 15.3,4,7,10,12

1 Great and wonderful are your deeds Lord I God ·
      the Al¡mighty:
   just and true are your I ways O I King · of the I nations.

2 Who shall not revere and praise your I name O I Lord:
   for I you a¡lone are I holy.

3 All nations shall come and worship I in your I presence:
   for your just I dealings · have I been re¡vealed.

4 To him who sits on the throne I and · to the I Lamb:
   be praise and honour glory and might
      for ever and I ever I   A–¡men.

11 URBS FORTITUDINIS

Isaiah 26. 1-4, 7, 8

1 We have a I strong I city:
   salvation will God apIpoint for I walls and I bulwarks.

2 Open I ye the I gates:
   that the righteous nation which keepeth the I
      truth may I enter I in.

3 Thou wilt keep him in perfect peace⌣
      whose mind is I stayed on I thee:
   beIcause he I trusteth · in I thee.

4 Trust ye in the I Lord for I ever:
   for our rock of I ages I is the I Lord.

5 The way of the I just is I uprightness:
   thou that art upright dost diIrect the I path · of the I
      just.

6 Yea in the way of thy judgments O Lord⌣
      have we I waited · for I thee:
   the desire of our soul is to thy Name   I
      and · to the reImembrance · of I thee.

   Glory to the Father and I to the I Son:
      and I to the I Holy I Spirit;

   as it was in the beIginning · is I now:
      and shall be for I ever I   A-Imen.

12 GLORIA IN EXCELSIS

1 Glory to | God · in the | highest:
and | peace · to his | people · on | earth.

2 Lord God heavenly King * Almighty God and Father
we worship you we | give you | thanks:
we | praise you | for your | glory.

3 Lord Jesus Christ only Son of the Father
Lord God | Lamb of | God:
you take away the sin of the | world * have | mercy |
on us.

4 You are seated at the right hand | of the | Father:
re|ceive | our | prayer.

5 For you a|lone · are the | Holy One:
you a|lone | are the | Lord.

6 You alone are the Most High   Jesus Christ   with the |
Holy | Spirit:
in the glory of God the | Father | A–|men.

13 SAVIOUR OF THE WORLD

Suitable for use in penitential seasons

1 Jesus Saviour of the world * come to us I in your I mercy:
    we look to I you to I save and I help us.

2 By your cross and your life laid down * you set your I
    people I free:
    we look to I you to I save and I help us.

3 When they were ready to perish you I saved ·
    your disIciples:
    we look to I you to I come to · our I help.

4 In the greatness of your mercy loose us I from our I
    chains:
    forgive the I sins of I all your I people.

†5 Make yourself known as our Saviour and I mighty ·
    DeIliverer:
    save and I help us · that I we may I praise you.

6 Come now and dwell with us I Lord Christ I Jesus:
    hear our I prayer · and be I with us I always.

7 And when you I come in · your I glory:
    make us to be one with you
    and to share the life of your I kingdom I A–Imen.

14 BLESS THE LORD

The Song of the Three 29-34

1 Bless the Lord the | God of · our | fathers:
    sing his | praise · and ex|alt him · for | ever.

2 Bless his holy and | glori·ous | name:
    sing his | praise · and ex|alt him · for | ever.

3 Bless him in his holy and | glori·ous | temple:
    sing his | praise · and ex|alt him · for | ever.

4 Bless him who be|holds the | depths:
    sing his | praise · and ex|alt him · for | ever.

5 Bless him seated be|tween the | cherubim:
    sing his | praise · and ex|alt him · for | ever.

6 Bless him on the | throne of · his | kingdom:
    sing his | praise · and ex|alt him · for | ever.

7 Bless him in the | heights of | heaven:
    sing his | praise · and ex|alt him · for | ever.

8 Bless the Father the Son and the | Holy | Spirit:
    sing his | praise · and ex|alt him · for | ever.

15 GLORY AND HONOUR

Revelation 4.11 and 5.9,10,13b

1 Glory and | honour · and | power:
   are yours by | right O | Lord our | God.

2 For you cre|ated | all things:
   and by your | will they | have their | being.

3 Glory and | honour · and | power:
   are yours by | right O | Lamb · for us | slain;

4 For by your blood you ransomed | men for | God:
   from every race and language
      from | every | people · and | nation.

5 To make them a | kingdom of | priests:
   to stand and | serve be|fore our | God.

6 To him who sits on the throne | and · to the | Lamb:
   be praise and honour   glory and might
      for ever and | ever | A–|men.

16 THE SONG OF CHRIST'S GLORY

Phil.2.6-11

1 Christ Jesus was in the | form of | God:
   but he did not | cling · to e|quality · with | God.

2 He emptied himself * taking the | form · of a | servant:
   and was | born · in the | likeness · of | men.

3 And being found in human form he | humbled · him|self:
   and became obedient unto death | even | death ·
      on a | cross.

4 Therefore God has | highly · ex|alted him:
   and bestowed on him the | name a·bove | every | name.

5 That at the name of Jesus every | knee should | bow:
   in heaven and on | earth and | under · the | earth.

6 And every tongue confess that Jesus | Christ is | Lord:
   to the glory of God the | Father | A–|men.

THE PSALTER

Glory to the Father and ǀ to the ǀ Son:
   and ǀ to the ǀ Holy ǀ Spirit;

as it was in the beǀginning is ǀ now:
   and shall be for ǀ ever ǀ   A-ǀmen.

For notes on chanting, see p. 105.

PSALM 1

1 Blessèd is the man who has not walked␣
    in the counsel | of the · un|godly:
  nor followed the way of sinners
    nor taken his | seat a|mongst the | scornful.

2 But his delight is in the | law · of the | Lord:
    and on that law will he | ponder | day and | night.

3 He is like a tree planted beside | streams of | water:
    that yields its | fruit in | due | season.

4 Its leaves also | shall not | wither:
    and look what|ever · he | does · it shall | prosper.

5 As for the ungodly * it is not | so with | them:
    they are like the | chaff · which the | wind | scatters.

6 Therefore the ungodly shall not stand | up · at the | judgment:
    nor sinners in the congre|gation | of the | righteous.

†7 For the Lord cares for the | way · of the | righteous:
    but the | way of · the un|godly · shall | perish.

PSALM 2

1 Why are the | nations · in | tumult:
    and why do the peoples | cherish · a | vain | dream?

2 The kings of the earth rise up
    and the rulers con|spire to|gether:
  against the Lord and a|gainst · his an|ointed | saying,

†3 'Let us break their | bonds a|sunder:
    let us throw | off their | chains | from us.'

4 He that dwells in heaven shall | laugh them · to | scorn:
    the Lord will | hold them | in de|rision.

5 Then will he speak to them in his wrath
    and terrify them | in his | fury:
  'I the Lord have set up my king on | Zion · my | holy | hill.'

6 I will announce the Lord's decree
    that which | he has | spoken:
  'You are my son   this | day have | I be|gotten you.

7 'Ask of me   and I will give you the nations for |
    your in|heritance:
  the uttermost parts of the | earth for |
    your pos|session.

†8 'You shall break them with a | rod of | iron:
  and shatter them in | pieces · like a | potter's | vessel.'

9 Now therefore be | wise O | kings:
  be advised   you that are | judges | of the | earth.

10 Serve the Lord with awe
    and govern yourselves in | fear and | trembling:
  lest he be angry and you | perish | in your | course.

†11 For his wrath is | quickly | kindled:
  blessèd are those that | turn to | him for | refuge.

PSALM 3

1 Lord how numerous | are my | enemies:
  many they | are that | rise a|gainst me.

2 Many there are that | talk of me · and | say:
  'There is no | help for · him | in his | God.'

3 But you Lord are about me | as a | shield:
  you are my glory   and the | lifter | up · of my | head.

4 I cry to the Lord with a | loud | voice:
  and he answers me | from his | holy | hill.

5 I lay myself | down and | sleep:
  I wake again be|cause the | Lord sus|tains me.

6 Therefore I will not be afraid⸺
    of the multitudes | of the | nations:
  who have set themselves a|gainst me · on | every |
    side.

7 Arise Lord   and deliver me | O my | God:
  for you will strike all my enemies upon the cheek
  you will | break the | teeth of · the un|godly.

8 Deliverance be|longs · to the | Lord:
  O let your | blessing · be up|on your | people.

PSALM 4

1 Answer me when I call O | God of · my |
    righteousness:
  when I was hard-pressed you set me free
    be gracious to me | now and | hear my | prayer.

2 Sons of men   how long will you turn my | glory ·
    to my | shame:
  how long will you love what is worthless
    and | seek | after | lies?

3 Know that the Lord has shown me his | wonder·ful |
    kindness:
  when I call to the | Lord | he will | hear me.

4 Tremble and | do no | sin:
  commune with your own heart up|on your | bed ·
    and be | still.

5 Offer the sacrifices | that are | right:
  and | put your | trust · in the | Lord.

6 There are many who say   'Who will | show us · any |
    good?:
  the light of your countenance O | Lord has | gone |
    from us.'

7 Yet you have given my | heart more | gladness:
  than they have when their corn | wine and |
    oil in|crease.

8 In peace I will lie | down and | sleep:
  for you alone Lord | make me | dwell in | safety.

PSALM 5

1 Hear my words O Lord   give | heed · to my | groaning:
  listen to my cry   you that are my | king | and my |
    God.

2 In the morning when I pray to you
    surely you will | hear my | voice:
  at daybreak I lay my prayers be|fore you · and | look |
    up.

3 For you are not a God who takes I pleasure · in I
   wickedness:
   nor can any I evil I dwell with I you.

4 The boastful cannot I stand in · your I sight:
   you hate all I those that I work I mischief.

5 Those who speak I lies · you desItroy:
   you abhor the treacherous O Lord
       and I those · that are I stained with I blood.

6 But because of your great goodness ⌣
   I will I come into ·˙ your I house:
   I will bow down toward your holy I
       temple · in I awe and I fear of you.

7 Lead me O Lord in your righteousness
       for my enemies I lie in I wait:
   make I straight your I way beIfore me.

8 For there is no I truth · in their I mouth:
   and within they are I eaten I up by I malice.

9 Their throat is an I open I sepulchre:
   and their tongue speaks I smooth and I flatter·ing I
       words.

10 Destroy them O God * let them fall by their I
       own conItriving:
   cast them out for their many offences
       for I they have · reIbelled aIgainst you.

11 But let all who put their trust in I you reIjoice:
   let them I shout with I joy for I ever.

12 Be the defender of those who I love your I name:
   let them exIult beIcause of I you.

†13 For you will bless O Lord the I man · that is I righteous:
   you will cover him with your I favour I as · with a I
       shield.

PSALM 6

1 O Lord rebuke me not in your I indigInation:
   nor chasten me I in your I fierce disIpleasure.

2 Have mercy upon me O Lord for I I am I weak:
   O Lord heal me for my I very I bones · are aIfraid.

3 My soul also is I greatly I troubled:
   and you Lord how I long will I you deIlay?

4 Turn again O Lord and deIliver · my I soul:
   O save me I for your I mercy's I sake.

5 For in death I no man · reImembers you:
   and who can I give you I thanks · from the I grave?

6 I am wearied I with my I groaning:
   every night I drown my bed with weeping
      and I water · my I couch · with my I tears.

†7 My eyes waste aIway for I sorrow:
   they grow dim beIcause of I all my I enemies.

8 Away from me all I you that · do I evil:
   for the Lord has I heard the I voice · of my I weeping.

9 The Lord has heard my I suppliIcation:
   the I Lord · will reIceive my I prayer.

†10 All my enemies shall be put to shame and I greatly ·
        disImayed:
   they shall turn back and be conIfounded I in a I
        moment.

PSALM 7

1 O Lord my God   to you have I I come for I shelter:
   save me from all who pursue me * O I save I and
      deIliver me,

2 Lest like lions they I tear my I throat:
   lest they carry me I off and I none can I save me.

3 O Lord my God   if I have I done · such a I thing:
   if there is any I wicked·ness I on my I hands,

4 If I have repaid with evil him that I was my I friend:
   or plundered my I enemy · withIout just I cause,

†5 Then let the enemy pursue me and | over|take me:
　　let him trample my life to the ground
　　　　and lay my | honour | in the | dust.

6 Arise O | Lord · in your | anger:
　　rise up in | wrath a|gainst my | adversaries.

7 Awake my God * you that or|dain | justice:
　　and let the assembly of the | peoples |
　　　　gather · a|bout you;

8 Take your seat | high a|bove them:
　　and sit in judgment O | Lord | over · the | nations.

9 Judge for me O Lord　according | to my | righteousness:
　　and | as · my in|tegrity · re|quires.

10 Let the wickedness of the ungodly cease
　　　　but es|tablish · the | righteous:
　　for you try the very hearts and minds of | men ⏜
　　　　O | righteous | God.

11 God is my | shield | over me:
　　he pre|serves the | true of | heart.

12 God is a | righteous | judge:
　　and God condemns | evil | every | day.

13 If a man does not turn he | whets his | sword:
　　he bends his | bow and | makes it | ready;

†14 He prepares the | instruments · of | death:
　　and makes his | arrows | darts of | fire.

15 See how the ungodly con|ceives | mischief:
　　how he swells with wickedness | and gives | birth to |
　　　lies.

16 He digs a pit and | hollows · it | out:
　　but falls himself into the | trap · he had | made for |
　　　others.

17 His mischief rebounds upon his | own | head:
　　and his violence comes | down · on his | own | pate.

18 I will thank the | Lord · for his | justice:
　　I will sing | praises · to the | Lord Most | High.

PSALM 8

1 O | Lord our | Governor:
   how glorious is your | name in | all the | earth!

2 Your majesty above the heavens is | yet re|counted:
   by the | mouths of | babes and | sucklings.

†3 You have founded a strong defence _
    a|gainst your | adversaries:
   to quell the | ene·my | and · the a|venger.

4 When I consider your heavens the | work of · your |
    fingers:
   the moon and the stars which | you have | set in |
    order,

5 What is man   that you should be | mindful | of him:
   or the son of | man that | you should | care for him?

6 Yet you have made him little | less · than a | god:
   and have | crowned him · with | glory · and | honour.

7 You have made him the | master · of your | handiwork:
   and have put all things in sub|jection · be|neath his |
    feet,

8 All | sheep and | oxen:
   and all the | creatures | of the | field,

9 The birds of the air and the | fish · of the | sea:
   and everything that moves _
    in the pathways | of the | great | waters.

†10 O | Lord our | Governor:
    how glorious is your | name in | all the | earth!

PSALM 9

1 I will give you thanks O Lord with my | whole | heart:
   I will tell of all the | wonders | you have | done.

2 I will re|joice · and be | glad in you:
   I will make my songs to your | name | O Most | High.

3 For my enemies are | driven | back:
   they stumble and | perish | at your | presence.

4 You have maintained my I cause · and my I right:
    you sat enIthroned · as a I righteous I judge.

5 You rebuked the heathen nations
    you brought the I wicked · to deIstruction:
    you blotted out their I name for I ever · and I ever.

6 The strongholds of the enemy are made a perpetual I
    desoIlation:
    you plucked up their cities ⌣
    and I even · their I memory · has I perished.

7 The Lord confounds them * but the Lord enIdures for I
    ever:
    he has I set up · his I throne for I judgment.

8 He shall judge the I world with I righteousness:
    and deal true I justice I to the I peoples.

9 The Lord is a strong tower to I him that · is opIpressed:
    he is a tower of I strength in I time of I need.

10 All who heed your name will I trust in I you:
    for you have never forIsaken I those that I seek you.

11 O sing praises to the Lord who I dwells in I Zion:
    tell among the peoples what I great things I he has I
    done.

12 For he that avenges blood has reImembered · the I poor:
    he has I not forIgotten · their I cry.

13 The Lord has been merciful toward me
    he saw what I I suffered · from my I foes:
    he raised me up aIgain · from the I gates of I death,

14 That I might tell all your praises in the I gates of I Zion:
    that I might reIjoice in I your deIliverance.

15 The nations have sunk into the pit they I dug for I
    others:
    in the very snare they I laid · is their I foot I taken;

16 The Lord has declared himself and upIheld the I right:
    the wicked are trapped in the I work · of their I own I
    hands.

17 The wicked shall be given ı over · to ı death:
    and all the nations ı that forıget ı God.

18 For the needy shall not always ı be forıgotten:
    nor shall the hope of the ı poor ı perish · for ı ever.

19 Arise Lord   let not ı man preıvail:
    let the ı nations · be ı judged beıfore you.

20 Put them in ı fear O ı Lord:
    and let the nations ı know · that they ı are but ı men.

PSALM 10

1 Why do you stand far ı off O ı Lord:
    why do you hide your ı face in ı time of ı need?

2 The ungodly in their pride ı persecute · the ı poor:
    let them be caught in the ı schemes they ı have
    deıvised.

3 For the ungodly man boasts of his ı heart's deısire:
    he grasps at profit   he ı spurns ·
    and blasıphemes the ı Lord.

4 He says in his arrogance ı 'God will · not aıvenge':
    'There is no ı God' is ı all his ı thought.

5 He is settled in ı all his ı ways:
    your statutes O Lord are far above him ı ⏝
    and he ı does not ı see.

6 He snorts defiance at his enemies
    he says in his heart 'I shall ı never · be ı shaken:
    I shall walk seıcure from ı any · man's ı curse.'

7 His mouth is full of opıpression · and deıceit:
    mischief and ı wickedness · lie ı under · his ı tongue.

8 He skulks aıbout · in the ı villages:
    and ı secret·ly ı murders · the ı innocent.

9 His eyes watch ı out · for the ı helpless:
    he lurks conıcealed · like a ı lion · in a ı thicket.

10 He lies in wait to ı seize up·on the ı poor:
    he lays hold on the poor man and ı drags him ı off ·
    in his ı net.

11 The upright are crushed and | humbled · be|fore him:
   and the helpless | fall in|to his | power.

12 He says in his heart | 'God · has for|gotten:
   he has covered his | face and | sees | nothing.'

13 Arise O Lord God   lift | up your | hand:
   for|get · not the | poor for | ever.

14 Why should the wicked man | spurn | God:
   why should he say in his heart | 'He will | not
      a|venge'?

15 Surely you see the | trouble · and the | sorrow:
   you look on   and will take it | into · your | own |
      hands.

16 The helpless commits him|self to | you:
   for you are the | helper | of the | fatherless.

†17 Break the | power of · the un|godly:
   search out his wickedness | till · it is | found no | more.

18 The Lord is king for | ever · and | ever:
   the heathen have | perished | from his | land.

19 You have heard the longing of the | meek O | Lord:
   you turned your | ear · to their | hearts' de|sire,

†20 To help the poor and fatherless | to their | right:
   that men may no more be | terri·fied | from their |
      land.

PSALM 11

1 In the Lord I have | found my | refuge:
   how then can you say to me |
      'Flee · like a | bird · to the | mountains;

2 'Look how the wicked bend their bows
      and notch the arrow up|on the | string:
   to shoot from the | darkness · at the | true of | heart;

3 'If the foundations | are des|troyed:
   what | can the | just man | do?'

4 The Lord is in his holy place
     the Lord is en|throned in | heaven:
  his eyes search out
     his glance | tries the | children · of | men.

5 He tries the | righteous · and the | wicked:
  and him that delights in | violence · his | soul ab|hors.

6 He will rain down coals of fire and brimstone __
     up|on the | wicked:
  a scorching wind shall | be their | cup to | drink.

†7 For the Lord is righteous and loves | righteous | acts:
  the | upright · shall | see his | face.

PSALM 12

1 Help Lord   for there is not one | godly · man | left:
  the faithful have vanished from a|mong the |
     children · of | men.

2 Everyone tells | lies · to his | neighbour:
  they flatter with their lips __
     but | speak · from a | double | heart.

3 If only the Lord would cut off all | flatter·ing | lips:
  and the | tongue that | speaks so | proudly!

4 They say 'By our tongues we | shall pre|vail:
  our lips are our servants   who is | lord | over | us?'

5 Because of the oppression of the poor
     because of the | groaning · of the | needy:
  'I will arise' says the Lord * 'and set them in safety __
     from | those that | snarl | after them.'

6 The words of the Lord are pure
     as silver re|fined · in a | crucible:
  as gold that is seven times | puri·fied | in the | fire.

7 You will surely | guard us · O | Lord:
  and shield us for ever from this | evil | gener|ation,

8 Though the ungodly strut on | every | side:
  though the vilest of men have | master·y |
     of man|kind.

PSALM 13

1 How long O Lord will you so | utterly · for|get me:
    how long will you | hide your | face | from me?

2 How long must I suffer anguish in my soul
        and be so grieved in my heart | day and | night:
    how long shall my | ene·my | triumph | over me?

3 Look upon me O Lord my | God and | answer me:
    lighten my | eyes · lest I | sleep in | death;

4 Lest my enemy say   'I have pre|vailed a|gainst him':
    lest my foes ex|ult | at my | overthrow.

5 Yet I put my trust in your un|failing | love:
    O let my heart re|joice in | your sal|vation.

6 And I will make my | song · to the | Lord:
    because he | deals so | bounti·fully | with me.

PSALM 14

1 The fool has said in his heart 'There | is no | God':
    they have all become vile and abominable in their __
        doings   there | is not | one that · does | good.

2 The Lord looked down from heaven upon the |
        children · of | men:
    to see if there were any who would act | wisely ·
        and | seek · after | God.

†3 But they have all turned out of the way
        they have all alike be|come cor|rupt:
    there is none that does | good | no not | one.

4 Are all the evildoers devoid of | under|standing:
    who eat up my people as men eat bread __
        and | do not | pray · to the | Lord?

5 They shall be | struck with | terror:
    for God is with the | compa·ny | of the | righteous.

6 Though they frustrate the poor man | in his | hopes:
    surely the | Lord | is his | refuge.

7 O that deliverance for Israel might come ǀ forth from ǀ
   Zion:
  when the Lord turns again the fortunes of his people
   then shall Jacob reǀjoice and ǀ Israel · be ǀ glad.

PSALM 15

1 Lord who may aǀbide in · your ǀ tabernacle:
  or who may dwell upǀon your ǀ holy ǀ hill?

2 He that leads an uncorrupt life
   and does the ǀ thing · which is ǀ right:
  who speaks the truth from his heart
   and has not ǀ slandered ǀ with his ǀ tongue;

3 He that has done no evil ǀ to his ǀ fellow:
  nor vented aǀbuse aǀgainst his ǀ neighbour;

4 In whose eyes the worthless ǀ have no ǀ honour:
  but he makes much of ǀ those that ǀ fear the ǀ Lord;

5 He that has ǀ sworn · to his ǀ neighbour:
  and will ǀ not go ǀ back · on his ǀ oath;

6 He that has not put his ǀ money · to ǀ usury:
  nor taken a ǀ bribe aǀgainst the ǀ innocent.

†7 He that ǀ does these ǀ things:
  shall ǀ never · be ǀ overǀthrown.

PSALM 16

1 Preserve ǀ me O ǀ God:
  for in ǀ you · have I ǀ taken ǀ refuge.

2 I have said to the Lord ǀ You are ǀ my lord:
  and all my ǀ good deǀpends on ǀ you.

3 As for those who are held ǀ holy · on the ǀ earth:
  the other ǀ gods · in whom ǀ men deǀlight,

4 Though the idols are many that ǀ men run ǀ after:
  their offerings of blood I will not offer
   nor take their ǀ name upǀon my ǀ lips.

5 The Lord is my appointed portion ǀ and my ǀ cup:
  you ǀ hold my ǀ lot · in your ǀ hands.

6 The share that has fallen to me is in | pleasant | places:
and a fair | land is | my pos|session.

7 I will bless the Lord who has | given · me | counsel:
at night also | he · has in|structed · my | heart.

8 I have set the Lord | always · be|fore me:
he is at my right | hand · and I | shall not | fall.

†9 Therefore my heart is glad and my | spirit · re|joices:
my flesh | also · shall | rest se|cure.

10 For you will not give me over to the | power of | death:
nor suffer your | faithful one · to | see the | Pit.

11 You will show me the | path of | life:
in your presence is the fulness of joy * and from ⌣
your right hand flow de|lights for | ever|more.

PSALM 17

1 Hear my just cause O Lord give | heed to · my | cry:
listen to my prayer that | comes from · no | lying |
lips.

2 Let judgment for me come | forth from · your | presence:
and let your | eyes dis|cern the | right.

3 Though you search my heart   and visit me | in the |
night-time:
though you try me by fire   you will | find no |
wicked·ness | in me.

4 My mouth does not transgress like the | mouth of |
others:
for I have | kept the | word of · your | lips.

†5 My steps have held firm in the way of | your
com|mands:
and my feet have not | stumbled | from your | paths.

6 I call upon you O God for you will | surely | answer:
incline your ear to | me and | hear my | words.

7 Show me the wonders of your steadfast love
O saviour of those who come to | you for | refuge:

who by your right hand deliver them ⌣
   from | those that · rise | up a|gainst them.

8 Keep me as the | apple · of your | eye:
   hide me under the | shadow | of your | wings,

9 From the onslaught | of the | wicked:
   from my enemies that en|circle me · to | take my |
   life.

10 They have closed their | hearts to | pity:
   and their | mouths speak | proud | things.

11 They advance upon me * they surround me on | every |
   side:
   watching how they may | bring me | to the | ground,

†12 Like a lion that is | greedy · for its | prey:
   like a lion's whelp | lurking · in | hidden | places.

13 Arise O Lord * stand in their way and | cast them |
   down:
   deliver me from the | wicked | by your | sword.

[14 Slay them by your hand O Lord
   slay them so that they | perish · from the | earth:
   de|stroy them · from a|mong the | living.]

15 But as for your cherished ones   let their bellies be ⌣
   filled and let their | sons be | satisfied:
   let them pass on their | wealth | to their | children.

(†)16 And I also shall see your face   because my | cause is |
   just:
   when I awake and see you as you | are I | shall be |
   satisfied.

PSALM 18

1 I love you O | Lord my | strength:
   O Lord my crag my | fortress · and | my de|liverer,

2 My God   the rock to which I | come for | refuge:
   my shield my mighty saviour | and my | high
   de|fence.

†3 I called to the Lord with | loud · lamen|tation:
   and I was | rescued | from my | enemies.

4 The waves of | death en|compassed me:
   and the floods of | chaos | over|whelmed me;

5 The cords of the grave | tightened · a|bout me:
   and the snares of | death lay | in my | path.

6 In my anguish I | called · to the | Lord:
   I cried for | help | to my | God.

7 From his temple he | heard my | voice:
   and my cry came | even | to his | ears.

8 The earth heaved and quaked
      the foundations of the | hills were | shaken:
   they | trembled · be|cause · he was | angry.

9 Smoke went | out · from his | nostrils:
   and a consuming | fire | from his | mouth.

10 He parted the heavens and | came | down:
   and there was | darkness | under · his | feet.

11 He rode upon the | cherubim · and | flew:
   he came swooping up|on the | wings · of the | wind.

12 He made the | darkness · his | covering:
   and his canopy was thick | cloud and | water·y |
      darkness.

13 Out of his clouds   from the | brightness · be|fore him:
   broke | hailstones · and | coals of | fire.

14 The Lord | thundered · in the | heavens:
   the Most | High | uttered · his | voice.

15 He let loose his arrows
      he scattered them on | every | side:
   he hurled down | lightnings · with the | roar · of the |
      thunderbolt.

16 The springs of the | sea · were un|covered:
   and the found|ations · of the | world laid | bare,

17 At your re|buke O | Lord:
   at the blast of the | breath of | your dis|pleasure.

18 He reached down from on | high and | took me:
    he drew me | out of · the | great | waters.

19 He delivered me from my | strongest | enemy:
    from my |foes · that were | mightier · than | I.

20 They confronted me in the | day of · my cal|amity:
    but the | Lord was | my up|holder.

21 He brought me out into a | place of | liberty:
    and rescued me be|cause · I de|lighted · his | heart.

22 The Lord rewarded me for my | righteous | dealing:
    he recompensed me according to the | cleanness |
        of my | hands,

23 Because I had kept to the | ways · of the | Lord:
    and had not turned from my | God to | do | evil.

24 For I had an eye to | all his | laws:
    and did not | put · his com|mandments | from me.

25 I was also | blameless · be|fore him:
    and I kept my|self from | wrong|doing.

†26 Therefore the Lord re|warded · my | innocence:
    because my hands were | unde|filed · in his | sight.

27 With the faithful you | show your·self | faithful:
    with the | blameless · you | show your·self | blameless;

28 With the | pure · you are | pure:
    but with the | crookèd · you | show yourself ·
        per|verse.

29 For you will save a | humble | people:
    but you bring down the | high looks | of the | proud.

30 You light my lamp O | Lord my | God:
    you make my | darkness | to be | bright.

†31 For with your help I can charge a | troop of | men:
    with the help of my God I can | leap a | city | wall.

32 The way of our God is perfect
        the word of the Lord has been | tried · in the | fire:
    he is a shield to | all that | trust in | him.

33 For who is I God · but the I Lord:
  or who is our I rock I but our I God?

34 It is God that I girded me · with I strength:
  that I made my I way I perfect.

35 He made my feet like the I feet · of a I hind:
  and set me sureIfooted · upIon the Imountains.

36 He taught my I hands to I fight:
  and my arms to I aim an I arrow · of I bronze.

37 You gave me the shield of I your salIvation:
  your right hand upheld me
    and your swift reIsponse has I made me I great.

38 You lengthened my I stride beIneath me:
  and my I ankles I did not I slip.

39 I pursued my enemies and I overItook them:
  nor did I turn again I till · I had I made an I
    end of them.

40 I smote them till they could I rise no I more:
  and they I fell beIneath my I feet.

41 You girded me with I strength · for the I battle:
  you threw I down my I adver·saries I under me.

42 You caused my enemies to I show their I backs:
  and I deIstroyed I those that I hated me.

43 They cried for help   but there was I none to I save
    them:
  they cried to the I Lord · but he I would not I answer.

44 I pounded them fine as dust beIfore the I wind:
  I trod them under I like the I mire · of the I streets.

45 You delivered me from the strife of the peoples
    you made me the I head · of the I nations:
  a people that I had not I known beIcame my I
    servants.

46 As soon as they heard me I they oIbeyed me:
  and aliens I humbled · themIselves beIfore me.

47 The strength of the aliens I withered · aIway:
  they came I falter·ing I from their I strongholds.

48 The Lord lives   and blessèd | be my | rock:
    exalted be the | God of | my sal|vation,

49 The God who sees to it that | I am · a|venged:
    who sub|dues the | peoples | under me.

50 You set me free from my enemies
       you put me out of | reach of · my at|tackers:
    you de|livered me · from | vio·lent | men.

51 For this will I give you thanks among the | nations · O |
       Lord:
    and sing | praises | to your | name,

†52 To him that gives great triumphs | to his | king:
    that deals so faithfully with his anointed
       with David and | with his | seed for | ever.

PSALM 19

1 The heavens declare the | glory · of | God:
    and the | firmament · pro|claims his | handiwork;

2 One day | tells it · to an|other:
    and night to | night com|muni·cates | knowledge.

3 There is no | speech or | language:
    nor | are their | voices | heard;

4 Yet their sound has gone out through | all the | world:
    and their | words · to the | ends · of the | earth.

5 There he has pitched a | tent · for the | sun:
    which comes out as a bridegroom from his chamber
       and rejoices like a | strong · man to | run his |
       course.

6 Its rising is at one end of the heavens
       and its circuit to their | farthest | bound:
    and nothing is | hidden | from its | heat.

7 The law of the Lord is perfect re|viving · the | soul:
    the command of the Lord is true | ⌣
       and makes | wise the | simple.

8 The precepts of the Lord are right ⌣
    and re|joice the | heart:

the commandment of the Lord is pure | ‿
   and gives | light · to the | eyes.

9 The fear of the Lord is clean and en|dures for | ever:
   the judgments of the Lord are unchanging‿
   and | righteous | every | one.

10 More to be desired are they than gold
   even | much fine | gold:
   sweeter also than honey
   than the | honey · that | drips · from the | comb.

11 Moreover by them is your | servant | taught:
   and in keeping them | there is | great re|ward.

12 Who can know his own un|witting | sins?:
   O cleanse me | from my | secret | faults.

13 Keep your servant also from presumptuous sins
   lest they get the | master·y | over me:
   so I shall be clean and | innocent · of | great of|fence.

14 May the words of my mouth and the meditation of my
   heart   be acceptable | in your | sight:
   O Lord my | strength and | my re|deemer.

PSALM 20

1 May the Lord hear you in the | day of | trouble:
   the God of Jacob | lift you | up to | safety.

2 May he send you his | help · from the | sanctuary:
   and be your | strong sup|port from | Zion.

3 May he remember | all your | offerings:
   and accept with | favour · your | burnt | sacrifices,

4 Grant you your | heart's de|sire:
   and ful|fil | all your | purposes.

†5 May we also rejoice in your victory
   and triumph in the | name of · our | God:
   the Lord per|form all | your pe|titions.

6 Now I know that the Lord will | save · his a|nointed:
   that he will answer him from his holy heaven
   with the victorious | strength · of his | right | hand.

7 Some put their trust in chariots and | some in | horses:
　　but we will trust in the | name · of the | Lord our |
　　　God.

8 They are brought | down and | fallen:
　　but we are made | strong and | stand | upright.

9 O Lord | save the | king:
　　and hear us | when we | call up|on you.

PSALM 21

1 The king shall rejoice in your | strength O | Lord:
　　he shall ex|ult in | your sal|vation.

2 You have given him his | heart's de|sire:
　　you have not de|nied him · the re|quest · of his | lips.

3 For you came to meet him with the | blessings ·
　　　of suc|cess:
　　and placed a crown of | gold up|on his | head.

4 He asked you for | life · and you | gave it him:
　　length of | days for | ever · and | ever.

5 Great is his glory because of | your sal|vation:
　　you have | clothed him · with | honour · and | majesty.

6 You have given him ever|lasting · fe|licity:
　　and made him | glad · with the | joy of · your |
　　　presence.

†7 For the king puts his | trust · in the | Lord:
　　and through the tender mercy of the Most High | _
　　　he shall | never · be | moved.

8 Your hand shall light up|on your | enemies:
　　and your right hand shall | find out | all who |
　　　hate you.

9 You will make them like a blazing furnace _
　　　in the | day of · your | coming:
　　the Lord will overwhelm them in his wrath _
　　　and | fire | shall con|sume them.

10 You will root out their offspring | from the | earth:
　　and their seed from a|mong the | children · of | men;

11 Because they have stirred up ǀ evil · aǀgainst you:
    and plotted mischief   ǀ which they ǀ cannot ·
       perǀform.

12 Therefore will you set your ǀ shoulder · toǀward them:
    and draw the string of the ǀ bow to ǀ strike at · their ǀ
       faces.

13 Arise O Lord in your ǀ great ǀ strength:
    and we will ǀ sing and ǀ praise your ǀ power.

PSALM 22

1 My God my God   why have ǀ you forǀsaken me:
    why are you so far from helping me
      and from the ǀ words ǀ of my ǀ groaning?

2 My God I cry to you by day   but you ǀ do not ǀ answer:
    and by night ǀ also · I ǀ take no ǀ rest.

3 But you conǀtinue ǀ holy:
    you that ǀ are the ǀ praise of ǀ Israel.

4 In you our ǀ fathers ǀ trusted:
    they ǀ trusted · and ǀ you deǀlivered them;

5 To you they cried and ǀ they were ǀ saved:
    they put their trust in you ǀ and were ǀ
      not conǀfounded.

6 But as for me   I am a worm and ǀ no ǀ man:
    the scorn of ǀ men · and deǀspised · by the ǀ people.

7 All those that see me ǀ laugh me · to ǀ scorn:
    they shoot out their lips at me and ǀ wag their ǀ heads ǀ
      saying,

8 'He trusted in the Lord   ǀ let him · deǀliver him:
    let him deǀliver him · if ǀ he deǀlights in him.'

9 But you are he that took me ǀ out of · the ǀ womb:
    that brought me to lie at ǀ peace · on my ǀ mother's ǀ
      breast.

10 On you have I been cast ǀ since my ǀ birth:
    you are my God ǀ even · from my ǀ mother's ǀ womb.

11 O go not from me   for trouble is ǀ hard at ǀ hand:
    and ǀ there is ǀ none to ǀ help.

12 Many I oxen · surIround me:
    fat bulls of Bashan close me I in on I every I side.

13 They gape I wide their I mouths at me:
    like I lions · that I roar and I rend.

14 I am poured out like water
       and all my bones are I out of I joint:
    my heart within my I breast · is like I melting I wax.

15 My mouth is dried I up · like a I potsherd:
    and my I tongue I clings · to my I gums.

16 My hands and my I feet are I withered:
    and you I lay me · in the I dust of I death.

17 For many dogs are I come aIbout me:
    and a band of evilIdoers I hem me I in.

18 I can count I all my I bones:
    they stand I staring · and I gazing · upIon me.

19 They part my I garments · aImong them:
    and cast I lots I for my I clothing.

20 O Lord do not I stand far I off:
    you are my helper   I hasten I to my I aid.

21 Deliver my I body · from the I sword:
    my I life · from the I power · of the I dogs;

22 O save me from the I lion's I mouth:
    and my afflicted soul from the I horns · of the I wild I
       oxen.

23 I will tell of your I name · to my I brethren:
    in the midst of the congreIgation I will I I praise you.

24 O praise the Lord all I you that I fear him:
    hold him in honour O seed of Jacob
       and let the seed of I Israel I stand in I awe of him.

†25 For he has not despised nor abhorred‿
       the poor man I in his I misery:
    nor did he hide his face from him
       but I heard him I when he I cried.

26 From you springs my praise in the I great ·
       congreIgation:
    I will pay my vows in the I sight of I all that I fear you;

155

27 The meek shall eat of the sacrifice I and be I satisfied:
and those who seek the Lord shall praise him
may their I hearts reljoice for I ever!

28 Let all the ends of the earth remember __
and I turn · to the I Lord:
and let all the families of the I nations I worship ·
belfore him.

29 For the kingdom I is the I Lord's:
and he shall be I ruler I over · the I nations.

30 How can those who sleep in the earth I do him I
homage:
or those that descend to the I dust bow I down belfore
him?

31 But he has saved my I life · for himlself:
and I my poslterity · shall I serve him.

†32 This shall be told of my Lord to a future I generlation:
and his righteousness declared__
to a people yet unlborn   that I he has I done it.

PSALM 23

1 The Lord I is my I shepherd:
therefore I can I I lack I nothing.

2 He will make me lie down in I green I pastures:
and I lead me · belside still I waters.

3 He will relfresh my I soul:
and guide me in right pathways I for his I name's I
sake.

4 Though I walk through the valley of the shadow of __
death   I will I fear no I evil:
for you are with me
your I rod · and your I staff I comfort me.

5 You spread a table before me
in the face of I those who I trouble me:
you have anointed my head with oil I and my I cup ·
will be I full.

6 Surely your goodness and loving-kindness__
will follow me * all the I days · of my I life:
and I shall dwell in the I house · of the I Lord for I
ever.

PSALM 24

1 The earth is the Lord's and I all · that is I in it:
   the compass of the I world and I those who I dwell
   therein.

2 For he has founded it up|on the I seas:
   and es|tablished it · up|on the I waters.

3 Who shall ascend the I hill · of the I Lord:
   or who shall I stand · in his I holy I place?

4 He that has clean hands and a I pure I heart:
   who has not set his soul upon idols
   nor I sworn his I oath · to a I lie.

5 He shall receive I blessing · from the I Lord:
   and recompense from the I God of I his sal|vation.

6 Of such a kind as this are I those who I seek him:
   those who seek your I face O I God of I Jacob.

7 Lift up your heads O you gates
   and be lifted up you ever|lasting I doors:
   and the King of I glory I shall come I in.

8 Who is the I King of I glory?:
   the Lord strong and mighty * the I Lord I mighty · in I
   battle.

9 Lift up your heads O you gates
   and be lifted up you ever|lasting I doors:
   and the King of I glory I shall come I in.

10 Who is the I King of I glory?:
   the Lord of hosts I he · is the I King of I glory.

PSALM 25

1 In you O Lord my God have I I put my I hope:
   in you have I trusted   let me not be ashamed
   nor let my I ene·mies I triumph I over me.

2 Let none who wait for you be I put to I shame:
   but let those that break faith__
   be con|founded · and I gain I nothing.

3 Show me your I ways O I Lord:
   and I teach me I your I paths.

4 Lead me in the ways of your | truth and | teach me:
    for you are the | God of | my sal|vation.

5 In you have I hoped | all the · day | long:
    be|cause of · your | goodness · O | Lord.

6 Call to mind your compassion and your |
      loving-|kindness:
    for | they are | from of | old.

7 Remember not the sins of my youth nor |
      my trans|gressions:
    but according | to your | mercy | think on me.

8 Good and upright | is the | Lord:
    therefore will he direct | sinners | in the | way.

†9 The meek he will guide in the | path of | justice:
    and | teach the | humble · his | ways.

10 All the paths of the Lord are | faithful · and | true:
    for those who keep his | covenant · and | his
      com|mandments.

11 For your name's | sake O | Lord:
    be merciful to my | sin   though | it is | great.

12 Who is he that | fears the | Lord?:
    him will the Lord direct in the | way that | he should |
      choose.

13 His soul shall | dwell at | ease:
    and his | children · shall in|herit · the | land.

14 The confidences of God belong to | those that | fear him:
    and his covenant shall | give them | under|standing.

15 My eyes are ever | looking · to the | Lord:
    for he will bring my | feet | out of · the | net.

16 Turn your face toward me | and be | gracious:
    for | I am · a|lone · and in | misery.

17 O free my | heart from | pain:
    and bring me | out of | my dis|tress.

18 Give heed to my af|fliction · and ad|versity:
    and for|give me | all my | sins.

19 Consider my enemies how I many · they I are:
  and they bear a I vio·lent I hate aIgainst me.

20 O keep my I life · and deIliver me:
  put me not to shame   for I I come to I you for I refuge.

21 Let innocence and integrity I be my I guard:
  for in I you I have I I hoped.

†22 O God deIliver I Israel:
  out of I all his I tribuIlation.

PSALM 26

1 Give judgment for me O Lord
    for I have walked in I my inItegrity:
  I have trusted in the I Lord and I not I wavered.

2 Put me to the test O I Lord and I prove me:
  try my I mind I and my I heart.

3 For your steadfast love has been beIfore my I eyes:
  and I I have I walked in · your I truth.

4 I have not I sat · with deIceivers:
  nor conIsorted I with the I hypocrites;

5 I hate the asIsembly · of the I wicked:
  I will not I sit I with the · unIgodly.

6 I wash my hands in I innocence · O I Lord:
  that I may I go aIbout your I altar,

†7 And lift up the I voice of I thanksgiving:
  to tell of I all your I marvel·lous I works.

8 Lord I love the house of your I habitIation:
  and the I place · where your I glory I dwells.

9 Do not sweep me aIway with I sinners:
  nor my I life with I men of I blood,

10 In whose hand is aIbominIation:
  and their right I hand is I full of I bribes.

11 As for me   I walk in I my inItegrity:
  O ransom me I and be I favourable · toIward me.

†12 My foot stands on an I even I path:
  I will bless the I Lord · in the I great · congreIgation.

PSALM 27

1 The Lord is my light and my salvation
    whom then I shall I I fear?:
  the Lord is the stronghold of my life
    of whom I shall I I be aIfraid?

2 When the wicked   even my enemies and my foes
    come upon me I to deIvour me:
  they shall I stumble I and I fall.

3 If an army encamp against me
    my heart shall I not · be aIfraid:
  and if war should rise aIgainst me I yet · will I I trust.

4 One thing I have asked from the Lord which I I
    will reIquire:
  that I may dwell in the house of the Lord I ⏑
    all the I days · of my I life,

†5 To see the fair I beauty · of the I Lord:
  and to I seek his I will · in his I temple.

6 For he will hide me under his shelter in the I day of I
    trouble:
  and conceal me in the shadow of his tent
    and set me I high upIon a I rock.

7 And now he will lift I up my I head:
  above my I ene·mies I round aIbout me.

†8 And I will offer sacrifices in his sanctuary with I
    exulItation:
  I will sing   I will sing I praises I to the I Lord.

9 O Lord hear my I voice · when I I cry:
  have I mercy · upIon me · and I answer me.

10 My heart has said of you I 'Seek his I face':
  your I face Lord I I will I seek.

11 Do not I hide your I face from me:
  or thrust your I servant · aIside · in disIpleasure;

12 For you have I been my I helper:
  do not cast me away or forsake me O I God of I
    my salIvation.

†13 Though my father and my | mother · for|sake me:
  the |Lord will | take me | up.

14 Teach me your | way O | Lord:
  and lead me in an even path | for they | lie in | wait for
  me.

15 Do not give me over to the | will of · my | enemies:
  for false witnesses have risen against me
  and | those who | breathe out | violence.

16 But I believe that I shall surely see the |
  goodness · of the | Lord:
  in the | land | of the | living.

17 O wait for the Lord   stand firm and he will |
  strengthen · your | heart:
  and | wait I | say · for the | Lord.

PSALM 28

1 To you will I cry O Lord my Rock
  be not | deaf · to my | prayer:
  lest if you turn away silent
  I become like those that go | down | to the | grave.

2 Hear the voice of my supplication —
  when I cry to | you for | help:
  when I lift up my hands —
  towards the | holi·est | place of · your | sanctuary.

3 Do not snatch me away with the ungodly
  with the | evil|doers:
  who speak peace to their neighbours
  but nourish | malice | in their | hearts.

4 Repay them ac|cording · to their | deeds:
  and according to the | wickedness · of |
  their en|deavours;

5 Requite them for the | work · of their | hands:
  and | give them | their de|serts.

6 For they pay no heed to the Lord's acts
  nor to the operation | of his | hands:
  therefore shall he break them | down · and not |
  build them | up.

7 Let the Lord's | name be | praised:
   for he has heard the | voice · of my | suppli|cation.

8 The Lord is my strength and my shield
      in him my heart trusts and | I am | helped:
   therefore my heart dances for joy
      and in my | song | will I | praise him.

9 The Lord is the | strength · of his | people:
   and a sure refuge for | his an|ointed | king.

10 O save your people * and give your | blessing · to your |
      own:
   be their shepherd and | bear them | up for | ever.

PSALM 29

1 Ascribe to the Lord you | sons of | heaven:
   ascribe to the | Lord | glory · and | might.

2 Ascribe to the Lord the honour | due · to his | name:
   O worship the Lord in the | beauty | of his | holiness.

3 The voice of the Lord is up|on the | waters:
   the God of glory thunders   the Lord up|on the |
      great | waters.

4 The voice of the Lord is mighty in | oper|ation:
   the voice of the | Lord · is a | glori·ous | voice.

5 The voice of the Lord | breaks the | cedar-trees:
   the Lord breaks in | pieces · the | cedars · of | Lebanon.

6 He makes them | skip · like a | calf:
   Lebanon and Sirion | like a | young wild | ox.

7 The voice of the Lord di|vides the | lightning-flash:
   the voice of the Lord whirls the sands of the desert
   the Lord | whirls the | desert · of | Kadesh.

8 The voice of the Lord rends the terebinth trees
      and strips | bare the | forests:
   in his | temple | all cry | 'Glory'.

9 The Lord sits enthroned a|bove the | water-flood:
   the Lord sits en|throned · as a | king for | ever.

10 The Lord will give | strength · to his | people:
   the Lord will give to his | people · the | blessing · of |
      peace.

1 I will exalt you O Lord
    for you have drawn me | up · from the | depths:
  and have not suffered my | foes to | triumph |
    over me.

2 O Lord my | God I | cried to you:
  and | you have | made me | whole.

†3 You brought me back O Lord from the | land of | silence:
  you saved my life‿
    from among | those that · go | down · to the | Pit.

4 Sing praises to the Lord all | you his | faithful ones:
  and give | thanks · to his | holy | name.

5 For if in his anger is havoc
    in his good | favour · is | life:
  heaviness may endure for a night
    but | joy comes | in the | morning.

6 In my prosperity I said   'I shall | never · be | moved:
  your goodness O Lord has | set me · on so | firm a |
    hill.'

7 Then you | hid your | face from me:
  and | I was | greatly · dis|mayed.

8 I cried to | you O | God:
  and made my petition | humbly | to my | Lord.

9 'What profit is there in my blood
    if I go | down · to the | Pit:
  can the dust give you thanks |‿
    or de|clare your | faithfulness?

†10 'Hear O | Lord · and be | merciful:
  O | Lord | be my | helper.'

11 You have turned my lamentation | into | dancing:
  you have put off my sackcloth and | girded | me with |
    joy,

12 That my heart may sing your praise and | never · be |
    silent:
  O Lord my God   I will | give you | thanks for | ever.

PSALM 31

1 To you Lord have I ǀ come for ǀ shelter:
 let me ǀ never · be ǀ put to ǀ shame.

2 O deliver me ǀ in your ǀ righteousness:
 incline your ear to me ǀ and be ǀ swift to ǀ save me.

3 Be for me a rock of refuge   a fortress ǀ to deǀfend me:
 for you are my ǀ high rock ǀ and my ǀ stronghold.

4 Lead me and guide me for your ǀ name's ǀ sake:
 bring me out of the net that they have secretly ⌐
  laid for me * for ǀ you ǀ are my ǀ strength.

5 Into your hands I comǀmit my ǀ spirit:
 you will redeem me ǀ O Lord ǀ God of ǀ truth.

6 I hate those that ǀ clutch vain ǀ idols:
 but my ǀ trust is ǀ in the ǀ Lord.

7 I will rejoice and be glad in your ǀ loving-ǀkindness:
 for you have looked on my distress
  and ǀ known me ǀ in adǀversity.

8 You have not given me over to the ǀ power · of the ǀ
  enemy:
 you have set my feet where ǀ I may ǀ walk at ǀ liberty.

9 Have mercy upon me O Lord   for ǀ I am · in ǀ trouble:
 my eye wastes away for grief
  my throat also ǀ and my ǀ inward ǀ parts.

10 For my life wears out in sorrow ⌐
  and my ǀ years with ǀ sighing:
 my strength fails me in my affliction
  and my ǀ bones ǀ are conǀsumed.

11 I am become the scorn of ǀ all my ǀ enemies:
 and my neighbours ǀ wag their ǀ heads · in deǀrision.

12 I am a thing of ǀ horror · to my ǀ friends:
 and those that see me in the ǀ street ǀ shrink ǀ from me.

13 I am forgotten like a dead man ǀ out of ǀ mind:
 I have beǀcome · like a ǀ broken ǀ vessel.

14 For I hear the ǀ whispering · of ǀ many:
 and ǀ fear · is on ǀ every ǀ side;

15 While they plot to|gether · a|gainst me:
  and scheme to | take a|way my | life.

16 But in you Lord have I | put my | trust:
  I have said | 'You |are my | God.'

17 All my days are | in your | hand:
  O deliver me from the power of my | enemies ·
    and | from my | persecutors.

18 Make your face to shine up|on your | servant:
  and save me | for your | mercy's | sake.

19 O Lord let me not be confounded ⌣
    for I have | called up|on you:
  but let the wicked be put to shame
    and brought to | silence | in the | grave.

20 Let the lying | lips be | dumb:
  that in pride and contempt ⌣
    speak such | insolence · a|gainst the | just.

21 O how plentiful is your goodness
    stored up for | those that | fear you:
  and prepared in the sight of men
    for all who | come to | you for | refuge.

22 You will hide them in the cover of your presence ⌣
    from the | plots of | men:
  you will shelter them in your refuge | ⌣
    from the | strife of | tongues.

23 Blessèd be the | Lord our | God:
  for he has wonderfully shown me his steadfast love
    when I was | as a | city · be|sieged.

24 When I was afraid I | said in · my | haste:
  'I am | cut off | from your | sight.'

25 But you heard the voice of my | suppli|cation:
  when I | cried to | you for | help.

26 Love the Lord all | you his | faithful ones:
  for the Lord guards the true
    but | fully · re|quites the | proud.

†27 Be strong and let your | heart take | courage:
  all | you that | hope · in the | Lord.

PSALM 32

1 Blessèd is he whose I sin · is forIgiven:
 whose inIiquity · is I put aIway.

2 Blessèd is the man to whom the Lord imIputes no I
  blame:
 and in whose I spirit · there I is no I guile.

3 For whilst I I held my I tongue:
 my bones wasted aIway · with my I daily ·
  comIplaining.

4 Your hand was heavy upon me I day and I night:
 and my moisture was dried I up · like a I drought in I
  summer.

5 Then I ackInowledged · my I sin to you:
 and my inIiquity · I I did not I hide;

6 I said 'I will confess my transIgressions · to the I Lord':
 and so you forgave the I wicked·ness I of my I sin.

7 For this cause shall everyone that is faithful ⸺
   make his prayer to you * in the I day of I trouble:
 and in the time of the great water-floods I ⸺
   they shall I not come I near him.

8 You are a place to hide me in
   you will preIserve me · from I trouble:
 you will surround me with deIliverance · on I every I
  side.

9 'I will instruct you
   and direct you in the way that I you should I go:
 I will fasten my eye upIon you · and I give you I
  counsel.

10 'Be not like horse or mule that have no I underIstanding:
 whose forward course must be I curbed with I bit and I
  bridle.'

11 Great tribulations remain I for the · unIgodly:
 but whoever puts his trust in the Lord
   mercy emIbraces him · on I every I side.

12 Rejoice in the Lord you righteous I and be I glad:
 and shout for joy all I you · that are I true of I heart.

PSALM 33

1 Rejoice in the | Lord you | righteous:
   for it be|fits the | just to | praise him.

2 Give the Lord thanks up|on the | harp:
   and sing his praise to the | lute of | ten | strings.

3 O sing him a | new | song:
   make sweetest | melody · with | shouts of | praise.

4 For the word of the | Lord is | true:
   and | all his | works are | faithful.

5 He loves | righteousness · and | justice:
   the earth is filled with the loving-|kindness | of the |
   Lord.

6 By the word of the Lord were the | heavens | made:
   and their numberless | stars · by the | breath of · his |
   mouth.

7 He gathered the waters of the sea as | in a | water-skin:
   and laid up the | deep | in his | treasuries.

8 Let the whole earth | fear the | Lord:
   and let all the inhabitants of the | world | stand in |
   awe of him.

9 For he spoke and | it was | done:
   he commanded | and it | stood | fast.

10 The Lord frustrates the | counsels · of the | nations:
   he brings to nothing the de|vices | of the | peoples.

11 But the counsels of the Lord shall en|dure for | ever:
   the purposes of his heart from gener|ation · to |
   gener|ation.

12 Blessèd is that nation whose | God · is the | Lord:
   the people he chose to | be his | own pos|session.

13 The Lord looks down from heaven
   and surveys all the | children · of | men:
   he considers from his dwelling-place ⎯
   all the in|habit·ants | of the | earth;

14 He who fashioned the | hearts of · them | all:
   and compre|hends all | that they | do.

15 A king is not saved by a | mighty | army:
    nor is a warrior de|livered · by | much | strength;

16 A horse is a vain hope to | save a | man:
    nor can he rescue | any · by his | great | power.

17 But the eye of the Lord is on | those that | fear him:
    on those that trust in | his un|failing | love,

18 To de|liver them · from | death:
    and to | feed them · in the | time of | dearth.

19 We have waited eagerly | for the | Lord:
    for | he is · our | help · and our | shield.

20 Surely our hearts shall re|joice in | him:
    for we have | trusted · in his | holy | name.

†21 Let your merciful kindness be up|on us · O | Lord:
    even as our | hope | is in | you.

PSALM 34

1 I will bless the | Lord con|tinually:
    his praise shall be | always | in my | mouth.

2 Let my soul | boast · of the | Lord:
    the humble shall | hear it | and re|joice.

3 O praise the | Lord with | me:
    let us ex|alt his | name to|gether.

4 For I sought the Lord's | help · and he | answered:
    and he | freed me · from | all my | fears.

5 Look towards him and be | bright with | joy:
    your | faces · shall | not · be a|shamed.

6 Here is a wretch who cried and the | Lord | heard him:
    and | saved him · from | all his | troubles.

7 The angel of the Lord encamps round | those who |
    fear him:
    and de|livers · them | in their | need.

8 O taste and see that the | Lord is | good:
    happy the | man who | hides in | him!

9 Fear the Lord all ǀ you his ǀ holy ones:
　for those who ǀ fear him ǀ never ǀ lack.

10 Lions may suffer ǀ want · and go ǀ hungry:
　but those who seek the ǀ Lord lack ǀ nothing ǀ good.

11 Come my children　ǀ listen · to ǀ me:
　and I will ǀ teach you · the ǀ fear · of the ǀ Lord.

12 Which of you ǀ relish·es ǀ life:
　wants ǀ time · to enǀjoy good ǀ things?

13 Keep your ǀ tongue from ǀ evil:
　and your ǀ lips from ǀ telling ǀ lies.

14 Turn from evil and ǀ do ǀ good:
　seek ǀ peace ǀ and purǀsue it.

15 The eyes of God are ǀ on the ǀ righteous:
　and his ǀ ears toǀwards their ǀ cry.

16 The Lord sets his face against ǀ wrongǀdoers:
　to root out their ǀ memo·ry ǀ from the ǀ earth.

17 The righteous cry　the ǀ Lord ǀ hears it:
　and ǀ frees them · from ǀ all · their afǀflictions.

18 The Lord is close to those who are ǀ broken-ǀhearted:
　and the ǀ crushed in ǀ spirit · he ǀ saves.

19 The trials of the ǀ righteous · are ǀ many:
　but our God deǀlivers · him ǀ from them ǀ all.

20 He guards ǀ all his ǀ bones:
　so ǀ that not ǀ one is ǀ broken.

21 Evil will ǀ slay the ǀ wicked:
　and those who hate the ǀ righteous · will ǀ be
　deǀstroyed.

22 The Lord ransoms the ǀ lives · of his ǀ servants:
　and none who hide in ǀ him will ǀ be deǀstroyed.

PSALM 35

1 Contend O Lord with those who conǀtend with ǀ me:
　fight against ǀ those that ǀ fight aǀgainst me.

2 Take up ∣ shield and ∣ buckler:
    and aᴵrise aᴵrise to ∣ help me.

3 Draw the spear
    and bar the way against ∣ those · that purᴵsue me:
    say to me ∣ 'I am ∣ your deᴵliverer.'

4 Let those that seek my life‿
    be put to ∣ shame · and disᴵgraced:
    let those that plot my destruction‿
    be ∣ turned ∣ back · and conᴵfounded.

5 Let them be like chaff beᴵfore the ∣ wind:
    with the ∣ angel · of the ∣ Lord ∣ driving them;

6 Let their way be ∣ dark and ∣ slippery:
    with the ∣ angel · of the ∣ Lord purᴵsuing.

7 For without cause‿
    they have secretly ∣ spread a ∣ net for me:
    without cause they have ∣ dug a ∣ pit · to enᴵtrap me.

8 Let sudden disᴵaster ∣ strike them:
    let the net that they have hidden catch them
    let them ∣ fall to ∣ their deᴵstruction.

9 Then shall my soul be ∣ joyful · in the ∣ Lord:
    and I will reᴵjoice in ∣ his deᴵliverance.

10 All my bones shall say ∣ 'Lord · who is ∣ like you?:
    for you deliver the poor man from him that is too‿
    strong for him * the poor and needy from ∣
    him that ∣ would deᴵspoil them.'

11 Malicious witnesses rise ∣ up aᴵgainst me:
    I am questioned about things of ∣ which I ∣ know ∣
    nothing.

12 They repay me ∣ evil · for ∣ good:
    I am as ∣ one beᴵreaved of · his ∣ children.

13 Yet when they were sick I ∣ put on ∣ sackcloth:
    I afᴵflicted · myᴵself with ∣ fasting.

14 And if my prayer returned unanswered ∣ to my ∣ bosom:
    I went about mourning
    as though for a ∣ brother ∣ or a · comᴵpanion;

15 I was bowed I down with I grief:
    as I though · for my I own I mother.

16 But when I stumbled   they rejoiced and gathered⌣
    together * they gathered toIgether · aIgainst me:
    as though they were strangers I never knew
    they I tore at · me I without I ceasing.

†17 When I I slipped they I mocked me:
    and I gnashed · at me I with their I teeth.

18 Lord how long will I you look I on?:
    take me from the evil they intend
    take me I from aImidst the I lions.

19 And I will give you thanks in the I great · congreIgation:
    I will I praise you · in the I throng · of the I people.

20 Let not those that wrongfully are my enemies I ⌣
    triumph I over me:
    let not those that hate me without cause I ⌣
    mock me I with their I eyes.

21 For they speak words that do not I make for I peace:
    they invent lies against those that are I quiet I in the I
    land.

22 They stretch their mouths to I jeer at me · and I say:
    'Aha aha! We have I seen I all that · we I wish!'

23 And you also have seen O Lord I do not · be I silent:
    O God I go not I far I from me.

24 Bestir yourself awake to I do me I right:
    to plead my I cause O I Lord my I God.

25 Judge me O Lord my God according I to your I
    righteousness:
    and let them I not reIjoice I over me.

26 Let them not say in their hearts 'We I have our I wish':
    let them not I say 'We I have deIstroyed him.'

27 Let those that rejoice at my hurt ⌣
    be disgraced and confounded I altoIgether:
    let those that lord it over me ⌣
    be I clothed in I shame · and disIhonour.

28 But let those that long for my vindication‿
      shout for | joy · and re|joice:
  let them say always that the Lord is great
      who takes such de|light · in his | servant's | good.

29 And my tongue shall | speak of · your | righteousness:
  and of your | praise | all the · day | long.

PSALM 36

1 The transgressor speaks‿
      from the wickedness in his | own | heart:
  there is no fear of | God be|fore his | eyes.

2 For he flatters himself in his | own | sight:
  he hates his in|iquity · to be | found | out.

3 The words of his mouth are wickedness | and de|ceit:
  he has ceased to act | wisely · and | do | good.

4 He plots mischief as he lies up|on his | bed:
  he has set himself on a path that is not good
      he | does not | spurn | evil.

5 Your unfailing kindness O Lord is | in the | heavens:
  and your faithfulness | reaches | to the | clouds.

6 Your righteousness is like the | strong | mountains:
  and your justice as the great deep
      you O Lord | save both | man and | beast.

7 How precious O God is your en|during | kindness:
  the children of men shall take refuge‿
      under the | shadow | of your | wings.

8 They shall be satisfied‿
      with the good things | of your | house:
  and you will give them drink‿
      from the | river · of | your de|lights.

9 For with you is the | well of | life:
  and in your | light shall | we see | light.

10 O continue your merciful kindness‿
      toward | those who | know you:
  and your righteous dealing‿
      to | those · that are | true of | heart.

11 Let not the foot of the | proud · come a|gainst me:
　　nor the hand of the un|godly | drive · me a|way.

12 There are they fallen 　| those who · do | evil:
　　they are thrust down and | shall not | rise a|gain.

PSALM 37

1 Do not | vie · with the | wicked:
　　or | envy | those that · do | wrong;

2 For they will soon | wither · like the | grass:
　　and fade a|way · like the | green | leaf.

3 Trust in the | Lord and · do | good:
　　and you shall dwell in the land⌣
　　　　and | feed in | safe | pastures.

4 Let the Lord be | your de|light:
　　and he will | grant you · your | heart's de|sire.

5 Commit your | way · to the | Lord:
　　trust | him and | he will | act.

6 He will make your righteousness⌣
　　　　shine as | clear · as the | light:
　　and your | inno·cence | as the | noonday.

7 Be still before the Lord * and wait | patient·ly | for him:
　　do not be vexed when a man prospers
　　　　when he puts his | evil | purposes · to | work.

8 Let go of anger and a|bandon | wrath:
　　let not envy | move you · to | do | evil.

9 For the wicked shall be | cut | down:
　　but those who wait for the | Lord · shall pos|sess the |
　　　　land.

10 In a little while the ungodly shall | be no | more:
　　you will look for him in his place⌣
　　　　but | he will | not be | found.

†11 But the meek shall pos|sess the | land:
　　and en|joy · the a|bundance · of | peace.

12 The ungodly man plots a|gainst the | righteous:
　　and | gnashes · at him | with his | teeth.

13 But the Lord shall | laugh him · to | scorn:
  for he sees that the | day · for his | overthrow · is |
    near.

14 The ungodly have drawn the sword and | strung the |
    bow:
  to strike down the poor and needy
    to slaughter | those that | walk in | innocence.

15 Their swords shall pierce their | own | hearts:
  and their | bows | shall be | broken.

16 Though the righteous man | has · but a | little:
  it is better than the great | wealth of | the un|godly.

17 For the strong arm of the ungodly | shall be | broken:
  but the | Lord up|holds the | righteous.

18 The Lord cares for the | lives · of the | innocent:
  and their heritage | shall be | theirs for | ever.

19 They shall not be put to shame in the | evil | days:
  but in time of famine | they shall | eat their | fill.

†20 As for the ungodly they shall perish
    they are the enemies | of the | Lord:
  like fuel in a furnace they shall | vanish · al|way in |
    smoke.

21 The ungodly man borrows but does | not re|pay:
  but the | righteous · is | gracious · and | gives.

22 Those who are blessed by God shall pos|sess the | land:
  but those whom he has | cursed · shall be | cut | down.

23 If a man's steps are | guided · by the | Lord:
  and | he de|lights in · his | way,

24 Though he stumble he shall | not fall | headlong:
  for the Lord | holds him | by the | hand.

25 I have been young and | now am | old:
  but I never saw the righteous man forsaken
    or his | children | begging · their | bread.

26 He is ever | gracious · and | lends:
  and his | children | shall be | blessed.

27 Turn from evil and | do | good:
    and you shall | dwell · in the | land for | ever.

28 For the | Lord loves | justice:
    he will | not for|sake his | faithful ones.

29 But the unjust shall be de|stroyed for | ever:
    and the children of the un|godly · shall be | cut |
    down.

30 The just shall pos|sess the | land:
    and they shall | dwell in | it for | ever.

31 The mouth of the righteous man | utters | wisdom:
    and his | tongue speaks | what is | right.

32 The law of his God is | in his | heart:
    and his | footsteps | will not | slip.

33 The ungodly man watches | out · for the | righteous:
    and | seeks oc|casion · to | slay him.

34 But the Lord will not abandon him | to his | power:
    nor let him be con|demned when | he is | judged.

†35 Wait for the Lord and | hold to · his | way:
    and he will | raise you up to possess the land
    to see the un|godly · when | they are · de|stroyed.

36 I have seen the ungodly in | terri·fying | power:
    spreading himself | like a · lux|uri·ant | tree;

37 I passed by again and | he was | gone:
    I searched for him | but · he could | not be | found.

38 Observe the blameless man and con|sider · the | upright:
    for the man of | peace shall | have pos|terity.

39 But transgressors shall be de|stroyed · alto|gether:
    and the posterity of the | wicked · shall be | cut |
    down.

40 Deliverance for the righteous shall | come · from the |
    Lord:
    he is their | strength in | time of | trouble.

41 The Lord will help them | and de|liver them:
    he will save them from the ungodly and deliver them
    because they | come to | him for | refuge.

PSALM 38

1 O Lord rebuke me not | in your | anger:
   nor chasten me | in your | fierce dis|pleasure.

2 For your arrows have been | aimed a|gainst me:
   and your hand has come | down | heavy · up|on me.

3 There is no health in my flesh⌣
      because of your | indig|nation:
   nor soundness in my bones by | reason | of my | sin.

4 The tide of my iniquities has gone | over · my | head:
   their weight is a burden too | heavy · for | me to | bear.

5 My wounds | stink and | fester:
   be|cause | of my | foolishness.

6 I am bowed down and | brought so | low:
   that I go | mourning | all the · day | long.

7 For my loins are filled with a | burning | pain:
   and there is no sound | part in | all my | body.

8 I am numbed and | stricken · to the | ground:
   I cry aloud in the | yearning | of my | heart.

9 O Lord   all I long for | is be|fore you:
   and my deep sighing | is not | hidden | from you.

10 My heart is in tumult   my | strength | fails me:
   and even the | light of · my | eyes has | gone from me.

11 My friends and my companions hold aloof from |
      my af|fliction:
   and my | kinsmen | stand far | off.

12 Those who seek my | life | strike at me:
   and those that desire my hurt spread evil tales
      and murmur | slanders | all the | day.

13 But I am like a deaf man and | hear | nothing:
   like one that is dumb who | does not | open · his |
      mouth.

14 So I have become as one who | cannot | hear:
   in whose | mouth · there is | no re|tort.

15 For in you Lord have I I put my I trust:
    and you will I answer me · O I Lord my I God.

16 For I prayed 'Let them never ex|ult I over me:
    those who turn arrogant I when my I foot I slips.'

17 Truly I am I ready · to I fall:
    and my I pain is I with me · con|tinually.

18 But I ac|knowledge · my I wickedness:
    and I am filled with I sorrow I at my I sin.

19 Those that are my enemies without cause are I great in I
        number:
    and those who hate me I wrongful|ly are I many.

20 Those also who repay evil for good I are a|gainst me:
    because I I seek I after I good.

†21 Forsake me not O Lord
      go not far I from me · my I God:
    hasten to my I help O I Lord · my sal|vation.

PSALM 39

1 I said 'I will keep watch over my ways⌣
      lest I I sin · with my I tongue:
    I will keep a guard on my mouth⌣
      while the I wicked · are I in my I sight.'

2 I held my tongue and I said I nothing:
    I kept I silent · but I found no I comfort.

3 My pain was increased my heart grew I
      hot with|in me:
    while I mused the fire blazed and I I spoke I with my I
      tongue;

4 'Lord let me I know my I end:
    and the I number I of my I days,

†5 'That I may know how I short my I time is:
    for you have made my days but a handsbreadth
    and my whole I span · is as I nothing · be|fore you.'

6 Surely every man though he stand secure I is but I
      breath:
    man I lives · as a I passing I shadow.

7 The riches he heaps are but a | puff of | wind:
 and he cannot | tell | who will | gather them.

8 And now Lord | what is · my | hope?:
 truly my | hope | is in | you.

9 O deliver me from | all · my trans|gressions:
 do not | make me · the | butt of | fools.

10 I was dumb   I did not | open · my | mouth:
 for surely | it was | your | doing.

11 Take away your | plague | from me:
 I am brought to an | end · by the | blows · of your |
  hand.

12 When with rebukes you chastise a | man for | sin:
 you cause his fair looks to dissolve in putrefaction
  surely | every · man | is but | breath.

13 Hear my prayer O Lord   and give | ear to · my | cry:
 be not | silent | at my | tears.

14 For I am but a | stranger · with | you:
 a passing guest as | all my | fathers | were.

15 Turn your eye from me   that I may | smile a|gain:
 before I go | hence and | am no | more.

PSALM 40

1 I waited patiently | for the | Lord:
 and he in|clined to me · and | heard my | cry.

2 He brought me up from the pit of roaring waters
  out of the | mire and | clay:
 and set my feet upon a | rock · and made | firm my |
  foothold.

3 And he has put a new | song · in my | mouth:
 even a song of | thanks·giving | to our | God.

4 Many shall | see it · and | fear:
 and shall | put their | trust · in the | Lord.

5 Blessèd is the man who has made the | Lord his | hope:
 who has not turned to the proud
  or to those who | wander | in de|ceit.

6 O Lord my God
    great are the wonderful things which you have ⌣
    done   and your thoughts which I are to|wards us:
  there is none to I be com|pared with I you;

†7 Were I to de|clare them · and I speak of them:
  they are more than I am I able I to ex|press.

8 Sacrifice and offering you do I not de|sire:
  but my I ears · you have I marked · for o|bedience;

9 Burnt-offering and sin-offering you have I not re|quired:
  then I said I I   Lo I I come.

10 In the scroll of the book it is written of me ⌣
    that I should I do your I will:
  O my God I long to do it * your I law de|lights my I
  heart.

11 I have declared your righteousness ⌣
    in the I great · congre|gation:
  I have not restrained my lips O I Lord ⌣
  and I that you I know.

12 I have not hidden your righteousness I in my I heart:
  I have spoken of your faithfulness I and of I
  your sal|vation.

13 I have not kept back your loving-kindness I and your I
  truth:
  from the I great I congre|gation.

14 O Lord do not withhold your I mercy I from me:
  let your loving-kindness and your I truth I ever ·
  pre|serve me.

15 For innumerable troubles have I come up|on me:
  my sins have overtaken me I and I I cannot I see.

16 They are more in number than the I hairs · of my I head:
  there|fore my I heart I fails me.

17 Be pleased O I Lord · to de|liver me:
  O I Lord make I haste to I help me.

18 Let those who seek my life to I take it · a|way:
  be put to shame and con|founded I alto|gether.

19 Let them be turned back and disgraced who | wish me |
    evil:
      let them be aghast for shame who |
      say to me · 'A|ha a|ha!'

20 Let all who seek you be joyful and |
      glad be|cause of you:
      let those who love your salvation say | always ·
      'The | Lord is | great.'

21 As for me I am | poor and | needy:
      but the | Lord will | care | for me.

†22 You are my helper and | my de|liverer:
      make no long de|lay O | Lord my | God.

PSALM 41

1 Blessèd is he that considers the | poor and | helpless:
      the Lord will deliver him | in the | day of | trouble.

2 The Lord will guard him and preserve his life
      he shall be counted | happy · in the | land:
      you will not give him | over · to the | will · of his |
      enemies.

†3 And if he lies sick on his bed the | Lord · will sus|tain
      him:
      if illness lays him | low · you will | over|throw it.

4 I said 'O Lord be | merciful · to|ward me:
      heal me for | I have | sinned a|gainst you.'

5 My enemies speak evil | of me | saying:
      'When will he die and his | name | perish · for |
      ever?'

6 And if one should come to see me he mouths |
      empty | words:
      while his heart gathers mischief
      and | when he · goes | out he | vents it.

7 All those that hate me whisper to|gether · a|gainst me:
      they de|vise | plots a|gainst me.

8 They say 'A deadly | thing has · got | hold of him:
      he will not get up a|gain from | where he | lies.'

9 Even my bosom friend in I whom I I trusted:
who shared my bread ' has I lifted · his I
heel aIgainst me.

10 But you O Lord be gracious and I raise me I up:
and I will repay them I what they I have deIserved.

11 By this will I I know that · you I favour me:
that my enemy I shall not I triumph I over me.

(†)12 Because of my innocence you I hold me I fast:
you have set me beIfore your I face for I ever.

(13 Blessèd be the Lord the I God of I Israel:
from everlasting to everlasting * I Amen I   A–Imen.)

PSALM 42

1 As a deer longs for the I running I brooks:
so longs my I soul for I you O I God.

2 My soul is thirsty for God * thirsty for the I living I
God:
when shall I I come and I see his I face?

3 My tears have been my food I day and I night:
while they ask me all day long I   'Where now I
is your I God?'

4 As I pour out my soul by myself I reImember I this:
how I went to the house of the Mighty One I ⌣
into · the I temple · of I God,

†5 To the shouts and I songs of · thanksIgiving:
a multitude I keeping I high I festival.

6 *Why are you so full of I heaviness · my I soul:
and I why · so unIquiet · withIin me?*

7 *O put your I trust in I God:
for I will praise him yet
who is my deIliver·er I and my I God.*

8 My soul is I heavy · withIin me:
therefore I will remember you from the land of
Jordan
from Mizar aImong the I hills of I Hermon.

181

9 Deep calls to deep in the ǀ roar of · your ǀ waters:
  all your waves and ǀ breakers ǀ have gone ǀ over me.

10 Surely the Lord will grant his loving mercy ǀ in the ǀ
   day-time:
   and in the night his song will be with me
   a ǀ prayer · to the ǀ God · of my ǀ life.

11 I will say to God my rock 'Why have ǀ
   you forǀgotten me:
   why must I go like a mourner beǀcause the ǀ enemy ·
   opǀpresses me?'

†12 Like a sword through my bones my ǀ enemies · have ǀ
   mocked me:
   while they ask me all day long ǀ 'Where now ǀ
   is your ǀ God?'

13 *Why are you so full of ǀ heaviness · my ǀ soul:*
   and ǀ why · so unǀquiet · withǀin me?

14 *O put your ǀ trust in ǀ God:*
   for I will praise him yet
   who is my deǀliver·er ǀ and my ǀ God.

PSALM 43

1 Give judgment for me O God
  take up my cause against an unǀgodly ǀ people:
  deliver me from deǀceitful · and ǀ wicked ǀ men.

2 For you are God my refuge why have you ǀ turned ·
  me aǀway:
  why must I go like a mourner ‿
  beǀcause the ǀ enemy · opǀpresses me?

3 O send out your light and your truth and ǀ let them ǀ
  lead me:
  let them guide me to your holy ǀ hill and ǀ to your ǀ
  dwelling.

4 Then I shall go to the altar of God
  to God my joy and ǀ my deǀlight:
  and to the harp I shall sing your ǀ praises · O ǀ
  God my ǀ God.

5 *Why are you so full of | heaviness · my | soul:*
   and | why · so un|quiet · with|in me?

6 *O put your | trust in | God:*
   for I will praise him yet
   who is my de|liver·er | and my | God.

PSALM 44

1 We have heard with our ears O God —
      our | fathers · have | told us:
   what things you did in their | time · in the | days of |
      old;

2 How by your own hand you drove out the nations —
      and | planted · us | in:
   how you crushed the peoples
      but caused | us to | root and | grow.

3 For it was not by their swords —
      that our fathers took pos|session · of the | land:
   nor did their own | arm | get them · the | victory,

4 But your right hand | your arm —
      and the | light of · your | countenance:
   be|cause · you de|lighted · in | them.

5 You are my | king · and my | God:
      who or|dained | victory · for | Jacob.

6 By your power we struck our | ene·mies | through:
      in your name we trod down | those that |
         rose a|gainst us.

7 For I did not | trust · in my | bow:
      nor | could my | sword | save me;

8 But it was you that delivered us | from our | enemies:
      and put our | adver·saries | to con|fusion.

†9 In God we made our boast | all the · day | long:
      we gave | thanks to · your | name with·out | ceasing.

10 But now you have cast us off and | brought us · to |
         shame:
      you | go not | out · with our | armies.

11 You have caused us to show our | backs · to the | enemy:
    so that our foes | plunder | us at | will.

12 You have given us like | sheep · to be | butchered:
    you have | scattered us · a|mong the | nations.

13 You have sold your | people · for | nothing:
    and | made a | profit·less | bargain.

14 You have made us a laughing-stock | to our | neighbours:
    mocked and held in de|rision · by | those a|bout us.

15 You have made us a byword a|mong the | nations:
    so that the peoples | toss their | heads in | scorn.

16 My disgrace is before me | all the | day:
    and | shame has | covered · my | face,

17 At the voice of the slanderer | and re|viler:
    at the sight of the | ene·my | and a|venger.

18 All this has come upon us   though we have | not for|gotten you:
    we have | not be|trayed your | covenant.

19 Our hearts have | not turned | back:
    nor have our steps | strayed | from your | paths.

20 And yet you have crushed us in the | haunt of | jackals:
    and covered us | with the | shadow · of | death.

21 If we had forgotten the | name of · our | God:
    or stretched out our hands in | prayer to · some | strange | god,

22 Would not God | search it | out?:
    for he knows the very | secrets | of the | heart.

23 But for your sake are we killed | all the · | day | long:
    we are | counted · as | sheep · for the | slaughter.

24 Rouse yourself O Lord | why · do you | sleep?:
    awake do not | cast us | off for | ever.

25 Why do you | hide your | face:
    and forget our | misery · and | our af|fliction?

26 Our souls are | bowed · to the | dust:
    our | bellies | cleave · to the | ground.

27 Arise O ∣ Lord to ∣ help us:
  and redeem us ∣ for your ∣ mercy's ∣ sake.

PSALM 45

1 My heart is astir with fine phrases
    I make my ∣ song · for a ∣ king:
  my tongue is the ∣ pen · of a ∣ ready ∣ writer.

2 You are the fairest of the sons of men
    grace ∣ flows · from your ∣ lips:
  therefore has God ∣ blessed you · for ∣ ever · and ∣
    ever.

3 Gird your sword upon your thigh O ∣ mighty ∣ warrior:
  in glory and majesty tread ∣ down your ∣ foes and ∣
    triumph!

4 Ride on in the ∣ cause of ∣ truth:
  and ∣ for the ∣ sake of ∣ justice.

5 Your right hand shall teach a ∣ terrible · in∣struction:
  peoples shall fall beneath you * your arrows shall be ⌣
    'sharp in the ∣ hearts · of the ∣ king's ∣ enemies.

6 Your throne is the throne of God ∣ it en∣dures for ∣
    ever:
  and the sceptre of your ∣ kingdom · is a ∣ righteous ∣
    sceptre.

7 You have loved righteousness and ∣ hated ∣ evil:
  therefore God your God * has anointed you ⌣
    with the oil of ∣ gladness · a∣bove your ∣ fellows.

8 All your garments are fragrant ⌣
    with myrrh ∣ aloes · and ∣ cassia:
  music from ivory ∣ pala·ces ∣ makes you ∣ glad.

†9 Kings' daughters are among your ∣ noble ∣ women:
  the queen is at your right ∣ hand in ∣ gold of ∣ Ophir.

10 Hear O daughter   consider and in∣cline your ∣ ear:
  forget your own ∣ people · and your ∣ father's ∣ house.

11 The king de∣sires your ∣ beauty:
  he is your lord   ∣ therefore · bow ∣ down be∣fore him.

†12 The richest among the people O | daughter · of | Tyre:
　　shall en|treat your | favour · with | gifts.

13 The king's daughter is all | glorious · with|in:
　　her clothing is em|broidered | cloth of | gold.

14 In robes of many colours she is led to | you O | king:
　　and after her the | virgins | that are | with her.

†15 They are led with | gladness · and re|joicing:
　　they enter the | palace | of the | king.

16 In place of your fathers | you shall · have | sons:
　　and make them princes | over | all the | land.

17 And I will make known your name to every |
　　　gener|ation:
　　therefore the peoples shall | give you | praise for |
　　　ever.

PSALM 46

1 God is our | refuge · and | strength:
　　a very | present | help in | trouble.

2 Therefore we will not fear though the | earth be | moved:
　　and though the mountains are | shaken · in the |
　　　midst · of the | sea;

†3 Though the waters | rage and | foam:
　　and though the mountains quake at the |
　　　rising | of the | sea.

4 There is a river whose streams make glad the | city · of |
　　　God:
　　the holy dwelling-place | of the | Most | High.

5 God is in the midst of her
　　　therefore she shall | not be | moved:
　　God will | help her · and at | break of | day.

6 The nations make uproar and the | kingdoms · are |
　　　shaken:
　　but God has lifted his | voice · and the | earth shall |
　　　tremble.

.7 *The Lord of | hosts is | with us:*
    the God of | Jacob | is our | stronghold.

8 Come then and see what the | Lord has | done:
    what destruction he has | brought up|on the | earth.

9 He makes wars to cease in | all the | world:
    he breaks the bow and shatters the spear
    and burns the | chari·ots | in the | fire.

10 'Be still and know that | I am | God:
    I will be exalted among the nations
    I will be ex|alted · up|on the | earth.'

11 *The Lord of | hosts is | with us:*
    the God of | Jacob | is our | stronghold.

PSALM 47

1 O clap your hands | all you | peoples:
    and cry aloud to | God with | shouts of | joy.

2 For the Lord Most High | is to · be | feared:
    he is a great | King · over | all the | earth.

3 He cast down | peoples | under us:
    and the | nations · be|neath our | feet.

4 He chose us a land for | our pos|session:
    that was the pride of | Jacob | whom he | loved.

5 God has gone up with the | sound · of re|joicing:
    and the | Lord · to the | blast · of the | horn.

6 O sing praises sing | praises · to | God:
    O sing praises sing | praises | to our | King.

7 For God is the King of | all the | earth:
    O | praise him · in a | well-wrought | psalm.

8 God has become the | King · of the | nations:
    he has taken his seat up|on his | holy | throne.

9 The princes of the peoples are | gathered · to|gether:
    with the | people · of the | God of | Abraham.

10 For the mighty ones of the earth␣
        are become the | servants · of | God:
  and | he is | greatly · ex|alted.

PSALM 48

1 Great is the Lord and | greatly · to be | praised:
  in the | city | of our | God.

2 High and beautiful is his | holy | hill:
  it is the | joy of | all the | earth.

†3 On Mount Zion where godhead truly dwells
        stands the city of the | Great | King:
  God is well known in her palaces | as a | sure de|fence.

4 For the kings of the | earth as|sembled:
  they gathered to|gether · and | came | on;

5 They saw they were | struck | dumb:
  they were a|stonished · and | fled in | terror.

6 Trembling took | hold on them · and | anguish:
  as on a | woman | in her | travail;

7 Like the breath of the | east | wind:
  that | shatters · the | ships of | Tarshish.

8 As we have heard so have we seen␣
        in the city of the | Lord of | hosts:
  in the city of our God␣
        which | God · has es|tablished · for | ever.

9 We have called to mind your loving-|kindness · O | God:
  in the | midst of | your | temple.

10 As your name is great O God so also | is your | praise:
  even to the | ends | of the | earth.

11 Your right hand is full of victory
        let Zion's | hill re|joice:
  let the daughters of Judah be | glad␣
        be|cause of · your | judgments.

12 Walk about Zion go round about her ␣
  and | count · all her | towers:

consider well her ramparts ǀ pass ǀ through her ǀ
    palaces;

13 That you may tell those who come after that ǀ such is ǀ
    God:
    our God for ever and ever * and ǀ he will ǀ guide us ·
    eǀternally.

PSALM 49

1 O hear this ǀ all you ǀ peoples:
    give ear all you inǀhabit·ants ǀ of the ǀ world,

2 All children of men and ǀ sons of ǀ Adam:
    both ǀ rich and ǀ poor aǀlike.

3 For my mouth shall ǀ speak ǀ wisdom:
    and the thoughts of my heart ⏤
        shall be ǀ full of ǀ underǀstanding.

4 I will incline my ǀ ear · to a ǀ riddle:
    and unfold the mystery to the ǀ sounds ǀ of the ǀ harp.

5 Why should I fear in the ǀ evil ǀ days:
    when the wickedness of ǀ my deǀceivers · surǀrounds
        me,

6 Though they trust to their ǀ great ǀ wealth:
    and boast of the aǀbundance ǀ of their ǀ riches?

7 No man may ǀ ransom · his ǀ brother:
    or give ǀ God a ǀ price ǀ for him,

8 So that he may ǀ live for ǀ ever:
    and ǀ never ǀ see the ǀ grave;

9 For to ransom men's ǀ lives · is so ǀ costly:
    that he must aǀbandon ǀ it for ǀ ever.

10 For we see that ǀ wise men ǀ die:
    and perish with the foolish and the ignorant ǀ
        leaving · their ǀ wealth to ǀ others.

†11 The tomb is their home for ever
        their dwelling-place throughout ǀ all · generǀations:
    though they called estates ǀ after · their ǀ own ǀ names.

12 A rich man without I under|standing:
    is I like the I beasts that I perish.

13 This is the I lot · of the I foolish:
    the end of those who are I pleased · with their I own I
       words.

14 They are driven like sheep into the grave ⌣
    and I death · is their I shepherd:
    they slip down I easi·ly I into · the I tomb.

15 Their bright forms shall wear a|way · in the I grave:
    and I lose their I former I glory.

†16 But God will I ransom · my I life:
    he will take me I from the I power · of the I grave.

17 Do not fear when a I man grows I rich:
    when the I wealth · of his I household · in|creases,

18 For he will take nothing a|way · when he I dies:
    nor will his I wealth go I down I after him.

19 Though he counts himself happy I while he I lives:
    and praises you I also I when you I prosper,

20 He will go to the company I of his I fathers:
    who will I never I see the I light.

†21 A rich man without I under|standing:
    is I like the I beasts that I perish.

PSALM 50

1 The Lord our God the I Mighty One · has I spoken:
    and summoned the earth * from the rising of ⌣
    the sun to its I setting I in the I west.

2 From Zion I perfect · in I beauty:
    God has I shone I out in I glory.

3 Our God is coming   he will I not keep I silent:
    before him is devouring fire
    and I tempest I whirls a|bout him.

4 He calls to the I heavens · a|bove:
    and to the earth so I he may I judge his I people.

5 'Gather to I me my I faithful ones:
  those who by sacrifice I made a I coven·ant I with me.'

6 The heavens shall proIclaim his I righteousness:
  for I God himIself is I judge.

7 'Listen my people and I I will I speak:
  O Israel I am God your God   and I I will I give my I testimony.

8 'It is not for your sacrifices that I I reIprove you:
  for your burnt-Iofferings · are I always · beIfore me.

9 'I will take no I bull · from your I farms:
  or I he-goat I from your I pens.

10 'For all the beasts of the forest beIlong to I me:
  and so do the I cattle · upIon the I mountains.

11 'I know all the I birds · of the I air:
  and the grasshoppers of the I field are I in my I sight.

12 'If I were hungry I I would not I tell you:
  for the whole world is I mine and I all · that is I in it.

13 'Do I eat the I flesh of I bulls:
  or I drink the I blood of I goats?

14 'Offer to God a sacrifice of I thanksIgiving:
  and pay your I vows · to the I Most I High.

†15 'Call upon me in the I day of I trouble:
  I will bring you out   and I you shall I glori·fy I me.'

16 But God I says · to the I wicked:
  'What have you to do with reciting my laws
  or taking my I coven·ant I on your I lips,

17 'Seeing you I loathe I discipline:
  and have I tossed my I words beIhind you?

18 'When you saw a thief you I went aIlong with him:
  and you I threw in · your I lot · with adIulterers.

19 'You have loosed your I mouth in I evil:
  and your I tongue strings I lies toIgether.

20 'You sit and speak aIgainst your I brother:
  and slander your I own I mother's I son.

191

21 'These things you have done   and I | held my | tongue:
    and you thought I was just such an|other |
       as your|self.

22 'But I | will con|vict you:
    and set before your | eyes what | you have | done.

23 'O consider this   you who for|get | God:
    lest I tear you in pieces   and | there be | no one · to |
       save you.

†24 'He honours me who brings sacrifice of | thanks|giving:
    and to him who keeps to my way ⌣
       I will | show the · sal|vation · of | God.'

PSALM 51

1 Have mercy on me O God in your en|during | goodness:
    according to the fulness of your compassion | ⌣
       blot out | my of|fences.

2 Wash me thoroughly | from my | wickedness:
    and | cleanse me | from my | sin.

3 For I acknowledge | my re|bellion:
    and my | sin is | ever · be|fore me.

4 Against you only have I sinned
    and done what is evil | in your | eyes:
    so you will be just in your sentence
    and | blameless | in your | judging.

5 Surely in wickedness I was | brought to | birth:
    and in | sin my | mother · con|ceived me.

6 You that desire truth in the | inward | parts:
    O teach me wisdom in the secret | places | of the |
       heart.

7 Purge me with hyssop and I | shall be | clean:
    wash me and I | shall be | whiter · than | snow.

8 Make me hear of | joy and | gladness:
    let the bones which | you have | broken · re|joice.

9 Hide your | face · from my | sins:
    and | blot out | all · my in|iquities.

10 Create in me a clean I heart O I God:
    and reInew a · right I spirit · withIin me.

11 Do not cast me I out · from your I presence:
    do not take your I holy I spirit I from me.

12 O give me the gladness of your I help aIgain:
    and supIport me · with a I willing I spirit.

†13 Then will I teach transIgressors · your I ways:
    and sinners shall I turn to I you aIgain.

14 O Lord God of my salvation deIliver me · from I
      bloodshed:
    and my I tongue shall I sing of · your I righteousness.

15 O Lord I open · my I lips:
    and my I mouth · shall proIclaim your I praise.

16 You take no pleasure in sacrifice or I I would I give it:
    burnt-Iofferings · you I do not I want.

17 The sacrifice of God is a I broken I spirit:
    a broken and contrite heart O God I you will I
      not deIspise.

18 In your graciousness do I good to I Zion:
    reIbuild the I walls · of JeIrusalem.

19 Then will you delight in right sacrifices
    in burnt-offerings I and obIlations:
    then will they offer young I bulls upIon your I altar.

PSALM 52

1 Why O man of power do you boast I all the · day I long:
    of mischief done to I him · that is I faithful · to I God?

2 You contrive deIstroying I slanders:
    your tongue is like a sharpened I
      razor· it I cuts deIceitfully.

3 You have loved evil I and not I good:
    to tell lies I rather · than to I speak the I truth.

4 You love all words that I may do I hurt:
    and I every · deIceit · of the I tongue.

5 But God will de|stroy you | utterly:
>> he will snatch you away and pluck you out of your ⁔
>> dwelling
>> he will up|root you · from the | land · of the | living.

6 The righteous shall | see it · and | fear:
>> they shall | laugh you · to | scorn and | say,

†7 'Behold   this is the man ⁔
>> who did not take | God · for his | strength:
>> but trusted in the abundance of his riches
>> and | found his | strength in | slander.'

8 As for me   I am like a green olive tree in the | house of |
>> God:
>> I will trust in the goodness of | God for | ever · and |
>> ever.

9 I will always give you thanks * for this was | your |
>> doing:
>> I will glorify your name before the faithful
>> for | it is | good to | praise you.

PSALM 53

1 The fool has said in his heart   'There | is no | God':
>> they have all become vile and abominable in their ⁔
>> wickedness * there | is not | one that · does | good.

2 God looked down from heaven upon the | children · of |
>> men:
>> to see if there were any who would act | wisely ·
>> and | seek · after | God.

3 But they have all turned aside
>> they have all alike be|come cor|rupt:
>> there is none that does | good | no not | one.

4 Are all the evildoers devoid of | under|standing:
>> who eat up my people as men eat bread
>> and | do not | pray to | God?

5 They shall be | struck with | terror:
>> for God will scatter the | bones | of the · un|godly.

6 They shall be ǀ put to · conǀfusion:
    because ǀ God ǀ has reǀjected them.

†7 O that deliverance for Israel might come ǀ forth from ǀ
    Zion:
    when the Lord turns again the fortunes of his people
    then shall Jacob reǀjoice and ǀ Israel · be ǀ glad.

PSALM 54

1 Save me O God by the ǀ power of · your ǀ name:
    and ǀ vindicate · me ǀ by your ǀ might.

2 Hear my ǀ prayer O ǀ God:
    and ǀ listen · to the ǀ words of · my ǀ mouth.

3 For the insolent have ǀ risen · aǀgainst me:
    ruthless men who have not set God beǀfore them ǀ ‿
    seek my ǀ life.

4 But surely ǀ God is · my ǀ helper:
    the Lord is the upǀholder ǀ of my ǀ life.

[5 Let evil recoil on those that ǀ would wayǀlay me:
    O deǀstroy them ǀ in your ǀ faithfulness!]

6 Then will I offer you sacrifice with a ǀ willing ǀ heart:
    I will praise your name O ǀ Lord for ǀ it is ǀ good.

[†]7 For you will deliver me from ǀ every ǀ trouble:
    my eyes shall see the ǀ downfall ǀ of my ǀ enemies.

PSALM 55

1 Hear my ǀ prayer O ǀ God:
    and do not hide yourǀself from ǀ my peǀtition.

2 Give heed to ǀ me and ǀ answer me:
    I am ǀ restless · in ǀ my comǀplaining.

3 I am in turmoil at the ǀ voice · of the ǀ enemy:
    at the ǀ onslaught ǀ of the ǀ wicked.

4 For they bring down disǀaster · upǀon me:
    they persecute ǀ me with ǀ bitter ǀ fury.

5 My heart ǀ writhes withǀin me:
    and the terrors of ǀ death have ǀ fallen · upǀon me.

6 Fear and trembling ı come upıon me:
  and ı horror ı overıwhelms me.

7 And I said 'O for the ı wings · of a ı dove:
  that I might fly aıway and ı find ı rest.

8 'Then I would ı flee far ı off:
  and make my ı lodging ı in the ı wilderness.

9 'I would hasten to ı find me · a ı refuge:
  out ı of the ı blast of ı slander,

10 'Out of the tempest of their ı calumny · O ı Lord:
  and ı far · from their ı double ı tongues.'

11 For I have seen violence and ı strife · in the ı city:
  day and night they go ı round it · upıon its ı walls.

12 Evil and wickedness ı are withıin it:
  iniquity is within it * oppression and fraud do ı
    not deıpart · from its ı streets.

13 It was not an enemy that reviled me
    or I ı might have ı borne it:
  it was not my foe that dealt so insolently with me
    or I might have ı hidden · myıself ı from him;

14 But it was you a ı man · like myıself:
  my companion ı and · my famıiliar ı friend.

†15 Together we enıjoyed sweet ı fellowship:
  in the ı house ı of our ı God.

[16 Let them pass aıway · in conıfusion:
  let death ı carry · them ı to desıtruction;

17 Let them go down aılive to ı Sheol:
  for evil is aımong them ı in their ı dwellings.]

18 But I will ı call to ı God:
  and the ı Lord my ı God will ı save me.

19 At evening at morning ı and at ı noon-day:
  I comıplain and ı groan aıloud.

20 And he will ı hear my ı voice:
  and ı ransom · my ı soul in ı peace,

21 From those that bear ǀ down upǀon me:
   for ǀ there are ǀ many · aǀgainst me.

22 God will hear and ǀ bring them ǀ low:
   he that ǀ is enǀthroned for ǀ ever.

23 For they do not ǀ keep their ǀ word:
   and they ǀ have no ǀ fear of ǀ God.

24 They lay violent hands ⏝
      on those that ǀ are at ǀ peace with them:
   they ǀ break ǀ solemn ǀ covenants.

25 Their mouths are smooth as butter
      but war is ǀ in their ǀ hearts:
   their words are softer than oil
      yet ǀ they are ǀ drawn ǀ swords.

26 Cast your burden on the Lord and ǀ
      he · will susǀtain you:
   he will never suffer the ǀ righteous ǀ man to ǀ stumble.

27 But as for them   you will bring them ǀ down O ǀ God:
   even ǀ to the ǀ depths · of the ǀ Pit.

†28 Bloodthirsty and deceitful men ⏝
      shall not live out ǀ half their ǀ days:
   but ǀ I will ǀ trust in ǀ you.

PSALM 56

1 Be merciful to me O God   for men are ǀ treading · me ǀ
      down:
   all day long my ǀ adver·sary ǀ presses · upǀon me.

2 My enemies tread me down ǀ all the ǀ day:
   for there are many that ǀ arrogant·ly ǀ
      fight aǀgainst me.

3 In the ǀ hour of ǀ fear:
   I will ǀ put my ǀ trust in ǀ you.

4 In God whose word I praise * in God I ǀ trust and ǀ
      fear not:
   what can ǀ flesh ǀ do to ǀ me?

5 All day long they afflict me ǀ with their ǀ words:
   and every thought is ǀ how to ǀ do me ǀ evil.

6 They stir up hatred | and con|ceal themselves:
   they watch my steps   while they | lie in |
      wait for · my | life.

7 Let there be | no es|cape for them:
   bring down the | peoples · in your | wrath O | God.

8 You have counted my anxious tossings
      put my | tears · in your | bottle:
   are not these things | noted | in your | book?

9 In the day that I call to you   my enemies shall | turn |
      back:
   this I | know   for | God is | with me.

10 In God whose word I praise * in God I | trust and |
      fear not:
   what can | man | do to | me?

11 To you O God must I per|form my | vows:
   I will pay the thank-|offer·ing | that is | due.

12 For you will deliver my soul from death_
      and my | feet from | falling:
   that I may walk before | God · in the | light · of the |
      living.

PSALM 57

1 Be merciful to me O | God be | merciful:
   for I | come to | you for | shelter;

2 And in the shadow of your wings will | I take | refuge:
   until these | troubles · are | over-|past.

3 I will call to | God Most | High:
   to the God who will ful|fil his | purpose | for me.

4 He will send from | heaven · and | save me:
   he will send forth his faithfulness and his_
      loving-kindness
   and rebuke | those · that would | trample · me | down.

5 For I lie amidst | raven·ing | lions:
   men whose teeth are spears and arrows
      and their | tongue a | sharpened | sword.

6 *Be exalted O God a\bove the | heavens:*
  and let your glory be | over | all the | earth.

7 They have set a net for my feet   and I am | brought |
    low:
   they have dug a pit before me
     but shall | fall · into | it them\selves.

8 My heart is fixed O God my | heart is | fixed:
   I will | sing and | make | melody.

9 Awake my soul   awake | lute and | harp:
   for | I · will a\waken · the | morning.

10 I will give you thanks O Lord a\mong the | peoples:
    I will sing your | praise a\mong the | nations.

11 For the greatness of your mercy | reaches · to the |
     heavens:
    and your | faithful·ness | to the | clouds.

12 *Be exalted O God a\bove the | heavens:*
   and let your glory be | over | all the | earth.

PSALM 58

[1 Do you indeed decree what is | just O | rulers:
   do you with uprightness | judge the | children · of |
     men?

 2 No   you work in the land with | evil | heart:
    you look on the violence | that your | hands have |
      wrought.

 3 The wicked are estranged | even · from the | womb:
    they are liars that go a\stray | from their | birth.

 4 They are venomous with the | venom · of | serpents:
    like the deaf | asp that | stops its | ears,

†5 And will not heed the | voice · of the | charmers:
    though the | binder · of | spells be | skilful.

 6 Break their teeth O | God · in their | mouths:
    shatter the jaws of the | young | lions · O | Lord.

 7 Let them dissolve and drain a\way like | water:
    let them be trodden down | let them | wither · like |
      grass,

8 Like a woman's miscarriage that melts and | passes ·
    a|way:
    like an abortive birth that | has not | seen the | sun.

9 Before they know it   let them be cut | down like |
    thorns:
    like brambles which a | man sweeps | angrily · a|side.

10 The righteous shall rejoice when he | sees the |
    vengeance:
    he will wash his feet in the | blood of | the un|godly.

11 And men will say   'There is re|ward · for the |
    righteous:
    there is indeed a | God who | judges · on | earth.']

PSALM 59

1 Deliver me from my | enemies · O | God:
    lift me to safety from | those that | rise a|gainst me;

2 O deliver me from the | evil|doers:
    and | save me · from | blood·thirsty | men.

3 For they lie in | wait · for my | life:
    savage men | stir up | violence · a|gainst me.

4 Not for my sin or my transgression O Lord
    not for any | evil · I have | done:
    do they run and take | up po|sition · a|gainst me.

(†)5 Arise to | meet me · and | see:
    you that are Lord of | hosts and | God of | Israel.

[6   Awake to punish | all the | nations:
    have no mercy on those that so | treacherous·ly | do |
    wrong.]

7 They return every evening   they | howl like | dogs:
    they | prowl a|round the | city.

8 Look how their | mouths | slaver:
    swords strike from their lips
    for they | say | 'Who will | hear it?'

9 But you O Lord will | laugh them · to | scorn:
    you will de|ride | all the | nations.

10 I will look to ǀ you · O my ǀ strength:
  for ǀ God is · my ǀ strong ǀ tower.

11 My God in his steadfastness will ǀ come to ǀ meet me:
  God will show me the ǀ downfall ǀ of my ǀ enemies.

12 Slay them not O Lord   lest my ǀ people · forǀget:
  but make them stagger by your ǀ power and ǀ
    bring them ǀ down.

13 Give them over to punishment * for the sin of their ⌣
    mouths for the ǀ words of · their ǀ lips:
  let them be ǀ taken ǀ in their ǀ pride.

[14 For the curses and lies that they have uttered
    O consume them ǀ in your ǀ wrath:
  consume them ǀ till they ǀ are no ǀ more;]

[†]15 That men may know that God ǀ rules · over ǀ Jacob:
  even to the ǀ ends ǀ of the ǀ earth.

16 They return every evening   they ǀ howl like ǀ dogs:
  they ǀ prowl aǀround the ǀ city.

17 They roam here and there ǀ looking · for ǀ food:
  and ǀ growl · if they ǀ are not ǀ filled.

18 But I will ǀ sing of · your ǀ might:
  I will sing aloud each ǀ morning ǀ of your ǀ goodness.

19 For you have been my ǀ strong ǀ tower:
  and a sure refuge in the ǀ day of ǀ my disǀtress.

†20 I will sing your praises ǀ O my ǀ strength:
  for ǀ God is · my ǀ strong ǀ tower.

PSALM 60

1 O God you have cast us ǀ off and ǀ broken us:
  you were enraged against us   ǀ O reǀstore us ·
    aǀgain!

2 You have caused the land to quake   you have ǀ rent it ǀ
    open:
  heal the rifts for the ǀ earth ǀ quivers · and ǀ breaks.

3 You have steeped your people in a ǀ bitter ǀ draught:
  you have given them a ǀ wine to ǀ make them ǀ
    stagger.

4 You have caused those that fear you to I take I flight:
    so that they I run I from the I bow.

†5 O save us by your right I hand and I answer us:
    that those whom you I love may I be deI livered.

6 God has said in his I holy I place:
    'I will exult and divide Shechem
        I will parcel I out the I valley · of I Succoth.

7 'Gilead is mine and MaI nasseh · is I mine:
    Ephraim is my helmet and I Judah · my I
        rod · of comI mand.

†8 'Moab is my wash-bowl over Edom will I I cast my I
    shoe:
    against Philistia I will I I shout in I triumph.'

9 Who will lead me into the I forti·fied I city:
    who will I bring me I into I Edom?

10 Have you not cast us I off O I God?:
    you I go not I out · with our I armies.

11 Give us your help aI gainst the I enemy:
    for I vain · is the I help·of I man.

12 By the power of our God we I shall do I valiantly:
    for it is he that will I tread I down our I enemies.

PSALM 61

1 Hear my loud I crying · O I God:
    and give I heed I to my I prayer.

2 From the ends of the earth I call to you⏝
        when my I heart I faints:
    O set me on the I rock · that is I higher · than I I.

3 For you have I been my I refuge:
    and my strong I tower aI gainst the I enemy.

4 I will dwell in your I tent for I ever:
    and find shelter in the I cover·ing I of your I wings.

5 For you have heard my ǀ vows O ǀ God:
    you have granted the desire of ǀ those that ǀ fear your ǀ
        name.

6 You will give the ǀ king long ǀ life:
    and his years shall endure through ǀ many ǀ
        generǀations.

7 He shall dwell before ǀ God for ǀ ever:
    loving-kindness and ǀ truth shall ǀ be his ǀ guard.

8 So will I ever sing praises ǀ to your ǀ name:
    while I ǀ daily · perǀform my ǀ vows.

PSALM 62

1 My soul waits in ǀ silence · for ⌈ God:
    for from ǀ him comes ǀ my salǀvation.

2 He only is my rock and ǀ my salǀvation:
    my strong tower   so that ǀ I shall ǀ never · be ǀ moved.

3 How long will you all plot against a ǀ
        man · to deǀstroy him:
    as though he were a leaning ǀ fence · or a ǀ buckling ǀ
        wall?

4 Their design is to thrust him from his height
        and their deǀlight · is in ǀ lies:
    they bless with their ǀ lips but ǀ inwardly · they ǀ curse.

5 Nevertheless my soul   wait in ǀ silence · for ǀ God:
    for from ǀ him ǀ comes my ǀ hope.

6 He only is my rock and ǀ my salǀvation:
    my strong tower   so that ǀ I shall ǀ not be ǀ moved.

7 In God is my deliverance ǀ and my ǀ glory:
    God is my strong ǀ rock ǀ and my ǀ shelter.

8 Trust in him at all times ǀ O my ǀ people:
    pour out your hearts before him   for ǀ God ǀ is our ǀ
        refuge.

9 The children of men are but breath
        the children of ǀ men · are a ǀ lie:
    place them in the scales and they fly upward
        they ǀ are as ǀ light as ǀ air.

10 Put no trust in extortion
      do not grow | worthless · by | robbery:
      if riches increase | set not · your | heart up|on them.

11 God has spoken once   twice have I | heard him | say:
      that | power be|longs to | God,

12 That to the Lord belongs a | constant | goodness:
      for you reward a man ac|cording | to his | works.

PSALM 63

1 O God | you are · my | God:
      eagerly | will I | seek | you.

2 My soul thirsts for you   my | flesh | longs for you:
      as a dry and thirsty | land · where no | water | is.

3 So it was when I beheld you | in the | sanctuary:
      and | saw your | power · and your | glory.

4 For your unchanging goodness is | better · than | life:
      there|fore my | lips shall | praise you.

5 And so I will bless you as | long as · I | live:
      and in your name will I | lift my | hands on | high.

6 My longing shall be satisfied__
      as with | marrow · and | fatness:
      my mouth shall | praise you · with ex|ultant | lips.

7 When I remember you up|on my | bed:
      when I meditate up|on you · in the | night | watches,

8 How you have | been my | helper:
      then I sing for joy in the | shadow | of your | wings,

†9 Then my | soul | clings to you:
      and | your right | hand up|holds me.

10 Those that seek my life are | marked · for de|struction:
      they shall go down to the deep | places | of the | earth.

11 They shall be de|livered · to the | sword:
      they shall | be a | portion · for | jackals.

†12 The king will rejoice in God
      and all who take oaths on his | name shall | glory:
      but the mouths of | liars | shall be | stopped.

PSALM 64

1 Hear my voice O God in I my com|plaining:
   preserve my I life from I fear · of the I enemy.

2 Hide me from the conspiracy I of the I wicked:
   from the I throng of I evil|doers,

3 Who sharpen their I tongues like I swords:
   who string the bow   who take I arrows · of I bitter I
   words,

4 To shoot from hiding at the I blameless I man:
   to strike at him I sudden·ly I and un|seen.

5 They are confirmed in an I evil I purpose:
   they confide it to one another while they lay the ⌣
   snares   I saying I 'Who will I see them?'

6 They hatch mischief   they hide a well-con|sidered I
   plan:
   for the mind and heart of I man is I very I deep.

7 But God will shoot at them with his I swift I arrows:
   they shall be I sudden·ly I struck I through.

8 The Lord will bring them down ⌣
   for what their I tongues have I spoken:
   and all that see it shall I toss their I heads in I scorn.

9 Then I all men · shall I fear:
   and tell what the Lord has I done and I ponder · his I
   works.

10 The righteous man shall rejoice in the Lord
   and find in I him his I refuge:
   and all the I upright · in I heart · shall ex|ult.

PSALM 65

1 You are to be praised O I God in I Zion:
   to you shall vows be paid I   you that I answer I
   prayer.

2 To you shall all flesh come to con|fess their I sins:
   when our misdeeds prevail against us I ⌣
   you will I purge · them a|way.

3 Blessèd is the man whom you choose
     and take to yourself to dwell with⏐in your ⏐ courts:
  we shall be filled with the good things ‿
     of your house ⏐ of your ⏐ holy ⏐ temple.

4 You will answer us in your righteousness ‿
     with terrible deeds O ⏐ God our ⏐ saviour:
  you that are the hope of all the ends of the earth ‿
     and ⏐ of the ⏐ distant ⏐ seas;

5 Who by your strength made ⏐ fast the ⏐ mountains:
  you ⏐ that are ⏐ girded · with ⏐ power;

6 Who stilled the raging of the seas ‿
     the ⏐ roaring · of the ⏐ waves:
  and the ⏐ tumult ⏐ of the ⏐ peoples.

7 Those who dwell at the ends of the earth ‿
     are a⏐fraid at · your ⏐ wonders:
  the dawn and the ⏐ even·ing ⏐ sing your ⏐ praises.

8 You tend the ⏐ earth and ⏐ water it:
  you ⏐ make it ⏐ rich and ⏐ fertile.

9 The river of God is ⏐ full of ⏐ water:
  and so providing for the earth ‿
     you pro⏐vide ⏐ grain for ⏐ men.

10 You drench its furrows   you level the ⏐ ridges ·
  be⏐tween:
  you soften it with showers and ⏐ bless its ⏐ early ⏐
  growth.

11 You crown the ⏐ year · with your ⏐ goodness:
  and the tracks where you have ⏐ passed ⏐ drip with ⏐
  fatness.

12 The pastures of the ⏐ wilderness · run ⏐ over:
  and the ⏐ hills are ⏐ girded· with ⏐ joy.

13 The meadows are ⏐ clothed with ⏐ sheep:
  and the valleys stand so thick with corn ‿
     they ⏐ shout for ⏐ joy and ⏐ sing.

PSALM 66

1 O shout with joy to God ǀ all the ǀ earth:
   sing to the honour of his name
     and give him ǀ glory ǀ as his ǀ praise.

2 Say to God   'How fearful ǀ are your ǀ works:
   because of your great might ⌣
     your ǀ enemies · shall ǀ cower · beǀfore you.'

3 All the ǀ earth shall ǀ worship you:
   and sing to you   and sing ǀ praises ǀ to your ǀ name.

4 Come then and see what ǀ God has ǀ done:
   how terrible are his ǀ dealings · with the ǀ
     children · of ǀ men.

5 He turned the sea into dry land
   they crossed the ǀ river · on ǀ foot:
   then ǀ were we ǀ joyful · beǀcause of him.

6 By his power he rules for ever
   his eyes keep ǀ watch · on the ǀ nations:
   and rebels shall ǀ never ǀ rise aǀgainst him.

7 O bless our ǀ God you ǀ peoples:
   and cause his ǀ praises ǀ to reǀsound,

8 Who has held our ǀ souls in ǀ life:
   who has not ǀ suffered · our ǀ feet to ǀ slip.

9 For you have ǀ proved us · O ǀ God:
   you have ǀ tried us · as ǀ silver · is ǀ tried.

10 You brought us ǀ into · the ǀ net:
   you laid sharp ǀ torment ǀ on our ǀ loins.

†11 You let men ride over our heads
   we went through ǀ fire and ǀ water:
   but you brought us out ǀ into · a ǀ place of ǀ liberty.

12 I will come into your house with ǀ burnt-ǀofferings:
   and ǀ I will ǀ pay you · my ǀ vows,

13 The vows that ǀ opened · my ǀ lips:
   that my mouth uttered ǀ when I ǀ was in ǀ trouble.

14 I will offer you burnt-offerings of fattened beasts
  with the sweet | smoke of | rams:
 I will sacrifice a | bull · and the | flesh of | goats.

15 Come then and hear all | you that · fear | God:
 and I will | tell what | he has | done for me.

16 I called to him | with my | mouth:
 and his | praise was | on my | tongue.

17 If I had cherished wickedness | in my | heart:
 the | Lord would | not have | heard me.

18 But | God has | heard me:
 he has | heeded · the | voice of · my | prayer.

19 Praise | be to | God:
 who has not turned back my prayer
  or his | steadfast | love | from me.

PSALM 67

1 Let God be gracious to | us and | bless us:
 and make his | face | shine up|on us,

2 That your ways may be | known on | earth:
 your liberating | power · a|mong all | nations.

3 Let the peoples | praise you · O | God:
 let | all the | peoples | praise you.

4 Let the nations be | glad and | sing:
 for you judge the peoples with integrity
  and govern the | nations · up|on | earth.

5 Let the peoples | praise you · O | God:
 let | all the | peoples | praise you.

6 Then the earth will | yield its | fruitfulness:
 and | God our | God will | bless us.

†7 God | shall | bless us:
 and all the | ends · of the | earth will | fear him.

PSALM 68

1 God shall arise   and his enemies ۱ shall be ۱ scattered:
   those that hate him shall ۱ flee be۱fore his ۱ face.

2 As smoke is dispersed   so shall ۱ they · be dis۱persed:
   as wax melts before a fire * so shall the wicked ۱ perish
   · at the ۱ presence · of ۱ God.

3 But the righteous shall be glad and ex۱ult be·fore ۱ God:
   they ۱ shall re۱joice with ۱ gladness.

4 O sing to God   sing praises ۱ to his ۱ name:
   glorify him that rode through the deserts * him⌣
   whose name is the Lord ۱ and ex۱ult be۱fore him.

5 He is the father of the fatherless
   he upholds the ۱ cause · of the ۱ widow:
   God ۱ in his ۱ holy ۱ dwelling place.

6 He gives the desolate a home to dwell in
   and brings the prisoners out ۱ into · pros۱perity:
   but rebels must ۱ dwell · in a ۱ barren ۱ land.

7 O God   when you went out be۱fore your ۱ people:
   when you ۱ marched ۱ through the ۱ wilderness,

8 The earth shook   the heavens ۱ poured down ۱ water:
   before the God of Sinai   before ۱ God the ۱ God of ۱
   Israel.

9 You showered down a generous ۱ rain O ۱ God:
   you prepared the land of your pos۱session · when ۱
   it was ۱ weary.

10 And there your ۱ people ۱ settled:
   in the place that your goodness O God⌣
   had made ۱ ready ۱ for the ۱ poor.

11 The Lord spoke the word * and great was the⌣
   company of those that ۱ carried · the ۱ tidings:
   'Kings with their armies are ۱ fleeing · are ۱ fleeing ·
   a۱way.

12 'Even the women at home may ۱ share · in the ۱ spoil:
   and will you sit ۱ idly · a۱mong the ۱ sheepfolds?

13 'There are images of doves ⌣
    whose wings are | covered · with | silver:
and their | pinions · with | shining | gold.'

14 When the Almighty | scattered | kings:
    they were like snow | falling · up|on Mount |
    Zalmon.

15 The mountain of Bashan is a | mighty | mountain:
    the mountain of Bashan is a | mountain · of | many |
    peaks.

16 O mountains of many peaks   why | look so |
    enviously:
at the mountain where God is pleased to dwell
    where the | Lord · will re|main for | ever?

17 The chariots of God are twice ten thousand ⌣
    and | thousands up·on | thousands:
the Lord came from Sinai | into · his | holy | place.

18 When you ascended the heights you led the enemy ⌣
    captive * you received | tribute · from | men:
but rebels shall not | dwell · in the | presence · of |
    God.

19 Blessèd be the Lord day by day
    who bears us | as his | burden:
he is the | God of | our de|liverance.

20 God is to us a | God who | saves:
    by God the Lord do | we es|cape | death.

[21 But God shall smite the | heads · of his | enemies:
    the hairy scalp of | those that | walk · in their | sins.

22 The Lord said 'I will bring them | back from | Bashan:
    I will bring them a|gain · from the | deep | sea';

[†]23 That you may dip your | feet in | blood:
    and the tongues of your | dogs ·
    in the | blood of · your | enemies.]

24 Your procession is | seen O | God:
    the procession of my | God and | King · in the |
    sanctuary.

25 The singers go before   the mulsicians · come I after:
    and around them the maidens I beating I on the I
       timbrels.

26 In their choirs they I bless I God:
    those that are sprung from the fount of I Israel I ⌣
       bless the I Lord.

27 There is the little tribe of I Benja·min I leading them:
    the throng of the princes of Judah   the princes of I
       Zebulun · and the I princes · of I Naphtali.

28 Give the command my God * in accordance I
      with your I power:
    that godlike I power wherelby you I act for us.

29 Give the command from your temple I at Jelrusalem:
    and I kings shall I bring you I tribute.

30 Rebuke the beast of the reeds
      the herd of bulls amidst the I brutish I peoples:
    tread down those that are greedy for silver
      scatter the I peoples · that I relish I war.

31 Let them bring I bronze from I Egypt:
    let the hands of the Nubians I carry · it I swiftly · to I
       God.

32 Sing to God you I kingdoms · of the I earth:
    O sing I praises I to the I Lord,

33 To him that rides upon the highest heavens
      that were I from · the belginning:
    who utters his voice which I is a I mighty I voice.

34 Ascribe power to God   whose majesty is I over I
      Israel:
    and his I might is I in the I clouds.

35 Terrible is God who comes from his I holy I place:
    the God of Israel who gives   power and strength⌣
      to his people * I Blessèd I be I God.

PSALM 69

1 Save I me O I God:
    for the waters have come up I even I to my I throat.

2 I sink in the deep mire I where no I footing is:
    I have come into deep waters I and the I
        flood sweeps I over me.

3 I am weary with crying out my I throat is I parched:
    my eyes fail with I watching · so I long · for my I God.

4 Those that hate me without cause
      are more in number than the I hairs · of my I head:
    those that would destroy me are many
      they oppose me wrongfully
        for I must restore I things · that I I never I took.

5 O God you I know my I foolishness:
    and my I sins · are not I hidden I from you.

6 Let not those who wait for you be shamed‿
      because of me O Lord I God of I hosts:
    let not those who seek you be disgraced on I ‿
      my account · O I God of I Israel.

7 For your sake have I I suffered · reIproach:
    and I shame has I covered · my I face.

8 I have become a stranger I to my I brothers:
    an alien I to my · own I mother's I sons.

9 Zeal for your house has I eaten · me I up:
    and the taunts of those who taunt I you have I
      fallen · on I me.

10 I afflicted myIself with I fasting:
    and that was I turned to I my reIproach.

11 I made I sackcloth · my I clothing:
    and I beIcame a I byword I to them.

12 Those who sit in the gate I talk of I me:
    and the I drunkards · make I songs aIbout me.

13 But to you Lord I I make my I prayer:
    at I an acIcepta·ble I time.

14 Answer me O God in your a|bundant | goodness:
　　and | with your | sure de|liverance.

15 Bring me out of the mire　so that I | may not | sink:
　　let me be delivered from my enemies⁔
　　　　and | from the | deep | waters.

16 Let not the flood overwhelm me
　　　　or the depths | swallow · me | up:
　　let not the | Pit · shut its | mouth up|on me.

17 Hear me O Lord　as your loving-|kindness · is | good:
　　turn to me　as | your com|passion · is | great.

18 Do not hide your | face · from your | servant:
　　for I am in trouble　| O be | swift to | answer me!

19 Draw near to me | and re|deem me:
　　O | ransom me · be|cause of · my | enemies!

20 You know | all their | taunts:
　　my adversaries are | all | in your | sight.

21 Insults have | broken · my | heart:
　　my shame and dis|grace are | past | healing.

22 I looked for someone to have pity on me
　　　　but | there was | no man:
　　for some to | comfort me · but | found | none.

†23 They gave me | poison · for | food:
　　and when I was thirsty they | gave me ⅃ vinegar · to |
　　　　drink.

[24 Let their table be|come a | snare:
　　and their sacri|fici·al | feasts a | trap.

25 Let their eyes be darkened　so that they | cannot | see:
　　and make their | loins | shake con|tinually.

26 Pour out your | wrath up|on them:
　　and let your fierce | anger | over|take them.

27 Let their | camp be | desolate:
　　and let | no man | dwell · in their | tents.

28 For they persecute him whom | you have | stricken:
　　and multiply the pain of | him whom | you have |
　　　　wounded.

29 Let them have punishment up|on | punishment:
   let them | not re|ceive · your for|giveness.

†30 Let them be blotted out of the | book · of the | living:
   let them not be written | down a|mong the |
   righteous.]

31 As for me I am | poor · and in | misery:
   O God let your de|liver·ance | lift me | up.

32 And I will praise the name of | God · in a | song:
   and | glori·fy | him with | thanksgiving.

33 And that will please the Lord | more · than an | ox:
   more than a bull with | horns and | cloven | hoof.

34 Consider this you that are | meek ·   and re|joice:
   seek God and | let your | heart be | glad.

35 For the Lord | listens · to the | poor:
   he does not despise his | servants | in cap|tivity.

36 Let the heavens and the | earth | praise him:
   the | seas and | all that | moves in them.

37 For God will | save | Zion:
   he will re|build the | cities · of | Judah.

38 His people shall live there and possess it
   the seed of his servants | shall in|herit it:
   and those who | love his | name shall | dwell in it.

PSALM 70

1 O God be | pleased · to de|liver me:
   O | Lord make | haste to | help me.

2 Let them be put to shame and confounded who |
   seek my | life:
   let them be turned back and dis|graced who |
   wish me | evil.

3 Let them turn a|way for | shame:
   who | say to me · 'A|ha a|ha!'

4 Let all who seek you be joyful and |
   glad be|cause of you:
   let those who love your salvation say |
   always | 'God is | great.'

5 As for me I am | poor and | needy:
　　O | God be | swift to | save me.

6 You are my helper and | my de|liverer:
　　O | Lord make | no de|lay.

PSALM 71

1 To you Lord have I | come for | shelter:
　　let me | never · be | put to | shame.

2 In your righteousness rescue | and de|liver me:
　　incline your | ear to | me and | save me.

3 Be for me a rock of refuge * a fortress | to de|fend me:
　　for you are my high | rock | and my | stronghold.

4 Rescue me O my God from the | hand · of the | wicked:
　　from the grasp of the | piti·less | and un|just.

5 For you Lord | are my | hope:
　　you are my confidence O | God · from my | youth |
　　　upward.

6 On you have I | leaned · since my | birth:
　　you are he that brought me out of my mother's womb
　　and my | praise · is of | you con|tinually.

7 I have become as a fearful | warning · to | many:
　　but | you are · my | strength · and my | refuge.

8 My mouth shall be | filled · with your | praises:
　　I shall sing of your | glory | all the · day | long.

9 Cast me not away in the | time of · old | age:
　　nor forsake me | when my | strength | fails.

10 For my enemies | speak a|gainst me:
　　and those that watch for my life ⏜
　　　con|spire to|gether | saying,

†11 'God | has for|saken him:
　　pursue him　take him　for | there is | none to | save
　　　him.'

12 Be not far | from me · O | God:
　　my | God make | haste to | help me.

13 Let my adversaries be confounded and | put to | shame:
    let those who seek my hurt ⌣
         be | covered · with | scorn · and dis|grace.

14 As for me   I will wait in | hope con|tinually:
    and I will | praise you | more and | more.

15 My mouth shall speak of your righteousness | all the |
         day:
    and tell of your salvation | though it · ex|ceeds my |
         telling.

16 I will begin with the mighty acts of the | Lord my | God:
    and declare your righteous | dealing | yours a|lone.

17 O God you have taught me from my | youth | upward:
    and to this day I pro|claim your | marvel·lous | works.

18 Forsake me not O God in my old age   when I am |
         grey-|headed:
    till I have shown the strength of your arm ⌣
         to future generations * and your | might to |
              those that · come | after.

19 Your righteousness O God | reaches · to the | heavens:
    great are the things that you have done
         O | God | who is | like you?

20 You have burdened me with many and bitter troubles
         O | turn · and re|new me:
    and raise me up a|gain · from the | depths · of the |
         earth.

21 Bless me beyond my | former | greatness:
    O | turn to me · a|gain and | comfort me.

22 Then will I praise you upon the lute ⌣
         for your faithfulness | O my | God:
    and sing your praises to the harp O | Holy | One of |
         Israel.

23 My lips shall re|joice in · my | singing:
    and my soul | also · for | you have | ransomed me.

†24 My tongue shall speak of your righteous dealing |
         all the · day | long:
    for they shall be put to shame and disgraced ⌣
         that | seek to | do me | evil.

PSALM 72

1 Give the king your I judgment · O I God:
  and your righteouness to the I son I of a I king.

2 That he may judge your I people I rightly:
  and the I poor · of the I land with I equity.

3 Let the mountains be laden with peace⌣
    beIcause of · his I righteousness:
  and the hills also with prosIperi·ty I for his I people.

4 May he give justice to the poor aImong the I people:
  and rescue the children of the I needy ·
    and I crush · the opIpressor.

5 May he live while the I sun enIdures:
  and while the moon gives light throughIout all I
    generIations.

6 May he come down like rain upon the I new-mown I
    fields:
  and as I showers · that I water · the I earth.

7 In his time shall I righteous·ness I flourish:
  and abundance of peace till the I moon shall I be no I
    more.

8 His dominion shall stretch from I sea to I sea:
  from the Great I River · to the I ends · of the I earth.

9 His adversaries shall bow I down beIfore him:
  and his I enemies · shall I lick the I dust.

10 The kings of Tarshish and of the isles shall I
     bring I tribute:
   the kings of Sheba and I Seba · shall I offer I gifts.

†11 All kings shall fall I down beIfore him:
   and all I nations I do him I service.

12 He will deliver the needy I when they I cry:
   and the I poor man · that I has no I helper.

13 He will pity the helpless I and the I needy:
   and I save the I lives · of the I poor.

†14 He will redeem them from op|pression · and | violence:
  and their blood shall be | precious | in his | sight.

15 Long may he live   and be given of the | gold of | Sheba:
  may prayer be made for him continually
    and men | bless him | every | day.

16 Let there be abundance of | wheat · in the | land:
  let it | flourish · on the | tops · of the | mountains;

†17 Let its ears grow fat like the | grain of | Lebanon:
  and its sheaves | thicken · like the | grass · of the |
    field.

18 Let his name | live for | ever:
  and en|dure as | long · as the | sun.

19 Let all peoples use his | name in | blessing:
  and all | nations | call him | blessèd.

(20 Blessèd be the Lord God the | God of | Israel:
  who a|lone does | great | wonders.

21 Blessèd be his glorious | name for | ever:
  and let the whole earth be filled with his glory |
    Amen | A-|men.)

PSALM 73

1 God is indeed | good to | Israel:
  to | those whose | hearts are | pure.

2 Nevertheless my feet were | almost | gone:
  my | steps had | well-nigh | slipped.

3 For I was filled with envy | at the | boastful:
  when I saw the un|godly · had | such tran|quillity.

4 For they | suffer · no | pain:
  and their | bodies · are | hale and | fat.

5 They come to no mis|fortune · like | other folk:
  nor | are they | plagued like | other men.

6 Therefore they put on ǀ pride · as a ǀ necklace:
    and clothe themselves in ǀ vio·lence ǀ as · in a ǀ
      garment.

7 Their eyes shine from ǀ folds of ǀ fatness:
    and they have ǀ all that ǀ heart could ǀ wish.

8 Their talk is ǀ malice · and ǀ mockery:
    and they hand down ǀ slanders ǀ from on ǀ high.

9 Their mouths blasǀpheme a·gainst ǀ heaven:
    and their tongues go ǀ to and ǀ fro on ǀ earth.

10 Therefore my ǀ people ǀ turn to them:
    and ǀ find in ǀ them no ǀ fault.

11 They say ǀ 'How can · God ǀ know:
    is there underǀstanding · in the ǀ Most ǀ High?'

12 Behold ǀ these are · the unǀgodly:
    yet they ǀ prosper · and inǀcrease in ǀ riches.

13 Was it for nothing then that I ǀ cleansed my ǀ heart:
    and ǀ washed my ǀ hands in ǀ innocence?

14 Have I been stricken all day ǀ long in ǀ vain:
    and reǀbuked ǀ every ǀ morning?

†15 If I had said ǀ 'I will · speak ǀ thus':
    I should have betrayed the ǀ fami·ly ǀ of your ǀ
      children.

16 Then I thought to underǀstand ǀ this:
    but it ǀ was too ǀ hard ǀ for me,

17 Till I went into the ǀ sanctuary · of ǀ God:
    and then I underǀstood · what their ǀ end will ǀ be.

18 For you set them in ǀ slipper·y ǀ places:
    and cause them to ǀ fall · from their ǀ treacher·ous ǀ
      footholds.

19 How suddenly they are ǀ laid ǀ waste:
    they come to an ǀ end   they ǀ perish · in ǀ terror.

†20 As with a dream when ǀ one aǀwakes:
    so when you rouse yourself O Lord ǀ ⌣
      you will · deǀspise their ǀ image.

21 When my ǀ heart was ǀ soured:
    and I was ǀ wounded ǀ to the ǀ core,

22 I was but | brutish · and | ignorant:
    no | better · than a | beast be|fore you.

23 Nevertheless I am | always | with you:
    for you hold me | by my | right | hand.

24 You will guide me | with your | counsel:
    and afterwards | you will | lead me · to | glory.

25 Whom have I in | heaven · but | you?:
    and there is no one upon earth⌣
       that I de|sire · in com|parison · with | you.

26 Though my flesh and my | heart | fail me:
    you O | God · are my | portion · for | ever.

27 Behold those who for|sake you · shall | perish:
    and all who whore after other | gods you |
       will de|stroy.

28 But it is good for 'me to draw | near to | God:
    I have made the Lord God my refuge
       and I will tell of | all that | you have | done.

PSALM 74

1 O Lord our God   why cast us | off so | utterly:
    why does your anger burn a|gainst the |
       sheep of · your | pasture?

2 Remember your congregation * whom you took⌣
    to your|self of | old:
    the people that you redeemed to be your own⌣
    possession
       and Mount | Zion · where | you have | dwelt.

3 Rouse yourself and go to the | utter | ruins:
    to all the harm that the | enemy · has | done · in the |
       sanctuary.

4 Your adversaries have made uproar⌣
    in the place appointed | for your | praise:
    they have set | up their | standards · in| triumph.

5 They have destroyed on | every | side:
    like those who take axes | up · to a | thicket · of | trees.

6 All the carved woodwork they have ׀ broken ׀ down:
and ׀ smashed it · with ׀ hammers · and ׀ hatchets.

7 They have set ׀ fire to · your ׀ sanctuary:
and defiled to the ground the ׀ dwelling-· place ׀
of your ׀ name.

8 They have said in their hearts 'Let us make ׀ havoc ׀
of them':
they have burned down ⌣
all the holy ׀ places · of ׀ God · in the ׀ land.

9 We see no signs * there is not one ׀ prophet ׀ left:
there is none who knows how ׀ long these ׀
things shall ׀ be.

10 How long shall the adversary ׀ taunt you · O ׀ God:
shall the enemy blas׀pheme your ׀ name for ׀ ever?

†11 Why do you hold ׀ back your ׀ hand:
why do you keep your ׀ right hand ׀ in your ׀ bosom?

12 Yet God is my ׀ king · from of ׀ old:
who wrought de׀liverance · up׀on the ׀ earth.

13 You divided the ׀ sea · by your ׀ might:
you shattered the heads of the ׀ dragons ׀ in the ׀
waters.

14 You crushed the ׀ heads · of Le׀viathan:
and gave him as food to the ׀ creatures · of the ׀
desert ׀ waste.

15 You cleft open ׀ spring and ׀ fountain:
you dried up the ׀ ever׀flowing ׀ waters.

16 The day is yours * and so also ׀ is the ׀ night:
you have es׀tablished · the ׀ moon · and the ׀ sun.

17 You set all the boundaries ׀ of the ׀ earth:
you cre׀ated ׀ winter · and ׀ summer.

18 Remember O Lord the ׀ taunts · of the ׀ enemy:
how a mindless ׀ people · have blas׀phemed your ׀
name.

19 Do not give to the wild beasts the ǀ soul that ǀ
    praises you:
    do not forget for ever the ǀ life of ǀ your afǀflicted.

20 Look on all that ǀ you have ǀ made:
    for it is full of darkness
        and ǀ violence · inǀhabits · the ǀ earth.

21 Let not the oppressed and reviled turn aǀway reǀjected:
    but let the poor and ǀ needy ǀ praise your ǀ name.

22 Arise O God * plead your ǀ own ǀ cause:
    remember how a mindless people ǀ taunt you ǀ all day
        ǀ long.

23 Do not forget the ǀ clamour · of your ǀ adversaries:
    or how the shouting of your ǀ
        enemies · asǀcends conǀtinually.

PSALM 75

1 We give you thanks O God we ǀ give you ǀ thanks:
    we call upon your name
        and tell of all the ǀ wonders ǀ you have ǀ done.

2 'I will surely apǀpoint a ǀ time:
    when I the ǀ Lord will ǀ judge with ǀ equity.

3 'Though the earth shake and ǀ all who ǀ dwell in it:
    it is ǀ I · that have ǀ founded · its ǀ pillars.

4 'I will say to the boasters ǀ "Boast no ǀ more":
    and to the wicked ǀ "Do not ǀ flaunt your ǀ horns;

†5 '"Do not flaunt your ǀ horns so ǀ high:
    or speak so ǀ proud and ǀ stiff-ǀnecked."'

6 For there is none from the east or ǀ from the ǀ west:
    or from the wilderness ǀ who can ǀ raise ǀ up;

7 But it is God who ǀ is the ǀ judge:
    who puts down ǀ one · and exǀalts anǀother.

8 For there is a cup in the ǀ Lord's ǀ hand:
    and the wine ǀ foams · and is ǀ richly ǀ mixed;

9 He gives it in turn to each of the ǀ wicked · of the ǀ earth:
    they drink it and ǀ drain it ǀ to the ǀ dregs.

10 But I will sing praises to the | God of | Jacob:
  I will | glorify · his | name for | ever.

11 All the horns of the | wicked · I will | break:
  but the horns of the | righteous · shall be | lifted | high.

PSALM 76

1 In Judah | God is | known:
  his | name is | great in | Israel.

2 At Salem | is his | tabernacle:
  and his | dwelling | is in | Zion.

3 There he broke in pieces the flashing | arrows · of the | bow:
  the shield the | sword · and the | weapons · of | battle.

4 Radiant in | light are | you:
  greater in majesty | than · the e|ternal | hills.

5 The valiant were dumbfounded they | sleep their | sleep:
  and all the men of | war have | lost their | strength.

6 At the blast of your voice O | God of | Jacob:
  both horse and | chariot · were | cast a|sleep.

7 Terrible are | you Lord | God:
  and who may stand be|fore you · when | you are | angry?

8 You caused your sentence to be | heard from | heaven:
  the earth | feared | and was still,

9 When God a|rose to | judgment:
  to | save · all the | meek · of the | earth.

10 For you crushed the | wrath of | man:
  you bridled the | remnant | of the | wrathful.

11 O make vows to the Lord your | God and | keep them:
  let all around him bring gifts ⌣
    to him that is | worthy | to be | feared.

12 For he cuts down the | fury · of | princes:
  and he is terrible to the | kings | of the | earth.

PSALM 77

1 I call to my God   I cry ǀ out toǀward him:
  I call to my God   and ǀ surely ǀ he will ǀ answer.

2 In the day of my distress I seek the Lord
   I stretch out my hands to ǀ him by ǀ night:
  my soul is poured out without ceasing
   it reǀfuses ǀ all ǀ comfort.

3 I think upon God and ǀ groan aǀloud:
  I ǀ muse · and my ǀ spirit ǀ faints.

4 You hold my ǀ eyelids ǀ open:
  I am so ǀ dazed · that I ǀ cannot ǀ flee.

5 I consider the ǀ times · that are ǀ past:
  I remember the ǀ years of ǀ long aǀgo.

6 At night I am ǀ grieved · to the ǀ heart:
  I ponder ǀ and my ǀ spirit · makes ǀ search;

7 'Will the Lord cast us ǀ off for ǀ ever:
  will he ǀ show us · his ǀ favour · no ǀ more?

8 'Is his mercy clean ǀ gone for ǀ ever:
  and his promise come to an ǀ end for ǀ all ·
   generǀations?

9 'Has God forǀgotten · to be ǀ gracious:
  has he shut up his ǀ pity ǀ in disǀpleasure?'

10 And I say * 'Has the right hand of the Most High ǀ
   lost its ǀ strength:
  has the ǀ arm · of the ǀ Lord ǀ changed?'

11 I will declare the mighty ǀ acts · of the ǀ Lord:
  I will call to ǀ mind your ǀ wonders · of ǀ old.

12 I will think on all that ǀ you have ǀ done:
  and ǀ meditate · upǀon your ǀ works.

13 Your way O ǀ God is ǀ holy:
  who is so ǀ great a ǀ god as ǀ our God?

14 You are the God that ǀ works ǀ wonders:
  you made known your ǀ power aǀmong the ǀ nations;

15 By your mighty arm you reǀdeemed your ǀ people:

the I children · of I Jacob · and I Joseph.

16 The waters saw you O God
    the waters saw you and I were aǀfraid:
    the I depths I also · were I troubled.

17 The clouds poured out water   the I heavens I spoke:
    and your I arrows I darted I forth.

18 The voice of your thunder was I heard · in the I
    whirlwind:
    your lightnings lit the world
    the I earth I shuddered · and I quaked.

19 Your way was in the sea * your path in the I great I
    waters:
    and your I footsteps I were not I seen.

20 You led your I people · like I sheep:
    by the I hand of I Moses · and I Aaron.

PSALM 78

1 Give heed to my teaching I O my I people:
    incline your I ears · to the I words of · my I mouth;

2 For I will open my I mouth · in a I parable:
    and expound the I mysteries · of I former I times.

3 What we have I heard and I known:
    what I our foreǀfathers · have I told us,

4 We will not hide from their children
    but declare to a generation I yet to I come:
    the praiseworthy acts of the Lord
    his I mighty · and I wonderful I works.

5 He established a law in Jacob
    and made a deǀcree in I Israel:
    which he commanded our foreǀfathers · to I
    teach their I children,

6 That future generations might know
    and the children I yet unǀborn:
    that they in turn might I teach it I to their I sons;

7 So that they might put their I confidence · in I God:
    and not forget his I works but I
    keep · his comǀmandments,

8 And not be as their forefathers
     a stubborn and re|bellious · gener|ation:
   a generation that did not set their heart aright
     whose spirit I was not I faithful · to I God.

9 The children of Ephraim I armed · with the I bow:
     turned I back · in the I day of I battle.

10 They did not keep God's covenant
     they refused to I walk in · his I law:
   they forgot what he had done
     and the I wonders I he had I shown them.

11 For he did marvellous things ⌣
     in the I sight of · their I fathers:
   in the land of Egypt I in the I country · of I Zoan.

12 He divided the sea and I let them · pass I through:
     he made the I waters · stand I up · in a I heap.

13 In the daytime he I led them · with a I cloud:
     and all night I long · with the I light of I fire.

14 He cleft I rocks · in the I wilderness:
   and gave them drink in abundance I ⌣
     as from I springs of I water.

†15 He brought streams I out of · the I rock:
     and caused the waters to I flow I down like I rivers.

16 But for all this they sinned yet I more a|gainst him:
     and rebelled against the Most I High I in the I desert.

17 They wilfully put I God · to the I test:
     and de|manded I food · for their I appetite.

18 They spoke against I God and I said:
     'Can God prepare a I table I in the I wilderness?

19 'He indeed struck the rock * so that the waters gushed ⌣
     and the I streams · over|flowed:
   but can he also give bread
     or provide I meat I for his I people?'

20 When the Lord heard it he was angry
     and a fire was kindled a|gainst I Jacob:
   his wrath I blazed a|gainst I Israel.

21 For they put no | trust in | God:
   nor would they be|lieve his | power to | save.

†22 Then he commanded the | clouds a|bove:
   and | opened · the | doors of | heaven.

23 He rained down manna for | them to | eat:
   and | gave them · the | grain of | heaven.

24 So men ate the | bread of | angels:
   and he | sent them | food · in a|bundance.

25 He stirred up the south east | wind · in the | heavens:
   and | guided · it | by his | power.

26 He rained down meat upon them | thick as | dust:
   and winged | birds · like the | sands · of the | sea.

27 He made them fall into the | midst of · their | camp:
   and | all a|bout their | tents.

28 So they ate and were | well-|filled:
   for he had | given · them | what · they de|sired.

29 But before they had | satisfied · their | craving:
   while the | food was | still in · their | mouths,

30 The anger of God | blazed · up a|gainst them:
   and he slew their strongest men
      and laid | low the | youth of | Israel.

31 But for all this they | sinned yet | more:
   and | put no | faith · in his | wonders.

32 So he ended their | days · like a | breath:
   and their | years with | sudden | terror.

33 When he struck them down | then they | sought him:
   they turned and | sought | eagerly · for | God.

34 They remembered that | God · was their | rock:
   that God Most | High was | their re|deemer.

35 But they lied to him | with their | mouths:
   and dis|sembled | with their | tongues;

36 For their hearts were not | fixed up|on him:
   nor | were they | true to · his | covenant.

37 Yet he being merciful
    forgave their iniquity and did ı not deıstroy them:
  many times he turned his anger aside
    and would not ı wholly · aırouse his ı fury.

38 He remembered that they ı were but ı flesh:
  like a wind that passes ı and does ı not reıturn.

39 How often they rebelled against him ı in theı
    wilderness:
  and ı grieved him ı in the ı desert!

40 Again and again they put ı God · to the ı test:
  and provoked the ı Holy ı One of ı Israel.

41 They did not reımember · his ı power:
  or the day when he reıdeemed them ı from the ı
    enemy;

43 How he wrought his ı signs in ı Egypt:
  his ı wonders · in the ı country · of ı Zoan.

43 For he turned their ı rivers · into ı blood:
  so that they ı could not ı drink · from the ı streams.

44 He sent swarms of ı flies · that deıvoured them:
  and ı frogs that ı laid them ı waste.

45 He gave their ı crops · to the ı locust:
  and the fruits of their ı labour ı to the ı grasshopper.

46 He struck down their ı vines with ı hailstones:
  and their ı syco·more ı trees with ı frost.

47 He gave up their ı cattle · to the ı hail:
  and their ı flocks · to the ı flash · of the ı lightning.

48 He loosed on them the fierceness of his anger
    his fury his indignation ı and disıtress:
  and these were his ı messen·gers ı of deıstruction.

49 He opened a ı path · for his ı fury:
  he would not spare them from death
    but gave ı up their ı lives · to the ı pestilence.

50 He struck down the ı firstborn · of ı Egypt:
  the firstfruits of their manhood ı ͟
    in the ı dwellings · of ı Ham.

51 As for his own people   he led them I out like I sheep:
  and guided them in the I wilder·ness I like a I flock.

52 He led them in safety   and they were I not a|fraid:
  but the I sea I covered · their I enemies.

53 He brought them to his I holy I land:
  to the mountains that his I own right I hand had I
  won.

54 He drove out the nations before them
    and apportioned their lands I as a · pos|session:
  and settled the tribes of I Israel I in their I tents.

55 But they rebelled against God Most High⌣
    and I put him · to the I test:
  they would I not o|bey · his com|mandments.

56 They turned back and dealt treacherously I ⌣
    like their I fathers:
  they turned aside I slack · as an I unstrung I bow.

57 They provoked him to anger with their I heathen I
    shrines:
  and moved him to jealousy I with their I carved I
  images.

58 God heard and was angry * he utterly re|jected I Israel:
  he forsook the tabernacle at Shiloh
    the I tent · where he I dwelt a·mong I men.

59 He gave the ark of his might I into · cap|tivity:
  and his glory I into · the I hands · of the I enemy.

60 He delivered his I people · to the I sword:
  and was enraged a|gainst his I own pos|session.

61 Fire de|voured the · young I men:
  there was I no one · to be|wail the I maidens;

62 Their priests I fell · by the I sword:
  and there was I none to I mourn · for the I widows.

63 Then the Lord awoke like a I man · out of I sleep:
  like a warrior that had been I over|come with I wine.

64 He struck the backs of his enemies ǀ as they ǀ fled:
　　and ǀ put them · to perǀpetu·al ǀ shame.

65 He rejected the ǀ family · of ǀ Joseph:
　　he reǀfused the ǀ tribe of ǀ Ephraim.

66 But he chose the ǀ tribe of ǀ Judah:
　　and the hill of ǀ Zion ǀ which he ǀ loved.

67 He built his sanctuary like the ǀ heights of ǀ heaven:
　　like the earth which ǀ he had ǀ founded · for ǀ ever.

68 He chose ǀ David · his ǀ servant:
　　and ǀ took him ǀ from the ǀ sheepfolds;

69 He brought him from ǀ following · the ǀ ewes:
　　to be the shepherd of his people Jacob
　　and of ǀ Israel · his ǀ own posǀsession.

70 So he tended them with ǀ upright ǀ heart:
　　and ǀ guided them · with ǀ skilful ǀ hand.

PSALM 79

1 O God the heathen have ǀ come in·to your ǀ land:
　　they have defiled your holy temple
　　they have made Jeǀrusalem · a ǀ heap of ǀ stones.

2 They have given the dead bodies of your servants ⌣
　　as food to the ǀ birds · of the ǀ air:
　　and the flesh of your faithful ones ⌣
　　to the wild ǀ beasts ǀ of the ǀ earth.

3 Their blood they have spilt like water ⌣
　　on every ǀ side · of Jeǀrusalem:
　　and ǀ there is ǀ none to ǀ bury them.

4 We have become a mockery ǀ to our ǀ neighbours:
　　the scorn and ǀ laughing-stock · of ǀ those aǀbout us.

5 How long O Lord shall your anger be ǀ so exǀtreme:
　　will your jealous ǀ fury ǀ burn like ǀ fire?

6 Pour out your wrath on the nations that ǀ do not ǀ know
　　you:
　　on the kingdoms that have not ǀ called upǀon your ǀ
　　name.

7 For they have delvoured | Jacob:
  and made his | dwelling-place · a | desollation.

8 Do not remember against us the sin of | former | times:
  but let your compassion hasten to meet us
    for we are | brought | very | low.

†9 Help us O God our saviour for the | honour · of your | name:
  O deliver us and expiate our | sins · for your | name's | sake.

[10 Why should the heathen say | 'Where is · their | God?':
  O let vengeance for the blood of your servants that ⌣ is shed
    be shown upon the | nations | in our | sight.]

11 Let the sorrowful sighing of the prisoners | come belfore you:
  and as your power is great reprieve |
    those conldemned to | die.

[12 For the taunts with which our neighbours ⌣
    have taunted | you O | Lord:
  repay them seven times | over | into · their | bosoms.]

13 So we that are your people and the sheep of your
    pasture shall give you | thanks for | ever:
  we will declare your praise in | every | generlation.

PSALM 80

1 Hear O Shepherd of Israel
    you that led | Joseph · like a | flock:
  you that are enthroned upon the cherubim | ⌣
    shine | out in | glory;

2 Before Ephraim Benjamin | and Manlasseh:
  stir up your | power and | come to | save us.

†3 *Restore us again O | Lord of | hosts:*
  show us the light of your countenance | ⌣
    and we | shall be | saved.

4 O Lord | God of | hosts:
  how long will you be | angry · at your | people's | prayer?

231

5 You have fed them with the | bread of | tears:
    and given them tears to | drink in | good | measure.

6 You have made us the victim | of our | neighbours:
    and our | ene·mies | laugh us · to | scorn.

7 *Restore us again O | Lord of | hosts:*
    show us the light of your countenance | ‿
      and we | shall be | saved.

8 You brought a | vine · out of | Egypt:
    you drove out the | nations · and | planted · it | in.

9 You cleared the | ground be|fore it:
    and it struck | root and | filled the | land.

10 The hills were | covered · with its | shadow:
    and its boughs were like the | boughs · of the | great |
      cedars.

11 It stretched out its | branches · to the | sea:
    and its tender | shoots · to the | Great | River.

12 Why then have you broken | down its | walls:
    so that every passer-|by can | pluck its | fruit?

13 The wild boar out of the woods | roots it | up:
    and the locusts from the | wild | places · de|vour it.

14 Turn to us again O | Lord of | hosts:
    look | down from | heaven · and | see.

15 Bestow your care up|on this | vine:
    the stock which your | own right | hand has | planted.

16 As for those that burn it with fire and | cut it | down:
    let them perish at the re|buke | of your | countenance.

17 Let your power rest on the man at your | right | hand:
    on that son of man whom you | made so | strong ·
      for your|self.

18 And so we shall | not turn | back from you:
    give us life   and we will | call up|on your | name.

19 *Restore us again O | Lord of | hosts:*
    show us the light of your countenance | ‿
      and we | shall be | saved.

PSALM 81

1 O sing joyfully to I God our I strength:
   shout in I triumph · to the I God of I Jacob.

2 Make music and I beat up·on the I drum:
   sound the I lute and · the mellodi·ous I harp.

3 Blow the ram's horn at the I new I moon:
   and at the full moon I of our I day of I festival.

4 For this was a I statute · for I Israel:
   a comImandment · of the I God of I Jacob,

†5 Which he laid on Joseph as a I solemn I charge:
   when he came I out of · the I land of I Egypt.

6 I heard a voice that I had not I known I saying:
   'I eased your shoulders of the burden
     and your I hands were I freed · from the I load.

7 'You called to me in trouble I and I I rescued you:
   I answered you from the secret place of my thunder
     I put you to the I test · at the I waters · ofI Meribah.

8 'Listen my people and I I · will adImonish you:
   O Israel if I only I you would I hear me.

9 'There shall be no strange I god aImong you:
   nor shall you bow I down · to an I ali·en I god.

†10 'I am the Lord your God
     who brought you up from the I land of I Egypt:
   open wide your I mouth and I I will I fill it.

11 'But my people would not I listen · to my I voice:
   and I Israel I would have I none of me.

12 'So I left them to the stubbornness I of their I hearts:
   to walk acIcording · to their I own deIsigns.

13 'If only my I people · would I listen:
   if Israel I would but I walk in · my I ways,

14 'I would soon put I down their I enemies:
   and turn my I hand aIgainst their I adversaries.

15 'Those that hate the Lord would I cringe beIfore him:
   and their I punishment · would I last for I ever.

16 'But Israel I would feed with the | finest | wheat:
   and satisfy you with | honey | from the | rocks.'

PSALM 82

1 God has stood up in the | council · of | heaven:
   in the midst of the | gods | he gives | judgment.

2 'How long will you | judge un|justly:
   and | favour · the | cause · of the | wicked?

3 'Judge for the | poor and | fatherless:
   vindicate the af|flicted | and op|pressed.

4 'Rescue the | poor and | needy:
   and | save them · from the | hands · of the | wicked.

5 'They do not know   they do not understand
      they walk a|bout in | darkness:
   all the found|ations · of the | earth are | shaken.

6 'Therefore I say | "Though · you are | gods:
   and all of you | sons · of the | Most | High,

7 '"Nevertheless you shall | die like | man:
   and | fall like | one of · the | princes."'

8 Arise O God and | judge the | earth:
   for you shall take all | nations · as | your pos|session.

PSALM 83

1 Hold not your | peace O | God:
   O God be not | silent | or un|moved.

2 See how your | enemies · make | uproar:
   how those that hate you have | lifted | up their |
      heads.

3 For they lay shrewd plots a|gainst your | people:
   they scheme against | those whom | you have |
      cherished.

4 'Come' they say 'let us destroy them
      that they may no | longer · be a | nation:
   that the very name of Israel may | be re|membered ·
      no | more.'

5 With one mind they con|spire to|gether:
　　they | make al|liance · a|gainst you,

6 The tribes of Edom | and the | Ishmaelites:
　　the people of | Moab | and the | Hagarites,

7 Gebal and | Ammon · and | Amalek:
　　Philistia | and · the in|habitants · of | Tyre;

8 Asshur | also · is | joined with them:
　　and lends a friendly | arm · to the | children · of | Lot.

9 Do to them as you | did to | Midian:
　　as to Sisera and Jabin | at the | river · of | Kishon,

10 Who were de|stroyed at | Endor:
　　and be|came like | dung · for the | earth.

11 Make their leaders as | Oreb · and | Zeeb:
　　and all their princes like | Zebah | and Zal|munna,

12 Who said 'Let us | take pos|session:
　　let us | seize the | pastures · of | God.'

13 Make them like | thistledown · my | God:
　　or like chaff | blown be|fore the | wind.

14 As fire con|suming · a | thicket:
　　or as flame that | sets the | hillsides · a|blaze,

15 Pursue them | with your | tempest:
　　and | terrify · them | with your | storm-wind.

16 Cover their faces with | shame O | Lord:
　　that | they may | seek your | name.

[17 Let them be disgraced and dis|mayed for | ever:
　　let them | be con|founded · and | perish,]

(†)18 That they may know that you whose | name · is the | Lord:
　　are alone the Most | High · over | all the | earth.

PSALM 84

1 How lovely | is your | dwelling-place:
   O | Lord | God of | hosts!

2 My soul has a desire and longing⌣
      to enter the | courts · of the | Lord:
   my heart and my flesh re|joice · in the | living | God.

3 The sparrow has found her a home   and the swallow⌣
      a nest where she may | lay her | young:
   even your altar   O Lord of | hosts my |
      King · and my | God.

4 Blessèd are those who | dwell in · your | house:
   they will | always · be | praising | you.

5 Blessèd is the man whose | strength · is in | you:
   in whose | heart · are the | highways · to | Zion;

6 Who going through the valley of dryness
      finds there a spring from | which to | drink:
   till the autumn | rain shall | clothe it · with | blessings.

†7 They go from | strength to | strength:
   they appear every one of them⌣
      before the | God of | gods in | Zion.

8 O Lord God of hosts | hear my | prayer:
   give | ear O | God of | Jacob.

9 Behold O God | him who · reigns | over us:
   and look upon the | face of | your a|nointed.

10 One day in your courts is | better · than a | thousand:
   I would rather stand at the threshold of the house⌣
      of my God
      than | dwell · in the | tents of · un|godliness.

11 For the Lord God is a rampart and a shield
      the Lord gives | favour · and | honour:
   and no good thing will he withhold⌣
      from | those who | walk in | innocence.

†12 O Lord | God of | hosts:
   blessèd is the man who | puts his | trust in | you.

PSALM 85

1 O Lord you were gracious | to your | land:
   you re|stored the | fortunes · of | Jacob.

2 You forgave the iniquity | of your | people:
   and | covered | all their | sin.

3 You put aside | all your | wrath:
   and turned away from your | fierce | indig|nation.

4 Return to us again O | God our | saviour:
   and | let your | anger | cease from us.

5 Will you be displeased with | us for | ever:
   will you stretch out your wrath⌣
      from one gener|ation | to an|other?

6 Will you not give us | life a|gain:
   that your | people | may re|joice in you?

†7 Show us your | mercy · O | Lord:
   and | grant us | your sal|vation.

8 I will hear what the Lord | God will | speak:
   for he will speak peace to his people * to his⌣
      faithful ones whose | hearts are | turned to | him.

9 Truly his salvation is near to | those that | fear him:
   and his | glory · shall | dwell · in our | land.

10 Mercy and truth are | met to|gether:
   righteousness and | peace have | kissed each | other;

11 Truth shall flourish | out of · the | earth:
   and righteousness | shall look | down from | heaven.

12 The Lord will also give us | all · that is | good:
   and our | land shall | yield its | plenty.

13 For righteousness shall | go be|fore him:
   and tread the | path be|fore his | feet.

PSALM 86

1 Incline your ear to me O ǀ God and ǀ answer me:
     for ǀ I am ǀ poor · and in ǀ misery.

2 Preserve my life for ǀ I am ǀ faithful:
     my God save your servant who ǀ puts his ǀ trust in ǀ
     you.

3 Be merciful to ǀ me O ǀ Lord:
     for I ǀ call to · you ǀ all the · day ǀ long.

4 O make glad the ǀ soul of · your ǀ servant:
     for I put my ǀ hope in ǀ you O ǀ Lord.

5 For you Lord are ǀ good · and forǀgiving:
     of great and continuing kindness ⌣
          to ǀ all who ǀ call upǀon you.

6 Hear my ǀ prayer O ǀ Lord:
     and give heed to the ǀ voice · of my ǀ suppliǀcation.

†7 In the day of my trouble I ǀ call upǀon you:
     for ǀ you will ǀ surely ǀ answer.

8 Among the gods there is none like ǀ you O ǀ Lord:
     nor are there ǀ any ǀ deeds like ǀ yours.

9 All the nations you have made ⌣
     shall come and ǀ worship · beǀfore you:
     O Lord they shall ǀ gloriǀfy your ǀ name.

10 For you are great and do ǀ marvel·lous ǀ things:
     and ǀ you aǀlone are ǀ God.

11 Show me your way O Lord and I will ǀ walk in · yourǀ
     truth:
     let my heart deǀlight to ǀ fear your ǀ name.

12 I will praise you O Lord my God with ǀ all my ǀ heart:
     and I will ǀ glorify · your ǀ name for ǀ ever.

13 For great is your abiding ǀ love toǀward me:
     and you have delivered my life ⌣
          from the ǀ lowest ǀ depths · of the ǀ grave.

14 Insolent men O God have ǀ risen · aǀgainst me:
     a band of ruthless men seek my life
          they have not set ǀ God beǀfore their ǀ eyes.

15 But you Lord are a God | gracious · and com|passionate:
    slow to anger | full of | goodness · and | truth.

16 Turn to me and be merciful
       give your | strength · to your | servant:
    and | save the | son of · your | handmaid.

17 Show me some token | of your | goodness:
    that those who hate me may see it and be ashamed
    because you Lord are my | helper | and my |
    comforter.

PSALM 87

1 He has founded it upon a | holy | hill:
    and the Lord loves the gates of Zion ⌣
       more than | all the | dwellings · of | Jacob.

2 Glorious things shall be | spoken · of | you:
    O Zion | city | of our | God.

3 I might speak of my kinsmen in Egypt | or in | Babylon:
    in Philistia Tyre or Nubia | where | each was | born.

4 But of Zion it | shall be | said:
       many were born in her
       he that is Most | High | has es|tablished her.

5 When the Lord draws up the record | of the | nations:
    he shall take note where | every | man was | born.

6 And the singers and the | dancers · to|gether:
    shall | make their | song · to your | name.

PSALM 88

1 O Lord my God I call for | help by | day:
    and by night also I | cry | out be|fore you.

2 Let my prayer come | into · your | presence:
    and turn your | ear · to my | loud | crying.

†3 For my soul is | filled with | trouble:
    and my life has come | even · to the | brink · of the |
    grave.

4 I am reckoned among those that go ⏐ down · to the ⏐ Pit:
   I am a ⏐ man that ⏐ has no ⏐ help.

5 I lie among the dead
      like the slain that ⏐ sleep · in the ⏐ grave:
   whom you remember no more
      who are cut ⏐ off ⏐ from your ⏐ power.

6 You have laid me in the ⏐ lowest ⏐ Pit:
   in darkness and ⏐ in the ⏐ water·y ⏐ depths.

7 Your wrath lies ⏐ heavy · up⏐on me:
   and all your ⏐ waves are ⏐ brought a⏐gainst me.

8 You have put my ⏐ friends far ⏐ from me:
   and made me to ⏐ be ab⏐horred ⏐ by them.

9 I am so fast in prison I ⏐ cannot · get ⏐ free:
   my eyes fail be⏐cause of ⏐ my af⏐fliction.

10 Lord I call to you ⏐ every ⏐ day:
   I stretch ⏐ out my ⏐ hands to⏐ward you.

11 Will you work ⏐ wonders · for the ⏐ dead:
   or will the shades rise ⏐ up a⏐gain to ⏐ praise you?

12 Shall your love be de⏐clared · in the ⏐ grave:
   or your faithfulness ⏐ in the ⏐ place · of de⏐struction?

13 Will your wonders be made ⏐ known · in the ⏐ dark:
      or your righteousness ⏿
      in the land where ⏐ all things ⏐ are for⏐gotten?

14 But to you Lord ⏐ will I ⏐ cry:
      early in the morning my ⏐ prayer shall ⏐
      come be⏐fore you.

15 O Lord why have ⏐ you re⏐jected me:
   why do you ⏐ hide your ⏐ face ⏐ from me?

16 I have been afflicted and wearied from my ⏐ youth ⏐
      upward:
   I am tossed high and ⏐ low   I ⏐ cease to ⏐ be.

17 Your fierce anger has ⏐ over⏐whelmed me:
   and your ⏐ terrors · have ⏐ put me · to ⏐ silence.

18 They surround me like a flood ⏐ all the · day ⏐ long:
   they close up⏐on me · from ⏐ every ⏐ side.

19 Friend and acquaintance you have put | far | from me:
    and kept my com|panions | from my | sight.

PSALM 89

1 Lord I will sing for ever of your | loving-|kindnesses:
    my mouth shall proclaim your faithfulness ⏜
        through|out all | gener|ations.

2 I have said of your loving-kindness ⏜
        that it is | built for | ever:
    you have established your | faithful·ness | in the |
    heavens.

3 The Lord said 'I have made a covenant | with my |
    chosen:
    I have sworn an | oath · to my | servant | David.

4 'I will establish your | line for | ever:
    and build up your | throne for | all · gener|ations.'

5 Let the heavens praise your | wonders · O | Lord:
    and let your faithfulness be sung ⏜
        in the as|sembly | of the | holy ones.

6 For who amidst the clouds can be com|pared · to the |
    Lord:
    or who is like the Lord a|mong the | sons of | heaven?

7 A God to be feared in the council | of the | holy ones:
    great and terrible above | all that | are a|round him.

8 O Lord God of hosts | who is like you?
    your power and your | faithfulness · are |
    all a|bout you.

9 You rule the | raging · of the | sea:
    when its | waves | surge you | still them.

10 You crushed Rahab | like a | carcase:
    you scattered your enemies | by your | mighty |
    arm.

11 The heavens are yours * so also | is the | earth:
    you founded the | world and | all · that is | in it.

12 You created the | north · and the | south:
　　Tabor and Mount | Hermon · shall |
　　　　sing of · your | name.

13 Mighty | is your | arm:
　　strong is your hand * and your right | hand is |
　　　　lifted | high.

14 Righteousness and justice are the foundation |
　　　　of your | throne:
　　loving-kindness and | faithfulness · at|tend your |
　　　　presence.

15 Happy the people who know the tri|umphal | shout:
　　who walk O | Lord · in the | light of · your |
　　　　countenance.

16 They rejoice all the day long be|cause of · your | name:
　　because of your | righteousness · they | are ex|alted.

17 For you are their glory | and their | strength:
　　and our heads are up|lifted | by your | favour.

18 Our king be|longs · to the | Lord:
　　he that rules over us to the | Holy | One of | Israel.

19 You spoke | once · in a | vision:
　　and | said | to your | faithful one,

20 'I have set a youth a|bove a | warrior:
　　I have exalted a | young man | out of · the | people.

21 'I have found my | servant | David:
　　and anointed him | with my | holy | oil.

22 'My hand | shall up|hold him:
　　and my | arm | shall | strengthen him.

23 'No enemy | shall de|ceive him:
　　no | evil | man shall | hurt him.

24 'I will crush his | adversaries · be|fore him:
　　and | strike down | those that | hate him.

25 'My faithfulness and loving-kindness | shall be |
　　　　with him:
　　and through my name his | head · shall be | lifted |
　　　　high.

26 'I will set the hand of his dominion ⌣
       upon the | Western | Sea:
    and his right hand shall stretch ⌣
       to the | streams of | Meso·po|tamia.

27 'He will call to me | "You · are my | Father:
    my God and the | Rock of | my sal|vation."

28 'I will make him my | first-born | son:
    and highest a|mong the | kings · of the | earth.

29 'I will ever maintain my loving-|kindness ·
       to|ward him:
    and my covenant | with him · shall | stand | firm.

30 'I will establish his | line for | ever:
    and his | throne · like the | days of | heaven.

31 'If his children for|sake my | law:
    and | will not | walk in · my | judgments;

32 'If they pro|fane my | statutes:
    and | do not | keep · my com|mandments,

33 'Then I will punish their re|bellion · with the | rod:
    and | their in|iquity · with | blows.

34 'But I will not cause my loving-|kindness · to |
       cease from him:
    nor will | I be|tray my | faithfulness.

35 'I will not pro|fane my | covenant:
    or alter | what has | passed from · my | lips.

36 'Once and for all I have | sworn · by my | holiness:
    I will | not prove | false to | David.

37 'His posterity shall en|dure for | ever:
    and his throne be | as the | sun be|fore me;

38 'Like the moon that is es|tablished · for | ever:
    and stands in the | heavens · for | ever|more.'

39 Yet you have been enraged a|gainst · your an|ointed:
    you have ab|horred him | and re|jected him.

40 You have spurned the covenant | with your | servant:
    and de|filed his | crown · to the | dust.

41 You have broken down | all his | walls:
   and | made his | strongholds | desolate.

42 All that pass | by | plunder him:
   he has be|come the | scorn of · his | neighbours.

43 You have exalted the right hand | of his | adversaries:
   and | gladdened | all his | enemies.

44 His bright sword you have | turned | backward:
   you have not en|abled him · to | stand · in the | battle.

45 You have brought his | lustre · to an | end:
   you have | cast his | throne · to the | ground.

46 You have cut short the | days of · his | youth:
   and | clothed him | with dis|honour.

47 How long O Lord will you hide your|self so | utterly:
   how long shall your | fury | burn like | fire?

48 Remember how I draw to my e|ternal | end:
   have you created | all man|kind for | nothing?

49 Where is the man who can live and | not see | death:
   who can deliver his | life · from the | power · of the | grave?

50 Where O Lord are your loving-|kindnesses · of | old:
   which you have vowed to | David | in your | faithfulness?

51 Remember O Lord how your servant | is re|viled:
   how I bear in my bosom the | onslaught | of the | peoples;

52 Remember how your | ene·mies | taunt:
   how they mock the | footsteps · of | your an|ointed.

(†)(53 Blessèd be the | Lord for | ever:
   A|men and | A—|men.)

PSALM 90

1 Lord you have I been our I refuge:
     from one gener|ation I to an|other.

2 Before the mountains were born
          or the earth and the world were I brought to I be:
     from eternity to et|erni·ty I you are I God.

3 You turn man| back · into I dust:
     saying   'Return to I dust you I sons of I Adam.'

4 For a thousand years in your sight ⌣
          are like I yester·day I passing:
     or I like one I watch · of the I night.

5 You cut them I short · like a I dream:
     like the fresh I grass I of the I morning;

6 In the morning it is I green and I flourishes:
     at evening it is I withered · and I dried I up.

7 And we are con|sumed · by your I anger:
     because of your indig|nation · we I cease to I be.

8 You have brought our in|iquities · be|fore you:
     and our secret I sins · to the I light of · your I
          countenance.

9 Our days decline be|neath your I wrath:
     and our years I pass a|way · like a I sigh.

10 The days of our life are three score years and ten
          or if we have I strength   four I score:
     the pride of our labours is but toil and sorrow
          for it passes quickly a|way and I we are I gone.

11 Who can know the I power of · your I wrath:
     who can know your indig|nation · like I those that I
          fear you?

12 Teach us so to I number · our I days:
     that we may ap|ply our I hearts to I wisdom.

13 Relent O Lord * how long will I you be I angry?:
     take I pity I on your I servants.

14 O satisfy us early | with your | mercy:
    that | all our days we | may re|joice and | sing.

15 Give us joy for all the days you | have af|flicted us:
    for the | years · we have | suffered · ad|versity.

16 Show your | servants · your | work:
    and let their | children | see your | glory.

†17 May the gracious favour of the Lord our |
    God · be up|on us:
    prosper the work of our hands
        O | prosper · the | work · of our | hands!

PSALM 91

1 He who dwells in the shelter of the | Most | High:
    who abides under the | shadow | of the · Al|mighty,

2 He will say to the Lord
    'You are my refuge | and my | stronghold:
    my | God in | whom I | trust.'

3 For he will deliver you from the | snare · of the | hunter:
    and | from the · de|stroying | curse.

4 He will cover you with his wings
    and you will be safe | under · his | feathers:
    his faithfulness will | be your | shield · and de|fence.

5 You shall not be afraid of any | terror · by | night:
    or of the | arrow · that | flies by | day,

6 Of the pestilence that walks a|bout in | darkness:
    or the | plague · that de|stroys at | noonday.

7 A thousand may fall beside you
    and ten thousand at your | right | hand:
    but | you it | shall not | touch;

8 Your own | eyes shall | see:
    and look on the re|ward | of the · un|godly.

9 The Lord him|self · is your | refuge:
    you have | made the · Most | High your | stronghold.

10 Therefore no | harm · will be|fall you:
    nor will any | scourge come | near your | tent.

11 For he will com⎪mand his ⎪ angels:
    to ⎪ keep you · in ⎪ all your ⎪ ways.

12 They will bear you ⎪ up · in their ⎪ hands:
    lest you dash your ⎪ foot a⎪gainst a ⎪ stone.

13 You will tread on the ⎪ lion · and the ⎪ adder:
    the young lion and the serpent ‿
      you will ⎪ trample ⎪ under ⎪ foot.

14 'He has set his love upon me
    and therefore I ⎪ will de⎪liver him:
    I will lift him out of danger be⎪cause · he has ⎪
      known my ⎪ name.

15 'When he calls upon me ⎪ I will ⎪ answer him:
    I will be with him in trouble
      I will ⎪ rescue him · and ⎪ bring him · to ⎪ honour.

16 'With long ⎪ life · I will ⎪ satisfy him:
    and ⎪ fill him · with ⎪ my sal⎪vation.'

PSALM 92

1 How good to give ⎪ thanks · to the ⎪ Lord:
    to sing praises to your ⎪ name ⎪ O Most ⎪ High,

2 To declare your ⎪ love · in the ⎪ morning:
    and at ⎪ night to ⎪ sing of · your ⎪ faithfulness,

†3 Upon the lute upon the lute of ⎪ ten ⎪ strings:
    and to the ⎪ melo·dy ⎪ of the ⎪ lyre.

4 For in all you have done O Lord you have ⎪ made me ⎪
      glad:
    I will sing for joy be⎪cause of · the ⎪ works · of your ⎪
      hands.

5 Lord how glorious ⎪ are your ⎪ works:
    your ⎪ thoughts are ⎪ very ⎪ deep.

6 The brutish do ⎪ not con⎪sider:
    and the ⎪ fool · cannot ⎪ under⎪stand

7 That though the wicked ⎪ sprout like ⎪ grass:
    and ⎪ all wrong⎪doers ⎪ flourish,

8 They flourish to be de|stroyed · for I ever:
   but you Lord are ex|alted · for I ever|more.

9 For behold   your enemies O Lord ⌣
      your I enemies · shall I perish:
   and all the workers of I wicked·ness I shall be I
      scattered.

10 You have lifted up my head
      like the horns of the I wild I oxen:
   I am an|ointed · with I fresh I oil;

11 My eyes have looked I down · on my I enemies:
   and my ears have heard the ruin ⌣
      of I those who · rose I up a|gainst me.

12 The righteous shall I flourish · like the I palm tree:
   they shall spread a|broad · like a I cedar · in I Lebanon;

13 For they are planted in the I house · of the I Lord:
   and flourish in the I courts of I our I God.

14 In old age they shall be I full of I sap:
   they shall be I sturdy · and I laden · with I branches;

15 And they will say that the I Lord is I just:
   the Lord my Rock in I whom is I no un|righteousness.

PSALM 93

1 The Lord is King * and has put on I robes of I glory:
   the Lord has put on his glory
      he has I girded · him|self with I strength.

2 He has made the I world so I firm:
   that it I cannot I be I moved.

3 Your throne is es|tablished · from of I old:
   you I are from I ever|lasting.

4 The floods have lifted up O Lord
      the floods have lifted I up their I voice:
   the I floods lift I up their I pounding.

5 But mightier than the sound of many waters
      than the mighty waters or the I breakers · of the I
         sea:
   the I Lord on I high is I mighty.

6 Your decrees are ǀ very ǀ sure:
  and holiness O Lord aǀdorns your ǀ house for ǀ ever.

PSALM 94

1 O Lord God to whom ǀ vengeance · beǀlongs:
  O God to whom vengeance beǀlongs shine ǀ out in ǀ
  glory.

2 Arise ǀ judge · of the ǀ earth:
  and requite the ǀ proud as ǀ they deǀserve.

3 Lord how ǀ long · shall the ǀ wicked:
  how ǀ long · shall the ǀ wicked ǀ triumph?

4 How long shall all evildoers ǀ pour out ǀ words:
  how ǀ long · shall they ǀ boast and ǀ flaunt themselves?

5 They crush your ǀ people · O ǀ Lord:
  they opǀpress your ǀ own posǀsession.

6 They murder the ǀ widow · and the ǀ alien:
  they ǀ put the ǀ fatherless · to ǀ death.

7 And they say 'The ǀ Lord · does not ǀ see:
  nor does the ǀ God of ǀ Jacob · conǀsider it.'

8 Consider this   you senseless aǀmong the ǀ people:
  fools ǀ when · will you ǀ underǀstand?

9 He who planted the ear   does ǀ he not ǀ hear:
  he who formed the ǀ eye   does ǀ he not ǀ see?

10 He who disciplines the nations will ǀ he not ǀ punish:
  has the ǀ teacher · of manǀkind no ǀ knowledge?

†11 The Lord knows the ǀ thoughts of ǀ man:
  he ǀ knows · that they ǀ are mere ǀ breath.

12 Blessèd is the man whom you ǀ discipline · O ǀ Lord:
  and ǀ teach ǀ from your ǀ law,

13 Giving him rest from ǀ days of ǀ misery:
  till a ǀ pit is ǀ dug · for the ǀ wicked.

14 The Lord will not cast ǀ off his ǀ people:
  nor ǀ will he · forǀsake his ǀ own.

15 For justice shall return to the | righteous | man:
    and with him to | all the | true of | heart.

16 Who will stand up for me a|gainst the | wicked:
    who will take my part a|gainst the | evil|doers?

17 If the Lord had not | been my | helper:
    I would soon have | dwelt · in the | land of | silence.

18 But when I said   'My | foot has | slipped':
    your | mercy · O | Lord was | holding me.

19 In all the | doubts · of my | heart:
    your consol|ations · de|lighted · my | soul.

20 Will you be any friend to the | court of | wickedness:
    that contrives | evil · by | means of | law?

21 They band together against the | life · of the | righteous:
    and con|demn | inno·cent | blood.

22 But the | Lord · is my | stronghold:
    my | God · is my | rock · and my | refuge.

23 Let him requite them for their wickedness
        and silence them | for their | evil:
    the | Lord our | God shall | silence them.

PSALM 95

1 O come let us sing | out · to the | Lord:
    let us shout in triumph to the | rock of | our sal|vation.

2 Let us come before his | face with | thanksgiving:
    and cry | out to · him | joyfully · in | psalms.

3 For the Lord is a | great | God:
    and a great | king a·bove | all | gods.

4 In his hand are the | depths · of the | earth:
    and the peaks of the | mountains · are | his | also.

†5 The sea is his and | he | made it:
    his hands | moulded | dry | land.

6 Come let us worship and | bow | down:
    and kneel be|fore the | Lord our | maker.

7 For he is the | Lord our | God:
    we are his | people · and the | sheep of · his | pasture.

8 Today if only you would hear his voice
      'Do not harden your | hearts · as at | Meribah:
    as on that day at | Massah | in the | wilderness;

9 'When your | fathers | tested me:
    put me to proof though | they had | seen my | works.

10 'Forty years long I loathed that gener|ation · and | said:
    "It is a people who err in their hearts
      for they | do not | know my | ways";

11 'Of whom I | swore · in my | wrath:
    "They | shall not | enter · my | rest." '

PSALM 96

1 O sing to the Lord a | new | song:
    sing to the | Lord | all the | earth.

2 Sing to the Lord and bless his | holy | name:
    proclaim the good news of his sal|vation · from |
      day to | day.

3 Declare his glory a|mong the | nations:
    and his | wonders · a|mong all | peoples.

4 For great is the Lord and | greatly · to be | praised:
    he is more to be | feared than | all | gods.

5 As for all the gods of the nations | they are · mere | idols:
    it is the | Lord who | made the | heavens.

6 Majesty and | glory · are be|fore him:
    beauty and | power are | in his | sanctuary.

7 Render to the Lord you families | of the | nations:
    render to the | Lord | glory · and | might.

8 Render to the Lord the honour | due · to his | name:
    bring offerings and | come in|to his | courts.

9 O worship the Lord in the beauty | of his | holiness:
    let the whole earth | stand in | awe of | him.

10 Say among the nations that the ǀ Lord is ǀ king:
    he has made the world so firm that it can never be ⌣
      moved * and he shall ǀ judge the ǀ peoples · with ǀ
      equity.

11 Let the heavens rejoice and let the ǀ earth be ǀ glad:
    let the sea ǀ roar and ǀ all that ǀ fills it;

12 Let the fields rejoice and ǀ every·thing ǀ in them:
    then shall all the trees of the wood ⌣
      shout with ǀ joy beǀfore the ǀ Lord;

†13 For he comes he comes to ǀ judge the ǀ earth:
    he shall judge the world with righteousness
      and the ǀ peoples ǀ with his ǀ truth.

PSALM 97

1 The Lord is king let the ǀ earth reǀjoice:
    let the ǀ multitude · of ǀ islands · be ǀ glad.

2 Clouds and darkness are ǀ round aǀbout him:
    righteousness and justice are the foundǀation ǀ of his ǀ
      throne.

3 Fire ǀ goes beǀfore him:
    and burns up his ǀ enemies · on ǀ every ǀ side.

4 His lightnings ǀ light the ǀ world:
    the ǀ earth ǀ sees it · and ǀ quakes.

5 The mountains melt like wax beǀfore his ǀ face:
    from before the face of the ǀ Lord of ǀ all the ǀ earth.

6 The heavens have proǀclaimed his ǀ righteousness:
    and all ǀ peoples · have ǀ seen his ǀ glory.

7 They are ashamed * all those who serve idols ⌣
    and glory in ǀ mere ǀ nothings:
    all ǀ gods bow ǀ down beǀfore him.

8 Zion heard and was glad * and the daughters of ǀ Judah ·
    reǀjoiced:
    beǀcause of · your ǀ judgments · O ǀ God.

9 For you Lord are most high over ǀ all the ǀ earth:
    you are exalted ǀ far a·bove ǀ all ǀ gods.

10 The Lord loves ǀ those that · hate ǀ evil:
    the Lord guards the life of the faithful
        and delivers them from the ǀ hand of ǀ the unǀgodly.

11 Light ǀ dawns · for the ǀ righteous:
    and ǀ joy · for the ǀ true of ǀ heart.

12 Rejoice in the ǀ Lord you ǀ righteous:
    and give ǀ thanks · to his ǀ holy ǀ name.

PSALM 98

1 O sing to the Lord a ǀ new ǀ song:
    for he has ǀ done ǀ marvel·lous ǀ things;

2 His right hand and his ǀ holy ǀ arm:
    they have ǀ got ǀ him the ǀ victory.

3 The Lord has made ǀ known · his salǀvation:
    he has revealed his just deǀliverance · in the ǀ sight of ·
        the ǀ nations.

4 He has remembered his mercy and faithfulness ⌣
        towards the ǀ house of ǀ Israel:
    and all the ends of the earth ⌣
        have seen the salǀvation ǀ of our ǀ God.

5 Shout with joy to the Lord ǀ all the ǀ earth:
    break into ǀ singing · and ǀ make ǀ melody.

6 Make melody to the Lord upǀon the ǀ harp:
    upon the harp and ǀ with the ǀ sounds of ǀ praise.

7 With trumpets ǀ and with ǀ horns:
    cry out in triumph beǀfore the ǀ Lord the ǀ king.

8 Let the sea roar and ǀ all that ǀ fills it:
    the good earth and ǀ those who ǀ live upǀon it.

9 Let the rivers ǀ clap their ǀ hands:
    and let the mountains ring out toǀgether · beǀfore the ǀ
        Lord;

10 For he comes to ǀ judge the ǀ earth:
    he shall judge the world with righteousness
        and the ǀ peoples ǀ with ǀ equity.

PSALM 99

1 The Lord is king   let the | nations | tremble:
    he is enthroned upon the cherubim | let the |
      earth | quake.

2 The Lord is | great in | Zion:
    he is | high a|bove all | nations.

3 Let them praise your great and | terri·ble | name:
    for | holy | is the | Lord.

4 The Mighty One is king and | loves | justice:
    you have established equity * you have dealt | ⌣
      righteousness · and | justice · in | Jacob.

†5 *O exalt the | Lord our | God:*
    and bow down before his | footstool · for | he is | holy.

6 Moses and Aaron among his priests
    and Samuel among those who call up|on his | name:
    they called to the | Lord | and he | answered.

7 He spoke to them from the | pillar · of | cloud:
    they kept to his teachings | and the | law · that he |
      gave them.

8 You answered them O | Lord our | God:
    you were a forgiving God to them
    and | pardoned · their | wrong|doing.

9 *O exalt the | Lord our | God:*
    and bow down towards his holy hill
      for the | Lord our | God is | holy.

PSALM 100

1 O shout to the Lord in triumph | all the | earth:
    serve the Lord with gladness
    and come before his | face with | songs of | joy.

2 Know that the Lord | he is | God:
    it is he who has made us and we are his
    we are his | people · and the | sheep of · his |
      pasture.

3 Come into his gates with thanksgiving
    and into his | courts with | praise:
    give thanks to him and | bless his | holy | name.

4 For the Lord is good * his loving mercy ǀ is for ǀ ever:
   his faithfulness throughǀout all ǀ generǀations.

PSALM 101

1 My song shall be of ǀ steadfastness · and ǀ justice:
   to ǀ you Lord ǀ will I ǀ sing.

2 I will be wise in the ǀ way of ǀ innocence:
   O ǀ when ǀ will you ǀ come to me?

3 I will walk withǀin my ǀ house:
   inǀ puriǀty of ǀ heart.

4 I will set nothing evil beǀfore my ǀ eyes:
   I hate the sin of backsliders　it shall ǀ get no ǀ hold ǀ
    on me.

†5 Crookedness of heart shall deǀpart ǀ from me:
   I will ǀ know ǀ nothing · of ǀ wickedness.

[6 The man who secretly slanders his neighbour I ǀ
    will deǀstroy:
   the proud look and the arrogant ǀ heart · I will ǀ
    not enǀdure.]

7 My eyes shall look to the faithful in the land
    and they shall ǀ make their ǀ home with me:
   one who walks in the way of innocence ǀ ⌣
    he shall ǀ minis·ter ǀ to me.

8 No man who practises deceit shall ǀ live in · my ǀ house:
   no one who utters ǀ lies shall ǀ stand in · my ǀ sight.

[9 Morning by morning I will destroy⌣
    all the ǀ wicked · of the ǀ land:
   and cut off all evildoers from the ǀ city ǀ of the ǀ Lord.]

PSALM 102

1 O Lord ǀ hear my ǀ prayer:
   and ǀ let my ǀ cry ǀ come to you.

2 Do not hide your face from me in the ǀ day of · my ǀ
    trouble:
   turn your ear to me
    and when I ǀ call be ǀ swift to ǀ answer.

3 For my days pass a|way like | smoke:
 and my bones | burn as | in a | furnace.

4 My heart is scorched and | withered · like | grass:
 and I for|get to | eat my | bread.

5 I am weary with the | sound of · my | groaning:
 my | bones stick | fast to · my | skin.

6 I have become like an | owl · in the | wilderness:
 like a | screech-owl · a|mong the | ruins.

7 I keep watch   and | flit · to and | fro:
 like a | sparrow · up|on a | housetop.

8 My enemies taunt me | all day | long:
 and those who | rave at me · make | oaths a|gainst me.

9 Surely I have eaten | ashes · for | bread:
 and | mingled · my | drink with | tears,

10 Because of your wrath and | indig|nation:
 for you have taken me | up and | tossed · me a|side.

†11 My days de|cline · like a | shadow:
 and I | wither · a|way like | grass.

12 But you Lord are en|throned for | ever:
 and your name shall be known through|out all | gener|ations.

13 You will arise and have | mercy up·on | Zion:
 for it is time to pity her   the ap|pointed | time has | come.

14 Your servants love | even · her | stones:
 and her | dust moves | them to | pity.

15 Then shall the nations fear your | name O | Lord:
 and all the | kings · of the | earth your | glory,

16 When the Lord has | built up | Zion:
 when he | shows him|self · in his | glory,

17 When he turns to the | prayer · of the | destitute:
 and does not de|spise their | suppli|cation.

†18 Let this be written down for | those who · come | after:
 and a people yet un|born will | praise the | Lord.

19 For the Lord has looked down from the ǀ height · of his ǀ
    holiness:
    from heaven he has ǀ looked upǀon the ǀ earth,

20 To hear the ǀ groaning · of the ǀ prisoner:
    to deliver ǀ those conǀdemned to ǀ die;

21 That they may proclaim the name of the ǀ Lord in ǀ Zion:
    and his ǀ praises ǀ in Jeǀrusalem,

22 When the nations are ǀ gathered · toǀgether:
    and the ǀ kingdoms · to ǀ serve the ǀ Lord.

23 He has broken my strength beǀfore my ǀ time:
    he has ǀ cut ǀ short my ǀ days.

24 Do not take me away O God in the ǀ midst of · my ǀ life:
    you whose years exǀtend through ǀ all · generǀations.

25 In the beginning you laid the foundǀations · of the ǀ
    earth:
    and the ǀ heavens · are the ǀ work of · your ǀ hands.

26 They shall perish but ǀ you · will enǀdure:
    they shall all grow old like a garment*like clothes ⌣
    you will change them and ǀ they shall ǀ pass aǀway.

27 But you are the ǀ same for ǀ ever:
    and your ǀ years will ǀ never ǀ fail.

28 The children of your servants shall ǀ rest seǀcure:
    and their seed shall be esǀtablished ǀ in your ǀ sight.

PSALM 103

1 Praise the Lord ǀ O my ǀ soul:
    and all that is within me ǀ praise his ǀ holy ǀ name.

2 Praise the Lord ǀ O my ǀ soul:
    and forǀget not ǀ all his ǀ benefits,

3 Who forgives ǀ all your ǀ sin:
    and ǀ heals ǀ all · your inǀfirmities,

4 Who redeems your ǀ life · from the ǀ Pit:
    and crowns you with ǀ mercy ǀ and comǀpassion;

†5 Who satisfies your being with I good I things:
    so that your I youth · is relnewed · like an I eagle's.

6 The Lord I works I righteousness:
    and justice for I all who I are oplpressed.

7 He made known his I ways to I Moses:
    and his I works · to the I children · of I Israel.

8 The Lord is full of comlpassion · and I mercy:
    slow to anger I and of I great I goodness.

9 He will not I always · be I chiding:
    nor will he I keep his I anger · for I ever.

10 He has not dealt with us aclcording · to our I sins:
    nor rewarded us aclcording I to our I wickedness.

11 For as the heavens are high albove the I earth:
    so great is his I mercy · over I those that I fear him;

12 As far as the east is I from the I west:
    so far has he I set our I sins I from us.

13 As a father is tender tolwards his I children:
    so is the Lord I tender · to I those that I fear him.

†14 For he knows of I what · we are I made:
    he relmembers · that we I are but I dust.

15 The days of man are I but as I grass:
    he flourishes I like a I flower · of the I field;

16 When the wind goes over it I it is I gone:
    and its I place will I know it · no I more.

17 But the merciful goodness of the Lord * endures for _
    ever and ever toward I those that I fear him:
    and his righteousness uplon their I children's I
    children;

18 Upon those who I keep his I covenant:
    and I remember · his comlmandments · to I do them.

19 The Lord has established his I throne in I heaven:
    and his I kingdom I rules · over I all.

20 Praise the Lord all you his angels   you that exlcel in I
    strength:

you that fulfil his word
    and obey the ˈvoice of ˈhis comˈmandment.

21 Praise the Lord all ˈyou his ˈhosts:
    his ˈservants · who ˈdo his ˈwill.

22 Praise the Lord all his works
    in all places of ˈhis doˈminion:
    praise the ˈLord ˈO my ˈsoul!

PSALM 104

1 Bless the Lord ˈO my ˈsoul:
    O Lord my ˈGod how ˈgreat you ˈare!

2 Clothed with ˈmajesty · and ˈhonour:
    wrapped in ˈlight as ˈin a ˈgarment.

3 You have stretched out the ˈheavens · like a ˈtent-cloth:
    and laid the beams of your ˈdwelling · upˈon their ˈwaters;

4 You make the ˈclouds your ˈchariot:
    and ˈride up · on the ˈwings · of the ˈwind;

5 You make the ˈwinds your ˈmessengers:
    and ˈflames of ˈfire your ˈministers;

6 You have set the earth on ˈits foundˈations:
    so ˈthat it · shall ˈnever · be ˈmoved.

7 The deep covered it ˈas · with a ˈmantle:
    the waters ˈstood aˈbove the ˈhills.

8 At your reˈbuke they ˈfled:
    at the voice of your ˈthunder · they ˈhurried · aˈway;

9 They went up to the mountains
    they went ˈdown · by the ˈvalleys:
    to the place which ˈyou · had apˈpointed ˈfor them.

10 You fixed a limit which they ˈmay not ˈpass:
    they shall not return aˈgain to ˈcover · the ˈearth.

11 You send springs ˈinto · the ˈgullies:
    which ˈrun beˈtween the ˈhills;

12 They give drink to every ˈbeast · of the ˈfield:
    and the wild ˈasses ˈquench their ˈthirst.

13 Beside them the birds of the air | build their | nests:
and | sing a|mong the | branches.

14 You water the mountains from your | dwelling · on |
high:
and the earth is | filled · by the | fruits of · your | work.

15 You cause the grass to | grow · for the | cattle:
and all green things for the | servants | of man|kind.

16 You bring food | out of · the | earth:
and wine that makes | glad the | heart of | man,

17 Oil to give him a | shining | countenance:
and | bread to | strengthen · his | heart.

18 The trees of the Lord are | well-|watered:
the cedars of | Lebanon · that | he has | planted,

19 Where the birds | build their | nests:
and the stork | makes her | home · in the | pine-tops.

20 The high hills are a refuge for the | wild | goats:
and the crags a | cover | for the | conies.

21 You created the moon to | mark the | seasons:
and the sun | knows the | hour · of its | setting.

22 You make darkness | and it · is | night:
in which all the beasts of the | forest | move by |
stealth.

23 The lions | roar · for their | prey:
seek|ing their | food from | God.

24 When the sun rises | they re|tire:
and | lay them·selves | down · in their | dens.

†25 Man goes | out · to his | work:
and to his | labour · un|til the | evening.

26 Lord how various | are your | works:
in wisdom you have made them all
and the | earth is | full of · your | creatures.

27 There is the wide im|measur·able | sea:
there move living things without | number |
great and | small;

28 There go the ships | to and | fro:
   and there is that Leviathan
      whom you | formed to | sport · in the | deep.

29 These all | look to | you:
   to give them their | food in | due | season.

30 When you give it to | them they | gather it:
   when you open your hand they are | satisfied · with |
      good | things.

31 When you hide your | face · they are | troubled:
   when you take away their breath‿
      they | die · and re|turn · to their | dust.

†32 When you send forth your spirit they | are cre|ated:
   and you re|new the | face · of the | earth.

33 May the glory of the Lord en|dure for | ever:
   may the | Lord re|joice · in his | works.

34 If he look upon the | earth · it shall | tremble:
   if he but touch the | mountains | they shall | smoke.

35 I will sing to the Lord as | long as · I | live:
   I will praise my | God · while I | have · any | being.

36 May my meditation be | pleasing | to him:
   for my | joy shall | be · in the | Lord.

†37 May sinners perish from the earth
   let the wicked | be no | more:
   bless the Lord O my soul
      O | praise | – the | Lord.

PSALM 105

1 O give thanks to the Lord   and call up|on his | name:
   tell among the | peoples · what | things · he has |
      done.

2 Sing to him O | sing | praises:
   and be telling of | all his | marvel·lous | works.

3 Exult in his | holy | name:
   and let those that seek the | Lord be | joyful · in | heart.

4 Seek the | Lord · and his | strength:
   O | seek his | face con|tinually.

5 Call to mind what wonders | he has | done:
   his marvellous acts   and the | judgments | of his |
      mouth,

6 O seed of | Abraham · his | servant:
   O | children · of | Jacob · his | chosen one.

7 For he is the | Lord our | God:
   and his judgments | are in | all the | earth.

8 He has remembered his | covenant · for | ever:
   the word that he ordained for a | thousand |
      gener|ations,

9 The covenant that he | made with | Abraham:
   the | oath · that he | swore to | Isaac,

10 And confirmed it to | Jacob · as a | statute:
   to Israel as an | ever|lasting | covenant,

11 Saying 'I will give you the | land of | Canaan:
   to be the | portion · of | your in|heritance',

12 And that when they | were but | few:
   little in number   and | ali·ens | in the | land.

13 They wandered from | nation · to | nation:
   from one people and | kingdom | to an|other.

14 He suffered no man to | do them | wrong:
   but re|proved · even | kings for · their | sake,

†15 Saying 'Touch not | my an|ointed:
   and | do my | prophets · no | harm.'

16 Then he called down a | famine · on the | land:
   and destroyed the | bread that | was their | stay.

17 But he had sent a | man a|head of them:
   Joseph | who was | sold · into | slavery,

18 Whose feet they | fastened · with | fetters:
   and thrust his | neck in·to a | hoop of | iron.

19 Till the time that his | words proved | true:
   he was | tested · by the | Lord's com|mand.

20 Then the king I sent and I loosed him:
    the ruler of I nations I set him I free;

21 He made him master I of his I household:
    and ruler I over I all · his posIsessions,

†22 To rebuke his I officers · at I will:
    and to I teach his I counsel·lors I wisdom.

23 Then Israel I came · into I Egypt:
    and Jacob I dwelt · in the I land of I Ham.

24 There the Lord made his I people I fruitful:
    too I numer·ous I for their I enemies,

25 Whose hearts he turned to I hate his I people:
    and to deal deIceitful·ly I with his I servants.

26 Then he sent I Moses · his I servant:
    and I Aaron · whom I he had I chosen.

27 Through them he I manifested · his I signs:
    and his I wonders · in the I land of I Ham.

28 He sent darkness I and it · was I dark:
    yet they would I not oIbey · his comImands.

29 He turned their I waters · into I blood:
    and I slew the I fish thereIin.

30 Their country I swarmed with I frogs:
    even the inner I chambers I of their I kings.

31 He spoke the word   and there came great I swarms of I flies:
    and I gnats with·in I all their I borders.

32 He sent them I storms of I hail:
    and darts of I fire I into · their I land.

33 He struck their I vines · and their I fig-trees:
    and shattered the I trees withIin their I borders.

34 He commanded   and there I came I grasshoppers:
    and young I locusts · withIout I number.

35 They ate up every green thing I in the I land:
    and deIvoured the I fruit · of the I soil.

36 He smote all the first-born ǀ in their ǀ land:
   the ǀ firstfruits · of ǀ all their ǀ manhood.

37 He brought Israel out with silver ǀ and with ǀ gold:
   and not one among their ǀ tribes was ǀ seen to ǀ
   stumble.

38 Egypt was ǀ glad · at their ǀ going:
   for dread of ǀ Israel · had ǀ fallen · upǀon them.

39 He spread out a ǀ cloud · for a ǀ covering:
   and ǀ fire to ǀ lighten · the ǀ night.

40 The people asked and he ǀ brought them ǀ quails:
   and satisfied them ǀ with the ǀ bread from ǀ heaven.

41 He opened a rock so that the ǀ waters ǀ gushed:
   and ran in the parched ǀ land ǀ like a ǀ river.

42 For he had remembered his ǀ holy ǀ word:
   that he gave to ǀ Abraǀham his ǀ servant.

43 So he led out his ǀ people · with reǀjoicing:
   his ǀ chosen ones · with ǀ shouts of ǀ joy;

44 He gave them the ǀ land · of the ǀ nations:
   and they took possession of the ǀ fruit ⌣
   of ǀ other · men's ǀ toil,

†45 So that they might ǀ keep his ǀ statutes:
   and faithfully obey his laws
   O ǀ praise ǀ – the ǀ Lord.

PSALM 106

1 Praise the Lord
   O give thanks to the Lord for ǀ he is ǀ good:
   and his ǀ mercy · enǀdures for ǀ ever.

2 Who can express the mighty ǀ acts · of the ǀ Lord:
   or ǀ fully ǀ voice his ǀ praise?

3 Blessèd are those who act acǀcording · to ǀ justice:
   who at ǀ all times ǀ do the ǀ right.

4 Remember me O Lord
   when you visit your people ǀ with your ǀ favour:

and come to me I also · with I your sal|vation,

†5 That I may see the prosperity I of your I chosen:
　　that I may rejoice with the rejoicing of your people
　　and exult with I those who I are your I own.

6 We have sinned I like our I fathers:
　　we have acted per|versely · and I done I wrong.

7 Our fathers when they I were in I Egypt:
　　took no I heed I of your I wonders;

8 They did not remember ⏝
　　　the multitude of your I loving-|kindnesses:
　　but they re|belled · at the I Red I Sea.

9 Nevertheless he saved them for his I name's I sake:
　　that he I might make I known his I power.

10 He commanded the Red Sea and it I dried I up:
　　and he led them through the I deep as I through a I
　　　desert.

11 He delivered them from the I hand · of their I adversary:
　　and redeemed them I from the I power · of the I
　　　enemy.

12 The waters closed over I their op|pressors:
　　so that not I one was I left a|live.

13 Then they be|lieved his I words:
　　and I sang him I songs of I praise.

14 But in a little while they forgot what I he had I done:
　　and would I wait · for his I counsel · no I more.

15 Greed took hold of them I in the I desert:
　　and they put I God · to the I test · in the I wilderness.

16 So he gave them that which I they de|sired:
　　but sent a I wasting I sickness · a|mong them.

17 Then they grew envious of Moses I in the I camp:
　　and of Aaron the I holy · one I of the I Lord;

18 Whereupon the earth opened and I swallowed · up I
　　　Dathan:
　　it closed over the I compan·y I of A|biram;

19 Fire flared out a|gainst their | number:
  and | flame de|voured · the un|godly.

20 At Horeb they | made themselves · a | calf:
  and bowed down in | worship | to an | image.

21 And so they exchanged the | glory · of | God:
  for the likeness of an | ox that | eats | hay.

22 They forgot God who | was their | saviour:
  that had done such | great | things in | Egypt,

23 Who had worked his wonders in the | land of | Ham:
  and his terrible | deeds · at the | Red | Sea.

†24 Therefore he | thought · to de|stroy them:
  had not Moses his servant stood before him in the ⌣
    breach * to turn a|way his |
      wrath · from de|stroying them.

25 Then they despised the | pleasant | land:
  and | put no | faith · in his | promise,

26 But murmured | in their | tents:
  and would not o|bey the | voice · of the | Lord.

27 So he lifted his hand to swear an | oath a|gainst them:
  that he would | strike them | down · in the |
    wilderness,

28 And cast out their children a|mong the | nations:
  and | scatter them · through | all the | lands.

29 Then they joined themselves to the | Baal · of | Peor:
  and ate things sacrificed to | gods that | have no | life.

30 They provoked him to anger with their | wanton | deeds:
  and | plague broke | out a|mong them.

31 Then stood up Phinehas and | inter|posed:
  and | so the | plague was | ended;

32 And that was counted to | him for | righteousness:
  throughout all gener|ations · for | ever|more.

33 They angered God also at the | waters · of | Meribah:
  so that Moses | suffered · for | their mis|deeds;

34 For they had em|bittered · his | spirit:
and he spoke | rashly | with his | lips.

35 They did not de|stroy the | peoples:
as the Lord had com|manded | them to | do,

36 But they mingled themselves | with the | heathen:
and | learned to | follow · their | ways.

37 They worshipped | foreign | idols:
and | these be|came their | snare,

38 So that they | sacrificed · their | sons:
and their | own | daughters · to | demons.

39 They shed | inno·cent | blood:
even the blood of their | own | sons and | daughters,

40 Whom they offered to the | idols · of | Canaan:
and the | land · was de|filed with | blood.

41 They made themselves | foul · by their | acts:
and with wanton deeds | whored · after | strange |
    gods.

42 Then was the wrath of the Lord kindled a|gainst his |
    people:
and he | loathed his | own pos|session;

43 He gave them into the | hands · of the | nations:
and their | adver·saries | ruled | over them.

44 Their enemies be|came · their op|pressors:
and they were brought into sub|jection · be|neath
    their | power.

45 Many a | time he | saved them:
but they rebelled against him to follow their own
    designs * and were brought | down |
        by their | wickedness.

46 Nevertheless he looked on | their dis|tress:
when he | heard their | loud | crying.

47 He remembered his | coven·ant | with them:
and relented   according to the a|bundance · * of his |
    loving-|kindness.

48 And he caused them ǀ to be ǀ pitied:
      even by ǀ those that ǀ held them ǀ captive.

(†)49 Save us O Lord our God
          and gather us from aǀmong the ǀ nations:
      that we may give thanks to your holy name
          and ǀ make our ǀ boast · in your ǀ praises.

(50 Blessèd be the Lord the God of Israel
          from everlasting to ǀ everǀlasting:
      and let all the people say Amen ǀ
          Praise ǀ – the ǀ Lord.)

PSALM 107

1 O give thanks to the Lord for ǀ he is ǀ good:
      for his loving ǀ mercy ǀ is for ǀ ever.

2 Let the Lord's reǀdeemed ǀ say so:
      whom he has redeemed from the ǀ hand ǀ of the ǀ
          enemy,

†3 And gathered in from every land
          from the east and ǀ from the ǀ west:
      from the ǀ north and ǀ from the ǀ south.

4 Some went astray in the wilderness and ǀ in the ǀ
          desert:
      and found no ǀ path to · an inǀhabit·ed ǀ city;

5 They were ǀ hungry · and ǀ thirsty:
      and their ǀ heart ǀ fainted · withǀin them.

6 Then they cried to the Lord in ǀ their disǀtress:
      and he ǀ took them ǀ out of · their ǀ trouble.

7 He led them by the ǀ right ǀ path:
      till they ǀ came to · an inǀhabit·ed ǀ city.

8 *Let them thank the ǀ Lord · for his ǀ goodness:*
      and for the wonders that he ǀ does · for the ǀ children · of ǀ
          men;

9 *For he ǀ satisfies · the ǀ thirsty:*
      and fills the ǀ hungry · with ǀ good ǀ things.

10 Some sat in darkness and in ǀ deadly ǀ shadow:
　　bound ǀ fast · in afǀfliction · and ǀ iron,

11 Because they had rebelled against the ǀ words of ǀ God:
　　and scorned the purposes ǀ of the ǀ Most ǀ High.

12 So he bowed down their ǀ hearts · with afǀfliction:
　　they tripped ǀ headlong · with ǀ none to ǀ help them.

13 Then they cried to the Lord in ǀ their disǀtress:
　　and he ǀ took them ǀ out of · their ǀ trouble.

†14 He brought them out from darkness and ǀ deadly ǀ
　　　shadow:
　　and ǀ broke their ǀ chains in ǀ two.

15 *Let them thank the ǀ Lord · for his ǀ goodness:*
　　and for the wonders that he ǀ does · for the ǀ children · of ǀ
　　　men;

16 *For he shatters the ǀ doors of ǀ bronze:*
　　and ǀ cleaves the ǀ bars of ǀ iron.

17 Fools were far ǀ gone · in transǀgression:
　　and beǀcause of · their ǀ sins · were afǀflicted.

18 They sickened at ǀ any ǀ food:
　　and had ǀ come · to the ǀ gates of ǀ death.

19 Then they cried to the Lord in ǀ their disǀtress:
　　and he ǀ took them ǀ out of · their ǀ trouble.

20 He sent his ǀ word and ǀ healed them:
　　and ǀ saved their ǀ life · from the ǀ Pit.

21 *Let them thank the ǀ Lord · for his ǀ goodness:*
　　and for the wonders that he ǀ does · for the ǀ children · of ǀ
　　　men;

22 *Let them offer sacrifices of ǀ thanksǀgiving:*
　　and tell what he has ǀ done with ǀ shouts of ǀ joy.

23 Those who go down to the ǀ sea in ǀ ships:
　　and follow their ǀ trade on ǀ great ǀ waters,

24 These men have seen the ǀ works of ǀ God:
　　and his ǀ wonders ǀ in the ǀ deep.

25 For he spoke and I raised the I storm-wind:
   and it lifted I high the I waves · of the I sea.

26 They go up to the sky   and down aIgain · to the I
      depths:
   their courage melts aIway · in the I face · of disIaster.

27 They reel and stagger like I drunken I men:
   and are I at their I wits' I end.

28 Then they cried to the Lord in I their disItress:
   and he I took them I out of · their I trouble.

29 He calmed the I storm · to a I silence:
   and the I waves · of the I sea were I stilled.

30 Then they were glad beIcause · they were I quiet:
   and he I brought them · to the I haven · they I
      longed for.

31 *Let them thank the I Lord · for his I goodness:*
   and for the wonders that he I does · for the I children · of I
      men;

32 *Let them exalt him in the asIsembly · of the I people:*
   and I praise him · in the I council · of I elders.

33 He turns the I rivers · into I desert:
   and springs of I water · into I thirsty I ground.

34 He makes of a fruitful land a I salty I waste:
   beIcause · its inIhabitants · are I evil.

35 He turns the wilderness into a I pool of I water:
   and parched I ground · into I flowing I springs.

36 And there he I settles · the I hungry:
   and they I build a I city · to I live in.

37 They sow fields and I plant I vineyards:
   which I give them I fruitful I harvest.

38 He blesses them   and they I multi·ply I greatly:
   he does not I let their I cattle · dimIinish.

39 But he pours conItempt up·on I princes:
   and makes them I stray · in the I pathless I desert;

40 They are weakened and I brought I low:

through | stress of · ad|versity · and | sorrow.

41 But he lifts the | poor · out of | misery:
and increases their | families · like | flocks of | sheep.

42 The upright shall | see it · and re|joice:
and all | wickedness · shall | shut its | mouth.

†43 Whoever is wise   let him ob|serve these | things:
and consider the loving-|kindness | of the | Lord.

PSALM 108

1 My heart is fixed O God my | heart is | fixed:
I will | sing and | make | melody.

2 Awake my soul   awake | lute and | harp:
for | I · will a|waken · the | morning.

3 I will give you thanks O Lord a|mong the | peoples:
I will sing your | praise a|mong the | nations.

4 For the greatness of your mercy | reaches · to the |
heavens:
and your | faithful·ness | to the | clouds.

5 Be exalted O God a|bove the | heavens:
and let your glory be | over | all the | earth;

6 That those whom you love may | be de|livered:
O save us by | your right | hand and | answer me.

7 God has said in his | holy | place:
'I will exult and divide Shechem
I will parcel | out the | valley · of | Succoth.

8 'Gilead is mine and Man|asseh · is | mine:
Ephraim is my helmet and | Judah · my | rod ·
of com|mand.

†9 'Moab is my wash-bowl   over Edom will I | cast my |
shoe:
against Philistia | will I | shout in | triumph.'

10 Who will lead me into the | forti·fied | city:
who will | bring me | into | Edom?

11 Have you not cast us I off O I God?:
  you I go not I out · with our I armies.

12 Give us your help aIgainst the I enemy:
  for I vain · is the I help of I man.

13 By the power of our God we I shall do I valiantly:
  for it is he that I will tread I down our I enemies.

PSALM 109

1 O God of my praise do I not be I silent:
  for evil and deceitful I mouths are I
    opened · aIgainst me.

2 They speak of me with I lying I tongues:
  they surround me with words of hatred
    they fight aIgainst me · withIout I cause.

3 In return for my friendship I they opIpose me:
  and I that for · no I fault of I mine.

4 They repay me I evil · for I good:
  and I hatred · for I my afIfection.

[5 Appoint an evil man to I stand aIgainst him:
  and let an adversary I be at · his I right I hand.

6 When he is judged let him be I found I guilty:
  let his prayer for I help be I counted · as I sin.

7 Let his I days be I few:
  and let another I take what I he has I hoarded.

8 Let his children be I made I fatherless:
  and his I wife beIcome a I widow.

9 Let his children be I vagabonds · and I beggars:
  let them seek alms I far · from their I own I homes.

10 Let the usurer exact I all · that he I has:
  and let strangers I plunder · the I fruit · of his I toil.

11 Let no man be I loyal · to I him:
  and let no one have I pity · on his I father·less I
    children.

12 Let his line beIcome exItinct:
  in one generation let their I name be I blotted I out.

13 Let the sins of his fathers be reˈmembered · by the ˈ
    Lord:
    and his mother's iniquity ˈ not be ˈ wiped aˈway.

14 Let their sins be constantly beˈfore the ˈ Lord:
    may he root out their ˈ memo·ry ˈ from the ˈ earth.

15 For he was a man that did not remember to ˈ show ˈ
    loyalty:
    but he persecuted the humble the poor and the ⌣
    crushed in spirit
    and ˈ sought to ˈ put them · to ˈ death.

16 He loved to curse * let curses ˈ fall on ˈ him:
    he took no pleasure in blessing
    so let ˈ it be ˈ far from ˈ him.

17 He clothed himself in cursing ˈ like a ˈ garment:
    so let it seep like water into his body
    and like ˈ oil ˈ into · his ˈ bones.

18 Let it be as the clothes he ˈ wraps aˈbout him:
    or like the ˈ girdle · that he ˈ wears each ˈ day.

[†]19 This is the Lord's recompense to ˈ
    those · that opˈpose him:
    to ˈ those that · speak ˈ evil · aˈgainst me.]

20 Act for me O Lord my God for your ˈ name's ˈ sake:
    and deliver me   as your ˈ steadfast ˈ love is ˈ good.

21 For I am ˈ poor and ˈ needy:
    and my ˈ heart ˈ writhes withˈin me.

22 I fade like a ˈ lengthen·ing ˈ shadow:
    I am ˈ shaken ˈ off · like a ˈ locust.

23 My knees are ˈ weak from ˈ fasting:
    my ˈ flesh grows ˈ lean and ˈ shrunken.

†24 I have become the ˈ scorn of · my ˈ enemies:
    and when they see me they ˈ toss their ˈ
    heads · in deˈrision.

25· Help me O ˈ Lord my ˈ God:
    and save me ˈ for your ˈ mercy's ˈ sake,

26 That men may know it was ǀ your ǀ hand:
    that ǀ you O ǀ Lord have ǀ done it.

27 Though they curse yet ǀ give me · your ǀ blessing:
    and those that come against me will be put to shame
    and your ǀ servant ǀ shall reǀjoice.

28 Let those that oppose me be ǀ covered · with disǀgrace:
    let them ǀ wear their ǀ shame · as a ǀ garment.

29 And I will give the Lord great ǀ thanks · with my ǀ
    mouth:
    and ǀ praise him · in the ǀ midst · of a ǀ multitude.

30 For the Lord will stand at the right ǀ hand · of the ǀ poor:
    to save him from ǀ those that ǀ would conǀdemn him.

PSALM 110

1 The Lord ǀ said to ǀ my lord:
    'Sit at my right hand
    until I ǀ make your ǀ enemies · your ǀ footstool.'

2 The Lord commits to you the sceptre ǀ of your ǀ power:
    reign from ǀ Zion · in the ǀ midst of · your ǀ enemies.

3 Noble are you * from the day of your birth upon the ǀ
    holy ǀ hill:
    radiant are you even from the womb
    in the ǀ morning ǀ dew of · your ǀ youth.

4 The Lord has sworn and will ǀ not turn ǀ back:
    'You are a priest for ever * after the ǀ order ǀ
    of Melǀchizedek.'

5 The king shall stand at your right ǀ hand O ǀ Lord:
    and shatter ǀ kings · in the ǀ day of · his ǀ wrath.

6 Glorious in majesty * he shall judge aǀmong the ǀ
    nations:
    and shatter heads ǀ over · a ǀ wide ǀ land.

†7 He shall slake his thirst from the brook beǀside the ǀ way:
    therefore shall ǀ he lift ǀ up his ǀ head.

PSALM 111

1 O praise the Lord
    I will praise the Lord with my ǀ whole ǀ heart:
  in the company of the upright
    and aǀmong the ǀ congreǀgation.

2 The works of the ǀ Lord are ǀ great:
  and studied by ǀ all who ǀ take deǀlight in them.

3 His deeds are maǀjestic · and ǀ glorious:
  and his ǀ righteous·ness ǀ stands for ǀ ever.

4 His marvellous acts have won him a name to ǀ
    be reǀmembered:
  the ǀ Lord is ǀ gracious · and ǀ merciful.

5 He gives food to ǀ those that ǀ fear him:
  he reǀmembers · his ǀ covenant · for ǀ ever.

6 He showed his people the ǀ power · of his ǀ acts:
  in giving them the ǀ herit·age ǀ of the ǀ heathen.

7 The works of his hands are ǀ faithful · and ǀ just:
  and ǀ all · his comǀmandments · are ǀ sure;

8 They stand firm for ǀ ever · and ǀ ever:
  they are done in ǀ faithful·ness ǀ and in ǀ truth.

9 He sent redemption to his people
    he ordained his ǀ covenant · for ǀ ever:
  holy is his name and ǀ worthy ǀ to be ǀ feared.

10 The fear of the Lord is the beginning of wisdom
    and of good understanding are those that ǀ keep ·
    his comǀmandments:
  his ǀ praise · shall enǀdure for ǀ ever.

PSALM 112

1 O praise the Lord
    Blessèd is the man who ǀ fears the ǀ Lord:
  and greatly deǀlights in ǀ his comǀmandments.

2 His children shall be ǀ mighty · in the ǀ land:
  a race of upright ǀ men who ǀ will be ǀ blessed.

3 Riches and plenty shall be ǀ in his ǀ house:
  and his ǀ righteous·ness ǀ stands for ǀ ever.

4 Light arises in darkness I for the I upright:
    gracious and merciful I is the I righteous I man.

5 It goes well with the man who acts I generously · and I
        lends:
    who I guides · his afIfairs with I justice.

6 Surely he shall I never · be I moved:
    the righteous shall be held in I everIlasting ·
        reImembrance.

7 He will not I fear bad I tidings:
    his heart is steadfast I trusting I in the I Lord.

8 His heart is confident and I will not I fear:
    he will see the I downfall I of his I enemies.

9 He gives I freely · to the I poor:
    his righteousness stands for ever
        his I head is · upIlifted · in I glory.

10 The wicked man shall see it I and be I angry:
    he shall gnash his teeth and consume away
        and the I hope · of the I wicked · shall I fail.

PSALM 113

1 Praise the Lord
        O sing praises you that I are his I servants:
    O I praise the I name · of the I Lord.

2 Let the name of the I Lord be I blessed:
    from this time I forward I and for I ever.

3 From the rising of the sun to its I going I down:
    let the I name · of the I Lord be I praised.

4 The Lord is exalted over I all the I nations:
    and his I glory · is aIbove the I heavens.

5 Who can be likened to the I Lord our I God:
    in I heaven · or upIon the I earth,

6 Who has his I dwelling · so I high:
    yet condescends to I look on I things beIneath?

7 He raises the I lowly · from theI dust:
    and lifts the I poor from I out of · the I dungheap;

8 He gives them a place a|mong the | princes:
    even among the | princes | of his | people.

†9 He causes the barren woman to | keep | house:
    and makes her a joyful mother of children |
        Praise | – the | Lord.

PSALM 114

1 When Israel came | out of | Egypt:
    and the house of Jacob from among a | people · of an |
        alien | tongue,

2 Judah be|came his | sanctuary:
    and | Israel | his do|minion.

3 The sea saw | that and | fled:
    Jor|dan was | driven | back.

4 The mountains | skipped like | rams:
    and the little | hills like | young | sheep.

5 What ailed you O | sea · that you | fled:
    O Jordan that | you were | driven | back?

6 You mountains that you | skipped like | rams:
    and you little | hills like | young | sheep?

7 Tremble O earth at the | presence · of the | Lord:
    at the | presence · of the | God of | Jacob,

8 Who turned the rock into a | pool of | water:
    and the flint-stone | into · a | welling | spring.

PSALM 115

1 Not to us O Lord not to us
        but to your name | give the | glory:
    for the sake of your faithfulness | and your |
        loving-|kindness.

2 Why should the heathen say | 'Where is · their | God?':
    our God is in heaven   he | does what|ever · he | wills.

3 As for their idols   they are | silver · and | gold:
    the | work · of a | man's | hand.

4 They have | mouths but | speak not:
    they have | eyes · but they | cannot | see.

5 They have ears yet I hear I nothing:
   they have I noses · but I cannot I smell.

6 Hands they have but handle nothing
   feet but they I do not I walk:
   they I make no I sound · with their I throats.

†7 Those who make them I shall be I like them:
   so shall I everyone · that I trusts in I them.

8 O Israel I trust · in the I Lord:
   he is your I help I and your I shield.

9 O house of Aaron I trust · in the I Lord:
   he is your I help I and your I shield.

10 You that fear the Lord I trust · in the I Lord:
   he is your I help I and your I shield.

11 The Lord has remembered us and I he will I bless us:
   he will bless the house of Israel
   he will I bless the I house of I Aaron.

12 He will bless all those that I fear the I Lord:
   both I high and I low to I gether.

13 May the Lord in I crease you I greatly:
   you I and your I children I after you.

14 The blessing of the I Lord · be up I on you:
   he that I made I heaven · and I earth.

15 As for the heavens I they · are the I Lord's:
   but the earth he has I given · to the I children · of I
   men.

16 The dead do not I praise the I Lord:
   nor do I any · that go I down to I silence.

17 But we will I bless the I Lord:
   both now and for evermore
   O I praise I – the I Lord.

PSALM 116

1 I love the Lord because he ǀ heard my ǀ voice:
   the ǀ voice of · my ǀ suppliǀcation;

2 Because he inǀclined his ǀ ear to me:
   in the ǀ day ǀ that I ǀ called to him.

3 The cords of death encompassed me
     the snares of the ǀ grave took ǀ hold on me:
   I ǀ was in ǀ anguish · and ǀ sorrow.

4 Then I called upon the ǀ name · of the ǀ Lord:
   'O ǀ Lord · I beǀseech you · deǀliver me!'

5 Gracious and righteous ǀ is the ǀ Lord:
   full of comǀpassion ǀ is our ǀ God.

6 The Lord preǀserves the ǀ simple:
   when ǀ I was · brought ǀ low he ǀ saved me.

7 Return O my ǀ soul · to your ǀ rest:
   for the ǀ Lord ǀ has reǀwarded you.

8 For you O Lord have delivered my ǀ soul from ǀ death:
   my eyes from ǀ tears · and my ǀ feet from ǀ falling.

†9 I will walk beǀfore the ǀ Lord:
   in the ǀ land ǀ of the ǀ living.

10 I believed that I would perish   I was ǀ brought · very ǀ low:
   I said in my haste ǀ 'All ǀ men are ǀ liars.'

11 How shall I reǀpay the ǀ Lord:
   for ǀ all his ǀ bene·fits ǀ to me?

12 I will take up the ǀ cup of · salǀvation:
   and ǀ call up·on the ǀ name · of the ǀ Lord.

13 I will pay my ǀ vows · to the ǀ Lord:
   in the ǀ presence · of ǀ all his ǀ people.

14 Grievous in the ǀ sight · of the ǀ Lord:
   is the ǀ death ǀ of his ǀ faithful ones.

15 O Lord I am your servant
     your servant and the ǀ son of · your ǀ handmaid:
   you ǀ have unǀloosed my ǀ bonds.

16 I will offer you a sacrifice of | thanks|giving:
    and | call up·on the | name · of the | Lord.

17 I will pay my | vows · to the | Lord:
    in the | presence · of | all his | people,

†18 In the courts of the | house · of the | Lord:
    even in your midst O Jerusalem |
        Praise | – the | Lord.

PSALM 117

1 O praise the Lord | all you | nations:
    O | praise him | all you | peoples.

2 For great is his loving-|kindness · to|ward us:
    and the faithfulness of the Lord endures for ever |
        Praise | – the | Lord.

PSALM 118

1 O give thanks to the Lord for | he is | good:
    his | mercy · en|dures for | ever.

2 Let Israel | now pro|claim:
    that his | mercy · en|dures for | ever.

3 Let the house of | Aaron · pro|claim:
    that his | mercy · en|dures for | ever.

4 Let those who fear the | Lord pro|claim:
    that his | mercy · en|dures for | ever.

5 In my danger I | called · to the | Lord:
    he | answered · and | set me | free.

6 The Lord is on my side I | shall not | fear:
    what can | man | do to | me?

7 The Lord is at my side | as my | helper:
    I shall see the | downfall | of my | enemies.

8 It is better to take refuge | in the | Lord:
    than to | put your | trust in | man;

†9 It is better to take refuge | in the | Lord:
    than to | put your | trust in | princes.

10 All the I nations · sur|rounded me:
    but in the name of the I Lord I I drove them I back.

11 They surrounded   they surrounded me on I every I
        side:
    but in the name of the I Lord I I drove them I back.

12 They swarmed about me like bees
        they blazed like fire a|mong the I thorns:
    in the name of the I Lord I I drove them I back.

13 I was pressed so hard that I I almost I fell:
    but the I Lord I was my I helper.

†14 The Lord is my I strength · and my I song:
    and has be|come I my sal|vation.

15 The sounds of I joy · and de|liverance:
    are I in the I tents · of the I righteous.

16 The right hand of the Lord does I mighty I things:
    the right hand of the I Lord I raises I up.

17 I shall not I die but I live:
    and pro|claim the I works · of the I Lord.

18 The Lord has I disciplined · me I hard:
    but he has not I given · me I over · to I death.

19 Open me the I gates of I righteousness:
    and I will enter and give I thanks I to the I Lord.

20 This is the I gate · of the I Lord:
    the I righteous I shall I enter it.

21 I will praise you I for you I answered me:
    and have be|come I my sal|vation.

22 The stone that the I builders · re|jected:
    has be|come the I head · of the I corner.

23 This is the I Lord's I doing:
    and it is I marvel·lous I in our I eyes.

24 This is the day that the I Lord has I made:
    let us re|joice I and be I glad in it.

25 O Lord I save us · we I pray:
    O Lord I send I us pros|perity.

26 Blessèd is he who comes in the ǀ name · of the ǀ Lord:
　　from the ǀ house · of the ǀ Lord we ǀ bless you.

27 The Lord is God　and he has ǀ given · us ǀ light:
　　guide the festal throng up to the ǀ horns ǀ of the ǀ altar.

28 You are my God and ǀ I will ǀ praise you:
　　you are my ǀ God I ǀ will exǀalt you.

†29 O give thanks to the Lord for ǀ he is ǀ good:
　　and his ǀ mercy · enǀdures for ǀ ever.

PSALM 119

1

1 Blessèd are those whose ǀ way is ǀ blameless:
　　who ǀ walk · in the ǀ law · of the ǀ Lord.

2 Blessèd are those who ǀ keep · his comǀmands:
　　and seek him ǀ with their ǀ whole ǀ heart;

3 Those who ǀ do no ǀ wrong:
　　but ǀ walk · in the ǀ ways of · our ǀ God.

4 For you Lord ǀ have comǀmanded us:
　　to perseǀvere in ǀ all your ǀ precepts.

5 If only my ǀ ways · were unǀerring:
　　towards the ǀ keeping ǀ of your ǀ statutes!

6 Then I should ǀ not · be aǀshamed:
　　when I ǀ looked on ǀ all · your comǀmandments.

7 I will praise you with sinǀcerity · of ǀ heart:
　　as I ǀ learn your ǀ righteous ǀ judgments.

8 I will ǀ keep your ǀ statutes:
　　O forǀsake me ǀ not ǀ utterly.

2

9 How shall a young man's ǀ path be ǀ pure:
　　unǀless he ǀ keep to · your ǀ word?

10 I have sought you with my ǀ whole ǀ heart:
　　let me not ǀ stray from ǀ your comǀmandments.

11 I have treasured your ǀ words · in my ǀ heart:
　　that I ǀ might not ǀ sin aǀgainst you.

12 Blessèd are ⏐ you Lord ⏐ God:
    O ⏐ teach me ⏐ your ⏐ statutes.

13 With my lips I ⏐ have been ⏐ telling:
    all the ⏐ judgments ⏐ of your ⏐ mouth;

14 And I find more joy in the way of ⏐ your com⏐mands:
    than in ⏐ all ⏐ manner · of ⏐ riches.

15 I will meditate ⏐ on your ⏐ precepts:
    and give ⏐ heed ⏐ to your ⏐ ways;

16 For my delight is wholly ⏐ in your ⏐ statutes:
    and I will ⏐ not for⏐get your ⏐ word.

3

17 O be bountiful to your servant that ⏐ I may ⏐ live:
    in o⏐bedi·ence ⏐ to your ⏐ word.

18 Take away the ⏐ veil · from my ⏐ eyes:
    that I may see the ⏐ wonders ⏐ of your ⏐ law.

19 I am but a ⏐ stranger · on the ⏐ earth:
    do not ⏐ hide · your com⏐mandments ⏐ from me.

20 My soul is con⏐sumed with ⏐ longing:
    for your ⏐ judgments ⏐ day and ⏐ night.

21 You have re⏐buked the ⏐ proud:
    and cursed are those who ⏐ stray from ⏐
        your com⏐mandments;

22 Turn away from me their re⏐proach and ⏐ scorn:
    for ⏐ I have ⏐ kept · your com⏐mands.

23 Though princes sit and plot to⏐gether · a⏐gainst me:
    your servant shall ⏐ medi·tate ⏐ on your ⏐ statutes:

24 For your commands are ⏐ my de⏐light:
    and they are ⏐ counsellors · in ⏐ my de⏐fence.

4

25 I am humbled ⏐ to the ⏐ dust:
    O give me life ac⏐cording ⏐ to your ⏐ word.

26 If I ex⏐amine · my ⏐ ways:
    surely you will answer me * O ⏐ teach me ⏐ your ⏐
        statutes!

27 Make me to understand the | way of · your | precepts:
    and I shall meditate | on your | marvel·lous | works.

28 My soul pines a|way for | sorrow:
    O raise me up ac|cording | to your | word.

29 Keep me far from the | way of · de|ception:
    and | grant me · the | grace of · your | law.

30 I have chosen the | way of | truth:
    and have | set your | judgments · be|fore me.

31 I hold fast to | your com|mands:
    O Lord let me | never | be con|founded.

32 Let me run the way of | your com|mandments:
    for | you will | liberate · my | heart.

5

33 Teach me O Lord the | way of · your | statutes:
    and I will | honour · it | to the | end.

34 Give me understanding | that I may | keep your | law:
    that I may keep it | with my | whole | heart.

35 Guide me in the path of | your com|mandments:
    for there|in is | my de|light.

36 Incline my heart to | your com|mands:
    and | not to | selfish | gain.

37 Turn away my eyes from | looking · on | vanities:
    as I walk in your | way | give me | life.

38 Make good your promise | to your | servant:
    the promise that en|dures for | all who | fear you.

39 Turn aside the | taunts · that I | dread:
    for your | judgments · are | very | good.

40 Lord I | long for · your | precepts:
    in your | righteous·ness | give me | life.

6

41 Let your loving mercy come to | me O | Lord:
    and your salvation ac|cording | to your | word.

42 Then I shall have an answer for |
    those · who re|proach me:
    for I | trust | in your | word.

43 Do not take the word of truth utterly | out of · my |
    mouth:
    for in your | judgments | is my | hope.

44 Let me keep your | law con|tinually:
    O | let me | keep it · for | ever.

45 And so I shall | walk at | liberty:
    be|cause · I have | sought your | precepts.

46 I shall speak of your com|mands be·fore | kings:
    and shall | not be | put to | shame.

47 My delight shall be in | your com|mandments:
    which | I have | greatly | loved;

48 I shall worship you with | outstretched | hands:
    and I shall | medi·tate | on your | statutes.

7

49 Remember your | word · to your | servant:
    on | which · you have | built my | hope.

50 This has been my comfort in | my af|fliction:
    for your | word has | brought me | life.

51 Though the proud have | laughed me · to | scorn:
    I have not | turned a|side from · your | law;

52 But I called to mind O Lord your | judgments · of | old:
    and in | them · I have | found · consol|ation.

53 I am seized with indignation | at the | wicked:
    for | they have · for|saken · your | law.

54 But your statutes have be|come my | songs:
    in the | house | of my | pilgrimage.

55 I think on your name O | Lord · in the | night:
    and | I ob|serve your | law;

56 This has | been · my re|ward:
    be|cause · I have | kept your | precepts.

8

57 The Lord I is my I portion:
  I have I promised · to I keep your I words.

58 I have sought your favour with my I whole I heart:
  O be gracious to me ac|cording I to your I word.

59 I have taken I stock of · my I ways:
  and have turned back my I feet to I your com|mands.

60 I made haste and did I not de|lay:
  to I keep I your com|mandments.

61 The snares of the I wicked · en|compassed me:
  but I did I not for|get your I law;

62 At midnight I rise to I give you I thanks:
  for the I righteous·ness I of your I judgments.

63 I am a friend to I all who I fear you:
  to I those who I keep your I precepts.

64 The earth O Lord is full of your I loving I mercy:
  O I teach me I your I statutes.

9

65 Lord you have done I good to · your I servant:
  in ac|cordance I with your I word.

66 O teach me right I judgment · and I knowledge:
  for I I I trust in I your com|mandments.

67 Before I was afflicted I I went a|stray:
  but I now I I I keep your I word.

68 You are good and you I do I good:
  O I teach me I your I statutes.

69 The proud have I smeared me · with I lies:
  but I will keep your precepts I with my I whole I heart.

70 Their hearts are I gross like I fat:
  but my de|light is I in your I law.

71 It is good for me that I I was · af|flicted:
  so I I might I learn your I statutes.

72 The law of your mouth is ǀ dearer · to ǀ me:
    than a ǀ wealth of ǀ gold and ǀ silver.

10

73 Your hands have ǀ made me · and ǀ fashioned me:
    O give me understanding⏝
      that ǀ I may ǀ learn · your comǀmandments.

74 Those who fear you shall see me ǀ and reǀjoice:
    for my ǀ hope is ǀ in your ǀ word.

75 I know Lord that your ǀ judgments · are ǀ right:
    and that in ǀ faithfulness · you ǀ have afǀflicted me.

76 Let your merciful kindness ǀ be my ǀ comfort:
    according to your ǀ promise ǀ to your ǀ servant.

77 O let your mercy come to me that ǀ I may ǀ live:
    for your ǀ law is ǀ my deǀlight.

78 Let the proud be shamed
    who steal my ǀ rights · through their ǀ lies:
    but I will ǀ medi·tate ǀ on your ǀ precepts.

79 Let those who fear you ǀ turn to ǀ me:
    and ǀ they shall ǀ know · your comǀmands.

80 O let my heart be ǀ sound in · your ǀ statutes:
    that I may ǀ never · be ǀ put to ǀ shame.

11

81 My soul languishes for ǀ your salǀvation:
    but my ǀ hope is ǀ in your ǀ word;

82 My eyes fail with ǀ watching · for your ǀ promise:
    saying 'O ǀ when ǀ will you ǀ comfort me?'

83 I am parched as a wineskin ǀ in the ǀ smoke:
    yet I do ǀ not forǀget your ǀ statutes.

84 How many are ǀ the days of · your ǀ servant:
    and ǀ when · will you ǀ judge my ǀ persecutors?

85 The proud have dug ǀ pitfalls ǀ for me:
    in deǀfiance ǀ of your ǀ law.

86 All your com|mandments · are | true:
    but they persecute me with lies * O | come | to my |
      help!

87 They have almost made an end of me | on the | earth:
    but I have | not for|saken · your | precepts.

88 In your merciful goodness | give me | life:
    that I may keep the com|mands | of your | mouth.

12

89 Lord your | word · is for | ever:
    it stands | firm | in the | heavens.

90 Your faithfulness abides from one gener|ation ·
      to an|other:
    firm as the | earth which | you have | made.

91 As for your judgments they stand | fast this | day:
    for | all things | are your | servants.

92 If your law had not been | my de|light:
    I would have | perished · in | my af|fliction.

93 I will never for|get your | precepts:
    for by | them · you have | given · me | life.

94 I am | yours O | save me:
    for | I have | sought your | precepts.

95 The wicked have lain in wait for me | to de|stroy me:
    but I | think on | your com|mands.

96 I have seen that all perfection | comes · to an | end:
    only your com|mandment | has no | bounds.

13

97 Lord how I | love your | law:
    it is my medi|tation | all the · day | long.

98 Your commandments have made me wiser | than my |
      enemies:
    for they re|main with | me for | ever.

99 I have more understanding than | all my | teachers:
    for I | study | your com|mands.

100 I am wiser | than the | agèd:
   be|cause · I have | kept your | precepts.

101 I have held back my feet from every | evil | path:
   that | I might | keep your | word;

102 I have not turned a|side from · your | judgments:
   for | you your|self are · my | teacher.

103 How sweet are your | words · to my | tongue:
   sweeter than | honey | to my | mouth.

104 Through your precepts I get | under|standing:
   therefore I | hate all | lying | ways.

14

105 Your word is a lantern | to my | feet:
   and a | light | to my | path.

106 I have vowed and | sworn an | oath:
   to | keep your | righteous | judgments.

107 I have been afflicted be|yond | measure:
   Lord give me life ac|cording | to your | word.

108 Accept O Lord the freewill offerings | of my | mouth:
   and | teach me | your | judgments.

109 I take my life in my | hands con|tinually:
   yet I do | not for|get your | law.

110 The wicked have | laid a | snare for me:
   but I | have not | strayed from · your | precepts.

111 Your commands are my in|heritance · for | ever:
   they | are the | joy of · my | heart.

112 I have set my heart to ful|fil your | statutes:
   always | even | to the | end.

15

113 I loathe those who are | double-|minded:
   but your | law | do I | love.

114 You are my shelter | and my | shield:
   and in your | word | is my | hope.

115 Away from me all | you that · do | evil:
    I will keep the com|mandments | of my | God.

116 Be my stay according to your word that | I may | live:
    and do not disap|point me | in my | hope.

117 Hold me up and I | shall be | safe:
    and I will ever de|light | in your | statutes.

118 You scorn all those who | swerve from · your | statutes:
    for their | calumnies · a|gainst me · are | lies;

119 All the ungodly of the earth you | count as | dross:
    therefore I | love | your com|mands.

120 My flesh | shrinks for | fear of you:
    and I am a|fraid | of your | judgments.

16

121 I have done what is | just and | right:
    O do not give me | over · to | my op|pressors.

122 Stand surety for your | servant's | good:
    let | not the | proud op|press me.

123 My eyes fail with watching for | your sal|vation:
    for the fulfilment | of your | righteous | word.

124 O deal with your servant according to your | loving |
        mercy:
    and | teach me | your | statutes.

125 I am your servant   O give me | under|standing:
    that | I may | know · your com|mands.

126 It is time for the | Lord to | act:
    for they | vio·late | your | law.

127 Therefore I | love · your com|mandments:
    more than gold | more · than the | finest | gold;

128 Therefore I straighten my paths by | all your | precepts:
    and I | hate all | lying | ways.

17

129 Wonderful are | your com|mands:
    and | therefore · my | soul | keeps them.

130 The unfolding of your | word gives | light:
    it gives under|standing | to the | simple.

131 I open my mouth and draw | in my | breath:
    for I | yearn for | your com|mandments.

132 O turn to me and be | merci·ful | to me:
    as is your way with | those who | love your | name.

133 Order my steps according | to your | word:
    that no evil | may get | master·y | over me.

134 Deliver me from | man's op|pression:
    that | I may | keep your | precepts.

135 Make your face shine up|on your | servant:
    and | teach me | your | statutes.

136 My eyes gush out with | streams of | water:
    because they | pay no | heed to · your | law.

18

137 Righteous are | you Lord | God:
    and | just are | your | judgments;

138 The commands that | you · have com|manded:
    are ex|ceeding·ly | righteous · and | true.

139 Zeal and indignation have | choked my | mouth:
    because my enemies | have for|gotten · your | words.

140 Your word has been | tried · in the | fire:
    and | therefore · your | servant | loves it.

141 I am small and of | no ac|count:
    but I have | not for|gotten · your | precepts.

142 Your righteousness is an ever|lasting | righteousness:
    and your | law | is the | truth.

143 Trouble and anguish have | taken | hold on me:
    but your com|mandments · are | my de|light.

144 The righteousness of your commands is | ever|lasting:
    O give me under|standing · and | I shall | live.

19

145 I call with my | whole | heart:
      hear me O Lord | I will | keep your | statutes. |

146 I cry out to | you O | save me:
      and | I will | heed · your com|mands.

147 Before the morning light I | rise · and I | call:
      for in your | word | is my | hope.

148 Before the night watch my | eyes | wake:
      that I may | meditate · up|on your | words.

149 Hear my voice O Lord in your | loving | mercy:
      and according to your | judgments | give me | life.

150 They draw near to me who mal|icious·ly | persecute me:
      but | they are | far from · your | law.

151 You Lord are | close at | hand:
      and | all · your com|mandments · are | true.

152 I have known long since from | your com|mands:
      that you have | founded | them for | ever.

20

153 Consider my affliction | and de|liver me:
      for I do | not for|get your | law.

154 Plead my cause and | set me | free:
      O give me life ac|cording | to your | word.

155 Salvation is | far · from the | wicked:
      for they | do not | seek your | statutes.

156 Numberless O Lord are your | tender | mercies:
      according to your | judgments | give me | life.

157 Many there are that persecute | me and | trouble me:
      but I have not | swerved from | your com|mands.

158 I am cut to the heart when I | see the | faithless:
      for they | do not | keep your | word.

159 Consider O Lord how I | love your | precepts:
      and in your | mercy | give me | life.

160 The sum of your | word is | truth:
      and all your righteous | judgments | stand for | ever.

21

161 Princes have persecuted me with|out a | cause:
   but my heart | stands in | awe of · your | word.

162 I am as | glad of · your | word:
   as | one who | finds rich | spoil.

163 Lies I | hate · and ab|hor:
   but your | law | do I | love.

164 Seven times a | day I | praise you:
   be|cause of · your | righteous | judgments.

165 Great is the peace of those who | love your | law:
   and | nothing · shall | make them | stumble.

166 Lord I have waited for | your sal|vation:
   and I have | done | your com|mandments.

167 My soul has heeded | your com|mands:
   and I | love them · be|yond | measure.

168 I have kept your precepts | and com|mands:
   for all my | ways are | open · be|fore you.

22

169 Let my cry | come to you · O | Lord:
   O give me understanding ac|cording | to your | word;

170 Let my supplication | come be|fore you:
   and deliver me ac|cording | to your | promise.

171 My lips shall pour | forth your | praise:
   be|cause you | teach me · your | statutes;

172 My tongue shall | sing of · your | word:
   for | all · your com|mandments · are | righteousness.

173 Let your hand be | swift to | help me:
   for | I have | chosen · your | precepts.

174 Lord I have longed for | your sal|vation:
   and your | law is | my de|light.

175 O let my soul live that | I may | praise you:
   and let your | judgments | be my | help.

176 I have gone astray like a | sheep · that is | lost:
   O seek your servant
      for I do | not for|get · your com|mandments.

PSALM 120

1 I call to the | Lord · in my | trouble:
    that | he may | answer | me.

2 O Lord deliver me from | lying | lips:
    and | from the | treacher·ous | tongue.

3 What will he do to you * and what more will he do⁓
        to you O | treacher·ous | tongue?:
    you are sharp as the arrows of a warrior
        that are | tempered · in | coals of | juniper.

4 Alas for me * I am like a | stranger · in | Meshech:
    like one who dwells a|midst the | tents of | Kedar.

5 My soul has | been too | long:
    among | those · who are | enemies · to | peace.

6 I am for peace   but | when I | speak of it:
    they | make them·selves | ready · for | war.

PSALM 121

1 I lift up my | eyes · to the | hills:
    but | where · shall I | find | help?

2 My help | comes · from the | Lord:
    who has | made | heaven · and | earth.

3 He will not suffer your | foot to | stumble:
    and he who watches | over · you | will not | sleep.

4 Be sure he who has | charge of | Israel:
    will | neither | slumber · nor | sleep.

5 The Lord him|self is · your | keeper:
    the Lord is your defence up|on your | right | hand;

6 The sun shall not | strike you · by | day:
    nor | shall the | moon by | night.

7 The Lord will defend you from | all | evil:
    it is | he · who will | guard your | life.

8 The Lord will defend your going out and your | coming |
        in:
    from this time | forward · for | ever|more.

PSALM 122

1 I was glad when they | said to | me:
   'Let us | go · to the | house · of the | Lord.'

2 And now our | feet are | standing:
   with|in your | gates · O Je|rusalem;

†3 Jerusalem which is | built · as a | city:
   where the | pilgrims | gather · in | unity.

4 There the tribes go up   the | tribes · of the | Lord:
   as he commanded Israel
      to give | thanks · to the | name · of the | Lord.

5 There are set | thrones of | judgment:
   the | thrones · of the | house of | David.

6 O pray for the | peace · of Je|rusalem:
   may | those who | love you | prosper.

7 Peace be with|in your | walls:
   and pros|peri·ty | in your | palaces.

8 For the sake of my brothers | and com|panions:
   I will | pray that | peace be | with you.

9 For the sake of the house of the | Lord our | God:
   I will | seek | for your | good.

PSALM 123

1 To you I lift | up my | eyes:
   you who are en|throned | in the | heavens.

2 As the eyes of servants look to the | hand of · their |
      master:
   or as the eyes of a maid to|ward the | hand of · her |
      mistress,

†3 So our eyes look to the | Lord our | God:
   un|til he | show us · his | mercy.

4 Have mercy upon us O Lord have | mercy · up|on us:
   for we have | had our | fill · of de|rision.

5 Our souls overflow with the mockery of | those at | ease:
   and with the | contempt | of the | proud.

PSALM 124

1 If the Lord had not been on our side
    now may | Israel | say:
  if the Lord had not been on our side —
    when | men rose | up a|gainst us,

2 Then they would have | swallowed us · a|live.
  when their | anger · was | kindled · a|gainst us.

3 Then the waters would have overwhelmed us
    and the | torrent · gone | over us:
  the raging waters | would have | gone clean | over us.

4 But praised | be the | Lord:
  who has not given us as a | prey | to their | teeth.

5 We have escaped like a bird from the | snare · of the |
    fowler:
  the snare is | broken · and | we have · gone | free.

6 Our help is in the | name · of the | Lord:
  who has | made | heaven · and | earth.

PSALM 125

1 Those who put their trust in the Lord —
    shall | be as · Mount | Zion:
  which cannot be | shaken · but en|dures for | ever.

2 As the mountains stand about Jerusalem
    so stands the Lord a|bout his | people:
  from this time | forward · for | ever|more.

3 For the sceptre of wickedness shall have no sway
    over the land apportioned | to the | righteous:
  lest the righteous | set their | hands to · do | evil.

4 Do good O Lord to | those · who are | good:
  to | those · that are | upright · in | heart.

†5 As for those who turn aside to crooked ways
    let the Lord lead them away with the | evil|doers:
  and in | Israel | let there · be | peace.

PSALM 126

1 When the Lord turned again the | fortunes · of | Zion:
   then were we like | men re|stored to | life.

2 Then was our mouth | filled with | laughter:
   and | our | tongue with | singing.

3 Then said they a|mong the | heathen:
   'The Lord has | done great | things for | them.'

4 Truly the Lord has done great | things for | us:
   and | therefore | we re|joiced.

5 Turn again our | fortunes · O | Lord:
   as the streams re|turn · to the | dry | south.

6 Those that | sow in | tears:
   shall | reap with | songs of | joy.

†7 He who goes out weeping | bearing · the | seed:
   shall come again in gladness | ⌣
     bringing · his | sheaves | with him.

PSALM 127

1 Unless the Lord | builds the | house:
   their labour | is but | lost that | build it.

2 Unless the Lord | keeps the | city:
   the | watchmen | watch in | vain.

3 It is in vain that you rise up early and go so late to rest
    eating the | bread of | toil:
   for the Lord bestows honour | and on | those ·
    whom he | loves.

4 Behold children are a heritage | from the | Lord:
   and the | fruit · of the | womb is · his | gift.

5 Like arrows in the | hand · of a | warrior:
   are the | sons · of a | man's | youth.

6 Happy the man who has his | quiver | full of them:
   he will not be put to shame
    when he confronts his | enem·ies | at the | gate.

PSALM 128

1 Blessèd is everyone who ǀ fears the ǀ Lord:
   and walks in the ǀ confine ǀ of his ǀ ways.

2 You will eat the ǀ fruit of · your ǀ labours:
   happy shall you ǀ be and ǀ all · shall go ǀ well with you.

3 Your wife withǀin your ǀ house:
   shall ǀ be · as a ǀ fruitful ǀ vine;

4 Your children aǀround your ǀ table:
   like the fresh ǀ shoots ǀ of the ǀ olive.

5 Behold thus shall the ǀ man be ǀ blessed:
   who ǀ lives · in the ǀ fear · of the ǀ Lord.

6 May the Lord so ǀ bless you · from ǀ Zion:
   that you see Jerusalem in prosperity ǀ ⌣
   all the ǀ days of · your ǀ life.

†7 May you see your ǀ children's ǀ children:
   and in ǀ Israel ǀ let there · be ǀ peace.

PSALM 129

1 Many a time from my youth upward have they ǀ
   fought aǀgainst me:
   now ǀ may ǀ Israel ǀ say,

2 Many a time from my youth upward have they ǀ
   fought aǀgainst me:
   but ǀ they have ǀ not preǀvailed.

3 They have scored my back as ǀ with a ǀ ploughshare:
   they have ǀ opened ǀ long ǀ furrows.

4 But the ǀ Lord is ǀ righteous:
   and he has cut me ǀ free · from the ǀ thongs · of the ǀ
   wicked.

5 They shall be confounded and ǀ turned ǀ backward:
   all ǀ those who ǀ hate ǀ Zion.

6 They shall be as the grass that grows upǀon the ǀ
   housetops:
   which withers before it ǀ comes to ǀ any ǀ good,

7 With which no reaper may ǀ fill his ǀ hand:
   nor the ǀ binder · of ǀ sheaves his ǀ bosom.

8 And none who pass by shall say to them
   'The blessing of the I Lord · be up|on you:
   we I bless you · in the I name · of the I Lord.'

PSALM 130

1 Out of the depths have I called to I you O I Lord:
   Lord I hear I my I voice;

2 O let your ears con|sider I well:
   the I voice · of my I suppli|cation.

3 If you Lord should note what I we do I wrong:
   who I then O I Lord could I stand?

4 But there is for|giveness · with I you:
   so that I you I shall be I feared.

5 I wait for the Lord * my I soul I waits for him:
   and I in his I word · is my I hope.

6 My soul I looks · for the I Lord:
   more than watchmen for the morning
      more I say than I watchmen I for the I morning.

7 O Israel trust in the Lord * for with the I Lord ·
   there is I mercy:
   and with I him is I ample · re|demption.

8 He will re|deem I Israel:
   from the I multi·tude I of his I sins.

PSALM 131

1 O Lord my I heart is · not I proud:
   nor I are my I eyes I haughty.

2 I do not busy myself in I great I matters:
   or in I things too I wonder·ful I for me.

3 But I have calmed and quieted my soul
   like a weaned child upon its I mother's I breast:
   like a child on its mother's breast I is my I
      soul with|in me.

4 O Israel I trust · in the I Lord:
   from this time I forward I and for I ever.

PSALM 132

1 Lord remember David and | all his | trouble:
how he swore an oath to the Lord
    and vowed to the | Mighty | One of | Jacob;

2 'I will not enter the | shelter · of my | house:
nor climb into the | comfort | of my | bed;

3 'I will not give | sleep to · my | eyes:
or | slumber | to my | eyelids,

4 'Till I find out a place for the | ark · of the | Lord:
a dwelling for the | Mighty | One of | Jacob.'

5 Lo we | heard of it · at | Ephrathah:
we | found it · in the | fields of | Ja-ar.

6 Let us go to the | place of · his | dwelling:
let us fall upon our | knees be|fore his | footstool.

7 Arise O Lord | into · your | resting-place:
you | and the | ark of · your | might.

8 Let your priests be | clothed with | righteousness:
and let your | faithful · ones | shout for | joy.

†9 For the sake of | David · your | servant:
do not turn away the | face of | your an|ointed.

10 The Lord has | sworn to | David:
an | oath · which he | will not | break;

11 'One who is the | fruit of · your | body:
I will | set up|on your | throne.

12 'If your children will keep my covenant
    and the com|mands · which I | teach them:
their children also shall sit up|on your | throne for |
    ever.'

13 For the Lord has chosen | Zion · for him|self:
he has de|sired it · for his | habi|tation.

14 'This shall be my | resting-place · for | ever:
here will I dwell   for | my de|light · is in | her.

15 'I will bless her pro|visions · with a|bundance:

I will | satisfy · her | poor with | bread.

16 'I will clothe her | priests with · sal|vation:
and her | faithful ones · shall | shout for | joy.

17 'There will I make a horn to sprout ⌣
for the | family · of | David:
I have prepared a | lamp for | my an|ointed.

†18 'As for his enemies I will | cover them · with | shame:
but upon his | head · shall his | crown be | bright.'

PSALM 133

1 Behold how good and how | lovely · it | is:
when brothers | live to|gether · in | unity.

2 It is fragrant as oil upon the head
that runs down | over · the | beard:
fragrant as oil upon the beard of Aaron
that ran down over the | collar | of his | robe.

3 It is like a | dew of | Hermon:
like the dew that falls up|on the | hill of | Zion.

4 For there the Lord has com|manded · his | blessing:
which is | life for | ever|more.

PSALM 134

1 Come bless the Lord   all you | servants · of the | Lord:
you that by night | stand · in the | house of · our | God.

2 Lift up your hands toward the holy place ⌣
and | bless the | Lord:
may the Lord bless you from Zion
the | Lord who · made | heaven · and | earth.

PSALM 135

1 Praise the Lord
praise the | name · of the | Lord:
praise him you | servants | of the | Lord,

2 Who stand in the | house · of the | Lord:
in the | courts · of the | house of · our | God.

3 Praise the Lord for the | Lord is | gracious:
   sing praises to his | name for | it is | good.

4 For the Lord has chosen Jacob | for him|self:
   and Israel | as his | own pos|session.

5 I know that the | Lord is | great:
   and that our | Lord · is a|bove all | gods.

6 He does whatever he wills * in heaven and up|on the | earth:
   in the seas and | in the | great | depths.

7 He brings up clouds from the | ends · of the | earth:
   he makes lightning for the rain
   and brings the | wind | out of · his | storehouses.

8 He struck down the | firstborn · of | Egypt:
   both | man and | beast a|like.

9 He sent signs and wonders into your | midst O | Egypt:
   against Pharaoh and a|gainst | all his | servants.

10 He struck down | great | nations:
   and | slew | mighty | kings,

11 Sihon king of the Amorites   and Og the | king of | Bashan:
   and | all the | princes · of | Canaan.

12 He made over their | land · as a | heritage:
   a | heritage · for | Israel · his | people.

13 O Lord your name shall en|dure for | ever:
   so shall your renown through|out all | gener|ations.

14 For the Lord will | vindicate · his | people:
   he will take | pity | on his | servants.

15 As for the idols of the nations
      they are but | silver · and | gold:
   the | work · of a | man's | hand.

16 They have | mouths but | speak not:
   they have | eyes · but they | cannot | see.

17 They have ears yet | hear | nothing:
   there is no | breath | in their | nostrils.

18 Those who make them ǀ shall be ǀ like them:
   so shall ǀ everyǀone that ǀ trusts in them.

19 Bless the Lord O ǀ house of ǀ Israel:
   bless the ǀ Lord O ǀ house of ǀ Aaron.

20 Bless the Lord O ǀ house of ǀ Levi:
   you that ǀ fear the · Lord ǀ bless the ǀ Lord.

†21 Blessèd be the ǀ Lord from ǀ Zion:
   he that dwells in Jerusalem ǀ
     Praise ǀ – the ǀ Lord.

PSALM 136

1 O give thanks to the Lord for ǀ he is ǀ good:
   for his ǀ mercy · enǀdures for ǀ ever.

2 O give thanks to the ǀ God of ǀ gods:
   for his ǀ mercy · enǀdures for ǀ ever.

†3 O give thanks to the ǀ Lord of ǀ lords:
   for his ǀ mercy · enǀdures for ǀ ever;

4 To him who alone does ǀ great ǀ wonders:
   for his ǀ mercy · enǀdures for ǀ ever;

5 Who by wisdom ǀ made the ǀ heavens:
   for his ǀ mercy · enǀdures for ǀ ever;

6 Who stretched out the earth upǀon the ǀ waters:
   for his ǀ mercy · enǀdures for ǀ ever;

7 Who made the ǀ great ǀ lights:
   for his ǀ mercy · enǀdures for ǀ ever,

8 The sun to ǀ rule the ǀ day:
   for his ǀ mercy · enǀdures for ǀ ever,

9 The moon and the stars to ǀ govern · the ǀ night:
   for his ǀ mercy · enǀdures for ǀ ever;

10 Who struck down Egypt ǀ and its ǀ firstborn:
   for his ǀ mercy · enǀdures for ǀ ever;

11 Who brought out Israel ǀ from aǀmong them:
   for his ǀ mercy · enǀdures for ǀ ever,

†12 With a strong hand and with I outstretched I arm:
    for his I mercy · en\dures for I ever;

13 Who divided the Red Sea into I two I parts:
    for his I mercy · en\dures for I ever,

14 And made Israel pass I through the I midst of it:
    for his I mercy · en\dures for I ever;

15 Who cast off Pharaoh and his host into the I Red I Sea:
    for his I mercy · en\dures for I ever;

16 Who led his people I through the I wilderness:
    for his I mercy · en\dures for I ever;

17 Who struck down I great I kings:
    for his I mercy · en\dures for I ever;

18 Who slew I mighty I kings:
    for his I mercy · en\dures for I ever,

19 Sihon I king · of the I Amorites:
    for his I mercy · en\dures for I ever,

20 And Og the I king of I Bashan:
    for his I mercy · en\dures for I ever;

21 Who made over their I land · as a I heritage:
    for his I mercy · en\dures for I ever,

22 As a heritage for I Israel · his I servant:
    for his I mercy · en\dures for I ever;

23 Who remembered us in our hu\mili\ation:
    for his I mercy · en\dures for I ever,

24 And delivered us I from our I enemies:
    for his I mercy · en\dures for I ever;

25 Who gives food to I all that I lives:
    for his I mercy · en\dures for I ever.

26 O give thanks to the I God of I heaven:
    for his I mercy · en\dures for I ever.

PSALM 137

1 By the waters of Babylon we sat I down and I wept:
   when I we reImembered I Zion.

2 As for our harps we I hung them I up:
   upon the I trees · that are I in that I land.

3 For there those who led us away captive ⌣
   reIquired of us · a I song:
   and those who had despoiled us demanded mirth
   saying 'Sing us I one of · the I songs of I Zion.'

*4 How can we sing the Lord's I song · in a I strange I land?

5 If I forget you I O JeIrusalem:
   let my right I hand forIget its I mastery.

6 Let my tongue cling to the I roof of · my I mouth:
   if I do not remember you
   if I do not prefer Jerusalem aIbove my I chief I joy.

[7 Remember O Lord against the Edomites ⌣
   the I day · of JeIrusalem:
   how they said 'Down with it   down with it I
   raze it · to I its foundIations.'

8 O daughter of Babylon   I you that · lay I waste:
   happy shall he be who serves I you as I you have ·
   served I us;

†9 Happy shall he be who I takes your I little ones:
   and I dashes them · aIgainst the I stones.]

* sung to the last four bars of the chant.

PSALM 138

1 I will give you thanks O Lord with my I whole I heart:
   even before the I gods · will I I sing your I praises.

2 I will bow down toward your holy temple
   and give I thanks to · your I name:
   because of your faithfulness and your loving-kindness
   for you have made your name and your I
   word suIpreme · over I all things.

3 At a time when I called to you you ǀ gave me ǀ answer:
  and put new ǀ strength withǀin my ǀ soul.

4 All the kings of the earth shall ǀ praise you · O ǀ Lord:
  for they have ǀ heard the ǀ words of · your ǀ mouth;

5 And they shall sing of the ǀ ways · of the ǀ Lord:
  that the ǀ glory · of the ǀ Lord is ǀ great.

6 For though the Lord is exalted   he looks upǀon the ǀ
     lowly:
  but he ǀ humbles · the ǀ proud · from aǀfar.

7 Though I walk in the midst of danger
     yet will you preǀserve my ǀ life:
  you will stretch out your hand⌣
     against the fury of my enemies
        and ǀ your right ǀ hand shall ǀ save me.

8 The Lord will complete his ǀ purpose ǀ for me:
  your loving-kindness O Lord endures for ever
     do not forsake the ǀ work · of your ǀ own ǀ hands.

PSALM 139

1 O Lord you have searched me ǀ out and ǀ known me:
  you know when I sit or when I stand
     you comprehend my ǀ thoughts ǀ long beǀfore.

2 You discern my path   and the places ǀ where I ǀ rest:
  you are acǀquainted · with ǀ all my ǀ ways.

3 For there is not a ǀ word · on my ǀ tongue:
  but you Lord ǀ know it ǀ altoǀgether.

4 You have encompassed me beǀhind · and beǀfore:
  and have ǀ laid your ǀ hand upǀon me.

†5 Such knowledge is too ǀ wonder·ful ǀ for me:
  so ǀ high · that I ǀ cannot · enǀdure it.

6 Where shall I ǀ go · from your ǀ spirit:
  or where shall I ǀ flee ǀ from your ǀ presence?

7 If I ascend into heaven ǀ you are ǀ there:
  if I make my bed in the grave ǀ you are ǀ there ǀ also.

8 If I spread out my wings toǀwards the ǀ morning:
  or dwell in the ǀ utter·most ǀ parts · of the ǀ sea,

9 Even there your ǀ hand shall ǀ lead me:
  and ǀ your right ǀ hand shall ǀ hold me.

10 If I say 'Surely the ǀ darkness · will ǀ cover me:
   and the ǀ night ǀ will enǀclose me',

11 The darkness is no darkness with you
     but the night is as ǀ clear · as the ǀ day:
   the darkness and the ǀ light are ǀ both aǀlike.

12 For you have created my ǀ inward ǀ parts:
   you knit me together ǀ in my ǀ mother's ǀ womb.

13 I will praise you for ǀ you are · to be ǀ feared:
   fearful are your ǀ acts and ǀ wonderful · your ǀ works.

14 You knew my soul * and my bones were not ǀ hidden ǀ
     from you:
   when I was formed in secret
     and ǀ woven · in the ǀ depths · of the ǀ earth.

15 Your eyes saw my limbs when they were ǀ
     yet imǀperfect:
   and in your book were ǀ all my ǀ members ǀ written;

†16 Day by ǀ day · they were ǀ fashioned:
    and not ǀ one was ǀ late in ǀ growing.

17 How deep are your thoughts to ǀ me O ǀ God:
   and how ǀ great ǀ is the ǀ sum of them!

18 Were I to count them
     they are more in number ǀ than the ǀ sand:
   were I to come to the ǀ end · I would ǀ still be ǀ
     with you.

[19 If only you would slay the ǀ wicked · O ǀ God:
   if only the men of ǀ blood · would deǀpart ǀ from me!

20 For they affront you ǀ by their ǀ evil:
   and your enemies exǀalt themǀselves aǀgainst you.

21 Do I not hate them O Lord that ǀ hate ǀ you:
   do I not loathe ǀ those · who reǀbel aǀgainst you?

22 I hate them with a ǀ perfect ǀ hatred:
   they ǀ have beǀcome my ǀ enemies.]

23 Search me out O God and | know my | heart:
  put me to the | proof and | know my | thoughts.

24 Look well lest there be any way of | wicked·ness |
    in me:
  and lead me in the | way · that is | ever|lasting.

PSALM 140

1 Deliver me O Lord from | evil | men:
  and pre|serve me · from | vio·lent | men,

2 Who devise mischief | in their | hearts:
  who stir up | enmi·ty | day by | day.

3 They have sharpened their | tongues · like a |
    serpent's:
  and the venom of | asps is | under · their | lips.

4 Keep me O Lord from the | power · of the | wicked:
  preserve me from violent men
    who think to | thrust me | from my | course.

5 The arrogant have laid a snare for me
    and rogues have | stretched the | net:
  they have set | traps a|long my | way.

6 But I have said to the Lord | 'You are · my | God':
  hear O | Lord the | voice of · my | pleading.

7 O Lord my God and my | sure | stronghold:
  you have covered my | head · in the | day of | battle.

8 Do not fulfil O Lord the de|sire · of the | wicked:
  nor further the | evil · that he | has de|vised.

[9 Let not those that beset me | lift their | heads:
  but let the mischief that is | on their | lips | bury
    them.

10 Let hot burning coals be | poured up|on them:
  let them be plunged into that miry pit __
    from | which · they shall | never · a|rise.

[†]11 Let no man of evil tongue find | footing · in the | land:
  the evil   the violent man   let him be |
    hunted | to the | end.]

12 I know that the Lord will work justice ǀ for ·
    the opǀpressed:
    and right ǀ judgments ǀ for the ǀ poor.

13 Surely the righteous shall have cause to ǀ praise your ǀ
    name:
    and the ǀ just shall ǀ dwell in · your ǀ sight.

PSALM 141

1 O Lord I call to you   make ǀ haste to ǀ help me:
    and ǀ hear my ǀ voice · when I ǀ cry.

2 Let my prayer be as ǀ incense · beǀfore you:
    and the lifting up of my ǀ hands · as the ǀ evening ǀ
    sacrifice.

3 Set a guard O ǀ Lord · on my ǀ mouth:
    and ǀ keep the ǀ door · of my ǀ lips.

4 Let not my heart incline to evil speech
    to join in wickedness with ǀ wrongǀdoers:
    let me not taste the ǀ pleasures ǀ of their ǀ table.

5 But let the righteous ǀ man chasǀtise me:
    and the ǀ faithful ǀ man reǀbuke me.

6 Let not the oil of the wicked anǀoint my ǀ head:
    for I pray to you ǀ still aǀgainst their ǀ wickedness.

7 They shall be cast down⌣
    by that Mighty One who ǀ is their ǀ judge:
    and how pleasing shall my ǀ words be ǀ to them ǀ then!

8 As when a farmer ǀ breaks the ǀ ground:
    so shall their bones lie ǀ scattered · at the ǀ mouth of ǀ
    Sheol.

9 But my eyes look to you O ǀ Lord my ǀ God:
    to you I come for refuge ǀ do not · pour ǀ out my ǀ
    life.

10 Keep me from the snare that ǀ they have ǀ laid for me:
    and from the ǀ traps · of the ǀ evilǀdoers.

†11 Let the wicked fall together into their ǀ own ǀ nets:
    whilst ǀ I pass ǀ safely ǀ by.

309

PSALM 142

1 I call to the Lord with a | loud | voice:
　　with loud | voice · I en|treat his | favour.

2 I pour out my com|plaint be|fore him:
　　and | tell him | all my | trouble.

3 When my spirit is faint within me you | know my | path:
　　in the way where I walk | ⌣
　　　they have | hidden · a | snare for me.

4 I look to my right | hand and I | see:
　　but | no | man will | know me:

5 All es|cape is | gone:
　　and | there is | no one · who | cares for me.

6 I call to you O Lord　I say | 'You are · my | refuge:
　　you are my | portion · in the | land · of the | living.'

7 Heed my loud crying　for I am | brought · very | low:
　　O save me from my persecutors | ⌣
　　　for they | are too | strong for me.

8 Bring me | out of · the | prison-house:
　　that | I may | praise your | name.

†9 When you have given me | my re|ward:
　　then will the | righteous | gather · a|bout me.

PSALM 143

1 Hear my | prayer O | Lord:
　　in your faithfulness consider my petition
　　　and in your | righteous·ness | give me | answer.

2 Bring not your servant | into | judgment:
　　for in your sight can | no man | living · be | justified.

3 For the enemy has pursued me
　　he has crushed my | life · to the | ground:
　　he has made me dwell in darkness ⌣
　　　like | those for | ever | dead.

4 Therefore my | spirit · grows | faint:
　　and my | heart · is ap|palled with|in me.

5 I remember the days of old
　　I think on all that | you have | done:

I con|sider · the | works of · your | hands.

6 I stretch out my | hands to|ward you:
   my soul yearns for you | like a | thirsty | land.

7 Be swift to hear me O Lord   for my | spirit | fails:
   hide not your face from me
      lest I be like | those who · go | down · to the | Pit.

8 O let me hear of your merciful kindness in the morning
      for my | trust · is in | you:
   show me the way that I should go
      for | you | are my | hope.

9 Deliver me from my | enemies · O | Lord:
   for I | run to | you for | shelter.

10 Teach me to do your will   for | you are · my | God:
   let your kindly spirit | lead me · in an | even | path.

†)11 For your name's sake O Lord pre|serve my | life:
   and for the sake of your righteousness | bring me |
      out of | trouble.

[12 In your merciful goodness slay my enemies
      and destroy all those that | come a|gainst me:
   for | truly · I | am your | servant.]

PSALM 144

1 Blessèd be the | Lord my | Rock:
   who teaches my hands to | war · and my | fingers · to |
      fight;

2 My strength and my stronghold
      my fortress and | my de|liverer:
   my shield to whom I come for refuge
      who sub|dues the | peoples | under me.

3 Lord what is man   that you should be |
      mindful | of him:
   or the son of man |that you | should con|sider him?

4 Man is but a |breath of | wind:
   his days are like a | shadow · that | passes · a|way.

5 Part the heavens O Lord and | come | down:
   touch the | mountains · and | they shall | smoke.

6 Dart forth your lightnings
    and scatter them on | every | side:
  let loose your | arrows · with the | roar · of the |
    thunderbolt.

7 Reach down your hand from on high
    rescue me and pluck me out of the | great | waters:
  out of the | hands | of the | aliens,

8 Whose | mouths speak | perjury:
  and their right hand | is a · right | hand of | falsehood.

9 I will sing you a new | song O | God:
  on the ten-stringed | lute · will I | sing your | praises.

10 You have given | victory · to | kings:
  and de|liverance · to | David · your | servant.

11 O save me from the | peril · of the | sword:
  pluck me out of the | hands | of the | aliens,

12 Whose | mouths speak | perjury:
  and their right hand | is a · right | hand of | falsehood.

13 Our sons in their youth shall be like | sturdy | plants:
  and our daughters as the | carved | corners · of |
    palaces.

14 Our barns shall be full and give food of | every | kind:
  the sheep shall lamb in our fields ⌣
  in | thousands · and | tens of | thousands.

15 Our cattle shall be heavy with calf
    there shall be no miscarriage or un|timely | birth:
  and no loud | crying | in our | streets.

16 Happy the people whose lot is | such as | this:
  happy that people who | have the | Lord for · their |
    God!

PSALM 145

1 I will exalt you O | God my | king:
  I will bless your | name for | ever · and | ever.

2 Every | day · will I | bless you:
  and praise your | name for | ever · and | ever.

3 Great is the Lord * and wonderfully ǀ worthy · to be ǀ
    praised:
    his greatness is ǀ past ǀ searching ǀ out.

4 One generation shall praise your ǀ works · to anǀother:
    and deǀclare your ǀ mighty ǀ acts.

5 As for me * I will be talking ⌣
    of the glorious splendour ǀ of your ǀ majesty:
    I will tell the ǀ story · of your ǀ marvel·lous ǀ works.

6 Men shall recount the power of your ǀ terri·ble ǀ deeds:
    and ǀ I will · proǀclaim your ǀ greatness.

†7 Their lips shall flow with the remembrance ⌣
    of your aǀbundant ǀ goodness:
    they shall ǀ shout for ǀ joy at · your ǀ righteousness.

8 The Lord is ǀ gracious · and comǀpassionate:
    slow to anger ǀ and of ǀ great ǀ goodness.

9 The Lord is ǀ loving · to ǀ every man:
    and his mercy is ǀ over ǀ all his ǀ works.

10 All creation ǀ praises you · O ǀ Lord:
    and your faithful ǀ servants ǀ bless your ǀ name.

11 They speak of the glory ǀ of your ǀ kingdom:
    and ǀ tell of · your ǀ great ǀ might,

†12 That all mankind may know your ǀ mighty ǀ acts:
    and the glorious ǀ splendour · of your ǀ kingdom.

13 Your kingdom is an everǀlasting ǀ kingdom:
    and your dominion enǀdures through ǀ all ·
    generǀations.

14 The Lord upholds all ǀ those who ǀ stumble:
    and raises up ǀ those · that are ǀ bowed ǀ down.

15 The eyes of all look to ǀ you in ǀ hope:
    and you give them their ǀ food in ǀ due ǀ season;

16 You open ǀ wide your ǀ hand:
    and fill all things ǀ living · with your ǀ bounte·ous ǀ
    gift.

17 The Lord is just in ǀ all his ǀ ways:
    and ǀ faithful · in ǀ all his ǀ dealings.

18 The Lord is near to all who | call up|on him:
　　to all who | call up|on him · in | truth.

19 He will fulfil the desire of | those that | fear him:
　　he will | hear their | cry and | save them.

20 The Lord preserves all | those that | love him:
　　but the wicked | he will | utterly · de|stroy.

†21 My mouth shall speak the | praises · of the | Lord:
　　and let all flesh bless his holy | name for |
　　　　ever · and | ever.

PSALM 146

1 Praise the Lord
　　praise the Lord | O my | soul:
　　while I | live · I will | praise the | Lord;

2 While I | have · any | being:
　　I will sing | praises | to my | God.

3 Put not your | trust in | princes:
　　nor in the sons of | men who | cannot | save.

4 For when their breath goes from them
　　they return a|gain · to the | earth:
　　and on that day | all their | thoughts | perish.

5 Blessèd is the man whose help is the | God of | Jacob:
　　whose hope is | in the | Lord his | God,

6 The God who made | heaven · and | earth:
　　the sea and | all | that is | in them,

†7 Who keeps | faith for | ever:
　　who deals justice to | those that | are op|pressed.

8 The Lord gives | food · to the | hungry:
　　and | sets the | captives | free.

9 The Lord gives | sight · to the | blind:
　　the Lord lifts up | those · that are | bowed | down.

10 The Lord | loves the | righteous:
　　the Lord cares for the | stranger | in the | land.

11 He upholds the | widow · and the | fatherless:
　　as for the way of the wicked he | turns it | upside |
　　　　down.

†12 The Lord shall be | king for | ever:
     your God O Zion shall reign through all generations |
          Praise | – the | Lord.

PSALM 147

1 O praise the Lord
        for it is good to sing praises | to our | God:
     and to | praise him · is | joyful · and | right.

2 The Lord is re|building · Je|rusalem:
     he is gathering together ⌣
          the | scattered | outcasts · of | Israel.

3 He heals the | broken · in | spirit:
     and | binds | up their | wounds.

4 He counts the | number · of the | stars:
     and | calls them | all by | name.

5 Great is our Lord and | great · is his | power:
     there is no | measuring · his | under|standing.

6 The Lord re|stores the | humble:
     but he brings down the | wicked | to the | dust.

7 O sing to the Lord a | song of | thanksgiving:
     sing praises to our | God up|on the | harp.

8 He covers the heavens with cloud
        and prepares | rain · for the | earth:
     and makes the grass to | sprout up|on the |
          mountains.

9 He gives the | cattle · their | food:
     and feeds the young | ravens · that | call | to him.

10 He takes no pleasure in the | strength · of a | horse:
     nor does he de|light in | any · man's | legs,

†11 But the Lord's delight is in | those that | fear him:
     who | wait in | hope · for his | mercy.

12 Praise the | Lord · O Je|rusalem:
     sing | praises · to your | God O | Zion.

13 For he has strengthened the | bars of · your | gates:
     and | blessed your | children · with|in you.

14 He makes peace with|in your | borders:
  and satisfies you | with the | finest | wheat.

15 He sends his com|mand · to the | earth:
  and his | word runs | very | swiftly.

16 He gives | snow like | wool:
  and | scatters · the | hoar-frost · like | ashes.

17 He sprinkles his ice like | morsels · of | bread:
  and the waters | harden | at his | frost.

†18 He sends out his | word and | melts them:
  he blows with his | wind · and the | waters | flow.

19 He made his word | known to | Jacob:
  his | statutes · and | judgments · to | Israel.

20 He has not dealt so with any | other | nation:
  nor have they knowledge of his laws |
    Praise | – the | Lord.

PSALM 148

1 Praise the Lord
    praise the | Lord from | heaven:
  O | praise him | in the | heights.

2 Praise him | all his | angels:
  O | praise him | all his | host.

3 Praise him | sun and | moon:
  praise him | all you | stars of | light.

4 Praise him you | highest | heaven:
  and you waters that | are a|bove the | heavens.

5 Let them praise the | name · of the | Lord:
  for he com|manded · and | they were | made.

6 He established them for | ever · and | ever:
  he made an ordinance which | shall not | pass a|way.

7 O praise the | Lord · from the | earth:
  praise him you sea-|monsters · and | all | deeps;

8 Fire and hail | mist and | snow:
  and storm-wind ful|filling | his com|mand;

9 Mountains and | all | hills:
   fruiting | trees and | all | cedars;

10 Beasts of the wild and | all | cattle:
   creeping | things and | winged | birds;

11 Kings of the earth and | all | peoples:
   princes and all | rulers | of the | world;

12 Young | men and | maidens:
   old | men and | children · to|gether.

13 Let them praise the | name · of the | Lord:
   for | his · name a|lone · is ex|alted.

14 His glory is above | earth and | heaven:
   and he has lifted | high the | horn · of his | people.

†15 Therefore he is the praise of | all his | servants:
   of the children of Israel   a people that is near him |
      Praise | – the | Lord.

PSALM 149

1 O praise the Lord
      and sing to the Lord a | new | song:
   O praise him in the as|sembly | of the | faithful.

2 Let Israel rejoice in | him that | made him:
   let the children of Zion be | joyful | in their | king.

3 Let them praise him | in the | dance:
   let them sing his praise with | timbrel | and with |
      harp.

4 For the Lord takes de|light · in his | people:
   he adorns the | meek with | his sal|vation.

5 Let his faithful ones ex|ult · in his | glory:
   let them sing for | joy up|on their | beds.

6 Let the high praises of God be | in their | mouths:
   and a | two-edged | sword · in their | hands,

7 To execute vengeance | on the | nations;
   and | chastisement · up|on the | peoples,

8 To bind their | kings in | chains:
   and their | nobles · with | fetters · of | iron,

†9 To visit upon them the judgment that ǀ is deǀcreed:
   such honour belongs to all his faithful servants ǀ
   Praise ǀ – the ǀ Lord.

PSALM 150

1 Praise the Lord
   O praise ǀ God · in his ǀ sanctuary:
   praise him in the ǀ firma·ment ǀ of his ǀ power.

2 Praise him for his ǀ mighty ǀ acts:
   praise him according to ǀ his aǀbundant ǀ goodness.

3 Praise him in the ǀ blast · of the ǀ ram's horn:
   praise him upǀon the ǀ lute and ǀ harp.

4 Praise him with the ǀ timbrel · and ǀ dances:
   praise him upǀon the ǀ strings and ǀ pipe.

5 Praise him on the ǀ high-·sounding ǀ cymbals:
   praise him upǀon the ǀ loud ǀ cymbals.

6 Let everything that has breath ǀ praise the ǀ Lord:
   O ǀ praise ǀ – the ǀ Lord!

COLLECTS
AND READINGS

COLLECTS AND READINGS

for Sundays, Principal Holy Days and Seasons

NOTES

(A) *General*

1 References are to the New International Version of the Bible; to the Revised Standard Version of the Bible, for the Apocrypha; and to the Liturgical Psalter (The Psalms: A New Translation for Worship). Psalter references to the Book of Common Prayer where these differ are given in brackets, for Sundays.

2 Verses are stated inclusively. The letter 'a' after a verse number signifies the first part of that verse and the letter 'b' the second part.

3 Verses printed in brackets are permitted additions at the discretion of the minister.

4 Readings should be announced in the order: Book, Chapter, Verse.

5 Appropriate liturgical colours are suggested. They are not mandatory. Traditional local uses may be followed.

(B) *Sunday Psalms and Readings*

1 The lectionary course begins with the Ninth Sunday before Christmas. When this occurs in a year with an even number the psalms and readings for YEAR 1 are followed. When this occurs in a year with an odd number the psalms and readings are for YEAR 2. The course begun continues until the Last Sunday after Pentecost following.

2 A set of psalms and readings is provided for each of the Sundays of Years 1 and 2 with certain exceptions. Each set has a psalm, an Old Testament reading and two New Testament readings and is to be used at all celebrations of the Holy Communion.

   When only two readings are used the Gospel is always read, and of the others the one marked with an asterisk* must not be omitted.

   This set is also for use if the principal service in a church is Morning or Evening Prayer. One of the New Testament readings may be omitted. Appropriate extensions or alternatives are indicated in brackets as suitable at Morning or Evening Prayer.

A short introduction may be given before a reading.

3 The second set of psalms and readings, to which reference is given, is for a second service in a church – for example at Evening Prayer if the principal set is used in the morning, or vice versa. It is permissible to use the readings of the principal set for the alternative year at such a second service if desired.

4 Where a portion of a psalm is appointed it is permissible to use the psalm more extensively or in full.

5 Any collect in this section may be used as an occasional prayer at the discretion of the minister.

9th SUNDAY BEFORE CHRISTMAS   *Green*

The Creation

COLLECT

Almighty God,
you created the heavens and the earth,
and made man in your own image:
Teach us to discern your hand in all your works,
and to serve you with reverence and thanksgiving;
through Jesus Christ our Lord.   **Amen.**

Year 1

PSALM 104.1–10 (PB 1–9)

OLD TESTAMENT*   *Genesis 1.1–3, 24–31a (1.1 – 2.3)*

In the beginning God created the heavens and the earth.
Now the earth was formless and empty, darkness was over
the surface of the deep, and the Spirit of God was hovering
over the waters.

And God said, 'Let there be light,' and there was light.

And God said, 'Let the land produce living creatures
according to their kinds: livestock, creatures that move along
the ground, and wild animals, each according to its kind.'
And it was so. God made the wild animals according to their
kinds, the livestock according to their kinds, and all the creatures that move along the ground according to their kinds.
And God saw that it was good.

Then God said, 'Let us make man in our image, in our likeness, and let them rule over the fish of the sea and the birds
of the air, over the livestock, over all the earth, and over all
the creatures that move along the ground.'

So God created man in his own image,
in the image of God he created him;
male and female he created them.

God blessed them and said to them, 'Be fruitful and
increase in number; fill the earth and subdue it. Rule over
the fish of the sea and the birds of the air and over every
living creature that moves on the ground.'

Then God said, 'I give you every seed-bearing plant on the
face of the whole earth and every tree that has fruit with seed

in it. They will be yours for food. And to all the beasts of the earth and all the birds of the air and all the creatures that move on the ground – everything that has the breath of life in it – I give every green plant for food.' And it was so.

God saw all that he had made, and it was very good.

EPISTLE *Colossians 1.15–20*

Christ is the image of the invisible God, the firstborn over all creation. For by him all things were created: things in heaven and on earth, visible and invisible, whether thrones or powers or rulers or authorities; all things were created by him and for him. He is before all things, and in him all things hold together. And he is the head of the body, the church; he is the beginning and the firstborn from among the dead, so that in everything he might have the supremacy. For God was pleased to have all his fulness dwell in him, and through him to reconcile to himself all things, whether things on earth or things in heaven, by making peace through his blood, shed on the cross.

GOSPEL *John 1.1–14 (–18)*

In the beginning was the Word, and the Word was with God, and the Word was God. He was with God in the beginning.

Through him all things were made; without him nothing was made that has been made. In him was life, and that life was the light of men. The light shines in the darkness, but the darkness has not understood it.

There came a man who was sent from God; his name was John. He came as a witness to testify concerning that light, so that through him all men might believe. He himself was not the light; he came only as a witness to the light. The true light that gives light to every man was coming into the world.

He was in the world, and though the world was made through him, the world did not recognize him. He came to that which was his own, but his own did not receive him. Yet to all who received him, to those who believed in his name, he gave the right to become children of God – children born not of natural descent, nor of human decision or a husband's will, but born of God.

The Word became flesh and lived for a while among us.

We have seen his glory, the glory of the one and only Son, who came from the Father, full of grace and truth.

Psalm 148; 150   Proverbs 8.1,22–31   Revelation 21.1–7,22–27

Year 2

PSALM 29

OLD TESTAMENT*   *Genesis 2. 4b–9, 15–25 (2.4b–25)*

When the LORD God made the earth and the heavens, no shrub of the field had yet appeared on the earth and no plant of the field had yet sprung up; the LORD God had not sent rain on the earth and there was no man to work the ground, but streams came up from the earth and watered the whole surface of the ground. And the LORD God formed man from the dust of the ground and breathed into his nostrils the breath of life, and man became a living being.

Now the LORD God had planted a garden in the east, in Eden; and there he put the man he had formed. And the LORD God made all kinds of trees grow out of the ground – trees that were pleasing to the eye and good for food. In the middle of the garden were the tree of life and the tree of the knowledge of good and evil.

The LORD God took the man and put him in the Garden of Eden to work it and take care of it. And the LORD God commanded the man, 'You are free to eat from any tree in the garden; but you must not eat from the tree of the knowledge of good and evil, for when you eat of it you will surely die.'

The LORD God said, 'It is not good for the man to be alone. I will make a helper suitable for him.'

Now the LORD God had formed out of the ground all the beasts of the field and all the birds of the air. He brought them to the man to see what he would name them; and whatever the man called each living creature, that was its name. So the man gave names to all the livestock, the birds of the air and all the beasts of the field.

But for Adam no suitable helper was found. So the LORD God caused the man to fall into a deep sleep; and while he was sleeping, he took one of the man's ribs and closed up the place with flesh. Then the LORD God made a woman from the rib he had taken out of the man, and he brought her to the man.

The man said,

'This is now bone of my bones and flesh of my flesh;
she shall be called "woman", for she was taken out of man.'

For this reason a man will leave his father and mother and be
united to his wife, and they will become one flesh.

The man and his wife were both naked, and they felt no
shame.

EPISTLE   *Revelation 4*

I, John, looked, and there before me was a door standing
open in heaven. And the voice I had first heard speaking to
me like a trumpet said, 'Come up here, and I will show you
what must take place after this.' At once I was in the Spirit,
and there before me was a throne in heaven with someone
sitting on it. And the one who sat there had the appearance
of jasper and carnelian. A rainbow, resembling an emerald,
encircled the throne. Surrounding the throne were twenty-
four other thrones, and seated on them were twenty-four
elders. They were dressed in white and had crowns of gold
on their heads. From the throne came flashes of lightning,
rumblings and peals of thunder. Before the throne, seven
lamps were blazing. These are the seven spirits of God. Also
before the throne there was what looked like a sea of glass,
clear as crystal.

In the centre, around the throne, were four living creatures, and they were covered with eyes, in front and behind.
The first living creature was like a lion, the second was like
an ox, the third had a face like a man, the fourth was like a
flying eagle. Each of the four living creatures had six wings
and was covered with eyes all around, even under his
wings. Day and night they never stop saying:

'Holy, holy, holy is the Lord God Almighty,
who was, and is, and is to come.'

Whenever the living creatures give glory, honour and thanks
to him who sits on the throne and who lives for ever and
ever, the twenty-four elders fall down before him who sits
on the throne, and worship him who lives for ever and ever.
They lay their crowns before the throne and say:

'You are worthy, our Lord and God,
to receive glory and honour and power,

for you created all things,
and by your will they were created
and have their being.'

GOSPEL *John 3.1–8 (–12)*

There was a man of the Pharisees named Nicodemus, a member of the Jewish ruling council. He came to Jesus at night and said, 'Rabbi, we know you are a teacher who has come from God. For no one could perform the miraculous signs you are doing if God were not with him.'

In reply Jesus declared, 'I tell you the truth, unless a man is born again, he cannot see the kingdom of God.'

'How can a man be born when he is old?' Nicodemus asked. 'Surely he cannot enter a second time into his mother's womb to be born!'

Jesus answered, 'I tell you the truth, unless a man is born of water and the Spirit, he cannot enter the kingdom of God. Flesh gives birth to flesh, but the Spirit gives birth to spirit. You should not be surprised at my saying, "You must be born again." The wind blows wherever it pleases. You hear its sound, but you cannot tell where it comes from or where it is going. So it is with everyone born of the Spirit.'

Psalm 104 *or* 104. 1–25 (PB 1–23) Job 38.1–21 and 42.1–6 Acts 14.8–17

8th SUNDAY BEFORE CHRISTMAS *Green*
The Fall

COLLECT

Heavenly Father,
whose blessed Son was revealed that he might destroy
the works of the devil,
and make us the sons of God
and heirs of eternal life:
Grant that we, having this hope,
may purify ourselves even as he is pure;
that, when he shall appear in power and great glory,
we may be made like him
in his eternal and glorious kingdom;
where he lives and reigns with you and the Holy Spirit,
one God, now and for ever.   **Amen.**

Year 1

PSALM 130

OLD TESTAMENT* *Genesis 4.1–10 (MP/EP Exodus 20.1–20)*

Adam lay with his wife Eve, and she conceived and gave birth to Cain. She said, 'With the help of the LORD I have brought forth a man.' Later she gave birth to his brother Abel.

Now Abel kept flocks, and Cain worked the soil. In the course of time Cain brought some of the fruits of the soil as an offering to the LORD. But Abel brought fat portions from some of the firstborn of his flock. The LORD looked with favour on Abel and his offering, but on Cain and his offering he did not look with favour. So Cain was very angry, and his face was downcast.

Then the LORD said to Cain, 'Why are you angry? Why is your face downcast? If you do what is right, will you not be accepted? But if you do not do what is right, sin is crouching at your door; it desires to have you, but you must master it.'

Now Cain said to his brother Abel, 'Let us go out to the field.' And while they were in the field, Cain attacked his brother Abel and killed him.

Then the LORD said to Cain, 'Where is your brother Abel?' 'I do not know,' he replied. 'Am I my brother's keeper?'

The LORD said, 'What have you done? Listen! Your brother's blood cries out to me from the ground.'

EPISTLE *1 John 3.9–18*

No one who is born of God will continue to sin, because God's seed remains in him; he cannot go on sinning, because he has been born of God. This is how we know who the children of God are and who the children of the devil are: Anyone who does not do what is right is not a child of God; neither is anyone who does not love his brother.

This is the message you heard from the beginning: We should love one another. Do not be like Cain, who belonged to the evil one and murdered his brother. And why did he murder him? Because his own actions were evil and his brother's were righteous. Do not be surprised, my brothers, if the world hates you. We know that we have passed from death to life, because we love our brothers. Anyone who does not love remains in death. Anyone who hates his brother is a murderer, and you know that no murderer has eternal life in him.

This is how we know what love is: Jesus Christ laid down his life for us. And we ought to lay down our lives for our brothers. If anyone has material possessions and sees his brother in need but has no pity on him, how can the love of God be in him? Dear children, let us not love with words or tongue but with actions and in truth.

GOSPEL *Mark 7.14–23 (1–23)*

Jesus called the crowd to him and said, 'Listen to me, everyone, and understand this. Nothing outside a man can make him "unclean" by going into him. Rather, it is what comes out of a man that makes him "unclean".'

After he had left the crowd and entered the house, his disciples asked him about this parable. 'Are you so dull?' he asked. 'Do you not see that nothing that enters a man from the outside can make him "unclean"? For it does not go into his heart but into his stomach, and then out of his body.' (In saying this, Jesus declared all foods "clean".)

He went on: 'What comes out of a man is what makes him "unclean." For from within, out of men's hearts, come evil thoughts, sexual immorality, theft, murder, adultery, greed, malice, deceit, lewdness, envy, slander, arrogance and folly. All these evils come from inside and make a man "unclean".'

Psalm 25   Isaiah 44.6–22   1 Corinthians 10.1–13 (–24)

Year 2

PSALM 10.13–20

OLD TESTAMENT* *Genesis 3.1–15 (–24)*

Now the serpent was more crafty than any of the wild animals the LORD God had made. He said to the woman, 'Did God really say, "You must not eat from any tree in the garden"?'

The woman said to the serpent, 'We may eat fruit from the trees in the garden, but God did say, "You must not eat fruit from the tree that is in the middle of the garden, and you must not touch it, or you will die." '

'You will not surely die,' the serpent said to the woman. 'For God knows that when you eat of it your eyes will be opened, and you will be like God, knowing good and evil.'

When the woman saw that the fruit of the tree was good for food and pleasing to the eye, and also desirable for gaining wisdom, she took some and ate it. She also gave some to her husband, who was with her, and he ate it. Then the eyes of both of them were opened, and they realized that they were naked; so they sewed fig leaves together and made coverings for themselves.

Then the man and his wife heard the sound of the LORD God as he was walking in the garden in the cool of the day, and they hid from the LORD God among the trees of the garden. But the LORD God called to the man, 'Where are you?'

He answered, 'I heard you in the garden, and I was afraid because I was naked; so I hid.'

And he said, 'Who told you that you were naked? Have you eaten from the tree that I commanded you not to eat from?'

The man said, 'The woman you put here with me – she gave me some fruit from the tree, and I ate it.'

Then the LORD God said to the woman, 'What is this you have done?'

The woman said, 'The serpent deceived me, and I ate.'

So the LORD God said to the serpent, 'Because you have done this,

'Cursed are you above all the livestock
and all the wild animals!
You will crawl on your belly
and you will eat dust all the days of your life.
And I will put enmity
between you and the woman,
and between your offspring and hers;
he will crush your head,
and you will strike his heel.'

EPISTLE *Romans 7.7–13 (–25)*

What shall we say, then? Is the law sin? Certainly not! Indeed I would not have known what sin was except through the law. For I would not have known what it was to covet if the law had not said, 'Do not covet.' But sin, seizing the opportunity afforded by the commandment, produced in me every kind of covetous desire. For apart from law, sin is dead. Once I was alive apart from law; but when the commandment came, sin sprang to life and I died. I found that the very commandment that was intended to bring life actually brought death. For sin, seizing the opportunity afforded by the commandment, deceived me, and through the commandment put me to death. So then, the law is holy, and the commandment is holy, righteous and good.

Did that which is good, then, become death to me? By no means! But in order that sin might be recognized as sin, it produced death in me through what was good, so that through the commandment sin might become utterly sinful.

GOSPEL   *John 3.13–21*

Jesus said, 'No one has ever gone into heaven except the one who came from heaven – the Son of Man. Just as Moses lifted up the snake in the desert, so the Son of Man must be lifted up, that everyone who believes in him may have eternal life.

'For God so loved the world that he gave his one and only Son, that whoever believes in him shall not perish but have eternal life. For God did not send his Son into the world to condemn the world, but to save the world through him. Whoever believes in him is not condemned, but whoever does not believe stands condemned already because he has not believed in the name of God's one and only Son. This is the verdict: Light has come into the world, but men loved darkness instead of light because their deeds were evil. Everyone who does evil hates the light, and will not come into the light for fear that his deeds will be exposed. But whoever lives by the truth comes into the light, so that it may be seen plainly that what he has done has been done through God.'

Psalm 139.1–18   Jeremiah 17.5–14   Romans 5.12–21

7th SUNDAY BEFORE CHRISTMAS   *Green*

The Election of God's People: Abraham

COLLECT

Almighty God
your chosen servant Abraham faithfully obeyed your call,
and rejoiced in your promise
to bless all the families of the earth in him:
Strengthen our faith, that in us your promise
may be fulfilled;
through Jesus Christ our Lord.   **Amen.**

Year 1

PSALM 1

OLD TESTAMENT*   *Genesis 12.1–9*

The LORD had said to Abram, 'Leave your country, your
people and your father's household and go to the land I will
show you.

'I will make you into a great nation
and I will bless you;
I will make your name great,
and you will be a blessing.
I will bless those who bless you,
and whoever curses you I will curse;
and all peoples on earth
will be blessed through you.'

So Abram left, as the LORD had told him; and Lot went
with him. Abram was seventy-five years old when he set out
from Haran. He took his wife Sarai, his nephew Lot, all the
possessions they had accumulated and the people they had
acquired in Haran, and they set out for the land of Canaan,
and they arrived there.

Abram travelled through the land as far as the site of the
great tree of Moreh at Shechem. The Canaanites were then
in the land, but the LORD appeared to Abram and said, 'To
your offspring I will give this land.' So he built an altar there
to the LORD, who had appeared to him.

From there he went on towards the hills east of Bethel and

pitched his tent, with Bethel on the west and Ai on the east. There he built an altar to the LORD and called on the name of the LORD. Then Abram set out and continued towards the Negev.

EPISTLE *Romans 4.13–25*

It was not through law that Abraham and his offspring received the promise that he would be heir of the world, but through the righteousness that comes by faith. For if those who live by law are heirs, faith has no value and the promise is worthless, because law brings wrath. And where there is no law there is no transgression.

Therefore, the promise comes by faith, so that it may be by grace and may be guaranteed to all Abraham's offspring – not only to those who are of the law but also to those who are of the faith of Abraham. He is the father of us all. As it is written: 'I have made you a father of many nations.' He is our father in the sight of God, in whom he believed – the God who gives life to the dead and calls things that are not as though they were.

Against all hope, Abraham in hope believed and so became the father of many nations, just as it had been said to him, 'So shall your offspring be.' Without weakening in his faith, he faced the fact that his body was as good as dead – since he was about a hundred years old – and that Sarah's womb was also dead. Yet he did not waver through unbelief regarding the promise of God, but was strengthened in his faith and gave glory to God, being fully persuaded that God had power to do what he had promised. This is why 'it was credited to him as righteousness.' The words 'it was credited to him' were written not for him alone, but also for us, to whom God will credit righteousness – for us who believe in him who raised Jesus our Lord from the dead. He was delivered over to death for our sins and was raised to life for our justification.

GOSPEL *John 8.51–59 (31–59)*

Jesus said, 'I tell you the truth, if a man keeps my word, he will never see death.'

At this the Jews exclaimed, 'Now we know that you are demon-possessed! Abraham died and so did the prophets, yet you say that if a man keeps your word, he will never taste death. Are you greater than our father Abraham? He died, and so did the prophets. Who do you think you are?'

Jesus replied, 'If I glorify myself, my glory means nothing. My Father, whom you claim as your God, is the one who glorifies me. Though you do not know him, I know him. If I said I did not, I would be a liar like you, but I do know him and keep his word. Your father Abraham rejoiced at the thought of seeing my day; he saw it and was glad.'

'You are not yet fifty years old,' the Jews said to him, 'and you have seen Abraham!'

'I tell you the truth,' Jesus answered, 'before Abraham was born, I am!' At this, they picked up stones to stone him, but Jesus hid himself, slipping away from the temple grounds.

Psalm 32;36   Genesis 18.1–19   Romans 9.1–13

Year 2

PSALM 105.1–11

OLD TESTAMENT*   *Genesis 22.1–18*

God tested Abraham. He said to him, 'Abraham!' 'Here I am,' he replied.

Then God said, 'Take your son, your only son Isaac, whom you love, and go to the region of Moriah. Sacrifice him there as a burnt offering on one of the mountains I will tell you about.'

Early the next morning Abraham got up and saddled his donkey. He took with him two of his servants and his son Isaac. When he had cut enough wood for the burnt offering, he set out for the place God had told him about. On the third day Abraham looked up and saw the place in the distance. He said to his servants, 'Stay here with the donkey while I and the boy go over there. We will worship and then we will come back to you.'

Abraham took the wood for the burnt offering and placed it on his son Isaac, and he himself carried the fire and the knife. As the two of them went on together, Isaac spoke up and said to his father Abraham, 'Father?'

'Yes, my son?' Abraham replied.

'The fire and wood are here,' Isaac said, 'but where is the lamb for the burnt offering?'

Abraham answered, 'God himself will provide the lamb for the burnt offering, my son.' And the two of them went on together.

When they reached the place God had told him about, Abraham built an altar there and arranged the wood on it. He bound his son Isaac and laid him on the altar, on top of the wood. Then he reached out his hand and took the knife to slay his son. But the angel of the LORD called out to him from heaven, 'Abraham! Abraham!'

'Here I am,' he replied.

'Do not lay a hand on the boy,' he said. 'Do not do anything to him. Now I know that you fear God, because you have not withheld from me your son, your only son.'

Abraham looked up and there in a thicket he saw a ram caught by its horns. He went over and took the ram and sacrificed it as a burnt offering instead of his son. So Abraham called that place 'The LORD will provide'. And to this day it is said, 'On the mountain of the LORD it will be provided.'

The angel of the LORD called to Abraham from heaven a second time and said, 'I swear by myself, declares the LORD, that because you have done this and have not withheld your son, your only son, I will surely bless you and make your descendants as numerous as the stars in the sky and as the sand on the seashore. Your descendants will take possession of the cities of their enemies, and through your offspring all nations on earth will be blessed, because you have obeyed me.'

EPISTLE *James 2.14–24 (–26)*

What good is it, my brothers, if a man claims to have faith but has no deeds? Can such faith save him? Suppose a brother or sister is without clothes and daily food. If one of you says to him, 'Go, I wish you well; keep warm and well fed,' but does nothing about his physical needs, what good is it? In the same way, faith by itself, if it is not accompanied by action, is dead.

But someone will say, 'You have faith; I have deeds.'

Show me your faith without deeds, and I will show you my faith by what I do. You believe that there is one God. Good! Even the demons believe that – and shudder.

You foolish man, do you want evidence that faith without deeds is useless? Was not our ancestor Abraham considered righteous for what he did when he offered his son Isaac on the altar? You see that his faith and his actions were working together, and his faith was made complete by what he did.

GOSPEL *Luke 20.9–17*

Jesus went on to tell the people this parable: 'A man planted a vineyard, rented it to some farmers and went away for a long time. At harvest time he sent a servant to the tenants so they would give him some of the fruit of the vineyard. But the tenants beat him and sent him away empty-handed. He sent another servant, but that one also they beat and treated shamefully and sent away empty-handed. He sent still a third, and they wounded him and threw him out.

'Then the owner of the vineyard said, "What shall I do? I will send my son, whom I love; perhaps they will respect him."

'But when the tenants saw him, they talked the matter over. "This is the heir," they said. "Let us kill him, and the inheritance will be ours." So they threw him out of the vineyard and killed him.

'What then will the owner of the vineyard do to them? He will come and kill those tenants and give the vineyard to others.'

When the people heard this, they said, 'May this never be!'

Jesus looked directly at them and asked, 'Then what is the meaning of that which is written:

' "The stone the builders rejected
has become the capstone."?'

Psalm 135 *or* 136   Isaiah 56.1–18   Galatians 3.1–14

6th SUNDAY BEFORE CHRISTMAS

Green

The Promise of Redemption: Moses

COLLECT

Lord God, Redeemer of Israel,
you sent your servant Moses
to lead your people out of slavery and affliction:
Deliver us from the tyranny of sin and death
and bring us to the promised land,
where we may live in perfect union
with you and the Holy Spirit;
through Jesus Christ our Lord.   **Amen.**

Year 1

PSALM   135.1–6

OLD TESTAMENT*   *Exodus 3.7–15 (2.23 – 3.20)*

The LORD said, 'I have indeed seen the misery of my people
in Egypt. I have heard them crying out because of their slave
drivers, and I am concerned about their suffering. So I have
come down to rescue them from the hand of the Egyptians
and to bring them up out of that land into a good and
spacious land, a land flowing with milk and honey – the
home of the Canaanites, Hittites, Amorites, Perizzites,
Hivites and Jebusites. And now the cry of the Israelites has
reached me, and I have seen the way the Egyptians are
oppressing them. So now, go. I am sending you to Pharaoh
to bring my people the Israelites out of Egypt.'

But Moses said to God, 'Who am I, that I should go to
Pharaoh and bring the Israelites out of Egypt?'

And God said, 'I will be with you. And this will be the sign
to you that it is I who have sent you: When you have brought
the people out of Egypt, you will worship God on this
mountain.'

Moses said to God, 'Suppose I go to the Israelites and say
to them, "The God of your fathers has sent me to you," and
they ask me, "What is his name?" Then what shall I tell
them?'

God said to Moses, 'I am who I am. This is what you are to
say to the Israelites: "I AM has sent me to you." '

God also said to Moses, 'Say to the Israelites, "The LORD, the God of your fathers – the God of Abraham, the God of Isaac and the God of Jacob – has sent me to you." This is my name for ever, the name by which I am to be remembered from generation to generation.'

EPISTLE   *Hebrews 3.1–6*

Holy brothers, who share in the heavenly calling, fix your thoughts on Jesus, the apostle and high priest whom we confess. He was faithful to the one who appointed him, just as Moses was faithful in all God's house. Jesus has been found worthy of greater honour than Moses, just as the builder of a house has greater honour than the house itself. For every house is built by someone, but God is the builder of everything. Moses was faithful as a servant in all God's house, testifying to what would be said in the future. But Christ is faithful as a son over God's house. And we are his house, if we hold on to our courage and the hope of which we boast.

GOSPEL   *John 6.25–35 (24–40)*

When the people found Jesus on the other side of the lake, they asked him, 'Rabbi, when did you get here?'

Jesus answered, 'I tell you the truth, you are looking for me, not because you saw miraculous signs but because you ate the loaves and had your fill. Do not work for food that spoils, but for food that endures to eternal life, which the Son of Man will give you. On him God the Father has placed his seal of approval.'

Then they asked him, 'What must we do to do the works God requires?'

Jesus answered, 'The work of God is this: to believe in the one he has sent.'

So they asked him, 'What miraculous sign then will you give that we may see it and believe you? What will you do? Our forefathers ate the manna in the desert; as it is written, "He gave them bread from heaven to eat." '

Jesus said to them, 'I tell you the truth, it is not Moses who has given you the bread from heaven, but it is my Father who gives you the true bread from heaven. For the bread of God is he who comes down from heaven and gives life to the world.'

'Sir,' they said, 'from now on give us this bread.'

Then Jesus declared, 'I am the bread of life. He who comes to me will never go hungry, and he who believes in me will never be thirsty.'

Psalm 66   Deuteronomy 18.15–22   Acts 3

Year 2

PSALM 77.11–20

OLD TESTAMENT*   *Exodus 6.2–8 (–13)*

God also said to Moses, 'I am the Lord. I appeared to Abraham, to Isaac and to Jacob as God Almighty, but by my name the Lord I did not make myself known to them. I also established my covenant with them to give them the land of Canaan, where they lived as aliens. Moreover, I have heard the groaning of the Israelites, whom the Egyptians are enslaving, and I have remembered my covenant.

'Therefore, say to the Israelites: "I am the Lord and I will bring you out from under the yoke of the Egyptians. I will free you from being slaves to them and will redeem you with an outstretched arm and with mighty acts of judgment. I will take you as my own people, and I will be your God. Then you will know that I am the Lord your God, who brought you out from under the yoke of the Egyptians. And I will bring you to the land I swore with uplifted hand to give to Abraham, to Isaac and to Jacob. I will give it to you as a possession. I am the Lord." '

EPISTLE   *Hebrews 11.17–31*

By faith Abraham, when God tested him, offered Isaac as a sacrifice. He who had received the promises was about to sacrifice his one and only son, even though God had said to him, 'It is through Isaac that your offspring will be reckoned.' Abraham reasoned that God could raise the dead, and figuratively speaking, he did receive Isaac back from death.

By faith Isaac blessed Jacob and Esau in regard to their future.

By faith Jacob, when he was dying, blessed each of Joseph's sons, and worshipped as he leaned on the top of his staff.

By faith Joseph, when his end was near, spoke about the exodus of the Israelites from Egypt and gave instructions about his bones.

By faith Moses' parents hid him for three months after he was born, because they saw he was no ordinary child, and they were not afraid of the king's edict.

By faith Moses, when he had grown up, refused to be known as the son of Pharaoh's daughter. He chose to be ill-treated along with the people of God rather than to enjoy the pleasures of sin for a short time. He regarded disgrace for the sake of Christ as of greater value than the treasures of Egypt, because he was looking ahead to his reward. By faith he left Egypt, not fearing the king's anger; he persevered because he saw him who is invisible. By faith he kept the Passover and the sprinkling of blood, so that the destroyer of the first-born would not touch the first-born of Israel.

By faith the people passed through the Red Sea as on dry land; but when the Egyptians tried to do so, they were drowned.

By faith the walls of Jericho fell, after the people had marched around them for seven days.

By faith the prostitute Rahab, because she welcomed the spies, was not killed with those who were disobedient.

GOSPEL *Mark 13.5–13 (1–13)*

Jesus said to his disciples: 'Watch out that no one deceives you. Many will come in my name, claiming, "I am he," and will deceive many. When you hear of wars and rumours of wars, do not be alarmed. Such things must happen, but the end is still to come. Nation will rise against nation, and kingdom against kingdom. There will be earthquakes in various places, and famines. These are the beginning of birth pains.

'You must be on your guard. You will be handed over to the local councils and flogged in the synagogues. On account of me you will stand before governors and kings as witnesses to them. And the gospel must first be preached to all nations. Whenever you are arrested and brought to trial, do not worry beforehand about what to say. Just say whatever is given you at the time, for it is not you speaking, but the Holy Spirit.

'Brother will betray brother to death, and a father his child. Children will rebel against their parents and have them put to death. All men will hate you because of me, but he who stands firm to the end will be saved.'

Psalm 106.1–15,42–50 (PB 1–14, 39–46)   Exodus 1.8–14,22 – 2.10
Hebrews 3

5th SUNDAY BEFORE CHRISTMAS
SUNDAY BEFORE ADVENT   *Green*

The Remnant of Israel

COLLECTS

Almighty God,
you have called your people to bear witness to you:
Give us grace to obey your commands
and keep us truly faithful,
that all nations may hear your voice,
return to you, and glorify your name;
through Jesus Christ our Lord.   **Amen.**

Stir up, O Lord,
the wills of your faithful people:
that, richly bearing the fruit of good works,
they may by you be richly rewarded;
through Jesus Christ our Lord.   **Amen.**

Year 1

PSALM 80.1–7

OLD TESTAMENT*   *1 Kings 19.9–18*

Elijah went into a cave on the mountain of God and spent the night.

And the word of the LORD came to him: 'What are you doing here, Elijah?'

He replied, 'I have been very zealous for the LORD God Almighty. The Israelites have rejected your covenant, broken down your altars, and put your prophets to death with the sword. I am the only one left, and now they are trying to kill me too.'

The LORD said, 'Go out and stand on the mountain in the presence of the LORD, for the LORD is about to pass by.'

Then a great and powerful wind tore the mountains apart and shattered the rocks before the LORD, but the LORD was not in the wind. After the wind there was an earthquake, but the LORD was not in the earthquake. After the earthquake came a fire, but the LORD was not in the fire. And after the fire came a gentle whisper. When Elijah heard it, he pulled his cloak over his face and went out and stood at the mouth of the cave.

Then a voice said to him, 'What are you doing here, Elijah?'

He replied, 'I have been very zealous for the LORD God Almighty. The Israelites have rejected your covenant, broken down your altars, and put your prophets to death with the sword. I am the only one left, and now they are trying to kill me too.'

The LORD said to him, 'Go back the way you came, and go to the Desert of Damascus. When you get there, anoint Hazael king over Aram. Also, anoint Jehu son of Nimshi king over Israel, and anoint Elisha son of Shaphat from Abel Meholah to succeed you as prophet. Jehu will put to death any who escape the sword of Hazael, and Elisha will put to death any who escape the sword of Jehu. Yet I reserve seven thousand in Israel – all whose knees have not bowed down to Baal and all whose mouths have not kissed him.'

EPISTLE *Romans 11.13–24 (1–24)*

I am talking to you Gentiles. Inasmuch as I am the apostle to the Gentiles, I make much of my ministry in the hope that I may somehow arouse my own people to envy and save some of them. For if their rejection is the reconciliation of the world, what will their acceptance be but life from the dead? If the part of the dough offered as firstfruits is holy, then the whole batch is holy; if the root is holy, so are the branches.

If some of the branches have been broken off, and you, though a wild olive shoot, have been grafted in among the others and now share in the nourishing sap from the olive root, do not boast over those branches. If you do, consider this: You do not support the root, but the root supports you. You will say then, 'Branches were broken off so that I could be grafted in.' Granted. But they were broken off because of unbelief, and you stand by faith. Do not be arrogant, but be afraid. For if God did not spare the natural branches, he will not spare you either.

Consider therefore the kindness and sternness of God: sternness to those who fell, but kindness to you, provided that you continue in his kindness. Otherwise, you also will be cut off. And if they did not persist in unbelief, they will be grafted in, for God is able to graft them in again. After all, if you were cut out of an olive tree that is wild by nature, and contrary to nature were grafted into a cultivated olive tree, how much more readily will these, the natural branches, be grafted into their own olive tree?

GOSPEL *Matthew 24.37–44*

Jesus said, 'As it was in the days of Noah, so it will be at the coming of the Son of Man. For in the days before the flood, people were eating and drinking, marrying and giving in marriage, up to the day Noah entered the ark; and they knew nothing about what would happen until the flood came and took them all away. That is how it will be at the coming of the Son of Man. Two men will be in the field; one will be taken and the other left. Two women will be grinding with a hand mill; one will be taken and the other left.

'Therefore keep watch, because you do not know on what day your Lord will come. But understand this: If the owner of the house had known at what time of night the thief was coming, he would have kept watch and would not have let his house be broken into. So you also must be ready, because the Son of Man will come at an hour when you do not expect him.'

Psalm 147 Genesis 18.20–33 Mark 13.14–37

Year 2

PSALM 80.8–19

OLD TESTAMENT* *Isaiah 10.20–23*

On the day of the LORD the remnant of Israel,
the survivors of the house of Jacob,
will no longer rely on him who struck them down
but will truly rely on the LORD,

the Holy One of Israel.
A remnant will return, a remnant of Jacob
will return to the Mighty God.
Though your people, O Israel, be like the sand by the sea,
only a remnant will return.
Destruction has been decreed,
overwhelming and righteous.
The Lord, the LORD Almighty, will carry out
the destruction decreed upon the whole land.

EPISTLE   *Romans 9.19–28*

One of you will say to me: 'Then why does God still blame
us? For who resists his will?' But who are you, O man, to talk
back to God? 'Shall what is formed say to him who formed it,
"Why did you make me like this?" ' Does not the potter have
the right to make out of the same lump of clay some pottery
for noble purposes and some for common use?

What if God, choosing to show his wrath and make his
power known, bore with great patience the objects of his
wrath – prepared for destruction? What if he did this to make
the riches of his glory known to the objects of his mercy,
whom he prepared in advance for glory – even us, whom he
also called, not only from the Jews but also from the Gentiles? As he says in Hosea:

'I will call them "my people" who are not my people;
and I will call her "my loved one" who is not my loved one,'

and,

'It will happen that in the very place where it was said to
    them,
"You are not my people,"
they will be called "sons of the living God".'

Isaiah cries out concerning Israel:

'Though the number of the Israelites be like the sand by the
    sea,
only the remnant will be saved.
For the Lord will carry out his sentence on earth with speed
    and finality.'

GOSPEL *Mark 13.14–23 (–37)*

Jesus said, 'When you see "the abomination that causes desolation" standing where it does not belong – let the reader understand – then let those who are in Judea flee to the mountains. Let no one on the roof of his house go down or enter the house to take anything out. Let no one in the field go back to get his cloak. How dreadful it will be in those days for pregnant women and nursing mothers! Pray that this will not take place in winter, because those will be days of distress unequalled from the beginning, when God created the world, until now – and never to be equalled again. If the Lord had not cut short those days, no one would survive. But for the sake of the elect, whom he has chosen, he has shortened them. At that time, if anyone says to you, "Look, here is the Christ!" or, "Look, there he is!" do not believe it. For false Christs and false prophets will appear and perform signs and miracles to deceive the elect – if that were possible. So be on your guard; I have told you everything ahead of time.'

Psalm 75;76   Genesis 6.5–22   1 Peter 3.8–22

4th SUNDAY BEFORE CHRISTMAS   ADVENT 1

Violet

The Advent Hope

COLLECT

Almighty God,
give us grace to cast away the works of darkness,
and put on the armour of light,
now in the time of this mortal life
in which your Son Jesus Christ
came to visit us in great humility;
So that, on the last day,
when he shall come again in his glorious majesty
to judge both the living and the dead,
we may rise to the life immortal,
through him who lives and reigns
with you and the Holy Spirit, now and for ever.   **Amen.**

This collect may be said daily in Advent.

Year 1

PSALM 50.1–6

OLD TESTAMENT* *Isaiah 52.7–10 (1–10)*

How beautiful on the mountains
are the feet of those who bring good news,
who proclaim peace,
who bring good tidings,
who proclaim salvation,
who say to Zion,
'Your God reigns!'
Listen! Your watchmen lift up their voices;
together they shout for joy.
When the LORD returns to Zion,
they will see it with their own eyes.
Burst into songs of joy together,
you ruins of Jerusalem,
for the LORD has comforted his people,
he has redeemed Jerusalem.
The LORD will lay bare his holy arm
in the sight of all the nations,
and all the ends of the earth will see
the salvation of our God.

EPISTLE *1 Thessalonians 5.1–11 (1–28)*

Now, brothers, about times and dates we do not need to
write to you, for you know very well that the day of the Lord
will come like a thief in the night. While people are saying,
'Peace and safety,' destruction will come on them suddenly,
as labour pains on a pregnant woman, and they will not
escape.

But you, brothers, are not in darkness so that this day
should surprise you like a thief. You are all sons of the light
and sons of the day. We do not belong to the night or to the
darkness. So then, let us not be like others, who are asleep,
but let us be alert and self-controlled. For those who sleep,
sleep at night, and those who get drunk, get drunk at night.
But since we belong to the day, let us be self-controlled,
putting on faith and love as a breastplate, and the hope of
salvation as a helmet. For God did not appoint us to suffer
wrath but to receive salvation through our Lord Jesus Christ.

He died for us so that, whether we are awake or asleep, we may live together with him. Therefore encourage one another and build each other up, just as in fact you are doing.

GOSPEL *Luke 21.25–33*

Jesus said to some of his disciples: 'There will be signs in the sun, moon and stars. On the earth, nations will be in anguish and perplexity at the roaring and tossing of the sea. Men will faint from terror, apprehensive of what is coming on the world, for the heavenly bodies will be shaken. At that time they will see the Son of Man coming in a cloud with power and great glory. When these things begin to take place, stand up and lift up your heads, because your redemption is drawing near.'

He told them this parable: 'Look at the fig-tree and all the trees. When they sprout leaves, you can see for yourselves and know that summer is near. Even so, when you see these things happening, you know that the kingdom of God is near.

'I tell you the truth, this generation will certainly not pass away until all these things have happened. Heaven and earth will pass away, but my words will never pass away.'

Psalm 18.1–32 (PB 1–31)   Isaiah 1.1–20   Luke 12.35–48

Year 2

PSALM 82

OLD TESTAMENT* *Isaiah 51.4–11*

'Listen to me, my people;
hear me, my nation:
The law will go out from me;
my justice will become a light to the nations.
My righteousness draws near speedily,
my salvation is on the way,
and my arm will bring justice to the nations.
The islands will look to me
and wait in hope for my arm.
Lift up your eyes to the heavens,
look at the earth beneath;

the heavens will vanish like smoke,
the earth will wear out like a garment
and its inhabitants die like flies.
But my salvation will last for ever,
my righteousness will never fail.

'Hear me, you who know what is right,
you people who have my law in your hearts:
Do not fear the reproach of men
or be terrified by their insults.
For the moth will eat them up like a garment;
the worm will devour them like wool.
But my righteousness will last for ever,
my salvation through all generations.'

Awake, awake! Clothe yourself with strength,
O arm of the LORD;
awake, as in days gone by, as in generations of old.
Was it not you who cut Rahab to pieces,
who pierced that monster through?
Was it not you who dried up the sea,
the waters of the great deep,
who made a road in the depths of the sea
so that the redeemed might cross over?
The ransomed of the LORD will return.
They will enter Zion with singing;
everlasting joy will crown their heads.
Gladness and joy will overtake them,
and sorrow and sighing will flee away.

EPISTLE *Romans 13.8–14*

Let no debt remain outstanding, except the continuing debt
to love one another, for he who loves his fellow man has
fulfilled the law. The commandments, 'Do not commit adultery,' 'Do not murder,' 'Do not steal,' 'Do not covet,' and
whatever other commandments there may be, are summed
up in this one rule: 'Love your neighbour as yourself.' Love
does no harm to its neighbour. Therefore love is the fulfilment of the law.

And do this, understanding the present time. The hour
has come for you to wake up from your slumber, because
our salvation is nearer now than when we first believed. The
night is nearly over; the day is almost here. So let us put

aside the deeds of darkness and put on the armour of light.
Let us behave decently, as in the daytime, not in orgies and
drunkenness, not in sexual immorality and debauchery, not
in dissension and jealousy. Rather, clothe yourselves with
the Lord Jesus Christ, and do not think about how to gratify
the desires of the sinful nature.

GOSPEL *Matthew 25.31–46*

Jesus said to his disciples:
'When the Son of Man comes in his glory, and all the angels
with him, he will sit on his throne in heavenly glory. All the
nations will be gathered before him, and he will separate the
people one from another as a shepherd separates the sheep
from the goats. He will put the sheep on his right and the
goats on his left.

'Then the King will say to those on his right, "Come, you
who are blessed by my Father; take your inheritance, the
kingdom prepared for you since the creation of the world.
For I was hungry and you gave me something to eat, I was
thirsty and you gave me something to drink, I was a stranger
and you invited me in, I needed clothes and you clothed me,
I was sick and you looked after me, I was in prison and you
came to visit me."

'Then the righteous will answer him, "Lord, when did we
see you hungry and feed you, or thirsty and give you something to drink? When did we see you a stranger and invite
you in, or needing clothes and clothe you? When did we see
you sick or in prison and go to visit you?"

'The King will reply, "I tell you the truth, whatever you
did for one of the least of these brothers of mine, you did for
me."

'Then he will say to those on his left, "Depart from me,
you who are cursed, into the eternal fire prepared for the
devil and his angels. For I was hungry and you gave me
nothing to eat, I was thirsty and you gave me nothing to
drink, I was a stranger and you did not invite me in, I
needed clothes and you did not clothe me, I was sick and in
prison and you did not look after me."

'They also will answer, "Lord, when did we see you
hungry or thirsty or a stranger or needing clothes or sick or
in prison, and did not help you?"

'He will reply, "I tell you the truth, whatever you did not

do for one of the least of these, you did not do for me.''

'Then they will go away to eternal punishment, but the righteous to eternal life.'

Psalm 68.1–20   Isaiah 2.10–22   Matthew 24.1–28

3rd SUNDAY BEFORE CHRISTMAS   ADVENT 2

Violet

The Word of God in the Old Testament

COLLECT

Blessed Lord,
who caused all holy Scriptures
to be written for our learning:
Help us so to hear them,
to read, mark, learn and inwardly digest them
that, through patience, and the comfort of your holy word,
we may embrace and for ever hold fast
the blessed hope of everlasting life,
which you have given us in our Saviour Jesus Christ.
Amen.

Year 1

PSALM 19.7–14 (PB 7–15)

OLD TESTAMENT*   *Isaiah 55.1–11 (–15)*

'Come, all you who are thirsty,
come to the waters;
and you who have no money, come, buy and eat!
Come, buy wine and milk without money and without cost.
Why spend money on what is not bread,
and your labour on what does not satisfy?
Listen, listen to me, and eat what is good,
and your soul will delight in the richest of fare.
Give ear and come to me;
hear me, that your soul may live.
I will make an everlasting covenant with you,
my unfailing kindnesses promised to David.
See, I have made him a witness to the peoples,
a leader and commander of the peoples.

Surely you will summon nations you know not,
and nations that do not know you will hasten to you,
because of the LORD your God,
the Holy One of Israel,
for he has endowed you with splendour.'

Seek the LORD while he may be found;
call on him while he is near.
Let the wicked forsake his way
and the evil man his thoughts.
Let him turn to the LORD and he will have mercy on him,
and to our God, for he will freely pardon.

'For my thoughts are not your thoughts,
neither are your ways my ways,'
declares the LORD.
'As the heavens are higher than the earth,
so are my ways higher than your ways
and my thoughts than your thoughts.
As the rain and the snow come down from heaven,
and do not return to it without watering the earth
and making it bud and flourish,
so that it yields seed for the sower and bread for the eater,
so is my word that goes out from my mouth:
It will not return to me empty,
but will accomplish what I desire
and achieve the purpose for which I sent it.'

EPISTLE *2 Timothy 3.14 – 4.5 (–8)*

Continue in what you have learned and have become convinced of, because you know those from whom you learned
it, and how from infancy you have known the holy Scriptures, which are able to make you wise for salvation through
faith in Christ Jesus. All Scripture is God-breathed and is
useful for teaching, rebuking, correcting and training in
righteousness, so that the man of God may be thoroughly
equipped for every good work.

In the presence of God and of Christ Jesus, who will judge
the living and the dead, and in view of his appearing and his
kingdom, I give you this charge: Preach the Word; be prepared in season and out of season; correct, rebuke and
encourage – with great patience and careful instruction. For
the time will come when men will not put up with sound

doctrine. Instead, to suit their own desires, they will gather around them a great number of teachers to say what their itching ears want to hear. They will turn their ears away from the truth and turn aside to myths. But you, keep your head in all situations, endure hardship, do the work of an evangelist, discharge all the duties of your ministry.

GOSPEL   *John 5.36–47*

Jesus said to the Jews, 'I have testimony weightier than that of John. For the very work that the Father has given me to finish and which I am doing, testifies that the Father has sent me. And the Father who sent me has himself testified concerning me. You have never heard his voice nor seen his form, nor does his word dwell in you, for you do not believe the one he sent. You diligently study the Scriptures because you think that by them you possess eternal life. These are the Scriptures that testify about me, yet you refuse to come to me to have life.

'I do not accept praise from men, but I know you. I know that you do not have the love of God in your hearts. I have come in my Father's name, and you do not accept me; but if someone else comes in his own name, you will accept him. How can you believe if you accept praise from one another, yet make no effort to obtain the praise that comes from the only God?

'But do not think I will accuse you before the Father. Your accuser is Moses, on whom your hopes are set. If you believed Moses, you would believe me, for he wrote about me. But since you do not believe what he wrote, how are you going to believe what I say?'

Psalm 119.137–152   1 Kings 22.1–28 (*or* 1–17)   Romans 10.5–17

Year 2

PSALM 119.129–136

OLD TESTAMENT*   *Isaiah 64.1–7 (–12)*

Oh, that you would rend the heavens and come down,
that the mountains would tremble before you!
As when fire sets twigs ablaze and causes water to boil,

come down to make your name known to your enemies
and cause the nations to quake before you!
For when you did awesome things that we did not expect,
you came down, and the mountains trembled before you.
Since ancient times no one has heard,
no ear has perceived,
no eye has seen any God besides you,
who acts on behalf of those who wait for him.
You come to the help of those who gladly do right,
who remember your ways.
But when we continued to sin against them,
you were angry.
How then can we be saved?
All of us have become like one who is unclean,
and all our righteous acts are like filthy rags;
we all shrivel up like a leaf,
and like the wind our sins sweep us away.
No one calls on your name
or strives to lay hold of you;
for you have hidden your face from us
and made us waste away because of our sins.

EPISTLE *Romans 15.4–13*

Everything that was written in the past was written to teach
us, so that through endurance and the encouragement of the
Scriptures we might have hope.

May the God who gives endurance and encouragement
give you a spirit of unity among yourselves as you follow
Christ Jesus, so that with one heart and mouth you may
glorify the God and Father of our Lord Jesus Christ.

Accept one another, then, just as Christ accepted you, in
order to bring praise to God. For I tell you that Christ has
become a servant of the Jews on behalf of God's truth, to
confirm the promises made to the patriarchs so that the Gentiles may glorify God for his mercy, as it is written:

'Therefore I will praise you among the Gentiles;
I will sing hymns to your name.'

Again, it says,

'Rejoice, O Gentiles, with his people.'

And again,

'Praise the Lord, all you Gentiles,
and sing praises to him, all you peoples.'

And again, Isaiah says,

'The root of Jesse will spring up,
one who will arise to rule over the nations;
the Gentiles will hope in him.'

May the God of hope fill you with all joy and peace as you trust in him, so that you may overflow with hope by the power of the Holy Spirit.

GOSPEL   *Luke 4.14–21 (–30)*

Jesus returned to Galilee in the power of the Spirit, and news about him spread through the whole countryside. He taught in their synagogues, and everyone praised him.

He went to Nazareth, where he had been brought up, and on the Sabbath day he went into the synagogue, as was his custom. And he stood up to read. The scroll of the prophet Isaiah was handed to him. Unrolling it, he found the place where it is written:

'The Spirit of the Lord is on me,
because he has anointed me to preach good news to the poor.
He has sent me to proclaim freedom for the prisoners
and recovery of sight for the blind,
to release the oppressed,
to proclaim the year of the Lord's favour.'

Then he rolled up the scroll, gave it back to the attendant and sat down. The eyes of everyone in the synagogue were fastened on him, and he said to them, 'Today this scripture is fulfilled in your hearing.'

Psalm 119.89–104   Jeremiah 36.9–32 (*or* 9–26)   Matthew 25.14–30

2nd SUNDAY BEFORE CHRISTMAS   ADVENT 3

Violet

The Forerunner

COLLECT

Almighty God,
you sent John the Baptist
to prepare the way for the coming of your Son:
Guide the ministers and stewards of your truth
to make our disobedient hearts obey the law of love;
that when Christ comes again in glory to judge the world
we may stand with confidence before him,
who lives and reigns with you and the Holy Spirit
now and for ever.   **Amen.**

Year 1

PSALM 126

OLD TESTAMENT*   *Isaiah 40.1–11*

Comfort, comfort my people, says your God.
Speak tenderly to Jerusalem, and proclaim to her
that her hard service has been completed,
that her sin has been paid for,
that she has received from the LORD's hand
double for all her sins.

A voice of one calling:
'In the desert prepare the way for the LORD;
make straight in the wilderness
a highway for our God.
Every valley shall be raised up,
every mountain and hill made low;
the rough ground shall become level,
the rugged places a plain.
And the glory of the LORD will be revealed,
and all mankind together will see it.
For the mouth of the LORD has spoken.'

A voice says, 'Cry out.'
And I said, 'What shall I cry?'
'All men are like grass,
and all their glory is like the flowers of the field.
The grass withers and the flowers fall,

because the breath of the LORD blows on them.
Surely the people are grass.
The grass withers and the flowers fall,
but the word of our God stands for ever.'

You who bring good tidings to Zion,
go up on a high mountain.
You who bring good tidings to Jerusalem,
lift up your voice with a shout,
lift it up, do not be afraid;
say to the towns of Judah,
'Here is your God!'
See, the Sovereign LORD comes with power,
and his arm rules for him.
See, his reward is with him,
and his recompense accompanies him.
He tends his flock like a shepherd:
He gathers the lambs in his arms
and carries them close to his heart;
he gently leads those that have young.

EPISTLE *1 Corinthians 4.1–5*

Men ought to regard us as servants of Christ and as those
entrusted with the secret things of God. Now it is required
that those who have been given a trust must prove faithful. I
care very little if I am judged by you or by any human court;
indeed, I do not even judge myself. My conscience is clear,
but that does not make me innocent. It is the Lord who
judges me. Therefore judge nothing before the appointed
time; wait till the Lord comes. He will bring to light what is
hidden in darkness and will expose the motives of men's
hearts. At that time each will receive his praise from God.

GOSPEL *John 1.19–28 (–34)*

Now this was John's testimony when the Jews of Jerusalem
sent priests and Levites to ask him who he was. He did not
fail to confess, but confessed freely, 'I am not the Christ.'
  They asked him, 'Then who are you? Are you Elijah?'
  He said, 'I am not.'
  'Are you the Prophet?'
  He answered, 'No'.
  Finally they said, 'Who are you? Give us an answer to take

back to those who sent us. What do you say about yourself?'

John replied in the words of Isaiah the prophet, 'I am the voice of one calling in the desert, "Make straight the way for the Lord." '

Now some Pharisees who had been sent questioned him, 'Why then do you baptize if you are not the Christ, nor Elijah, nor the Prophet?'

'I baptize with water,' John replied, 'but among you stands one you do not know. He is the one who comes after me, the thongs of whose sandals I am not worthy to untie.'

This all happened at Bethany on the other side of the Jordan, where John was baptizing.

Psalm 80   Amos 7   Luke 1.1–25

Year 2

BENEDICTUS   (MP/EP PSALM 126)

OLD TESTAMENT*   *Malachi 3.1–5 (and ch.4)*

'See, I will send my messenger, who will prepare the way before me. Then suddenly the LORD you are seeking will come to his temple; the messenger of the covenant, whom you desire, will come,' says the LORD Almighty.

But who can endure the day of his coming? Who can stand when he appears? For he will be like a refiner's fire or a launderer's soap. He will sit as a refiner and purifier of silver; he will purify the Levites and refine them like gold and silver. Then the LORD will have men who will bring offerings in righteousness, and the offerings of Judah and Jerusalem will be acceptable to the LORD, as in days gone by, as in former years.

'So I will come near to you for judgment. I will be quick to testify against sorcerers, adulterers and perjurers, against those who defraud labourers of their wages, who oppress the widows and the fatherless, and deprive aliens of justice, but do not fear me,' says the LORD Almighty.

EPISTLE   *Philippians 4.4–9 (–23)*

Rejoice in the Lord always. I will say it again: Rejoice! Let your gentleness be evident to all. The Lord is near. Do not be anxious about anything, but in everything, by prayer and petition, with thanksgiving, present your requests to God. And the peace of God, which transcends all understanding, will guard your hearts and your minds in Christ Jesus.

Finally, brothers, whatever is true, whatever is noble, whatever is right, whatever is pure, whatever is lovely, whatever is admirable – if anything is excellent or praiseworthy – think about such things. Whatever you have learned or received or heard from me, or seen in me – put it into practice. And the God of peace will be with you.

GOSPEL *Matthew 11.2–15 (–19)*

When John heard in prison what Christ was doing, he sent his disciples to ask him, 'Are you the one who was to come, or should we expect someone else?'

Jesus replied, 'Go back and report to John what you hear and see: The blind receive sight, the lame walk, those who have leprosy are cured, the deaf hear, the dead are raised, and the good news is preached to the poor. Blessed is the man who does not fall away on account of me.'

As John's disciples were leaving, Jesus began to speak to the crowd about John: 'What did you go out into the desert to see? A reed swayed by the wind? If not, what did you go out to see? A man dressed in fine clothes? No, those who wear fine clothes are in kings' palaces. Then what did you go out to see? A prophet? Yes, I tell you, and more than a prophet. This is the one about whom it is written:

"I will send my messenger ahead of you,
who will prepare your way before you."

'I tell you the truth: Among those born of women there has not risen anyone greater than John the Baptist; yet he who is least in the kingdom of heaven is greater than he. From the days of John the Baptist until now, the kingdom of heaven has been forcefully advancing, and forceful men lay hold of it. For all the Prophets and the Law prophesied until John. And if you are willing to accept it, he is the Elijah who was to come. He who has ears, let him hear.'

Psalm 11;14   1 Kings 18.17–39   Luke 3.1–20

SUNDAY BEFORE CHRISTMAS ADVENT 4 *Violet*
The Annunciation

COLLECT

Heavenly Father,
you chose the Blessed Virgin Mary
to be the mother of the promised Saviour:
Fill us with your grace,
that in all things we may accept your holy will
and with her rejoice in your salvation;
through Jesus Christ our Lord. **Amen.**

Year 1

PSALM 45.10–17(PB 11–18)

OLD TESTAMENT* *Isaiah 11.1–9 (10.33 – 11.10)*

A shoot will come up from the stump of Jesse;
from his roots a Branch will bear fruit.
The Spirit of the LORD will rest on him –
the Spirit of wisdom and of understanding,
the Spirit of counsel and of power,
the Spirit of knowledge and of the fear of the LORD –
and he will delight in the fear of the LORD.

He will not judge by what he sees with his eyes,
or decide by what he hears with his ears;
but with righteousness he will judge the needy,
with justice he will give decisions for the poor of the earth.
He will strike the earth with the rod of his mouth;
with the breath of his lips he will slay the wicked.
Righteousness will be his belt
and faithfulness the sash round his waist.

The wolf will live with the lamb,
the leopard will lie down with the goat,
the calf and the lion and the yearling together;
and a little child will lead them.
The cow will feed with the bear,
their young will lie down together,
and the lion will eat straw like the ox.
The infant will play near the hole of the cobra,

and the young child put his hand into the viper's nest.
They will neither harm nor destroy
on all my holy mountain,
for the earth will be full of the knowledge of the LORD
as the waters cover the sea.

EPISTLE   *1 Corinthians 1.26–31*

Brothers, think of what you were when you were called. Not
many of you were wise by human standards; not many were
influential; not many were of noble birth. But God chose the
foolish things of the world to shame the wise; God chose the
weak things of the world to shame the strong. He chose the
lowly things of this world and the despised things – and the
things that are not – to nullify the things that are, so that no
one may boast before him. It is because of him that you are in
Christ Jesus, who has become for us wisdom from God – that
is, our righteousness, holiness and redemption. Therefore,
as it is written: 'Let him who boasts boast in the Lord.'

GOSPEL   *Luke 1.26–38a*

In the sixth month, God sent the angel Gabriel to Nazareth, a
town in Galilee, to a virgin pledged to be married to a man
named Joseph, a descendant of David. The virgin's name
was Mary. The angel went to her and said, 'Greetings, you
who are highly favoured! The Lord is with you.'

Mary was greatly troubled at his words and wondered
what kind of greeting this might be. But the angel said to
her, 'Do not be afraid, Mary, you have found favour with
God. You will be with child and give birth to a son, and you
are to give him the name Jesus. He will be great and will be
called the Son of the Most High. The Lord God will give him
the throne of his father David, and he will reign over the
house of Jacob for ever; his kingdom will never end.'

'How will this be,' Mary asked the angel, 'since I am a
virgin?'

The angel answered, 'The Holy Spirit will come upon you,
and the power of the Most High will overshadow you. So the
holy one to be born will be called the Son of God. Even Elizabeth your relative is going to have a child in her old age, and
she who was said to be barren is in her sixth month. For
nothing is impossible with God.'

'I am the Lord's servant,' Mary answered. 'May it be to me as you have said.'

Psalm 40   1 Samuel 1.1–20   Luke 1.39–55

Year 2

MAGNIFICAT   (MP/EP PSALM 45. 10–17; PB 11–18)

OLD TESTAMENT*   *Zechariah 2.10–13(1–13)*

'Shout and be glad, O Daughter of Zion. For I am coming, and I will live among you,' declares the LORD. 'Many nations will be joined with the LORD in that day and will become my people. I will live among you and you will know that the LORD Almighty has sent me to you. The LORD will inherit Judah as his portion in the holy land and will again choose Jerusalem. Be still before the LORD, all mankind, because he has roused himself from his holy dwelling.'

EPISTLE   *Revelation 21.1–7 (20.11 – 21.7)*

I, John, saw a new heaven and a new earth, for the first heaven and the first earth had passed away, and there was no longer any sea. I saw the Holy City, the new Jerusalem, coming down out of heaven from God, prepared as a bride beautifully dressed for her husband. And I heard a loud voice from the throne saying, 'Now the dwelling of God is with men, and he will live with them. They will be his people, and God himself will be with them and be their God. He will wipe every tear from their eyes. There will be no more death or mourning or crying or pain, for the old order of things has passed away.'

He who was seated on the throne said, 'I am making everything new!' Then he said, 'Write this down, for these words are trustworthy and true.'

He said to me: 'It is done. I am the Alpha and the Omega, the Beginning and the End. To him who is thirsty I will give to drink without cost from the spring of the water of life. He who overcomes will inherit all this, and I will be his God and he will be my son.'

GOSPEL *Matthew 1.18–23*

This is how the birth of Jesus Christ came about. His mother Mary was pledged to be married to Joseph, but before they came together, she was found to be with child through the Holy Spirit. Because Joseph her husband was a righteous man and did not want to expose her to public disgrace, he had in mind to divorce her quietly.

But after he had considered this, an angel of the Lord appeared to him in a dream and said, 'Joseph son of David, do not be afraid to take Mary home as your wife, because what is conceived in her is from the Holy Spirit. She will give birth to a son, and you are to give him the name Jesus, because he will save his people from their sins.'

All this took place to fulfil what the Lord had said through the prophet. 'The virgin will be with child and will give birth to a son, and they will call him Immanuel' – which means, 'God with us'.

Psalm 113;123;131   Jeremiah 33.10–16   Revelation 22.6–21

CHRISTMAS EVE   *Violet*

If Christmas Eve falls on a Sunday, the readings for that Sunday are used.

COLLECT

Almighty God,
you make us glad with the yearly remembrance
of the birth of your only Son Jesus Christ:
Grant that as we joyfully receive him for our redeemer,
we may with sure confidence behold him
when he shall come to be our judge;
who lives and reigns with you and the Holy Spirit
one God, now and ever.   **Amen.**

Years 1 and 2

PSALM 89.1–7 (1–18)

OLD TESTAMENT* *Isaiah 62.1–5*

For Zion's sake I will not keep silent,

for Jerusalem's sake I will not remain quiet,
till her righteousness shines out like the dawn,
her salvation like a blazing torch.
The nations will see your righteousness,
and all kings your glory;
you will be called by a new name
that the mouth of the LORD will bestow.
You will be a crown of splendour in the LORD's hand,
a royal diadem in the hand of your God.
No longer will they call you Deserted,
or name your land Desolate.
But you will be called Hephzibah,
and your land Beulah,
for the LORD will take delight in you,
and your land will be married.
As a young man marries a maiden,
so will your sons marry you;
as a bridegroom rejoices over his bride,
so will your God rejoice over you.

EPISTLE *Acts 13.16–25*

Standing up, Paul motioned with his hand and said:

'Men of Israel and you Gentiles who worship God, listen
to me! The God of the people of Israel chose our fathers and
made the people prosper during their stay in Egypt. With
mighty power he led them out of that country and endured
their conduct forty years in the desert. He overthrew seven
nations in Canaan and gave their land to his people as their
inheritance. All this took about four hundred and fifty years.

'After this, God gave them judges until the time of Samuel
the prophet. Then the people asked for a king, and he gave
them Saul son of Kish, of the tribe of Benjamin, who ruled
forty years. After removing Saul, he made David their king.
He testified concerning him: "I have found David son of
Jesse a man after my own heart; he will do everything I want
him to do." From this man's descendants God has brought
to Israel the Saviour Jesus, as he promised. Before the
coming of Jesus, John preached repentance and baptism to
all the people of Israel. As John was completing his work, he
said: "Who do you think I am? I am not that one. No, but he
is coming after me, whose sandals I am not worthy to
untie." '

GOSPEL *Luke 1.67–79*

Zechariah was filled with the Holy Spirit and prophesied:

'Praise be to the Lord, the God of Israel,
because he has come and has redeemed his people.
He has raised up a horn of salvation for us
in the house of his servant David
(as he said through his holy prophets of long ago),
salvation from our enemies
and from the hand of all who hate us—
to show mercy to our fathers
and to remember his holy covenant,
the oath he swore to our father Abraham:
to rescue us from the hand of our enemies,
and to enable us to serve him without fear
in holiness and righteousness before him all our days.
And you, my child, will be called a prophet of the Most
   High;
for you will go on before the Lord to prepare the way for
   him,
to give his people the knowledge of salvation
through the forgiveness of their sins,
because of the tender mercy of our God,
by which the rising sun will come to us from heaven
to shine on those living in darkness
and in the shadow of death,
to guide our feet into the path of peace.'

Morning Prayer
Psalm 137;138   Isaiah 58   Romans 1.1–7

Evening Prayer
Psalm 85   Isaiah 32.1–8   John 13.1–17

CHRISTMAS DAY

White or Gold

The Birth of Christ

COLLECTS

Eternal God,
who made this most holy night to shine
with the brightness of your one true light:
Bring us who have known the revelation of that light on
    earth
to see the radiance of your heavenly glory;
through Jesus Christ our Lord.   **Amen.**

This may be used at midnight or early morning.

Almighty God,
in the birth of your Son
you have poured on us the new light of your incarnate
    Word,
and shown us the fulness of your love:
Help us to walk in his light and dwell in his love
that we may know the fulness of his joy;
who lives and reigns with you and the Holy Spirit,
one God, now and for ever.   **Amen.**

or

All praise to you,
almighty God and heavenly King,
who sent your Son into the world
to take our nature upon him
and to be born of a pure virgin:
Grant that, as we are born again in him,
so he may continually dwell in us,
and reign on earth as he reigns in heaven
with you and the Holy Spirit
now and for ever.   **Amen.**

Years 1 and 2

PSALM 85 *or* 96 *or* 98

OLD TESTAMENT *Isaiah 9.2–7*

The people walking in darkness
have seen a great light;
on those living in the land of the shadow of death
a light has dawned.
You have enlarged the nation
and increased their joy;
they rejoice before you
as people rejoice at the harvest,
as men rejoice when dividing the plunder.
For as in the day of Midian's defeat,
you have shattered the yoke that burdens them,
the bar across their shoulders,
the rod of their oppressor.
Every warrior's boot used in battle
and every garment rolled in blood
will be destined for burning,
will be fuel for the fire.
For to us a child is born,
to us a son is given,
and the government will be on his shoulders.
And he will be called
Wonderful Counsellor, Mighty God,
Everlasting Father, Prince of Peace.
Of the increase of his government and peace
there will be no end.
He will reign on David's throne
and over his kingdom,
establishing and upholding it
with justice and righteousness
from that time on and for ever.
The zeal of the LORD Almighty
will accomplish this.

or
Isaiah 62.10–12

Pass through, pass through the gates!
Prepare the way for the people.
Build up, build up the highway!
Remove the stones.
Raise a banner for the nations.

The LORD has made proclamation

to the ends of the earth:
'Say to the Daughter of Zion,
"See your Saviour comes!
See, his reward is with him,
and his recompense accompanies him." '
They will be called The Holy People,
The Redeemed of the LORD;
and you will be called Sought After,
The City No Longer Deserted.

or
Micah 5.2–4

'But you, Bethlehem Ephrathah,
though you are small among the clans of Judah,
out of you will come for me
one who will be ruler over Israel,
whose origins are from of old,
from ancient times.'
Therefore Israel will be abandoned
until the time when she who is in labour gives birth
and the rest of his brothers return
to join the Israelites.
He will stand and shepherd his flock
in the strength of the LORD,
in the majesty of the name of the LORD his God.
And they will live securely, for then his greatness
will reach to the ends of the earth.
And he will be their peace.

EPISTLE   *Titus 2.11–14 and 3.3–7*

The grace of God that brings salvation has appeared to all
men. It teaches us to say 'No' to ungodliness and worldly
passions, and to live self-controlled, upright and godly lives
in this present age, while we wait for the blessed hope – the
glorious appearing of our great God and Saviour, Jesus
Christ, who gave himself for us to redeem us from all
wickedness and to purify for himself a people that are his
very own, eager to do what is good.

At one time we too were foolish, disobedient, deceived
and enslaved by all kinds of passions and pleasures. We
lived in malice and envy, being hated and hating one
another. But when the kindness and love of God our Saviour

appeared, he saved us, not because of righteous things we had done, but because of his mercy. He saved us through the washing of rebirth and renewal by the Holy Spirit, whom he poured out on us generously through Jesus Christ our Saviour, so that, having been justified by his grace, we might become heirs having the hope of eternal life.

or
1 John 4.7–14

Dear friends, let us love one another, for love comes from God. Everyone who loves has been born of God and knows God. Whoever does not love does not know God, because God is love. This is how God showed his love among us: He sent his one and only Son into the world that we might live through him. This is love: not that we loved God, but that he loved us and sent his Son as an atoning sacrifice for our sins. Dear friends, since God so loved us, we also ought to love one another. No one has ever seen God; but if we love each other, God lives in us and his love is made complete in us.

We know that we live in him and he in us, because he has given us of his Spirit. And we have seen and testify that the Father has sent his Son to be the Saviour of the world.

or
Hebrews 1.1–5 (–12)

In the past God spoke to our forefathers through the prophets at many times and in various ways, but in these last days he has spoken to us by his Son, whom he appointed heir of all things, and through whom he made the universe. The Son is the radiance of God's glory and the exact representation of his being, sustaining all things by his powerful word. After he had provided purification for sins, he sat down at the right hand of the Majesty in heaven. So he became as much superior to the angels as the name he has inherited is superior to theirs.

For to which of the angels did God ever say,

'You are my Son;
today I have become your Father'?

Or again,

'I will be his Father,
and he will be my Son'?

GOSPEL*   *Luke 2.1–14 (–20)*

In those days Caesar Augustus issued a decree that a census should be taken of the entire Roman world. (This was the first census that took place while Quirinius was governor of Syria.) And everyone went to his own town to register.

So Joseph also went up from the town of Nazareth in Galilee to Judea, to Bethlehem the town of David, because he belonged to the house and line of David. He went there to register with Mary, who was pledged to be married to him and was expecting a child. While they were there, the time came for the baby to be born, and she gave birth to her firstborn, a son. She wrapped him in strips of cloth and placed him in a manger, because there was no room for them in the inn.

And there were shepherds living out in the fields near by, keeping watch over their flocks at night. An angel of the Lord appeared to them, and the glory of the Lord shone around them, and they were terrified. But the angel said to them, 'Do not be afraid. I bring you good news of great joy that will be for all the people. Today in the town of David a Saviour has been born to you; he is Christ the Lord. This will be a sign to you: You will find a baby wrapped in strips of cloth and lying in a manger.'

Suddenly a great company of the heavenly host appeared with the angel, praising God and saying,

'Glory to God in the highest,
and on earth peace to men on whom his favour rests.'

or
Luke 2.8–20

There were shepherds living out in the fields near by, keeping watch over their flocks at night. An angel of the Lord appeared to them, and the glory of the Lord shone around them, and they were terrified. But the angel said to them, 'Do not be afraid. I bring you good news of great joy that will be for all the people. Today in the town of David a Saviour has been born to you; he is Christ the Lord. This will be a sign to you: You will find a baby wrapped in strips of cloth and lying in a manger.'

Suddenly a great company of the heavenly host appeared with the angel, praising God and saying,

'Glory to God in the highest,
and on earth peace to men on whom his favour rests.'

When the angels had left them and gone into heaven, the shepherds said to one another, 'Let us go to Bethlehem and see this thing that has happened, which the Lord has told us about.'

So they hurried off and found Mary and Joseph, and the baby, who was lying in the manger. When they had seen him, they spread the word concerning what had been told them about this child, and all who heard it were amazed at what the shepherds said to them. But Mary treasured up all these things and pondered them in her heart. The shepherds returned, glorifying and praising God for all the things they had heard and seen, which were just as they had been told.

or
John 1.1–14

In the beginning was the Word, and the Word was with God, and the Word was God. He was with God in the beginning.

Through him all things were made; without him nothing was made that has been made. In him was life, and that life was the light of men. The light shines in the darkness, but the darkness has not understood it.

There came a man who was sent from God; his name was John. He came as a witness to testify concerning that light, so that through him all men might believe. He himself was not the light; he came only as a witness to the light. The true light that gives light to every man was coming into the world.

He was in the world, and though the world was made through him, the world did not recognize him. He came to that which was his own, but his own did not receive him. Yet to all who received him, to those who believed in his name, he gave the right to become children of God – children born not of natural descent, nor of human decision or a husband's will, but born of God.

The Word became flesh and lived for a while among us. We have seen his glory, the glory of the one and only Son, who came from the Father, full of grace and truth.

Morning Prayer
Psalm 19   Isaiah 35   John 3.16–21

Evening Prayer
Psalm 8;110   Isaiah 65.17–25   1 John 1.1–9

SUNDAY AFTER CHRISTMAS DAY   *White*

Year 1

The Incarnation

COLLECT

Almighty God
who wonderfully created us in your image,
and yet more wonderfully restored us
through your Son Jesus Christ:
Grant that as he came to share our humanity,
so we may share the life of his divinity;
who lives and reigns with you and the Holy Spirit,
one God, now and for ever.   **Amen.**

PSALM 2

OLD TESTAMENT   *Isaiah 7.10–14*

The LORD spoke to Ahaz and said, 'Ask the LORD your God
for a sign, whether in the deepest depths or in the highest
heights.'

But Ahaz said, 'I will not ask; I will not put the LORD to the
test.'

Then Isaiah said, 'Hear now, you house of David! Is it not
enough to try the patience of men? Will you try the patience
of my God also? Therefore the LORD himself will give you a
sign: The virgin will be with child and will give birth to a son,
and will call him Immanuel.'

EPISTLE   *Galatians 4.1–7*

What I am saying is that as long as the heir is a child, he is no
different from a slave, although he owns the whole estate.
He is subject to guardians and trustees until the time set by
his father. So also, when we were children, we were in
slavery under the basic principles of the world. But when the
time had fully come, God sent his Son, born of a woman,
born under law, to redeem those under law, that we might
receive the full rights of sons. Because you are sons, God
sent the Spirit of his Son into our hearts, the Spirit who calls
out, '*Abba*, Father.' So you are no longer a slave, but a son;
and since you are a son, God has made you also an heir.

GOSPEL* *John 1.14–18*

The Word became flesh and lived for a while among us. We have seen his glory, the glory of the one and only Son, who came from the Father, full of grace and truth.

John testifies concerning him. He cries out, saying, 'This was he of whom I said, "He who comes after me has surpassed me because he was before me." ' From the fullness of his grace we have all received one blessing after another. For the law was given through Moses: grace and truth came through Jesus Christ. No one has ever seen God, but God the only Son, who is at the Father's side, has made him known.

Psalm 132   Isaiah 40.18–31   Col. 1.1-20

When Christmas Day falls on a Wednesday and The Presentation of Christ falls on a Sunday the readings for Year 1 are to be used on this Sunday.

Year 2

The Presentation

COLLECT

Almighty God,
your Son Jesus Christ was presented in the Temple
and acclaimed the glory of Israel
and the light of the nations:
Grant that in him we may be presented to you,
and in the world reflect his glory;
through Jesus Christ our Lord.   **Amen.**

PSALM 116.11–18 (PB 11–16)

OLD TESTAMENT   *1 Samuel 1.20–28*

In the course of time Hannah conceived and gave birth to a son. She named him Samuel, saying, 'Because I asked the Lord for him.'

When the man Elkanah went up with all his family to offer the annual sacrifice to the Lord and to fulfil his vow, Hannah did not go. She said to her husband, 'After the boy is weaned, I will take him and present him before the Lord and he will live there always.'

'Do what seems best to you,' Elkanah her husband told her. 'Stay here until you have weaned him; only may the LORD make good his word.' So the woman stayed at home and nursed her son until she had weaned him.

After he was weaned, she took the boy with her, young as he was, along with a three-year-old bull, an ephah of flour and a skin of wine, and brought him to the house of the LORD at Shiloh. When they had slaughtered the bull, they brought the boy to Eli, and she said to him, 'As surely as you live, my lord, I am the woman who stood here beside you praying to the LORD. I prayed for this child, and the LORD has granted me what I asked of him. So now I give him to the LORD. For his whole life he shall be given over to the LORD.' And he worshipped the LORD there.

EPISTLE *Romans 12.1–8 (–17)*

I urge you, brothers, in view of God's mercy, to offer your bodies as living sacrifices, holy and pleasing to God – which is your spiritual worship. Do not conform any longer to the pattern of this world, but be transformed by the renewing of your mind. Then you will be able to test and approve what God's will is – his good, pleasing and perfect will.

For by the grace given me I say to every one of you: Do not think of yourself more highly than you ought, but rather think of yourself with sober judgment, in accordance with the measure of faith God has given you. Just as each of us has one body with many members, and these members do not all have the same function, so in Christ we who are many form one body, and each member belongs to all the others. We have different gifts, according to the grace given us. If a man's gift is prophesying, let him use it in proportion to his faith. If it is serving, let him serve; if it is teaching, let him teach; if it is encouraging, let him encourage; if it is contributing to the needs of others, let him give generously; if it is leadership, let him govern diligently; if it is showing mercy, let him do it cheerfully.

GOSPEL* *Luke 2.22–40*

When the time of their purification according to the Law of Moses had been completed, Joseph and Mary took Jesus to Jerusalem to present him to the Lord (as it is written in the Law of the Lord, 'Every firstborn male is to be consecrated to the Lord'), and to offer a sacrifice in keeping with what is said in the Law of the Lord: 'a pair of doves or two young pigeons.'

Now there was a man in Jerusalem called Simeon, who was righteous and devout. He was waiting for the consolation of Israel, and the Holy Spirit was upon him. It had been revealed to him by the Holy Spirit that he would not die before he had seen the Lord's Christ. Moved by the Spirit, he went into the temple courts. When the parents brought in the child Jesus to do for him what the custom of the Law required, Simeon took him in his arms and praised God, saying:

'Sovereign Lord, as you have promised,
you now dismiss your servant in peace.
For my eyes have seen your salvation,
which you have prepared in the sight of all people,
a light for revelation to the Gentiles
and for glory to your people Israel.'

The child's father and mother marvelled at what was said about him. Then Simeon blessed them and said to Mary, his mother: 'This child is destined to cause the falling and rising of many in Israel, and to be a sign that will be spoken against, so that the thoughts of many hearts will be revealed. And a sword will pierce your own soul too.'

There was also a prophetess, Anna, the daughter of Phanuel, of the tribe of Asher. She was very old; she had lived with her husband seven years after her marriage, and then was a widow until she was eighty-four. She never left the temple but worshipped night and day, fasting and praying. Coming up to them at that very moment, she gave thanks to God and spoke about the child to all who were looking forward to the redemption of Jerusalem.

When Joseph and Mary had done everything required by the Law of the Lord, they returned to Galilee to their own town of Nazareth. And the child grew and became strong; he was filled with wisdom, and the grace of God was upon him.

Psalm 84;122   Haggai 2.1–9   Luke 2.41–52

CHRISTMAS 2

Year 1

'My Father's House'

COLLECT

Heavenly Father,
whose blessed Son shared at Nazareth
the life of an earthly home:
Help us to live as the holy family,
united in love and obedience,
and bring us at last to our home in heaven;
through Jesus Christ our Lord.   **Amen.**

PSALM 27.1–8 (PB1–7)

OLD TESTAMENT *Ecclesiasticus 3.2–7*

The Lord honoured the father above the children,
and he confirmed the right of the mother over her sons.
Whoever honours his father atones for sins,
and whoever glorifies his mother is like one who lays up
    treasure.
Whoever honours his father will be gladdened by his own
    children,
and when he prays he will be heard.
Whoever glorifies his father will have long life,
and whoever obeys the Lord will refresh his mother;
he will serve his parents as his masters.

or

Exodus 12.21–27

Moses summoned all the elders of Israel and said to them,
'Go at once and select the animals for your families and
slaughter the Passover lamb. Take a bunch of hyssop, dip it
into the blood in the basin and put some of the blood on the
top and on both sides of the door-frame. Not one of you shall
go out of the door of his house until morning. When the
LORD goes through the land to strike down the Egyptians, he
will see the blood on the top and sides of the door-frame and
will pass over that doorway, and he will not permit the
destroyer to enter your houses and strike you down.

'Obey these instructions as a lasting ordinance for you and your descendants. When you enter the land that the LORD will give you as he promised, observe this ceremony. And when your children ask you, "What does this ceremony mean to you?" then tell them, "It is the Passover sacrifice to the LORD, who passed over the houses of the Israelites in Egypt and spared our homes when he struck down the Egyptians." ' Then the people bowed down and worshipped.

EPISTLE   *Romans 8.11–17*

If the Spirit of him who raised Jesus from the dead is living in you, he who raised Christ from the dead will also give life to your mortal bodies through his Spirit, who lives in you.

Therefore, brothers, we have an obligation – but it is not to the sinful nature, to live according to it. For if you live according to the sinful nature, you will die; but if by the Spirit you put to death the misdeeds of the body, you will live, because those who are led by the Spirit of God are sons of God. For you did not receive a spirit that makes you a slave again to fear, but you received the Spirit of sonship. And by him we cry, '*Abba*, Father'. The Spirit himself testifies with our spirit that we are God's children. Now if we are children, then we are heirs – heirs of God and co-heirs with Christ, if indeed we share in his sufferings in order that we may also share in his glory.

GOSPEL*   *Luke 2.41–52*

Every year his parents went to Jerusalem for the Feast of the Passover. When he was twelve years old, they went up to the Feast, according to the custom. After the Feast was over, while his parents were returning home, the boy Jesus stayed behind in Jerusalem, but they were unaware of it. Thinking he was in their company, they travelled on for a day. Then they began looking for him among their relatives and friends. When they did not find him, they went back to Jerusalem to look for him. After three days they found him in the temple courts, sitting among the teachers, listening to them and asking them questions. Everyone who heard him was amazed at his understanding and his answers. When his parents saw him, they were astonished. His mother said to him, 'Son, why have you treated us like this? Your father and I have been anxiously searching for you.'

'Why were you searching for me?' he asked 'Did you not know I had to be in my Father's house?' But they did not understand what he was saying to them.

Then he went down to Nazareth with them and was obedient to them. But his mother treasured all these things in her heart. And Jesus grew in wisdom and stature, and in favour with God and men.

Psalm 89.19–38 (20–36)   1 Samuel 1   John 4.19–26

Year 2

The Light of the World

COLLECT

Eternal God,
by the shining of a star
you led the wise men to the worship of your Son:
Grant that all the nations of the earth
may be guided by his light,
so that the whole world may behold your glory;
through Jesus Christ our Lord.   **Amen.**

PSALM 67

OLD TESTAMENT   *Isaiah 60.1–6*

'Arise, shine, for your light has come,
and the glory of the LORD rises upon you.
See, darkness covers the earth
and thick darkness is over the peoples,
but the LORD rises upon you
and his glory appears over you.
Nations will come to your light,
and kings to the brightness of your dawn.

'Lift up your eyes and look about you:
All assemble and come to you;
your sons come from afar,
and your daughters are carried on the arm.
Then you will look and be radiant,
your heart will throb and swell with joy;
the wealth on the seas will be brought to you,

to you the riches of the nations will come.
Herds of camels will cover your land,
young camels of Midian and Ephah.
And all from Sheba will come,
bearing gold and incense
and proclaiming the praise of the LORD.'

EPISTLE   *Revelation 21.22 – 22.5*

I, John, did not see a temple in the city, because the Lord
God Almighty and the Lamb are its temple. The city does not
need the sun or the moon to shine on it, for the glory of God
gives it light, and the Lamb is its lamp. The nations will walk
by its light, and the kings of the earth will bring their splendour into it. On no day will its gates ever be shut, for there
will be no night there. The glory and honour of the nations
will be brought into it. Nothing impure will ever enter it, nor
will anyone who does what is shameful or deceitful, but only
those whose names are written in the Lamb's book of life.

Then the angel showed me the river of the water of life, as
clear as crystal, flowing from the throne of God and of the
Lamb down the middle of the great street of the city. On
each side of the river stood the tree of life, bearing twelve
crops of fruit, yielding its fruit every month. And the leaves
of the tree are for the healing of the nations. No longer will
there be any curse. The throne of God and of the Lamb will
be in the city, and his servants will serve him. They will see
his face, and his name will be on their foreheads. They will
not need the light of a lamp or the light of the sun, for the
Lord God will give them light. And they will reign for ever
and ever.

GOSPEL*   *Matthew 2.1–12, 19–23*

After Jesus was born in Bethlehem in Judea, during the time
of King Herod, Magi from the east came to Jerusalem and
asked, 'Where is the one who has been born king of the
Jews? We saw his star in the east and have come to worship
him.'

When King Herod heard this he was disturbed, and all Jerusalem with him. When he had called together all the
people's chief priests and teachers of the law, he asked them
where the Christ was to be born. 'In Bethlehem in Judea,'
they replied 'for this is what the prophet has written:

' "But you, Bethlehem, in the land of Judah,
are by no means least among the rulers of Judah;
for out of you will come a ruler
who will be the shepherd of my people Israel." '

Then Herod called the Magi secretly and found out from them the exact time the star had appeared. He sent them to Bethlehem and said, 'Go and make a careful search for the child. As soon as you find him, report to me, so that I too may go and worship him.'

After they had heard the king, they went on their way, and the star they had seen in the east went ahead of them until it stopped over the place where the child was. When they saw the star, they were overjoyed. On coming to the house, they saw the child with his mother Mary, and they bowed down and worshipped him. Then they opened their treasures and presented him with gifts of gold and of incense and of myrrh. And having been warned in a dream not to go back to Herod, they returned to their country by another route.

After Herod died, an angel of the Lord appeared in a dream to Joseph in Egypt and said, 'Get up, take the child and his mother and go to the land of Israel, for those who were trying to take the child's life are dead.'

So he got up, took the child and his mother and went to the land of Israel. But when he heard that Archelaus was reigning in Judea in place of his father Herod, he was afraid to go there. Having been warned in a dream, he withdrew to the district of Galilee, and he went and lived in a town called Nazareth. So was fulfilled what was said through the prophets: 'He will be called a Nazarene.'

Psalm 85;87   Isaiah 60:13–22   1 Corinthians 2

The Epiphany takes precedence of Christmas 2. Christmas 2 does not occur when The Epiphany falls on Friday, Saturday or Sunday.

THE EPIPHANY OF OUR LORD   *White*
6 January

COLLECT

O God, the giver of light,
you led the wise men to worship your Son:
Bring all men to the light of your truth,
that the world may be filled with your glory;
through Jesus Christ our Lord,
who lives and reigns with you and the Holy Spirit
now and for ever.   **Amen.**

Years 1 and 2

PSALM 72.1–8 *or* 72.10–21 (PB 10–19)

OLD TESTAMENT   *Isaiah 49.1–6*

Listen to me, you islands;
hear this you distant nations:
Before I was born the LORD called me;
from my birth he has made mention of my name.
He made my mouth like a sharpened sword,
in the shadow of his hand he hid me;
he made me into a polished arrow
and concealed me in his quiver.
He said to me, 'You are my servant,
Israel, in whom I will display my splendour.'
But I said, 'I have laboured to no purpose;
I have spent my strength in vain and for nothing.
Yet what is due to me is in the LORD's hand,
and my reward is with my God.'

And now the LORD says –
he who formed me in the womb to be his servant
to bring Jacob back to him
and gather Israel to himself,
for I am honoured in the eyes of the LORD
and my God has been my strength –
he says:
'It is too small a thing for you to be my servant
to restore the tribes of Jacob
and bring back those of Israel I have kept.

I will also make you a light for the Gentiles,
that you may bring my salvation to the ends of the earth.'

For this reason I, Paul, the prisoner of Christ Jesus for the sake of you Gentiles, pray to God.

Surely you have heard about the administration of God's grace that was given to me for you, that is, the mystery made known to me by revelation, as I have already written briefly. In reading this, then, you will be able to understand my insight into the mystery of Christ, which was not made known to men in other generations as it has now been revealed by the Spirit to God's holy apostles and prophets. This mystery is that through the gospel the Gentiles are heirs together with Israel, members together of one body, and sharers together in the promise in Christ Jesus.

I became a servant of this gospel by the gift of God's grace given me through the working of his power. Although I am less than the least of all God's people, this grace was given me: to preach to the Gentiles the unsearchable riches in Christ, and to make plain to everyone the administration of this mystery, which for ages past was kept hidden in God, who created all things. His intent was that now, through the church, the manifold wisdom of God should be made known to the rulers and authorities in the heavenly realms, according to his eternal purpose which he accomplished in Christ Jesus our Lord. In him and through faith in him we may approach God with freedom and confidence.

After Jesus was born in Bethlehem in Judea, during the time of King Herod, Magi from the east came to Jerusalem and asked, 'Where is the one who has been born king of the Jews? We saw his star in the east and have come to worship him.'

When King Herod heard this he was disturbed, and all Jerusalem with him. When he had called together all the people's chief priests and teachers of the law, he asked them where the Christ was to be born. 'In Bethlehem in Judea,' they replied, 'for this is what the prophet has written:

"But you, Bethlehem, in the land of Judah,
are by no means least among the rulers of Judah;

for out of you will come a ruler
who will be the shepherd of my people Israel." '

Then Herod called the Magi secretly and found out from
them the exact time the star had appeared. He sent them to
Bethlehem and said, 'Go and make a careful search for the
child. As soon as you find him, report to me, so that I too
may go and worship him.'

After they had heard the king, they went on their way,
and the star they had seen in the east went ahead of them
until it stopped over the place where the child was. When
they saw the star, they were overjoyed. On coming to the
house, they saw the child with his mother Mary, and they
bowed down and worshipped him. Then they opened their
treasures and presented him with gifts of gold and of incense
and of myrrh. And having been warned in a dream not to go
back to Herod, they returned to their country by another
route.

Year 1
Psalm 2;8   Isaiah 42.1–9   John 1.29–34

Year 2
Psalm 96;97   Isaiah 49.7–13   John 2.1–11

EPIPHANY 1   *White on Sunday*
                                       Green on weekdays

The Baptism of Jesus

COLLECT

Almighty God,
who anointed Jesus at his baptism with the Holy Spirit
and revealed him as your beloved Son:
Inspire us, your children,
who are born of water and the Spirit,
to surrender our lives to your service,
that we may rejoice to be called sons of God;
through Jesus Christ our Lord.   **Amen.**

Year 1

PSALM 36.5–10

OLD TESTAMENT *1 Samuel 16.1–13a (MP/EP   Joshua 3)*

The LORD said to Samuel, 'How long will you mourn for Saul, since I have rejected him as king over Israel? Fill your horn with oil and be on your way; I am sending you to Jesse of Bethlehem. I have chosen one of his sons to be king.'

But Samuel said, 'How can I go? Saul will hear about it and kill me.'

The LORD said, 'Take a heifer with you and say, "I have come to sacrifice to the LORD." Invite Jesse to the sacrifice, and I will show you what to do. You are to anoint for me the one I indicate.'

Samuel did what the LORD said. When he arrived at Bethlehem, the elders of the town trembled when they met him. They asked, 'Do you come in peace?'

Samuel replied, 'Yes, in peace; I have come to sacrifice to the LORD. Consecrate yourselves and come to the sacrifice with me.' Then he consecrated Jesse and his sons and invited them to the sacrifice.

When they arrived, Samuel saw Eliab and thought, 'Surely the LORD's anointed stands here before the LORD.'

But the LORD said to Samuel, 'Do not consider his appearance or his height, for I have rejected him. The LORD does not look at the things man looks at. Man looks at the outward appearance, but the LORD looks at the heart.'

Then Jesse called Abinadab and made him pass in front of Samuel. But Samuel said, 'The LORD has not chosen this one either.' Jesse then made Shammah pass by, but Samuel said, 'Nor has the LORD chosen this one.' Jesse made seven of his sons pass before Samuel, but Samuel said to him, 'The LORD has not chosen these.' So he asked Jesse, 'Are these all the sons you have?'

'There is still the youngest,' Jesse answered, 'but he is tending the sheep.'

Samuel said, 'Send for him; we will not sit down until he arrives.'

So he sent and had him brought in. He was ruddy, with a fine appearance and handsome features.

Then the LORD said, 'Rise and anoint him; he is the one.'

So Samuel took the horn of oil and anointed him in the

presence of his brothers, and from that day on the Spirit of the LORD came upon David in power.

EPISTLE *Acts 10.34–38a*

Peter began to speak: 'I now realize how true it is that God does not show favouritism but accepts men from every nation who fear him and do what is right. This is the message God sent to the people of Israel, telling the good news of peace through Jesus Christ, who is Lord of all. You know what has happened throughout Judea, beginning in Galilee after the baptism that John preached – how God anointed Jesus of Nazareth with the Holy Spirit and power.'

GOSPEL* *Matthew 3.13–17 (1–17)*

Jesus came from Galilee to the Jordan to be baptized by John. But John tried to deter him, saying, 'I need to be baptized by you, and do you come to me?'

Jesus replied, 'Let it be so now; it is proper for us to do this to fulfil all righteousness.' Then John consented.

As soon as Jesus was baptized, he went up out of the water. At that moment heaven was opened, and he saw the Spirit of God descending like a dove and lighting on him. And a voice from heaven said, 'This is my Son, whom I love; with him I am well pleased.'

Psalm 46;47   Isaiah 61   Acts 18.24 – 19.6

Year 2

PSALM 89.19–30 (PB 20–30)

OLD TESTAMENT *Isaiah 42.1–7*

'Here is my servant, whom I uphold,
my chosen one in whom I delight;
I will put my Spirit on him
and he will bring justice to the nations.
He will not shout or cry out,
or raise his voice in the streets.
A bruised reed he will not break,
and a smouldering wick he will not snuff out.
In faithfulness he will bring forth justice;
he will not falter or be discouraged

till he establishes justice on earth.
In his law the islands will put their hope.'

This is what God the LORD says –
he who created the heavens and stretched them out,
who spread out the earth
and all that comes out of it,
who gives breath to its people,
and life to those who walk on it:
'I, the LORD, have called you in righteousness;
I will take hold of your hand.
I will keep you and will make you
to be a covenant for the people
and a light for the Gentiles,
to open eyes that are blind,
to free captives from prison
and to release from the dungeon those who sit in darkness.'

EPISTLE   *Ephesians 2.1–10*

As for you, you were dead in your transgressions and sins,
in which you used to live when you followed the ways of
this world and of the ruler of the kingdom of the air,
the spirit who is now at work in those who are disobedient. All
of us also lived among them at one time, gratifying the crav-
ings of our sinful nature and following its desires and
thoughts. Like the rest, we were by nature objects of wrath.
But because of his great love for us, God, who is rich in
mercy, made us alive with Christ even when we were dead
in transgressions – it is by grace you have been saved. And
God raised us up with Christ and seated us with him in the
heavenly realms in Christ Jesus, in order that in the coming
ages he might show the incomparable riches of his grace
expressed in his kindness to us in Christ Jesus. For it is by
grace you have been saved, through faith – and this not from
yourselves, it is the gift of God – not by works, so that no one
can boast. For we are God's workmanship, created in Christ
Jesus to do good works, which God prepared in advance for
us to do.

GOSPEL*   *John 1.29–34*

John saw Jesus coming towards him and said, 'Look, the
Lamb of God, who takes away the sin of the world! This is
the one I meant when I said, "A man who comes after me

has surpassed me because he was before me." I myself did not know him but the reason I came baptizing with water was that he might be revealed to Israel.'

Then John gave this testimony: 'I saw the Spirit come down from heaven as a dove and remain on him. I would not have known him, except that the one who sent me to baptize with water told me, "The man on whom you see the Spirit come down and remain is he who will baptize with the Holy Spirit." I have seen and I testify that this is the Son of God.'

Psalm 29;30   Genesis 8.15 – 9.17   Mark 1.1–13

EPIPHANY 2   *Green*

The First Disciples

COLLECT

Almighty God,
by your grace alone we have been accepted,
and called to your service:
Strengthen and inspire us by your Holy Spirit,
and make us worthy of our calling;
through Jesus Christ our Lord.   **Amen.**

Year 1

PSALM 100

OLD TESTAMENT   *Jeremiah 1.4–10 (–19)*

The word of the LORD came to me, saying,

'Before I formed you in the womb I knew you,
before you were born I set you apart;
I appointed you as a prophet to the nations.'

'Ah, Sovereign LORD,' I said, 'I do not know how to speak; I am only a child.'

But the LORD said to me, 'Do not say, "I am only a child." You must go to everyone I send you to and say whatever I command you. Do not be afraid of them, for I am with you and will rescue you,' declares the LORD.

Then the LORD reached out his hand and touched my

mouth and said to me, 'Now, I have put my words in your mouth. See, today I appoint you over nations and kingdoms to uproot and tear down, to destroy and overthrow, to build and to plant.'

EPISTLE   *Acts 26.1,9–20*

Agrippa said to Paul, 'You have permission to speak for yourself.'

So Paul motioned with his hand and began his defence:

'I too was convinced that I ought to do all that was possible to oppose the name of Jesus of Nazareth. And that is just what I did in Jerusalem. On the authority of the chief priests I put many of the saints in prison, and when they were put to death, I cast my vote against them. Many a time I went from one synagogue to another to have them punished, and I tried to force them to blaspheme. In my obsession against them, I even went to foreign cities to persecute them.

'On one of these journeys I was going to Damascus with the authority and commission of the chief priests. About noon, O king, as I was on the road, I saw a light from heaven, brighter than the sun, blazing around me and my companions. We all fell to the ground, and I heard a voice saying to me in Aramaic, "Saul, Saul, why do you persecute me? It is hard for you to kick against the goads."

'Then I asked, "Who are you, Lord?"

' "I am Jesus, whom you are persecuting," the Lord replied. "Now get up and stand on your feet. I have appeared to you to appoint you as a servant and as a witness of what you have seen of me and what I will show you. I will rescue you from your own people and from the Gentiles. I am sending you to open their eyes and turn them from darkness to light, and from the power of Satan to God, so that they may receive forgiveness of sins and a place among those who are sanctified by faith in me."

'So then, King Agrippa, I was not disobedient to the vision from heaven. First to those in Damascus, then to those in Jerusalem and in all Judea, and to the Gentiles also, I preached that they should repent and turn to God and prove their repentance by their deeds.'

GOSPEL*   *Mark 1.14–20   (MP/EP   Luke 5.1–11)*

After John was put in prison, Jesus went into Galilee, proclaiming the good news of God. 'The time has come,' he said. 'The kingdom of God is near. Repent and believe the good news!'

As Jesus walked beside the Sea of Galilee, he saw Simon and his brother Andrew casting a net into the lake, for they were fishermen. 'Come, follow me,' Jesus said, 'and I will make you fishers of men.' At once they left their nets and followed him.

When he had gone a little farther, he saw James son of Zebedee and his brother John in a boat, preparing their nets. Without delay he called them, and they left their father Zebedee in the boat with the hired men and followed him.

Psalm 15;16   Ezekiel 2.1–7;3.4–11   Matthew 10.1–22

Year 2

PSALM 145.1–12

OLD TESTAMENT   *1 Samuel 3.1–10 (3.1–4,1a)*

The boy Samuel ministered before the LORD under Eli. In those days the word of the LORD was rare; there were not many visions.

One night Eli, whose eyes were becoming so weak that he could barely see, was lying down in his usual place. The lamp of God had not yet gone out, and Samuel was lying down in the temple of the LORD, where the ark of God was. Then the LORD called Samuel.

Samuel answered, 'Here I am.' And he ran to Eli and said, 'Here I am; you called me.'

But Eli said, 'I did not call; go back and lie down.' So he went and lay down.

Again the LORD called 'Samuel!' And Samuel got up and went to Eli and said, 'Here I am; you called me.'

'My son,' Eli said, 'I did not call; go back and lie down.'

Now Samuel did not yet know the LORD. The word of the LORD had not yet been revealed to him.

The LORD called Samuel a third time, and Samuel got up and went to Eli and said, 'Here I am; you called me.'

Then Eli realized that the LORD was calling to the boy. So Eli told Samuel, 'Go and lie down, and if he calls you, say, "Speak, LORD, for your servant is listening." ' So Samuel went and lay down in his place.

The LORD came and stood there, calling as at the other times, 'Samuel! Samuel!'

Then Samuel said, 'Speak, for your servant is listening.'

EPISTLE *Galatians 1.11–24*

I want you to know, brothers, that the gospel I preached is not something that man made up. I did not receive it from any man, nor was I taught it; rather, I received it by revelation from Jesus Christ.

For you have heard of my previous way of life in Judaism, how intensely I persecuted the church of God and tried to destroy it. I was advancing in Judaism beyond many Jews of my own age, and was extremely zealous for the traditions of my fathers. But when God, who set me apart from birth and called me by his grace, was pleased to reveal his Son in me so that I might preach him among the Gentiles, I did not consult any man, nor did I go up to Jerusalem to see those who were apostles before I was, but I went immediately into Arabia and later returned to Damascus.

Then after three years, I went up to Jerusalem to get acquainted with Peter and stayed with him fifteen days. I saw none of the other apostles – only James, the Lord's brother. I assure you before God that what I am writing you is no lie. Later I went to Syria and Cilicia. I was personally unknown to the churches of Judea that are in Christ. They only heard the report: 'The man who formerly persecuted us is now preaching the faith he once tried to destroy.' And they praised God because of me.

GOSPEL* *John 1.35–51*

The next day John, who had been baptizing at Bethany, was there again with two of his disciples. When he saw Jesus passing by, he said, 'Look, the Lamb of God!'.

When the two disciples heard him say this, they followed Jesus. Turning around, Jesus saw them following and asked, 'What do you want?'

They said, 'Rabbi' (which means Teacher), 'where are you staying?'

'Come,' he replied, 'and you will see.'

So they went and saw where he was staying, and spent that day with him. It was about the tenth hour.

Andrew, Simon Peter's brother, was one of the two who

heard what John had said and who had followed Jesus. The first thing Andrew did was to find his brother Simon and tell him, 'We have found the Messiah' (that is, the Christ).

Then he brought Simon to Jesus, who looked at him and said, 'You are Simon son of John. You will be called Cephas' (which, when translated, is Peter).

The next day Jesus decided to leave for Galilee. Finding Philip, he said to him, 'Follow me.'

Philip, like Andrew and Peter, was from the town of Bethsaida. Philip found Nathanael and told him, 'We have found the one Moses wrote about in the Law, and about whom the prophets also wrote – Jesus of Nazareth, the son of Joseph.'

'Nazareth! Can anything good come from there?' Nathanael asked.

'Come and see,' said Philip.

When Jesus saw Nathanael approaching, he said of him, 'Here is a true Israelite, in whom there is nothing false.'

'How do you know me?' Nathanael asked.

Jesus answered, 'I saw you while you were still under the fig-tree before Philip called you.'

Then Nathanael declared, 'Rabbi, you are the Son of God; you are the King of Israel.'

Jesus said, 'You believe because I told you I saw you under the fig-tree. You shall see greater things than that.' He then added, ' I tell you the truth, you shall see heaven open, and the angels of God ascending and descending on the Son of Man.'

Psalm 121;126   1 Kings 20.1–29   Matthew 13.44–58

EPIPHANY 3 *Green*

Signs of Glory

COLLECT

Almighty God,
whose Son revealed in signs and miracles
the wonder of your saving love:
Enrich your people with your heavenly grace,
and in all our weakness
sustain us by your mighty power;
through Jesus Christ our Lord.   **Amen.**

Year 1

PSALM 46

OLD TESTAMENT *Exodus 33.12–23 (7–23)*

Moses said to the LORD, 'You have been telling me, "Lead these people," but you have not let me know whom you will send with me. You have said, "I know you by name and you have found favour with me." If I have found favour in your eyes, teach me your ways so I may know you and continue to find favour with you. Remember that this nation is your people.'

The LORD replied, 'My Presence will go with you, and I will give you rest.'

Then Moses said to him, 'If your Presence does not go with us, do not send us up from here. How will anyone know that you are pleased with me and with your people unless you go with us? What else will distinguish me and your people from all the other people on the face of the earth?'

And the LORD said to Moses, 'I will do the very thing you have asked, because I am pleased with you and I know you by name.'

Then Moses said, 'Now show me your glory.'

And the LORD said, 'I will cause all my goodness to pass in front of you, and I will proclaim my name, the LORD, in your presence. I will have mercy on whom I will have mercy, and I will have compassion on whom I will have compassion. But,' he said, 'you cannot see my face, for no one may see me and live.'

Then the LORD said, 'There is a place near me where you may stand on a rock. When my glory passes by, I will put you in a cleft in the rock and cover you with my hand until I have passed by. Then I will remove my hand and you will see my back; but my face must not be seen.'

EPISTLE *1 John 1.1–7*

That which was from the beginning, which we have heard, which we have seen with our eyes, which we have looked at and our hands have touched – this we proclaim concerning the Word of life. The life appeared; we have seen it and testify to it, and we proclaim to you the eternal life, which was with the Father and has appeared to us. We proclaim to you what we have seen and heard, so that you also may have fellowship with us. And our fellowship is with the Father and with his Son, Jesus Christ. We write this to make our joy complete.

This is the message we have heard from him and declare to you: God is light; in him there is no darkness at all. If we claim to have fellowship with him yet walk in the darkness, we lie and do not live by the truth. But if we walk in the light, as he is in the light, we have fellowship with one another, and the blood of Jesus, his Son, purifies us from every sin.

GOSPEL* *John 2.1–11*

On the third day a wedding took place at Cana in Galilee. Jesus' mother was there, and Jesus and his disciples had also been invited to the wedding. When the wine was gone, Jesus' mother said to him, 'They have no more wine.'

'Dear woman, why do you involve me?' Jesus replied, 'My time has not yet come.'

His mother said to the servants, 'Do whatever he tells you.'

Nearby stood six stone water jars, the kind used by the Jews for ceremonial washing, each holding from twenty to thirty gallons.

Jesus said to the servants, 'Fill the jars with water'; so they filled them to the brim.

Then he told them, 'Now draw some out and take it to the master of the banquet.'

They did so, and the master of the banquet tasted the water that had been turned into wine. He did not realize where it had come from, though the servants who had drawn the water knew. Then he called the bridegroom aside and said, 'Everyone brings out the choice wine first and then the cheaper wine after the guests have had too much to drink; but you have saved the best till now.'

This, the first of his miraculous signs, Jesus performed in Cana of Galilee. He thus revealed his glory, and his disciples put their faith in him.

Psalm 135 *or* 136   Isaiah 26.1–9   John 4.43–54

Year 2

PSALM 107.1–9

OLD TESTAMENT   *Deuteronomy 8.1–6 (–10)*

Moses said to Israel, 'Be careful to follow every command I am giving you today, so that you may live and increase and may enter and possess the land that the LORD promised on oath to your forefathers. Remember how the LORD your God led you all the way in the desert these forty years, to humble you and to test you in order to know what was in your heart, whether or not you would keep his commands. He humbled you, causing you to hunger and then feeding you with manna, which neither you nor your fathers had known, to teach you that man does not live on bread alone but on every word that comes from the mouth of the LORD. Your clothes did not wear out and your feet did not swell during these forty years. Know then in your heart that as a man disciplines his son, so the LORD your God disciplines you.

'Observe the commands of the LORD your God, walking in his ways and revering him.'

EPISTLE   *Philippians 4.10–20*

I rejoice greatly in the Lord that at last you have renewed your concern for me. Indeed, you have been concerned, but you had no opportunity to show it. I am not saying this because I am in need, for I have learned to be content whatever the circumstances. I know what it is to be in need, and I know what it is to have plenty. I have learned the secret of being content in any and every situation, whether well fed or hungry, whether living in plenty or in want. I can do everything through him who gives me strength.

Yet it was good of you to share in my troubles. Moreover, as you Philippians know, in the early days of your acquaintance with the gospel, when I set out from Macedonia, not one church shared with me in the matter of giving and receiving, except you only; for even when I was in Thessalonica, you sent me aid again and again when I was in need. Not that I am looking for a gift, but I am looking for what may be credited to your account. I have received full payment and even more; I am amply supplied, now that I have received from Epaphroditus the gifts you sent. They are a fragrant offering, an acceptable sacrifice, pleasing to God. And my God will meet all your needs according to his glorious riches in Christ Jesus.

To our God and Father be glory for ever and ever. Amen.

GOSPEL* *John 6.1–14 (–21)*

Jesus crossed to the far shore of the Sea of Galilee (that is, the Sea of Tiberias), and a great crowd of people followed him because they saw the miraculous signs he had performed on the sick. Then Jesus went up on the hillside and sat down with his disciples. The Jewish Passover Feast was near.

When Jesus looked up and saw a great crowd coming towards him, he said to Philip, 'Where shall we buy bread for these people to eat?' He asked this only to test him, for he already had in mind what he was going to do.

Philip answered him, 'Eight months' wages would not buy enough bread for each one to have a bite!'

Another of his disciples, Andrew, Simon Peter's brother, spoke up, 'Here is a boy with five small barley loaves and two small fish, but how far will they go among so many?'

Jesus said, 'Make the people sit down.' There was plenty of grass in that place, and the men sat down, about five thousand of them. Jesus then took the loaves, gave thanks, and distributed to those who were seated as much as they wanted. He did the same with the fish.

When they had all had enough to eat, he said to his disciples, 'Gather the pieces that are left over. Let nothing be wasted.' So they gathered them and filled twelve baskets with the pieces of the five barley loaves left over by those who had eaten.

After the people saw the miraculous sign that Jesus did, they began to say: 'Surely this is the Prophet who is to come into the world.'

Psalm 33   Nehemiah 13.15–22   John 5.1–21

EPIPHANY 4   *Green*
The New Temple

COLLECT

Almighty God,
in Christ you make all things new:
Transform the poverty of our nature
by the riches of your grace,
and in the renewal of our lives
make known your heavenly glory;
through Jesus Christ our Lord.   **Amen.**

Year 1

PSALM 48.9–13 (PB 8–13)

OLD TESTAMENT   *1 Kings 8.22–30 (–34 and 9.1–3)*

Solomon stood before the altar of the LORD in front of the whole assembly of Israel, spread out his hands towards heaven and said:

'O LORD, God of Israel, there is no God like you in heaven above or on earth below – you who keep your covenant of love with your servants who continue wholeheartedly in your way. You have kept your promise to your servant David my father; with your mouth you have promised and with your hand you have fulfilled it – as it is today.

'Now LORD, God of Israel, keep for your servant David my father the promises you made to him when you said, "You shall never fail to have a man to sit before me on the throne of Israel, if only your sons are careful in all they do to walk before me as you have done." And now, O God of Israel, let your word that you promised your servant David my father come true.

'But will God really dwell on earth? The heavens, even the highest heaven, cannot contain you. How much less this temple I have built! Yet give attention to your servant's prayer and his plea for mercy, O LORD my God. Hear the cry and the prayer that your servant is praying in your presence this day. May your eyes be open towards this temple night and day, this place of which you said, "My Name shall be there," so that you will hear the prayer your servant prays towards this place. Hear the supplication of your servant and of your people Israel when they pray towards this place. Hear from heaven, your dwelling-place, and when you hear, forgive.'

EPISTLE   *1 Corinthians 3.10–17*

By the grace God has given me, I laid a foundation as an expert builder, and someone else is building on it. But each one should be careful how he builds. For no one can lay any foundation other than the one already laid, which is Jesus Christ. If any man builds on this foundation using gold, silver, costly stones, wood, hay or straw, his work will be shown for what it is, because the Day will bring it to light. It will be revealed with fire, and the fire will test the quality of each man's work. If what he has built survives, he will receive his reward. If it is burned up, he will suffer loss; he himself will be saved, but only as one escaping through the flames.

Do you not know that you yourselves are God's temple and that God's Spirit lives in you? If anyone destroys God's temple, God will destroy him; for God's temple is sacred, and you are that temple.

GOSPEL*   *John 2.13–22 (–25)*

When it was almost time for the Jewish Passover, Jesus went up to Jerusalem. In the temple courts he found men selling cattle, sheep and doves, and others sitting at tables exchanging money. So he made a whip out of cords, and drove all from the temple area, both sheep and cattle; he scattered the coins of the money changers and overturned their tables. To those who sold doves he said, 'Get these out of here! How dare you turn my Father's house into a market!'

His disciples remembered that it is written, 'Zeal for your house will consume me.'

Then the Jews demanded of him, 'What miraculous sign can you show us to prove your authority to do all this?'

Jesus answered them, 'Destroy this temple, and I will raise it again in three days.'

The Jews replied, 'It has taken forty-six years to build this temple, and you are going to raise it in three days?' But the temple he had spoken of was his body. After he was raised from the dead, his disciples recalled what he had said. Then they believed the Scripture and the words that Jesus had spoken.

Psalm 34   1 Samuel 21.1–6   Matthew 12.1–21

Year 2

PSALM 84.1–7

OLD TESTAMENT   *Jeremiah 7.1–11   (MP/EP   Exodus 19.10–25)*

This is the word that came to Jeremiah from the LORD: 'Stand at the gate of the LORD's house and there proclaim this message:

' "Hear the word of the LORD, all you people of Judah who come through these gates to worship the LORD. This is what the LORD Almighty, the God of Israel, says: Reform your ways and your actions, and I will let you live in this place. Do not trust in deceptive words and say, 'This is the temple of the LORD, the temple of the LORD, the temple of the LORD!' If you really change your ways and your actions and deal with each other justly, if you do not oppress the alien, the fatherless or the widow and do not shed innocent blood in this place, and if you do not follow other gods to your own harm, then I will let you live in this place, in the land I gave to your forefathers for ever and ever. But look, you are trusting in deceptive words that are worthless.

' "Will you steal and murder, commit adultery and perjury, burn incense to Baal and follow other gods you have not known, and then come and stand before me in this house, which bears my Name, and say, 'We are safe' – safe to do all these detestable things? Has this house, which bears my Name, become a den of robbers to you? But I have been watching! declares the LORD." '

EPISTLE   *Hebrews 12.18–29 (14–29)*

You have not come to a mountain that can be touched and that is burning with fire; to darkness, gloom and storm; to a trumpet blast or to such a voice speaking words, so that those who heard it begged that no further word be spoken to them, because they could not bear what was commanded: 'If even an animal touches the mountain, it must be stoned.'

The sight was so terrifying that Moses said, 'I am trembling with fear.'

But you have come to Mount Zion, to the heavenly Jerusalem, the city of the living God. You have come to thousands upon thousands of angels in joyful assembly, to the church of the first-born, whose names are written in heaven. You have come to God, the judge of all men, to the spirits of righteous men made perfect, to Jesus the mediator of a new covenant, and to the sprinkled blood that speaks a better word than the blood of Abel.

See to it that you do not refuse him who speaks. If they did not escape when they refused him who warned them on earth, how much less will we, if we turn away from him who warns us from heaven? At that time his voice shook the earth, but now he has promised, 'Once more I will shake not only the earth but also the heavens.' The words 'once more' indicate the removing of what can be shaken – that is, created things – so that what cannot be shaken may remain.

Therefore, since we are receiving a kingdom that cannot be shaken, let us be thankful, and so worship God acceptably with reverence and awe, for our God is a consuming fire.

GOSPEL* *John 4.19–26*

The Samaritan woman said to Jesus, 'Sir, I can see that you are a prophet. Our fathers worshipped on this mountain, but you Jews claim that the place where we must worship is in Jerusalem.'

Jesus declared, 'Believe me, woman, a time is coming when you will worship the Father neither on this mountain nor in Jerusalem. You Samaritans worship what you do not know; we worship what we do know, for salvation is from the Jews. Yet a time is coming and has now come when the true worshippers will worship the Father in spirit and truth, for they are the kind of worshippers the Father seeks. God is spirit, and his worshippers must worship in spirit and in truth.'

The woman said, 'I know that Messiah' (called Christ) 'is coming. When he comes, he will explain everything to us.'

Then Jesus declared, 'I who speak to you am he.'

Psalm 50   Zechariah 8.1–7   Acts 15.1–21

398

EPIPHANY 5

The Wisdom of God

COLLECT

Give us, Lord, we pray
the spirit to think and do always
those things that are right;
that we, who can do no good thing without you,
may have power to live
according to your holy will;
through Jesus Christ our Lord. **Amen.**

Years 1 and 2

PSALM 36 *or* 49.1–12

OLD TESTAMENT *Proverbs 2.1–9 (–15)*

My son, if you accept my words
and store up my commands within you,
turning your ear to wisdom and applying your heart to
   understanding,
and if you call out for insight
and cry aloud for understanding,
and if you look for it as for silver
and search for it as for hidden treasure,
then you will understand the fear of the LORD
and find the knowledge of God.
For the LORD gives wisdom,
and from his mouth come knowledge and understanding.
He holds victory in store for the upright,
he is a shield to those whose walk is blameless,
for he guards the course of the just
and protects the way of his faithful ones.
Then you will understand what is right and just
and fair – every good path.

or

Ecclesiasticus 42.15–25

I will now call to mind the works of the Lord,
and will declare what I have seen.
By the words of the Lord his works are done.
The sun looks down on everything with its light,
and the work of the Lord is full of his glory.
The Lord has not enabled his holy ones
to recount all his marvellous works,
which the Lord the Almighty has established
that the universe may stand firm in his glory.
He searches out the abyss, and the hearts of men,
and considers their crafty devices.
For the Most High knows all that may be known,
and he looks into the signs of the age.
He declares what has been and what is to be,
and he reveals the tracks of hidden things.
No thought escapes him, and not one word is hidden from
   him.
He has ordained the splendours of his wisdom,
and he is from everlasting to everlasting.
Nothing can be added or taken away,
and he needs no one to be his counsellor.
How greatly to be desired are all his works,
and how sparkling they are to see!
All these things live and remain for ever
for every need, and all are obedient.
All things are twofold, one opposite the other,
and he has made nothing incomplete.
One confirms the good things of the other,
and who can have enough of beholding his glory?

EPISTLE *1 Corinthians 3.18–23*

Do not deceive yourselves. If any one of you thinks he is
wise by the standards of this age, he should become a 'fool'
so that he may become wise. For the wisdom of this world is
foolishness in God's sight. As it is written: 'He catches the
wise in their craftiness', and again, 'The Lord knows that the
thoughts of the wise are futile.' So then, no more boasting
about men! All things are yours, whether Paul or Apollos or
Cephas or the world or life or death or the present or the

future – all are yours, and you are of Christ, and Christ is of God.

GOSPEL* *Matthew 12.38–42*

Some of the Pharisees and teachers of the law said to Jesus, 'Teacher, we want to see a miraculous sign from you.'

He answered, 'A wicked and adulterous generation asks for a miraculous sign! But none will be given it except the sign of the prophet Jonah. For as Jonah was three days and three nights in the belly of a huge fish, so the Son of Man will be three days and three nights in the heart of the earth. The men of Nineveh will stand up at the judgment with this generation and condemn it; for they repented at the preaching of Jonah, and now one greater than Jonah is here. The Queen of the South will rise at the judgment with this generation and condemn it; for she came from the ends of the earth to listen to Solomon's wisdom, and now one greater than Solomon is here.'

Year 1
Psalm 119.121–136   Jeremiah 10.1–16   1 Timothy 3.14 – 4.10

Year 2
Psalm 92   Job 12 *or* Wisdom 7.28 – 8.9   1 Corinthians 1.18–25

EPIPHANY 6   *Green*

Parables

COLLECT

Heavenly Father,
your Son taught us in parables:
Enable your Church to speak
to the minds of people of every generation
by constantly renewing us through the Holy Spirit
that we may fully proclaim the everlasting Gospel;
through Jesus Christ our Lord.   **Amen.**

Years 1 and 2

PSALM 43 *or* 25.1–10 (PB 1–9)

OLD TESTAMENT *2 Samuel 12.1–10*

The LORD sent Nathan to David. When he came to him, he said, 'There were two men in a certain town, one rich and the other poor. The rich man had a very large number of sheep and cattle, but the poor man had nothing except one little ewe lamb that he had bought. He raised it, and it grew up with him and his children. It shared his food, drank from his cup and even slept in his arms. It was like a daughter to him.

'Now a traveller came to the rich man, but the rich man refrained from taking one of his own sheep or cattle to prepare a meal for the traveller who had come to him. Instead, he took the ewe lamb that belonged to the poor man and prepared it for the one who had come to him.'

David burned with anger against the man and said to Nathan, 'As surely as the LORD lives, the man who did this deserves to die! He must pay for that lamb four times over, because he did such a thing and had no pity.'

Then Nathan said to David, 'You are the man! This is what the LORD, the God of Israel, says: "I anointed you king over Israel, and I delivered you from the hand of Saul. I gave your master's house to you, and your master's wives into your arms. I gave you the house of Israel and Judah. And if all this had been too little, I would have given you even more. Why did you despise the word of the LORD by doing what is evil in his eyes? You struck down Uriah the Hittite with the sword of the Ammonites. Now, therefore, the sword shall never depart from your house, because you despised me and took the wife of Uriah the Hittite to be your own."'

EPISTLE *Romans 1.18–25*

The wrath of God is being revealed from heaven against all the godlessness and wickedness of men who suppress the truth by their wickedness, since what may be known about God is plain to them, because God has made it plain to them. For since the creation of the world God's invisible qualities – his eternal power and divine nature – have been clearly seen, being understood from what has been made, so that men are without any excuse.

For although they knew God, they neither glorified him as God nor gave thanks to him, but their thinking became futile and their foolish hearts were darkened. Although they claimed to be wise, they became fools and exchanged the glory of the immortal God for images made to look like mortal man and birds and animals and reptiles.

Therefore God gave them over in the sinful desires of their hearts to sexual impurity for the degrading of their bodies with one another. They exchanged the truth of God for a lie, and worshipped and served created things rather than the Creator – who is forever praised.   Amen.

GOSPEL* *Matthew 13.24–30*

Jesus told another parable: 'The kingdom of heaven is like a man who sowed good seed in his field. But while everyone was sleeping, his enemy came and sowed weeds among the wheat, and went away. When the wheat sprouted and formed heads, then the weeds also appeared.

'The owner's servants came to him and said, "Sir, did you not sow good seed in your field? Where then did the weeds come from?"

' "An enemy did this," he replied.

'The servants asked him, "Do you want us to go and pull them up?"

' "No," he answered, "because while you are pulling the weeds, you may root up the wheat with them. Let both grow together until the harvest. At that time I will tell the harvesters: "First collect the weeds and tie them in bundles to be burned, then gather the wheat and bring it into my barn." '

Year 1
Psalm 127;128;133   Isaiah 5.1–7 (–16)   John 15.1–11

Year 2
Psalm 75;76   Proverbs 1.20–33   James 3

9th SUNDAY BEFORE EASTER
SEPTUAGESIMA

Christ the Teacher

COLLECT

Eternal God,
whose Son Jesus Christ is for all mankind
the way, the truth and the life:
Grant that we may walk in his way,
rejoice in his truth and share his risen life;
who lives and reigns
with you and the Holy Spirit,
one God, now and for ever.   **Amen.**

Year 1

PSALM 103.1–13

OLD TESTAMENT   *Isaiah 30.18–21*

The LORD longs to be gracious to you;
he rises to show you compassion.
For the LORD is a God of justice.
Blessed are all who wait for him!

O people of Zion, who live in Jerusalem, you will weep no
more. How gracious he will be when you cry for help! As
soon as he hears, he will answer you. Although the Lord
gives you the bread of adversity and the water of affliction,
your teachers will be hidden no more; with your own eyes
you will see them. Whether you turn to the right or to the
left, your ears will hear a voice behind you, saying, 'This is
the way; walk in it.'

EPISTLE   *1 Corinthians 4.8–13*

Already you have all you want! Already you have become
rich! You have become kings – and that without us! How I
wish that you really had become kings so that we might be
kings with you! For it seems to me that God has put us
apostles on display at the end of the procession, like men
condemned to die in the arena. We have been made a spectacle to the whole universe, to angels as well as to men. We

are fools for Christ, but you are so wise in Christ! We are weak, but you are strong! You are honoured, we are dishonoured! To this very hour we go hungry and thirsty, we are in rags, we are brutally treated, we are homeless. We work hard with our own hands. When we are cursed, we bless; when we are persecuted, we endure it; when we are slandered, we answer kindly. Up to this moment we have become the scum of the earth, the refuse of the world.

GOSPEL*   *Matthew 5.1–12*

When Jesus saw the crowds, he went up on a mountainside and sat down. His disciples came to him, and he began to teach them, saying:

'Blessed are the poor in spirit,
for theirs is the kingdom of heaven.
Blessed are those who mourn,
for they will be comforted.
Blessed are the meek,
for they will inherit the earth.
Blessed are those who hunger and thirst for righteousness,
for they will be filled.
Blessed are the merciful,
for they will be shown mercy.
Blessed are the pure in heart,
for they will see God.
Blessed are the peacemakers,
for they will be called sons of God.
Blessed are those who are persecuted because of righteousness,
for theirs is the kingdom of heaven.

'Blessed are you when people insult you, persecute you and falsely say all kinds of evil against you because of me. Rejoice and be glad, because great is your reward in heaven, for in the same way they persecuted the prophets who were before you.'

Psalm 71   Deuteronomy 5.1–21   Luke 13.22–35

Year 2

PSALM 34.11–18

OLD TESTAMENT   *Proverbs 3.1–8 (–18)*

My son, do not forget my teaching,
but keep my commands in your heart,
for they will prolong your life many years
and bring you prosperity.

Let love and faithfulness never leave you;
bind them around your neck,
write them on the tablet of your heart.
Then you will win favour and a good name
in the sight of God and man.

Trust in the LORD with all your heart
and lean not on your own understanding;
in all your ways acknowledge him,
and he will make your paths straight.

Do not be wise in your own eyes;
fear the LORD and shun evil.
This will bring health to your body
and nourishment to your bones.

EPISTLE   *1 Corinthians 2.1–10*

When I came to you, brothers, I did not come with eloquence
or superior wisdom as I proclaimed to you the testimony
about God. For I resolved to know nothing while I was with
you except Jesus Christ and him crucified. I came to you in
weakness and fear, and with much trembling. My message
and my preaching were not with wise and persuasive words,
but with a demonstration of the Spirit's power, so that your
faith might not rest on men's wisdom, but on God's power.

We do, however, speak a message of wisdom among the
mature, but not the wisdom of this age or of the rulers of this
age, who are coming to nothing. No, we speak of God's
secret wisdom, a wisdom that has been hidden and that God
destined for our glory before time began. None of the rulers
of this age understood it, for if they had, they would not
have crucified the Lord of glory. However, as it is written:

'No eye has seen, no ear has heard,

no mind has conceived
what God has prepared for those who love him'

but God has revealed it to us by his Spirit.

The Spirit searches all things, even the deep things of God.

GOSPEL* *Luke 8.4–15 (MP/EP Mark 4.1–20)*

While a large crowd was gathering and people were coming to Jesus from town after town, he told this parable: 'A farmer went out to sow his seed. As he was scattering the seed, some fell along the path; it was trampled on, and the birds of the air ate it up. Some fell on rock, and when it came up, the plants withered because they had no moisture. Other seed fell among thorns, which grew up with it and choked the plants. Still other seed fell on good soil. It came up and yielded a crop, a hundred times more than was sown.'

When he said this, he called out, 'He who has ears to hear, let him hear.'

His disciples asked him what this parable meant. He said, 'The knowledge of the secrets of the kingdom of God has been given to you, but to others I speak in parables, so that,

' "though seeing, they may not see;
though hearing, they may not understand."

'This is the meaning of the parable: The seed is the word of God. Those along the path are the ones who hear, and then the devil comes and takes away the word from their hearts, so that they cannot believe and be saved. Those on the rock are the ones who receive the word with joy when they hear it, but they have no root. They believe for a while, but in the time of testing they fall away. The seed that fell among thorns stands for those who hear, but as they go on their way they are choked by life's worries, riches and pleasures, and they do not mature. But the seed on good soil stands for those with a noble and good heart, who hear the word, retain it, and by persevering produce a crop.'

Psalm 73   Job 28 (*or* 28.9–28)   Luke 6.20–38

8th SUNDAY BEFORE EASTER
SEXAGESIMA

Christ the Healer

COLLECT

Almighty and everlasting God,
whose Son Jesus Christ healed the sick
and restored them to wholeness of life:
Look with compassion on the anguish of the world
and heal the afflictions of all your people;
through our Lord and Saviour Jesus Christ,
who lives and reigns with you and the Holy Spirit,
one God, now and for ever.   **Amen.**

Year 1

PSALM 147.1–11

OLD TESTAMENT   *Zephaniah 3.14–20   (MP/EP   2 Kings 20)*

Sing, O Daughter of Zion;
shout aloud, O Israel!
Be glad and rejoice with all your heart,
O Daughter of Jerusalem!
The LORD has taken away your punishment,
he has turned back your enemy.
The LORD, the King of Israel is with you;
never again will you fear any harm.
On that day they will say to Jerusalem,
'Do not fear, O Zion;
do not let your hands hang limp.
The LORD your God is with you,
he is mighty to save.
He will take great delight in you,
he will quiet you with his love,
he will rejoice over you with singing.'

'The sorrows for the appointed feasts
I will remove from you;
they are a burden and a reproach to you.
At that time I will deal
with all who oppressed you;

I will rescue the lame
and gather those who have been scattered.
I will give them praise and honour
in every land where they were put to shame.
At that time I will gather you;
at that time I will bring you home.
I will give you honour and praise
among all the peoples of the earth
when I restore your fortunes
before your very eyes,'
says the LORD.

EPISTLE *James 5.13–16a*

Is any one of you in trouble? He should pray. Is any one
happy? Let him sing songs of praise. Is any one of you sick?
He should call the elders of the church to pray over him and
anoint him with oil in the name of the Lord. And the prayer
offered in faith will make the sick person well; the Lord will
raise him up. If he has sinned, he will be forgiven. Therefore
confess your sins to each other and pray for each other so
that you may be healed.

GOSPEL* *Mark 2.1–12 (–20)*

When Jesus entered Capernaum, the people heard that he
had come home. So many gathered that there was no room
left, not even outside the door, and he preached the word to
them. Some men came, bringing to him a paralytic, carried
by four of them. Since they could not get him to Jesus
because of the crowd, they made an opening in the roof
above Jesus and, after digging through it, lowered the mat
the paralysed man was lying on. When Jesus saw their faith,
he said to the paralytic, 'Son, your sins are forgiven.'

Now some teachers of the law were sitting there, thinking
to themselves, 'Why does this fellow talk like that? He is
blaspheming! Who can forgive sins but God alone?'

Immediately Jesus knew in his spirit that this was what
they were thinking in their hearts, and he said to them,
'Why are you thinking these things? Which is easier: to say
to the paralytic, "Your sins are forgiven," or to say, "Get up,
take your mat and walk"? But that you may know that the
Son of Man has authority on earth to forgive sins. . .' He
said to the paralytic, 'I tell you, get up, take your mat and go

409

home.' He got up, took his mat and walked out in full view of them all. This amazed everyone and they praised God, saying, 'We have never seen anything like this!'

Psalm 139.1–18   2 Kings 4.8–37   Mark 1.21–45

Year 2

PSALM 131

OLD TESTAMENT   *2 Kings 5.1–14 (–27)*

Now Naaman was commander of the army of the king of Aram. He was a great man in the sight of his master and highly regarded, because through him the LORD had given victory to Aram. He was a valiant soldier, but he had leprosy.

Now bands from Aram had gone out and had taken captive a young girl from Israel, and she served Naaman's wife. She said to her mistress, 'If only my master would see the prophet who is in Samaria! He would cure him of his leprosy.'

Naaman went to his master and told him what the girl from Israel had said. 'By all means, go,' the king of Aram replied. 'I will send a letter to the king of Israel.' So Naaman left, taking with him ten talents of silver, six thousand shekels of gold and ten sets of clothing. The letter that he took to the king of Israel read: 'With this letter I am sending my servant Naaman to you so that you may cure him of his leprosy.'

As soon as the king of Israel read the letter, he tore his robes and said, 'Am I God? Can I kill and bring back to life? Why does this fellow send someone to me to be cured of his leprosy? See how he is trying to pick a quarrel with me!'

When Elisha the man of God heard that the king of Israel had torn his robes, he sent him this message: 'Why have you torn your robes? Have the man come to me and he will know that there is a prophet in Israel.' So Naaman went with his horses and chariots and stopped at the door of Elisha's house. Elisha sent a messenger to say to him, 'Go, wash yourself seven times in the Jordan, and your flesh will be restored and you will be cleansed.'

But Naaman went away angry and said, 'I thought that he would surely come out to me and stand and call on the name of the LORD his God, wave his hand over the spot and cure me of my leprosy. Are not Abana and Pharpar, the rivers of Damascus, better than any of the waters of Israel? Could I not wash in them and be cleansed?' So he turned and went off in a rage.

Naaman's servants went to him and said, 'My father, if the prophet had told you to do some great thing, would you not have done it? How much more then, when he tells you, "Wash and be cleansed"?' So he went down and dipped himself in the Jordan seven times, as the man of God had told him, and his flesh was restored and became clean like that of a young boy.

EPISTLE   *2 Corinthians 12.1–10*

I must go on boasting. Although there is nothing to be gained, I will go on to visions and revelations from the Lord. I know a man in Christ who fourteen years ago was caught up to the third heaven. Whether it was in the body or out of the body I do not know – God knows. And I know that this man – whether in the body or apart from the body I do not know, but God knows – was caught up to Paradise. He heard inexpressible things, things that man is not permitted to tell. I will boast about a man like that, but I will not boast about myself, except about my weaknesses. Even if I should choose to boast, I would not be a fool, because I would be speaking the truth. But I refrain, so no one will think more of me than is warranted by what I do or say.

To keep me from becoming conceited because of these surpassingly great revelations, there was given me a thorn in my flesh, a messenger of Satan, to torment me. Three times I pleaded with the Lord to take it away from me. But he said to me, 'My grace is sufficient for you, for my power is made perfect in weakness.' Therefore I will boast all the more gladly about my weaknesses, so that Christ's power may rest on me. That is why, for Christ's sake, I delight in weaknesses, in insults, in hardships, in persecutions, in difficulties. For when I am weak, then I am strong.

GOSPEL*   *Mark 7.24–37*

Jesus went to the vicinity of Tyre. He entered a house and did not want anyone to know it; yet he could not keep his presence secret. In fact, as soon as she heard about him, a woman whose little daughter was possessed by an evil spirit came and fell at his feet. The woman was a Greek, born in Syrian Phoenicia. She begged Jesus to drive the demon out of her daughter.

'First let the children eat all they want,' he told her, 'for it is not right to take the children's bread and toss it to their dogs.'

'Yes, Lord,' she replied, 'but even the dogs under the table eat the children's crumbs'.

Then he told her, 'For such a reply, you may go; the demon has left your daughter.'

She went home and found her child lying on the bed, and the demon gone.

Then Jesus left the vicinity of Tyre and went through Sidon, down to the Sea of Galilee and into the region of the Decapolis. There some people brought a man to him who was deaf and could hardly talk, and they begged him to place his hand on the man.

After he took him aside, away from the crowd, Jesus put his fingers into the man's ears. Then he spat and touched the man's tongue. He looked up to heaven and with a deep sigh said to him, '*Ephphatha!*' (which means, 'Be opened!'). At this, the man's ears were opened, his tongue was loosened and he began to speak plainly.

Jesus commanded them not to tell anyone. But the more he did so, the more they kept talking about it. People were overwhelmed with amazement. 'He has done everything well,' they said. 'He even makes the deaf hear and the dumb speak.'

Psalm 137.1–6;146   Numbers 21.4–9   John 9 (*or* 9.1–25)

7th SUNDAY BEFORE EASTER
QUINQUAGESIMA

Green or Violet

Christ the Friend of Sinners

COLLECT

Merciful Lord,
grant to your faithful people pardon and peace;
that we may be cleansed from all our sins
and serve you with a quiet mind;
through Jesus Christ our Lord.   **Amen.**

Year 1

PSALM 32

OLD TESTAMENT   *Hosea 14.1–7*

Return, O Israel, to the LORD your God.
Your sins have been your downfall!
Take words with you and return to the LORD.
Say to him:
'Forgive all our sins
and receive us graciously,
that we may offer the fruit of our lips.
Assyria cannot save us;
we will not mount war-horses.
We will never again say "Our gods"
to what our own hands have made,
for in you the fatherless find compassion.'

'I will heal their waywardness
and love them freely,
for my anger has turned away from them.
I will be like the dew to Israel;
he will blossom like a lily.
Like a cedar of Lebanon
he will send down his roots;
his young shoots will grow.
His splendour will be like an olive tree,
his fragrance like a cedar of Lebanon.
Men will dwell again in his shade.
He will flourish like the grain.
He will blossom like a vine,
and his fame will be like the wine from Lebanon.'

EPISTLE   *Philemon 1–16 (–23)*

Paul, a prisoner of Christ Jesus, and Timothy our brother,
   To Philemon our dear friend and fellow-worker, to Apphia
our sister, to Archippus our fellow-soldier and to the church
that meets in your home:
   Grace to you and peace from God our Father and the Lord
Jesus Christ.
   I always thank my God as I remember you in my prayers,
because I hear about your faith in the Lord Jesus and your

413

love for all the saints. I pray that you may be active in sharing your faith, so that you will have a full understanding of every good thing we have in Christ. Your love has given me great joy and encouragement, because you, brother, have refreshed the hearts of the saints.

Therefore, although in Christ I could be bold and order you to do what you ought to do, yet I appeal to you on the basis of love. I then, as Paul – an old man and now also a prisoner of Christ Jesus – I appeal to you for my son Onesimus, who became my son while I was in chains. Formerly he was useless to you, but now he has become useful both to you and to me.

I am sending him – who is my very heart – back to you. I would have liked to keep him with me so that he could take your place in helping me while I am in chains for the gospel. But I did not want to do anything without your consent, so that any favour you do will be spontaneous and not forced. Perhaps the reason he was separated from you for a little while was that you might have him back for good – no longer as a slave, but better than a slave, as a dear brother. He is very dear to me but even dearer to you, both as a man and as a brother in the Lord.

GOSPEL* *Mark 2.13–17*

Once again Jesus went out beside the lake. A large crowd came to him, and he began to teach them. As he walked along, he saw Levi son of Alphaeus sitting at the tax collector's booth. 'Follow me,' Jesus told him, and Levi got up and followed him.

While Jesus was having dinner at Levi's house, many tax collectors and 'sinners' were eating with him and his disciples, for there were many who followed him. When the teachers of the law who were Pharisees saw him eating with the 'sinners' and tax collectors, they asked his disciples: 'Why does he eat with tax collectors and "sinners"?'

On hearing this, Jesus said to them, 'It is not the healthy who need a doctor, but the sick. I have not come to call the righteous, but sinners.'

Psalm 56;57   Jeremiah 13.1–11   Luke 7.36 – 8.3

Year 2

PSALM 119.65–72

OLD TESTAMENT *Numbers 15.32–36 (27–36)*

While the Israelites were in the desert, a man was found gathering wood on the Sabbath day. Those who found him gathering wood brought him to Moses and Aaron and the whole assembly, and they kept him in custody, because it was not clear what should be done to him. Then the LORD said to Moses, 'The man must die. The whole assembly must stone him outside the camp.' So the assembly took him outside the camp and stoned him to death, as the LORD commanded Moses.

or

Isaiah 57.15–21

This is what the high and lofty One says—
he who lives for ever, whose name is holy:
'I live in a high and holy place,
but also with him who is contrite and lowly in spirit,
to revive the spirit of the lowly
and to revive the heart of the contrite.
I will not accuse for ever,
nor will I always be angry,
for then the spirit of man
would grow faint before me—
the breath of man that I have created.
I was enraged by his sinful greed;
I punished him, and hid my face in anger,
yet he kept on his wilful ways.
I have seen his ways, but I will heal him;
I will guide him and restore comfort to him,
creating praise on the lips of the mourners in Israel.
Peace, peace, to those far and near,'
says the LORD. 'And I will heal them.'
But the wicked are like the tossing sea,
which cannot rest,
whose waves cast up mire and mud.
'There is no peace,' says my God, 'for the wicked.'

EPISTLE *Colossians 1.18–23*

Christ is the head of the body, the church; he is the beginning and the firstborn from among the dead, so that in everything he might have the supremacy. For God was pleased to have all his fulness dwell in him, and through him to reconcile to himself all things, whether things on earth or things in heaven, by making peace through his blood, shed on the cross.

Once you were alienated from God and were enemies in your minds because of your evil behaviour. But now he has reconciled you by Christ's physical body through death to present you holy in his sight, without blemish and free from accusation – if you continue in your faith, established and firm, not moved from the hope held out in the gospel. This is the gospel that you heard and that has been proclaimed to every creature under heaven, and of which I, Paul, have become a servant.

GOSPEL* *John 8.2–11*

Jesus appeared again in the temple courts, where all the people gathered around him, and he sat down to teach them. The teachers of the law and the Pharisees brought in a woman caught in adultery. They made her stand before the group and said to Jesus, 'Teacher, this woman was caught in the act of adultery. In the Law Moses commanded us to stone such women. Now what do you say?' They were using this question as a trap, in order to have a basis for accusing him.

But Jesus bent down and started to write on the ground with his finger. When they kept on questioning him, he straightened up and said to them, 'If any one of you is without sin, let him be the first to throw a stone at her.' Again he stooped down and wrote on the ground.

At this, those who heard began to go away one at a time, the older ones first, until only Jesus was left, with the woman still standing there. Jesus straightened up and asked her, 'Woman, where are they? Has no one condemned you?'

'No one, sir,' she said.

'Then neither do I condemn you,' Jesus declared. 'Go now and leave your life of sin.'

Psalm 103   Jeremiah 30.1–3,10–22   Luke 13.1–17

ASH WEDNESDAY   *Violet*

COLLECT

Almighty and everlasting God,
you hate nothing that you have made,
and you forgive the sins of all who are penitent:
Create and make in us new and contrite hearts,
that we may be truly sorry for our sins,
and obtain from you, the God of all mercy,
perfect remission and forgiveness:
through Jesus Christ our Lord.   **Amen.**

This collect may be said daily in Lent.

Years 1 and 2

PSALM 6 *or* 51.1–17 *or* 90.1–12

OLD TESTAMENT   *Isaiah 58.1–8*

The Lord says,

'Shout it aloud, do not hold back.
Raise your voice like a trumpet.
Declare to my people their rebellion
and to the house of Jacob their sins.
For day after day they seek me out;
they seem eager to know my ways,
as if they were a nation that does what is right
and has not forsaken the commands of its God.
They ask me for just decisions
and seem eager for God to come near them.
"Why have we fasted," they say,
"and you have not seen it?
Why have we humbled ourselves,
and you have not noticed?"

'Yet on the day of your fasting, you do as you please
and exploit all your workers.
Your fasting ends in quarrelling and strife,
and in striking each other with wicked fists.
You cannot fast as you do today
and expect your voice to be heard on high.
Is this the kind of fast I have chosen,
only a day for a man to humble himself?

417

Is it only for bowing one's head like a reed
and for lying on sackcloth and ashes?
Is that what you call a fast,
a day acceptable to the LORD?

'Is not this the kind of fasting I have chosen:
to loose the chains of injustice
and untie the cords of the yoke,
to set the oppressed free
and break every yoke?
Is it not to share your food with the hungry
and to provide the poor wanderer with shelter –
when you see the naked, to clothe him,
and not to turn away from your own flesh and blood?
Then your light will break forth like the dawn,
and your healing will quickly appear;
then your righteousness will go before you,
and the glory of the LORD will be your rearguard.'

or

Joel 2.12–17

'Even now,' declares the LORD,
'return to me with all your heart,
with fasting and weeping and mourning.'

Rend your heart and not your garments.
Return to the LORD your God,
for he is gracious and compassionate,
slow to anger and abounding in love,
and he relents from sending calamity.
Who knows but that he may turn and have pity
and leave behind a blessing –
grain offerings and drink offerings
for the LORD your God.

Blow the trumpet in Zion,
declare a holy fast, call a sacred assembly.
Gather the people, consecrate the assembly;
bring together the elders, gather the children,
those nursing at the breast.
Let the bridegroom leave his room
and the bride her chamber.
Let the priests, who minister before the LORD,

weep between the temple porch and the altar.
Let them say, 'Spare your people, O LORD.
Do not make your inheritance an object of scorn,
a byword among the nations.
Why should they say among the peoples,
"Where is their God?" '

or

Amos 5.6–15

Seek the LORD and live,
or he will sweep through the house of Joseph like a fire;
it will devour,
and Bethel will have no one to quench it.
You who turn justice into bitterness
and cast righteousness to the ground

(he who made the Pleiades and Orion,
who turns blackness into dawn
and darkens day into night,
who calls for the waters of the sea
and pours them out over the face of the land –
the LORD is his name –
he flashes destruction on the stronghold
and brings the fortified city to ruin),

you hate the one who reproves in court
and despise him who tells the truth.
You trample on the poor
and force him to give you corn.
Therefore, though you have built stone mansions,
you will not live in them;
though you have planted lush vineyards,
you will not drink their wine.
For I know how many are your offences
and how great your sins.
You oppress the righteous and take bribes
and you deprive the poor of justice in the courts.
Therefore the prudent man keeps quiet in such times,
for the times are evil.

Seek good, not evil,
that you may live.
Then the LORD God Almighty will be with you,

just as you say he is.
Hate evil, love good;
maintain justice in the courts.
Perhaps the LORD God Almighty will have mercy
on the remnant of Joseph.

EPISTLE *1 Corinthians 9.24–27*

Do you not know that in a race all the runners run, but only
one gets the prize? Run in such a way as to get the prize.
Everyone who competes in the games goes into strict
training. They do it to get a crown that will not last; but we
do it to get a crown that will last for ever. Therefore I do not
run like a man running aimlessly; I do not fight like a man
beating the air. No, I beat my body and make it my slave so
that after I have preached to others, I myself will not be disqualified for the prize.

or

James 4.1–10

What causes fights and quarrels among you? Do they not
come from your desires that battle within you? You want
something but do not get it. You kill and covet, but you
cannot have what you want. You quarrel and fight. You do
not have, because you do not ask God. When you ask, you
do not receive, because you ask with wrong motives, that
you may spend what you get on your pleasures.

You adulterous people, do you not know that friendship
with the world is hatred towards God? Anyone who chooses
to be a friend of the world becomes an enemy of God. Or do
you think Scripture says without reason that the spirit he
caused to live in us tends towards envy, but he gives us
more grace? That is why Scripture says:

'God opposes the proud
but gives grace to the humble.'

Submit yourselves, then, to God. Resist the devil, and he
will flee from you. Come near to God and he will come near
to you. Wash your hands, you sinners, and purify your
hearts, you double-minded. Grieve, mourn and wail.
Change your laughter to mourning and your joy to gloom.
Humble yourselves before the Lord, and he will lift you up.

GOSPEL* *Matthew 6.16–21*

Jesus said:

'When you fast, do not look sombre as the hypocrites do, for they disfigure their faces to show men they are fasting. I tell you the truth, they have received their reward in full. But when you fast, put oil on your head and wash your face, so that it will not be obvious to men that you are fasting, but only to your Father, who is unseen; and your Father, who sees what is done in secret, will reward you.

'Do not store up for yourselves treasures on earth, where moth and rust destroy, and where thieves break in and steal. But store up for yourselves treasures in heaven, where moth and rust do not destroy, and where thieves do not break in and steal. For where your treasure is, there your heart will be also.'

or

Luke 18.9–14

To some who were confident of their own righteousness and looked down on everybody else, Jesus told this parable.

'Two men went up to the temple to pray, one a Pharisee and the other a tax collector. The Pharisee stood up and prayed about himself: "God, I thank you that I am not like all other men – robbers, evildoers, adulterers – or even like this tax collector. I fast twice a week and give a tenth of all I get."

'But the tax collector stood at a distance. He would not even look up to heaven, but beat his breast and said, "God, have mercy on me, a sinner."

'I tell you that this man, rather than the other, went home justified before God. For everyone who exalts himself will be humbled, and he who humbles himself will be exalted.'

Year 1
Psalm 102   Daniel 9.3–19   1 Timothy 6.6–19

Year 2
Psalm 38   Isaiah 1.11–20   Matthew 16.21–28

6th SUNDAY BEFORE EASTER   LENT 1   *Violet*

The King and the Kingdom: Temptation

COLLECT

Almighty God,
whose Son Jesus Christ
fasted forty days in the wilderness,
was tempted as we are, and yet did not sin:
Give us grace to discipline ourselves
in obedience to your Spirit,
and, as you know our weakness,
so may we know your saving power;
through Jesus Christ our Lord.   **Amen.**

Year 1

PSALM 119.1–8

OLD TESTAMENT   *Genesis 2.7–9 and 3.1–7*
                        (MP/EP   Deuteronomy 30.11–20)

The LORD God formed man from the dust of the ground and
breathed into his nostrils the breath of life, and man became
a living being.

Now the LORD God had planted a garden in the east, in
Eden; and there he put the man he had formed. And the
LORD God made all kinds of trees grow out of the ground –
trees that were pleasing to the eye and good for food. In the
middle of the garden were the tree of life and the tree of the
knowledge of good and evil.

Now the serpent was more crafty than any of the wild
animals the LORD God had made. He said to the woman,
'Did God really say, "You must not eat from any tree in the
garden"?'

The woman said to the serpent, 'We may eat fruit from the
trees in the garden, but God did say, "You must not eat fruit
from the tree that is in the middle of the garden, and you
must not touch it, or you will die." '

'You will not surely die,' the serpent said to the woman.
'For God knows that when you eat of it your eyes will be
opened, and you will be like God, knowing good and evil.'

When the woman saw that the fruit of the tree was good

for food and pleasing to the eye, and also desirable for gaining wisdom, she took some and ate it. She also gave some to her husband, who was with her, and he ate it. Then the eyes of both of them were opened, and they realized that they were naked; so they sewed fig leaves together and made coverings for themselves.

EPISTLE *Hebrews 2.14–18 (5–18)*

Since the children of God's family have flesh and blood, Jesus too shared in their humanity so that by his death he might destroy him who holds the power of death – that is, the devil – and free those who all their lives were held in slavery by their fear of death. For surely it is not angels he helps, but Abraham's descendants. For this reason he had to be made like his brothers in every way, in order that he might become a merciful and faithful high priest in service to God, and that he might make atonement for the sins of the people. Because he himself suffered when he was tempted, he is able to help those who are being tempted.

GOSPEL* *Matthew 4.1–11*

Jesus was led by the Spirit into the desert to be tempted by the devil. After fasting forty days and forty nights, he was hungry. The tempter came to him and said, 'If you are the Son of God, tell these stones to become bread.'

Jesus answered, 'It is written: "Man does not live on bread alone, but on every word that comes from the mouth of God." '

Then the devil took him to the holy city and made him stand on the highest point of the temple. 'If you are the Son of God,' he said, 'throw yourself down. For it is written:

' "He will command his angels concerning you,
and they will lift you up in their hands,
so that you will not strike your foot against a stone." '

Jesus answered him, 'It is also written: "Do not put the Lord your God to the test." '

Again, the devil took him to a very high mountain and showed him all the kingdoms of the world and their splendour. 'All this I will give you,' he said, 'if you will bow down and worship me.'

Jesus said to him, 'Away from me, Satan! For it is written:

"Worship the Lord your God, and serve him only." '

Then the devil left him, and angels came and attended him.

Psalm 119.9–24   1 Samuel 26   Luke 22.1–23

Year 2

PSALM 91.1–12

OLD TESTAMENT   *Genesis 4.1–10   (MP/EP   Deuteronomy 6)*

Adam lay with his wife Eve, and she conceived and gave birth to Cain. She said, 'With the help of the LORD I have brought forth a man.' Later she gave birth to his brother Abel.

Now Abel kept flocks, and Cain worked the soil. In the course of time Cain brought some of the fruits of the soil as an offering to the LORD. But Abel brought fat portions from some of the firstborn of his flock. The LORD looked with favour on Abel and his offering, but on Cain and his offering he did not look with favour. So Cain was very angry, and his face was downcast.

Then the LORD said to Cain, 'Why are you angry? Why is your face downcast? If you do what is right, will you not be accepted? But if you do not do what is right, sin is crouching at your door; it desires to have you, but you must master it.'

Now Cain said to his brother Abel, 'Let us go out to the field.' And while they were in the field, Cain attacked his brother Abel and killed him.

Then the LORD said to Cain, 'Where is your brother Abel?'

'I do not know,' he replied. 'Am I my brother's keeper?'

The LORD said, 'What have you done? Listen! Your brother's blood cries out to me from the ground.'

EPISTLE   *Hebrews 4.12–16 (1–16)*

The word of God is living and active. Sharper than any double-edged sword, it penetrates even to dividing soul and spirit, joints and marrow; it judges the thoughts and attitudes of the heart. Nothing in all creation is hidden from God's sight. Everything is uncovered and laid bare before the eyes of him to whom we must give account.

Therefore, since we have a great high priest who has gone

through the heavens, Jesus the Son of God, let us hold firmly to the faith we profess. For we do not have a high priest who is unable to sympathize with our weaknesses, but we have one who has been tempted in every way, just as we are – yet was without sin. Let us then approach the throne of grace with confidence, so that we may receive mercy and find grace to help us in our time of need.

GOSPEL* *Luke 4.1–13*

Jesus, full of the Holy Spirit, returned from the Jordan and was led by the Spirit in the desert, where for forty days he was tempted by the devil. He ate nothing during those days, and at the end of them he was hungry.

The devil said to him, 'If you are the Son of God, tell this stone to become bread.'

Jesus answered, 'It is written: "Man does not live on bread alone." '

The devil led him up to a high place and showed him in an instant all the kingdoms of the world. And he said to him, 'I will give you all their authority and splendour, for it has been given to me, and I can give it to anyone I want to. So if you worship me, it will be yours.'

Jesus answered, 'It is written: "Worship the Lord your God and serve him only." '

The devil led him to Jerusalem and made him stand on the highest point of the temple. 'If you are the Son of God,' he said, 'throw yourself down from here. For it is written:

' "He will command his angels concerning you
to guard you carefully;
they will lift you up in their hands,
so that you will not strike your foot against a stone." '

Jesus answered, 'It says: "Do not put the Lord your God to the test." '

When the devil had finished all this tempting, he left him until an opportune time.

Psalm 51   Exodus 17.1–13   Matthew 26.1–30

5th SUNDAY BEFORE EASTER   LENT 2   *Violet*

The King and the Kingdom: Conflict

COLLECT

Lord God Almighty,
your Son prayed for his disciples,
that in all the conflicts of the world
you would deliver them from the power of the devil:
Strengthen us to resist every assault and temptation,
and to follow you, the only God;
through Jesus Christ our Lord.   **Amen.**

Year 1

PSALM 119.33–40

OLD TESTAMENT   *Genesis 6.11–22   (MP/EP   2 Kings 6.8–23)*

Now the earth was corrupt in God's sight and was full of violence. God saw how corrupt the earth had become, for all the people on earth had corrupted their ways. So God said to Noah, 'I am going to put an end to all people, for the earth is filled with violence because of them. I am surely going to destroy both them and the earth. So make yourself an ark of cypress wood; make rooms in it and coat it with pitch inside and out. This is how you are to build it: The ark is to be 450 . feet long, 75 feet wide and 45 feet high. Make a roof for it and finish the ark to within 18 inches of the top. Put a door in the side of the ark and make lower, middle and upper decks. I am going to bring floodwaters on the earth to destroy all life under the heavens, every creature that has the breath of life in it. Everything on earth will perish. But I will establish my covenant with you, and you will enter the ark – you and your sons and your wife and your sons' wives with you. You are to bring into the ark two of all living creatures, male and female, to keep them alive with you. Two of every kind of bird, of every kind of animal and of every kind of creature that moves along the ground will come to you to be kept alive. You are to take every kind of food that is to be eaten and store it away as food for you and for them.'

Noah did everything just as God commanded him.

EPISTLE *1 John 4.1–6*

Dear friends, do not believe every spirit, but test the spirits to see whether they are from God, because many false prophets have gone out into the world. This is how you can recognize the Spirit of God: Every spirit that acknowledges that Jesus Christ has come in the flesh is from God, but every spirit that does not acknowledge Jesus is not from God. This is the spirit of the antichrist, which you have heard is coming and even now is already in the world.

You, dear children, are from God and have overcome them, because the one who is in you is greater than the one who is in the world. They are from the world and therefore speak from the viewpoint of the world, and the world listens to them. We are from God, and whoever knows God listens to us; but whoever is not from God does not listen to us. This is how we recognize the Spirit of truth and the spirit of falsehood.

GOSPEL* *Luke 19.41–48 (– 20.8)*

As Jesus approached Jerusalem and saw the city, he wept over it and said, 'If you, even you, had only known on this day what would bring you peace – but now it is hidden from your eyes. The days will come upon you when your enemies will build an embankment against you and encircle you and hem you in on every side. They will dash you to the ground, you and the children within your walls. They will not leave one stone on another, because you did not recognize the time of God's coming to you.'

Then he entered the temple area and began driving out those who were selling. 'It is written,' he said to them, ' "My house will be a house of prayer"; but you have made it "a den of robbers".'

Every day he was teaching at the temple. But the chief priests, the teachers of the law and the leaders among the people were trying to kill him. Yet they could not find any way to do it, because all the people hung on his words.

Psalm 119.73–88 Genesis 37.1–28 Luke 22.24–53 (*or* 39–53)

Year 2

PSALM 18.18–26 (PB 17–25)

OLD TESTAMENT   *Genesis 7.17–24   (MP/EP   Isaiah 35)*

For forty days the flood kept coming on the earth, and as the waters increased they lifted the ark high above the earth. The waters rose and increased greatly on the earth, and the ark floated on the surface of the water. They rose greatly on the earth, and all the high mountains under the entire heavens were covered. The waters rose and covered the mountains to a depth of more than twenty feet. Every living thing that moved on the earth perished – birds, livestock, wild animals, all the creatures that swarm over the earth, and all mankind. Everything on dry land that had the breath of life in its nostrils died. Every living thing on the face of the earth was wiped out; men and animals and the creatures that move along the ground and the birds of the air were wiped from the earth. Only Noah was left, and those with him in the ark.

The waters flooded the earth for a hundred and fifty days.

EPISTLE   *1 John 3.1–10*

How great is the love the Father has lavished on us, that we should be called children of God! And that is what we are! The reason the world does not know us is that it did not know him. Dear friends, now we are children of God, and what we will be has not yet been made known. But we know that when he appears, we shall be like him, for we shall see him as he is. Everyone who has this hope in him purifies himself, just as he is pure.

Everyone who sins breaks the law; in fact, sin is lawlessness. But you know that he appeared so that he might take away our sins. And in him is no sin. No one who lives in him keeps on sinning. No one who continues to sin has either seen him or known him.

Dear children, do not let anyone lead you astray. He who does what is right is righteous, just as he is righteous. He who does what is sinful is of the devil, because the devil has been sinning from the beginning. The reason the Son of God appeared was to destroy the devil's work. No one who is born of God will continue to sin, because God's seed remains in him; he cannot go on sinning, because he has been born of God. This is how we know who the children of God are and who the children of the devil are: Anyone who does not do what is right is not a child of God; neither is anyone who does not love his brother.

GOSPEL* *Matthew 12.22–32 (MP/EP Luke 11.14–26)*

They brought Jesus a demon-possessed man who was blind and dumb, and Jesus healed him, so that he could both talk and see. All the people were astonished and said, 'Could this be the Son of David?'

But when the Pharisees heard this, they said, 'It is only by Beelzebub, the prince of demons, that this fellow drives out demons.'

Jesus knew their thoughts and said to them, 'Every kingdom divided against itself will be ruined, and every city or household divided against itself will not stand. If Satan drives out Satan, he is divided against himself. How then can his kingdom stand? And if I drive out demons by Beelzebub, by whom do your people drive them out? So then, they will be your judges. But if I drive out demons by the Spirit of God, then the kingdom of God has come upon you.

'Or again, how can anyone enter a strong man's house and carry off his possessions unless he first ties up the strong man? Then he can rob his house.

'He who is not with me is against me, and he who does not gather with me scatters. And so I tell you, every sin and blasphemy will be forgiven men, but the blasphemy against the Spirit will not be forgiven. Anyone who speaks a word against the Son of Man will be forgiven, but anyone who speaks against the Holy Spirit will not be forgiven, either in this age or in the age to come.'

Psalm 74   Amos 3   Matthew 26.31–56

4th SUNDAY BEFORE EASTER   LENT 3   *Violet*

The King and the Kingdom: Suffering

COLLECT

Lord God,
your Son Jesus Christ suffered
before he entered his glory:
Make us willing to deny ourselves,
take up the cross, and follow in his footsteps,
that we may share in his eternal joy;
who lives and reigns with you
and the Holy Spirit, now and for ever.   **Amen.**

Year 1

PSALM 119.97–104

OLD TESTAMENT   *Genesis 22.1–13   (MP/EP   Isaiah 59.9–20)*

The time came when God tested Abraham. He said to him,
'Abraham!' 'Here I am,' he replied.

Then God said, 'Take your son, your only son Isaac,
whom you love, and go to the region of Moriah. Sacrifice
him there as a burnt offering on one of the mountains I will
tell you about.'

Early the next morning Abraham got up and saddled his
donkey. He took with him two of his servants and his son
Isaac. When he had cut enough wood for the burnt offering,
he set out for the place God had told him about. On the third
day Abraham looked up and saw the place in the distance.
He said to his servants, 'Stay here with the donkey while I
and the boy go over there. We will worship and then we will
come back to you.'

Abraham took the wood for the burnt offering and placed
it on his son Isaac, and he himself carried the fire and the
knife. As the two of them went on together, Isaac spoke up
and said to his father Abraham, 'Father?'

'Yes, my son?' Abraham replied.

'The fire and wood are here,' Isaac said, 'but where is the
lamb for the burnt offering?'

Abraham answered, 'God himself will provide the lamb
for the burnt offering, my son.' And the two of them went

on together.

When they reached the place God had told him about, Abraham built an altar there and arranged the wood on it. He bound his son Isaac and laid him on the altar, on top of the wood. Then he reached out his hand and took the knife to slay his son. But the angel of the LORD called out to him from heaven, 'Abraham! Abraham!'

'Here I am,' he replied.

'Do not lay a hand on the boy,' he said, 'Do not do anything to him. Now I know that you fear God, because you have not withheld from me your son, your only son.'

Abraham looked up and there in a thicket he saw a ram caught by its horns. He went over and took the ram and sacrificed it as a burnt offering instead of his son.

EPISTLE *Colossians 1.24–29 (– 2.7)*

Now I rejoice in what was suffered for you, and I fill up in my flesh what is still lacking in regard to Christ's afflictions, for the sake of his body, which is the church. I have become its servant by the commission God gave me to present to you the word of God in its fulness – the mystery that has been kept hidden for ages and generations, but is now disclosed to the saints. To them God has chosen to make known among the Gentiles the glorious riches of this mystery, which is Christ in you, the hope of glory.

We proclaim him, admonishing and teaching everyone with all wisdom, so that we may present everyone perfect in Christ. To this end I labour, struggling with all his energy, which so powerfully works in me.

GOSPEL* *Luke 9.18–27*

Once when Jesus was praying in private and his disciples were with him, he asked them, 'Who do the crowds say I am?'

They replied, 'Some say John the Baptist; others say Elijah; and still others, that one of the prophets of long ago has come back to life.'

'But what about you?' he asked. 'Who do you say I am?'

Peter answered, 'The Christ of God.'

Jesus strictly warned them not to tell this to anyone. And he said, 'The Son of Man must suffer many things and be rejected by the elders, chief priests and teachers of the law, and he must be killed and on the third day be raised to life.'

Then he said to them all: 'If anyone would come after me, he must deny himself and take up his cross daily and follow me. For whoever wants to save his life will lose it, but whoever loses his life for me will save it. What good is it for a man to gain the whole world, and yet lose or forfeit his very self? If anyone is ashamed of me and my words, the Son of Man will be ashamed of him when he comes in his glory and in the glory of the Father and of the holy angels. I tell you the truth, some who are standing here will not taste death before they see the kingdom of God.'

Psalm 119.105–120   Exodus 5.1 – 6.1   Luke 22.54–71

Year 2

PSALM 115.1–7 (PB 1–8)

OLD TESTAMENT   *Genesis 12.1–9   (MP/EP   Isaiah 45.14–25)*

The LORD said to Abram, 'Leave your country, your people and your father's household and go to the land I will show you.

'I will make you into a great nation
and I will bless you;
I will make your name great,
and you will be a blessing.
I will bless those who bless you,
and whoever curses you I will curse;
and all peoples on earth
will be blessed through you.'

So Abram left, as the LORD had told him; and Lot went with him. Abram was seventy-five years old when he set out from Haran. He took his wife Sarai, his nephew Lot, all the possessions they had accumulated and the people they had acquired in Haran, and they set out for the land of Canaan, and they arrived there.

Abram travelled through the land as far as the site of the great tree of Moreh at Shechem. The Canaanites were then in the land, but the LORD appeared to Abram and said, 'To your offspring I will give this land.' So he built an altar there to the LORD, who had appeared to him.

From there he went on towards the hills east of Bethel and pitched his tent, with Bethel on the west and Ai on the east. There he built an altar to the LORD and called on the name of the LORD. Then Abram set out and continued towards the Negev.

EPISTLE   *1 Peter 2.19–25   (MP/EP   Acts 12.1–17a)*

It is commendable if a man bears up under the pain of unjust suffering because he is conscious of God. But how is it to your credit if you receive a beating for doing wrong and endure it? But if you suffer for doing good and you endure it, this is commendable before God. To this you were called, because Christ suffered for you, leaving you an example, that you should follow in his steps.

'He committed no sin,
and no deceit was found in his mouth.'

When they hurled their insults at him, he did not retaliate; when he suffered, he made no threats. Instead, he entrusted himself to him who judges justly. He himself bore our sins in his body on the tree, so that we might die to sins and live for righteousness; by his wounds you have been healed. For you were like sheep going astray, but now you have returned to the Shepherd and Overseer of your souls.

GOSPEL*   *Matthew 16.13–28*

When Jesus came to the region of Caesarea Philippi, he asked his disciples, 'Who do people say the Son of Man is?'

They replied, 'Some say John the Baptist; others say Elijah; and still others, Jeremiah or one of the prophets.'

'But what about you?' he asked. 'Who do you say I am?'

Simon Peter answered, 'You are the Christ, the Son of the living God.'

Jesus replied, 'Blessed are you, Simon son of Jonah, for this was not revealed to you by man, but by my Father in heaven. And I tell you that you are Peter, and on this rock I will build my church, and the gates of Hades will not overcome it. I will give you the keys of the kingdom of heaven; whatever you bind on earth will be bound in heaven, and whatever you loose on earth will be loosed in heaven.' Then he warned his disciples not to tell anyone that he was the Christ.

From that time on Jesus began to explain to his disciples that he must go to Jerusalem and suffer many things at the hands of the elders, chief priests and teachers of the law, and that he must be killed and on the third day be raised to life.

Peter took him aside and began to rebuke him. 'Never, Lord!' he said. 'This shall never happen to you!'

Jesus turned and said to Peter 'Out of my sight, Satan! You are a stumbling block to me; you do not have in mind the things of God, but the things of men.'

Then Jesus said to his disciples, 'If anyone would come after me, he must deny himself and take up his cross and follow me. For whoever wants to save his life will lose it, but whoever loses his life for me will find it. What good will it be for a man if he gains the whole world, yet forfeits his soul? Or what can a man give in exchange for his soul? For the Son of Man is going to come in his Father's glory with his angels, and then he will reward each person according to what he has done. I tell you the truth, some who are standing here will not taste death before they see the Son of Man coming in his kingdom.'

Psalm 31   Job 2   Matthew 26.57–75

3rd SUNDAY BEFORE EASTER   LENT 4 *Violet*

The King and the Kingdom: Transfiguration

COLLECT
Almighty Father,
whose Son was revealed in majesty
before he suffered death upon the cross:
Give us faith to perceive his glory,
that we may be strengthened to suffer with him,
and be changed into his likeness
from glory to glory;
who lives and reigns with you and the Holy Spirit,
one God, now and for ever.   **Amen.**

Year 1

PSALM 119.153–160

OLD TESTAMENT *Exodus 34.29–35 (1–5, 29–35)*

When Moses came down from Mount Sinai with the two tablets of the Testimony in his hands, he was not aware that his face was radiant because he had spoken with the LORD. When Aaron and all the Israelites saw Moses, his face was radiant, and they were afraid to come near him. But Moses called to them; so Aaron and all the leaders of the community came back to him, and he spoke to them.

Afterwards all the Israelites came near him, and he gave them all the commands the LORD had given him on Mount Sinai.

When Moses finished speaking to them, he put a veil over his face. But whenever he entered the LORD's presence to speak with him, he removed the veil until he came out. And when he came out and told the Israelites what he had been commanded, they saw that his face was radiant. Then Moses would put the veil back over his face until he went in to speak with the LORD.

EPISTLE *2 Corinthians 3.4–18 (1–18)*

This is our confidence through Christ before God. Not that we are competent to claim anything for ourselves, but our competence comes from God. He has made us competent as ministers of a new covenant – not of the letter but of the Spirit; for the letter kills, but the Spirit gives life.

Now if the ministry that brought death, which was engraved in letters on stone, came with glory, so that the Israelites could not look steadily at the face of Moses because of its glory, fading though it was, will not the ministry of the Spirit be even more glorious? If the ministry that condemns men is glorious, how much more glorious is the ministry that brings righteousness! For what was glorious has no glory now in comparison with the surpassing glory. And if what was fading away came with glory, how much greater is the glory of that which lasts!

Therefore, since we have such a hope, we are very bold. We are not like Moses, who would put a veil over his face to keep the Israelites from gazing at it while the radiance was

fading away. But their minds were made dull, for to this day
the same veil remains when the old covenant is read. It has
not been removed, because only in Christ is it taken away.
Even to this day when Moses is read, a veil covers their
hearts. But whenever anyone turns to the Lord, the veil is
taken away. Now the Lord is the Spirit, and where the Spirit
of the Lord is, there is freedom. And we, who with unveiled
faces all reflect the Lord's glory, are being transformed into
his likeness with ever-increasing glory, which comes from
the Lord, who is the Spirit.

GOSPEL* *Luke 9.28–36*

Jesus took Peter, John and James with him and went up on
to a mountain to pray. As he was praying, the appearance of
his face changed, and his clothes became as bright as a flash
of lightning. Two men, Moses and Elijah, appeared in glorious splendour, talking with Jesus. They spoke about his
departure, which he was about to bring to fulfilment at Jerusalem. Peter and his companions were very sleepy, but
when they became fully awake, they saw his glory and the
two men standing with him. As the men were leaving Jesus,
Peter said to him, 'Master, it is good for us to be here. Let us
put up three shelters – one for you, one for Moses and one
for Elijah.' (He did not know what he was saying.)

While he was speaking, a cloud appeared and enveloped
them, and they were afraid as they entered the cloud. A
voice came from the cloud, saying, 'This is my Son, whom I
have chosen; listen to him.' When the voice had spoken,
they found that Jesus was alone. The disciples kept this to
themselves, and told no one at that time what they had seen.

Psalm 119.161–176   Exodus 24   Luke 23.1–25

Year 2

PSALM 18.27–38 (PB 26–37)

OLD TESTAMENT   *Exodus 3.1–6   (MP/EP   1 Kings 19.1–18)*

Now Moses was tending the flock of Jethro his father-in-law,
the priest of Midian, and he led the flock to the far side of the
desert and came to Horeb, the mountain of God. There the
angel of the LORD appeared to him in flames of fire from

within a bush. Moses saw that though the bush was on fire it did not burn up. So Moses thought, 'I will go over and see this strange sight – why the bush does not burn up.'

When the LORD saw that he had gone over to look, God called to him from within the bush, 'Moses, Moses!'

And Moses said, 'Here I am.'

'Do not come any closer,' God said. 'Take off your sandals, for the place where you are standing is holy ground.' Then he said, 'I am the God of your father, the God of Abraham, the God of Isaac and the God of Jacob.' At this, Moses hid his face, because he was afraid to look at God.

EPISTLE *2 Peter 1.16–19 (1–19)*

We did not follow cleverly invented stories when we told you about the power and coming of our Lord Jesus Christ, but we were eye-witnesses of his majesty. For he received honour and glory from God the Father when the voice came to him from the Majestic Glory, saying, 'This is my Son, whom I love; with him I am well pleased.' We ourselves heard this voice that came from heaven when we were with him on the sacred mountain.

And we have the word of the prophets made more certain, and you will do well to pay attention to it, as to a light shining in a dark place, until the day dawns and the morning star rises in your hearts.

GOSPEL* *Matthew 17.1–13*

Jesus took with him Peter, James and John the brother of James, and led them up a high mountain by themselves. There he was transfigured before them. His face shone like the sun, and his clothes became as white as the light. Just then there appeared before them Moses and Elijah, talking with Jesus.

Peter said to Jesus, 'Lord, it is good for us to be here. If you wish, I will put up three shelters – one for you, one for Moses and one for Elijah.'

While he was still speaking, a bright cloud enveloped them, and a voice from the cloud said, 'This is my Son, whom I love; with him I am well pleased. Listen to him!'

When the disciples heard this, they fell face down to the ground, terrified. But Jesus came and touched them. 'Get up,' he said. 'Do not be afraid.' When they looked up, they saw no one except Jesus.

As they were coming down the mountain, Jesus instructed them, 'Do not tell anyone what you have seen, until the Son of Man has been raised from the dead.'

The disciples asked him, 'Why then do the teachers of the law say that Elijah must come first?'

Jesus replied, 'To be sure, Elijah comes and will restore all things. But I tell you, Elijah has already come, and they did not recognize him, but have done to him everything they wished. In the same way the Son of Man is going to suffer at their hands.' Then the disciples understood that he was talking to them about John the Baptist.

Psalm 23;27   Isaiah 52.13 – 53.6   Matthew 27.1–32

For Mothering Sunday readings, see page 752.

2nd SUNDAY BEFORE EASTER
LENT 5 (PASSION SUNDAY) *Violet*
The King and the Kingdom: Victory

COLLECT

Grant, O merciful Father,
that, as you saved mankind
by the cross and passion of your Son Jesus Christ;
so, trusting in the power of his sacrifice,
we may share in the glory of his victory;
through Jesus Christ our Lord.   **Amen.**

Year 1

PSALM 76.1–9

OLD TESTAMENT   *Exodus 6.2–13   (MP/EP   Isaiah 63.1–16)*

God said to Moses, 'I am the LORD. I appeared to Abraham, to Isaac and to Jacob as God Almighty, but by my name the LORD I did not make myself known to them. I also established my covenant with them to give them the land of Canaan, where they lived as aliens. Moreover, I have heard the groaning of the Israelites, whom the Egyptians are enslaving, and I have remembered my covenant.

'Therefore, say to the Israelites: "I am the LORD and I will bring you out from under the yoke of the Egyptians. I will free you from being slaves to them and will redeem you with an outstretched arm and with mighty acts of judgment. I will take you as my own people, and I will be your God. Then you will know that I am the LORD your God, who brought you out from under the yoke of the Egyptians. And I will bring you to the land I swore with uplifted hand to give to Abraham, to Isaac and to Jacob. I will give it to you as a possession. I am the LORD." '

Moses reported this to the Israelites, but they did not listen to him because of their discouragement and cruel bondage.

Then the LORD said to Moses, 'Go, tell Pharaoh king of Egypt to let the Israelites go out of his country.'

But Moses said to the LORD, 'If the Israelites will not listen to me, why would Pharaoh listen to me, since I speak with faltering lips?'

Now the LORD spoke to Moses and Aaron about the Israelites and Pharaoh king of Egypt, and he commanded them to bring the Israelites out of Egypt.

EPISTLE   *Colossians 2.8–15*

See to it that no one takes you captive through hollow and deceptive philosophy, which depends on human tradition and the basic principles of this world rather than on Christ.

For in Christ all the fulness of the Deity lives in bodily form, and you have been given fulness in Christ, who is the head over every power and authority. In him you were also circumcised, in the putting off of the sinful nature, not with a circumcision done by the hands of men but with the circumcision done by Christ, having been buried with him in baptism and raised with him through your faith in the power of God, who raised him from the dead.

When you were dead in your sins and in the uncircumcision of your sinful nature, God made you alive with Christ. He forgave us all our sins, having cancelled the written code, with its regulations, that was against us and that stood opposed to us; he took it away, nailing it to the cross. And having disarmed the powers and authorities, he made a public spectacle of them, triumphing over them by the cross.

GOSPEL* *John 12.20–32 (–36a)*

Now there were some Greeks among those who went up to worship at the Feast. They came to Philip, who was from Bethsaida in Galilee, with a request. 'Sir,' they said, 'we would like to see Jesus.' Philip went to tell Andrew; Andrew and Philip in turn told Jesus.

Jesus replied, 'The hour has come for the Son of Man to be glorified. I tell you the truth, unless an ear of wheat falls to the ground and dies, it remains only a single seed. But if it dies, it produces many seeds. The man who loves his life will lose it, while the man who hates his life in this world will keep it for eternal life. Whoever serves me must follow me; and where I am, my servant also will be. My Father will honour the one who serves me.

'Now my heart is troubled, and what shall I say? "Father, save me from this hour"? No, it was for this very reason I came to this hour. Father, glorify your name!'

Then a voice came from heaven, 'I have glorified it, and will glorify it again.' The crowd that was there and heard it said it had thundered; others said an angel had spoken to him.

Jesus said, 'This voice was for your benefit, not mine. Now is the time for judgment on this world; now the prince of this world will be driven out. But I, when I am lifted up from the earth, will draw all men to myself.'

Psalm 66   Lamentations 3.19–33   Luke 23.26–49

Year 2

PSALM 22.23–29 (PB 22–28)

OLD TESTAMENT   *Jeremiah 31.31–34 (27–37)*

'The time is coming,' declares the LORD,
'when I will make a new covenant
with the house of Israel
and with the house of Judah.
It will not be like the covenant
I made with their forefathers

when I took them by the hand
to lead them out of Egypt,
because they broke my covenant,
though I was a husband to them,'
declares the LORD.

'This is the covenant that I will make with the house of Israel
after that time,' declares the LORD.
'I will put my law in their minds
and write it on their hearts.
I will be their God,
and they will be my people.
No longer will a man teach his neighbour,
or a man his brother, saying, "Know the LORD,"
because they will all know me,
from the least of them to the greatest,'
declares the LORD.
'For I will forgive their wickedness
and will remember their sins no more.'

EPISTLE *Hebrews 9.11–14*

When Christ came as high priest of the good things that are
already here, he went through the greater and more perfect
tabernacle that is not man-made, that is to say, not a part of
this creation. He did not enter by means of the blood of goats
and calves; but he entered the Most Holy Place once for all
by his own blood, having obtained eternal redemption. The
blood of goats and bulls and the ashes of a heifer sprinkled
on those who are ceremonially unclean sanctify them so that
they are outwardly clean. How much more, then, will the
blood of Christ, who through the eternal Spirit offered
himself unblemished to God, cleanse our consciences from
acts that lead to death, so that we may serve the living God!

GOSPEL* *Mark 10.32–45*

Jesus and his disciples were on their way up to Jerusalem,
with Jesus leading the way, and the disciples were astonished, while those who followed were afraid. Again he took
the Twelve aside and told them what was going to happen to
him. 'We are going up to Jerusalem,' he said, 'and the Son of
Man will be betrayed to the chief priests and teachers of the
law. They will condemn him to death and will turn him over

to the Gentiles, who will mock him and spit on him, flog him and kill him. Three days later he will rise.'

Then James and John, the sons of Zebedee, came to him. 'Teacher,' they said, 'We want you to do for us whatever we ask.'

'What do you want me to do for you?' he asked.

They replied, 'Let one of us sit at your right and the other at your left in your glory.'

'You do not know what you are asking,' Jesus said. 'Can you drink the cup I drink or be baptized with the baptism I am baptized with?'

'We can,' they answered.

Jesus said to them, 'You will drink the cup I drink and be baptized with the baptism I am baptized with, but to sit at my right or left is not for me to grant. These places belong to those for whom they have been prepared.'

When the ten heard about this, they became indignant with James and John. Jesus called them together and said, 'You know that those who are regarded as rulers of the Gentiles lord it over them, and their high officials exercise authority over them. Not so with you. Instead, whoever wants to become great among you must be your servant, and whoever wants to be first must be slave of all. For even the Son of Man did not come to be served, but to serve, and to give his life as a ransom for many.'

Psalm 130;143.1–11   Isaiah 53.7–12   Matthew 27.33–54

PALM SUNDAY   LENT 6 *Violet or Red*

The Way of the Cross

COLLECT

Almighty and everlasting God,
in your tender love towards mankind
you sent your Son our Saviour Jesus Christ
to take our human nature,
and to suffer death upon the cross;
Grant that following the example
of his patience and humility
we may be made partakers of his resurrection;
through Jesus Christ our Lord.   **Amen.**

Years 1 and 2

PSALM 22.1–11 *or* 24 *or* 69.1–9 *or* 45.1–7 (PB 1–8)

OLD TESTAMENT *Isaiah 50.4–9a*

The Sovereign LORD has given me an instructed tongue,
to know the word that sustains the weary.
He wakens me morning by morning,
wakens my ear to listen like one being taught.
The Sovereign LORD has opened my ears,
and I have not been rebellious;
I have not drawn back.
I offered my back to those who beat me,
my cheeks to those who pulled out my beard;
I did not hide my face
from mocking and spitting.
Because the Sovereign LORD helps me,
I will not be disgraced.
Therefore have I set my face like flint,
and I know I will not be put to shame.
He who vindicates me is near.
Who then will bring charges against me?
Let us face each other!
Who is my accuser?
Let him confront me!
It is the Sovereign LORD who helps me.
Who is he that will condemn me?

or

Zechariah 9.9–12

Rejoice greatly; O Daughter of Zion!
Shout, daughter of Jerusalem!
See, your king comes to you,
righteous and having salvation,
gentle and riding on a donkey,
on a colt, the foal of a donkey.
I will take away the chariots from Ephraim
and the war-horses from Jerusalem,
and the battle-bow will be broken.
He will proclaim peace to the nations.
His rule will extend from sea to sea
and from the River to the ends of the earth.

443

As for you, because of the blood of my covenant with you,
I will free your prisoners from the waterless pit.
Return to your fortress, O prisoners of hope;
even now I announce that I will restore twice as much to
  you.

EPISTLE   *Philippians 2.5–11*

Your attitude should be the same as
that of Christ Jesus:
Who, being in very nature God,
did not consider equality with God something to be grasped,
but made himself nothing,
taking the very nature of a servant,
being made in human likeness.
And being found in appearance as a man,
he humbled himself
and became obedient to death –
even death on a cross!
Therefore God exalted him to the highest place
and gave him the name that is above every name,
that at the name of Jesus every knee should bow,
in heaven and on earth and under the earth,
and every tongue confess that Jesus Christ is Lord,
to the glory of God the Father.

or

1 Corinthians 1.18–25

The message of the cross is foolishness to those who are
perishing, but to us who are being saved it is the power of
God. For it is written:

'I will destroy the wisdom of the wise;
the intelligence of the intelligent I will frustrate.'

  Where is the wise man? Where is the scholar? Where is the
philosopher of this age? Has not God made foolish the
wisdom of the world? For since in the wisdom of God the
world through its wisdom did not know him, God was
pleased through the foolishness of what was preached to
save those who believe. Jews demand miraculous signs and
Greeks look for wisdom, but we preach Christ crucified: a
stumbling block to Jews and foolishness to Gentiles, but to

those whom God has called, both Jews and Greeks, Christ the power of God and the wisdom of God. For the foolishness of God is wiser than man's wisdom, and the weakness of God is stronger than man's strength.

GOSPEL* *Mark 14.32 – 15.41*

A shorter reading, Mark 15.1–41, may be used at Holy Communion when it is not desired to read the whole Passion.

Jesus and his disciples went to a place called Gethsemane, and Jesus said to his disciples, 'Sit here while I pray.' He took Peter, James and John along with him, and he began to be deeply distressed and troubled. 'My soul is overwhelmed with sorrow to the point of death,' he said to them. 'Stay here and keep watch.'

Going a little farther, he fell to the ground and prayed that if possible the hour might pass from him. '*Abba*, Father,' he said, 'everything is possible for you. Take this cup from me. Yet not what I will, but what you will.'

Then he returned to his disciples and found them sleeping, 'Simon,' he said to Peter, 'are you asleep? Could you not keep watch for one hour? Watch and pray so that you will not fall into temptation. The spirit is willing, but the body is weak.'

Once more he went away and prayed the same thing. When he came back, he again found them sleeping, because their eyes were heavy. They did not know what to say to him.

Returning the third time, he said to them, 'Are you still sleeping and resting? Enough! The hour has come. Look, the Son of Man is betrayed into the hands of sinners. Rise! Let us go! Here comes my betrayer!'

Just as he was speaking, Judas, one of the Twelve, appeared. With him was a crowd armed with swords and clubs, sent from the chief priests, the teachers of the law and the elders.

Now the betrayer had arranged a signal with them: 'The one I kiss is the man; arrest him and lead him away under guard.' Going at once to Jesus, Judas said, 'Rabbi!' and kissed him. The men seized Jesus and arrested him. Then one of those standing near drew his sword and struck the servant of the high priest, cutting off his ear.

'Am I leading a rebellion,' said Jesus, 'that you have come out with swords and clubs to capture me? Every day I was with you, teaching in the temple courts, and you did not arrest me. But the Scriptures must be fulfilled.' Then everyone deserted him and fled.

A young man, wearing nothing but a linen garment, was following Jesus. When they seized him, he fled naked, leaving his garment behind.

They took Jesus to the high priest, and all the other chief priests, elders and teachers of the law came together. Peter followed him at a distance right into the courtyard of the high priest. There he sat with the guards and warmed himself at the fire.

The chief priests and the whole Sanhedrin were looking for evidence against Jesus so that they could put him to death, but they did not find any. Many testified falsely against him, but their statements did not agree.

Then some stood up and gave this false testimony against him: 'We heard him say, "I will destroy this man-made temple and in three days will build another, not made by man." ' Yet even then their testimony did not agree.

Then the high priest stood up before them and asked Jesus, 'Are you not going to answer? What is this testimony that these men are bringing against you?' But Jesus remained silent and gave no answer.

Again the high priest asked him, 'Are you the Christ, the Son of the Blessed One?'

'I am,' said Jesus. 'And you will see the Son of Man sitting at the right hand of the Mighty One and coming on the clouds of heaven.'

The high priest tore his clothes. 'Why do we need any more witnesses?' he asked. 'You have heard the blasphemy. What do you think?'

They all condemned him as worthy of death. Then some began to spit at him; they blindfolded him, struck him with their fists, and said, 'Prophesy!' And the guards took him and beat him.

While Peter was below in the courtyard, one of the servant girls of the high priest came by. When she saw Peter warming himself, she looked closely at him.

'You also were with that Nazarene, Jesus,' she said.

But he denied it. 'I do not know or understand what

you are talking about,' he said, and went out into the entrance.

When the servant girl saw him there, she said again to those standing around, 'This fellow is one of them.' Again he denied it.

After a little while, those standing near said to Peter, 'Surely you are one of them, for you are a Galilean.'

He began to call down curses on himself, and he swore to them, 'I do not know this man you are talking about.'

Immediately the cock crowed the second time. Then Peter remembered the word Jesus had spoken to him: 'Before the cock crows twice you will disown me three times.' And he broke down and wept.

Very early in the morning, the chief priests, with the elders, the teachers of the law and the whole Sanhedrin, reached a decision. They bound Jesus, led him away and turned him over to Pilate.

'Are you the king of the Jews?' asked Pilate.

'Yes, it is as you say', Jesus replied.

The chief priests accused him of many things. So again Pilate asked him, 'Are you not going to answer? See how many things they are accusing you of.'

But Jesus still made no reply, and Pilate was amazed.

Now it was the custom at the Feast to release a prisoner whom the people requested. A man called Barabbas was in prison with the insurrectionists who had committed murder in the uprising. The crowd came up and asked Pilate to do for them what he usually did.

'Do you want me to release to you the king of the Jews?' asked Pilate, knowing it was out of envy that the chief priests had handed Jesus over to him. But the chief priests stirred up the crowd to have Pilate release Barabbas instead.

'What shall I do, then, with the one you call the king of the Jews?' Pilate asked them.

'Crucify him!' they shouted.

'Why? What crime has he committed?' asked Pilate.

But they shouted all the louder, 'Crucify him!'

Wanting to satisfy the crowd, Pilate released Barabbas to them. He had Jesus flogged, and handed him over to be crucified.

The soldiers led Jesus away into the palace (that is, the

Praetorium) and called together the whole company of soldiers. They put a purple robe on him, then wove a crown of thorns and set it on him. And they began to call out to him, 'Hail, King of the Jews!' Again and again they struck him on the head with a staff and spat on him. Falling on their knees, they worshipped him. And when they had mocked him, they took off the purple robe and put his own clothes on him. Then they led him out to crucify him.

A certain man from Cyrene, Simon, the father of Alexander and Rufus, was passing by on his way in from the country, and they forced him to carry the cross. They brought Jesus to the place called Golgotha (which means The Place of the Skull). Then they offered him wine mixed with myrrh, but he did not take it. And they crucified him. Dividing up his clothes, they cast lots to see what each would get.

It was the third hour when they crucified him. The written notice of the charge against him read: THE KING OF THE JEWS. They crucified two robbers with him, one on his right and one on his left. Those who passed by hurled insults at him, shaking their heads and saying, 'So! You who are going to destroy the temple and build it in three days, come down from the cross and save yourself!'

In the same way the chief priests and the teachers of the law mocked him among themselves. 'He saved others,' they said, 'but he cannot save himself! Let this Christ, this King of Israel, come down now from the cross, that we may see and believe.' Those crucified with him also heaped insults on him.

At the sixth hour darkness came over the whole land until the ninth hour. And at the ninth hour Jesus cried out in a loud voice, '*Eloi, Eloi, lama sabachthani?*' – which means, 'My God, my God, why have you forsaken me?'

When some of those standing near heard this, they said, 'Listen, he is calling Elijah.'

One man ran, filled a sponge with wine vinegar, put it on a stick, and offered it to Jesus to drink. 'Leave him alone now. Let us see if Elijah comes to take him down,' he said.

With a loud cry, Jesus breathed his last.

The curtain of the temple was torn in two from top to bottom. And when the centurion, who stood there in front of Jesus, heard his cry and saw how he died, he said, 'Surely this man was the Son of God!'

Some women were watching from a distance. Among them were Mary Magdalene, Mary the mother of James the younger and of Joses, and Salome. In Galilee these women had followed him and cared for his needs. Many other women who had come up with him to Jerusalem were also there.

or

Matthew 21.1–13

Jesus and his disciples approached Jerusalem, and when they came to Bethphage on the Mount of Olives, he sent two disciples, saying to them, 'Go to the village ahead of you, and at once you will find a donkey tied there, with her colt by her. Untie them and bring them to me. If anyone says anything to you, tell him that the Lord needs them, and he will send them right away.'

This took place to fulfil what was spoken through the prophet:

'Say to the Daughter of Zion,
"See, your king comes to you,
gentle and riding on a donkey,
on a colt, the foal of a donkey." '

The disciples went and did as Jesus had instructed them. They brought the donkey and the colt, placed their cloaks on them, and Jesus sat on them. A very large crowd spread their cloaks on the road, while others cut branches from the trees and spread them on the road. The crowds that went ahead of him and those that followed shouted,

'Hosanna to the Son of David!'

'Blessed is he who comes in the name of the Lord!'

'Hosanna in the highest!'

When Jesus entered Jerusalem, the whole city was stirred and asked, 'Who is this?'

The crowds answered, 'This is Jesus, the prophet from Nazareth in Galilee.'

Jesus entered the temple area and drove out all who were buying and selling there. He overturned the tables of the

449

money-changers and the benches of those selling doves. 'It is written,' he said to them, ' "My house will be called a house of prayer," but you are making it a "den of robbers".'

Year 1
Psalm 61;62   Jeremiah 7.1–11 *or* Exodus 11   Luke 19.29–48

Year 2
Psalm 22.1–22 (PB 1–21)   Isaiah 5.1–7   Mark 12.1–12

MONDAY IN HOLY WEEK   *Violet or Red*

COLLECT

Almighty God
whose most dear Son went not up to joy
but first he suffered pain,
and entered not into glory
before he was crucified:
Mercifully grant that we,
walking in the way of his cross,
may find it none other
than the way of life and peace;
through Jesus Christ our Lord.   **Amen.**

PSALM 55.1–8 (PB1–7) *or* 9–15 (PB8–15)

OLD TESTAMENT   *Isaiah 42.1–7*

'Here is my servant, whom I uphold,
my chosen one in whom I delight;
I will put my Spirit on him
and he will bring justice to the nations.
He will not shout or cry out,
or raise his voice in the streets.
A bruised reed he will not break,
and a smouldering wick he will not snuff out.
In faithfulness he will bring forth justice;
he will not falter or be discouraged
till he establishes justice on earth.
In his law the islands will put their hope.'

This is what God the LORD says–
he who created the heavens and stretched them out,
who spread out the earth and all that comes out of it,

who gives breath to its people,
and life to those who walk on it:
'I, the LORD, have called you in righteousness;
I will take hold of your hand.
I will keep you and will make you
to be a covenant for the people
and a light for the Gentiles,
to open eyes that are blind,
to free captives from prison
and to release from the dungeon those who sit in darkness.'

EPISTLE   *Hebrews 2.9–18*

We see Jesus, who was made a little lower than the angels, now crowned with glory and honour because he suffered death, so that by the grace of God he might taste death for everyone.

In bringing many sons to glory, it was fitting that God, for whom and through whom everything exists, should make the author of their salvation perfect through suffering. Both the one who makes men holy and those who are made holy are of the same family. So Jesus is not ashamed to call them brothers. He says,

'I will declare your name to my brothers;
in the presence of the congregation I will sing your praises.'

And again,

'I will put my trust in him.'

And again he says,

'Here am I, and the children God has given me.'

Since the children have flesh and blood, he too shared in their humanity so that by his death he might destroy him who holds the power of death – that is, the devil – and free those who all their lives were held in slavery by their fear of death. For surely it is not angels he helps, but Abraham's descendants. For this reason he had to be made like his brothers in every way, in order that he might become a merciful and faithful high priest in service to God, and that he might make atonement for the sins of the people. Because he himself suffered when he was tempted, he is able to help those who are being tempted.

Year 1

GOSPEL* *Matthew 26.1–30*

When Jesus had finished all he wanted to say, he told his disciples, 'As you know, the Passover is two days away – and the Son of Man will be handed over to be crucified.'

Then the chief priests and the elders of the people assembled in the palace of the high priest, whose name was Caiaphas, and they plotted to arrest Jesus in some sly way and kill him. 'But not during the Feast,' they said, 'or there may be a riot among the people.'

While Jesus was in Bethany in the home of a man known as Simon the Leper, a woman came to him with an alabaster jar of very expensive perfume, which she poured on his head as he was reclining at the table.

When the disciples saw this, they were indignant. 'Why this waste?' they asked. 'This perfume could have been sold at a high price and the money given to the poor.'

Aware of this, Jesus said to them, 'Why are you bothering this woman? She has done a beautiful thing to me. The poor you will always have with you, but you will not always have me. When she poured this perfume on my body, she did it to prepare me for burial. I tell you the truth, wherever this gospel is preached throughout the world, what she has done will also be told, in memory of her.'

Then one of the Twelve – the one called Judas Iscariot – went to the chief priests and asked, 'What are you willing to give me if I hand him over to you?' So they counted out for him thirty silver coins. From then on Judas watched for an opportunity to hand him over.

On the first day of the Feast of Unleavened Bread, the disciples came to Jesus and asked, 'Where do you want us to make preparations for you to eat the Passover?'

He replied, 'Go into the city to a certain man and tell him, "The Teacher says: My appointed time is near. I am going to celebrate the Passover with my disciples at your house." ' So the disciples did as Jesus had directed them and prepared the Passover.

When evening came, Jesus was reclining at the table with the Twelve. And while they were eating, he said, 'I tell you the truth, one of you will betray me.'

They were very sad and began to say to him one after the

other, 'Surely not I, Lord?'

Jesus replied, 'The one who has dipped his hand into the bowl with me will betray me. The Son of Man will go just as it is written about him. But woe to that man who betrays the Son of Man! It would be better for him if he had not been born.'

Then Judas, the one who would betray him, said, 'Surely not I, Rabbi?'

Jesus answered, 'Yes, it is you.'

While they were eating, Jesus took bread, gave thanks and broke it, and gave it to his disciples, saying, 'Take and eat; this is my body.'

Then he took the cup, gave thanks and offered it to them, saying, 'Drink from it, all of you. This is my blood of the covenant, which is poured out for many for the forgiveness of sins. I tell you, I will not drink of this fruit of the vine from now on until that day when I drink it anew with you in my Father's kingdom.'

When they had sung a hymn, they went out to the Mount of Olives.

Year 2

GOSPEL* *Luke 22.1–38*

Now the Feast of Unleavened Bread, called the Passover, was approaching, and the chief priests and the teachers of the law were looking for some way to get rid of Jesus, for they were afraid of the people. Then Satan entered Judas, called Iscariot, one of the Twelve. And Judas went to the chief priests and the officers of the temple guard and discussed with them how he might betray Jesus. They were delighted and agreed to give him money. He consented, and watched for an opportunity to hand Jesus over to them when no crowd was present.

Then came the day of Unleavened Bread on which the Passover lamb had to be sacrificed. Jesus sent Peter and John, saying, 'Go and make preparations for us to eat the Passover.'

'Where do you want us to prepare for it?' they asked.

He replied, 'As you enter the city, a man carrying a jar of water will meet you. Follow him to the house that he enters, and say to the owner of the house, "The Teacher asks:

Where is the guest room, where I may eat the Passover with my disciples?" He will show you a large upper room, all furnished. Make preparations there.'

They left and found things just as Jesus had told them. So they prepared the Passover.

When the hour came, Jesus and his apostles reclined at the table. And he said to them, 'I have eagerly desired to eat this Passover with you before I suffer. For I tell you, I will not eat it again until it finds fulfilment in the kingdom of God.'

After taking the cup, he gave thanks and said, 'Take this and divide it among you. For I tell you I will not drink again of the fruit of the vine until the kingdom of God comes.'

And he took bread, gave thanks and broke it, and gave it to them, saying, 'This is my body given for you; do this in remembrance of me.'

In the same way, after the supper he took the cup, saying, 'This cup is the new covenant in my blood, which is poured out for you. But the hand of him who is going to betray me is with mine on the table. The Son of Man will go as it has been decreed, but woe to that man who betrays him.' They began to question among themselves which of them it might be who would do this.

Also a dispute arose among them as to which of them was considered to be greatest. Jesus said to them, 'The kings of the Gentiles lord it over them; and those who exercise authority over them call themselves Benefactors. But you are not to be like that. Instead, the greatest among you should be like the youngest, and the one who rules like the one who serves. For who is greater, the one who is at the table or the one who serves? Is it not the one who is at the table? But I am among you as one who serves. You are those who have stood by me in my trials. And I confer on you a kingdom, just as my Father conferred one on me, so that you may eat and drink at my table in my kingdom and sit on thrones, judging the twelve tribes of Israel.

'Simon, Simon, Satan has asked to sift you as wheat. But I have prayed for you, Simon, that your faith may not fail. And when you have turned back, strengthen your brothers.'

But he replied, 'Lord, I am ready to go with you to prison and to death.'

Jesus answered, 'I tell you, Peter, before the cock crows today, you will deny three times that you know me.'

Then Jesus asked them, 'When I sent you without purse,

bag or sandals, did you lack anything?'

'Nothing,' they answered.

He said to them, 'But now if you have a purse, take it and also a bag; and if you do not have a sword, sell your cloak and buy one. It is written: "And he was numbered with the transgressors"; and I tell you that this must be fulfilled in me. Yes, what is written about me is reaching its fulfilment.'

The disciples said, 'See, Lord, here are two swords.'

'That is enough,' he replied.

Morning Prayer
Psalm 41   Lamentations 1.1–12a   John 14.1–14 (–31)

Evening Prayer
Psalm 25   Lamentations 2.8–19   John 14.15–31 *or* Galatians 6.11–18

TUESDAY IN HOLY WEEK   *Violet or Red*

COLLECT

O God, who by the passion of your blessed Son
made an instrument of shameful death
to be for us the means of life:
Grant us so to glory in the cross of Christ,
that we may gladly suffer pain and loss
for the sake of your Son our Saviour Jesus Christ;
who lives and reigns with you and the Holy Spirit,
one God, now and for ever.   **Amen.**

PSALM 55.18–26 (PB 17–25) *or* 13

OLD TESTAMENT   *Isaiah 49.1–6*

Listen to me, you islands;
hear this you distant nations:
Before I was born the LORD called me;
from my birth he has made mention of my name.
He made my mouth like a sharpened sword,
in the shadow of his hand he hid me;
he made me into a polished arrow
and concealed me in his quiver.
He said to me, 'You are my servant,
Israel, in whom I will display my splendour.'

But I said, 'I have laboured to no purpose;
I have spent my strength in vain and for nothing.
Yet what is due to me is in the LORD's hand,
and my reward is with my God.'

And now the LORD says —
he who formed me in the womb to be his servant
to bring Jacob back to him
and gather Israel to himself,
for I am honoured in the eyes of the LORD
and my God has been my strength —
he says:
'It is too small a thing for you to be my servant
to restore the tribes of Jacob
and bring back those of Israel I have kept.
I will also make you a light for the Gentiles,
that you may bring my salvation to the ends of the earth.'

EPISTLE *Hebrews 8.1–6*

The point of what we are saying is this: We do have such a high priest, who sat down at the right hand of the throne of the Majesty in heaven, and who serves in the sanctuary, the true tabernacle set up by the Lord, not by man.

Every high priest is appointed to offer both gifts and sacrifices and so it was necessary for this one also to have something to offer. If he were on earth, he would not be a priest, for there are already men who offer the gifts described by the law. They serve at a sanctuary that is a copy and shadow of what is in heaven. This is why Moses was warned when he was about to build the tabernacle: 'See to it that you make everything according to the pattern shown you on the mountain.' But the ministry Jesus has received is as superior to theirs as the covenant of which he is mediator is superior to the old one, and it is founded on better promises.

Year 1

GOSPEL* *Matthew 26.31–75*

Jesus said to his disciples, 'This very night you will all fall away on account of me, for it is written:

' "I will strike the shepherd,
and the sheep of the flock will be scattered."

But after I have risen, I will go ahead of you into Galilee.'

Peter replied, 'Even if all fall away on account of you, I never will.'

'I tell you the truth,' Jesus answered, 'this very night, before the cock crows, you will disown me three times.'

But Peter declared, 'Even if I have to die with you, I will never disown you.' And all the other disciples said the same.

Then Jesus went with his disciples to a place called Gethsemane, and he said to them, 'Sit here while I go over there and pray.' He took Peter and the two sons of Zebedee along with him, and he began to be sorrowful and troubled. Then he said to them, 'My soul is overwhelmed with sorrow to the point of death. Stay here and keep watch with me.'

Going a little farther, he fell with his face to the ground and prayed, 'My Father, if it is possible, may this cup be taken from me. Yet not as I will, but as you will.'

Then he returned to his disciples and found them sleeping. 'Could you men not keep watch with me for one hour?' he asked Peter. 'Watch and pray so that you will not fall into temptation. The spirit is willing, but the body is weak.'

He went away a second time and prayed, 'My Father, if it is not possible for this cup to be taken away unless I drink it, may your will be done.'

When he came back, he again found them sleeping, because their eyes were heavy. So he left them and went away once more and prayed the third time, saying the same thing.

Then he returned to the disciples and said to them, 'Are you still sleeping and resting? Look, the hour is near, and the Son of Man is betrayed into the hands of sinners. Rise, let us go! Here comes my betrayer!'

While he was still speaking, Judas, one of the Twelve, arrived. With him was a large crowd armed with swords and clubs, sent from the chief priests and the elders of the people. Now the betrayer had arranged a signal with them: 'The one I kiss is the man; arrest him.' Going at once to Jesus, Judas said, 'Greetings, Rabbi!' and kissed him.

Jesus replied, 'Friend, do what you came for.'

Then the men stepped forward, seized Jesus and arrested him. With that, one of Jesus' companions reached for his sword, drew it out and struck the servant of the high priest, cutting off his ear.

'Put your sword back in its place,' Jesus said to him, 'for all who draw the sword will die by the sword. Do you think I cannot call on my Father, and he will at once put at my disposal more than twelve legions of angels? But how then would the Scriptures be fulfilled that say it must happen in this way?'

At that time Jesus said to the crowd, 'Am I leading a rebellion, that you have come out with swords and clubs to capture me? Every day I sat in the temple courts teaching, and you did not arrest me. But this has all taken place that the writings of the prophets might be fulfilled.' Then all the disciples deserted him and fled.

Those who had arrested Jesus took him to Caiaphas, the high priest, where the teachers of the law and the elders had assembled. But Peter followed him at a distance, right up to the courtyard of the high priest. He entered and sat down with the guards to see the outcome.

The chief priests and the whole Sanhedrin were looking for false evidence against Jesus so that they could put him to death. But they did not find any, though many false witnesses came forward.

Finally two came forward and declared, 'This fellow said, "I am able to destroy the temple of God and rebuild it in three days." '

Then the high priest stood up and said to Jesus, 'Are you not going to answer? What is this testimony that these men are bringing against you?' But Jesus remained silent.

The high priest said to him, 'I charge you under oath by the living God: Tell us if you are the Christ, the Son of God.'

'Yes, it is as you say,' Jesus replied. 'But I say to all of you: In future you will see the Son of Man sitting at the right hand of the Mighty One and coming on the clouds of heaven.'

Then the high priest tore his clothes and said, 'He has spoken blasphemy! Why do we need any more witnesses? Look, now you have heard the blasphemy. What do you think?'

'He is worthy of death,' they answered.

Then they spat in his face and struck him with their fists. Others slapped him and said, 'Prophesy to us, Christ. Who hit you?'

Now Peter was sitting out in the courtyard, and a servant girl came to him. 'You also were with Jesus of Galilee,' she said.

But he denied it before them all. 'I do not know what you

are talking about,' he said.

Then he went out to the gateway, where another girl saw him and said to the people there, 'This fellow was with Jesus of Nazareth.'

He denied it again, with an oath: 'I do not know the man!'

After a little while, those standing there went up to Peter and said, 'Surely you are one of them, for your accent gives you away.'

Then he began to call down curses on himself and he swore to them, 'I do not know the man!'

Immediately a cock crowed.

Then Peter remembered the word Jesus had spoken: 'Before the cock crows, you will disown me three times.' And he went outside and wept bitterly.

Year 2

GOSPEL* *Luke 22.39–71*

Jesus went out as usual to the Mount of Olives, and his disciples followed him. On reaching the place, he said to them, 'Pray that you will not fall into temptation.' He withdrew about a stone's throw beyond them, knelt down and prayed, 'Father, if you are willing, take this cup from me; yet not my will, but yours be done.' An angel from heaven appeared to him and strengthened him. And being in anguish, he prayed more earnestly, and his sweat was like drops of blood falling to the ground.

When he rose from prayer and went back to the disciples, he found them asleep, exhausted from sorrow. 'Why are you sleeping?' he asked them. 'Get up and pray so that you will not fall into temptation.'

While he was still speaking a crowd came up, and the man who was called Judas, one of the Twelve, was leading them. He approached Jesus to kiss him, but Jesus asked him, 'Judas, are you betraying the Son of Man with a kiss?'

When Jesus' followers saw what was going to happen, they said, 'Lord, should we strike with our swords?' And one of them struck the servant of the high priest, cutting off his right ear.

But Jesus answered, 'No more of this!' And he touched the man's ear and healed him.

Then Jesus said to the chief priests, the officers of the

temple guard, and the elders, who had come for him, 'Am I leading a rebellion, that you have come with swords and clubs? Every day I was with you in the temple courts, and you did not lay a hand on me. But this is your hour – when darkness reigns.'

Then seizing him, they led him away and took him into the house of the high priest. Peter followed at a distance. But when they had kindled a fire in the middle of the courtyard and had sat down together, Peter sat down with them. A servant girl saw him seated there in the firelight. She looked closely at him and said, 'This man was with him.'

But he denied it. 'Woman, I do not know him,' he said.

A little later someone else saw him and said, 'You also are one of them.'

'Man, I am not!' Peter replied.

About an hour later another asserted, 'Certainly this fellow was with him, for he is a Galilean.'

Peter replied, 'Man, I do not know what you are talking about!' Just as he was speaking, the cock crowed. The Lord turned and looked straight at Peter. Then Peter remembered the word the Lord had spoken to him: 'Before the cock crows today, you will disown me three times.' And he went outside and wept bitterly.

The men who were guarding Jesus began mocking and beating him. They blindfolded him and demanded, 'Prophesy! Who hit you?' And they said many other insulting things to him.

At daybreak the council of the elders of the people, both the chief priests and teachers of the law, met together, and Jesus was led before them. 'If you are the Christ,' they said, 'tell us.'

Jesus answered, 'If I tell you, you will not believe me, and if I asked you, you would not answer. But from now on, the Son of Man will be seated at the right hand of the mighty God.'

They all asked, 'Are you then the Son of God?'

He replied, 'You are right in saying I am.'

Then they said, 'Why do we need any more testimony? We have heard it from his own lips.'

Morning Prayer
Psalm 27   Lamentations 3.1–18 (–30)   John 15.1–17 (–27)

Evening Prayer
Psalm 69.1–16   Lamentations 3.40–51   John 15.18–27 *or* Romans 5.6–11

WEDNESDAY IN HOLY WEEK   *Violet or Red*

COLLECT

Lord God,
whose blessed Son our Saviour
gave his back to the smiters,
and did not hide his face from shame:
Give us grace to endure
the sufferings of this present time,
with sure confidence in the glory that shall be revealed;
through Jesus Christ your Son our Lord.   **Amen.**

PSALM 54 *or* 102.1–11

OLD TESTAMENT   *Isaiah 50.4–9a*

The Sovereign LORD has given me an instructed tongue,
to know the word that sustains the weary.
He wakens me morning by morning,
wakens my ear to listen like one being taught.
The Sovereign LORD has opened my ears,
and I have not been rebellious;
I have not drawn back.
I offered my back to those who beat me,
my cheeks to those who pulled out my beard;
I did not hide my face from mocking and spitting.
Because the Sovereign LORD helps me,
I will not be disgraced.
Therefore have I set my face like flint,
and I know I will not be put to shame.
He who vindicates me is near.
Who then will bring charges against me?
Let us face each other!
Who is my accuser?
Let him confront me!
It is the Sovereign LORD who helps me.
Who is he that will condemn me?

EPISTLE   *1 Peter 2.19–25*

It is commendable if a man bears up under the pain of unjust
suffering because he is conscious of God. But how is it to
your credit if you receive a beating for doing wrong and

endure it? But if you suffer for doing good and you endure it, this is commendable before God. To this you were called, because Christ suffered for you, leaving you an example, that you should follow in his steps.

'He committed no sin,
and no deceit was found in his mouth.'

When they hurled their insults at him, he did not retaliate; when he suffered, he made no threats. Instead, he entrusted himself to him who judges justly. He himself bore our sins in his body on the tree, so that we might die to sins and live for righteousness; by his wounds you have been healed. For you were like sheep going astray, but now you have returned to the Shepherd and Overseer of your souls.

Year 1

GOSPEL* *Matthew 27.1–56*

Early in the morning, all the chief priests and the elders of the people came to the decision to put Jesus to death. They bound him, led him away and turned him over to Pilate, the governor.

When Judas, who had betrayed him, saw that Jesus was condemned, he was seized with remorse and returned the thirty silver coins to the chief priests and the elders. 'I have sinned,' he said, ' for I have betrayed innocent blood.'

'What is that to us?' they replied. 'That is your responsibility.'

So Judas threw the money into the temple and left. Then he went away and hanged himself.

The chief priests picked up the coins and said, 'It is against the law to put this into the treasury, since it is blood money.' So they decided to use the money to buy the potter's field as a burial place for foreigners. That is why it has been called the Field of Blood to this day. Then what was spoken by Jeremiah the prophet was fulfilled: 'They took the thirty silver coins, the price set on him by the people of Israel, and they used them to buy the potter's field, as the Lord commanded me.'

Meanwhile Jesus stood before the governor, and the governor asked him, 'Are you the king of the Jews?'

'Yes, it is as you say,' Jesus replied.

When he was accused by the chief priests and the elders, he gave no answer. Then Pilate asked him, 'Do you not hear how many things they are accusing you of?' But Jesus made no reply, not even to a single charge – to the great amazement of the governor.

Now it was the governor's custom at the Feast to release a prisoner chosen by the crowd. At that time they had a notorious prisoner, called Barabbas. So when the crowd had gathered, Pilate asked them, 'Which one do you want me to release to you: Barabbas, or Jesus who is called Christ?' For he knew it was out of envy that they had handed Jesus over to him.

While Pilate was sitting on the judge's seat, his wife sent him this message: 'Do not have anything to do with that innocent man, for I have suffered a great deal today in a dream because of him.'

But the chief priests and the elders persuaded the crowd to ask for Barabbas and to have Jesus executed.

'Which of the two do you want me to release to you?' asked the governor.

'Barabbas,' they answered.

'What shall I do, then, with Jesus who is called Christ?' Pilate asked.

They all answered, 'Crucify him!'

'Why? What crime has he committed?' asked Pilate.

But they shouted all the louder, 'Crucify him!'

When Pilate saw that he was getting nowhere, but that instead an uproar was starting, he took water and washed his hands in front of the crowd. 'I am innocent of this man's blood,' he said. 'It is your responsibility!'

All the people answered, 'Let his blood be on us and on our children!'

Then he released Barabbas to them. But he had Jesus flogged, and handed him over to be crucified.

Then the governor's soldiers took Jesus into the Praetorium and gathered the whole company of soldiers around him. They stripped him and put a scarlet robe on him, and then wove a crown of thorns and set it on his head. They put a staff in his right hand and knelt in front of him and mocked him. 'Hail, King of the Jews!' they said. They spat on him, and took the staff and struck him on the head again and again. After they had mocked him, they took off the robe and put his own clothes on him. Then they led him away to crucify him.

As they were going out, they met a man from Cyrene, named Simon, and they forced him to carry the cross. They came to a place called Golgotha (which means The Place of the Skull). There they offered him wine to drink, mixed with gall; but after tasting it, he refused to drink it. When they had crucified him, they divided up his clothes by casting lots. And sitting down, they kept watch over him there. Above his head they placed the written charge against him: THIS IS JESUS, THE KING OF THE JEWS. Two robbers were crucified with him, one on his right and one on his left. Those who passed by hurled insults at him, shaking their heads and saying, 'You who are going to destroy the temple and build it in three days, save yourself! Come down from the cross, if you are the Son of God!'

In the same way the chief priests, the teachers of the law and the elders mocked him. 'He saved others,' they said, 'but he cannot save himself! He is the king of Israel! Let him come down now from the cross, and we will believe in him. He trusts in God. Let God rescue him now if he wants him, for he said, "I am the Son of God." ' In the same way the robbers who were crucified with him also heaped insults on him.

From the sixth hour until the ninth hour darkness came over all the land. About the ninth hour Jesus cried out in a loud voice, '*Eloi, Eloi, lama sabachthani?*' – which means, 'My God, my God, why have you forsaken me?'

When some of those standing there heard this, they said, 'He is calling Elijah.'

Immediately one of them ran and got a sponge. He filled it with wine vinegar, put it on a stick, and offered it to Jesus to drink. But the rest said, 'Leave him alone. Let us see if Elijah comes to save him.'

And when Jesus had cried out again in a loud voice, he gave up his spirit.

At that moment the curtain of the temple was torn in two from top to bottom. The earth shook and the rocks split. The tombs broke open and the bodies of many holy people who had died were raised to life. They came out of the tombs, and after Jesus' resurrection they went into the holy city and appeared to many people.

When the centurion and those with him who were guarding Jesus saw the earthquake and all that had happened, they were terrified, and exclaimed, 'Surely he was the Son of God!'

Many women were there, watching from a distance. They had followed Jesus from Galilee to care for his needs. Among them were Mary Magdalene, Mary the mother of James and Joseph, and the mother of Zebedee's sons.

Year 2

GOSPEL* *Luke 23.1–49*

The whole company of the chief priests and teachers of the law arose and led Jesus off to Pilate. And they began to accuse him, saying, 'We have found this man subverting our nation. He opposes payment of taxes to Caesar and claims to be Christ, a king.'

So Pilate asked Jesus, 'Are you the king of the Jews?'

'Yes, it is as you say,' Jesus replied.

Then Pilate announced to the chief priests and the crowd, 'I find no basis for a charge against this man.'

But they insisted, 'He stirs up the people all over Judea by his teaching. He started in Galilee and has come all the way here.'

On hearing this, Pilate asked if the man was a Galilean. When he learned that Jesus was under Herod's jurisdiction, he sent him to Herod, who was also in Jerusalem at that time.

When Herod saw Jesus, he was greatly pleased, because for a long time he had been wanting to see him. From what he had heard about him, he hoped to see him perform some miracle. He plied him with many questions, but Jesus gave him no answer. The chief priests and the teachers of the law were standing there, vehemently accusing him. Then Herod and his soldiers ridiculed and mocked him. Dressing him in an elegant robe, they sent him back to Pilate. That day Herod and Pilate became friends – before this they had been enemies.

Pilate called together the chief priests, the rulers and the people, and said to them, 'You brought me this man as one who was inciting the people to rebellion. I have examined him in your presence and have found no basis for your charges against him. Neither has Herod, for he sent him back to us; as you can see, he has done nothing to deserve death. Therefore, I will punish him and then release him.'

With one voice they cried out, 'Away with this man! Release Barabbas to us!' (Barabbas had been thrown into prison for an insurrection in the city, and for murder.)

Wanting to release Jesus, Pilate appealed to them again. But they kept shouting, 'Crucify him! Crucify him!'

For the third time he spoke to them: 'Why? What crime has this man committed? I have found in him no grounds for the death penalty. Therefore I will have him punished and then release him.'

But with loud shouts they insistently demanded that he be crucified, and their shouts prevailed. So Pilate decided to grant their demand. He released the man who had been thrown into prison for insurrection and murder, the one they asked for, and surrendered Jesus to their will.

As they led him away, they seized Simon from Cyrene, who was on his way in from the country, and put the cross on him and made him carry it behind Jesus. A large number of people followed him, including women who mourned and wailed for him. Jesus turned and said to them, 'Daughters of Jerusalem, do not weep for me; weep for yourselves and for your children. For the time will come when you will say, "Blessed are the barren women, the wombs that never bore and the breasts that never nursed!" Then

' "they will say to the mountains, 'Fall on us!'
and to the hills, 'Cover us!' "'

'For if men do these things when the tree is green, what will happen when it is dry?'

Two other men, both criminals, were also led out with him to be executed. When they came to the place called The Skull, there they crucified him, along with the criminals – one on his right, the other on his left. Jesus said, 'Father, forgive them, for they do not know what they are doing.' And they divided up his clothes by casting lots.

The people stood watching, and the rulers even sneered at him. They said, 'He saved others; let him save himself if he is the Christ of God, the Chosen One.'

The soldiers also came up and mocked him. They offered him wine vinegar and said, 'If you are the king of the Jews, save yourself.'

There was a written notice above him, which read: THIS IS

THE KING OF THE JEWS.

One of the criminals who hung there hurled insults at him: 'Are you not the Christ? Save yourself and us!'

But the other criminal rebuked him. 'Do you not fear God,' he said, 'since you are under the same sentence? We are punished justly, for we are getting what our deeds deserve. But this man has done nothing wrong.'

Then he said, 'Jesus, remember me when you come into your kingdom.'

Jesus answered him, 'I tell you the truth, today you will be with me in paradise.'

It was now about the sixth hour, and darkness came over the whole land until the ninth hour, for the sun stopped shining. And the curtain of the temple was torn in two. Jesus called out with a loud voice, 'Father, into your hands I commit my spirit.' When he had said this, he breathed his last.

The centurion, seeing what had happened, praised God and said, 'Surely this was a righteous man.' When all the people who had gathered to witness this sight saw what took place, they beat their breasts and went away. But all those who knew him, including the women who had followed him from Galilee, stood at a distance, watching these things.

Morning Prayer
Psalm 31   Jeremiah 11.18–20   John 16.1–15 (–33)

Evening Prayer
Psalm 88   Isaiah 63.1–9   John 16.16–33 or Romans 5.12–19

MAUNDY THURSDAY

Violet or Red
White at Holy Communion

The Lord's Supper

COLLECTS

Almighty and heavenly Father,
we thank you that in this wonderful sacrament
you have given us the memorial
of the passion of your Son Jesus Christ:
Grant us so to reverence
the sacred mysteries of his body and blood,
that we may know within ourselves
and show forth in our lives
the fruits of his redemption;
who lives and reigns with you and the Holy Spirit,
one God, now and for ever. **Amen.**

Almighty God,
your Son Jesus Christ washed the disciples' feet:
Give us the will to be the servants of others
as he was the servant of all;
who gave up his life and died for us,
yet is alive and reigns with you and the Holy Spirit,
one God, now and for ever. **Amen.**

PSALM 116.11–18 (PB 11–16) *or* 26

OLD TESTAMENT *Exodus 12.1–14*

The LORD said to Moses and Aaron in Egypt, 'This month is
to be for you the first month, the first month of your year.
Tell the whole community of Israel that on the tenth day of
this month each man is to take a lamb for his family, one for
each household. If any household is too small for a whole
lamb, they must share one with their nearest neighbour,
having taken into account the number of people there are.
You are to determine the amount of lamb needed in accordance with what each person will eat. The animals you choose
must be year-old males without defect, and you may take
them from the sheep or the goats. Take care of them until the
fourteenth day of the month, when all the people of the
community of Israel must slaughter them at twilight.
Then they are to take some of the blood and put it on the

sides and tops of the door-frames of the houses where they eat the lambs. That night they are to eat the meat roasted over the fire, along with bitter herbs, and bread made without yeast. Do not eat the meat raw or cooked in water, but roast it over the fire – head, legs and inner parts. Do not leave any of it till morning; if some is left till morning, you must burn it. This is how you are to eat it: with your cloak tucked into your belt, your sandals on your feet and your staff in your hand. Eat it in haste; it is the LORD's Passover.

'On that same night I will pass through Egypt and strike down every firstborn – both men and animals – and I will bring judgment on all the gods of Egypt; I am the LORD. The blood will be a sign for you on the houses where you are; and when I see the blood, I will pass over you. No destructive plague will touch you when I strike Egypt.

'This is a day you are to commemorate; for the generations to come you shall celebrate it as a festival to the LORD – a lasting ordinance.'

EPISTLE* *1 Corinthians 11.23–29*

I received from the Lord what I also passed on to you: The Lord Jesus, on the night he was betrayed, took bread, and when he had given thanks, he broke it and said, 'This is my body, which is for you; do this in remembrance of me.' In the same way, after supper he took the cup, saying, 'This cup is the new covenant in my blood; do this, whenever you drink it, in remembrance of me.' For whenever you eat this bread and drink this cup, you proclaim the Lord's death until he comes.

Therefore, whoever eats the bread or drinks the cup of the Lord in an unworthy manner will be guilty of sinning against the body and blood of the Lord. A man ought to examine himself before he eats of the bread and drinks of the cup. For anyone who eats and drinks without recognizing the body of the Lord eats and drinks judgment on himself.

GOSPEL *John 13.1–15*

It was just before the Passover Feast. Jesus knew that the time had come for him to leave this world and go to the Father. Having loved his own who were in the world, he now showed them the full extent of his love.

The evening meal was being served, and the devil had

already prompted Judas Iscariot, son of Simon, to betray Jesus. Jesus knew that the Father had put all things under his power, and that he had come from God and was returning to God; so he got up from the meal, took off his outer clothing, and wrapped a towel round his waist. After that, he poured water into a basin and began to wash his disciples' feet, drying them with the towel that was wrapped around him.

He came to Simon Peter, who said to him, 'Lord, are you going to wash my feet?'

Jesus replied, 'You do not realize now what I am doing, but later you will understand.'

'No,' said Peter, 'you shall never wash my feet.'

Jesus answered, 'Unless I wash you, you have no part with me.'

'Then, Lord,' Simon Peter replied, 'not just my feet but my hands and my head as well!'

Jesus answered, 'A person who has had a bath needs only to wash his feet; his whole body is clean. And you are clean, though not every one of you.' For he knew who was going to betray him, and that was why he said not every one was clean.

When he had finished washing their feet, he put on his clothes and returned to his place. 'Do you understand what I have done for you?' he asked them. 'You call me "Teacher" and "Lord", and rightly so, for that is what I am. Now that I, your Lord and Teacher, have washed your feet, you also should wash one another's feet. I have set you an example that you should do as I have done for you.'

Morning Prayer
Psalm 39   Exodus 24.1–11   John 17

Evening Prayer
Psalm 42;43   Leviticus 16.2–24   John 13.16–35 *or* Ephesians 2.11–18

GOOD FRIDAY

The Death of Christ

COLLECT

Almighty Father,
look with mercy on this your family,
for which our Saviour Jesus Christ
was content to be betrayed,
and given up into the hands of wicked men,
and to suffer death on the cross;
who lives and reigns with you and the Holy Spirit,
one God, now and for ever.   **Amen.**

PSALM 22.14–22 (PB 14–21) *or* 69.17–23 (PB 17–22)

OLD TESTAMENT   *Isaiah 52.13 – 53.12*

See, my servant will act wisely;
he will be raised and lifted up and highly exalted.
Just as there were many who were appalled at him–
his appearance was so disfigured beyond that of any man
and his form marred beyond human likeness–
so will he sprinkle many nations,
and kings will shut their mouths because of him.
For what they were not told, they will see,
and what they have not heard, they will understand.

Who has believed our message
and to whom has the arm of the LORD been revealed?
He grew up before him like a tender shoot,
and like a root out of dry ground.
He had no beauty or majesty to attract us to him,
nothing in his appearance that we should desire him.
He was despised and rejected by men,
a man of sorrows, and familiar with suffering.
Like one from whom men hide their faces.

Surely he took up our infirmities
and carried our sorrows,
yet we considered him stricken by God,
smitten by him, and afflicted.
But he was pierced for our transgressions,
he was crushed for our iniquities;

the punishment that brought us peace was upon him,
and by his wounds we are healed.
We all, like sheep, have gone astray,
each of us has turned to his own way;
and the LORD has laid on him the iniquity of us all.

He was oppressed and afflicted,
yet he did not open his mouth;
he was led like a lamb to the slaughter,
and as a sheep before her shearers is silent,
so he did not open his mouth.
By oppression and judgment, he was taken away.
And who can speak of his descendants?
For he was cut off from the land of the living;
for the transgression of my people he was stricken.
He was assigned a grave with the wicked,
and with the rich in his death,
though he had done no violence,
nor was any deceit in his mouth.

Yet it was the LORD's will to crush him and cause him to
    suffer,
and though the LORD makes his life a guilt offering,
he will see his offspring and prolong his days,
and the will of the LORD will prosper in his hand.
After the suffering of his soul,
he will see the light of life and be satisfied;
by his knowledge my righteous servant will justify many,
and he will bear their iniquities.
Therefore I will give him a portion among the great,
and he will divide the spoils with the strong,
because he poured out his life unto death,
and was numbered with the transgressors.
For he bore the sin of many,
and made intercession for the transgressors.

EPISTLE *Hebrews 10.1–25 (or 12–22)*

The law is only a shadow of the good things that are coming
– not the realities themselves. For this reason it can never, by
the same sacrifices repeated endlessly year after year, make
perfect those who draw near to worship. If it could, would
they not have stopped being offered? For the worshippers
would have been cleansed once for all, and would no longer

have felt guilty for their sins. But those sacrifices are an annual reminder of sins, because it is impossible for the blood of bulls and goats to take away sins.

Therefore, when Christ came into the world, he said,

'Sacrifice and offering you did not desire,
but a body you prepared for me;
with burnt offerings and sin offerings
you were not pleased.
Then I said, "Here I am – it is written about me in the scroll –
I have come to do your will, O God." '

First he said, 'Sacrifices and offerings, burnt offerings and sin offerings you did not desire, nor were you pleased with them' (although the law required them to be made). Then he said, 'Here I am, I have come to do your will.' He sets aside the first to establish the second. And by that will, we have been made holy through the sacrifice of the body of Jesus Christ once for all.

Day after day every priest stands and performs his religious duties; again and again he offers the same sacrifices, which can never take away sins. But when this priest had offered for all time one sacrifice for sins, he sat down at the right hand of God. Since that time he waits for his enemies to be made his footstool, because by one sacrifice he has made perfect for ever those who are being made holy.

The Holy Spirit also testifies to us about this. First he says:

'This is the covenant I will make with them
after that time, says the Lord.
I will put my laws in their hearts,
and I will write them on their minds.'

Then he adds:

'Their sins and lawless acts
I will remember no more.'

And where these have been forgiven, there is no longer any sacrifice for sin.

Therefore, brothers, since we have confidence to enter the Most Holy Place by the blood of Jesus, by a new and living way opened for us through the curtain, that is, his body, and since we have a great priest over the house of God, let us draw near to God with a sincere heart in full assurance of faith, having our hearts sprinkled to cleanse us from a guilty conscience and having our bodies washed with pure water. Let us hold unswervingly to the hope we profess, for he who promised is faithful. And let us consider how we may spur one another on towards love and good deeds. Let us not give up meeting together, as some are in the habit of doing, but let us encourage one another – and all the more as you see the Day approaching.

or

Hebrews 4.14–16 and 5.7–9

Since we have a great high priest who has gone through the heavens, Jesus the Son of God, let us hold firmly to the faith we profess. For we do not have a high priest who is unable to sympathize with our weaknesses, but we have one who has been tempted in every way, just as we are – yet was without sin. Let us then approach the throne of grace with confidence, so that we may receive mercy and find grace to help us in our time of need.

During the days of Jesus' life on earth, he offered up prayers and petitions with loud cries and tears to the one who could save him from death, and he was heard because of his reverent submission. Although he was a son, he learned obedience from what he suffered and, once made perfect, he became the source of eternal salvation for all who obey him.

GOSPEL* *John 18.1–19.37 (or 19.1–37)*

When he had finished praying, Jesus left with his disciples and crossed the Kidron Valley. On the other side there was an olive grove, and he and his disciples went into it.

Now Judas, who betrayed him, knew the place, because Jesus had often met there with his disciples. So Judas came to the grove, guiding a detachment of soldiers and some officials from the chief priests and Pharisees. They were carrying torches, lanterns and weapons.

Jesus, knowing all that was going to happen to him, went out and asked them, 'Who is it you want?'

'Jesus of Nazareth,' they replied.

'I am he,' Jesus said. (And Judas the traitor was standing there with them.) When Jesus said, 'I am he,' they drew back and fell to the ground.

Again he asked them, 'Who is it you want?'

And they said, 'Jesus of Nazareth.'

'I told you that I am he,' Jesus answered. 'If you are looking for me, then let these men go.' This happened so that the words he had spoken would be fulfilled: 'I have not lost one of those you gave me.'

Then Simon Peter, who had a sword, drew it and struck the high priest's servant, cutting off his right ear. (The servant's name was Malchus.)

Jesus commanded Peter, 'Put your sword away! Shall I not drink the cup the Father has given me?'

Then the detachment of soldiers with its commander and the Jewish officials arrested Jesus. They bound him and brought him first to Annas, who was the father-in-law of Caiaphas, the high priest that year. Caiaphas was the one who had advised the Jews that it would be good if one man died for the people.

Simon Peter and another disciple were following Jesus. Because this disciple was known to the high priest, he went with Jesus into the high priest's courtyard, but Peter had to wait outside at the door. The other disciple, who was known to the high priest, came back, spoke to the girl on duty there and brought Peter in.

'Surely you are not another of this man's disciples?' the girl at the door asked Peter.

He replied, 'I am not.'

It was cold, and the servants and officials stood around a fire they had made to keep warm. Peter also was standing with them, warming himself.

Meanwhile, the high priest questioned Jesus about his disciples and his teaching.

'I have spoken openly to the world,' Jesus replied. 'I always taught in synagogues or at the temple, where all the Jews come together. I said nothing in secret. Why question me? Ask those who heard me. Surely they know what I said.'

When Jesus said this, one of the officials near by struck him in the face. 'Is that any way to answer the high priest?' he demanded.

'If I said something wrong,' Jesus replied, 'testify as to what is wrong. But if I spoke the truth, why did you strike me?' Then Annas sent him, still bound, to Caiaphas the high priest.

As Simon Peter stood warming himself, he was asked, 'Surely you are not another of his disciples?'

He denied it, saying, 'I am not.'

One of the high priest's servants, a relative of the man whose ear Peter had cut off, challenged him, 'Did I not see you with him in the olive grove?' Again Peter denied it, and at that moment a cock began to crow.

Then the Jews led Jesus from Caiaphas to the palace of the Roman governor. By now it was early morning, and to avoid ceremonial uncleanness the Jews did not enter the palace; they wanted to be able to eat the Passover. So Pilate came out to them and asked, 'What charges are you bringing against this man?'

'If he were not a criminal,' they replied, 'we would not have handed him over to you.'

Pilate said, 'Take him yourselves and judge him by your own law.'

'But we have no right to execute anyone,' the Jews objected. This happened so that the words Jesus had spoken indicating the kind of death he was going to die would be fulfilled.

Pilate then went back inside the palace, summoned Jesus and asked him, 'Are you the king of the Jews?'

'Is that your own idea,' Jesus asked, 'or did others talk to you about me?'

'Do you think I am a Jew?' Pilate replied, 'It was your people and your chief priests who handed you over to me. What is it you have done?'

Jesus said, 'My kingdom is not of this world. If it were, my servants would fight to prevent my arrest by the Jews. But now my kingdom is from another place.'

'You are a king, then!' said Pilate.

Jesus answered, 'You are right in saying I am a king. In fact, for this reason I was born, and for this I came into the world, to testify to the truth. Everyone on the side of truth listens to me.'

'What is truth?' Pilate asked. With this he went out again to the Jews and said, 'I find no basis for a charge against him. But it is your custom for me to release to you one prisoner at the time of the Passover. Do you want me to release "the king of the Jews"?'

They shouted back, 'No, not him! Give us Barabbas!' Now Barabbas had taken part in a rebellion.

Then Pilate took Jesus and had him flogged. The soldiers twisted together a crown of thorns and put it on his head. They clothed him in a purple robe and went up to him again and again, saying, 'Hail, O king of the Jews!' And they struck him in the face.

Once more Pilate came out and said to the Jews, 'Look, I am bringing him out to you to let you know that I find no basis for a charge against him.' When Jesus came out wearing the crown of thorns and the purple robe, Pilate said to them, 'Here is the man!'

As soon as the chief priests and their officials saw him, they shouted, 'Crucify! Crucify!'

But Pilate answered, 'You take him and crucify him. As for me, I find no basis for a charge against him.'

The Jews insisted, 'We have a law, and according to that law he must die, because he claimed to be the Son of God.'

When Pilate heard this, he was even more afraid, and he went back inside the palace. 'Where do you come from?' he asked Jesus, but Jesus gave him no answer. 'Do you refuse to speak to me?' Pilate said. 'Do you not realize I have power either to free you or to crucify you?'

Jesus answered, 'You would have no power over me if it were not given to you from above. Therefore the one who handed me over to you is guilty of a greater sin.'

From then on, Pilate tried to set Jesus free, but the Jews kept shouting, 'If you let this man go, you are no friend of Caesar. Anyone who claims to be a king opposes Caesar.'

When Pilate heard this, he brought Jesus out and sat down on the judge's seat at a place known as The Stone Pavement (which in Aramaic is Gabbatha). It was the day of Preparation of Passover Week, about the sixth hour.

'Here is your king,' Pilate said to the Jews.

But they shouted, 'Take him away! Take him away! Crucify him!'

'Shall I crucify your king?' Pilate asked.

'We have no king but Caesar,' the chief priests answered.

Finally Pilate handed him over to them to be crucified.

So the soldiers took charge of Jesus. Carrying his own cross, he went out to The Place of the Skull (which in Aramaic is called Golgotha). Here they crucified him, and with him two others – one on each side and Jesus in the middle.

Pilate had a notice prepared and fastened to the cross. It read, JESUS OF NAZARETH, THE KING OF THE JEWS. Many of the Jews read this sign, for the place where Jesus was crucified was near the city, and the sign was written in Aramaic, Latin and Greek. The chief priests of the Jews protested to Pilate, 'Do not write "The King of the Jews," but that this man claimed to be king of the Jews.'

Pilate answered, 'What I have written, I have written.'

When the soldiers crucified Jesus, they took his clothes, dividing them into four shares, one for each of them, with the undergarment remaining. This garment was seamless, woven in one piece from top to bottom.

'Let us not tear it,' they said to one another. 'Let us decide by lot who will get it.'

This happened that the Scripture might be fulfilled which said,

'They divided my garments among them
and cast lots for my clothing.'

So this is what the soldiers did.

Near the cross of Jesus stood his mother, his mother's sister, Mary the wife of Clopas, and Mary of Magdala. When Jesus saw his mother there, and the disciple whom he loved standing near by, he said to his mother, 'Dear woman, here is your son,' and to the disciple, 'Here is your mother.' From that time on, this disciple took her into his home.

Later, knowing that all was now completed, and so that the Scripture would be fulfilled, Jesus said, 'I am thirsty.' A jar of wine vinegar was there, so they soaked a sponge in it, put the sponge on a stalk of the hyssop plant, and lifted it to Jesus' lips. When he had received the drink, Jesus said, 'It is finished,' With that, he bowed his head and gave up his spirit.

Now it was the day of Preparation, and the next day was to be a special Sabbath. Because the Jews did not want the bodies left on the crosses during the Sabbath, they asked Pilate to have the legs broken and the bodies taken down.

The soldiers therefore came and broke the legs of the first man who had been crucified with Jesus, and then those of the other. But when they came to Jesus and found that he was already dead, they did not break his legs. Instead, one of the soldiers pierced Jesus' side with a spear, bringing a sudden flow of blood and water. The man who saw it has given testimony, and his testimony is true. He knows that he tells the truth, and he testifies so that you also may believe. These things happened so that the Scripture would be fulfilled, 'Not one of his bones will be broken,' and, as another Scripture says, 'They will look on the one they have pierced.'

Morning Prayer
Psalm 40 *or* 40.1–14   Genesis 22.1–18   John 18 *or* Mark 15.21–41

Evening Prayer
Psalm 130;143.1–11   Lamentations 5.15–22   John 19.38–42
or Colossians 1.18–23

EASTER EVE

COLLECT

Grant, Lord,
that we who are baptized
into the death of your Son Jesus Christ,
may die to sin, and be buried with him;
and that through the grave, and the gate of death,
we may come to our joyful resurrection;
through him who died and rose again for us,
our Lord and Saviour Jesus Christ.   **Amen.**

PSALM 16.8–11 (PB 9–12) *or* 23

OLD TESTAMENT   *Job 14.1–14*

Job said:
'Man born of woman
is of few days and full of trouble.
He springs up like a flower and withers away;
like a fleeting shadow, he does not endure.
Do you fix your eye on such a one?
Will you bring him before you for judgment?

479

Who can bring what is pure from the impure?
No one!
Man's days are determined;
you have decreed the number of his months
and have set limits he cannot exceed.
So look away from him and let him alone,
till he has put in his time like a hired man.

'At least there is hope for a tree:
If it is cut down, it will sprout again,
and its new shoots will not fail.
Its roots may grow old in the ground
and its stump die in the soil,
yet at the scent of water it will bud
and put forth shoots like a plant.
But man dies and is laid low;
he breathes his last and is no more.
As water disappears from the sea
or a river bed becomes parched and dry,
so man lies down and does not rise;
till the heavens are no more, men will not awake
or be roused from their sleep.

'If only you would hide me in the grave
and conceal me till your anger has passed!
If only you would set me a time
and then remember me!
If a man dies, will he live again?
All the days of my hard service
I will wait for my renewal to come.'

EPISTLE   *1 Peter 3.17–22*

It is better, if it is God's will, to suffer for doing good than for doing evil. For Christ died for sins once for all, the righteous for the unrighteous, to bring you to God. He was put to death in the body but made alive by the Spirit, through whom also he went and preached to the spirits in prison who disobeyed long ago when God waited patiently in the days of Noah while the ark was being built. In it only a few people, eight in all, were saved through water, and this water symbolizes baptism that now saves you also – not the removal of dirt from the body but the pledge of a good conscience towards God. It saves you by the resurrection of

Jesus Christ, who has gone into heaven and is at God's right hand – with angels, authorities and powers in submission to him.

GOSPEL* *Matthew 27.57–66*

As evening approached, there came a rich man from Arimathea, named Joseph, who had himself become a disciple of Jesus. Going to Pilate, he asked for Jesus' body, and Pilate ordered that it be given to him. Joseph took the body, wrapped it in a clean linen cloth, and placed it in his own new tomb that he had cut out of the rock. He rolled a big stone in front of the entrance to the tomb and went away. Mary Magdalene and the other Mary were sitting there across from the tomb.

The next day, the one after Preparation Day, the chief priests and the Pharisees went to Pilate. 'Sir,' they said, 'we remember that while he was still alive that deceiver said, "After three days I will rise again." So give the order for the tomb to be made secure until the third day. Otherwise, his disciples may come and steal the body and tell the people that he has been raised from the dead. This last deception will be worse than the first.'

'Take a guard,' Pilate answered. 'Go, make the tomb as secure as you know how.' So they went and made the tomb secure by putting a seal on the stone and posting the guard.

or
John 2.18–22

The Jews demanded of Jesus, 'What miraculous sign can you show us to prove your authority to do all this?'

Jesus answered them, 'Destroy this temple, and I will raise it again in three days.'

The Jews replied, 'It has taken forty-six years to build this temple, and you are going to raise it in three days?' But the temple he had spoken of was his body. After he was raised from the dead, his disciples recalled what he had said. Then they believed the Scripture and the words that Jesus had spoken.

Morning Prayer
Psalm 142   Hosea 6.1–6   1 Peter 4.1–6

Evening Prayer
Psalm 116   Job 19.21–27   1 John 5.5–12

EASTER DAY

White

The Resurrection of Christ

COLLECT

All praise to you, our God and Father,
you raised your Son in triumph from the grave
conquering sin and death,
and opening for all mankind the way to eternal life:
Grant us so to die daily to sin
that we may rise and live with him
in the joy of his resurrection;
who lives and reigns with you and the Holy Spirit,
one God, now and for ever.   **Amen.**

or

Almighty God,
who through your only begotten Son Jesus Christ
overcame death and opened to us
the gate of everlasting life:
Grant that we who celebrate with joy
the day of our Lord's resurrection
may be raised from the death of sin
by your life-giving Spirit;
through Jesus Christ our Lord
who lives and reigns with you and the Holy Spirit,
one God, now and for ever.   **Amen.**

Years 1 and 2

PSALM 118.14–24 *or* Easter Anthems *or* Psalm 114

OLD TESTAMENT   *Isaiah 12*

In that day you will say:

'I will praise you, O LORD.
Although you were angry with me,
your anger has turned away
and you have comforted me.
Surely God is my salvation;
I will trust and not be afraid.
The LORD, the LORD, is my strength and my song;
he has become my salvation.'

With joy you will draw water from the wells of salvation.

In that day you will say:

'Give thanks to the LORD, call on his name;
make known among the nations what he has done,
and proclaim that his name is exalted.
Sing to the LORD, for he has done glorious things;
let this be known to all the world.
Shout aloud and sing for joy, people of Zion,
for great is the Holy One of Israel among you.'

or

Exodus 14.15–22 (–31)

The LORD said to Moses, 'Why are you crying out to me? Tell the Israelites to move on. Raise your staff and stretch out your hand over the sea to divide the water so that the Israelites can go through the sea on dry ground. I will harden the hearts of the Egyptians so that they will go in after them. And I will gain glory through Pharaoh and all his army, through his chariots and his horsemen. The Egyptians will know that I am the LORD when I gain glory through Pharaoh, his chariots and his horsemen.'

Then the angel of God, who had been travelling in front of Israel's army, withdrew and went behind them. The pillar of cloud also moved from in front and stood behind them, coming between the armies of Egypt and Israel. Throughout the night the cloud brought darkness to the one side and light to the other; so neither went near the other all night long.

Then Moses stretched out his hand over the sea, and all that night the LORD drove the sea back with a strong east wind and turned it into dry land. The waters were divided, and the Israelites went through the sea on dry ground, with a wall of water on their right and on their left.

or

Isaiah 43.16–21

This is what the LORD says –
he who made a way through the sea,
a path through the mighty waters,
who drew out the chariots and horses,

the army and reinforcements together,
and they lay there, never to rise again,
extinguished, snuffed out like a wick:
'Forget the former things;
do not dwell on the past.
See, I am doing a new thing!
Now it springs up; do you not perceive it?
I am making a way in the desert
and streams in the wasteland.
The wild animals honour me, the jackals and the owls,
because I provide water in the desert
and streams in the wasteland,
to give drink to my people, my chosen,
the people I formed for myself
that they may proclaim my praise.'

EPISTLE   *Revelation 1.10–18*

On the Lord's Day, I, John, was in the Spirit, and I heard
behind me a loud voice like a trumpet, which said: 'Write on
a scroll what you see and send it to the seven churches: to
Ephesus, Smyrna, Pergamum, Thyatira, Sardis, Philadel-
phia and Laodicea.'

I turned round to see the voice that was speaking to me.
And when I turned I saw seven golden lampstands, and
among the lampstands was someone 'like a son of man,'
dressed in a robe reaching down to his feet and with a
golden sash round his chest. His head and hair were white
like wool, as white as snow, and his eyes were like blazing
fire. His feet were like bronze glowing in a furnace, and his
voice was like the sound of rushing waters. In his right hand
he held seven stars, and out of his mouth came a sharp
double-edged sword. His face was like the sun shining in all
its brilliance.

When I saw him, I fell at his feet as though dead. Then he
placed his right hand on me and said: 'Do not be afraid. I am
the First and the Last. I am the Living One; I was dead, and
behold I am alive for ever and ever! And I hold the keys of
death and Hades.'

or

1 Corinthians 15.12–20

If it is preached that Christ has been raised from the dead, how can some of you say that there is no resurrection of the dead? If there is no resurrection of the dead, then not even Christ has been raised. And if Christ has not been raised, our preaching is useless and so is your faith. More than that, we are then found to be false witnesses about God, for we have testified about God that he raised Christ from the dead. But he did not raise him if in fact the dead are not raised. For if the dead are not raised, then Christ has not been raised either. And if Christ has not been raised, your faith is futile; you are still in your sins. Then those also who have fallen asleep in Christ are lost. If only for this life we have hope in Christ, we are to be pitied more than all men.

But Christ has indeed been raised from the dead, the first fruits of those who have fallen asleep.

or

Colossians 3.1–11

Since, then, you have been raised with Christ, set your hearts on things above, where Christ is seated at the right hand of God. Set your minds on things above, not on earthly things. For you died, and your life is now hidden with Christ in God. When Christ, who is your life, appears, then you also will appear with him in glory.

Put to death, therefore, whatever belongs to your earthly nature: sexual immorality, impurity, lust, evil desires and greed, which is idolatry. Because of these, the wrath of God is coming. You used to walk in these ways, in the life you once lived. But now you must rid yourselves of all such things as these: anger, rage, malice, slander and filthy language from your lips. Do not lie to each other, since you have taken off your old self with its practices and have put on the new self, which is being renewed in knowledge in the image of its Creator. Here there is no Greek or Jew, circumcised or uncircumcised, barbarian, Scythian, slave or free, but Christ is all, and is in all.

GOSPEL*   *Matthew 28.1–10*

After the Sabbath, at dawn on the first day of the week, Mary Magdalene and the other Mary went to look at the tomb.

There was a violent earthquake, for an angel of the Lord came down from heaven and, going to the tomb, rolled back the stone and sat on it. His appearance was like lightning, and his clothes were white as snow. The guards were so afraid of him that they shook and became like dead men.

The angel said to the women, 'Do not be afraid, for I know that you are looking for Jesus, who was crucified. He is not here; he has risen, just as he said. Come and see the place where he lay. Then go quickly and tell his disciples: "He has risen from the dead and is going ahead of you into Galilee. There you will see him." Now I have told you.'

So the women hurried away from the tomb, afraid yet filled with joy, and ran to tell his disciples. Suddenly Jesus met them. 'Greetings,' he said. They came to him, clasped his feet and worshipped him. Then Jesus said to them, 'Do not be afraid. Go and tell my brothers to go to Galilee; there they will see me.'

or

John 20.1–10 (–18)

Early on the first day of the week, while it was still dark, Mary of Magdala went to the tomb and saw that the stone had been removed from the entrance. So she came running to Simon Peter and the other disciple, the one Jesus loved, and said, 'They have taken the Lord out of the tomb, and we do not know where they have put him!'

So Peter and the other disciple started for the tomb. Both were running, but the other disciple outran Peter and reached the tomb first. He bent over and looked in at the strips of linen lying there but did not go in. Then Simon Peter, who was behind him, arrived and went into the tomb. He saw the strips of linen lying there, as well as the burial cloth that had been around Jesus' head. The cloth was folded up by itself, separate from the linen. Finally the other disciple, who had reached the tomb first, also went inside. He saw and believed. (They still did not understand from Scripture that Jesus had to rise from the dead.)

Then the disciples went back to their homes.

or

Mark 16.1–8

When the Sabbath was over, Mary Magdalene, Mary the mother of James, and Salome bought spices so that they might go to anoint Jesus' body. Very early on the first day of the week, just after sunrise, they were on their way to the tomb and they asked each other, 'Who will roll the stone away from the entrance of the tomb?'

But when they looked up, they saw that the stone, which was very large, had been rolled away. As they entered the tomb, they saw a young man dressed in a white robe sitting on the right side, and they were alarmed.

'Do not be alarmed,' he said. 'You are looking for Jesus the Nazarene, who was crucified. He has risen! He is not here. See the place where they laid him. But go, tell his disciples and Peter, "He is going ahead of you into Galilee. There you will see him, just as he told you." '

Trembling and bewildered, the women went out and fled from the tomb. They said nothing to anyone, because they were afraid.

Morning Prayer
Psalm 113;114;117   Isaiah 12   Romans 6.3–14

Evening Prayer
Psalm 118   Exodus 14.5–31   John 20.11–23

MONDAY IN EASTER WEEK   *White*

COLLECT

Almighty God,
your Son Jesus Christ after his resurrection
appeared to his disciples on the Emmaus Road,
and made himself known in the breaking of bread:
Open our eyes that we may know him
in all his redeeming work;
who lives and reigns with you and the Holy Spirit,
one God, now and for ever.   **Amen**

EASTER ANTHEMS *or* TE DEUM Part 2

OLD TESTAMENT *Isaiah 42.10–16*

Sing to the LORD a new song,
his praise from the ends of the earth,
you who go down to the sea, and all that is in it,
you islands, and all who live in them.
Let the desert and its towns raise their voices;
let the settlements where Kedar lives rejoice.
Let the people of Sela sing for joy;
let them shout from the mountaintops.
Let them give glory to the LORD
and proclaim his praise in the islands.
The LORD will march out like a mighty man,
like a warrior he will stir up his zeal;
with a shout he will raise the battle cry
and will triumph over his enemies.

'For a long time I have kept silent.
I have been quiet and held myself back.
But now, like a woman in childbirth,
I cry out, I gasp and pant.
I will lay waste the mountains and hills
and dry up all their vegetation;
I will turn rivers into islands and dry up the pools.
I will lead the blind by ways they have not known,
along unfamiliar paths I will guide them;
I will turn the darkness into light before them
and make the rough places smooth.
These are the things I will do;
I will not forsake them.'

EPISTLE *1 Peter 1.1–12*

Peter, an apostle of Jesus Christ,

To God's elect, strangers in the world, scattered
throughout Pontus, Galatia, Cappadocia, Asia and Bithynia,
who have been chosen according to the foreknowledge of
God the Father, by the sanctifying work of the Spirit, for
obedience to Jesus Christ and sprinkling by his blood:

Grace and peace be yours in abundance.

Praise be to the God and Father of our Lord Jesus Christ!
In his great mercy he has given us new birth into a living
hope through the resurrection of Jesus Christ from the dead,
and into an inheritance that can never perish, spoil or fade –

kept in heaven for you, who through faith are shielded by God's power until the coming of the salvation that is ready to be revealed in the last time. In this you greatly rejoice, though now for a little while you may have had to suffer grief in all kinds of trials. These have come so that your faith – of greater worth than gold, which perishes even though refined by fire – may be proved genuine and may result in praise, glory and honour when Jesus Christ is revealed. Though you have not seen him, you love him; and even though you do not see him now, you believe in him and are filled with an inexpressible and glorious joy, for you are receiving the goal of your faith, the salvation of your souls.

Concerning this salvation, the prophets, who spoke of the grace that was to come to you, searched intently and with the greatest care, trying to find out the time and circumstances to which the Spirit of Christ in them was pointing when he predicted the sufferings of Christ and the glories that would follow. It was revealed to them that they were not serving themselves but you, when they spoke of the things that have now been told you by those who have preached the gospel to you by the Holy Spirit sent from heaven. Even angels long to look into these things.

GOSPEL* *Luke 24.13–35*

Now that same day two of the disciples were going to a village called Emmaus, about seven miles from Jerusalem. They were talking with each other about everything that had happened. As they talked and discussed these things with each other, Jesus himself came up and walked along with them; but they were kept from recognizing him.

He asked them, 'What are you discussing together as you walk along?'

They stood still, their faces downcast. One of them, named Cleopas, asked him, 'Are you the only one living in Jerusalem who does not know the things that have happened there in these days?'

'What things?' he asked.

'About Jesus of Nazareth,' they replied. 'He was a prophet, powerful in word and deed before God and all the people. The chief priests and our rulers handed him over to be sentenced to death, and they crucified him; but we had hoped that he was the one who was going to redeem Israel.

And what is more, it is the third day since all this took place. In addition, some of our women amazed us. They went to the tomb early this morning but did not find his body. They came and told us that they had seen a vision of angels, who said he was alive. Then some of our companions went to the tomb and found it just as the women had said, but him they did not see.'

He said to them, 'How foolish you are, and how slow of heart to believe all that the prophets have spoken! Did not the Christ have to suffer these things and then enter his glory?' And beginning with Moses and all the Prophets, he explained to them what was said in all the Scriptures concerning himself.

As they approached the village to which they were going, Jesus acted as if he were going further. But they urged him strongly, 'Stay with us, for it is nearly evening; the day is almost over.' So he went in to stay with them.

When he was at the table with them, he took bread, gave thanks, broke it and began to give it to them. Then their eyes were opened and they recognized him, and he disappeared from their sight. They asked each other, 'Were not our hearts burning within us while he talked with us on the road and opened the Scriptures to us?'

They got up and returned at once to Jerusalem. There they found the Eleven and those with them, assembled together and saying, 'It is true! The Lord has risen and has appeared to Simon.' Then the two told what had happened on the way, and how Jesus was recognized by them when he broke the bread.

Morning Prayer
Psalm 120;121   Exodus 12.14–36   Colossians 3.1–11

Evening Prayer
Psalm 122;123   Isaiah 25.1–9   Luke 24.1–12

TUESDAY IN EASTER WEEK *White*

PSALM 16.8–11 (PB 8–12) *or* 30

OLD TESTAMENT *Micah 7.7–20*

I keep watch for the LORD
I wait in hope for God my Saviour;
my God will hear me.
Do not gloat over me, my enemy!
Though I have fallen, I will rise.
Though I sit in darkness,
the LORD will be my light.
Because I have sinned against him,
I will bear the LORD's wrath,
until he pleads my case
and establishes my right.
He will bring me out into the light;
I will see his justice.
Then my enemy will see it and will be covered with shame,
she who said to me,
'Where is the LORD your God?'
My eyes will see her downfall;
even now she will be trampled underfoot
like mire in the streets.
The day for building your walls will come,
the day for extending your boundaries.
In that day people will come to you
from Assyria and the cities of Egypt,
even from Egypt to the Euphrates
and from sea to sea
and from mountain to mountain.
The earth will become desolate because of its inhabitants,
as the result of their deeds.

Shepherd your people with your staff,
the flock of your inheritance,
which lives by itself in a forest,
in fertile pasture-lands.
Let them feed in Bashan and Gilead
as in days long ago.
'As in the days when you came out of Egypt,
I will show them my wonders.'

Nations will see and be ashamed,
deprived of all their power.
They will lay their hands on their mouths
and their ears will become deaf.
They will lick dust like a snake,
like creatures that crawl on the ground.
They will come trembling out of their dens;
they will turn in fear to the LORD our God
and will be afraid of you.
Who is a God like you,
who pardons sin and forgives the transgression
of the remnant of his inheritance?
You do not stay angry for ever
but delight to show mercy.
You will again have compassion on us;
you will tread our sins underfoot
and hurl all our iniquities into the depths of the sea.
You will be true to Jacob,
and show mercy to Abraham,
as you pledged on oath to our fathers
in days long ago.

EPISTLE   *1 Peter 1.13–25*

Prepare your minds for action; be self-controlled; set your hope fully on the grace to be given you when Jesus Christ is revealed. As obedient children, do not conform to the evil desires you had when you lived in ignorance. But just as he who called you is holy, so be holy in all you do; for it is written, 'Be holy, because I am holy.'

Since you call on a Father who judges each man's work impartially, live your lives as strangers here in reverent fear. For you know that it was not with perishable things such as silver or gold that you were redeemed from the empty way of life handed down to you from your forefathers, but with the precious blood of Christ, a lamb without blemish or defect. He was chosen before the creation of the world, but was revealed in these last times for your sake. Through him you believed in God, who raised him from the dead and glorified him, and so your faith and hope are in God.

Now that you have purified yourselves by obeying the truth so that you have sincere love for your brothers, love one another deeply, from the heart. For you have been born again, not of perishable seed, but of imperishable, through the living and enduring word of God. For,

'All men are like grass,
and all their glory is like the flowers of the field;
the grass withers and the flowers fall,
but the word of the Lord stands for ever.'

And this is the word that was preached to you.

GOSPEL* *Luke 24.36–49*

Jesus himself stood among the disciples and said to them, 'Peace be with you.'

They were startled and frightened, thinking they saw a ghost. He said to them, 'Why are you troubled, and why do doubts rise in your minds? Look at my hands and my feet. It is I myself! Touch me and see; a ghost does not have flesh and bones, as you see I have.'

When he had said this, he showed them his hands and feet. And while they still did not believe it because of joy and amazement, he asked them, 'Do you have anything here to eat?' They gave him a piece of broiled fish, and he took it and ate it in their presence.

He said to them, 'This is what I told you while I was still with you: Everything must be fulfilled that is written about me in the Law of Moses, the Prophets and the Psalms.'

Then he opened their minds so that they could understand the Scriptures. He told them, 'This is what is written: The Christ will suffer and rise from the dead on the third day, and repentance and forgiveness of sins will be preached in his name to all nations, beginning at Jerusalem. You are witnesses of these things. I am going to send you what my Father has promised; but stay in the city until you have been clothed with power from on high.'

Morning Prayer
Psalm 124;125   Exodus 12.37–51   Matthew 28.1–15

Evening Prayer
Psalm 126;127   Isaiah 26.1–19   Philippians 1.19–26

WEDNESDAY IN EASTER WEEK *White*

PSALM 111 *or* 112

OLD TESTAMENT *1 Kings 17.17–24*

The son of the woman who owned the house in Zarephath became ill. He grew worse and worse, and finally stopped breathing. She said to Elijah, 'What do you have against me, man of God? Did you come to remind me of my sin and kill my son?'

'Give me your son,' Elijah replied. He took him from her arms, carried him to the upper room where he was staying, and laid him on his bed. Then he cried out to the LORD, 'O LORD my God, have you brought tragedy also upon this widow I am staying with, by causing her son to die?' Then he stretched himself out on the boy three times and cried to the LORD, 'O LORD my God, let this boy's life return to him!'

The LORD heard Elijah's cry, and the boy's life returned to him, and he lived. Elijah picked up the child and carried him down from the room into the house. He gave him to his mother and said, 'Look, your son is alive!'

Then the woman said to Elijah, 'Now I know that you are a man of God and that the word of the LORD from your mouth is the truth.'

EPISTLE *1 Peter 2.1–10*

Rid yourselves of all malice and all deceit, hypocrisy, envy, and slander of every kind. Like newborn babies, crave pure spiritual milk, so that by it you may grow up in your salvation, now that you have tasted that the Lord is good.

As you come to him, the living Stone – rejected by men but chosen by God and precious to him – you also, like living stones, are being built into a spiritual house to be a holy priesthood, offering spiritual sacrifices acceptable to God through Jesus Christ. For in Scripture it says:

'See, I lay a stone in Zion,
a chosen and precious corner stone,
and the one who trusts in him
will never be put to shame.'

Now to you who believe, this stone is precious. But to those who do not believe,

'The stone the builders rejected
has become the capstone,'

and,

'A stone that causes men to stumble
and a rock that makes them fall.'

They stumble because they disobey the message – which is also what they were destined for.

But you are a chosen people, a royal priesthood, a holy nation, a people belonging to God, that you may declare the praises of him who called you out of darkness into his wonderful light. Once you were not a people, but now you are the people of God; once you had not received mercy, but now you have received mercy.

GOSPEL* *John 20.24–31*

Thomas (called Didymus), one of the Twelve, was not with the disciples when Jesus came. When the other disciples told him that they had seen the Lord, he declared, 'Unless I see the nail marks in his hands and put my finger where the nails were, and put my hand into his side, I will not believe it.'

A week later his disciples were in the house again, and Thomas was with them. Though the doors were locked, Jesus came and stood among them, and said, 'Peace be with you!' Then he said to Thomas, 'Put your finger here; see my hands. Reach out your hand and put it into my side. Stop doubting and believe.'

Thomas answered, 'My Lord and my God!'

Then Jesus told him, 'Because you have seen me, you have believed; blessed are those who have not seen and yet have believed.'

Jesus did many other miraculous signs in the presence of his disciples, which are not recorded in this book. But these are written that you may believe that Jesus is the Christ, the Son of God, and that by believing you may have life in his name.

Morning Prayer
Psalm 128;129   Exodus 13.1–16   Matthew 28.16–20

Evening Prayer
Psalm 130;131   Isaiah 61   1 Thessalonians 4.13–18

THURSDAY IN EASTER WEEK

PSALM 113 *or* **114**

OLD TESTAMENT *Jeremiah 31.1–14*

'At that time,' declares the LORD, 'I will be the God of all the clans of Israel, and they will be my people.'

This is what the LORD says:

'The people who survive the sword
will find favour in the desert;
I will come to give rest to Israel.'

The LORD appeared to us in the past, saying:

'I have loved you with an everlasting love;
I have drawn you with loving-kindness.
I will build you up again
and you will be rebuilt, O Virgin Israel.
Again you will take up your tambourines
and go out to dance with the joyful.
Again you will plant vineyards
on the hills of Samaria;
the farmers will plant them
and enjoy their fruit.
There will be a day when watchmen cry out
on the hills of Ephraim,
"Come, let us go up to Zion,
to the LORD our God." '

This is what the LORD says:

'Sing with joy for Jacob;
shout for the greatest of the nations.
Make your praises heard, and say,
"O LORD, save your people,
the remnant of Israel."
See, I will bring them from the land of the north
and gather them from the ends of the earth.
Among them will be the blind and the lame,
expectant mothers and women in labour;
a great throng will return.
They will come with weeping;
they will pray as I bring them back.
I will lead them beside streams of water

on a level path where they will not stumble,
because I am Israel's father,
and Ephraim is my firstborn son.

'Hear the word of the LORD O nations;
proclaim it in distant coastlands:
"He who scattered Israel will gather them
and will watch over his flock like a shepherd."
For the LORD will ransom Jacob
and redeem them from the hand of those stronger than they.
They will come and shout for joy on the heights of Zion;
they will rejoice in the bounty of the LORD –
the corn, the new wine and the oil,
the young of the flocks and herds.
They will be like a well-watered garden,
and they will sorrow no more.
Then maidens will dance and be glad,
young men and old as well.
I will turn their mourning into gladness;
I will give them comfort and joy instead of sorrow.
I will satisfy the priests with abundance,
and my people will be filled with my bounty,'

declares the LORD.

EPISTLE   *1 Peter 2.11–25*

Dear friends, I urge you, as aliens and strangers in the world, to abstain from sinful desires, which war against your soul. Live such good lives among the pagans that, though they accuse you of doing wrong, they may see your good deeds and glorify God on the day he visits us.

Submit yourselves for the Lord's sake to every authority instituted among men: whether to the king, as the supreme authority, or to governors, who are sent by him to punish those who do wrong and to commend those who do right. For it is God's will that by doing good you should silence the ignorant talk of foolish men. Live as free men, but do not use your freedom as a cover-up for evil; live as servants of God. Show proper respect to everyone: Love the brotherhood of believers, fear God, honour the king.

Slaves, submit yourselves to your masters with all respect, not only to those who are good and considerate, but also to those who are harsh. For it is commendable if a man bears up under the pain of unjust suffering because he is conscious of God. But how is it to your credit if you receive a beating for doing wrong and endure it? But if you suffer for doing good and you endure it, this is commendable before God. To this you were called, because Christ suffered for you, leaving you an example, that you should follow in his steps.

'He committed no sin,
and no deceit was found in his mouth.'

When they hurled their insults at him, he did not retaliate; when he suffered, he made no threats. Instead, he entrusted himself to him who judges justly. He himself bore our sins in his body on the tree, so that we might die to sins and live for righteousness; by his wounds you have been healed. For you were like sheep going astray, but now you have returned to the Shepherd and Overseer of your souls.

GOSPEL* *John 21.1–14*

Jesus appeared again to his disciples by the Sea of Tiberias. It happened this way: Simon Peter, Thomas (called Didymus), Nathanael from Cana in Galilee, the sons of Zebedee, and two other disciples were together. 'I am going out to fish,' Simon Peter told them, and they said, 'We will go with you.' So they went out and got into the boat, but that night they caught nothing.

Early in the morning, Jesus stood on the shore, but the disciples did not realize that it was Jesus.

He called out to them, 'Friends, have you not any fish?'

'No,' they answered.

He said, 'Throw your net on the right side of the boat and you will find some.' When they did, they were unable to haul the net in because of the large number of fish.

Then the disciple whom Jesus loved said to Peter, 'It is the Lord!' As soon as Simon Peter heard him say, 'It is the Lord,' he wrapped his outer garment around him (for he had taken it off) and jumped into the water. The other disciples followed in the boat, towing the net full of fish, for they were not far from shore, about a hundred yards. When they landed, they saw a fire of burning coals there with fish on it, and some bread.

Jesus said to them, 'Bring some of the fish you have just caught.'

Simon Peter climbed aboard and dragged the net ashore. It was full of large fish, one hundred and fifty-three of them, but even with so many the net was not torn. Jesus said to them, 'Come and have breakfast.' None of the disciples dared ask him, 'Who are you?' They knew it was the Lord. Jesus came, took the bread and gave it to them, and did the same with the fish. This was now the third time Jesus appeared to his disciples after he was raised from the dead.

Morning Prayer
Psalm 132   Exodus 13.17–14.14   Revelation 7.9–17

Evening Prayer
Psalm 133;134   Song of Solomon 2.8–17   Mark 16

FRIDAY IN EASTER WEEK   *White*

PSALM 115 *or* 116.1–9

OLD TESTAMENT   *Ezekiel 37.1–14*

The hand of the LORD was upon me, and he brought me out by the Spirit of the LORD and set me in the middle of a valley; it was full of bones. He led me to and fro among them, and I saw a great many bones on the floor of the valley, bones that were very dry. He asked me, 'Son of man, can these bones live?'

I said, 'O Sovereign LORD, you alone know.'

Then he said to me, 'Prophesy to these bones and say to them, "Dry bones, hear the word of the LORD. This is what the Sovereign LORD says to these bones: I will make breath enter you, and you will come to life. I will attach tendons to you and make flesh come upon you and cover you with skin; I will put breath in you, and you will come to life. Then you will know that I am the LORD." '

So I prophesied as I was commanded. And as I was prophesying, there was a noise, a rattling sound, and the bones came together, bone to bone. I looked, and tendons and flesh appeared on them and skin covered them, but there was no breath in them.

Then he said to me, 'Prophesy to the breath; prophesy, son of man, and say to it, "This is what the Sovereign LORD says: Come from the four winds, O breath, and breathe into these slain, that they may live." ' So I prophesied as he commanded me, and breath entered them; they came to life and stood up on their feet – a vast army.

Then he said to me: 'Son of man, these bones are the whole house of Israel. They say, "Our bones are dried up and our hope is gone; we are cut off." Therefore prophesy and say to them: "This is what the Sovereign LORD says: O my people, I am going to open your graves and bring you up from them; I will bring you back to the land of Israel. Then you, my people, will know that I am the LORD, when I open your graves and bring you up from them. I will put my Spirit in you and you will live, and I will settle you in your own land. Then you will know that I the LORD have spoken, and I have done it, declares the LORD." '

EPISTLE *1 Peter 3.1–12*

Wives, be submissive to your husbands so that, if any of them do not believe the word, they may be won over without talk by the behaviour of their wives, when they see the purity and reverence of your lives. Your beauty should not come from outward adornment, such as braided hair and the wearing of gold jewellery and fine clothes. Instead, it should be that of your inner self, the unfading beauty of a gentle and quiet spirit, which is of great worth in God's sight. For this is the way the holy women of the past who put their hope in God used to make themselves beautiful. They were submissive to their own husbands, like Sarah, who obeyed Abraham and called him her master. You are her daughters if you do what is right and do not give way to fear.

Husbands, in the same way be considerate as you live with your wives, and treat them with respect as the weaker partner and as heirs with you of the gracious gift of life, so that nothing will hinder your prayers. Finally, all of you, live in harmony with one another; be sympathetic, love as brothers, be compassionate and humble. Do not repay evil with evil or insult with insult, but with blessing, because to this you were called so that you may inherit a blessing. For,

'Whoever would love life and see good days
must keep his tongue from evil
and his lips from deceitful speech.
He must turn from evil and do good;

he must seek peace and pursue it.
For the eyes of the Lord are on the righteous
and his ears are attentive to their prayer,
but the face of the Lord is against those who do evil.'

GOSPEL* *John 21.15–17*

When they had finished eating, Jesus said to Simon Peter,
'Simon son of John, do you truly love me more than these?'

'Yes, Lord,' he said, 'you know that I love you.'

Jesus said, 'Feed my lambs.'

Again Jesus said, 'Simon son of John, do you truly love
me?'

He answered, 'Yes, Lord, you know that I love you.'

Jesus said, 'Take care of my sheep.'

The third time he said to him, 'Simon son of John, do you
love me?'

Peter was hurt because Jesus asked him the third time, 'Do
you love me?' He said, 'Lord, you know all things; you know
that I love you.'

Jesus said, 'Feed my sheep.'

Morning Prayer
Psalm 135   Exodus 14.15–31   Luke 8.41–56

Evening Prayer
Psalm 136   Zephaniah 3.14–20   Acts 17.16–31

SATURDAY IN EASTER WEEK   White

PSALM 118

OLD TESTAMENT   *Job 14.1–14*

Job said:
'Man born of woman
is of few days and full of trouble.
He springs up like a flower and withers away;
like a fleeting shadow, he does not endure.
Do you fix your eye on such a one?
Will you bring him before you for judgment?
Who can bring what is pure from the impure?
No one!
Man's days are determined;

you have decreed the number of his months
and have set limits he cannot exceed.
So look away from him and let him alone,
till he has put in his time like a hired man.

'At least there is hope for a tree:
If it is cut down, it will sprout again,
and its new shoots will not fail.
Its roots may grow old in the ground
and its stump die in the soil,
yet at the scent of water it will bud
and put forth shoots like a plant.
But man dies and is laid low;
he breathes his last and is no more.
As water disappears from the sea
or a river bed becomes parched and dry,
so man lies down and does not rise;
till the heavens are no more, men will not awake
or be roused from their sleep.

'If only you would hide me in the grave
and conceal me till your anger has passed!
If only you would set me a time
and then remember me!
If a man dies, will he live again?
All the days of my hard service
I will wait for my renewal to come.'

EPISTLE *1 Peter 4.1–11*

Since Christ suffered in his body, arm yourselves also with
the same attitude, because he who has suffered in his body is
done with sin. As a result, he does not live the rest of his
earthly life for evil human desires, but rather for the will of
God. For you have spent enough time in the past doing what
pagans choose to do – living in debauchery, lust, drunkenness, orgies, carousing and detestable idolatry. They think it
strange that you do not plunge with them into the same
flood of dissipation, and they heap abuse on you. But they
will have to give account to him who is ready to judge the
living and the dead. For this is the reason the gospel was
preached even to those who are now dead, so that they
might be judged according to men in regard to the body, but
live according to God in regard to the spirit.

The end of all things is near. Therefore be clear minded and self-controlled so that you can pray. Above all, love each other deeply, because love covers over a multitude of sins. Offer hospitality to one another without grumbling. Each one should use whatever gift he has received to serve others, faithfully administering God's grace in its various forms. If anyone speaks, he should do it as one speaking the very words of God. If anyone serves, he should do it with the strength God provides, so that in all things God may be praised through Jesus Christ. To him be the glory and the power for ever and ever. Amen.

GOSPEL* *John 21.20–25*

Peter turned and saw that the disciple whom Jesus loved was following them. (This was the one who had leaned back against Jesus at the supper and had said, 'Lord, who is going to betray you?') When Peter saw him, he asked, 'Lord, what about him?'

Jesus answered, 'If I want him to remain alive until I return, what is that to you? You must follow me.' Because of this, the rumour spread among the brothers that this disciple would not die. But Jesus did not say that he would not die; he only said, 'If I want him to remain alive until I return, what is that to you?'

This is the disciple who testifies to these things and who wrote them down. We know that his testimony is true.

Jesus did many other things as well. If every one of them were written down, I suppose that even the whole world would not have room for the books that would be written.

Morning Prayer
Psalm 137;138   Exodus 15.1–21   Luke 16.19–31

Evening Prayer
Psalm 139   Zechariah 8.1–8   Acts 26.1–23

EASTER 1

COLLECT

Merciful Father,
you gave Jesus Christ to be for us the bread of life,
that those who come to him should never hunger:
Draw us to our Lord in faith and love,
that we may eat and drink with him,
at his table in his kingdom,
where he lives and reigns with you and the Holy Spirit,
now and for ever. **Amen.**

Year 1

The Upper Room

PSALM 145.1–12

OLD TESTAMENT *Exodus 15.1–11 (MP/EP Isaiah 51.1–16)*

Moses and the Israelites sang this song to the LORD:

'I will sing to the LORD
for he is highly exalted.
The horse and its rider
he has hurled into the sea.
The LORD is my strength and my song;
he has become my salvation.
He is my God, and I will praise him,
my father's God, and I will exalt him.
The LORD is a warrior;
the LORD is his name.
Pharaoh's chariots and his army
he has hurled into the sea.
The best of Pharaoh's officers
are drowned in the Red Sea.
The deep waters have covered them;
they sank to the depths like a stone.

'Your right hand, O LORD,
was majestic in power.
Your right hand, O LORD,
shattered the enemy.
In the greatness of your majesty
you threw down those who opposed you.

You unleashed your burning anger;
it consumed them like stubble.
By the blast of your nostrils
the waters piled up.
The surging waters stood firm like a wall;
the deep waters congealed in the heart of the sea.

'The enemy boasted,
"I will pursue, I will overtake them.
I will divide the spoils;
I will gorge myself on them.
I will draw my sword
and my hand will destroy them."
But you blew with your breath,
and the sea covered them.
They sank like lead in the mighty waters.

'Who among the gods is like you, O LORD?
Who is like you–
majestic in holiness,
awesome in glory,
working wonders?'

EPISTLE   *1 Peter 1.3–9*

Praise be to the God and Father of our Lord Jesus Christ! In his great mercy he has given us new birth into a living hope through the resurrection of Jesus Christ from the dead, and into an inheritance that can never perish, spoil or fade – kept in heaven for you, who through faith are shielded by God's power until the coming of the salvation that is ready to be revealed in the last time. In this you greatly rejoice, though now for a little while you may have had to suffer grief in all kinds of trials. These have come so that your faith – of greater worth than gold, which perishes even though refined by fire – may be proved genuine and may result in praise, glory and honour when Jesus Christ is revealed. Though you have not seen him, you love him; and even though you do not see him now, you believe in him and are filled with an inexpressible and glorious joy, for you are receiving the goal of your faith, the salvation of your souls.

GOSPEL*   *John 20.19–29 (–31)*

On the evening of that first day of the week, when the dis-

505

ciples were together, with the doors locked for fear of the Jews, Jesus came and stood among them and said, 'Peace be with you!' After he said this, he showed them his hands and side. The disciples were overjoyed when they saw the Lord.

Again Jesus said, 'Peace be with you! As the Father has sent me, I am sending you.' And with that he breathed on them and said, 'Receive the Holy Spirit. If you forgive anyone his sins, they are forgiven; if you do not forgive them, they are not forgiven.'

Now Thomas (called Didymus), one of the Twelve, was not with the disciples when Jesus came. When the other disciples told him that they had seen the Lord, he declared, 'Unless I see the nail marks in his hands and put my finger where the nails were, and put my hand into his side, I will not believe it.'

A week later his disciples were in the house again, and Thomas was with them. Though the doors were locked, Jesus came and stood among them, and said, 'Peace be with you!' Then he said to Thomas, 'Put your finger here; see my hands. Reach out your hand and put it into my side. Stop doubting and believe.'

Thomas answered, 'My Lord and my God!'

Then Jesus told him, 'Because you have seen me, you have believed; blessed are those who have not seen and yet have believed.'

Psalm 30;48   Deuteronomy 4.25–40   Revelation 2.1–11

Year 2

The Bread of Life

PSALM 34.1–10

OLD TESTAMENT   *Exodus 16.2–15*

In the desert the whole community grumbled against Moses and Aaron. The Israelites said to them, 'If only we had died by the LORD's hand in Egypt! There we sat round pots of meat and ate all the food we wanted, but you have brought us out into this desert to starve this entire assembly to death.'

Then the LORD said to Moses, 'I will rain down bread from

heaven for you. The people are to go out each day and gather enough for that day. In this way I will test them and see whether they will follow my instructions. On the sixth day they are to prepare what they bring in, and that is to be twice as much as they gather on the other days.'

So Moses and Aaron said to all the Israelites, 'In the evening you will know that it was the LORD who brought you out of Egypt, and in the morning you will see the glory of the LORD, because he has heard your grumbling against him. Who are we, that you should grumble against us?' Moses also said, 'You will know that it was the LORD when he gives you meat to eat in the evening and all the bread you want in the morning, because he has heard your grumbling against him. Who are we? You are not grumbling against us, but against the LORD.'

Then Moses told Aaron, 'Say to the entire Israelite community, "Come before the LORD, for he has heard your grumbling." '

While Aaron was speaking to the whole Israelite community, they looked towards the desert, and there was the glory of the LORD appearing in the cloud.

The LORD said to Moses, 'I have heard the grumbling of the Israelites. Tell them, "At twilight you will eat meat, and in the morning you will be filled with bread. Then you will know that I am the LORD your God." '

That evening quail came and covered the camp, and in the morning there was a layer of dew around the camp. When the dew was gone, thin flakes like frost on the ground appeared on the desert floor. When the Israelites saw it, they said to each other, 'What is it?' For they did not know what it was.

Moses said to them, 'It is the bread the LORD has given you to eat.'

EPISTLE *1 Corinthians 15.53–58 (51–58)*

The perishable must clothe itself with the imperishable, and the mortal with immortality. When the perishable has been clothed with the imperishable, and the mortal with immortality, then the saying that is written will come true: 'Death has been swallowed up in victory.'

'Where, O death, is your victory?
Where, O death, is your sting?'

The sting of death is sin, and the power of sin is the law. But thanks be to God! He gives us the victory through our Lord Jesus Christ.

Therefore, my dear brothers, stand firm. Let nothing move you. Always give yourselves fully to the work of the Lord, because you know that your labour in the Lord is not in vain.

GOSPEL* *John 6.32–40 (24–51)*

Jesus said, 'I tell you the truth, it is not Moses who has given you the bread from heaven, but it is my Father who gives you the true bread from heaven. For the bread of God is he who comes down from heaven and gives life to the world.'

'Sir,' they said, 'from now on give us this bread.'

Then Jesus declared, 'I am the bread of life. He who comes to me will never go hungry, and he who believes in me will never be thirsty. But as I told you, you have seen me and still you do not believe. All that the Father gives me will come to me, and whoever comes to me I will never drive away. For I have come down from heaven not to do my will but to do the will of him who sent me. And this is the will of him who sent me, that I shall lose none of all that he has given me, but raise them up at the last day. For my Father's will is that everyone who looks to the Son and believes in him shall have eternal life, and I will raise him up at the last day.'

Psalm 115   Deuteronomy 11.1–15   2 Corinthians 4.5–18

EASTER 2   *White*

Year 1

The Emmaus Road

COLLECT

Almighty God,
your Son Jesus Christ after his resurrection
appeared to his disciples on the Emmaus Road,
and made himself known in the breaking of bread:
Open our eyes that we may know him
in all his redeeming work;
who lives and reigns with you and the Holy Spirit,
one God, now and for ever.   **Amen.**

PSALM 111

OLD TESTAMENT   *Isaiah 25.6–9 (1–9)*

On this mountain the Lord Almighty will prepare
a feast of rich food for all peoples,
a banquet of aged wine –
the best of meats and the finest of wines.
On this mountain he will destroy
the shroud that enfolds all peoples,
the sheet that covers all nations;
he will swallow up death for ever.
The Sovereign Lord will wipe away the tears
from all faces;
he will remove the disgrace of his people
from all the earth.
The Lord has spoken.

In that day they will say,

'Surely this is our God;
we trusted in him, and he saved us.
This is the Lord, we trusted in him;
let us rejoice and be glad in his salvation.'

EPISTLE   *Revelation 19.6–9*

I, John, heard what sounded like a great multitude, like the
roar of rushing waters and like loud peals of thunder,
shouting:

'Hallelujah!
For our Lord God Almighty reigns.
Let us rejoice and be glad
and give him glory!
For the wedding of the Lamb has come,
and his bride has made herself ready.
Fine linen, bright and clean,
was given her to wear.'

(Fine linen stands for the righteous acts of the saints.)

Then the angel said to me, 'Write: "Blessed are those who
are invited to the wedding supper of the Lamb!" ' And he
added, 'These are the true words of God.'

GOSPEL* *Luke 24.13–35*

Now that same day two of the disciples were going to a village called Emmaus, about seven miles from Jerusalem. They were talking with each other about everything that had happened. As they talked and discussed these things with each other, Jesus himself came up and walked along with them; but they were kept from recognizing him.

He asked them, 'What are you discussing together as you walk along?'

They stood still, their faces downcast. One of them, named Cleopas, asked him, 'Are you the only one living in Jerusalem who does not know the things that have happened there in these days?'

'What things?' he asked.

'About Jesus of Nazareth,' they replied. 'He was a prophet, powerful in word and deed before God and all the people. The chief priests and our rulers handed him over to be sentenced to death, and they crucified him; but we had hoped that he was the one who was going to redeem Israel. And what is more, it is the third day since all this took place. In addition, some of our women amazed us. They went to the tomb early this morning but did not find his body. They came and told us that they had seen a vision of angels, who said he was alive. Then some of our companions went to the tomb and found it just as the women had said, but him they did not see.'

He said to them, 'How foolish you are, and how slow of heart to believe all that the prophets have spoken! Did not the Christ have to suffer these things and then enter his glory?' And beginning with Moses and all the Prophets, he explained to them what was said in all the Scriptures concerning himself.

As they approached the village to which they were going, Jesus acted as if he were going further. But they urged him strongly, 'Stay with us, for it is nearly evening; the day is almost over.' So he went in to stay with them.

When he was at the table with them, he took bread, gave thanks, broke it and began to give it to them. Then their eyes were opened and they recognized him, and he disappeared from their sight. They asked each other, 'Were not our hearts burning within us while he talked with us on the road and opened the Scriptures to us?'

They got up and returned at once to Jerusalem. There they

found the Eleven and those with them, assembled together and saying, 'It is true! The Lord has risen and has appeared to Simon.' Then the two told what had happened on the way, and how Jesus was recognized by them when he broke the bread.

Psalm 49.1–16   Exodus 32.1–14,30–35   Luke 7.11–17

Year 2

The Good Shepherd

COLLECT

Merciful Father,
you gave your Son Jesus Christ to be the good shepherd,
and in his love for us to give his life and rise again:
Keep us always under his protection,
and give us grace to follow in his steps:
through Jesus Christ our Lord.   **Amen.**

PSALM 23

OLD TESTAMENT   *Ezekiel 34.7–15 (1–16)*

You shepherds, hear the word of the LORD: As surely as I live, declares the Sovereign LORD, because my flock lacks a shepherd and so has been plundered and has become food for all the wild animals, and because my shepherds did not search for my flock but cared for themselves rather than for my flock, therefore, O shepherds, hear the word of the LORD: This is what the Sovereign LORD says: I am against the shepherds and will hold them accountable for my flock. I will remove them from tending the flock so that the shepherds can no longer feed themselves. I will rescue my flock from their mouths, and it will no longer be food for them.

For this is what the Sovereign LORD says: I myself will search for my sheep and look after them. As a shepherd looks after his scattered flock when he is with them, so will I look after my sheep. I will rescue them from all the places where they were scattered on a day of clouds and darkness. I will bring them out from the nations and gather them from the countries, and I will bring them into their own land. I will pasture them on the mountains of Israel, in the ravines

511

and in all the settlements in the land. I will tend them in a good pasture, and the mountain heights of Israel will be their grazing land. There they will lie down in good grazing land, and there they will feed in a rich pasture on the mountains of Israel. I myself will tend my sheep and make them lie down, declares the Sovereign LORD. I will search for the lost and bring back the strays.

EPISTLE *1 Peter 5.1–11 (–14)*

To the elders among you, I appeal as a fellow elder, a witness of Christ's sufferings and one who also will share in the glory to be revealed: Be shepherds of God's flock that is under your care, serving as overseers – not because you must, but because you are willing, as God wants you to be; not greedy for money, but eager to serve; not lording it over those entrusted to you, but being examples to the flock. And when the Chief Shepherd appears, you will receive the crown of glory that will never fade away.

Young men, in the same way be submissive to those who are older. Clothe yourselves with humility towards one another, because,

'God opposes the proud
but gives grace to the humble.'

Humble yourselves, therefore, under God's mighty hand, that he may lift you up in due time. Cast all your anxiety on him because he cares for you.

Be self-controlled and alert. Your enemy the devil prowls around like a roaring lion looking for someone to devour. Resist him, standing firm in the faith, because you know that your brothers throughout the world are undergoing the same kind of sufferings.

And the God of all grace, who called you to his eternal glory in Christ, after you have suffered a little while, will himself restore you and make you strong, firm and steadfast. To him be the power for ever and ever. Amen.

GOSPEL* *John 10.7–16 (1–18)*

Jesus said, 'I tell you the truth, I am the gate for the sheep. All who ever came before me were thieves and robbers, but the sheep did not listen to them. I am the gate; whoever enters through me will be saved. He will come in and go out,

and find pasture. The thief comes only to steal and kill and
destroy; I have come that they may have life, and have it to
the full.

'I am the good shepherd. The good shepherd lays down
his life for the sheep. The hired hand is not the shepherd
who owns the sheep. So when he sees the wolf coming, he
abandons the sheep and runs away. Then the wolf attacks
the flock and scatters it. The man runs away because he is a
hired hand and cares nothing for the sheep.

'I am the good shepherd; I know my sheep and my sheep
know me – just as the Father knows me and I know the
Father – and I lay down my life for the sheep. I have other
sheep that are not of this sheep pen. I must bring them also.
They too will listen to my voice, and there shall be one flock
and one shepherd.'

Psalm 2;8   Ezra 1.1–18   Revelation 2.12–29

EASTER 3

COLLECT

Almighty God,
you raised your Son from death
to be the resurrection and the life for all believers:
Raise us to true life in him,
that we may seek the things which are above,
where Christ reigns with you and the Holy Spirit,
for ever.   **Amen.**

Year 1

The Lakeside

PSALM 16

OLD TESTAMENT   *Isaiah 61.1–7*

The Spirit of the Sovereign Lord is on me,
because the Lord has anointed me
to preach good news to the poor.
He has sent me to bind up the broken-hearted,
to proclaim freedom for the captives
and release for the prisoners,

to proclaim the year of the LORD's favour
and the day of vengeance of our God,
to comfort all who mourn,
and provide for those who grieve in Zion –
to bestow on them a crown of beauty
instead of ashes,
the oil of gladness
instead of mourning,
and a garment of praise
instead of a spirit of despair.
They will be called oaks of righteousness,
a planting of the LORD
for the display of his splendour.
They will rebuild the ancient ruins
and restore the places long devastated;
they will renew the ruined cities
that have been devastated for generations.
Aliens will shepherd your flocks;
foreigners will work your fields and vineyards.
And you will be called priests of the LORD,
you will be named ministers of our God.
You will feed on the wealth of nations,
and in their riches you will boast.

Instead of their shame
my people will receive a double portion,
and instead of disgrace
they will rejoice in their inheritance;
and so they will inherit a double portion in their land,
and everlasting joy will be theirs.

EPISTLE *1 Corinthians 15.1–11*

Now, brothers, I want to remind you of the gospel I preached to you, which you received and on which you have taken your stand. By this gospel you are saved, if you hold firmly to the word I preached to you. Otherwise, you have believed in vain.

For what I received I passed on to you as of first importance: that Christ died for our sins according to the Scriptures, that he was buried, that he was raised on the third day according to the Scriptures, and that he appeared to Peter, and then to the Twelve. After that, he appeared to more than five hundred of the brothers at the same time, most of whom are still living, though some have fallen asleep. Then he appeared to James, then to all the apostles, and last of all he appeared to me also, as to one abnormally born.

For I am the least of the apostles and do not even deserve to be called an apostle, because I persecuted the church of God. But by the grace of God I am what I am, and his grace to me was not without effect. No, I worked harder than all of them – yet not I, but the grace of God that was with me. Whether, then, it was I or they, this is what we preach, and this is what you believed.

GOSPEL* *John 21.1–14*

Jesus appeared again to his disciples by the Sea of Tiberias. It happened this way: Simon Peter, Thomas (called Didymus), Nathanael from Cana in Galilee, the sons of Zebedee, and two other disciples were together. 'I am going out to fish,' Simon Peter told them, and they said, 'We will go with you.' So they went out and got into the boat, but that night they caught nothing.

Early in the morning, Jesus stood on the shore, but the disciples did not realize that it was Jesus.

He called out to them, 'Friends, have you not any fish?'

'No,' they answered.

He said, 'Throw your net on the right side of the boat and you will find some.' When they did, they were unable to haul the net in because of the large number of fish.

Then the disciple whom Jesus loved said to Peter, 'It is the Lord!' As soon as Simon Peter heard him say, 'It is the Lord,' he wrapped his outer garment around him (for he had taken it off) and jumped into the water. The other disciples followed in the boat, towing the net full of fish, for they were not far from shore, about a hundred yards. When they landed, they saw a fire of burning coals there with fish on it, and some bread.

Jesus said to them, 'Bring some of the fish you have just caught.'

Simon Peter climbed aboard and dragged the net ashore. It was full of large fish, one hundred and fifty-three of them, but even with so many the net was not torn. Jesus said to them, 'Come and have breakfast.' None of the disciples dared ask him, 'Who are you?' They knew it was the Lord. Jesus came, took the bread and gave it to them, and did the

same with the fish. This was now the third time Jesus
appeared to his disciples after he was raised from the dead.

Psalm 126   Numbers 22.1–35 (*or* 1–20)   Acts 17.16–34

Year 2

The Resurrection and the Life

PSALM 30

OLD TESTAMENT   *1 Kings 17.17–24 (8–24)*

The son of the woman who owned the house in Zarephath
became ill. He grew worse and worse, and finally stopped
breathing. She said to Elijah, 'What do you have against me,
man of God? Did you come to remind me of my sin and kill
my son?'

'Give me your son,' Elijah replied. He took him from her
arms, carried him to the upper room where he was staying,
and laid him on his bed. Then he cried out to the LORD, 'O
LORD my God, have you brought tragedy also upon this
widow I am staying with, by causing her son to die?' Then
he stretched himself out on the boy three times and cried to
the LORD, 'O LORD my God, let this boy's life return to him!'

The LORD heard Elijah's cry, and the boy's life returned to
him, and he lived. Elijah picked up the child and carried him
down from the room into the house. He gave him to his
mother and said, 'Look, your son is alive!'

Then the woman said to Elijah, 'Now I know that you are a
man of God and that the word of the LORD from your mouth
is the truth.'

EPISTLE   *Colossians 3.1–11*

Since, then, you have been raised with Christ, set your
hearts on things above, where Christ is seated at the right
hand of God. Set your minds on things above, not on earthly
things. For you died, and your life is now hidden with Christ
in God. When Christ, who is your life, appears, then you
also will appear with him in glory.

Put to death, therefore, whatever belongs to your earthly
nature: sexual immorality, impurity, lust, evil desires and
greed, which is idolatry. Because of these, the wrath of God

is coming. You used to walk in these ways, in the life you once lived. But now you must rid yourselves of all such things as these: anger, rage, malice, slander and filthy language from your lips. Do not lie to each other, since you have taken off your old self with its practices and have put on the new self, which is being renewed in knowledge in the image of its Creator. Here there is no Greek or Jew, circumcised or uncircumcised, barbarian, Scythian, slave or free, but Christ is all, and is in all.

GOSPEL* *John 11.17–27 (–44)*

On his arrival, Jesus found that Lazarus had already been in the tomb for four days. Bethany was less than two miles from Jerusalem, and many Jews had come to Martha and Mary to comfort them in the loss of their brother. When Martha heard that Jesus was coming, she went out to meet him, but Mary stayed at home.

'Lord,' Martha said to Jesus, 'if you had been here, my brother would not have died. But I know that even now God will give you whatever you ask.'

Jesus said to her, 'Your brother will rise again.'

Martha answered, 'I know he will rise again in the resurrection at the last day.'

Jesus said to her, 'I am the resurrection and the life. He who believes in me will live, even though he dies; and whoever lives and believes in me will never die. Do you believe this?'

'Yes, Lord,' she told him, 'I believe that you are the Christ, the Son of God, who was to come into the world.'

Psalm 18.1–32 (PB 1–31) Ezra 3 Revelation 3.1–13

EASTER 4

COLLECT

Almighty God,
you have given us your Son Jesus Christ
to be the way, the truth and the life:
Help us in faith to follow him as your apostles did,
and bring us to eternal life;
through Jesus Christ our Lord.   **Amen.**

Year 1

The Charge to Peter

PSALM 33.1–12

OLD TESTAMENT   *Isaiah 62.1–5 (1–12)*

For Zion's sake I will not keep silent,
for Jerusalem's sake I will not remain quiet,
till her righteousness shines out like the dawn,
her salvation like a blazing torch.
The nations will see your righteousness,
and all kings your glory;
you will be called by a new name
that the mouth of the LORD will bestow.
You will be a crown of splendour in the LORD's hand,
a royal diadem in the hand of your God.
No longer will they call you Deserted,
or name your land Desolate.
But you will be called Hephzibah,
and your land Beulah,
for the LORD will take delight in you,
and your land will be married.
As a young man marries a maiden,
so will your sons marry you;
as a bridegroom rejoices over his bride,
so will your God rejoice over you.

EPISTLE   *Revelation 3.14–22*

To the angel of the church in Laodicea write:

These are the words of the Amen, the faithful and true witness, the ruler of God's creation. I know your deeds, that you are neither cold nor hot. I wish you were either one or the other! So, because you are lukewarm – neither hot nor cold – I am about to spit you out of my mouth. You say, 'I am rich; I have acquired wealth and do not need a thing.' But you do not realise that you are wretched, pitiful, poor, blind and naked. I counsel you to buy from me gold refined in the fire, so that you can become rich; and white clothes to wear, so that you can cover your shameful nakedness; and salve to put on your eyes, so that you can see.

Those whom I love I rebuke and discipline. So be earnest, and repent. Here I am! I stand at the door and knock. If anyone hears my voice and opens the door, I will go in and eat with him, and he with me.

To him who overcomes, I will give the right to sit with me on my throne, just as I overcame and sat down with my Father on his throne. He who has an ear, let him hear what the Spirit says to the churches.

GOSPEL*   *John 21.15–22 (–25)*

When they had finished eating, Jesus said to Simon Peter, 'Simon son of John, do you truly love me more than these?'

'Yes, Lord,' he said, 'you know that I love you.'

Jesus said, 'Feed my lambs.'

Again Jesus said, 'Simon son of John, do you truly love me?'

He answered, 'Yes, Lord, you know that I love you.'

Jesus said, 'Take care of my sheep.'

The third time he said to him, 'Simon son of John, do you love me?'

Peter was hurt because Jesus asked him the third time, 'Do you love me?' He said, 'Lord, you know all things; you know that I love you.'

Jesus said, 'Feed my sheep. I tell you the truth, when you were younger you dressed yourself and went where you wanted; but when you are old you will stretch out your hands, and someone else will dress you and lead you where you do not want to go.' Jesus said this to indicate the kind of death by which Peter would glorify God. Then he said to him, 'Follow me!'

Peter turned and saw that the disciple whom Jesus loved
was following them. (This was the one who had leaned back
against Jesus at the supper and had said, 'Lord, who is going
to betray you?') When Peter saw him, he asked, 'Lord, what
about him?'

Jesus answered, 'If I want him to remain alive until I
return, what is that to you? You must follow me.'

Psalm 77   Nehemiah 1   1 Corinthians 15.1–28

Year 2

The Way, the Truth and the Life

PSALM 37.23–32

OLD TESTAMENT   *Proverbs 4.10–19 (1–19)*

Listen, my son, accept what I say,
and the years of your life will be many.
I guide you in the way of wisdom
and lead you along straight paths.
When you walk, your steps will not be hampered;
when you run, you will not stumble.
Hold on to instruction, do not let it go;
guard it well, for it is your life.
Do not set foot on the path of the wicked
or walk in the way of evil men.
Avoid it, do not travel on it;
turn from it and go on your way.
For they cannot sleep till they do evil;
they are robbed of slumber
till they make someone fall.
They eat the bread of wickedness
and drink the wine of violence.
The path of the righteous is like the first gleam of dawn,
shining ever brighter till the full light of day.
But the way of the wicked is like deep darkness;
they do not know what makes them stumble.

EPISTLE   *2 Corinthians 4.13 – 5.5 (–15)*

It is written: 'I believed; therefore I have spoken.' With that same spirit of faith we also believe and therefore speak, because we know that the one who raised the Lord Jesus from the dead will also raise us with Jesus and will bring us with you in his presence. All this is for your benefit, so that the grace that is reaching more and more people may cause thanksgiving to overflow to the glory of God.

Therefore we do not lose heart. Though outwardly we are wasting away, yet inwardly we are being renewed day by day. For our light and momentary troubles are achieving for us an eternal glory that far outweighs them all. So we fix our eyes not on what is seen, but on what is unseen. For what is seen is temporary, but what is unseen is eternal.

Now we know that if the earthly tent we live in is destroyed, we have a building from God, an eternal house in heaven, not built by human hands. Meanwhile we groan, longing to be clothed with our heavenly dwelling, because when we are clothed, we will not be found naked. For while we are in this tent, we groan and are burdened, because we do not wish to be unclothed but to be clothed with our heavenly dwelling, so that what is mortal may be swallowed up by life. Now it is God who has made us for this very purpose and has given us the Spirit as a deposit, guaranteeing what is to come.

GOSPEL* *John 14.1–11*

Jesus said to his disciples, 'Do not let your hearts be troubled. Trust in God; trust also in me. In my Father's house are many rooms; if it were not so, I would have told you. I am going there to prepare a place for you. And if I go and prepare a place for you, I will come back and take you to be with me that you also may be where I am. You know the way to the place where I am going.'

Thomas said to him, 'Lord, we do not know where you are going, so how can we know the way?'

Jesus answered, 'I am the way and the truth and the life. No one comes to the Father except through me. If you really knew me, you would know my Father as well. From now on, you do know him and have seen him.'

Philip said, 'Lord, show us the Father and that will be enough for us.'

Jesus answered: 'Do you not know me, Philip, even after I have been among you such a long time? Anyone who has seen me has seen the Father. How can you say, ''Show us the Father''? Do you not believe that I am in the Father, and that the Father is in me? The words I say to you are not just my own. Rather, it is the Father, living in me, who is doing his work. Believe me when I say that I am in the Father and the Father is in me; or at least believe on the evidence of the miracles themselves.'

Psalm 57;63.1 – 9 Numbers 22.36 – 23.12 Luke 16.19–31

EASTER 5   *White*

Going to the Father

COLLECT

Lord Jesus Christ,
you returned to the glory of your Father,
and sent the Holy Spirit to be with us for ever:
May we, knowing his presence and power,
be led into the way of truth
and come to the glory of your kingdom;
where you live and reign
with the Father and the Holy Spirit,
one God, now and for ever. **Amen.**

Year 1

PSALM 84

OLD TESTAMENT *Hosea 6.1–6*

'Come, let us return to the LORD.
He has torn us to pieces but he will heal us;
he has injured us
but he will bind up our wounds.
After two days he will revive us;
on the third day he will restore us,
that we may live in his presence.
Let us acknowledge the LORD;
let us press on to acknowledge him.
As surely as the sun rises, he will appear;
he will come to us like the winter rains,

like the spring rains that water the earth.

'What can I do with you, Ephraim?
What can I do with you, Judah?
Your love is like the morning mist,
like the early dew that disappears.
Therefore I cut you in pieces with my prophets,
I killed you with the words of my mouth;
my judgments flashed like lightning upon you.
For I desire mercy, not sacrifice,
and acknowledgment of God rather than burnt offerings.'

EPISTLE   *1 Corinthians 15.21–28 (20–28,35–38)*

Since death came through a man, the resurrection of the dead comes also through a man. For as in Adam all die, so in Christ all will be made alive. But each in his own turn: Christ, the firstfruits; then, when he comes, those who belong to him. Then the end will come, when he hands over the kingdom to God the Father after he has destroyed all dominion, authority and power. For he must reign until he has put all his enemies under his feet. The last enemy to be destroyed is death. For he 'has put everything under his feet.' Now when it says that 'everything' has been put under him, it is clear that this does not include God himself, who put everything under Christ. When he has done this, then the Son himself will be made subject to him who put everything under him, so that God may be all in all.

GOSPEL*   *John 16.25–33*

Jesus said to his disciples, 'Though I have been speaking figuratively, a time is coming when I will no longer use this kind of language but will tell you plainly about my Father. In that day you will ask in my name. I am not saying that I will ask the Father on your behalf. No, the Father himself loves you because you have loved me and have believed that I came from God. I came from the Father and entered the world; now I am leaving the world and going back to the Father.'

Then Jesus' disciples said, 'Now you are speaking clearly and without figures of speech. Now we can see that you know all things and that you do not even need to have anyone ask you questions. This makes us believe that you came from God.'

'You believe at last!' Jesus answered. 'But a time is coming, and has come, when you will be scattered, each to his own home. You will leave me all alone. Yet I am not alone, for my Father is with me.

'I have told you these things, so that in me you may have peace. In this world you will have trouble. But take heart! I have overcome the world.'

Psalm 65;67   Deuteronomy 28.1–14   Luke 10.38 – 11.13

Year 2

PSALM 15

OLD TESTAMENT   *Deuteronomy 34*

Moses climbed Mount Nebo from the plains of Moab to the top of Pisgah, across from Jericho. There the LORD showed him the whole land – from Gilead to Dan, all of Naphtali, the territory of Ephraim and Manasseh, all the land of Judah as far as the western sea, the Negev and the whole region from the Valley of Jericho, the City of Palms, as far as Zoar. Then the LORD said to him, 'This is the land I promised on oath to Abraham, Isaac and Jacob when I said, "I will give it to your descendants." I have let you see it with your eyes, but you will not cross over into it.'

And Moses the servant of the LORD died there in Moab, as the LORD had said. He buried him in Moab, in the valley opposite Beth Peor, but to this day no one knows where his grave is. Moses was a hundred and twenty years old when he died, yet his eyes were not weak nor his strength gone. The Israelites grieved for Moses in the plains of Moab thirty days, until the time of weeping and mourning was over.

Now Joshua son of Nun was filled with the spirit of wisdom because Moses had laid his hands on him. So the Israelites listened to him and did what the LORD had commanded Moses.

Since then no prophet has risen in Israel like Moses, whom the LORD knew face to face, who did all those miraculous signs and wonders the LORD sent him to do in Egypt – to Pharaoh and to all his officials and to his whole land. For no one has ever shown the mighty power or performed the awesome deeds that Moses did in the sight of all Israel.

EPISTLE   *Romans 8.28–39*

We know that in all things God works for the good of those
who love him, who have been called according to his
purpose. For those God foreknew he also predestined to be
conformed to the likeness of his Son, that he might be the
firstborn among many brothers. And those he predestined,
he also called; those he called, he also justified; those he
justified, he also glorified.

What, then, shall we say in response to this? If God is for
us, who can be against us? He who did not spare his own
Son, but gave him up for us all – how will he not also, along
with him, graciously give us all things? Who will bring any
charge against those whom God has chosen? It is God who
justifies. Who is he that condemns? Christ Jesus, who died –
more than that, who was raised to life – is at the right hand
of God and is also interceding for us. Who shall separate us
from the love of Christ? Shall trouble or hardship or persecution or famine or nakedness or danger or sword? As it is
written:

'For your sake we face death all day long;
we are considered as sheep to be slaughtered.'

No, in all these things we are more than conquerors through
him who loved us. For I am convinced that neither death nor
life, neither angels nor demons, neither the present nor the
future, nor any powers, neither height nor depth, nor anything else in all creation, will be able to separate us from the
love of God that is in Christ Jesus our Lord.

GOSPEL*   *John 16.12–24*

Jesus said to his disciples, 'I have much more to say to you,
more than you can now bear. But when he, the Spirit of
truth, comes, he will guide you into all truth. He will not
speak on his own; he will speak only what he hears, and he
will tell you what is yet to come. He will bring glory to me by
taking from what is mine and making it known to you. All
that belongs to the Father is mine. That is why I said the
Spirit will take from what is mine and make it known to you.

'In a little while you will see me no more, and then after a
little while you will see me.'

Some of his disciples said to one another, 'What does he

525

mean by saying, "In a little while you will see me no more, and then after a little while you will see me," and "Because I am going to the Father"?' They kept asking, 'What does he mean by "a little while"? We do not understand what he is saying.'

Jesus saw that they wanted to ask him about this, so he said to them, 'Are you asking one another what I meant when I said, "In a little while you will see me no more, and then after a little while you will see me"? I tell you the truth, you will weep and mourn while the world rejoices. You will grieve, but your grief will turn to joy. A woman giving birth to a child has pain because her time has come; but when her baby is born she forgets the anguish because of her joy that a child is born into the world. So with you: Now is your time of grief, but I will see you again and you will rejoice, and no one will take away your joy. In that day you will no longer ask me anything. I tell you the truth, my Father will give you whatever you ask in my name. Until now you have not asked for anything in my name. Ask and you will receive, and your joy will be complete.'

Psalm 107.1–32   Nehemiah 2   Matthew 13.24–43

ROGATION DAYS

White

COLLECT

Almighty Father,
you have provided the resources of the world
to maintain the life of your children,
and have so ordered our life
that we are dependent on one another:
Bless us in our daily work,
and, as you have given us the knowledge to produce plenty,
so give us the will
to bring it within the reach of all;
through Jesus Christ our Lord.   **Amen.**

or

Almighty God,
whose will it is that the earth
should bear its fruits in their season:

Direct the labours of those who work on the land,
that they may employ the resources of nature
to your glory,
for our own well-being
and for the relief of those in need;
through Jesus Christ our Lord.   **Amen.**

MONDAY

PSALM 107.1–9 *or* 121

OLD TESTAMENT   *Job 28.1–11*

Job said:
'There is a mine for silver
and a place where gold is refined.
Iron is taken from the earth,
and copper is smelted from ore.
Man puts an end to the darkness;
he searches the farthest recesses
for ore in the blackest darkness.
Far from where people dwell he cuts a shaft,
in places forgotten by the foot of man;
far from men he dangles and sways.
The earth, from which food comes,
is transformed below as by fire:
sapphires come from its rocks,
and its dust contains nuggets of gold.
No bird of prey knows that hidden path,
no falcon's eye has seen it.
Proud beasts do not set foot on it,
and no lion prowls there.
Man's hand assaults the flinty rock
and lays bare the roots of the mountains.
He tunnels through the rock;
his eyes see all its treasures.
He searches the sources of the rivers
and brings hidden things to light.'

EPISTLE   *2 Thessalonians 3.6–13*

In the name of the Lord Jesus Christ, we command you,
brothers, to keep away from every brother who is idle and

does not live according to the teaching you received from us. For you yourselves know how you ought to follow our example. We were not idle when we were with you, nor did we eat anyone's food without paying for it. On the contrary, we worked night and day, labouring and toiling so that we would not be a burden to any of you. We did this, not because we do not have the right to such help, but in order to make ourselves a model for you to follow. For even when we were with you, we gave you this rule: 'If a man will not work, he shall not eat.'

We hear that some among you are idle. They are not busy; they are busybodies. Such people we command and urge in the Lord Jesus Christ, to settle down and earn the bread they eat. And as for you, brothers, never tire of doing what is right.

GOSPEL* *Matthew 6.1–15*

Jesus said: 'Be careful not to do your "acts of righteousness" before men, to be seen by them. If you do, you will have no reward from your Father in heaven.

'So when you give to the needy, do not announce it with trumpets, as the hypocrites do in the synagogues and on the streets, to be honoured by men. I tell you the truth, they have received their reward in full. But when you give to the needy, do not let your left hand know what your right hand is doing, so that your giving may be in secret. Then your Father, who sees what is done in secret, will reward you.

'But when you pray, do not be like the hypocrites, for they love to pray standing in the synagogues and on the street corners to be seen by men. I tell you the truth, they have received their reward in full. When you pray, go into your room, close the door and pray to your Father, who is unseen. Then your Father, who sees what is done in secret, will reward you. And when you pray, do not keep on babbling like pagans, for they think they will be heard because of their many words. Do not be like them, for your Father knows what you need before you ask him.

'This is how you should pray:

' "Our Father in heaven,
hallowed be your name,
your kingdom come,
your will be done

on earth as it is in heaven.
Give us today our daily bread.
Forgive us our debts,
as we also have forgiven our debtors.
And lead us not into temptation,
but deliver us from the evil one.''

'For if you forgive men when they sin against you, your heavenly Father will also forgive you. But if you do not forgive men their sins, your Father will not forgive your sins.'

Morning Prayer
Psalm 54;55   Deuteronomy 7.6–13   Matthew 6.19–34

Evening Prayer
Psalm 56;57   Joel 2.21–27   Acts 14.8–18

TUESDAY

PSALM 107.1–9 *or* 121

OLD TESTAMENT   *Deuteronomy 8.1–10*

Be careful to follow every command I am giving you today, so that you may live and increase and may enter and possess the land that the LORD promised on oath to your forefathers. Remember how the LORD your God led you all the way in the desert these forty years, to humble you and to test you in order to know what was in your heart, whether or not you would keep his commands. He humbled you, causing you to hunger and then feeding you with manna, which neither you nor your fathers had known, to teach you that man does not live on bread alone but on every word that comes from the mouth of the LORD. Your clothes did not wear out and your feet did not swell during these forty years. Know then in your heart that as a man disciplines his son, so the LORD your God disciplines you.

Observe the commands of the LORD your God, walking in his ways and revering him. For the LORD your God is bringing you into a good land – a land with streams and pools of water, with springs flowing in the valleys and hills; a land with wheat and barley, vines and fig trees, pomegranates, olive oil and honey; a land where bread will not be scarce and you will lack nothing; a land where the rocks are iron and you can dig copper out of the hills.

When you have eaten and are satisfied, praise the LORD your God for the good land he has given you.

Philippians 4.4–7

Rejoice in the Lord always. I will say it again: Rejoice! Let your gentleness be evident to all. The Lord is near. Do not be anxious about anything, but in everything, by prayer and petition, with thanksgiving, present your requests to God. And the peace of God, which transcends all understanding, will guard your hearts and your minds in Christ Jesus.

GOSPEL* *Luke 11.5–13*

Jesus said, 'Suppose one of you has a friend, and he goes to him at midnight and says, "Friend, lend me three loaves of bread, because a friend of mine on a journey has come to me, and I have nothing to set before him."

'Then the one inside answers, "Do not bother me. The door is already locked, and my children are with me in bed. I cannot get up and give you anything." I tell you, though he will not get up and give him the bread because he is his friend, yet because of the man's persistence he will get up and give him as much as he needs.

'So I say to you: Ask and it will be given to you; seek and you will find; knock and the door will be opened to you. For everyone who asks receives; he who seeks finds; and to him who knocks, the door will be opened.

'Which of you fathers, if your son asks for a fish, will give him a snake instead? Or if he asks for an egg, will give him a scorpion? If you then, though you are evil, know how to give good gifts to your children, how much more will your Father in heaven give the Holy Spirit to those who ask him!'

Morning Prayer
Psalm [58];59   Deuteronomy 11.8–21   James 5.1–18

Evening Prayer
Psalm 60;61   Haggai 1.1–11   2 Corinthians 9

WEDNESDAY

PSALM 107.1–9 *or* 121

OLD TESTAMENT   *1 Kings 8.35–40*

Solomon prayed, 'When the heavens are shut up and there is no rain because your people have sinned against you, and when they pray towards this place and confess your name and turn from their sin because you have afflicted them, then hear from heaven and forgive the sin of your servants, your people Israel. Teach them the right way to live, and send rain on the land you gave your people for an inheritance.

'When famine or plague comes to the land, or blight or mildew, locusts or grasshoppers, or when an enemy besieges them in any of their cities, whatever disaster or disease may come, and when a prayer or plea is made by any of your people Israel – each one aware of the afflictions of his own heart, and spreading out his hands towards this temple – then hear from heaven, your dwelling-place. Forgive and act; deal with each man according to all he does, since you know his heart (for you alone know the hearts of all men), so that they will fear you all the time they live in the land you gave our fathers.'

EPISTLE   *1 John 5.12–15*

He who has the Son has life; he who does not have the Son of God does not have life.

I write these things to you who believe in the name of the Son of God so that you may know that you have eternal life. This is the assurance we have in approaching God: that if we ask anything according to his will, he hears us. And if we know that he hears us – whatever we ask – we know that we have what we asked of him.

GOSPEL*   *Mark 11.22–24*

'Have faith in God,' Jesus said to his disciples. 'I tell you the truth, if anyone says to this mountain, "Go, throw yourself into the sea," and does not doubt in his heart but believes that what he says will happen, it will be done for him. There-

fore I tell you, whatever you ask for in prayer, believe that
you have received it, and it will be yours.'

Morning Prayer
Psalm 62;63   Jeremiah 14.1–9   John 6.22–40

Evening Prayer
Psalm 93;99   Ezekiel 1.4–5,26–28 *or* Song of the Three 29–37
Colossians 2.20 – 3.4

THE ASCENSION DAY
White

COLLECT

Almighty God,
as we believe your only begotten Son
our Lord Jesus Christ
to have ascended into the heavens:
Grant that we may in heart and mind also ascend
and with him continually dwell;
who is alive and reigns with you and the Holy Spirit,
one God, now and for ever.   **Amen.**

PSALM 8 *or* 21.1–7

OLD TESTAMENT   *Daniel 7.9–14*

'As I, Daniel, looked,
thrones were set in place,
and the Ancient of Days took his seat.
His clothing was as white as snow;
the hair of his head was white like wool.
His throne was flaming with fire,
and its wheels were all ablaze.
A river of fire was flowing,
 coming out from before him.
Thousands upon thousands attended him;
ten thousand times ten thousand stood before him.
The court was seated,
and the books were opened.

   'Then I continued to watch because of the boastful words
the horn was speaking. I kept looking until the beast was
slain and its body destroyed and thrown into the blazing
fire. (The other beasts had been stripped of their authority,

but were allowed to live for a period of time.)

'In my vision at night I looked, and there before me was one like a son of man, coming with the clouds of heaven. He approached the Ancient of Days and was led into his presence. He was given authority, glory and sovereign power; all peoples, nations and men of every language worshipped him. His dominion is an everlasting dominion that will not pass away, and his kingdom is one that will never be destroyed.'

EPISTLE* *Acts 1.1–11*

In my former book, Theophilus, I wrote about all that Jesus began to do and to teach until the day he was taken up to heaven, after giving instructions through the Holy Spirit to the apostles he had chosen. After his suffering, he showed himself to these men and gave many convincing proofs that he was alive. He appeared to them over a period of forty days and spoke about the kingdom of God. On one occasion, while he was eating with them, he gave them this command: 'Do not leave Jerusalem, but wait for the gift my Father promised, which you have heard me speak about. For John baptized with water, but in a few days you will be baptized with the Holy Spirit.'

So when they met together, they asked him, 'Lord, are you at this time going to restore the kingdom to Israel?'

He said to them: 'It is not for you to know the times or dates the Father has set by his own authority. But you will receive power when the Holy Spirit comes on you; and you will be my witnesses in Jerusalem, and in all Judea and Samaria, and to the ends of the earth.'

After he said this, he was taken up before their very eyes, and a cloud hid him from their sight.

They were looking intently up into the sky as he was going, when suddenly two men dressed in white stood beside them. 'Men of Galilee,' they said, 'why do you stand here looking into the sky? This same Jesus, who has been taken from you into heaven, will come back in the same way you have seen him go into heaven.'

GOSPEL *Matthew 28.16–20*

The eleven disciples went to Galilee, to the mountain where Jesus had told them to go. When they saw him, they worshipped him; but some doubted. Then Jesus came to them and said, 'All authority in heaven and on earth has been given to me. Therefore go and make disciples of all nations, baptizing them in the name of the Father and of the Son and of the Holy Spirit, and teaching them to obey everything I have commanded you. And surely I will be with you always, to the very end of the age.'

Year 1
Psalm 96;97   2 Samuel 23.1–5   Hebrews 1.1–24 (*Morning Prayer only*)

Year 2
Psalm 15;24   Isaiah 52.7–12   Hebrews 2.5–18 (*Evening Prayer only*)

EASTER 6
SUNDAY AFTER ASCENSION DAY   *White*
The Ascension of Christ

COLLECT

Eternal God, the King of Glory,
you have exalted your only Son
in great triumph to your kingdom in heaven:
Leave us not comfortless,
but send your Holy Spirit to strengthen us
and exalt us to the place
where Christ is gone before,
and where with you and the Holy Spirit
he is worshipped and glorified,
now and for ever.   **Amen.**

Year 1

PSALM 24

OLD TESTAMENT *Daniel 7.9–14*

'As I, Daniel, looked,
thrones were set in place,
and the Ancient of Days took his seat.
His clothing was as white as snow;
the hair of his head was white like wool.
His throne was flaming with fire,

and its wheels were all ablaze.
A river of fire was flowing,
coming out from before him.
Thousands upon thousands attended him;
ten thousand times ten thousand stood before him.
The court was seated,
and the books were opened.

'Then I continued to watch because of the boastful words
the horn was speaking. I kept looking until the beast was
slain and its body destroyed and thrown into the blazing
fire. (The other beasts had been stripped of their authority,
but were allowed to live for a period of time.)

'In my vision at night I looked, and there before me was
one like a son of man, coming with the clouds of heaven. He
approached the Ancient of Days and was led into his presence. He was given authority, glory and sovereign power; all
peoples, nations and men of every language worshipped
him. His dominion is an everlasting dominion that will not
pass away, and his kingdom is one that will never be
destroyed.'

EPISTLE *Ephesians 1.15–23*

For this reason, ever since I heard about your faith in the
Lord Jesus and your love for all the saints, I have not
stopped giving thanks for you, remembering you in my
prayers. I keep asking that the God of our Lord Jesus Christ,
the glorious Father, may give you the Spirit of wisdom and
revelation, so that you may know him better. I pray also that
the eyes of your heart may be enlightened in order that you
may know the hope to which he has called you, the riches of
his glorious inheritance in the saints, and his incomparably
great power for us who believe. That power is like the
working of his mighty strength, which he exerted in Christ
when he raised him from the dead and seated him at his
right hand in the heavenly realms, far above all rule and
authority, power and dominion, and every title that can be
given, not only in the present age but also in the one to
come. And God placed all things under his feet and
appointed him to be head over everything for the church,
which is his body, the fulness of him who fills everything in
every way.

GOSPEL* *Luke 24.45–53*

Jesus opened their minds so that they could understand the Scriptures. He told them, 'This is what is written: The Christ will suffer and rise from the dead on the third day, and repentance and forgiveness of sins will be preached in his name to all nations, beginning at Jerusalem. You are witnesses of these things. I am going to send you what my Father has promised; but stay in the city until you have been clothed with power from on high.' When he had led them out to the vicinity of Bethany, he lifted up his hands and blessed them. While he was blessing them, he left them and was taken up into heaven. Then they worshipped him and returned to Jerusalem with great joy. And they stayed continually at the temple, praising God.

Psalm 108;110   Jeremiah 31.1–13   Philippians 2.1–18

Year 2

PSALM 47

OLD TESTAMENT   *2 Kings 2.1–15*

When the Lord was about to take Elijah up to heaven in a whirlwind, Elijah and Elisha were on their way from Gilgal. Elijah said to Elisha, 'Stay here; the Lord has sent me to Bethel.'

But Elisha said, 'As surely as the Lord lives and as you live, I will not leave you.' So they went down to Bethel.

The company of the prophets at Bethel came out to Elisha and asked, 'Do you know that the Lord is going to take your master from you today?'

'Yes, I know,' Elisha replied, 'but do not speak of it.'

Then Elijah said to him, 'Stay here, Elisha; the Lord has sent me to Jericho.'

And he replied, 'As surely as the Lord lives and as you live, I will not leave you.' So they went to Jericho.

The company of the prophets at Jericho went up to Elisha and asked him, 'Do you know that the Lord is going to take your master from you today?'

'Yes, I know,' he replied, 'but do not speak of it.'

Then Elijah said to him, 'Stay here; the Lord has sent me to the Jordan.'

And he replied, 'As surely as the LORD lives and as you live, I will not leave you.' So the two of them walked on.

Fifty men of the company of the prophets went and stood at a distance, facing the place where Elijah and Elisha had stopped at the Jordan. Elijah took his cloak, rolled it up and struck the water with it. The water divided to the right and to the left, and the two of them crossed over on dry ground.

When they had crossed, Elijah said to Elisha, 'Tell me, what can I do for you before I am taken from you?'

'Let me inherit a double portion of your spirit,' Elisha replied.

'You have asked a difficult thing,' Elijah said, 'yet if you see me when I am taken from you, it will be yours – otherwise not.'

As they were walking along and talking together, suddenly a chariot of fire and horses of fire appeared and separated the two of them, and Elijah went up to heaven in a whirlwind. Elisha saw this and cried out, 'My father! My father! The chariots and horsemen of Israel!' And Elisha saw him no more. Then he took hold of his own clothes and tore them apart.

He picked up the cloak that had fallen from Elijah and went back and stood on the bank of the Jordan. Then he took the cloak that had fallen from him and struck the water with it. 'Where now is the LORD, the God of Elijah?' he asked. When he struck the water, it divided to the right and to the left, and he crossed over.

The company of the prophets from Jericho, who were watching, said, 'The spirit of Elijah is resting on Elisha.' And they went to meet him and bowed to the ground before him.

EPISTLE *Ephesians 4.1–13*

As a prisoner for the Lord, then, I urge you to live a life worthy of the calling you have received. Be completely humble and gentle; be patient, bearing with one another in love. Make every effort to keep the unity of the Spirit through the bond of peace. There is one body and one Spirit – just as you were called to one hope when you were called – one Lord, one faith, one baptism; one God and Father of all, who is over all and through all and in all.

But to each one of us grace has been given as Christ apportioned it. This is why it says:

'When he ascended on high,
he led captives in his train
and gave gifts to men.'

(What does 'he ascended' mean except that he also
descended to the lower, earthly regions? He who descended
is the very one who ascended higher than all the heavens, in
order to fill the whole universe.) It was he who gave some to
be apostles, some to be prophets, some to be evangelists,
and some to be pastors and teachers, to prepare God's
people for works of service, so that the body of Christ may
be built up until we all reach unity in the faith and in the
knowledge of the Son of God and become mature, attaining
to the whole measure of the fulness of Christ.

GOSPEL* *Luke 24.45–53 (MP/EP John 17)*

Jesus opened the disciples' minds so that they could understand the Scriptures. He told them, 'This is what is written:
The Christ will suffer and rise from the dead on the third
day, and repentance and forgiveness of sins will be preached
in his name to all nations, beginning at Jerusalem. You are
witnesses of these things. I am going to send you what my
Father has promised; but stay in the city until you have been
clothed with power from on high.'

   When he had led them out to the vicinity of Bethany, he
lifted up his hands and blessed them. While he was blessing
them, he left them and was taken up into heaven. Then they
worshipped him and returned to Jerusalem with great joy.
And they stayed continually at the temple, praising God.

Psalm 138;150 Isaiah 65.17–25 Revelation 5

PENTECOST WHITSUNDAY   *Red*

The Gift of the Spirit

COLLECT

Almighty God,
at this time you taught the hearts of your faithful people
by sending to them the light of your Holy Spirit:
Guide us by the same Spirit
to have a right judgment in all things,
and evermore to rejoice in his holy comfort;
through Jesus Christ our Saviour,
who lives and reigns with you
in the unity of the same Holy Spirit,
one God, now and for ever.   **Amen.**

or

Almighty God,
who on the day of Pentecost
sent the Holy Spirit to the disciples,
filling them with joy
and with boldness to preach the Gospel:
Send us out in the power of the same Spirit
to witness to your truth,
and to draw all men to the fire of your love;
through Jesus Christ our Lord.   **Amen.**

Year 1

PSALM 122

OLD TESTAMENT *Genesis 11.1–9 (MP/EP Ezekiel 37.1–14)*

Now the whole world had one language and a common
speech. As men moved eastwards, they found a plain in
Shinar and settled there.

They said to each other, 'Come, let us make bricks and
bake them thoroughly.' They used brick instead of stone,
and tar instead of mortar. Then they said, 'Come, let us build
ourselves a city, with a tower that reaches to the heavens, so
that we may make a name for ourselves and not be scattered
over the face of the whole earth.'

But the LORD came down to see the city and the tower that

the men were building. The LORD said, 'If as one people speaking the same language they have begun to do this, then nothing they plan to do will be impossible for them. Come, let us go down and confuse their language so they will not understand each other.'

So the LORD scattered them from there over all the earth, and they stopped building the city. That is why it was called Babel – because there the LORD confused the language of the whole world. From there the LORD scattered them over the face of the whole earth.

EPISTLE* *Acts 2.1–11 (–21)*

When the day of Pentecost came, they were all together in one place. Suddenly a sound like the blowing of a violent wind came from heaven and filled the whole house where they were sitting. They saw what seemed to be tongues of fire that separated and came to rest on each of them. All of them were filled with the Holy Spirit and began to speak in other tongues as the Spirit enabled them.

Now there were staying in Jerusalem God-fearing Jews from every nation under heaven. When they heard this sound, a crowd came together in bewilderment, because each one heard them speaking in his own language. Utterly amazed, they asked: 'Are not all these men who are speaking Galileans? Then how is it that each of us hears them in his own native language? Parthians, Medes and Elamites; residents of Mesopotamia, Judea and Cappadocia, Pontus and Asia, Phrygia and Pamphylia, Egypt and the parts of Libya near Cyrene; visitors from Rome (both Jews and converts to Judaism); Cretans and Arabs – we hear them declaring the wonders of God in our own tongues!'

GOSPEL *John 14.15–26*

Jesus said, 'If you love me, you will obey what I command. And I will ask the Father, and he will give you another Counsellor to be with you for ever – the Spirit of truth. The world cannot accept him, because it neither sees him nor knows him. But you know him, for he lives with you and will be in you. I will not leave you as orphans; I will come to you. Before long, the world will not see me any more, but you will see me. Because I live, you also will live. On that day you will realize that I am in my Father, and you are in me, and I am in you. Whoever has my commands and obeys them, he is the one who loves me. He who loves me will be loved by my Father, and I too will love him and show myself to him.'

Then Judas (not Judas Iscariot) said, 'But, Lord, why do you intend to show yourself to us and not to the world?'

Jesus replied, 'If anyone loves me, he will obey my teaching. My Father will love him, and we will come to him and make our home with him. He who does not love me will not obey my teaching. These words you hear are not my own; they belong to the Father who sent me.

'All this I have spoken while still with you. But the Counsellor, the Holy Spirit, whom the Father will send in my name, will teach you all things and will remind you of everything I have said to you.'

Psalm 68.1–20   Joel 2.21–32a   Romans 8.1–17

Year 2

PSALM 35.5–10

OLD TESTAMENT   *Exodus 19.16–24   (MP/EP   Joel 2.21–32a)*

On the morning of the third day there was thunder and lightning, with a thick cloud over the mountain, and a very loud trumpet blast. Everyone in the camp trembled. Then Moses led the people out of the camp to meet with God, and they stood at the foot of the mountain. Mount Sinai was covered with smoke, because the LORD descended on it in fire. The smoke billowed up from it like smoke from a furnace, the whole mountain trembled violently, and the sound of the trumpet grew louder and louder. Then Moses spoke and the voice of God answered him.

The LORD descended to the top of Mount Sinai and called Moses to the top of the mountain. So Moses went up and the LORD said to him, 'Go down and warn the people so they do not force their way through to see the LORD and many of them perish. Even the priests, who approach the LORD, must consecrate themselves, or the LORD will break out against them.'

Moses said to the LORD, 'The people cannot come up Mount Sinai, because you yourself warned us, "Put limits

541

around the mountain and set it apart as holy." '

The LORD replied, 'Go down and bring Aaron up with you. But the priests and the people must not force their way through to come up to the LORD, or he will break out against them.'

EPISTLE* *Acts 2.1–11 (–21)*

When the day of Pentecost came, they were all together in one place. Suddenly a sound like the blowing of a violent wind came from heaven and filled the whole house where they were sitting. They saw what seemed to be tongues of fire that separated and came to rest on each of them. All of them were filled with the Holy Spirit and began to speak in other tongues as the Spirit enabled them.

Now there were staying in Jerusalem God-fearing Jews from every nation under heaven. When they heard this sound, a crowd came together in bewilderment, because each one heard them speaking in his own language. Utterly amazed, they asked: 'Are not all these men who are speaking Galileans? Then how is it that each of us hears them in his own native language? Parthians, Medes and Elamites; residents of Mesopotamia, Judea and Cappadocia, Pontus and Asia, Phrygia and Pamphylia, Egypt and the parts of Libya near Cyrene; visitors from Rome – (both Jews and converts to Judaism); Cretans and Arabs – we hear them declaring the wonders of God in our own tongues!'

GOSPEL *John 20.19–23*

On the evening of that first day of the week, when the disciples were together, with the doors locked for fear of the Jews, Jesus came and stood among them and said, 'Peace, be with you!' After he said this, he showed them his hands and side. The disciples were overjoyed when they saw the Lord.

Again Jesus said, 'Peace be with you! As the Father has sent me, I am sending you.' And with that he breathed on them and said, 'Receive the Holy Spirit. If you forgive anyone his sins, they are forgiven; if you do not forgive them, they are not forgiven.'

Psalm 104   Ezekiel 37.1–14   Romans 8.18–27

PENTECOST 1   TRINITY SUNDAY

The Holy Trinity

COLLECT

Almighty and eternal God,
you have revealed yourself
as Father, Son and Holy Spirit,
one holy and undivided Trinity,
and live and reign in the perfect unity of love:
Keep us in this faith,
that we may know you in all your ways,
and evermore rejoice in your eternal glory,
who are three Persons in one God,
now and for ever.   **Amen.**

Years 1 and 2

PSALM 93 *or* 97

OLD TESTAMENT   *Isaiah 6.1–8*

In the year that King Uzziah died, I saw the LORD seated on a
throne, high and exalted, and the train of his robe filled the
temple. Above him were seraphs, each with six wings: With
two wings they covered their faces, with two they covered
their feet, and with two they were flying. And they were
calling to one another:

'Holy, holy, holy is the LORD Almighty;
the whole earth is full of his glory.'

At the sound of their voices the doorposts and thresholds
shook and the temple was filled with smoke.
   'Woe to me!' I cried. 'I am ruined! For I am a man of
unclean lips, and I live among a people of unclean lips, and
my eyes have seen the King, the LORD Almighty.'
   Then one of the seraphs flew to me with a live coal in his
hand, which he had taken with tongs from the altar. With it
he touched my mouth and said, 'See, this has touched your
lips; your guilt is taken away and your sin atoned for.'
   Then I heard the voice of the LORD saying, 'Whom shall I
send? And who will go for us?'
   And I said, 'Here am I. Send me!'

EPISTLE* *Ephesians 1.3–14*

Praise be to the God and Father of our Lord Jesus Christ, who has blessed us in the heavenly realms with every spiritual blessing in Christ. For he chose us in him before the creation of the world to be holy and blameless in his sight. In love he predestined us to be adopted as his sons through Jesus Christ, in accordance with his pleasure and will – to the praise of his glorious grace, which he has freely given us in the One he loves. In him we have redemption through his blood, the forgiveness of sins, in accordance with the riches of God's grace that he lavished on us with all wisdom and understanding. And he made known to us the mystery of his will according to his good pleasure, which he purposed in Christ, to be put into effect when the times will have reached their fulfilment – to bring all things in heaven and on earth together under one head, even Christ.

In him we were also chosen, having been predestined according to the plan of him who works out everything in conformity with the purpose of his will, in order that we, who were the first to hope in Christ, might be for the praise of his glory. And you also were included in Christ when you heard the word of truth, the gospel of your salvation. Having believed, you were marked in him with a seal, the promised Holy Spirit, who is a deposit guaranteeing our inheritance until the redemption of those who are God's possession – to the praise of his glory.

GOSPEL *John 14.8–17*

Philip said to Jesus, 'Lord, show us the Father and that will be enough for us.'

Jesus answered: 'Do you not know me, Philip, even after I have been among you such a long time? Anyone who has seen me has seen the Father. How can you say, "Show us the Father"? Do you not believe that I am in the Father, and that the Father is in me? The words I say to you are not just my own. Rather, it is the Father, living in me, who is doing his work. Believe me when I say that I am in the Father and the Father is in me; or at least believe on the evidence of the miracles themselves. I tell you the truth, anyone who has faith in me will do what I have been doing. He will do even greater things than these, because I am going to the Father. And I will do whatever you ask in my name, so that the Son may bring glory to the Father. You may ask me for anything in my name, and I will do it.

'If you love me, you will obey what I command. And I will ask the Father, and he will give you another Counsellor to be with you for ever – the Spirit of truth. The world cannot accept him, because it neither sees him nor knows him. But you know him, for he lives with you and will be in you.'

Psalm 29; 33   Exodus 34.1–10   Acts 2.22–36
or Psalm 145   Isaiah 40.12–31   Mark 1.1–13

PENTECOST 2   TRINITY 1   *Green*

COLLECT

Almighty and eternal God,
you have called us to be your people:
Bring us to closer unity and fellowship
with you and one another,
so that every member of your Church
may serve you in holiness and truth;
through our Lord and Saviour Jesus Christ.   **Amen.**

Year 1

The People of God

PSALM 95.1–7

OLD TESTAMENT   *Exodus 19.1–6 (–11)*

In the third month after the Israelites left Egypt – on the very day – they came to the Desert of Sinai. After they set out from Rephidim, they entered the Desert of Sinai, and Israel camped there in the desert in front of the mountain.

Then Moses went up to God, and the Lord called to him from the mountain and said, 'This is what you are to say to the house of Jacob and what you are to tell the people of Israel: "You yourselves have seen what I did to Egypt, and how I carried you on eagles' wings and brought you to myself. Now if you obey me fully and keep my covenant, then out of all nations you will be my treasured possession. Although the whole earth is mine, you will be for me a kingdom of priests and a holy nation." These are the words you are to speak to the Israelites.'

EPISTLE* *1 Peter 2.1–10*

Rid yourselves of all malice and all deceit, hypocrisy, envy, and slander of every kind. Like newborn babies, crave pure spiritual milk, so that by it you may grow up in your salvation, now that you have tasted that the Lord is good.

As you come to him, the living Stone – rejected by men but chosen by God and precious to him – you also, like living stones, are being built into a spiritual house to be a holy priesthood, offering spiritual sacrifices acceptable to God through Jesus Christ. For in Scripture it says:

'See, I lay a stone in Zion,
a chosen and precious corner stone,
and the one who trusts in him
will never be put to shame.'

Now to you who believe, this stone is precious. But to those who do not believe,

'The stone the builders rejected
has become the capstone,'

and,

'A stone that causes men to stumble
and a rock that makes them fall.'

They stumble because they disobey the message – which is also what they were destined for.

But you are a chosen people, a royal priesthood, a holy nation, a people belonging to God, that you may declare the praises of him who called you out of darkness into his wonderful light. Once you were not a people, but now you are the people of God; once you had not received mercy, but now you have received mercy.

GOSPEL *John 15.1–5*

Jesus said, 'I am the true vine and my Father is the gardener. He cuts off every branch in me that bears no fruit, while every branch that does bear fruit he trims clean so that it will be even more fruitful. You are already clean because of the word I have spoken to you. Remain in me, and I will remain in you. No branch can bear fruit by itself; it must remain in the vine. Neither can you bear fruit unless you remain in me.

'I am the vine; you are the branches. If a man remains in

me and I in him, he will bear much fruit; apart from me you can do nothing.'

Psalm 85;133   Deuteronomy 30.1–10   Matthew 18.10–22

Year 2

The Church's Unity and Fellowship

PSALM 135.1–6

OLD TESTAMENT   *2 Samuel 7.4–16 (1–17)*

The word of the LORD came to Nathan, saying:

'Go and tell my servant David, "This is what the LORD says: Are you the one to build me a house to dwell in? I have not dwelt in a house from the day I brought the Israelites up out of Egypt to this day. I have been moving from place to place with a tent as my dwelling. Wherever I have moved with all the Israelites, did I ever say to any of their rulers whom I commanded to shepherd my people Israel, 'Why have you not built me a house of cedar?' "

'Now then, tell my servant David, "This is what the LORD Almighty says: I took you from the pasture and from following the flock to be ruler over my people Israel. I have been with you wherever you have gone, and I have cut off all your enemies from before you. Now I will make your name great, like the names of the greatest men of the earth. And I will provide a place for my people Israel and will plant them so that they can have a home of their own and no longer be disturbed. Wicked people shall not oppress them any more, as they did at the beginning and have done ever since the time I appointed leaders over my people Israel. I will also give you rest from all your enemies.

' "The LORD declares to you that the LORD himself will establish a house for you: When your days are over and you rest with your fathers, I will raise up your offspring to succeed you, who will come from your own body, and I will establish his kingdom. He is the one who will build a house for my Name, and I will establish the throne of his kingdom for ever. I will be his father, and he shall be my son. When he does wrong, I will punish him with the rod of men, with floggings inflicted by men. But my love will never be taken away from him, as I took it away from Saul, whom I removed from before you. Your house and your kingdom shall endure for ever before me; your throne shall be established for ever." '

Acts 2.37–47

When the people heard this, they were cut to the heart and said to Peter and the other apostles, 'Brothers, what shall we do?'

Peter replied, 'Repent and be baptized, every one of you, in the name of Jesus Christ so that your sins may be forgiven. And you will receive the gift of the Holy Spirit. The promise is for you and your children and for all who are far off – for all whom the Lord our God will call.'

With many other words he warned them; and he pleaded with them. 'Save yourselves from this corrupt generation.' Those who accepted his message were baptized, and about three thousand were added to their number that day.

They devoted themselves to the apostles' teaching and to the fellowship, to the breaking of bread and to prayer. Everyone was filled with awe, and many wonders and miraculous signs were done by the apostles. All the believers were together and had everything in common. Selling their possessions and goods, they gave to anyone as he had need. Every day they continued to meet together in the temple courts. They broke bread in their homes and ate together with glad and sincere hearts, praising God and enjoying the favour of all the people. And the Lord added to their number daily those who were being saved.

GOSPEL *Luke 14.15–24 (7–24)*

One of those at the table with Jesus said to him, 'Blessed is the man who will eat at the feast in the kingdom of God.'

Jesus replied: 'A certain man was preparing a great banquet and invited many guests. At the time of the banquet he sent his servant to tell those who had been invited, "Come, for everything is now ready."

'But they all alike began to make excuses. The first said, "I have just bought a field, and I must go and see it. Please excuse me."

'Another said, "I have just bought five yoke of oxen, and I am on my way to try them out. Please excuse me."

'Still another said, "I have just got married, so I cannot come."

'The servant came back and reported this to his master. Then the owner of the house became angry and ordered his servant, "Go out quickly into the streets and alleys of the town and bring in the poor, the crippled, the blind and the lame."

' "Sir," the servant said, "what you ordered has been done, but there is still room."

'Then the master told his servant, "Go out to the roads and country lanes and make them come in, so that my house will be full. I tell you, not one of those men who were invited will get a taste of my banquet." '

Psalm 89.1–18 (PB 1–19)   Ezekiel 37.15–28   Ephesians 2.11–22

PENTECOST 3   TRINITY 2   *Green*

COLLECT

Lord God our Father
through our Saviour Jesus Christ
you have assured mankind of eternal life,
and in baptism have made us one with him:
Deliver us from the death of sin,
and raise us to new life in your love,
in the fellowship of the Holy Spirit,
by the grace of our Lord Jesus Christ.   **Amen.**

Year 1

The Life of the Baptized

PSALM 44.1–9

OLD TESTAMENT   *Deuteronomy 6.17–25 (10–25)*

Be sure to keep the commands of the LORD your God and the stipulations and decrees he has given you. Do what is right and good in the LORD's sight, so that it may go well with you and you may go in and take over the good land that the LORD promised on oath to your forefathers, thrusting out all your enemies before you, as the LORD said.

In the future, when your son asks you, 'What is the meaning of the stipulations, decrees and laws the LORD our God has commanded you?' tell him: 'We were slaves of Pharaoh in Egypt, but the LORD brought us out of Egypt with a mighty hand. Before our eyes the LORD sent miraculous signs and wonders – great and terrible – upon Egypt and Pharaoh and his whole household. But he brought us out from there to bring us in and give us the land that he promised on oath to our forefathers. The LORD commanded us to obey all these decrees and to fear the LORD our God, so that we might always prosper and be kept alive, as is the case today. And if we are careful to obey all this law before the LORD our God, as he has commanded us, that will be our righteousness.'

EPISTLE* *Romans 6.3–11*

Do you not know that all of us who were baptized into Christ Jesus were baptized into his death? We were therefore buried with him through baptism into death in order that, just as Christ was raised from the dead through the glory of the Father, we too may live a new life.

If we have been united with him in his death, we will certainly also be united with him in his resurrection. For we know that our old self was crucified with him so that the body of sin might be rendered powerless, that we should no longer be slaves to sin – because anyone who has died has been freed from sin.

Now if we died with Christ, we believe that we will also live with him. For we know that since Christ was raised from the dead, he cannot die again; death no longer has mastery over him. The death he died, he died to sin once for all; but the life he lives, he lives to God.

In the same way, count yourselves dead to sin but alive to God in Christ Jesus.

GOSPEL *John 15.5–11*

Jesus said, 'I am the vine; you are the branches. If a man remains in me and I in him, he will bear much fruit; apart from me you can do nothing. If anyone does not remain in me, he is like a branch that is thrown away and withers; such branches are picked up, thrown into the fire and burned. If you remain in me and my words remain in you, ask what-

ever you wish, and it will be given you. This is to my
Father's glory, that you bear much fruit, showing yourselves
to be my disciples.

'As the Father has loved me, so have I loved you. Now
remain in my love. If you obey my commands, you will
remain in my love, just as I have obeyed my Father's commands and remain in his love. I have told you this so that my
joy may be in you and that your joy may be complete.'

Psalm 11;20   Micah 3.5–12   Matthew 5.27–48

Year 2

The Church's Confidence in Christ

PSALM 150

OLD TESTAMENT   *Deuteronomy 8.11–20*

Be careful that you do not forget the LORD your God, failing
to observe his commands, his laws and his decrees that I am
giving you this day. Otherwise, when you build fine houses
and settle down, and when your herds and flocks grow large
and your silver and gold increase and all you have is multi-
plied, then your heart will become proud and you will forget
the LORD your God, who brought you out of Egypt, out of
the land of slavery. He led you through the vast and dreadful desert, that thirsty and waterless land, with its venomous
snakes and scorpions. He brought you water out of hard
rock. He gave you manna to eat in the desert, something
your fathers had never known, to humble and to test you so
that in the end it might go well with you. You may say to
yourself, 'My power and the strength of my hands have produced this wealth for me.' But remember the LORD your
God, for it is he who gives you the ability to produce wealth,
and so confirms his covenant, which he swore to your forefathers, as it is today.

If you ever forget the LORD your God and follow other
gods and worship and bow down to them, I testify against
you today that you will surely be destroyed. Like the nations
the LORD destroyed before you, so you will be destroyed for
not obeying the LORD your God.

EPISTLE* *Acts 4.8–12 (1–22)*

Peter, filled with the Holy Spirit, said: 'Rulers and elders of the people! If we are being called to account today for an act of kindness shown to a cripple and are asked how he was healed, then know this, you and everyone else in Israel: It is by the name of Jesus Christ of Nazareth, whom you crucified but whom God raised from the dead, that this man stands before you completely healed. He is

' "the stone you builders rejected,
which has become the capstone."

Salvation is found in no one else, for there is no other name under heaven given to men by which we must be saved.'

GOSPEL *Luke 8.41–56*

A man named Jairus, a ruler of the synagogue, came and fell at Jesus' feet, pleading with him to come to his house because his only daughter, a girl of about twelve, was dying.

As Jesus was on his way, the crowds almost crushed him. And a woman was there who had been subject to bleeding for twelve years, but no one could heal her. She came up behind him and touched the edge of his cloak, and immediately her bleeding stopped.

'Who touched me?' Jesus asked.

When they all denied it, Peter said, 'Master, the people are crowding and pressing against you.'

But Jesus said 'Someone touched me; I know that power has gone out from me.'

Then the woman, seeing that she could not go unnoticed, came trembling and fell at his feet. In the presence of all the people, she told why she had touched him and how she had been instantly healed. Then he said to her, 'Daughter, your faith has healed you. Go in peace.'

While Jesus was still speaking, someone came from the house of Jairus, the synagogue ruler. 'Your daughter is dead,' he said. 'Do not bother the teacher any more.'

Hearing this, Jesus said to Jairus, 'Do not be afraid; just believe, and she will be healed.'

When he arrived at the house of Jairus, he did not let anyone go in with him except Peter, John and James, and the child's father and mother. Meanwhile, all the people were wailing and mourning for her. 'Stop wailing,' Jesus said,

'She is not dead but asleep.'

They laughed at him, knowing that she was dead. But he took her by the hand and said, 'My child, get up!' Her spirit returned, and at once she stood up. Then Jesus told them to give her something to eat. Her parents were astonished, but he ordered them not to tell anyone what had happened.

Psalm 32;36   Isaiah 32.1–8   Mark 4.21–41

PENTECOST 4   TRINITY 3 *Green*

COLLECT

Father,
you have sent the Spirit of your Son into our hearts,
and called us to the glorious liberty of your children:
Give us grace to use our freedom in your service,
and in our lives to follow in the footsteps
of our Lord and Master, Jesus Christ,
who lives and reigns with you and the Holy Spirit,
one God, now and ever.   **Amen.**

Year 1

The Freedom of the Sons of God

PSALM 63.1–9

OLD TESTAMENT *Deuteronomy 7.6–11 (1–11)*

You are a people holy to the LORD your God. The LORD your God has chosen you out of all the peoples on the face of the earth to be his people, his treasured possession.

The LORD did not set his affection on you and choose you because you were more numerous than other peoples, for you were the fewest of all peoples. But it was because the LORD loved you and kept the oath he swore to your forefathers that he brought you out with a mighty hand and redeemed you from the land of slavery, from the power of Pharaoh king of Egypt. Know therefore that the LORD your God is God; he is the faithful God, keeping his covenant of love to a thousand generations of those who love him and keep his commands. But those who hate him he will repay to their face by destruction; he will not be slow to repay to their face those who hate him.

Therefore, take care to follow the commands, decrees and laws I give you today.

EPISTLE* *Galatians 3.23 – 4.7*

Before this faith came, we were held prisoners by the law, locked up until faith should be revealed. So the law was put in charge to lead us to Christ that we might be justified by faith. Now that faith has come, we are no longer under the supervision of the law.

You are all sons of God through faith in Christ Jesus, for all of you who were baptized into Christ have been clothed with Christ. There is neither Jew nor Greek, slave nor free, male nor female, for you are all one in Christ Jesus. If you belong to Christ, then you are Abraham's seed, and heirs according to the promise.

What I am saying is that as long as the heir is a child, he is no different from a slave, although he owns the whole estate. He is subject to guardians and trustees until the time set by his father. So also, when we were children, we were in slavery under the basic principles of the world. But when the time had fully come, God sent his Son, born of a woman, born under law, to redeem those under law, that we might receive the full rights of sons. Because you are sons, God sent the Spirit of his Son into our hearts, the Spirit who calls out, '*Abba*, Father.' So you are no longer a slave, but a son; and since you are a son, God has made you also an heir.

GOSPEL *John 15.12–17 (–27)*

Jesus said, 'My command is this: Love each other as I have loved you. Greater love has no one than this, that he lay down his life for his friends. You are my friends if you do what I command. I no longer call you servants, because a servant does not know his master's business. Instead, I have called you friends, for everything that I learned from my Father I have made known to you. You did not choose me, but I chose you to go and bear fruit – fruit that will last. Then the Father will give you whatever you ask in my name. This is my command: Love each other.'

Psalm 42;43   Ezekiel 18.1–4,19–32   Romans 14.1 – 15.3

Year 2

The Church's Ministry to the Individual

PSALM 67

OLD TESTAMENT *Isaiah 63.7–14 (MP/EP Joshua 24.1–5,15–31)*

I will tell of the kindnesses of the Lord,
the deeds for which he is to be praised,
according to all the Lord has done for us–
yes, the many good things he has done
for the house of Israel,
according to his compassion and many kindnesses.
He said, 'Surely they are my people,
sons who will not be false to me';
and so he became their Saviour.
In all their distress he too was distressed,
and the angel of his presence saved them.
In his love and mercy he redeemed them;
he lifted them up and carried them
all the days of old.
Yet they rebelled
and grieved his Holy Spirit.
So he turned and became their enemy
and he himself fought against them.
Then his people recalled the days of old,
the days of Moses and his people,–
where is he who brought them through the sea,
with the shepherd of his flock?
Where is he who set
his Holy Spirit among them,
who sent his glorious arm of power
to be at Moses' right hand,
who divided the waters before them,
to gain for himself everlasting renown,
who led them through the depths?
Like a horse in open country,
they did not stumble;
like cattle that go down to the plain,
they were given rest by the Spirit of the Lord.
This is how you guided your people
to make for yourself a glorious name.

EPISTLE* *Acts 8.26–38 (–40)*

Now an angel of the Lord said to Philip, 'Go south to the road – the desert road – that goes down from Jerusalem to Gaza.' So he started out, and on his way he met an Ethiopian eunuch, an important official in charge of all the treasury of Candace, queen of the Ethiopians. This man had gone to Jerusalem to worship, and on his way home was sitting in his chariot reading the book of Isaiah the prophet. The Spirit told Philip, 'Go to that chariot and stay near it.'

Then Philip ran up to the chariot and heard the man reading Isaiah the prophet. 'Do you understand what you are reading?' Philip asked.

'How can I,' he said, 'unless someone explains it to me?' So he invited Philip to come up and sit with him.

The eunuch was reading this passage of Scripture:

'He was led like a sheep to the slaughter,
and as a lamb before the shearer is silent,
so he did not open his mouth.
In his humiliation he was deprived of justice.
Who can speak of his descendants?
For his life was taken from the earth.'

The eunuch asked Philip, 'Tell me, please, who is the prophet talking about, himself or someone else?' Then Philip began with that very passage of Scripture and told him the good news about Jesus.

As they travelled along the road, they came to some water and the eunuch said, 'Look, here is water. Why should I not be baptized?' And he ordered the chariot to stop. Then both Philip and the eunuch went down into the water and Philip baptized him.

GOSPEL *Luke 15.1–10*

Now the tax collectors and 'sinners' were all gathering around to hear Jesus. But the Pharisees and the teachers of the law muttered, 'This man welcomes sinners, and eats with them.'

Then Jesus told them this parable: 'Suppose one of you has a hundred sheep and loses one of them. Does he not leave the ninety-nine in the open country and go after the lost sheep until he finds it? And when he finds it, he joyfully puts it on his shoulders and goes home. Then he calls his friends and neighbours together and says, "Rejoice with me; I have found my lost sheep." I tell you that in the same way there is more rejoicing in heaven over one sinner who repents than over ninety-nine righteous persons who do not need to repent.

'Or suppose a woman has ten silver coins and loses one. Does she not light a lamp, sweep the house and search carefully until she finds it? And when she finds it, she calls her friends and neighbours together and says, "Rejoice with me; I have found my lost coin." In the same way, I tell you, there is rejoicing in the presence of the angels of God over one sinner who repents.'

Psalm 147   1 Kings 10.1–13   John 4.1–26 (*or* 1–42)

PENTECOST 5   TRINITY 4   *Green*

COLLECT

Father,
your love reaches out to all mankind,
and you have commanded us to follow
   your Son our Saviour:
Give us grace to do your will,
and to share in your Church's mission
to proclaim the gospel of your love to all the world;
through Jesus Christ our Lord.   **Amen.**

Year 1

The New Law

PSALM 119.57–64

OLD TESTAMENT   *Exodus 20.1–17*

God spoke all these words:

'I am the LORD your God, who brought you out of Egypt, out of the land of slavery.

'You shall have no other gods before me.

'You shall not make for yourself an idol in the form of anything in heaven above or on the earth beneath or in the waters below. You shall not bow down to them or worship

557

them; for I, the LORD your God, am a jealous God, punishing the children for the sin of the fathers to the third and fourth generation of those who hate me, but showing love to thousands who love me and keep my commandments.

'You shall not misuse the name of the LORD your God, for the LORD will not hold anyone guiltless who misuses his name.

'Remember the Sabbath day by keeping it holy. Six days you shall labour and do all your work, but the seventh day is a Sabbath to the LORD your God. On it you shall not do any work, neither you, nor your son or daughter, nor your manservant or maidservant, nor your animals, nor the alien within your gates. For in six days the LORD made the heavens and the earth, the sea, and all that is in them, but he rested on the seventh day. Therefore the LORD blessed the Sabbath day and made it holy.

'Honour your father and your mother, so that you may live long in the land the LORD your God is giving you.

'You shall not murder,

'You shall not commit adultery.

'You shall not steal.

'You shall not give false testimony against your neighbour.

'You shall not covet your neighbour's house. You shall not covet your neighbour's wife, or his manservant or maidservant, his ox or donkey, or anything that belongs to your neighbour.'

EPISTLE* *Ephesians 5.1–10*

Be imitators of God, therefore, as dearly loved children and live a life of love, just as Christ loved us and gave himself up for us as a fragrant offering and sacrifice to God.

But among you there must not be even a hint of sexual immorality, or of any kind of impurity, or of greed, because these are improper for God's holy people. Nor should there be obscenity, foolish talk or coarse joking, which are out of place, but rather thanksgiving. For of this you can be sure: No immoral, impure or greedy person – such a man is an idolater – has any inheritance in the kingdom of Christ and of God. Let no one deceive you with empty words, for because of such things God's wrath comes on those who are disobedient. Therefore do not be partners with them.

For you were once darkness, but now you are light in the Lord. Live as children of light (for the fruit of the light consists in all goodness, righteousness and truth) and find out what pleases the Lord.

GOSPEL *Matthew 19.16–26 (–30)*

A man came up to Jesus and asked, 'Teacher, what good thing must I do to get eternal life?'

'Why do you ask me about what is good?' Jesus replied. 'There is only One who is good. If you want to enter life, obey the commandments.'

'Which ones?' the man inquired.

Jesus replied, ' "Do not murder, do not commit adultery, do not steal, do not give false testimony, honour your father and mother," and "love your neighbour as yourself." '

'All these I have kept,' the young man said. 'What do I still lack?'

Jesus answered, 'If you want to be perfect, go, sell your possessions and give to the poor, and you will have treasure in heaven. Then come, follow me.'

When the young man heard this, he went away sad, because he had great wealth.

Then Jesus said to his disciples, 'I tell you the truth, it is hard for a rich man to enter the kingdom of heaven. Again I tell you, it is easier for a camel to go through the eye of a needle than for a rich man to enter the kingdom of God.'

When the disciples heard this, they were greatly astonished and asked, 'Who then can be saved?'

Jesus looked at them and said, 'With man this is impossible, but with God all things are possible.'

Psalm 119.41–56 Jonah 3; 4 Acts 13.1–13

Year 2

The Church's Mission to All Men

PSALM 119.89–96

OLD TESTAMENT *Ruth 1.8–17,22*
                                (MP/EP 2 Kings 6.24,25;7.3–20)

Naomi said to her two daughters-in-law, 'Go back, each of you, to your mother's home. May the LORD show kindness to you, as you have shown to your dead and to me. May the LORD grant that each of you will find rest in the home of another husband.'

Then she kissed them and they wept aloud and said to her, 'We will go back with you to your people.'

But Naomi said, 'Return home, my daughters. Why would you come with me? Am I going to have any more sons, who could become your husbands? Return home, my daughters; I am too old to have another husband. Even if I thought there was still hope for me – even if I had a husband tonight and then gave birth to sons – would you wait until they grew up? Would you remain unmarried for them? No, my daughters. It is more bitter for me than for you, because the LORD's hand has gone out against me!'

At this they wept again. Then Orpah kissed her mother-in-law good-bye, but Ruth clung to her.

'Look,' said Naomi, 'your sister-in-law is going back to her people and her gods. Go back with her.'

But Ruth replied, 'Do not urge me to leave you or to turn back from you. Where you go I will go, and where you stay I will stay. Your people will be my people and your God my God. Where you die I will die, and there I will be buried. May the LORD deal with me, be it ever so severely, if anything but death separates you and me.'

So Naomi returned from Moab accompanied by Ruth the Moabitess, her daughter-in-law, arriving in Bethlehem as the barley harvest was beginning.

EPISTLE* *Acts 11.4–18 (1–18)*

Peter began and explained everything precisely as it had happened: 'I was in the city of Joppa praying, and in a trance I saw a vision. I saw something like a large sheet being let down from heaven by its four corners, and it came down to where I was. I looked into it and saw four-footed animals of the earth, wild beasts, reptiles, and birds of the air. Then I heard a voice telling me, "Get up, Peter. Kill and eat."

'I replied, "Surely not, Lord! Nothing impure or unclean has ever entered my mouth."

'The voice spoke from heaven a second time, "Do not call anything impure that God has made clean." This happened three times, and then it was all pulled up to heaven again.

'Just then three men who had been sent to me from

Caesarea stopped at the house where I was staying. The Spirit told me to have no hesitation about going with them. These six brothers also went with me, and we entered the man's house. He told us how he had seen an angel appear in his house and say, "Send to Joppa for Simon who is called Peter. He will bring you a message through which you and all your household will be saved."

'As I began to speak, the Holy Spirit came on them as he had come on us at the beginning. Then I remembered what the Lord had said, "John baptized with water, but you will be baptized with the Holy Spirit." So if God gave them the same gift as he gave us, who believed in the Lord Jesus Christ, who was I to think that I could oppose God!'

When they heard this, they had no further objections and praised God, saying, 'So then, God has even granted the Gentiles repentance unto life.'

GOSPEL *Luke 10.1–12*

The Lord appointed seventy-two others and sent them two by two ahead of him to every town and place where he was about to go. He told them, 'The harvest is plentiful, but the workers are few. Ask the Lord of the harvest, therefore, to send out workers into his harvest field. Go! I am sending you out like lambs among wolves. Do not take a purse or bag or sandals; and do not greet anyone on the road.

'When you enter a house, first say, "Peace to this house." If a man of peace is there, your peace will rest on him; if not, it will return to you. Stay in that house, eating and drinking whatever they give you, for the worker deserves his wages. Do not move round from house to house.

'When you enter a town and are welcomed, eat what is set before you. Heal the sick who are there and tell them, "The kingdom of God is near you." But when you enter a town and are not welcomed, go into its streets and say, "Even the dust of your town that sticks to our feet we wipe off against you. Yet be sure of this: The kingdom of God is near." I tell you, it will be more bearable on that day for Sodom than for that town.'

Psalm 67;98   Nehemiah 8.1–12   Luke 11.37–54

PENTECOST 6   TRINITY 5 *Green*

The New Man

COLLECT

Almighty God,
without you we are not able to please you:
Mercifully grant that your Holy Spirit
may in all things direct and rule our hearts;
through Jesus Christ our Lord.   **Amen.**

Year 1

PSALM 112

OLD TESTAMENT   *Exodus 24.3–11   (MP/EP   2 Kings 22)*

When Moses went and told the people all the LORD's words
and laws, they responded with one voice, 'Everything the
LORD has said we will do.' Moses then wrote down everything the LORD had said.

He got up early the next morning and built an altar at the
foot of the mountain and set up twelve stone pillars repre-
senting the twelve tribes of Israel. Then he sent young
Israelite men, and they offered burnt offerings and sacrificed
young bulls as fellowship offerings to the LORD. Moses took
half of the blood and put it in bowls, and the other half he
sprinkled on the altar. Then he took the Book of the Covenant and read it to the people. They responded 'We will do
everything the LORD has said; we will obey.'

Moses then took the blood, sprinkled it on the people and
said, 'This is the blood of the covenant that the LORD has
made with you in accordance with all these words.'

Moses and Aaron, Nadab and Abihu, and the seventy
elders of Israel went up and saw the God of Israel. Under his
feet was something like a pavement made of sapphire, clear
as the sky itself. But God did not raise his hand against these
leaders of the Israelites; they saw God, and they ate and
drank.

EPISTLE*   *Colossians 3.12–17*

As God's chosen people, holy and dearly loved, clothe yourselves with compassion, kindness, humility, gentleness and

patience. Bear with each other and forgive whatever griev-
ances you may have against one another. Forgive as the Lord
forgave you. And over all these virtues put on love, which
binds them all together in perfect unity.

Let the peace of Christ rule in your hearts, since as
members of one body you were called to peace. And be
thankful. Let the word of Christ dwell in you richly as you
teach and admonish one another with all wisdom, and as
you sing psalms, hymns and spiritual songs with gratitude
in your hearts to God. And whatever you do, whether in
word or deed, do it all in the name of the Lord Jesus, giving
thanks to God the Father through him.

GOSPEL *Luke 15.11–32*

Jesus said, 'There was a man who had two sons. The
younger one said to his father, "Father, give me my share of
the estate." So he divided his property between them.

'Not long after that, the younger son got together all he
had, set off for a distant country and there squandered his
wealth in wild living. After he had spent everything, there
was a severe famine in that whole country, and he began to
be in need. So he went and hired himself out to a citizen of
that country, who sent him to his fields to feed pigs. He
longed to fill his stomach with the pods that the pigs were
eating, but no one gave him anything.

'When he came to his senses, he said, "How many of my
father's hired men have food to spare, and here I am starving
to death! I will set out and go back to my father and say to
him: Father, I have sinned against heaven and against you. I
am no longer worthy to be called your son; make me like one
of your hired men." So he got up and went to his father.

'But while he was still a long way off, his father saw him
and was filled with compassion for him; he ran to his son,
threw his arms around him and kissed him.

'The son said to him "Father, I have sinned against heaven
and against you. I am no longer worthy to be called your
son."

'But the father said to his servants, "Quick! Bring the best
robe and put it on him. Put a ring on his finger and sandals
on his feet. Bring the fattened calf and kill it. Let us have a
feast and celebrate. For this son of mine was dead and is
alive again; he was lost and is found." So they began to
celebrate.

'Meanwhile, the older son was in the field. When he came near the house, he heard music and dancing. So he called one of the servants and asked him what was going on. "Your brother has come," he replied, "and your father has killed the fattened calf because he has him back safe and sound."

'The older brother became angry and refused to go in. So his father went out and pleaded with him. But he answered his father, "Look! All these years I have been slaving for you and never disobeyed your orders. Yet you never gave me even a young goat so I could celebrate with my friends. But when this son of yours who has squandered your property with prostitutes comes home, you kill the fattened calf for him!'

' "My son," the father said, "you are always with me, and everything I have is yours. But we had to celebrate and be glad, because this brother of yours was dead and is alive again; he was lost and is found." '

Psalm 77   2 Samuel 12.1–18a (–23)   Acts 9.1–22

Year 2

PSALM 1

OLD TESTAMENT   *Micah 6.1–8   (MP/EP   Daniel 1)*

Listen to what the LORD says:

'Stand up, plead your case before the mountains;
let the hills hear what you have to say.
Hear, O mountains, the LORD's accusation;
listen, you everlasting foundations of the earth.
For the LORD has a case against his people;
he is lodging a charge against Israel.

'My people, what have I done to you?
How have I burdened you? Answer me.
I brought you up out of Egypt
and redeemed you from the land of slavery.
I sent Moses to lead you,
also Aaron and Miriam.
My people, remember what Balak
king of Moab counselled
and what Balaam son of Beor answered.
Remember your journey from Shittim to Gilgal,

that you may know the righteous acts of the LORD.'

With what shall I come before the LORD
and bow down before the exalted God?
Shall I come before him with burnt offerings,
with calves a year old?
Will the LORD be pleased with thousands of rams,
with ten thousand rivers of oil?
Shall I offer my firstborn for my transgression,
the fruit of my body for the sin of my soul?
He has showed you, O man, what is good.
And what does the LORD require of you?
To act justly and to love mercy
and to walk humbly with your God.

EPISTLE* *Ephesians 4.17–32*

I tell you this, and insist on it in the Lord, that you must no longer live as the Gentiles do, in the futility of their thinking. They are darkened in their understanding and separated from the life of God because of the ignorance that is in them due to the hardening of their hearts. Having lost all sensitivity, they have given themselves over to sensuality so as to indulge in every kind of impurity, with a continual lust for more.

You, however, did not come to know Christ that way. Surely you heard of him and were taught in him in accordance with the truth that is in Jesus. You were taught, with regard to your former way of life, to put off your old self, which is being corrupted by its deceitful desires; to be made new in the attitude of your minds; and to put on the new self, created to be like God in true righteousness and holiness.

Therefore each of you must put off falsehood and speak truthfully to his neighbour, for we are all members of one body. 'In your anger do not sin': Do not let the sun go down while you are still angry, and do not give the devil a foothold. He who has been stealing must steal no longer, but must work, doing something useful with his own hands, that he may have something to share with those in need.

Do not let any unwholesome talk come out of your mouths, but only what is helpful for building others up according to their needs, that it may benefit those who listen. And do not grieve the Holy Spirit of God, with whom you were sealed for the day of redemption. Get rid of all bitterness, rage and anger, brawling and slander, along with every form of malice. Be kind and compassionate to one another, forgiving each other, just as in Christ God forgave you.

GOSPEL *Mark 10.46–52*

As Jesus and his disciples, together with a large crowd, were leaving the city of Jericho, a blind man, Bartimaeus (that is, the Son of Timaeus), was sitting by the roadside begging. When he heard that it was Jesus of Nazareth, he began to shout, 'Jesus, Son of David, have mercy on me!'

Many rebuked him and told him to be quiet, but he shouted all the more, 'Son of David, have mercy on me!'

Jesus stopped and said, 'Call him.'

So they called to the blind man, 'Cheer up! On your feet! He is calling you.' Throwing his cloak aside, he jumped to his feet and came to Jesus.

'What do you want me to do for you?' Jesus asked him.

The blind man said, 'Rabbi, I want to see.'

'Go,' said Jesus, 'your faith has healed you.' Immediately he received his sight and followed Jesus along the road.

Psalm 102   Isaiah 43.14 – 44.5   Mark 2.18 – 3.6

PENTECOST 7   TRINITY 6   *Green*

The More Excellent Way

COLLECT

Lord, you have taught us
that all our doings without love are worth nothing:
Send your Holy Spirit
and pour into our hearts
that most excellent gift of love,
the true bond of peace and of all virtues,
for without love
whoever lives is counted dead before you.
Grant this for the sake of your only Son
our Lord and Saviour Jesus Christ.   **Amen.**

566

Year 1

PSALM 62

OLD TESTAMENT   *Hosea 11.1–9*

'When Israel was a child, I loved him,
and out of Egypt I called my son.
But the more I called Israel,
the further they went from me.
They sacrificed to the Baals
and they burned incense to images.
It was I who taught Ephraim to walk,
taking them by the arms;
but they did not realize it was I who healed them.
I led them with cords of human kindness,
with ties of love;
I lifted the yoke from their neck
and bent down to feed them.

'Will they not return to Egypt
and will not Assyria rule over them
because they refuse to repent?
Swords will flash in their cities,
will destroy the bars of their gates
and put an end to their plans.
My people are determined to turn from me.
Even if they call to the Most High,
he will by no means exalt them.

'How can I give you up, Ephraim?
How can I hand you over, Israel?
How can I treat you like Admah?
How can I make you like Zeboiim?
My heart is changed within me;
all my compassion is aroused.
I will not carry out my fierce anger,
nor devastate Ephraim again.
For I am God, and not man—
the Holy One among you.
I will not come in wrath.'

EPISTLE* *1 Corinthians 12.27 – 13.13*

You are the body of Christ, and each one of you is a part of it. And in the church God has appointed first of all apostles, second prophets, third teachers, then workers of miracles, also those having gifts of healing, those able to help others, those with gifts of administration, and those speaking in different kinds of tongues. Are all apostles? Are all prophets? Are all teachers? Do all work miracles? Do all have gifts of healing? Do all speak in tongues? Do all interpret? But eagerly desire the greater gifts.

And now I will show you the most excellent way.

If I speak in the tongues of men and of angels, but have not love, I am only a resounding gong or a clanging cymbal. If I have the gift of prophecy and can fathom all mysteries and all knowledge, and if I have a faith that can move mountains, but have not love, I am nothing. If I give all I possess to the poor and surrender my body to the flames, but have not love, I gain nothing.

Love is patient, love is kind. It does not envy, it does not boast, it is not proud. It is not rude, it is not self-seeking, it is not easily angered, it keeps no record of wrongs. Love does not delight in evil but rejoices with the truth. It always protects, always trusts, always hopes, always perseveres.

Love never fails. But where there are prophecies, they will cease; where there are tongues, they will be stilled; where there is knowledge, it will pass away. For we know in part and we prophesy in part, but when perfection comes, the imperfect disappears. When I was a child, I talked like a child, I thought like a child, I reasoned like a child. When I became a man, I put childish ways behind me. Now we see but a poor reflection; then we shall see face to face. Now I know in part; then I shall know fully, even as I am fully known.

And now these three remain: faith, hope and love. But the greatest of these is love.

GOSPEL *Matthew 18.21–35*

Peter came to Jesus and asked, 'Lord, how many times shall I forgive my brother when he sins against me? Up to seven times?'

Jesus answered, 'I tell you, not seven times, but seventy-seven times.

'Therefore, the kingdom of heaven is like a king who wanted to settle accounts with his servants. As he began the settlement, a man who owed him ten thousand talents was brought to him. Since he was not able to pay, the master ordered that he and his wife and his children and all that he had be sold to repay the debt.

'The servant fell on his knees before him. ''Be patient with me,'' he begged, ''and I will pay back everything.'' The servant's master took pity on him, cancelled the debt and let him go.

'But when that servant went out, he found one of his fellow servants who owed him a hundred denarii. He grabbed him and began to choke him. ''Pay back what you owe me!'' he demanded.

'His fellow servant fell to his knees and begged him, ''Be patient with me, and I will pay you back.''

'But he refused. Instead, he went off and had the man thrown into prison until he could pay the debt. When the other servants saw what had happened, they were greatly distressed and went and told their master everything that had happened.

'Then the master called the servant in. ''You wicked servant,'' he said, ''I cancelled all that debt of yours because you begged me to. Should you not have had mercy on your fellow servant just as I had on you?'' In anger his master turned him over to the jailers until he should pay back all he owed.

'This is how my heavenly Father will treat each of you unless you forgive your brother from your heart.'

Psalm 81 Genesis 50.15–26 1 John 2.1–17

Year 2

PSALM 103.8–18

OLD TESTAMENT *Deuteronomy 10.12 – 11.1*

And now, O Israel, what does the LORD your God ask of you but to fear the LORD your God, to walk in all his ways, to love him, to serve the LORD your God with all your heart and with all your soul, and to observe the LORD's commands and decrees that I am giving you today for your own good?

To the LORD your God belong the heavens, even the highest heavens, the earth and everything in it. Yet the LORD set his affection on your forefathers and loved them, and he chose you, their descendants, above all the nations, as it is today. Circumcise your hearts, therefore, and do not be stiffnecked any longer. For the LORD your God is God of gods and LORD of lords, the great God, mighty and awesome, who shows no partiality and accepts no bribes. He defends the cause of the fatherless and the widow, and loves the alien, giving him food and clothing. And you are to love those who are aliens, for you yourselves were aliens in Egypt. Fear the LORD your God and serve him. Hold fast to him and take your oaths in his name. He is your praise; he is your God, who performed for you those great and awesome wonders you saw with your own eyes. Your forefathers who went down into Egypt were seventy in all, and now the LORD your God has made you as numerous as the stars in the sky.

Love the LORD your God and keep his requirements, his decrees, his laws and his commands always.

EPISTLE* *Romans 8.1–11*

There is now no condemnation for those who are in Christ Jesus, because through Christ Jesus the law of the Spirit of life set me free from the law of sin and death. For what the law was powerless to do in that it was weakened by the sinful nature, God did by sending his own Son in the likeness of sinful man to be a sin offering. And so he condemned sin in sinful man, in order that the righteous requirements of the law might be fully met in us, who do not live according to the sinful nature but according to the Spirit.

Those who live according to the sinful nature have their minds set on what that nature desires; but those who live in accordance with the Spirit have their minds set on what the Spirit desires. The mind of sinful man is death, but the mind controlled by the Spirit is life and peace, because the sinful mind is hostile to God. It does not submit to God's law, nor can it do so. Those controlled by the sinful nature cannot please God.

You, however, are controlled not by the sinful nature but by the Spirit, if the Spirit of God lives in you. And if anyone does not have the Spirit of Christ, he does not belong to

Christ. But if Christ is in you, your body is dead because of sin, yet your spirit is alive because of righteousness. And if the Spirit of him who raised Jesus from the dead is living in you, he who raised Christ from the dead will also give life to your mortal bodies through his Spirit, who lives in you.

GOSPEL *Mark 12.28–34 (–44)*

One of the teachers of the law came and heard Jesus and the Sadducees debating. Noticing that Jesus had given them a good answer, he asked him, 'Of all the commandments, which is the most important?'

'The most important one,' answered Jesus, 'is this: "Hear, O Israel, the Lord our God, the Lord is one. Love the Lord your God with all your heart and with all your soul and with all your mind and with all your strength." The second is this: "Love your neighbour as yourself." There is no commandment greater than these.'

'Well said, teacher,' the man replied. 'You are right in saying that God is one and there is no other but him. To love him with all your heart, with all your understanding and with all your strength, and to love your neighbour as yourself is more important than all burnt offerings and sacrifices.'

When Jesus saw that he had answered wisely, he said to him, 'You are not far from the kingdom of God.' And from then on no one dared ask him any more questions.

Psalm 99;100;101 Deuteronomy 24.10–22 1 John 3.13–24

PENTECOST 8   TRINITY 7   *Green*

The Fruit of the Spirit

COLLECT

Almighty God,
who sent your Holy Spirit
to be the life and light of your Church:
Open our hearts to the riches of his grace,
that we may bring forth the fruit of the Spirit
in love and joy and peace;
through Jesus Christ our Lord.   **Amen.**

Year 1

PSALM 25.1–10 (PB1–9)

OLD TESTAMENT *Ezekiel 36.24–28 (MP/EP Proverbs 8.1–17)*

I will take you out of the nations; I will gather you from all
the countries and bring you back into your own land. I will
sprinkle clean water on you, and you will be clean; I will
cleanse you from all your impurities and from all your idols.
I will give you a new heart and put a new spirit in you; I will
remove from you your heart of stone and give you a heart of
flesh. And I will put my Spirit in you and move you to follow
my decrees and be careful to keep my laws. You will be my
people, and I will be your God.

EPISTLE* *Galatians 5.16–25*

Live by the Spirit, and you will not gratify the desires of the
sinful nature. For the sinful nature desires what is contrary
to the Spirit, and the Spirit what is contrary to the sinful
nature. They are in conflict with each other, so that you do
not do what you want. But if you are led by the Spirit, you
are not under law.

The acts of the sinful nature are obvious: sexual
immorality, impurity and debauchery; idolatry and witch-
craft; hatred, discord, jealousy, fits of rage, selfish ambition,
dissensions, factions and envy; drunkenness, orgies, and
the like. I warn you, as I did before, that those who live like
this will not inherit the kingdom of God.

But the fruit of the Spirit is love, joy, peace, patience,
kindness, goodness, faithfulness, gentleness and self-
control. Against such things there is no law. Those who
belong to Christ Jesus have crucified the sinful nature with
its passions and desires. Since we live by the Spirit, let us
keep in step with the Spirit.

GOSPEL *John 15.16–27 (MP/EP Luke 6.39–49)*

Jesus said, 'You did not choose me, but I chose you to go and
bear fruit – fruit that will last. Then the Father will give you
whatever you ask in my name. This is my command: Love
each other.

'If the world hates you, keep in mind that it hated me first.

If you belonged to the world, it would love you as its own. As it is, you do not belong to the world, but I have chosen you out of the world. That is why the world hates you. Remember the words I spoke to you: "No servant is greater than his master." If they persecuted me, they will persecute you also. If they obeyed my teaching, they will obey yours also. They will treat you this way because of my name, for they do not know the One who sent me. If I had not come and spoken to them, they would not be guilty of sin. Now, however, they have no excuse for their sin. He who hates me hates my Father as well. If I had not done among them what no one else did, they would not be guilty of sin. But now they have seen these miracles, and yet they have hated both me and my Father. But this is to fulfil what is written in their Law: "They hated me without reason."

'When the Counsellor comes, whom I will send to you from the Father, the Spirit of truth who goes out from the Father, he will testify about me; but you also must testify, for you have been with me from the beginning.'

Psalm 73   Numbers 11.16–17,24–29   Acts 8.4–25

Year 2

PSALM 27.1–8 (PB 1–7)

OLD TESTAMENT   *Ezekiel 37.1–14   (MP/EP   Isaiah 32.9–18)*

The hand of the LORD was upon me, and he brought me out by the Spirit of the LORD and set me in the middle of a valley; it was full of bones. He led me to and fro among them, and I saw a great many bones on the floor of the valley, bones that were very dry. He asked me, 'Son of man, can these bones live?'

I said, 'O Sovereign LORD, you alone know.'

Then he said to me, 'Prophesy to these bones and say to them, "Dry bones, hear the word of the LORD! This is what the Sovereign LORD says to these bones: I will make breath enter you, and you will come to life. I will attach tendons to you and make flesh come upon you and cover you with skin; I will put breath in you, and you will come to life. Then you will know that I am the LORD." '

So I prophesied as I was commanded. And as I was prophesying, there was a noise, a rattling sound, and the bones came together, bone to bone. I looked, and tendons and flesh appeared on them and skin covered them, but there was no breath in them.

Then he said to me, 'Prophesy to the breath; prophesy, son of man, and say to it, "This is what the Sovereign LORD says: Come from the four winds, O breath, and breathe into these slain, that they may live." ' So I prophesied as he commanded me, and breath entered them; they came to life and stood up on their feet – a vast army.

Then he said to me: 'Son of man, these bones are the whole house of Israel. They say, "Our bones are dried up and our hope is gone; we are cut off." Therefore prophesy and say to them: "This is what the Sovereign LORD says: O my people, I am going to open your graves and bring you up from them; I will bring you back to the land of Israel. Then you, my people, will know that I am the LORD, when I open your graves and bring you up from them. I will put my Spirit in you and you will live, and I will settle you in your own land. Then you will know that I the LORD have spoken, and I have done it, declares the LORD." '

EPISTLE* *1 Corinthians 12.4–13 (1–31a)*

There are different kinds of gifts, but the same Spirit. There are different kinds of service, but the same Lord. There are different kinds of working, but the same God works all of them in all men.

Now to each one the manifestation of the Spirit is given for the common good. To one there is given through the Spirit the message of wisdom, to another the message of knowledge by means of the same Spirit, to another gifts of healing by that one Spirit, to another miraculous powers, to another prophecy, to another the ability to distinguish between spirits, to another the ability to speak in different kinds of tongues, and to still another the interpretation of tongues. All these are the work of one and the same Spirit, and he gives them to each man, just as he determines.

The body is a unit, though it is made up of many parts; and though all its parts are many, they form one body. So it is with Christ. For we were all baptized by one Spirit into one body – whether Jews or Greeks, slave or free – and we were all given the one Spirit to drink.

GOSPEL *Luke 6.27–38*

Jesus said, 'I tell you who hear me: Love your enemies, do good to those who hate you, bless those who curse you, pray for those who ill-treat you. If someone strikes you on one cheek, turn to him the other also. If someone takes your cloak, do not stop him from taking your tunic. Give to everyone who asks you, and if anyone takes what belongs to you, do not demand it back. Do to others as you would have them do to you.

'If you love those who love you, what credit is that to you? Even "sinners" love those who love them. And if you do good to those who are good to you, what credit is that to you? Even "sinners" do that. And if you lend to those from whom you expect repayment, what credit is that to you? Even "sinners" lend to "sinners", expecting to be repaid in full. But love your enemies, do good to them, and lend to them without expecting to get anything back. Then your reward will be great, and you will be sons of the Most High, because he is kind to the ungrateful and wicked. Be merciful, just as your Father is merciful.

'Do not judge, and you will not be judged. Do not condemn, and you will not be condemned. Forgive, and you will be forgiven. Give, and it will be given to you. A good measure, pressed down, shaken together and running over, will be poured into your lap. For with the measure you use, it will be measured to you.'

Psalm 91   Exodus 35.20 – 36.7   1 Corinthians 14.1–19

PENTECOST 9   TRINITY 8

The Armour of God

Green

COLLECT

Almighty God
you call us to your service:
Give us strength to put on the armour you provide
that we may resist the assaults of the devil,
and ever trust in the salvation
which you have promised us
in Jesus Christ our Lord.   **Amen.**

Year 1

PSALM 18.1–7

OLD TESTAMENT *Joshua 1.1–9*

After the death of Moses the servant of the LORD, the LORD said to Joshua son of Nun, Moses' assistant: 'Moses my servant is dead. Now then, you and all these people, get ready to cross the Jordan River into the land I am about to give to them – to the Israelites. I will give you every place where you set your foot, as I promised Moses. Your territory will extend from the desert and from Lebanon to the great river, the Euphrates – all the Hittite country – and to the Great Sea on the west. No one will be able to stand up against you all the days of your life. As I was with Moses, so I will be with you; I will never leave you or forsake you.

'Be strong and courageous, because you will lead these people to inherit the land I swore to their forefathers to give them. Be strong and very courageous. Be careful to obey all the law my servant Moses gave you; do not turn from it to the right or to the left, that you may be successful wherever you go. Do not let this Book of the Law depart from your mouth; meditate on it day and night, so that you may be careful to do everything written in it. Then you will be prosperous and successful. Have I not commanded you? Be strong and courageous. Do not be terrified; do not be discouraged, for the LORD your God will be with you wherever you go.'

EPISTLE *Ephesians 6.10–20 (–24)*

Finally, be strong in the Lord and in his mighty power. Put on the full armour of God so that you can take your stand against the devil's schemes. For our struggle is not against flesh and blood, but against the rulers, against the authorities, against the powers of this dark world and against the spiritual forces of evil in the heavenly realms. Therefore put on the full armour of God, so that when the day of evil comes, you may be able to stand your ground, and after you have done everything, to stand. Stand firm then, with the belt of truth buckled around your waist, with the breastplate of righteousness in place, and with your feet fitted with the readiness that comes from the gospel of peace. In addition to all this, take up the shield of faith, with which you can extinguish all the flaming arrows of the evil one. Take the helmet of salvation and the sword of the Spirit, which is the word of God. And pray in the Spirit on all occasions with all kinds of prayers and requests. With this in mind, be alert and always keep on praying for all the saints.

Pray also for me, that whenever I open my mouth, words may be given me so that I will fearlessly make known the mystery of the gospel, for which I am an ambassador in chains. Pray that I may declare it fearlessly, as I should.

GOSPEL *John 17.11b–19*

Jesus prayed, 'Holy Father, protect those whom you gave me by the power of your name – the name you gave me – so that they may be one as we are one. While I was with them, I protected them and kept them safe by that name you gave me. None has been lost except the one doomed to destruction so that Scripture would be fulfilled.

'I am coming to you now, but I say these things while I am still in the world, so that they may have the full measure of my joy within them. I have given them your word and the world has hated them, for they are not of the world any more than I am of the world. My prayer is not that you take them out of the world but that you protect them from the evil one. They are not of the world, even as I am not of it. Sanctify them by the truth; your word is truth. As you sent me into the world, I have sent them into the world. For them I sanctify myself, that they too may be truly sanctified.'

Psalm 90   Nehemiah 4.7–23   Matthew 6.1–18

Year 2

PSALM 18.32–38 (PB 31–37)

OLD TESTAMENT *1 Samuel 17.37–50 (1.11,32–51)*

David said to Saul, 'The LORD who delivered me from the paw of the lion and the paw of the bear will deliver me from the hand of this Philistine.'

Saul said to David, 'Go, and the LORD be with you.'

Then Saul dressed David in his own tunic. He put a coat of armour on him and a bronze helmet on his head. David fastened on his sword over the tunic and tried walking around, because he was not used to them.

'I cannot go in these,' he said to Saul, 'because I am not used to them.' So he took them off. Then he took his staff in his hand, chose five smooth stones from the stream, put them in the pouch of his shepherd's bag and, with his sling in his hand, approached the Philistine.

Meanwhile, the Philistine, with his shield-bearer in front of him, kept coming closer to David. He looked David over and saw that he was only a boy, ruddy and handsome, and he despised him. He said to David, 'Am I a dog, that you come at me with sticks?' And the Philistine cursed David by his gods. 'Come here,' he said, 'and I will give your flesh to the birds of the air and the beasts of the field!'

David said to the Philistine, 'You come against me with sword and spear and javelin, but I come against you in the name of the LORD Almighty, the God of the armies of Israel, whom you have defied. This day the LORD will hand you over to me, and I will strike you down and cut off your head. Today I will give the carcasses of the Philistine army to the birds of the air and the beasts of the earth, and the whole world will know that there is a God in Israel. All those gathered here will know that it is not by sword or spear that the LORD saves; for the battle is the LORD's, and he will give all of you into our hands.'

As the Philistine moved closer to attack him, David ran quickly towards the battle line to meet him. Reaching into his bag and taking out a stone, he slung it and struck the Philistine on the forehead. The stone sank into his forehead, and he fell face down on the ground.

So David triumphed over the Philistine with a sling and a stone; without a sword in his hand he struck down the Philistine and killed him.

EPISTLE* *2 Corinthians 6.3–10 (1–10)*

We put no stumbling block in anyone's path, so that our ministry will not be discredited. Rather, as servants of God we commend ourselves in every way: in great endurance; in troubles, hardships, and distresses; in beatings, imprisonments and riots; in hard work, sleepless nights and hunger; in purity, understanding, patience and kindness; in the Holy Spirit and in sincere love; in truthful speech and in the power of God; with weapons of righteousness in the right hand and in the left; through glory and dishonour, bad report and good report; genuine, yet regarded as impostors; known, yet regarded as unknown; dying, and yet we live on; beaten, and yet not killed; sorrowful, yet always rejoicing; poor, yet making many rich; having nothing, and yet possessing everything.

GOSPEL   *Mark 9.14–29*

When Jesus, with Peter, James and John, came to the other disciples, they saw a large crowd around them and the teachers of the law arguing with them. As soon as all the people saw Jesus, they were overwhelmed with wonder and ran to greet him.

'What are you arguing with them about?' he asked.

A man in the crowd answered, 'Teacher, I brought you my son, who is possessed by a spirit that has robbed him of speech. Whenever it seizes him, it throws him to the ground. He foams at the mouth, gnashes his teeth and becomes rigid. I asked your disciples to drive out the spirit, but they could not.'

'O unbelieving generation,' Jesus replied, 'how long shall I stay with you? How long shall I put up with you? Bring the boy to me.'

So they brought him. When the spirit saw Jesus, it immediately threw the boy into a convulsion. He fell to the ground and rolled around, foaming at the mouth.

Jesus asked the boy's father, 'How long has he been like this?'

'From childhood,' he answered. 'It has often thrown him into fire or water to kill him. But if you can do anything, take pity on us and help us.'

' "If you can"?' said Jesus. 'Everything is possible for him who believes.'

Immediately the boy's father exclaimed, 'I do believe; help me overcome my unbelief!'

When Jesus saw that a crowd was running to the scene, he rebuked the evil spirit. 'You deaf and dumb spirit,' he said, 'I command you, come out of him and never enter him again.'

The spirit shrieked, convulsed him violently and came out. The boy looked so much like a corpse that many said, 'He is dead.' But Jesus took him by the hand and lifted him to his feet, and he stood up.

After Jesus had gone indoors, his disciples asked him privately, 'Why could we not drive it out?'

He replied, 'This kind can come out only by prayer.'

Psalm 24;46   2 Samuel 1.1–12,17–27   1 Timothy 6.6–21

PENTECOST 10   TRINITY 9 *Green*
The Mind of Christ

COLLECT

Lord Jesus Christ,
you humbled yourself in taking the form of a servant,
and in obedience died on the cross for our salvation:
Give us the mind to follow you
and proclaim you as Lord and King,
to the glory of God the Father.   **Amen.**

Year 1

PSALM 71.1–8 (PB 1–7)

OLD TESTAMENT   *Job 42.1–6 (38.1–11 and 42.1–6)*

Job replied to the LORD:

'I know that you can do all things;
no plan of yours can be thwarted.
You asked, "Who is this that obscures my counsel without
    knowledge?"
Surely I spoke of things I did not understand,
things too wonderful for me to know.

'You said, "Listen now, and I will speak;
I will question you, and you shall answer me."
My ears had heard of you
but now my eyes have seen you.
Therefore I despise myself and repent in dust and ashes.'

EPISTLE*   *Philippians 2.1–11*

If you have any encouragement from being united with
Christ, if any comfort from his love, if any fellowship with

the Spirit, if any tenderness and compassion, then make my joy complete by being like-minded, having the same love, being one in spirit and purpose. Do nothing out of selfish ambition or vain conceit, but in humility consider others better than yourselves. Each of you should look not only to your own interest, but also to the interests of others.

Your attitude should be the same as that of Christ Jesus:

Who, being in very nature God,
did not consider equality with God something to be grasped,
but made himself nothing,
taking the very nature of a servant,
being made in human likeness.
And being found in appearance as a man,
he humbled himself
and became obedient to death –
even death on a cross!

Therefore God exalted him to the highest place
and gave him the name that is above every name,
that at the name of Jesus every knee should bow,
in heaven and on earth and under the earth,
and every tongue confess that Jesus Christ is Lord,
to the glory of God the Father.

GOSPEL *John 13.1–15 (–20)*

It was just before the Passover Feast. Jesus knew that the time had come for him to leave this world and go to the Father. Having loved his own who were in the world, he now showed them the full extent of his love.

The evening meal was being served, and the devil had already prompted Judas Iscariot, son of Simon, to betray Jesus. Jesus knew that the Father had put all things under his power, and that he had come from God and was returning to God; so he got up from the meal, took off his outer clothing, and wrapped a towel round his waist. After that, he poured water into a basin and began to wash his disciples' feet, drying them with the towel that was wrapped around him.

He came to Simon Peter, who said to him, 'Lord, are you going to wash my feet?'

Jesus replied, 'You do not realize now what I am doing, but later you will understand.'

'No,' said Peter, 'you shall never wash my feet.'

Jesus answered, 'Unless I wash you, you have no part with me.'

'Then, Lord,' Simon Peter replied, 'not just my feet but my hands and my head as well!'

Jesus answered, 'A person who has had a bath needs only to wash his feet; his whole body is clean. And you are clean, though not every one of you.' For he knew who was going to betray him, and that was why he said not every one was clean.

When he had finished washing their feet, he put on his clothes and returned to his place. 'Do you understand what I have done for you?' he asked them. 'You call me "Teacher" and "Lord," and rightly so, for that is what I am. Now that I, your Lord and Teacher, have washed your feet, you also should wash one another's feet. I have set you an example that you should do as I have done for you.'

Psalm 19   1 Samuel 18.1–16   Mark 9.30–50

Year 2

PSALM 73.23–28

OLD TESTAMENT   *1 Samuel 24.9–17 (1–17)*

David said to Saul, 'Why do you listen when men say, "David is bent on harming you"? This day you have seen with your own eyes how the Lᴏʀᴅ gave you into my hands in the cave. Some urged me to kill you, but I spared you; I said "I will not lift my hand against my master, because he is the Lᴏʀᴅ's anointed." See, my father, look at this piece of your robe in my hand! I cut the corner off your robe but did not kill you. Now understand and recognize that I am not guilty of wrongdoing or rebellion. I have not wronged you, but you are hunting me down to take my life. May the Lᴏʀᴅ judge between you and me. And may the Lᴏʀᴅ avenge the wrongs you have done to me, but my hand will not touch you. As the old saying goes, "From evildoers come evil deeds," so my hand will not touch you.

'Against whom has the king of Israel come out? Whom are you pursuing? A dead dog? A flea? May the Lᴏʀᴅ be our judge and decide between us. May he consider my cause and uphold it; may he vindicate me by delivering me from your hand.'

When David finished saying this, Saul asked, 'Is that your voice, David my son?' And he wept aloud. 'You are more righteous than I,' he said. 'You have treated me well, but I have treated you badly.'

EPISTLE* *Galatians 6.1–10 (–18)*

Brothers, if someone is caught in a sin, you who are spiritual should restore him gently. But watch yourself, or you also may be tempted. Carry each other's burdens, and in this way you will fulfil the law of Christ. If anyone thinks he is something when he is nothing, he deceives himself. Each one should test his own actions. Then he can take pride in himself, without comparing himself to somebody else, for each one should carry his own load.

Anyone who receives instruction in the word must share all good things with his instructor.

Do not be deceived: God cannot be mocked. A man reaps what he sows. The one who sows to please his sinful nature, from that nature will reap destruction; the one who sows to please the Spirit, from the Spirit will reap eternal life. Let us not become weary in doing good, for at the proper time we will reap a harvest if we do not give up. Therefore, as we have opportunity, let us do good to all people, especially to those who belong to the family of believers.

GOSPEL *Luke 7.36–50*

Now one of the Pharisees invited Jesus to have dinner with him, so he went to the Pharisee's house and reclined at the table. When a woman who had lived a sinful life in that town learned that Jesus was eating at the Pharisee's house, she brought an alabaster jar of perfume, and as she stood behind him at his feet weeping, she began to wet his feet with her tears. Then she wiped them with her hair, kissed them and poured perfume on them.

When the Pharisee who had invited him saw this, he said to himself, 'If this man were a prophet, he would know who is touching him and what kind of woman she is – that she is a sinner.'

Jesus answered him, 'Simon, I have something to tell you.'

'Tell me, teacher,' he said.

'Two men owed money to a certain money-lender. One owed him five hundred denarii, and the other fifty. Neither of them had the money to pay him back, so he cancelled the debts of both. Now which of them will love him more?'

Simon replied, 'I suppose the one who had the bigger debt cancelled.'

'You have judged correctly,' Jesus said.

Then he turned towards the woman and said to Simon, 'Do you see this woman? I came into your house. You did not give me any water for my feet, but she wet my feet with her tears and wiped them with her hair. You did not give me a kiss, but this woman, from the time I entered, has not stopped kissing my feet. You did not put oil on my head, but she has poured perfume on my feet. Therefore, I tell you, her many sins have been forgiven – for she loved much. But he who has been forgiven little loves little.'

Then Jesus said to her, 'Your sins are forgiven.'

The other guests began to say among themselves, 'Who is this who even forgives sins?'

Jesus said to the woman, 'Your faith has saved you; go in peace.'

Psalm 1;4   2 Samuel 9   Matthew 6.19–34

PENTECOST 11   TRINITY 10 *Green*

The Serving Community

COLLECT

Almighty Father,
whose Son Jesus Christ has taught us
that what we do for the least of our brethren
we do also for him:
Give us the will to be the servant of others
as he was the servant of all,
who gave up his life and died for us,
but is alive and reigns with you and the Holy Spirit,
one God, now and for ever. **Amen.**

Year 1

PSALM 31.21–27

OLD TESTAMENT   *Isaiah 42.1–7 (–12)*

'Here is my servant, whom I uphold,
my chosen one in whom I delight;
I will put my Spirit on him
and he will bring justice to the nations.
He will not shout or cry out,
or raise his voice in the streets.
A bruised reed he will not break,
and a smouldering wick he will not snuff out.
In faithfulness he will bring forth justice;
he will not falter or be discouraged
till he establishes justice on earth.
In his law the islands will put their hope.'

This is what God the LORD says–
he who created the heavens and stretched them out,
who spread out the earth and all that comes out of it,
who gives breath to its people,
and life to those who walk on it:

'I, the LORD, have called you in righteousness;
I will take hold of your hand.
I will keep you and will make you
to be a covenant for the people
and a light for the Gentiles,
to open eyes that are blind,
to free captives from prison
and to release from the dungeon those who sit in darkness.'

EPISTLE*   *2 Corinthians 4.1–10*

Since through God's mercy we have this ministry, we do not
lose heart. Rather, we have renounced secret and shameful
ways; we do not use deception, nor do we distort the word
of God. On the contrary, by setting forth the truth plainly we
commend ourselves to every man's conscience in the sight of
God. And even if our gospel is veiled, it is veiled to those
who are perishing. The god of this age has blinded the
minds of unbelievers, so that they cannot see the light of the
gospel of the glory of Christ, who is the image of God. For

we do not preach ourselves, but Jesus Christ as Lord, and ourselves as your servants for Jesus' sake. For God, who said, 'Let light shine out of darkness,' made his light shine in our hearts to give us the light of the knowledge of the glory of God in the face of Christ.

But we have this treasure in jars of clay to show that this all-surpassing power is from God and not from us. We are hard pressed on every side, but not crushed; perplexed, but not in despair; persecuted, but not abandoned; struck down, but not destroyed. We always carry around in our body the death of Jesus, so that the life of Jesus may also be revealed in our body.

GOSPEL *John 13.31–35 (21–50)*

Jesus said, 'Now is the Son of Man glorified and God is glorified in him. If God is glorified in him, then God will glorify the Son in himself, and will glorify him at once.

'My children, I will be with you only a little longer. You will look for me, and just as I told the Jews, so I tell you now: Where I am going, you cannot come.

'A new commandment I give you: Love one another. As I have loved you, so you must love one another. All men will know that you are my disciples if you love one another.'

Psalm 123;124;125   Exodus 18.13–26   Acts 6

Year 2

PSALM 40.1–7

OLD TESTAMENT *1 Chronicles 29.1–9 (–16)*

King David said to the whole assembly: 'My son Solomon, the one whom God has chosen, is young and inexperienced. The task is great, because this palatial building is not for man but for the LORD God. With all my resources I have provided for the temple of my God – gold for the gold work, silver for the silver, bronze for the bronze, iron for the iron and wood for the wood, as well as onyx for the settings, turquoise, stones of various colours, and all kinds of fine stone and marble – all of these in large quantities. Besides, in my devotion to the temple of my God I now give my personal treasures of gold and silver for the temple of my God, over and above everything I have provided for this holy temple: three thousand talents of gold (gold of Ophir) and seven thousand talents of refined silver, for the overlaying of the walls of the building, for the gold work and the silver work, and for all the work to be done by the craftsmen. Now, who is willing to consecrate himself today to the LORD?'

Then the leaders of families, the officers of the tribes of Israel, the commanders of thousands and commanders of hundreds, and the officials in charge of the king's work gave willingly. They gave towards the work on the temple of God five thousand talents and ten thousand darics of gold, ten thousand talents of silver, eighteen thousand talents of bronze and a hundred thousand talents of iron. Any who had precious stones gave them to the treasury of the temple of the LORD in the custody of Jahiel the Gershonite. The people rejoiced at the willing response of their leaders, for they had given freely and wholeheartedly to the LORD. David the king also rejoiced greatly.

EPISTLE*   *Philippians 1.1–11*

Paul and Timothy, servants of Christ Jesus.

To all the saints in Christ Jesus at Philippi, together with the overseers and deacons:

Grace and peace to you from God our Father and the Lord Jesus Christ.

I thank my God every time I remember you. In all my prayers for all of you, I always pray with joy because of your partnership in the gospel from the first day until now, being confident of this, that he who began a good work in you will carry it on to completion until the day of Christ Jesus.

It is right for me to feel this way about all of you, since I have you in my heart; for whether I am in chains or defending and confirming the gospel, all of you share in God's grace with me. God can testify how I long for all of you with the affection of Christ Jesus.

And this is my prayer: that your love may abound more and more in knowledge and depth of insight, so that you may be able to discern what is best and may be pure and blameless until the day of Christ, filled with the fruit of righteousness that comes through Jesus Christ – to the glory and praise of God.

GOSPEL *Matthew 20.1–16 (MP/EP Luke 17.5–10)*

Jesus said to his disciples, 'The kingdom of heaven is like a landowner who went out early in the morning to hire men to work in his vineyard. He agreed to pay them a denarius for the day and sent them into his vineyard.

'About the third hour he went out and saw others standing in the market-place doing nothing. He told them, "You also go and work in my vineyard, and I will pay you whatever is right." So they went.

'He went out again about the sixth hour and the ninth hour and did the same thing. About the eleventh hour he went out and found still others standing around. He asked them, "Why have you been standing here all day long doing nothing?"

' "Because no one has hired us," they answered.

'He said to them, "You also go and work in my vineyard."

'When evening came, the owner of the vineyard said to his foreman, "Call the workers and pay them their wages, beginning with the last ones hired and going on to the first."

'The workers who were hired about the eleventh hour came and each received a denarius. So when those came who were hired first, they expected to receive more. But each one of them also received a denarius. When they received it, they began to grumble against the landowner. "These men who were hired last worked only one hour," they said, "and you have made them equal to us who have borne the burden of the work and the heat of the day."

'But he answered one of them, "Friend, I am not being unfair to you. Did you not agree to work for a denarius? Take your pay and go. I want to give the man who was hired last the same as I gave you. Do I not have the right to do what I want with my own money? Or are you envious because I am generous?"

'So the last will be first, and the first will be last.'

Psalm 82;112   1 Kings 12.1–10   2 Corinthians 9

PENTECOST 12   TRINITY 11   *Green*

The Witnessing Community

COLLECT

Eternal Father,
you gave your apostles grace
to believe and to proclaim your word:
Grant that your Church may love and preach
the word which they believed,
and give to all men grace to come to you, the only God;
through Jesus Christ our Lord.   **Amen.**

Year 1

PSALM 96.1–6 (–13)

OLD TESTAMENT   *Isaiah 49.1–6 (–13)*

Listen to me, you islands;
hear this you distant nations:
Before I was born the LORD called me;
from my birth he has made mention of my name.
He made my mouth like a sharpened sword,
in the shadow of his hand he hid me;
he made me into a polished arrow
and concealed me in his quiver.
He said to me, 'You are my servant,
Israel, in whom I will display my splendour.'
But I said, 'I have laboured to no purpose;
I have spent my strength in vain and for nothing.
Yet what is due to me is in the LORD's hand,
and my reward is with my God.'

And now the LORD says—
he who formed me in the womb to be his servant
to bring Jacob back to him
and gather Israel to himself,
for I am honoured in the eyes of the LORD
and my God has been my strength—
he says:
'It is too small a thing for you to be my servant
to restore the tribes of Jacob
and bring back those of Israel I have kept.

I will also make you a light for the Gentiles,
that you may bring my salvation to the ends of the earth.'

EPISTLE*   *2 Corinthians 5.14 – 6.2 (5.11 – 6.2)*

Christ's love compels us, because we are convinced that one
died for all, and therefore all died. And he died for all, that
those who live should no longer live for themselves but for
him who died for them and was raised again.

So from now on we regard no one from a worldly point of
view. Though we once regarded Christ in this way, we do so
no longer. Therefore, if anyone is in Christ, he is a new
creation; the old has gone, the new has come! All this is from
God, who reconciled us to himself through Christ and gave
us the ministry of reconciliation: that God was reconciling
the world to himself in Christ, not counting men's sins
against them. And he has committed to us the message of
reconciliation. We are therefore Christ's ambassadors, as
though God were making his appeal through us. We implore
you on Christ's behalf: Be reconciled to God. God made him
who had no sin to be sin for us, so that in him we might
become the righteousness of God.

As God's fellow workers we urge you not to receive God's
grace in vain. For he says,

'In the time of my favour I heard you,
and in the day of salvation I helped you.'

I tell you, now is the time of God's favour, now is the day of
salvation.

GOSPEL   *John 17.20–26*

After speaking to his disciples, Jesus looked towards heaven
and prayed, 'My prayer is not for them alone. I pray also for
those who will believe in me through their message, that all
of them may be one, Father, just as you are in me and I am in
you. May they also be in us so that the world may believe
that you have sent me. I have given them the glory that you
gave me, that they may be one as we are one: I in them and
you in me. May they be brought to complete unity to let the
world know that you sent me and have loved them even as
you have loved me.

'Father, I want those you have given me to be with me
where I am, and to see my glory, the glory you have given

me because you loved me before the creation of the world.

'Righteous Father, though the world does not know you, I know you, and they know that you have sent me. I have made you known to them, and will continue to make you known in order that the love you have for me may be in them and that I myself may be in them.'

Psalm 145;150   Ezekiel 33.1–9,30–33   Acts 16.1–15

Year 2

PSALM 96.7–13 (1–13)

OLD TESTAMENT   *Micah 4.1–5   (MP/EP   Jonah 1 and 2)*

In the last days
the mountain of the LORD's temple will be established
as chief among the mountains;
it will be raised above the hills,
and peoples will stream to it.

Many nations will come and say,
'Come, let us go up to the mountain of the LORD,
to the house of the God of Jacob.
He will teach us his ways,
so that we may walk in his paths.'
The law will go out from Zion,
the word of the LORD from Jerusalem.
He will judge between many peoples
and will settle disputes for strong nations far and wide.
They will beat their swords into ploughshares
and their spears into pruning hooks.
Nation will not take up sword against nation,
nor will they train for war any more.
Every man will sit under his own vine
and under his own fig-tree,
and no one will make them afraid,
for the LORD Almighty has spoken.
All the nations may walk in the name of their gods;
we will walk in the name of the LORD
our God for ever and ever.

EPISTLE* *Acts 17.22–34 (MP/EP Acts 28)*

Paul then stood up in the meeting of the Areopagus and said: 'Men of Athens! I see that in every way you are very religious. For as I walked round and observed your objects of worship, I even found an altar with this inscription: TO AN UNKNOWN GOD. Now what you worship as something unknown I am going to proclaim to you.

'The God who made the world and everything in it is the Lord of heaven and earth and does not live in temples built by hands. And he is not served by human hands, as if he needed anything, because he himself gives all men life and breath and everything else. From one man he made every nation of men, that they should inhabit the whole earth; and he determined the times set for them and the exact places where they should live. God did this so that men would seek him and perhaps reach out for him and find him, though he is not far from each one of us. "For in him we live and move and have our being." As some of your own poets have said, "We are his offspring."

'Therefore since we are God's offspring, we should not think that the divine being is like gold or silver or stone – an image made by man's design and skill. In the past God overlooked such ignorance, but now he commands all people everywhere to repent. For he has set a day when he will judge the world with justice by the man he has appointed. He has given proof of this to all men by raising him from the dead.'

When they heard about the resurrection of the dead, some of them sneered, but others said, 'We want to hear you again on this subject.' At that, Paul left the Council. A few men became followers of Paul and believed. Among them was Dionysius, a member of the Areopagus, also a woman named Damaris, and a number of others.

GOSPEL *Matthew 5.13–16*

Jesus said, 'You are the salt of the earth. But if the salt loses its saltiness, how can it be made salty again? It is no longer good for anything, except to be thrown out and trampled by men.

'You are the light of the world. A city on a hill cannot be hidden. Neither do people light a lamp and put it under a bowl. Instead they put it on its stand, and it gives light to everyone in the house. In the same way, let your light shine before men, that they may see your good deeds and praise your Father in heaven.'

Psalm 34   Amos 5.14–24 (*or* 6–24)   Romans 15.14–29

PENTECOST 13   TRINITY 12

Green

The Suffering Community

COLLECT

Lord God,
your blessed Son our Saviour
gave his back to the smiters
and did not hide his face from shame:
Give us grace to endure the sufferings of the present time
with sure confidence in the glory that shall be revealed;
through Jesus Christ our Lord.   **Amen.**

Year 1

PSALM 31.1–5 (PB 1–6)

OLD TESTAMENT   *Isaiah 50.4–9a*

The Sovereign LORD has given me an instructed tongue,
to know the word that sustains the weary.
He wakens me morning by morning,
wakens my ear to listen like one being taught.
The Sovereign LORD has opened my ears,
and I have not been rebellious;
I have not drawn back.
I offered my back to those who beat me,
my cheeks to those who pulled out my beard;
I did not hide my face
from mocking and spitting.
Because the Sovereign LORD helps me,
I will not be disgraced.
Therefore have I set my face like flint,
and I know I will not be put to shame.
He who vindicates me is near.
Who then will bring charges against me?

Let us face each other!
Who is my accuser?
Let him confront me!
It is the Sovereign LORD who helps me.
Who is he that will condemn me?

EPISTLE *Acts 7.54 – 8.1   (MP/EP   1 Peter 4)*

When the Sanhedrin heard Stephen, they were furious and gnashed their teeth at him. But Stephen, full of the Holy Spirit, looked up to heaven and saw the glory of God, and Jesus standing at the right hand of God. 'Look,' he said. 'I see heaven open and the Son of Man standing at the right hand of God.'

At this they covered their ears and, yelling at the top of their voices, they all rushed at him, dragged him out of the city and began to stone him. Meanwhile, the witnesses laid their clothes at the feet of a young man named Saul.

While they were stoning him, Stephen prayed, 'Lord Jesus, receive my spirit.' Then he fell on his knees and cried out, 'Lord, do not hold this sin against them.' When he had said this, he fell asleep.

And Saul was there, giving approval to his death.

On that day a great persecution broke out against the church at Jerusalem, and all except the apostles were scattered throughout Judea and Samaria.

GOSPEL *John 16.1–11*

Jesus said, 'All this I have told you so that you will not go astray. They will put you out of the synagogue; in fact, a time is coming when anyone who kills you will think he is offering a service to God. They will do such things because they have not known the Father or me. I have told you this, so that when the time comes you will remember that I warned you. I did not tell you this at first because I was with you.

'Now I am going to him who sent me, yet none of you asks me, "Where are you going?" Because I have said these things, you are filled with grief. But I tell you the truth: It is for your good that I am going away. Unless I go away, the Counsellor will not come to you; but if I go, I will send him to you. When he comes, he will convict the world of guilt in regard to sin and righteousness and judgment: in regard to sin, because men do not believe in me; in regard to right-eousness, because I am going to the Father, where you can see me no longer; and in regard to judgment, because the prince of this world now stands condemned.'

Psalm 130; 137.1–6 2 Kings 19.8–19 Acts 16.16–40

Year 2

PSALM 43

OLD TESTAMENT *Jeremiah 20.7–11a (1–11a)*

O LORD, you deceived me, and I was deceived;
you overpowered me and prevailed.
I am ridiculed all day long;
everyone mocks me.
Whenever I speak, I cry out
proclaiming violence and destruction.
So the word of the LORD has brought me
insult and reproach all day long.
But if I say, 'I will not mention him
or speak any more in his name,'
his word is in my heart like a burning fire,
shut up in my bones.
I am weary of holding it in;
indeed, I cannot.
I hear many whispering,
'Terror on every side!
Report him! Let us report him!'
All my friends are waiting for me to slip, saying,
'Perhaps he will be deceived;
then we will prevail over him
and take our revenge on him.'
But the LORD is with me like a mighty warrior;
so my persecutors will stumble and not prevail.

EPISTLE* *Acts 20.17–35 (–38)*

From Miletus, Paul sent to Ephesus for the elders of the church. When they arrived, he said to them: 'You know how I lived the whole time I was with you, from the first day I came into the province of Asia. I served the Lord with great humility and with tears, although I was severely tested by the plots of the Jews. You know that I have not hesitated to preach anything that would be helpful to you but have taught you publicly and from house to house. I have declared to both Jews and Greeks that they must turn to God in repentance and have faith in our Lord Jesus.

'And now, compelled by the Spirit, I am going to Jerusalem, not knowing what will happen to me there. I only know that in every city the Holy Spirit warns me that prison and hardships are facing me. However, I consider my life worth nothing to me, if only I may finish the race and complete the task the Lord Jesus has given me – the task of testifying the gospel of God's grace.

'Now I know that none of you among whom I have gone about preaching the kingdom will ever see me again. Therefore, I declare to you today that I am innocent of the blood of all men. For I have not hesitated to proclaim to you the whole will of God. Guard yourselves and all the flock of which the Holy Spirit has made you overseers. Be shepherds of the church of God, which he bought with his own blood. I know that after I leave, savage wolves will come in among you and will not spare the flock. Even from your own number men will arise and distort the truth in order to draw away disciples after them. So be on your guard! Remember that for three years I never stopped warning each of you night and day with tears.

'Now I commit you to God and to the word of his grace, which can build you up and give you an inheritance among all those who are sanctified. I have not coveted anyone's silver or gold or clothing. You yourselves know that these hands of mine supplied my own needs and the needs of my companions. In everything I did, I showed you that by this kind of hard work we must help the weak, remembering the words the Lord Jesus himself said: "It is more blessed to give than to receive." '

GOSPEL *Matthew 10.16–22*

Jesus said to the disciples, 'I am sending you out like sheep among wolves. Therefore be as shrewd as snakes and as innocent as doves. But be on your guard against men; they will hand you over to the local councils and flog you in their synagogues. On my account you will be brought before governors and kings as witnesses to them and to the Gentiles. But when they arrest you, do not worry about what to say or how to say it. At that time you will be given what to say, for it will not be you speaking, but the Spirit of your Father speaking through you.

'Brother will betray brother to death, and a father his child; children will rebel against their parents and have them put to death. All men will hate you because of me, but he who stands firm to the end will be saved.'

Psalm 22.1–22 (PB 1–21)   Isaiah 49.13–23   Matthew 11.20–29

PENTECOST 14   TRINITY 13   *Green*
The Family

COLLECT

God our Father,
your Son Jesus Christ lived in a family at Nazareth:
Grant that in our families on earth
we may so learn to love and to live together
that we may rejoice as one family
in your heavenly home;
through Jesus Christ our Lord.   **Amen.**

Year 1

PSALM 127

OLD TESTAMENT   *Proverbs 31.10–31*

A wife of noble character who can find?
She is worth far more than rubies.
Her husband has full confidence in her
and lacks nothing of value.
She brings him good, not harm,
all the days of her life.
She selects wool and flax
and works with eager hands.
She is like the merchant ships,
bringing her food from afar.
She gets up while it is still dark;
she provides food for her family
and portions for her servant girls.

She considers a field and buys it;
out of her earnings she plants a vineyard.
She sets about her work vigorously;
her arms are strong for her tasks.
She sees that her trading is profitable,
and her lamp does not go out at night.
In her hand she holds the distaff
and grasps the spindle with her fingers.
She opens her arms to the poor
and extends her hands to the needy.
When it snows, she has no fear for her household;
for all of them are clothed in scarlet.
She makes coverings for her bed;
she is clothed in fine linen and purple.
Her husband is respected at the city gate,
where he takes his seat among the elders of the land.
She makes linen garments and sells them,
and supplies the merchants with sashes.
She is clothed with strength and dignity;
she can laugh at the days to come.
She speaks with wisdom,
and faithful instruction is on her tongue.
She watches over the affairs of her household
and does not eat the bread of idleness.
Her children arise and call her blessed;
her husband also, and he praises her:
'Many women do noble things,
but you surpass them all.'
Charm is deceptive, and beauty is fleeting;
but a woman who fears the LORD is to be praised.
Give her the reward she has earned,
and let her works bring her praise at the city gate.

EPISTLE* *Ephesians 5.25 – 6.4 (MP/EP 1 Corinthians 1.1–18)*

Husbands, love your wives, just as Christ loved the church
and gave himself up for her to make her holy, cleansing her
by the washing with water through the word, and to present
her to himself as a radiant church, without stain or wrinkle
or any other blemish, but holy and blameless. In this same
way, husbands ought to love their wives as their own
bodies. He who loves his wife loves himself. After all, no one
ever hated his own body, but he feeds and cares for it, just as

Christ does the church – for we are members of his body. 'For this reason a man will leave his father and mother and be united to his wife, and the two will become one flesh.' This is a profound mystery – but I am talking about Christ and the church. However, each one of you also must love his wife as he loves himself, and the wife must respect her husband.

Children, obey your parents in the Lord, for this is right. 'Honour your father and mother' – which is the first commandment with a promise – 'that it may go well with you and that you may enjoy life on the earth.'

Fathers, do not exasperate your children; instead, bring them up in the training and instruction of the Lord.

GOSPEL   *Mark 10.2–16*

Some Pharisees came and tested Jesus by asking, 'Is it lawful for a man to divorce his wife?'

'What did Moses command you?' he replied.

They said, 'Moses permitted a man to write a certificate of divorce and send her away.'

'It was because your hearts were hard that Moses wrote you this law,' Jesus replied. 'But at the beginning of creation God "made them male and female". "For this reason a man will leave his father and mother and be united to his wife, and the two will become one flesh". So they are no longer two, but one. Therefore what God has joined together, let man not separate.'

When they were in the house again, the disciples asked Jesus about this. He answered, 'Anyone who divorces his wife and marries another woman commits adultery against her. And if she divorces her husband and marries another man, she commits adultery.'

People were bringing little children to Jesus to have him touch them, but the disciples rebuked them. When Jesus saw this, he was indignant. He said to them, 'Let the little children come to me, and do not hinder them, for the kingdom of God belongs to such as these. I tell you the truth, anyone who will not receive the kingdom of God like a little child will never enter it.' And he took the children in his arms, put his hands on them and blessed them.

Psalm 103   Genesis 29.1–20   2 Timothy 1.1–14

Year 2

PSALM 128

OLD TESTAMENT *Genesis 45.1–15 (1–28)*

Joseph could no longer control himself before all his attendants, and he cried out, 'Make everyone leave my presence!' So there was no one with Joseph when he made himself known to his brothers. And he wept so loudly that the Egyptians heard him, and Pharaoh's household heard about it.

Joseph said to his brothers, 'I am Joseph! Is my father still living?' But his brothers were not able to answer him, because they were terrified at his presence.

Then Joseph said to his brothers, 'Come close to me.' When they had done so, he said, 'I am your brother Joseph, the one you sold into Egypt! And now, do not be distressed and do not be angry with yourselves for selling me here, because it was to save lives that God sent me ahead of you. For two years now there has been famine in the land, and for the next five years there will not be ploughing and reaping. But God sent me ahead of you to preserve for you a remnant on earth and to save your lives by a great deliverance.

'So then, it was not you who sent me here, but God. He made me father to Pharaoh, lord of his entire household and ruler of all Egypt. Now hurry back to my father and say to him, "This is what your son Joseph says: God has made me lord of all Egypt. Come down to me; do not delay. You shall live in the region of Goshen and be near me – you, your children and grandchildren, your flocks and herds, and all you have. I will provide for you there, because five years of famine are still to come. Otherwise you and your household and all who belong to you will become destitute."

'You can see for yourselves, and so can my brother Benjamin, that it is really I who am speaking to you. Tell my father about all the honour accorded me in Egypt and about everything you have seen. And bring my father down here quickly.'

Then he threw his arms around his brother Benjamin and wept, and Benjamin embraced him, weeping. And he kissed all his brothers and wept over them. Afterwards his brothers talked with him.

EPISTLE* *Ephesians 3.14–21*

I kneel before the Father, from whom his whole family in heaven and on earth derives its name. I pray that out of his glorious riches he may strengthen you with power through his Spirit in your inner being, so that Christ may dwell in your hearts through faith. And I pray that you, being rooted and established in love, may have power, together with all the saints, to grasp how wide and long and high and deep is the love of Christ, and to know this love that surpasses knowledge – that you may be filled to the measure of all the fulness of God.

Now to him who is able to do immeasurably more than all we ask or imagine, according to his power that is at work within us, to him be glory in the church and in Christ Jesus throughout all generations, for ever and ever! Amen.

GOSPEL *Luke 11.1–13 (MP/EP Luke 2.41–52)*

One day Jesus was praying in a certain place. When he finished, one of his disciples said to him, 'Lord, teach us to pray, just as John taught his disciples.'

He said to them, 'When you pray, say:

' "Father,
hallowed be your name,
your kingdom come.
Give us each day our daily bread.
Forgive us our sins,
for we also forgive everyone who sins against us.
And lead us not into temptation." '

Then he said to them, 'Suppose one of you has a friend, and he goes to him at midnight and says, "Friend, lend me three loaves of bread, because a friend of mine on a journey has come to me, and I have nothing to set before him."

'Then the one inside answers, "Do not bother me. The door is already locked, and my children are with me in bed. I cannot get up and give you anything." I tell you, though he will not get up and give him the bread because he is his friend, yet because of the man's persistence he will get up and give him as much as he needs.

'So I say to you: Ask and it will be given to you; seek and you will find; knock and the door will be opened to you. For everyone who asks receives; he who seeks finds; and to him who knocks, the door will be opened.

'Which of you fathers, if your son asks for a fish, will give him a snake instead? Or if he asks for an egg, will give him a scorpion? If you then, though you are evil, know how to give good gifts to your children, how much more will your Father in heaven give the Holy Spirit to those who ask him!'

Psalm 45   Genesis 47.1–12   Colossians 3.12–21

PENTECOST 15   TRINITY 14 *Green*

Those in Authority

COLLECT

Lord God,
you are the source of all power and might:
Govern the hearts and minds of those in authority,
that peace and justice may flourish on earth,
and your Church may ever serve you in godliness and joy;
through Jesus Christ our Lord.   **Amen.**

Year 1

PSALM 82

OLD TESTAMENT   *Isaiah 45.1–7 (–13)*

'This is what the LORD says to his anointed,
to Cyrus, whose right hand I take hold of
to subdue nations before him
and to strip kings of their armour,
to open the doors before him
so that gates will not be shut:
I will go before you
and will level the mountains;
I will break down gates of bronze
and cut through bars of iron.
I will give you the treasures of darkness,
riches stored in secret places,
so that you may know that I am the LORD,
the God of Israel, who calls you by name.
For the sake of Jacob my servant,
of Israel my chosen,

I call you by name
and bestow on you a title of honour,
though you do not acknowledge me.
I am the LORD, and there is no other;
apart from me there is no God.
I will strengthen you,
though you have not acknowledged me,
so that from the rising of the sun
to the place of its setting
men may know there is none besides me.
I am the LORD, and there is no other.
I form the light and create darkness,
I bring prosperity and create disaster;
I, the LORD, do all these things.'

EPISTLE* *Romans 13.1–7*

Everyone must submit himself to the governing authorities, for there is no authority except that which God has established. The authorities that exist have been established by God. Consequently, he who rebels against the authority is rebelling against what God has instituted, and those who do so will bring judgment on themselves. For rulers hold no terror for those who do right, but for those who do wrong. Do you want to be free from fear of the one in authority? Then do what is right and he will commend you. For he is God's servant to do you good. But if you do wrong, be afraid, for he does not bear the sword for nothing. He is God's servant, an agent of wrath to bring punishment on the wrongdoer. Therefore, it is necessary to submit to the authorities, not only because of possible punishment but also because of conscience.

This is also why you pay taxes, for the authorities are God's servants, who give their full time to governing. Give everyone what you owe him: If you owe taxes, pay taxes; if revenue, then revenue; if respect, then respect; if honour, then honour.

GOSPEL *Matthew 22.15–22 (1–33)*

The Pharisees went out and laid plans to trap Jesus in his words. They sent their disciples to him along with the Herodians. 'Teacher,' they said, 'we know you are a man of integrity and that you teach the way of God in accordance with the truth. You are not swayed by men, because you pay no attention to who they are. Tell us then, what is your opinion? Is it right to pay taxes to Caesar or not?'

But Jesus, knowing their evil intent, said, 'You hypocrites, why are you trying to trap me? Show me the coin used for paying the tax.' They brought him a denarius, and he asked them, 'Whose portrait is this? And whose inscription?'

'Caesar's,' they replied.

Then he said to them, 'Give to Caesar what is Caesar's, and to God what is God's.'

When they heard this, they were amazed. So they left him and went away.

Psalm 50   Daniel 5   Acts 25.1–12

Year 2

PSALM 20

OLD TESTAMENT   *1 Kings 3.4–15*

King Solomon went to Gibeon to offer sacrifices, for that was the most important high place, and Solomon offered a thousand burnt offerings on the altar. At Gibeon the Lord appeared to Solomon during the night in a dream, and God said, 'Ask for whatever you want me to give you.'

Solomon answered, 'You have shown great kindness to your servant, my father David, because he was faithful to you and righteous and upright in heart. You have continued this great kindness to him and have given him a son to sit on his throne this very day.

'Now, O Lord my God, you have made your servant king in place of my father David. But I am only a little child and do not know how to carry out my duties. Your servant is here among the people you have chosen, a great people, too numerous to count or number. So give your servant a discerning heart to govern your people and to distinguish between right and wrong. For who is able to govern this great people of yours?'

The Lord was pleased that Solomon had asked for this. So God said to him, 'Since you have asked for this and not for long life or wealth for yourself, nor have asked for the death of your enemies but for discernment in administering justice, I will do what you have asked. I will give you a wise and discerning heart, so that there will never have been anyone like you, nor will there ever be. Moreover, I will give you what you have not asked for – both riches and honour – so that in your lifetime you will have no equal among kings. And if you walk in my ways and obey my statutes and commands as David your father did, I will give you a long life.' Then Solomon awoke – and he realized that it had been a dream.

He returned to Jerusalem, stood before the ark of the Lord's covenant and sacrificed burnt offerings and fellowship offerings. Then he gave a feast for all his court.

EPISTLE* *1 Timothy 2.1–7 (1.12 – 2.8)*

I urge, first of all, that requests, prayers, intercession and thanksgiving be made for everyone – for kings and all those in authority, that we may live peaceful and quiet lives in all godliness and holiness. This is good, and pleases God our Saviour, who wants all men to be saved and to come to a knowledge of the truth. For there is one God and one mediator between God and men, the man Christ Jesus, who gave himself as a ransom for all men – the testimony given in its proper time. And for this purpose I was appointed a herald and an apostle – I am telling the truth, I am not lying – and a teacher of the true faith to the Gentiles.

GOSPEL *Matthew 14.1–12*

At that time Herod the tetrarch heard the reports about Jesus, and he said to his attendants, 'This is John the Baptist; he has risen from the dead! That is why miraculous powers are at work in him.'

Now Herod had arrested John and bound him and put him in prison because of Herodias, his brother Philip's wife, for John had been saying to him: 'It is not lawful for you to have her.' Herod wanted to kill John, but he was afraid of the people, because they considered him a prophet.

On Herod's birthday the daughter of Herodias danced for them and pleased Herod so much that he promised with an oath to give her whatever she asked. Prompted by her mother, she said, 'Give me here on a platter the head of John the Baptist.' The king was distressed, but because of his oaths and his dinner guests, he ordered that her request be granted and had John beheaded in the prison. His head was brought in on a platter and given to the girl, who carried it to her mother. John's disciples came and took his body and buried it. Then they went and told Jesus.

Psalm 72   1 Samuel 8.4–22a   1 Peter 2.11–25

PENTECOST 16   TRINITY 15   *Green*

The Neighbour

COLLECT

Heavenly Father,
you have taught us that in loving you and our fellow-men
we keep your commandments:
Give us the spirit of grace and peace
that we, united to one another in brotherly love,
may serve you with our whole heart;
through Jesus Christ our Lord.   **Amen.**

Year 1

PSALM 34.1–10

OLD TESTAMENT   *Leviticus 19.9–18 (1–4;9–18)*

When you reap the harvest of your land, do not reap to the very edges of your field or gather the gleanings of your harvest. Do not go over your vineyard a second time or pick up the grapes that have fallen. Leave them for the poor and the alien. I am the LORD your God.

Do not steal.

Do not lie.

Do not deceive one another.

Do not swear falsely by my name and so profane the name of your God. I am the LORD.

Do not defraud your neighbour or rob him.

Do not hold back the wages of a hired man overnight.

Do not curse the deaf or put a stumbling-block in front of the blind, but fear your God. I am the LORD.

Do not pervert justice; do not show partiality to the poor

or favouritism to the great, but judge your neighbour fairly.

Do not go about spreading slander among your people.

Do not do anything that endangers your neighbour's life. I am the LORD.

Do not hate your brother in your heart. Rebuke your neighbour frankly so that you will not share in his guilt.

Do not seek revenge or bear a grudge against one of your people, but love your neighbour as yourself. I am the LORD.

EPISTLE* *Romans 12.9–21*

Love must be sincere. Hate what is evil; cling to what is good. Be devoted to one another in brotherly love. Honour one another above yourselves. Never be lacking in zeal, but keep your spiritual fervour, serving the Lord. Be joyful in hope, patient in affliction, faithful in prayer. Share with God's people who are in need. Practise hospitality.

Bless those who persecute you; bless and do not curse. Rejoice with those who rejoice; mourn with those who mourn. Live in harmony with one another. Do not be proud, but be willing to associate with people of low position. Do not be conceited.

Do not repay anyone evil for evil. Be careful to do what is right in the eyes of everybody. If it is possible, as far as it depends on you, live at peace with everyone. Do not take revenge, my friends, but leave room for God's wrath, for it is written: 'It is mine to avenge; I will repay,' says the Lord. On the contrary:

'If your enemy is hungry, feed him;
if he is thirsty, give him something to drink.
In doing this, you will heap burning coals on his head.'

Do not be overcome by evil; but overcome evil with good.

GOSPEL *Luke 10.25–37*

On one occasion an expert in the law stood up to test Jesus. 'Teacher,' he asked, 'what must I do to inherit eternal life?'

'What is written in the Law?' he replied. 'How do you read it?'

He answered: ' "Love the Lord your God with all your heart and with all your soul and with all your strength and with all your mind"; and, "Love your neighbour as yourself." '

607

'You have answered correctly,' Jesus replied. 'Do this and you will live.'

But he wanted to justify himself, so he asked Jesus, 'And who is my neighbour?'

In reply Jesus said: 'A man was going down from Jerusalem to Jericho, when he fell into the hands of robbers. They stripped him of his clothes, beat him and went away, leaving him half-dead. A priest happened to be going down the same road, and when he saw the man, he passed by on the other side. So too, a Levite, when he came to the place and saw him, passed by on the other side. But a Samaritan, as he travelled, came where the man was; and when he saw him, he took pity on him. He went to him and bandaged his wounds, pouring on oil and wine. Then he put the man on his own donkey, brought him to an inn and took care of him. The next day he took out two silver coins and gave them to the innkeeper. "Look after him," he said, "and when I return, I will reimburse you for any extra expense you may have."

'Which of these three do you think was a neighbour to the man who fell into the hands of robbers?'

The expert in the law replied, 'The one who had mercy on him.'

Jesus told him, 'Go and do likewise.'

Psalm 107.1–32   1 Kings 21 (*or* 1–23)   Matthew 7.1–12

Year 2

PSALM 34.11–18

OLD TESTAMENT *Deuteronomy 15.7–11 (1–18)*

If there is a poor man among your brothers in any of the towns of the land that the LORD your God is giving you, do not be hard-hearted or tight-fisted towards your poor brother. Rather be open-handed and freely lend him whatever he needs. Be careful not to harbour this wicked thought: 'The seventh year, the year for cancelling debts, is near,' so that you do not show ill will towards your needy brother and give him nothing. He may then appeal to the LORD against you, and you will be found guilty of sin. Give generously to him and do so without a grudging heart; then because of this the LORD your God will bless you in all your work and in everything you put your hand to. There will always be poor people in the land. Therefore I command you to be open-handed towards your brothers and towards the poor and needy in your land.

EPISTLE* *1 John 4.15–21 (7–21)*

If anyone acknowledges that Jesus is the Son of God, God lives in him and he in God. And so we know and rely on the love God has for us.

God is love. Whoever lives in love lives in God, and God in him. Love is made complete among us so that we will have confidence on the day of judgment, because in this world we are like him. There is no fear in love. But perfect love drives out fear, because fear has to do with punishment. The man who fears is not made perfect in love.

We love because he first loved us. If anyone says, 'I love God,' yet hates his brother, he is a liar. For anyone who does not love his brother, whom he has seen, cannot love God, whom he has not seen. And he has given us this command: Whoever loves God must also love his brother.

GOSPEL *Luke 16.19–31*

Jesus said, 'There was a rich man who was dressed in purple and fine linen and lived in luxury every day. At his gate was laid a beggar named Lazarus, covered with sores and longing to eat what fell from the rich man's table. Even the dogs came and licked his sores.

'The time came when the beggar died and the angels carried him to Abraham's side. The rich man also died and was buried. In hell, where he was in torment, he looked up and saw Abraham far away, with Lazarus by his side. So he called to him, "Father Abraham, have pity on me and send Lazarus to dip the tip of his finger in water and cool my tongue, because I am in agony in this fire."

'But Abraham replied, "Son, remember that in your life-time you received your good things, while Lazarus received bad things, but now he is comforted here and you are in agony. And besides all this, between us and you a great chasm has been fixed, so that those who want to go from here to you cannot, nor can anyone cross over from there to us."

'He answered, "Then I beg you, father, send Lazarus to my father's house, for I have five brothers. Let him warn them, so that they will not also come to this place of torment."

'Abraham replied, "They have Moses and the Prophets; let them listen to them."

' "No, father Abraham," he said, "but if someone from the dead goes to them, they will repent."

'He said to him, "If they do not listen to Moses and the Prophets, they will not be convinced even if someone rises from the dead." '

Psalm 41;133   Proverbs 25.6–22   James 2.1–13

PENTECOST 17   TRINITY 16 *Green*
The Proof of Faith

COLLECT

Lord of all power and might,
author and giver of all good things:
Graft in our hearts the love of your name,
increase in us true religion,
nourish us with all goodness,
and of your great mercy keep us in the same;
through Jesus Christ our Lord.   **Amen.**

Year 1

PSALM 56

OLD TESTAMENT   *Jeremiah 7.1–11   (MP/EP   Joshua 14.6–14)*

This is the word that came to Jeremiah from the LORD: 'Stand at the gate of the LORD's house and there proclaim this message:

' "Hear the word of the LORD, all you people of Judah who come through these gates to worship the LORD. This is what the LORD Almighty, the God of Israel, says: Reform your ways and your actions, and I will let you live in this place. Do not trust in deceptive words and say, 'This is the temple of the LORD, the temple of the LORD, the temple of the LORD!'

If you really change your ways and your actions and deal with each other justly, if you do not oppress the alien, the fatherless or the widow and do not shed innocent blood in this place, and if you do not follow other gods to your own harm, then I will let you live in this place, in the land I gave to your forefathers for ever and ever. But look, you are trusting in deceptive words that are worthless.

' "Will you steal and murder, commit adultery and perjury, burn incense to Baal and follow other gods you have not known, and then come and stand before me in this house, which bears my Name, and say, 'We are safe' – safe to do all these detestable things? Has this house, which bears my Name, become a den of robbers to you? But I have been watching! declares the LORD." '

EPISTLE* *James 1.16–27 (MP/EP Acts 19.21–41)*

Do not be deceived, my dear brothers. Every good and perfect gift is from above, coming down from the Father of the heavenly lights, who does not change like shifting shadows. He chose to give us birth through the word of truth, that we might be a kind of firstfruits of all he created.

My dear brothers, take note of this: Everyone should be quick to listen, slow to speak and slow to become angry, for man's anger does not bring about the righteous life that God desires. Therefore, get rid of all moral filth and the evil that is so prevalent, and humbly accept the word planted in you, which can save you.

·Do not merely listen to the word, and so deceive yourselves. Do what it says. Anyone who listens to the word but does not do what it says is like a man who looks at his face in a mirror and, after looking at himself, goes away and immediately forgets what he looks like. But the man who looks intently into the perfect law that gives freedom, and continues to do this, not forgetting what he has heard, but doing it – he will be blessed in what he does.

If anyone considers himself religious and yet does not keep a tight rein on his tongue, he deceives himself and his religion is worthless. Religion that God our Father accepts as pure and faultless is this: to look after orphans and widows in their distress and to keep oneself from being polluted by the world.

GOSPEL   *Luke 17.11–19*

Now on his way to Jerusalem, Jesus travelled along the border between Samaria and Galilee. As he was going into a village, ten men who had leprosy met him. They stood at a distance and called out in a loud voice, 'Jesus, Master, have pity on us!'

When he saw them, he said, 'Go, show yourselves to the priests.' And as they went, they were cleansed.

One of them, when he saw he was healed, came back, praising God in a loud voice. He threw himself at Jesus' feet and thanked him – and he was a Samaritan.

Jesus asked, "Were not all ten cleansed? Where are the other nine? Was no one found to return and give praise to God except this foreigner?' Then he said to him, 'Rise and go; your faith has made you well.'

Psalm 91;93   Judges 7.1–8,19–23 (*or* 1–23)   John 7.1–24

Year 2

PSALM 57

OLD TESTAMENT   *Jeremiah 32.6–15 (1–15)*

Jeremiah said, 'The word of the Lᴏʀᴅ came to me: Hanamel son of Shallum your uncle is going to come to you and say, "Buy my field at Anathoth, because as nearest relative it is your right and duty to buy it."

'Then, just as the Lᴏʀᴅ had said, my cousin Hanamel came to me in the courtyard of the guard and said, "Buy my field at Anathoth in the territory of Benjamin. Since it is your right to redeem it and possess it, buy it for yourself."

'I knew that this was the word of the Lᴏʀᴅ; so I bought the field at Anathoth from my cousin Hanamel and weighed out for him seventeen shekels of silver. I signed and sealed the deed, had it witnessed, and weighed out the silver on the scales. I took the deed of purchase – the sealed copy containing the terms and conditions, as well as the unsealed copy – and I gave this deed to Baruch son of Neriah, the son of Mahseiah, in the presence of my cousin Hanamel and of the witnesses who had signed the deed and of all the Jews sitting in the courtyard of the guard.

'In their presence I gave Baruch these instructions: "This is what the LORD Almighty, the God of Israel, says: Take these documents, both the sealed and unsealed copies of the deed of purchase, and put them in a clay jar so that they will last a long time. For this is what the LORD Almighty, the God of Israel, says: Houses, fields and vineyards will again be bought in this land." '

We who are Jews by birth and not "Gentile sinners" know that a man is not justified by observing the law, but by faith in Jesus Christ. So we, too, have put our faith in Christ Jesus that we may be justified by faith in Christ and not by observing the law, because by observing the law no one will be justified.

If, while we seek to be justified in Christ, it becomes evident that we ourselves are sinners, does that mean that Christ promotes sin? Absolutely not! If I rebuild what I destroyed, I prove that I am a lawbreaker. For through the law I died to the law so that I might live for God. I have been crucified with Christ and I no longer live, but Christ lives in me. The life I live in the body, I live by faith in the Son of God, who loved me and gave himself for me. I do not set aside the grace of God, for if righteousness could be gained through the law, Christ died for nothing!

You foolish Galatians! Who has bewitched you? Before your very eyes Jesus Christ was clearly portrayed as crucified. I would like to learn just one thing from you: Did you receive the Spirit by observing the law, or by believing what you heard? Are you so foolish? After beginning with the Spirit, are you now trying to attain your goal by human effort? Have you suffered so much for nothing – if it really was for nothing? Does God give you his Spirit and work miracles among you because you observe the law, or because you believe what you heard?

Consider Abraham: 'He believed God, and it was credited to him as righteousness.' Understand, then, that those who believe are children of Abraham. The Scripture foresaw that God would justify the Gentiles by faith, and announced the gospel in advance to Abraham: 'All nations will be blessed through you.' So those who have faith are blessed along with Abraham, the man of faith.

GOSPEL   *Luke 7.1–10   (MP/EP   Luke 14.25–35)*

When Jesus had finished saying all this in the hearing of the people, he entered Capernaum. There a centurion's servant, whom his master valued highly, was sick and about to die. The centurion heard of Jesus and sent some elders of the Jews to him, asking him to come and heal his servant. When they came to Jesus, they pleaded earnestly with him, 'This man deserves to have you do this, because he loves our nation and has built our synagogue.' So Jesus went with them.

He was not far from the house when the centurion sent friends to say to him: 'Lord, do not trouble yourself, for I do not deserve to have you come under my roof. That is why I did not even consider myself worthy to come to you. But say the word, and my servant will be healed. For I myself am a man under authority, with soldiers under me. I tell this one, "Go", and he goes; and that one, "Come", and he comes. I say to my servant, "Do this", and he does it.'

When Jesus heard this, he was amazed at him, and turning to the crowd following him, he said, 'I tell you, I have not found such great faith even in Israel.' Then the men who had been sent returned to the house and found the servant well.

Psalm 19;20   Joshua 5.13 – 6.20   John 6.51–69

PENTECOST 18   TRINITY 17   *Green*

The Offering of Life

COLLECT

Almighty God,
you have made us for yourself,
and our hearts are restless
till they find their rest in you:
Teach us to offer ourselves to your service,
that here we may have your peace,
and in the world to come may see you face to face;
through Jesus Christ our Lord.   **Amen.**

Year 1

PSALM 145.14–21

OLD TESTAMENT *Deuteronomy 26.1–11 (MP/EP Haggai 1)*

When you have entered the land that the LORD your God is
giving you as an inheritance and have taken possession of it
and settled in it, take some of the firstfruits of all that you
produce from the soil of the land that the LORD your God is
giving you and put them in a basket. Then go to the place
that the LORD your God will choose as a dwelling for his
Name and say to the priest in office at the time, 'I declare
today to the LORD your God that I have come to the land that
the LORD swore to our forefathers to give us.' The priest shall
take the basket from your hands and set it down in front of
the altar of the LORD your God. Then you shall declare before
the LORD your God: 'My father was a wandering Aramean,
and he went down into Egypt with a few people and lived
there and became a great nation, powerful and numerous.
But the Egyptians ill-treated us and made us suffer, putting
us to hard labour. Then we cried out to the LORD, the God of
our fathers, and the LORD heard our voice and saw our
misery, toil and oppression. So the LORD brought us out of
Egypt with a mighty hand and an outstretched arm, with
great terror and with miraculous signs and wonders. He
brought us to this place and gave us this land, a land flowing
with milk and honey; and now I bring the firstfruits of the

soil that you, O Lᴏʀᴅ, have given me.' Place the basket before the Lᴏʀᴅ your God and bow down before him. And you and the Levites and the aliens among you shall rejoice in all the good things the Lᴏʀᴅ your God has given to you and your household.

EPISTLE*   *2 Corinthians 8.1–9*

We want you to know about the grace that God has given the Macedonian churches. Out of the most severe trial, their overflowing joy and their extreme poverty welled up in rich generosity. For I testify that they gave as much as they were able, and even beyond their ability. Entirely on their own, they urgently pleaded with us for the privilege of sharing in this service to the saints. And they did not do as we expected, but they gave themselves first to the Lord and then to us in keeping with God's will. So we urged Titus, since he had earlier made a beginning, to bring also to completion this act of grace on your part. But just as you excel in everything – in faith, in speech, in knowledge, in complete earnestness and in your love for us – see that you also excel in this grace of giving.

I am not commanding you, but I want to test the sincerity of your love by comparing it with the earnestness of others. For you know the grace of our Lord Jesus Christ, that though he was rich, yet for your sakes he became poor, so that you through his poverty might become rich.

GOSPEL   *Matthew 5.17–26*

Jesus said, 'Do not think that I have come to abolish the Law or the Prophets; I have not come to abolish them but to fulfil them. I tell you the truth, until heaven and earth disappear, not the smallest letter, not the least stroke of a pen, will by any means disappear from the Law until everything is accomplished. Anyone who breaks one of the least of these commandments and teaches others to do the same will be called least in the kingdom of heaven, but whoever practises and teaches these commands will be called great in the kingdom of heaven. For I tell you that unless your righteousness surpasses that of the Pharisees and the teachers of the law, you will certainly not enter the kingdom of heaven.

'You have heard that it was said to the people long ago. "Do not murder, and anyone who murders will be subject to judgment.'' But I tell you that anyone who is angry with his brother will be subject to judgment. Again, anyone who says to his brother, "Raca", is answerable to the Sanhedrin. But anyone who says, "You fool!" will be in danger of the fire of hell.

'Therefore, if you are offering your gift at the altar and there remember that your brother has something against you, leave the gift there in front of the altar. First go and be reconciled to your brother; then come and offer your gift.

'Settle matters quickly with your adversary who is taking you to court. Do it while you are still with him on the way, or he may hand you over to the judge, and the judge may hand you over to the officer, and you may be thrown into prison. I tell you the truth, you will not get out until you have paid the last penny.'

Psalm 118 Ecclesiastes 11 *and* 12 Luke 12.1–21

Year 2

PSALM 90.13–17 (1–17)

OLD TESTAMENT *Nehemiah 6.1–16*

When word came to Sanballat, Tobiah, Geshem the Arab and the rest of our enemies that I had rebuilt the wall and not a gap was left in it – though up to that time I had not set the doors in the gates – Sanballat and Geshem sent me this message: 'Come, let us meet together in one of the villages on the plain of Ono.'

But they were scheming to harm me; so I sent messengers to them with this reply: 'I am carrying on a great project and cannot go down. Why should the work stop while I leave it and go down to you?' Four times they sent me the same message, and each time I gave them the same answer.

Then, the fifth time, Sanballat sent his assistant to me with the same message, and in his hand was an unsealed letter in which was written:

'It is reported among the nations – and Geshem says it is true – that you and the Jews are plotting to revolt, and there-fore you are building the wall. Moreover, according to these reports you are about to become their king and have even appointed prophets to make this proclamation about you in

Jerusalem: "There is a king in Judah!" Now this report will get back to the king; so come, let us confer together.'

I sent him this reply: 'Nothing like what you are saying is happening; you are just making it up out of your head.'

They were all trying to frighten us, thinking, 'Their hands will get too weak for the work, and it will not be completed.'

But I prayed, 'Now strengthen my hands.'

One day I went to the house of Shemaiah son of Delaiah, the son of Mehetabel, who was shut in at his home. He said, 'Let us meet in the house of God, inside the temple, and let us close the temple doors, because men are coming to kill you – by night they are coming to kill you.'

But I said, 'Should a man like me run away? Or should one like me go into the temple to save his life? I will not go!' I realized that God had not sent him, but that he had prophesied against me because Tobiah and Sanballat had hired him. He had been hired to intimidate me so that I would commit a sin by doing this, and then they would give me a bad name to discredit me.

Remember Tobiah and Sanballat, O my God, because of what they have done; remember also the prophetess Noadiah and the rest of the prophets who have been trying to intimidate me.

So the wall was completed on the twenty-fifth of Elul, in fifty-two days. When all our enemies heard about this and all the surrounding nations saw it, our enemies lost their self-confidence, because they realized that this work had been done with the help of our God.

or

Ecclesiasticus 38.24–34

The wisdom of the scribe depends on the opportunity of
   leisure;
and he who has little business may become wise.
How can he become wise who handles the plough,
and who glories in the shaft of a goad,
who drives oxen and is occupied with their work,
and whose talk is about bulls?
He sets his heart on ploughing furrows,
and is careful about fodder for the heifers.
So too is every craftsman and master workman
who labours by night as well as by day;

those who cut the signet of seals,
each is diligent in making a great variety;
he sets his heart on painting a lifelike image,
and he is careful to finish his work.
So too is the smith sitting by the anvil,
intent upon his handiwork in iron;
the breath of the fire melts his flesh,
and he wastes away in the heat of the furnace;
he inclines his ear to the sound of the hammer,
and his eyes are on the pattern of the object.
He sets his heart on finishing his handiwork,
and he is careful to complete its decoration.
So too is the potter sitting at his work
and turning the wheel with his feet;
he is always deeply concerned over his work,
and all his output is by number.
He moulds the clay with his arm
and makes it pliable with his feet;
he sets his heart to finish the glazing,
and he is careful to clean the furnace.
All these rely upon their hands,
and each is skilful in his work.
Without them a city cannot be established,
and men can neither sojourn nor live there.
Yet they are not sought out for the council of the people,
nor do they attain eminence in the public assembly.
They do not sit in the judge's seat,
nor do they understand the sentence of judgment;
they cannot expound discipline or judgment,
and they are not found using proverbs.
But they keep stable the fabric of the world,
and their prayer is in the practice of their trade.

EPISTLE*   *1 Peter 4.7–11   (MP/EP   Romans 12)*

The end of all things is near. Therefore be clear minded and self-controlled so that you can pray. Above all, love each other deeply, because love covers over a multitude of sins. Offer hospitality to one another without grumbling. Each one should use whatever gift he has received to serve others, faithfully administering God's grace in its various forms. If anyone speaks, he should do it as one speaking the very words of God. If anyone serves, he should do it with the strength God provides, so that in all things God may be praised through Jesus Christ. To him be the glory and the power for ever and ever. Amen.

GOSPEL *Matthew 25.14–30*

Jesus said, 'The kingdom of heaven will be like a man going on a journey, who called his servants and entrusted his property to them. To one he gave five talents of money, to another two talents, and to another one talent, each according to his ability. Then he went on his journey. The man who had received the five talents went at once and put his money to work and gained five more. So also, the one with the two talents gained two more. But the man who had received the one talent went off, dug a hole in the ground and hid his master's money.

'After a long time the master of those servants returned and settled accounts with them. The man who had received the five talents brought the other five. "Master," he said, "you entrusted me with five talents. See, I have gained five more."

'His master replied, "Well done, good and faithful servant! You have been faithful with a few things; I will put you in charge of many things. Come and share your master's happiness!"

'The man with the two talents also came. "Master," he said, "you entrusted me with two talents; see, I have gained two more."

'His master replied, "Well done, good and faithful servant! You have been faithful with a few things; I will put you in charge of many things. Come and share your master's happiness!"

'Then the man who had received the one talent came. "Master," he said, "I knew that you are a hard man, harvesting where you have not sown and gathering where you have not scattered seed. So I was afraid and went out and hid your talent in the ground. See, here is what belongs to you."

'His master replied, "You wicked, lazy servant! So you knew that I harvest where I have not sown and gather where I have not scattered seed? Well then, you should have put my money on deposit with the bankers, so that when I returned I would have received it back with interest.

' "Take the talent from him and give it to the one who has

the ten talents. For everyone who has will be given more, and he will have an abundance. Whoever does not have, even what he has will be taken from him. And throw that worthless servant outside, into the darkness, where there will be weeping and gnashing of teeth." '

Psalm 116   Jeremiah 26.1–16   Philippians 1.12–26

PENTECOST 19   TRINITY 18 *Green*

The Last Sunday after Pentecost takes precedence.

The Life of Faith

COLLECT

Almighty God,
you alone can order
the unruly wills and affections of sinful men:
Grant that your people may love what you command,
and desire what you promise;
that in all the various changes of the world
our hearts may ever there be fixed
where true joys are to be found;
through Jesus Christ our Lord.   **Amen.**

Year 1

PSALM 139.1–11

OLD TESTAMENT   *Genesis 28.10–22*

Jacob left Beersheba and set out for Haran. When he reached a certain place, he stopped for the night because the sun had set. Taking one of the stones there, he put it under his head and lay down to sleep. He had a dream in which he saw a stairway resting on the earth, with its top reaching to heaven, and the angels of God were ascending and descending on it. There above it stood the LORD, and he said: 'I am the LORD, the God of your father Abraham and the God of Isaac. I will give you and your descendants the land on which you are lying. Your descendants will be like the dust of the earth, and you will spread out to the west and to the east, to the north and to the south. All peoples on earth will be blessed through you and your offspring. I am with you

and will watch over you wherever you go, and I will bring
you back to this land. I will not leave you until I have done
what I have promised you.'

When Jacob awoke from his sleep, he thought, 'Surely the
LORD is in this place, and I was not aware of it.' He was
afraid and said, 'How awesome is this place! This is none
other than the house of God; this is the gate of heaven.'

Early the next morning Jacob took the stone he had placed
under his head and set it up as a pillar and poured oil on top
of it. He called that place Bethel, though the city used to be
called Luz.

Then Jacob made a vow, saying, 'If God will be with me
and will watch over me on this journey I am taking and will
give me food to eat and clothes to wear so that I return safely
to my father's house, then the LORD will be my God. This
stone that I have set up as a pillar will be God's house, and of
all that you give me I will give you a tenth.'

EPISTLE* *Hebrews 11.1–2 and 8–16 (1–16)*

Now faith is being sure of what we hope for and certain of
what we do not see. This is what the ancients were commended for.

By faith Abraham, when called to go to a place he would
later receive as his inheritance, obeyed and went, even
though he did not know where he was going. By faith he
made his home in the promised land like a stranger in a
foreign country; he lived in tents, as did Isaac and Jacob,
who were heirs with him of the same promise. For he was
looking forward to the city with foundations, whose archi-
tect and builder is God.

By faith Abraham, even though he was past age – and
Sarah herself was barren – was enabled to become a father
because he considered him faithful who had made the
promise. And so from this one man, and he as good as dead,
came descendants, as numerous as the stars in the sky and
as countless as the sand on the seashore.

All these people were still living by faith when they died.
They did not receive the things promised; they only saw
them and welcomed them from a distance. And they
admitted that they were aliens and strangers on earth.
People who say such things show that they are looking for a
country of their own. If they had been thinking of the

country they had left, they would have had opportunity to return. Instead, they were longing for a better country – a heavenly one. Therefore God is not ashamed to be called their God, for he has prepared a city for them.

GOSPEL *Matthew 6.24–34*

Jesus said, 'No one can serve two masters. Either he will hate the one and love the other, or he will be devoted to the one and despise the other. You cannot serve both God and Money.

'Therefore I tell you, do not worry about your life, what you will eat or drink; or about your body, what you will wear. Is not life more important than food, and the body more important than clothes? Look at the birds of the air; they do not sow or reap or store away in barns, and yet your heavenly Father feeds them. Are you not much more valuable than they? Who of you by worrying can add a single hour to his life?

'And why do you worry about clothes? See how the lilies of the field grow. They do not labour or spin. Yet I tell you that not even Solomon in all his splendour was dressed like one of these. If that is how God clothes the grass of the field, which is here today and tomorrow is thrown into the fire, will he not much more clothe you, O you of little faith? So do not worry, saying, "What shall we eat?" or "What shall we wear?" For the pagans run after all these things, and your heavenly Father knows that you need them. But seek first his kingdom and his righteousness, and all these things will be given to you as well. Therefore do not worry about tomorrow, for tomorrow will worry about itself. Each day has enough trouble of its own.'

Psalm 37.1–22   Job 23.1–12   2 Corinthians 1.1–22

Year 2

PSALM 65.1–7 (PB 1–8)

OLD TESTAMENT *Daniel 6.10–23 (1–23)*

When Daniel learned that the decree had been published, he went home to his upstairs room where the windows opened towards Jerusalem. Three times a day he got down on his knees and prayed, giving thanks to his God, just as he had done before. Then these men went as a group and found Daniel praying and asking God for help. So they went to the king and spoke to him about his royal decree: 'Did you not publish a decree that during the next thirty days anyone who prays to any god or man except to you, O king, would be thrown into the lions' den?'

The king answered, 'The decree stands – in accordance with the laws of the Medes and Persians, which cannot be repealed.'

Then they said to the king, 'Daniel, who is one of the exiles from Judah, pays no attention to you, O king, or to the decree you put in writing. He still prays three times a day.' When the king heard this, he was greatly distressed; he was determined to rescue Daniel and made every effort until sundown to save him.

Then the men went as a group to the king and said to him, 'Remember, O king, that according to the law of the Medes and Persians no decree or edict that the king issues can be changed.'

So the king gave the order, and they brought Daniel and threw him into the lions' den. The king said to Daniel, 'May your God, whom you serve continually, rescue you!'

A stone was brought and placed over the mouth of the den, and the king sealed it with his own signet ring and with the rings of his nobles, so that Daniel's situation might not be changed. Then the king returned to his palace and spent the night without eating and without any entertainment being brought to him. And he could not sleep.

At the first light of dawn, the king got up and hurried to the lions' den. When he came near the den, he called to Daniel in an anguished voice, 'Daniel, servant of the living God, has your God, whom you serve continually, been able to rescue you from the lions?'

Daniel answered, 'O king, live for ever! My God sent his angel, and he shut the mouths of the lions. They have not hurt me, because I was found innocent in his sight. Nor have I ever done any wrong before you, O king.'

The king was overjoyed and gave orders to lift Daniel out of the den. And when Daniel was lifted from the den, no wound was found on him, because he had trusted in his God.

EPISTLE* *Romans 5.1–11*

Since we have been justified through faith, we have peace with God through our Lord Jesus Christ, through whom we have gained access by faith into this grace in which we now stand. And we rejoice in the hope of the glory of God. Not only so, but we also rejoice in our sufferings, because we know that suffering produces perseverance; perseverance, character; and character, hope. And hope does not disappoint us, because God has poured out his love into our hearts by the Holy Spirit, whom he has given us.

You see, at just the right time, when we were still powerless, Christ died for the ungodly. Very rarely will anyone die for a righteous man, though for a good man someone might possibly dare to die. But God demonstrates his own love for us in this: While we were still sinners, Christ died for us.

Since we have now been justified by his blood, how much more shall we be saved from God's wrath through him! For if, when we were God's enemies, we were reconciled to him through the death of his Son, how much more, having been reconciled, shall we be saved through his life! Not only is this so, but we also rejoice in God through our Lord Jesus Christ, through whom we have now received reconciliation.

GOSPEL *Luke 19.1–10 (18.35 – 19.10)*

Jesus entered Jericho and was passing through. A man was there by the name of Zacchaeus; he was a chief tax collector and was wealthy. He wanted to see who Jesus was, but being a short man he could not, because of the crowd. So he ran ahead and climbed a sycamore-fig tree to see him, since Jesus was coming that way.

When Jesus reached the spot, he looked up and said to him, 'Zacchaeus, come down immediately. I must stay at your house today.' So he came down at once and welcomed him gladly.

All the people saw this and began to mutter, 'He has gone to be the guest of a "sinner." '

But Zacchaeus stood up and said to the Lord, 'Look, Lord! Here and now I give half of my possessions to the poor, and if I have cheated anybody out of anything, I will pay back four times the amount.'

Jesus said to him, 'Today salvation has come to this house,

because this man, too, is a son of Abraham. For the Son of Man came to seek and to save what was lost.'

Psalm 85;111   Joshua 23   2 Corinthians 11.16–31

PENTECOST 20   TRINITY 19   *Green*

The Last Sunday after Pentecost takes precedence.

Endurance

COLLECT

Almighty God,
your Son has opened for us
a new and living way into your presence:
Give us pure hearts and steadfast wills
to worship you in spirit and in truth;
through Jesus Christ our Lord.   **Amen.**

Year 1

PSALM 37.35–41

OLD TESTAMENT   *Daniel 3.13–26 (1–30)*

Furious with rage, Nebuchadnezzar summoned Shadrach, Meshach and Abednego. So these men were brought before the king, and Nebuchadnezzar said to them, 'Is it true, Shadrach, Meshach and Abednego, that you do not serve my gods or worship the image of gold I have set up? Now when you hear the sound of the horn, flute, zither, lyre, harp, pipes and all kinds of music, if you are ready to fall down and worship the image I made, very good. But if you do not worship it, you will be thrown immediately into a blazing furnace. Then what god will be able to rescue you from my hand?'

Shadrach, Meshach and Abednego replied to the king, 'O Nebuchadnezzar, we do not need to defend ourselves before you in this matter. If we are thrown into the blazing furnace, the God we serve is able to save us from it, and he will rescue us from your hand, O king. But even if he does not, we want you to know, O king, that we will not serve your gods or worship the image of gold you have set up.'

Then Nebuchadnezzar was furious with Shadrach, Meshach and Abednego, and his attitude towards them changed. He ordered the furnace to be heated seven times hotter than usual and commanded some of the strongest soldiers in his army to tie up Shadrach, Meshach and Abednego and throw them into the blazing furnace. So these men, wearing their robes, trousers, turbans and other clothes, were bound and thrown into the blazing furnace. The king's command was so urgent and the furnace so hot that the flames of the fire killed the men who took up Shadrach, Meshach and Abednego, and these three men, firmly tied, fell into the blazing furnace.

Then King Nebuchadnezzar leaped to his feet in amazement and asked his advisers, 'Was it not three men that we tied up and threw into the fire?'

They replied, 'Certainly, O king.'

He said, 'Look! I see four men walking around in the fire, unbound and unharmed, and the fourth looks like a son of the gods.'

Nebuchadnezzar then approached the opening of the blazing furnace and shouted, 'Shadrach, Meshach and Abednego, servants of the Most High God, come out! Come here!'

So Shadrach, Meshach and Abednego came out of the fire.

EPISTLE* *Romans 8.18 – 25 (MP/EP Hebrews 11.32–12.2)*

I consider that our present sufferings are not worth comparing with the glory that will be revealed in us. The creation waits in eager expectation for the sons of God to be revealed. For the creation was subjected to frustration, not by its own choice, but by the will of the one who subjected it, in hope that the creation itself will be liberated from its bondage to decay and brought into the glorious freedom of the children of God.

We know that the whole creation has been groaning as in the pains of childbirth right up to the present time. Not only so, but we ourselves, who have the firstfruits of the Spirit, groan inwardly as we wait eagerly for our adoption as sons, the redemption of our bodies. For in this hope we were saved. But hope that is seen is no hope at all. Who hopes for what he already has? But if we hope for what we do not yet have, we wait for it patiently.

GOSPEL   *Luke 9.51–62*

As the time approached for Jesus to be taken up to heaven, he resolutely set out for Jerusalem, and he sent messengers on ahead. They went into a Samaritan village to get things ready for him, but the people there did not welcome him, because he was heading for Jerusalem. When the disciples James and John saw this, they asked, 'Lord, do you want us to call fire down from heaven to destroy them?' But Jesus turned and rebuked them, and they went to another village.

As they were walking along the road, a man said to him, 'I will follow you wherever you go.'

Jesus replied, 'Foxes have holes and birds of the air have nests but the Son of Man has no place to lay his head.'

He said to another man, 'Follow me.'

But the man replied, 'Lord, first let me go and bury my father.'

Jesus said to him, 'Let the dead bury their own dead, but you go and proclaim the kingdom of God.'

Still another said, 'I will follow you, Lord; but first let me go back and say good-bye to my family.'

Jesus replied, 'No one who puts his hand to the plough and looks back is fit for service in the kingdom of God.'

Psalm 51   Job 1   2 Timothy 2.1–19

Year 2

PSALM 121

OLD TESTAMENT   *Genesis 32.22–30 (3–30)*

Jacob got up and took his two wives, his two maidservants and his eleven sons and crossed the ford of the Jabbok. After he had sent them across the stream, he sent over all his possessions. So Jacob was left alone, and a man wrestled with him till daybreak. When the man saw that he could not overpower him, he touched the socket of Jacob's hip so that his hip was wrenched as he wrestled with the man. Then the man said, 'Let me go, for it is daybreak.'

But Jacob replied, 'I will not let you go unless you bless me.'

The man asked him, 'What is your name?'

'Jacob,' he answered.

Then the man said, 'Your name will no longer be Jacob, but Israel, because you have struggled with God and with men and have overcome.'

Jacob said, 'Please tell me your name.'

But he replied, 'Why do you ask my name?' Then he blessed him there.

So Jacob called the place Peniel, saying, 'It is because I saw God face to face, and yet my life was spared.'

EPISTLE* *1 Corinthians 9.19–27 (MP/EP Acts 27.1–25 or 13–25)*

Though I am free and belong to no man, I make myself a slave to everyone, to win as many as possible. To the Jews I became like a Jew, to win the Jews. To those under the law I became like one under the law (though I myself am not under the law), so as to win those under the law. To those not having the law I became like one not having the law (though I am not free from God's law but am under Christ's law), so as to win those not having the law. To the weak I became weak, to win the weak. I have become all things to all men so that by all possible means I might save some. I do all this for the sake of the gospel, that I may share in its blessings.

Do you not know that in a race all the runners run, but only one gets the prize? Run in such a way as to get the prize. Everyone who competes in the games goes into strict training. They do it to get a crown that will not last; but we do it to get a crown that will last for ever. Therefore I do not run like a man running aimlessly; I do not fight like a man beating the air. No, I beat my body and make it my slave so that after I have preached to others, I myself will not be disqualified for the prize.

GOSPEL *Matthew 7.13–27*

Jesus said, 'Enter through the narrow gate. For wide is the gate and broad is the road that leads to destruction, and many enter through it. But small is the gate and narrow the road that leads to life, and only a few find it.

'Watch out for false prophets. They come to you in sheep's clothing, but inwardly they are ferocious wolves. By their fruit you will recognize them. Do people pick grapes from thorn-bushes, or figs from thistles? Likewise every good tree bears good fruit, but a bad tree bears bad fruit. A good tree cannot bear bad fruit, and a bad tree cannot bear good fruit. Every tree that does not bear good fruit is cut down and thrown into the fire. Thus, by their fruit you will recognize them.

'Not everyone who says to me, "Lord, Lord," will enter the kingdom of heaven, but only he who does the will of my Father who is in heaven. Many will say to me on that day, "Lord, Lord, did we not prophesy in your name, and in your name drive out demons and perform many miracles?" Then I will tell them plainly, "I never knew you. Away from me, you evildoers!"

'Therefore everyone who hears these words of mine and puts them into practice is like a wise man who built his house on the rock. The rain came down, the streams rose, and the winds blew and beat against that house; yet it did not fall, because it had its foundation on the rock. But everyone who hears these words of mine and does not put them into practice is like a foolish man who built his house on sand. The rain came down, the streams rose, and the winds blew and beat against that house, and it fell with a great crash.'

Psalm 39   Jeremiah 38.1–13   James 1.1–15

PENTECOST 21   TRINITY 20   *Green*

The Last Sunday after Pentecost takes precedence.

The Christian Hope

COLLECT

Eternal Father,
whose Son Jesus Christ
ascended to the throne of heaven
that he might rule all things as Lord:
Keep the Church in the unity of the Spirit
and in the bond of peace,
and bring the whole created order
to worship at his feet;
who lives and reigns with you and the Holy Spirit,
one God, now and for ever.   **Amen.**

Year 1

PSALM 126

OLD TESTAMENT *Habbakuk 2.1–4 (–14)*

I will stand at my watch
and station myself on the ramparts;
I will look to see what the Lord will say to me,
and what answer I am to give to this complaint.
Then the Lᴏʀᴅ replied:

'Write down the revelation
and make it plain on tablets
so that a herald may run with it.
For the revelation awaits an appointed time;
it speaks of the end
and will not prove false.
Though it linger, wait for it;
it will certainly come and will not delay.

'See, he is puffed up;
his desires are not upright–
but the righteous will live by his faith.'

EPISTLE* *Acts 26.1–8*

Agrippa said to Paul, 'You have permission to speak for
yourself.'

So Paul motioned with his hand and began his defence:

'King Agrippa, I consider myself fortunate to stand before
you today as I make my defence against all the accusations of
the Jews, and especially so because you are well acquainted
with all the Jewish customs and controversies. Therefore, I
beg you to listen to me patiently.

'The Jews all know the way I have lived ever since I was a
child, from the beginning of my life in my own country, and
also in Jerusalem. They have known me for a long time and
can testify, if they are willing, that according to the strictest
sect of our religion, I lived as a Pharisee. And now it is
because of my hope in what God has promised our fathers
that I am on trial today. This is the promise our twelve tribes
are hoping to see fulfilled as they earnestly serve God day
and night. O King, it is because of this hope that the Jews are
accusing me. Why should any of you consider it incredible
that God raises the dead?'

GOSPEL *Luke 18.1–8 (–14)*

Jesus told his disciples a parable to show them that they should always pray and not give up. He said: 'In a certain town there was a judge who neither feared God nor cared about men. And there was a widow in that town who kept coming to him with the plea, "Grant me justice against my adversary."

'For some time he refused. But finally he said to himself, "Even though I do not fear God or care about men, yet because this widow keeps bothering me, I will see that she gets justice, so that she will not eventually wear me out with her coming!" '

And the Lord said, 'Listen to what the unjust judge says. And will not God bring about justice for his chosen ones, who cry out to him day and night? Will he keep putting them off? I tell you, he will see that they get justice, and quickly. However, when the Son of Man comes, will he find faith on the earth?'

Psalm 23;24 *or* 78.1–24   Ezekiel 34.11–24   2 Peter 3

Year 2

PSALM 11

OLD TESTAMENT *Ezekiel 12.21–28*

The word of the LORD came to me: 'Son of man, what is this proverb you have in the land of Israel: "The days go by and every vision comes to nothing"? Say to them, "This is what the Sovereign LORD says: I am going to put an end to this proverb, and they will no longer quote it in Israel." Say to them, "The days are near when every vision will be fulfilled. For there will be no more false visions or flattering divinations among the people of Israel. But I the LORD will speak what I will, and it shall be fulfilled without delay. For in your days, you rebellious house, I will fulfil whatever I say, declares the Sovereign LORD.' "

The word of the LORD came to me: 'Son of man, the house of Israel is saying, "The vision he sees is for many years from now, and he prophesies about the distant future."

'Therefore say to them, "This is what the Sovereign LORD says: None of my words will be delayed any longer; whatever I say will be fulfilled, declares the Sovereign LORD.' "

EPISTLE* *1 Peter 1.13–21 (3–21)*

Prepare your minds for action; be self-controlled; set your hope fully on the grace to be given you when Jesus Christ is revealed. As obedient children, do not conform to the evil desires you had when you lived in ignorance. But just as he who has called you is holy, so be holy in all you do; for it is written, 'Be holy, because I am holy.'

Since you call on a Father who judges each man's work impartially, live your lives as strangers here in reverent fear. For you know that it was not with perishable things such as silver or gold that you were redeemed from the empty way of life handed down to you from your forefathers, but with the precious blood of Christ, a lamb without blemish or defect. He was chosen before the creation of the world, but was revealed in these last times for your sake. Through him you believed in God, who raised him from the dead and glorified him, and so your faith and hope are in God.

GOSPEL *John 11.17–27*

On his arrival at Bethany, Jesus found that Lazarus had already been in the tomb for four days. Bethany was less than two miles from Jerusalem, and many Jews had come to Martha and Mary to comfort them in the loss of their brother. When Martha heard that Jesus was coming, she went out to meet him, but Mary stayed at home.

'Lord,' Martha said to Jesus, 'if you had been here, my brother would not have died. But I know that even now God will give you whatever you ask.'

Jesus said to her, 'Your brother will rise again.'

Martha answered, 'I know he will rise again in the resurrection at the last day.'

Jesus said to her, 'I am the resurrection and the life. He who believes in me will live, even though he dies; and whoever lives and believes in me will never die. Do you believe this?'

'Yes, Lord,' she told him, 'I believe that you are the Christ, the Son of God, who was to come into the world.'

Psalm 15;16   Job 4.1; 5.1–16   Hebrews 10.19–30

PENTECOST 22   TRINITY 21

Green

The Last Sunday after Pentecost takes precedence.

The Two Ways

COLLECT

Almighty God,
you gave your Son Jesus Christ
to break the power of evil:
Free us from all darkness and temptation,
and bring us to eternal light and joy;
through the power of him
who lives and reigns with you and the Holy Spirit,
one God, now and ever.   **Amen.**

Years 1 and 2

PSALM 119.1–8 *or* 112

OLD TESTAMENT   *Deuteronomy 11.18–28*

Fix these words of mine in your hearts and minds; tie them
as symbols on your hands and bind them on your foreheads.
Teach them to your children, talking about them when you
sit at home and when you walk along the road, when you lie
down and when you get up. Write them on the door frames
of your houses and on your gates, so that your days and the
days of your children may be many in the land that the LORD
swore to give your forefathers, as many as the days that the
heavens are above the earth.

If you carefully observe all these commands I am giving
you to follow – to love the LORD your God, to walk in all his
ways and to hold fast to him – then the LORD will drive out
all these nations before you, and you will dispossess nations
larger and stronger than you. Every place where you set
your foot will be yours: from the desert to Lebanon, and
from the Euphrates River to the western sea. No man will be
able to stand against you. The LORD your God, as he
promised you, will put the terror and fear of you on the
whole land, wherever you go.

See, I am setting before you today a blessing and a curse –
the blessing if you obey the commands of the LORD your God
that I am giving you today; the curse if you disobey the com-

mands of the LORD your God and turn from the way that I command you today by following other gods, which you have not known.

EPISTLE* *1 John 2.22–29*

Who is the liar? It is the man who denies that Jesus is the Christ. Such a man is the antichrist – he denies the Father and the Son. No one who denies the Son has the Father; whoever acknowledges the Son has the Father also.

See that what you have heard from the beginning remains in you. If it does, you also will remain in the Son and in the Father. And this is what he promised us – even eternal life.

I am writing these things to you about those who are trying to lead you astray. As for you, the anointing you received from him remains in you, and you do not need anyone to teach you. But as his anointing teaches you about all things and as that anointing is real, not counterfeit – just as it has taught you, remain in him.

And now, dear children, continue in him, so that when he appears we may be confident and unashamed before him at his coming.

If you know that he is righteous, you know that everyone who does what is right has been born of him.

GOSPEL *Luke 16.1–9*

Jesus told his disciples:

'There was a rich man whose manager was accused of wasting his possessions. So he called him in and asked him, "What is this I hear about you? Give an account of your management, because you cannot be manager any longer."

'The manager said to himself, "What shall I do now? My master is taking away my job. I am not strong enough to dig, and I am ashamed to beg – I know what I will do so that, when I lose my job here, people will welcome me into their houses."

'So he called in each one of his master's debtors. He asked the first, "How much do you owe my master?"

' "Eight hundred gallons of olive oil," he replied.

'The manager told him, "Take your bill, sit down quickly, and make it four hundred."

'Then he asked the second, "And how much do you owe?"

' "A thousand bushels of wheat," he replied.

'He told him, "Take your bill and make it eight hundred."

'The master commended the dishonest manager because he had acted shrewdly. For the people of this world are more shrewd in dealing with their own kind than are the people of the light. I tell you, use worldly wealth to gain friends for yourself, so that when it is gone, you will be welcomed into eternal dwellings.'

Psalm 40   Jeremiah 6.16–21   Mark 3.7–35

LAST SUNDAY AFTER PENTECOST *Green*

The last Sunday after Pentecost takes precedence of Pentecost 18 to Pentecost 22

Citizens of Heaven

COLLECT

Merciful God,
you have prepared for those who love you
such good things as pass man's understanding:
Pour into our hearts such love towards you,
that we, loving you above all things,
may obtain your promises,
which exceed all that we can desire;
through Jesus Christ our Lord.   **Amen.**

Year 1

PSALM 15

OLD TESTAMENT   *Jeremiah 29.1,4–14 (1–14)*

This is the text of the letter that the prophet Jeremiah sent from Jerusalem to the surviving elders among the exiles and to the priests, the prophets and all the other people Nebuchadnezzar had carried into exile from Jerusalem to Babylon.

This is what the Lord Almighty, the God of Israel, says to all those I carried into exile from Jerusalem to Babylon: 'Build houses and settle down; plant gardens and eat what they produce. Marry and have sons and daughters; find wives for your sons and give your daughters in marriage, so that they too may have sons and daughters. Increase in number there; do not decrease. Also, seek the peace and prosperity of the city to which I have carried you into exile. Pray to the LORD for it, because if it prospers, you too will prosper.' Yes, this is what the LORD Almighty, the God of Israel, says: 'Do not let the prophets and diviners among you deceive you. Do not listen to the dreams you encourage them to have. They are prophesying lies to you in my name. I have not sent them,' declares the LORD.

This is what the LORD says: 'When seventy years are completed for Babylon, I will come to you and fulfil my gracious promise to bring you back to this place. For I know the plans I have for you,' declares the LORD, 'plans to prosper you and not to harm you, plans to give you hope and a future. Then you will call upon me and come and pray to me, and I will listen to you. You will seek me and find me when you seek me with all your heart. I will be found by you,' declares the LORD, 'and will bring you back from captivity. I will gather you from all the nations and places where I have banished you,' declares the LORD, 'and will bring you back to the place from which I carried you into exile.'

EPISTLE* *Philippians 3.7–21*

But whatever was to my profit I now consider loss for the sake of Christ. What is more, I consider everything a loss compared to the surpassing greatness of knowing Christ Jesus my Lord, for whose sake I have lost all things. I consider them rubbish, that I may gain Christ and be found in him, not having a righteousness of my own that comes from the law, but that which is through faith in Christ – the righteousness that comes from God and is by faith. I want to know Christ and the power of his resurrection and the fellowship of sharing in his death, and so, somehow, to attain to the resurrection from the dead.

Not that I have already obtained all this, or have already been made perfect, but I press on to take hold of that for which Christ Jesus took hold of me. Brothers, I do not consider myself yet to have taken hold of it. But one thing I do: Forgetting what is behind and straining towards what is ahead, I press on towards the goal to win the prize for which God has called me heavenwards in Christ Jesus.

All of us who are mature should take such a view of

things. And if on some point you think differently, that too God will make clear to you. Only let us live up to what we have already attained.

Join with others in following my example, brothers, and take note of those who live according to the pattern we gave you. For, as I have often told you before and now say again even with tears, many live as enemies of the cross of Christ. Their destiny is destruction, their god is their stomach, and their glory is in their shame. Their mind is on earthly things. But our citizenship is in heaven. And we eagerly await a Saviour from there, the Lord Jesus Christ, who, by the power that enables him to bring everything under his control, will transform our lowly bodies so that they will be like his glorious body.

GOSPEL *John 17.1–10*

On the night that he was betrayed, Jesus looked toward heaven and prayed:

'Father, the time has come. Glorify your Son, that your Son may glorify you. For you granted him authority over all people that he might give eternal life to all those you have given him. Now this is eternal life: that they may know you, the only true God, and Jesus Christ, whom you have sent. I have brought you glory on earth by completing the work you gave me to do. And now, Father, glorify me in your presence with the glory I had with you before the world began.

'I have revealed you to those whom you gave me out of the world. They were yours; you gave them to me and they have obeyed your word. Now they know that everything you have given me comes from you. For I gave them the words you gave me and they accepted them. They knew with certainty that I came from you, and they believed that you sent me. I pray for them. I am not praying for the world, but for those you have given me, for they are yours. All I have is yours, and all you have is mine. And glory has come to me through them.'

Psalm 89.1–18 (PB 1–19)   Daniel 10.2–19   Revelation 1.1–18

Year 2

PSALM 146

OLD TESTAMENT   *Isaiah 33.17–22 (13–22)*

Your eyes will see the king in his beauty
and view a land that stretches afar.
In your thoughts you will ponder the former terror:
'Where is that chief officer?
Where is the one who took the revenue?
Where is the officer in charge of the towers?'
You will see those arrogant people no more,
those people of an obscure speech,
with their strange, incomprehensible tongue.
Look upon Zion, the city of our festivals;
your eyes will see Jerusalem,
a peaceful abode, a tent that will not be moved;
its stakes will never be pulled up,
nor any of its ropes broken.
There the LORD will be our Mighty One.
It will be like a place of broad rivers and streams.
No galley with oars will ride them,
no mighty ship will sail them.
For the LORD is our judge;
the LORD is our lawgiver;
the LORD is our king,
it is he who will save us.

EPISTLE*   *Revelation 7.2–4,9–17*

I, John, saw another angel coming up from the east, having
the seal of the living God. He called out in a loud voice to the
four angels who had been given power to harm the land and
the sea: 'Do not harm the land or the sea or the trees until we
put a seal on the foreheads of the servants of our God.' Then
I heard the numbers of those who were sealed: one hundred
and forty-four thousand from all the tribes of Israel.

After this I looked and there before me was a great multitude that no one could count, from every nation, tribe,
people and language, standing before the throne and in
front of the Lamb. They were wearing white robes and were
holding palm branches in their hands. And they cried out in
a loud voice:

'Salvation belongs to our God,
who sits on the throne,
and to the Lamb.'

All the angels were standing around the throne and around
the elders and the four living creatures. They fell down on
their faces before the throne and worshipped God, saying:

'Amen!
Praise and glory
and wisdom and thanks and honour
and power and strength
be to our God for ever and ever.
Amen!'

Then one of the elders asked me, 'These in white robes –
who are they, and where did they come from?'

I answered, 'Sir, you know.'

And he said, 'These are they who have come out of the
great tribulation; they have washed their robes and made
them white in the blood of the Lamb. Therefore

'they are before the throne of God
and serve him day and night in his temple;
and he who sits on the throne will spread his tent over them.
Never again will they hunger:
never again will they thirst.
The sun will not beat upon them,
nor any scorching heat.
For the Lamb at the centre of the throne will be their
    shepherd;
he will lead them to springs of living water.
And God will wipe away every tear from their eyes.'

GOSPEL *Matthew 25.1–13 (24.45–25.13)*

Jesus said, 'At that time the kingdom of heaven will be like
ten virgins who took their lamps and went out to meet the
bridegroom. Five of them were foolish and five were wise.
The foolish ones took their lamps but did not take any oil
with them. The wise, however, took oil in jars along with
their lamps. The bridegroom was a long time in coming, and
they all became drowsy and fell asleep.

'At midnight the cry rang out: "Here is the bridegroom!
Come out to meet him!"'

'Then all the virgins woke up and trimmed their lamps. The foolish ones said to the wise, "Give us some of your oil; our lamps are going out."

' "No," they replied, "there may not be enough for both us and you. Instead, go to those who sell oil and buy some for yourselves."

'But while they were on their way to buy the oil, the bridegroom arrived. The virgins who were ready went in with him to the wedding banquet. And the door was shut

'Later the others also came. "Sir! Sir!" they said, "Open the door for us!"

'But he replied, "I tell you the truth, I do not know you."

'Therefore keep watch, because you do not know the day or the hour.'

Psalm 84;122   Ezekiel 11.14–21   Hebrews 13.1–21

COLLECTS AND READINGS

for Saints' Days and Holy Days

The first printed set of psalms and readings is to be used at Holy Communion.

The other sets of readings may be used at Morning Prayer or Evening Prayer on the day, or at Evening Prayer on the preceding day. If readings for the holy day are used on the preceding evening, readings from the weekday course are to be used at Evening Prayer on the day.

THE NAMING OF JESUS
White

1 January

COLLECTS

Father Almighty,
you named your Son Jesus
because he came to bring salvation to the world:
Fulfil the promise of his holy Name,
and in your mercy save us from our sins;
through him who lives and reigns
with you and the Holy Spirit,
one God, for ever.   **Amen.**

New Year

Eternal Lord God,
we give you thanks for bringing us,
through the changes of time
to the beginning of another year:
Forgive us the sins we have committed
in the year that is past,
and help us to spend the remainder of our days
to your honour and glory;
through Jesus Christ our Lord.   **Amen.**

PSALM 8 *or* 62.1–8

643

OLD TESTAMENT *Isaiah 9.2,6–7*

The people walking in darkness
have seen a great light;
on those living in the land of the shadow of death
a light has dawned.
For to us a child is born,
to us a son is given,
and the government will be on his shoulders.
And he will be called
Wonderful Counsellor, Mighty God,
Everlasting Father, Prince of Peace.
Of the increase of his government and peace
there will be no end.
He will reign on David's throne
and over his kingdom,
establishing and upholding it
with justice and righteousness
from that time on and for ever.
The zeal of the LORD Almighty
will accomplish this.

EPISTLE *Acts 4.8–12*

Peter, filled with the Holy Spirit, said to them: 'Rulers and elders of the people! If we are being called to account today for an act of kindness shown to a cripple and are asked how he was healed, then know this, you and everyone else in Israel: It is by the name of Jesus Christ of Nazareth, whom you crucified but whom God raised from the dead, that this man stands before you completely healed. He is

' "the stone you builders rejected,
which has become the capstone."

Salvation is found in no one else, for there is no other name under heaven given to men by which we must be saved.'

GOSPEL *Luke 2.15–21*

When the angels had left them and gone into heaven, the shepherds said to one another, 'Let us go to Bethlehem and see this thing that has happened, which the Lord has told us about.'

So they hurried off and found Mary and Joseph, and the

baby who was lying in the manger. When they had seen him, they spread the word concerning what had been told them about this child, and all who heard it were amazed at what the shepherds said to them. But Mary treasured up all these things and pondered them in her heart. The shepherds returned, glorifying and praising God for all the things they had heard and seen, which were just as they had been told.

On the eighth day, when it was time to circumcise him, he was named Jesus, the name the angel had given him before he had been conceived.

Psalm 115   Joshua 1.1–9   Acts 3.1–16
Psalm 148   Jeremiah 23.1–6   Romans 10.5–13

For the use of these, and other additional readings for Saints' Days and Holy Days, see note on p. 643.

THE CONVERSION OF SAINT PAUL   *White*

25 January

COLLECT

Almighty God,
you caused the light of the gospel
to shine throughout the world
through the preaching of your servant Saint Paul:
Grant that we who celebrate his wonderful conversion
may follow him in bearing witness to your truth;
through Jesus Christ our Lord.   **Amen.**

PSALM 126 *or* 67

OLD TESTAMENT   *1 Kings 19.15–21*

The LORD said to Elijah 'Go back the way you came, and go to the Desert of Damascus. When you get there, anoint Hazael king over Aram. Also, anoint Jehu son of Nimshi king over Israel, and anoint Elisha son of Shaphat from Abel Meholah to succeed you as prophet. Jehu will put to death any who escape the sword of Hazael, and Elisha will put to death any who escape the sword of Jehu. Yet I reserve seven thousand in Israel – all whose knees have not bowed down to Baal and all whose mouths have not kissed him.'

So Elijah went from there and found Elisha son of Shaphat. He was ploughing with twelve yoke of oxen, and he himself was driving the twelfth pair. Elijah went up to him and threw his cloak around him. Elisha then left his oxen and ran after Elijah. 'Let me kiss my father and mother good-bye,' he said, 'and then I will come with you.'

'Go back,' Elijah replied. 'What have I done to you?'

So Elisha left him and went back. He took his yoke of oxen and slaughtered them. He burned the ploughing equipment to cook the meat and gave it to the people, and they ate. Then he set out to follow Elijah and became his attendant.

EPISTLE *Acts 9.1–22*

Saul was still breathing out murderous threats against the Lord's disciples. He went to the high priest and asked him for letters to the synagogues in Damascus, so that if he found any there who belonged to the Way, whether men or women, he might take them as prisoners to Jerusalem. As he neared Damascus on his journey, suddenly a light from heaven flashed around him. He fell to the ground and heard a voice say to him, 'Saul, Saul, why do you persecute me?'

'Who are you, Lord?' Saul asked.

'I am Jesus, whom you are persecuting,' he replied. 'Now get up and go into the city, and you will be told what you must do.'

The men travelling with Saul stood there speechless; they heard the sound but did not see anyone. Saul got up from the ground, but when he opened his eyes he could see nothing. So they led him by the hand into Damascus. For three days he was blind, and did not eat or drink anything.

In Damascus there was a disciple named Ananias. The Lord called to him in a vision, 'Ananias!'

'Yes, Lord,' he answered.

The Lord told him, 'Go to the house of Judas on Straight Street and ask for a man from Tarsus named Saul, for he is praying. In a vision he has seen a man named Ananias come and place his hands on him to restore his sight.'

'Lord,' Ananias answered, 'I have heard many reports about this man and all the harm he has done to your saints in Jerusalem. And he has come here with authority from the chief priests to arrest all who call on your name.'

But the Lord said to Ananias, 'Go! This man is my chosen

instrument to carry my name before the Gentiles and their kings and before the people of Israel. I will show him how much he must suffer for my name.'

Then Ananias went to the house and entered it. Placing his hands on Saul, he said, 'Brother Saul, the Lord – Jesus, who appeared to you on the road as you were coming here – has sent me so that you may see again and be filled with the Holy Spirit.' Immediately, something like scales fell from Saul's eyes, and he could see again. He got up and was baptized, and after taking some food, he regained his strength.

Saul spent several days with the disciples in Damascus. At once he began to preach in the synagogues that Jesus is the Son of God. All those who heard him were astonished and asked, 'Is he not the man who caused havoc in Jerusalem among those who call on this name? And has he not come here to take them as prisoners to the chief priests?' Yet Saul grew more and more powerful and baffled the Jews living in Damascus by proving that Jesus is the Christ.

GOSPEL   *Matthew 19.27–30*

Peter said to Jesus, 'We have left everything to follow you! What then will there be for us?'

Jesus said to them, 'I tell you the truth, at the renewal of all things, when the Son of Man sits on his glorious throne, you who have followed me will also sit on twelve thrones, judging the twelve tribes of Israel. And everyone who has left houses or brothers or sisters or father or mother or children or fields for my sake will receive a hundred times as much and will inherit eternal life. But many who are first will be last, and many who are last will be first.'

Psalm 18.22–35 (PB 21–33)   Ezekiel 3.22–27 *or* Ecclesiasticus 39.1 – 10
Colossians 1.24 – 2.7

Psalm 119.41–56   Isaiah 56.1–8   Philippians 3.1–14

SAINT BRIGID
1 February

COLLECT

Father,
we rejoice today
in the fellowship of your blessed servant Brigid,
and we give you thanks for her life of devoted service:
Inspire us with new life and light,
and give us perseverance to serve you all our days;
through Jesus Christ our Lord.   **Amen.**

PSALM 134

OLD TESTAMENT   *Hosea 6.1–4*

Come, let us return to the LORD.
He has torn us to pieces
but he will heal us;
he has injured us
but he will bind up our wounds.
After two days he will revive us;
on the third day he will restore us,
that we may live in his presence.
Let us acknowledge the LORD;
let us press on to acknowledge him.
As surely as the sun rises,
he will appear;
he will come to us like the winter rains,
like the spring rains that water the earth.

What can I do with you, Ephraim?
What can I do with you, Judah?
Your love is like the morning mist,
like the early dew that disappears.

EPISTLE   *1 John 1.1–4*

That which was from the beginning, which we have heard,
which we have seen with our eyes, which we have looked at
and our hands have touched – this we proclaim concerning
the Word of life. The life appeared; we have seen it and
testify to it, and we proclaim to you the eternal life, which

was with the Father and has appeared to us. We proclaim to you what we have seen and heard, so that you also may have fellowship with us. And our fellowship is with the Father and with his Son, Jesus Christ. We write this to make our joy complete.

GOSPEL *John 10.7–16*

Jesus said, 'I tell you the truth, I am the gate for the sheep. All who ever came before me were thieves and robbers, but the sheep did not listen to them. I am the gate; whoever enters through me will be saved. He will come in and go out, and find pasture. The thief comes only to steal and kill and destroy; I have come that they may have life, and have it to the full.

'I am the good shepherd. The good shepherd lays down his life for the sheep. The hired hand is not the shepherd who owns the sheep. So when he sees the wolf coming, he abandons the sheep and runs away. Then the wolf attacks the flock and scatters it. The man runs away because he is a hired hand and cares nothing for the sheep.

'I am the good shepherd; I know my sheep and my sheep know me – just as the Father knows me and I know the Father – and I lay down my life for the sheep. I have other sheep that are not of this sheep pen. I must bring them also. They too will listen to my voice, and there shall be one flock and one shepherd.'

Psalm 138   Isaiah 40.1–5   1 Corinthians 1.26–31

Psalm 123;131   Isaiah 61.10 – 62.5   3 John 2–8

THE PRESENTATION OF CHRIST
IN THE TEMPLE

White

2 February

COLLECT

Almighty Father,
your Son Jesus Christ was presented in the Temple
and acclaimed the glory of Israel
and the light of the nations:
Grant that we may be presented to you.
and serve you with pure and loving hearts;
through Jesus Christ our Lord.   **Amen.**

PSALM 48 *or* NUNC DIMITTIS

OLD TESTAMENT   *Malachi 3.1–5*

'See, I will send my messenger, who will prepare the way
before me. Then suddenly the LORD you are seeking will
come to his temple; the messenger of the covenant, whom
you desire, will come,' says the LORD Almighty.

But who can endure the day of his coming? Who can stand
when he appears? For he will be like a refiner's fire or a launderer's soap. He will sit as a refiner and purifier of silver; he
will purify the Levites and refine them like gold and silver.
Then the LORD will have men who will bring offerings in
righteousness, and the offerings of Judah and Jerusalem will
be acceptable to the LORD, as in days gone by, as in former
years.

'So I will come near to you for judgment. I will be quick to
testify against sorcerers, adulterers and perjurers, against
those who defraud labourers of their wages, who oppress
the widows and the fatherless, and deprive aliens of justice,
but do not fear me,' says the LORD Almighty.

EPISTLE   *1 Peter 2.1–10*

Rid yourselves of all malice and all deceit, hypocrisy, envy,
and slander of every kind. Like newborn babies, crave pure
spiritual milk, so that by it you may grow up in your salvation, now that you have tasted that the Lord is good. As
you come to him, the living Stone – rejected by men but
chosen by God and precious to him – you also, like living

stones, are being built into a spiritual house to be a holy priesthood, offering spiritual sacrifices acceptable to God through Jesus Christ. For in Scripture it says:

'See, I lay a stone in Zion,
a chosen and precious corner stone,
and the one who trusts in him
will never be put to shame.'

Now to you who believe, this stone is precious. But to those who do not believe,

'The stone the builders rejected
has become the capstone,'

and,

A stone that causes men to stumble
and a rock that makes them fall.'

They stumble because they disobey the message – which is also what they were destined for. But you are a chosen people, a royal priesthood, a holy nation, a people belonging to God, that you may declare the praises of him who called you out of darkness into his wonderful light. Once you were not a people, but now you are the people of God; once you had not received mercy, but now you have received mercy.

GOSPEL   *Luke 2.22–35*

When the time of their purification according to the Law of Moses had been completed, Joseph and Mary took Jesus to Jerusalem to present him to the Lord (as it is written in the Law of the Lord, 'Every firstborn male is to be consecrated to the Lord'), and to offer a sacrifice in keeping with what is said in the Law of the Lord: 'a pair of doves or two young pigeons.'

Now there was a man in Jerusalem called Simeon, who was righteous and devout. He was waiting for the consolation of Israel, and the Holy Spirit was upon him. It had been revealed to him by the Holy Spirit that he would not die before he had seen the Lord's Christ. Moved by the Spirit, he went into the temple courts. When the parents brought in the child Jesus to do for him what the custom of the Law required, Simeon took him in his arms and praised God, saying:

'Sovereign Lord, as you have promised,
you now dismiss your servant in peace.
For my eyes have seen your salvation,
which you have prepared in the sight of all people,
a light for revelation to the Gentiles
and for glory to your people Israel.'

The child's father and mother marvelled at what was said
about him. Then Simeon blessed them and said to Mary, his
mother: 'This child is destined to cause the falling and rising
of many in Israel, and to be a sign that will be spoken
against, so that the thoughts of many hearts will be revealed.
And a sword will pierce your own soul too.'

Psalm 122;123   Haggai 2.1–9   Hebrews 10.1–10

Psalm 42;43   1 Samuel 1.20–28   Romans 12.1–8

SAINT PATRICK   *White*
17 March

COLLECT

Almighty God,
in your providence you chose your servant Patrick,
to be the apostle of the Irish people,
to baptize those who were wandering
in darkness and error
and to bring them to the true light
and knowledge of your Word:
Keep us in that light
and bring us to everlasting life;
through Jesus Christ our Lord.   **Amen.**

PSALM 145.1–13

OLD TESTAMENT   *Tobit 13.1b–7*

Blessed is God who lives for ever,
and blessed is his kingdom.
For he afflicts, and he shows mercy;
he leads down to Hades, and brings up again,
and there is no one who can escape his hand.
Acknowledge him before the nations, O sons of Israel;

for he has scattered us among them.
Make his greatness to be known there,
and exalt him in the presence of all the living;
because he is our Lord and God,
he is our Father for ever.
He will afflict us for our iniquities;
and again he will show mercy,
and will gather you from among the nations
among whom you have been scattered.
If you turn to him with all your heart
and with all your soul,
to do what is right before him,
then he will turn to you
and will not hide his face from you.
But see what he will do with you;
give thanks to him with your full voice.
Praise the Lord of righteousness,
and exalt the King of the ages.
I give him thanks in the land of my captivity,
and I show his power and majesty to a land of sinners.
Turn back you sinners, and do right before him;
who knows if he will accept you and have mercy on you?
I exalt my God;
my soul exalts the King of heaven,
and will rejoice in his majesty.

or

Deuteronomy 32.1–9

Listen, O heavens, and I will speak;
hear, O earth, the words of my mouth.
Let my teaching fall like rain
and my words descend like dew,
like showers on new grass,
like abundant rain on tender plants.

I will proclaim the name of the LORD.
Oh, praise the greatness of our God!
He is the Rock, his works are perfect,
and all his ways are just.
A faithful God who does no wrong,
upright and just is he.

They have acted corruptly towards him;

653

to their shame they are no longer his children,
but a warped and crooked generation.
Is this the way you repay the LORD,
O foolish and unwise people?
Is he not your Father, your Creator,
who made you and formed you?

Remember the days of old;
consider the generations long past.
Ask your father and he will tell you,
your elders, and they will explain to you.
When the Most High gave the nations their inheritance,
when he divided all mankind,
he set up boundaries for the peoples
according to the number of the sons of Israel.
For the LORD's portion is his people,
Jacob his allotted inheritance.

EPISTLE   *2 Corinthians 4.1–12*

Since through God's mercy we have this ministry, we do not
lose heart. Rather, we have renounced secret and shameful
ways; we do not use deception, nor do we distort the word
of God. On the contrary, by setting forth the truth plainly we
commend ourselves to every man's conscience in the sight of
God. And even if our gospel is veiled, it is veiled to those
who are perishing. The god of this age has blinded the
minds of unbelievers, so that they cannot see the light of the
gospel of the glory of Christ, who is the image of God. For
we do not preach ourselves, but Jesus Christ as Lord, and
ourselves as your servants for Jesus' sake. For God, who
said, 'Let light shine out of darkness,' made his light shine in
our hearts to give us the light of the knowledge of the glory
of God in the face of Christ.

But we have this treasure in jars of clay to show that this
all-surpassing power is from God and not from us. We are
hard pressed on every side, but not crushed; perplexed, but
not in despair; persecuted, but not abandoned; struck down,
but not destroyed. We always carry around in our body the
death of Jesus, so that the life of Jesus may also be revealed
in our body. For we who are alive are always being given
over to death for Jesus' sake, so that his life may be revealed
in our mortal body. So then, death is at work in us, but life is
at work in you.

GOSPEL *John 4.31–38*

His disciples urged Jesus, 'Rabbi, eat something.'

But he said to them, 'I have food to eat that you know nothing about.'

Then his disciples said to each other, 'Could someone have brought him food!'

'My food,' said Jesus, 'is to do the will of him who sent me and to finish his work. Do you not say, "Four months more and then the harvest"? I tell you, open your eyes and look at the fields! They are ripe for harvest. Even now the reaper draws his wages, even now he harvests the crop for eternal life, so that the sower and the reaper may be glad together. Thus the saying "One sows and another reaps" is true. I sent you to reap what you have not worked for. Others have done the hard work, and you have reaped the benefits of their labour.'

Psalm 106.1–5   Isaiah 51.1–8   Acts 16.6–10

Psalm 96   Isaiah 8.19 – 9.2   Luke 6.20–31

THE ANNUNCIATION OF OUR LORD
TO THE BLESSED VIRGIN MARY *White*
25 March

COLLECT

Heavenly Father,
you chose the Blessed Virgin Mary
to be the mother of the promised Saviour,
and proclaimed the good news by the message of an angel:
Fill us with the abundance of your grace,
that, through the saving work of Christ,
we may be brought to the glory of his resurrection;
who lives and reigns with you and the Holy Spirit,
one God, for ever. **Amen.**

PSALM 113 *or* 131

OLD TESTAMENT *Isaiah 52.7–10*

How beautiful on themountains
are the feet of those who bring good news,

who proclaim peace,
who bring good tidings,
who proclaim salvation,
who say to Zion, 'Your God reigns!'
Listen! Your watchmen lift up their voices;
together they shout for joy.
When the LORD returns to Zion,
they will see it with their own eyes.
Burst into songs of joy together,
you ruins of Jerusalem,
for the LORD has comforted his people,
he has redeemed Jerusalem.
The LORD will lay bare his holy arm
in the sight of all the nations,
and all the ends of the earth
will see the salvation of our God.

EPISTLE   *Galatians 4.1–5*

What I am saying is that as long as the heir is a child, he is no
different from a slave, although he owns the whole estate.
He is subject to guardians and trustees until the time set by
his father. So also, when we were children, we were in
slavery under the basic principles of the world. But when the
time had fully come, God sent his Son, born of a woman,
born under law, to redeem those under law, that we might
receive the full rights of sons.

GOSPEL   *Luke 1.26–38a*

In the sixth month, God sent the angel Gabriel to Nazareth, a
town in Galilee, to a virgin pledged to be married to a man
named Joseph, a descendant of David. The virgin's name
was Mary. The angel went to her and said, 'Greetings, you
who are highly favoured! The Lord is with you.'

Mary was greatly troubled at his words and wondered
what kind of greeting this might be. But the angel said to
her, 'Do not be afraid, Mary, you have found favour with
God. You will be with child and give birth to a son, and you
are to give him the name Jesus. He will be great and will be
called the Son of the Most High. The Lord God will give him
the throne of his father David, and he will reign over the
house of Jacob for ever; his kingdom will never end.'

'How will this be,' Mary asked the angel, 'since I am a

virgin?'

The angel answered, 'The Holy Spirit will come upon you, and the power of the Most High will overshadow you. So the holy one to be born will be called the Son of God. Even Elizabeth your relative is going to have a child in her old age, and she who was said to be barren is in her sixth month. For nothing is impossible with God.'

'I am the Lord's servant,' Mary answered. 'May it be to me as you have said.'

Psalm 85   1 Samuel 2.1–10   Hebrews 2.5–18

Psalm 111   Genesis 3.8–15   Romans 5.12–21

SAINT MARK
25 April

Red

COLLECT

Almighty God,
you have enlightened your holy Church
through the inspired witness
of your evangelist Saint Mark:
Grant that we, being firmly grounded
in the truth of the gospel,
may be faithful to its teaching
both in word and deed;
through Jesus Christ our Lord.   **Amen.**

PSALM 45.1–5 (PB1–6) *or* 119.9–16

OLD TESTAMENT *Proverbs 15.28–33*

The heart of the righteous weighs its answers,
but the mouth of the wicked gushes evil.

The LORD is far from the wicked
but he hears the prayer of the righteous.

A cheerful look brings joy to the heart,
and good news gives health to the bones.

He who listens to a life-giving rebuke
will be at home among the wise.

He who ignores discipline despises himself,
but whoever heeds correction gains understanding.

The fear of the Lᴏʀᴅ teaches a man wisdom,
and humility comes before honour.

EPISTLE   *Ephesians 4.7–16*

To each one of us grace has been given as Christ apportioned it. This is why it says:

'When he ascended on high,
he led captives in his train
and gave gifts to men.'

(What does 'he ascended' mean except that he also descended to the lower, earthly regions? He who descended is the very one who ascended higher than all the heavens, in order to fill the whole universe.) It was he who gave some to be apostles, some to be prophets, some to be evangelists, and some to be pastors and teachers, to prepare God's people for works of service, so that the body of Christ may be built up until we all reach unity in the faith and in the knowledge of the Son of God and become mature, attaining to the whole measure of the fulness of Christ.

Then we will no longer be infants, tossed back and forth by the waves, and blown here and there by every wind of teaching and by the cunning and craftiness of men in their deceitful scheming. Instead, speaking the truth in love, we will in all things grow up into him who is the head, that is, Christ. From him the whole body, joined and held together by every supporting ligament, grows and builds itself up in love, as each part does its work.

GOSPEL   *Mark 13.5–13*

Jesus said to his disciples: 'Watch out that no one deceives you. Many will come in my name, claiming, "I am he," and will deceive many. When you hear of wars and rumours of wars, do not be alarmed. Such things must happen, but the end is still to come. Nation will rise against nation, and kingdom against kingdom. There will be earthquakes in various places, and famines. These are the beginning of birth pains.

'You must be on your guard. You will be handed over to

the local councils and flogged in the synagogues. On account of me you will stand before governors and kings as witnesses to them. And the gospel must first be preached to all nations. Whenever you are arrested and brought to trial, do not worry beforehand about what to say. Just say whatever is given you at the time, for it is not you speaking, but the Holy Spirit.

'Brother will betray brother to death, and a father his child. Children will rebel against their parents and have them put to death. All men will hate you because of me, but he who stands firm to the end will be saved.'

Psalm 19   Isaiah 62.6–12 *or* Ecclesiasticus 51.13–30   2 Timothy 4.1–11

Psalm 96   Ezekiel 1.4–14   Acts 15.35–41

SAINT PHILIP AND SAINT JAMES   *Red*
1 May

COLLECT

Almighty God,
to know you is eternal life:
Teach us to know your Son Jesus Christ
as the way, the truth and the life,
that we may follow the steps
of your apostles Philip and James
and walk in the way that leads to your eternal kingdom;
through Jesus Christ our Lord.   **Amen.**

PSALM 33.1–5 *or* 25.1–10 (PB 1–9)

OLD TESTAMENT   *Proverbs 4.10–18*

Listen, my son, accept what I say,
and the years of your life will be many.
I guide you in the way of wisdom
and lead you along straight paths.
When you walk, your steps will not be hampered;
when you run, you will not stumble.
Hold on to instruction, do not let it go;
guard it well, for it is your life.
Do not set foot on the path of the wicked

or walk in the way of evil men.
Avoid it, do not travel on it;
turn from it and go on your way.
For they cannot sleep till they do evil;
they are robbed of slumber till they make someone fall.
They eat the bread of wickedness
and drink the wine of violence.
The path of the righteous is like the first gleam of dawn,
shining ever brighter till the full light of day.

EPISTLE *Ephesians 1.3–14*

Praise be to the God and Father of our Lord Jesus Christ,
who has blessed us in the heavenly realms with every spiritual blessing in Christ. For he chose us in him before the
creation of the world to be holy and blameless in his sight. In
love he predestined us to be adopted as his sons through
Jesus Christ, in accordance with his pleasure and will – to the
praise of his glorious grace, which he has freely given us in
the One he loves. In him we have redemption through his
blood, the forgiveness of sins, in accordance with the riches
of God's grace that he lavished on us with all wisdom and
understanding. And he made known to us the mystery of
his will according to his good pleasure, which he purposed
in Christ, to be put into effect when the times will have
reached their fulfilment – to bring all things in heaven and
on earth together under one head, even Christ.

In him we were also chosen, having been predestined
according to the plan of him who works out everything in
conformity with the purpose of his will, in order that we,
who were the first to hope in Christ, might be for the praise
of his glory. And you also were included in Christ when you
heard the word of truth, the gospel of your salvation.
Having believed, you were marked in him with a seal, the
promised Holy Spirit, who is a deposit guaranteeing our
inheritance until the redemption of those who are God's
possession – to the praise of his glory.

GOSPEL *John 14.1–14*

Jesus said, 'Do not let your hearts be troubled. Trust in God;
trust also in me. In my Father's house are many rooms; if it
were not so, I would have told you. I am going there to
prepare a place for you. And if I go and prepare a place for

you, I will come back and take you to be with me that you also may be where I am. You know the way to the place where I am going.'

Thomas said to him, 'Lord, we do not know where you are going, so how can we know the way?'

Jesus answered, 'I am the way and the truth and the life. No one comes to the Father except through me. If you really knew me, you would know my Father as well. From now on, you do know him and have seen him.'

Philip said, 'Lord, show us the Father and that will be enough for us.'

Jesus answered: 'Do you not know me, Philip, even after I have been among you such a long time? Anyone who has seen me has seen the Father. How can you say, "Show us the Father"? Do you not believe that I am in the Father, and that the Father is in me? The words I say to you are not just my own. Rather, it is the Father, living in me, who is doing his work. Believe me when I say that I am in the Father and the Father is in me; or at least believe on the evidence of the miracles themselves. I tell you the truth, anyone who has faith in me will do what I have been doing. He will do even greater things than these, because I am going to the Father. And I will do whatever you ask in my name, so that the Son may bring glory to the Father. You may ask me for anything in my name, and I will do it.'

Psalm 27   Job 23.1–12   Acts 2.37–47

Psalm 119.137–152   Isaiah 30.15–21   John 1.43–51

SAINT MATTHIAS   *Red*
14 May

COLLECT

Almighty God,
you chose your faithful servant Matthias
to make up the number of the Twelve:
Preserve your Church from false apostles,
and by the ministry of faithful pastors and teachers
keep us steadfast in your truth;
through Jesus Christ our Lord.   **Amen.**

PSALM 16.1–6 (PB1–7) *or* 80.8–15

OLD TESTAMENT *1 Samuel 2.27–35*

A man of God came to Eli and said to him, ''This is what the LORD says: ''Did I not clearly reveal myself to your father's house when they were in Egypt under Pharaoh? I chose your father out of all the tribes of Israel to be my priest, to go up to my altar, to burn incense, and to wear an ephod in my presence. I also gave your father's house all the offerings made with fire by the Israelites. Why do you scorn my sacrifice and offering that I prescribed for my dwelling? Why do you honour your sons more than me by fattening yourselves on the choice parts of every offering made by my people Israel?''

'Therefore the LORD, the God of Israel, declares: ''I promised that your house and your father's house would minister before me for ever.'' But now the LORD declares: ''Far be it from me! Those who honour me I will honour, but those who despise me will be disdained. The time is coming when I will cut short your strength and the strength of your father's house, so that there will not be an old man in your family line and you will see distress in my dwelling. Although good will be done to Israel, in your family line there will never be an old man. Every one of you that I do not cut off from my altar will be spared only to blind your eyes with tears and to grieve your heart, and all your descendants will die in the prime of life.

' ''And what happens to your two sons, Hophni and Phinehas, will be a sign to you – they will both die on the same day. I will raise up for myself a faithful priest, who will do according to what is in my heart and mind. I will firmly establish his house, and he will minister before my anointed one always.'' '

EPISTLE *Acts 1.15–17, 20–26*

In those days Peter stood up among the believers (a group numbering about a hundred and twenty) and said, 'Brothers, the Scripture had to be fulfilled which the Holy Spirit spoke long ago through the mouth of David concerning Judas, who served as guide for those who arrested Jesus – he was one of our number and shared in this ministry.

'For it is written in the book of Psalms,

' "May his place be deserted;
let there be no one to dwell in it,"

and,

' "May another take his place of leadership."

'Therefore it is necessary to choose one of the men who have been with us the whole time the Lord Jesus went in and out among us, beginning from John's baptism to the time when Jesus was taken up from us. For one of these must become a witness with us of his resurrection.'

So they proposed two men: Joseph called Barsabbas (also known as Justus) and Matthias. Then they prayed 'Lord, you know everyone's heart. Show us which of these two you have chosen to take over this apostolic ministry, which Judas left to go where he belongs.' Then they drew lots, and the lot fell to Matthias; so he was added to the eleven apostles.

GOSPEL *John 15.1–11*

Jesus said, 'I am the true vine and my Father is the gardener. He cuts off every branch in me that bears no fruit, while every branch that does bear fruit he trims clean so that it will be even more fruitful. You are already clean because of the word I have spoken to you. Remain in me, and I will remain in you. No branch can bear fruit by itself; it must remain in the vine. Neither can you bear fruit unless you remain in me.

'I am the vine; you are the branches. If a man remains in me and I in him, he will bear much fruit; apart from me you can do nothing. If anyone does not remain in me, he is like a branch that is thrown away and withers; such branches are picked up, thrown into the fire and burned. If you remain in me and my words remain in you, ask whatever you wish, and it will be given you. This is to my Father's glory, that you bear much fruit, showing yourselves to be my disciples.

'As the Father has loved me, so have I loved you. Now remain in my love. If you obey my commands, you will remain in my love, just as I have obeyed my Father's commands and remain in his love. I have told you this so that my joy may be in you and that your joy may be complete.'

Psalm 33   Isaiah 22.15–22   Matthew 7.15–27

Psalm 92   1 Samuel 16.1–13a   1 Corinthians 4.1–7

THE VISITATION
OF THE BLESSED VIRGIN MARY
31 May

COLLECT

Almighty God,
by your grace Elizabeth rejoiced with Mary,
and hailed her as the mother of the Lord:
Fill us with your grace
that we may acclaim her Son Jesus as our Saviour
and rejoice to be called his brethren;
through him who lives and reigns
with you and the Holy Spirit,
one God, now and for ever.   **Amen.**

PSALM 113 or 131

OLD TESTAMENT *Zechariah 2.10–13*

'Shout and be glad, O Daughter of Zion. For I am coming,
and I will live among you,' declares the LORD. 'Many nations
will be joined with the LORD in that day and will become my
people. I will live among you and you will know that the
LORD Almighty has sent me to you. The LORD will inherit
Judah as his portion in the holy land and will again choose
Jerusalem. Be still before the LORD, all mankind, because he
has roused himself from his holy dwelling.'

EPISTLE *Galatians 4.1–5*

What I am saying is that as long as the heir is a child, he is no
different from a slave, although he owns the whole estate.
He is subject to guardians and trustees until the time set by
his father. So also, when we were children, we were in
slavery under the basic principles of the world. But when the
time had fully come, God sent his Son, born of a woman,
born under law, to redeem those under law, that we might
receive the full rights of sons.

GOSPEL *Luke 1.39–49 (–56)*

At that time Mary got ready and hurried to a town in the hill
country of Judah, where she entered Zechariah's home and

greeted Elizabeth. When Elizabeth heard Mary's greeting, the baby leaped in her womb, and Elizabeth was filled with the Holy Spirit. In a loud voice she exclaimed: 'Blessed are you among women, and blessed is the child you will bear! But why am I so favoured, that the mother of my Lord should come to me? As soon as the sound of your greeting reached my ears, the baby in my womb leaped for joy. Blessed is she who has believed that what the Lord has said to her will be accomplished!'

And Mary said:

'My soul praises the Lord
and my spirit rejoices in God my Saviour,
for he has been mindful of the humble state of his servant.
From now on all generations will call me blessed,
for the Mighty One has done great things for me –
holy is his name.'

Psalm 146   Zephaniah 3.14–18a   Colossians 3.12–17

Psalm 23   1 Samuel 2.1–10   Hebrews 2.11–18

SAINT COLUMBA
9 June

White

COLLECT

O God, you called your servant Columba
from among the princes of this land
to be a herald and evangelist of your kingdom:
Grant that your Church,
remembering his faith and courage,
may so proclaim the gospel,
that all men will come to know your Son as their Saviour,
and serve him as their King;
who lives and reigns with you and the Holy Spirit,
one God, now and for ever.   **Amen.**

PSALM 34.9–15

OLD TESTAMENT *Micah 4.1–5*

In the last days
the mountain of the LORD's temple will be established
as chief among the mountains;
it will be raised above the hills,
and peoples will stream to it.

Many nations will come and say,

'Come, let us go up to the mountain of the LORD,
to the house of the God of Jacob.
He will teach us his ways,
so that we may walk in his paths.'
The law will go out from Zion,
the word of the LORD from Jerusalem.
He will judge between many peoples
and will settle disputes for strong nations far and wide.
They will beat their swords into ploughshares
and their spears into pruning hooks.
Nation will not take up sword against nation,
nor will they train for war any more.
Every man will sit under his own vine
and under his own fig-tree,
and no one will make them afraid,
for the LORD Almighty has spoken.
All the nations may walk
in the name of their gods;
we will walk in the name of the LORD
our God for ever and ever.

EPISTLE *Romans 15.1–6*

We who are strong ought to bear with the failings of the weak and not to please ourselves. Each of us should please his neighbour for his good, to build him up. For even Christ did not please himself but, as it is written: 'The insults of those who insult you have fallen on me.' For everything that was written in the past was written to teach us, so that through endurance and the encouragement of the Scriptures we might have hope.

May the God who gives endurance and encouragement give you a spirit of unity among yourselves as you follow Christ Jesus, so that with one heart and mouth you may glorify the God and Father of our Lord Jesus Christ.

GOSPEL   *John 12.20–26*

Now there were some Greeks among those who went up to worship at the Feast. They came to Philip, who was from Bethsaida in Galilee, with a request. 'Sir,' they said, 'we would like to see Jesus.' Philip went to tell Andrew; Andrew and Philip in turn told Jesus.

Jesus replied, 'The hour has come for the Son of Man to be glorified. I tell you the truth, unless an ear of wheat falls to the ground and dies, it remains only a single seed. But if it dies, it produces many seeds. The man who loves his life will lose it, while the man who hates his life in this world will keep it for eternal life. Whoever serves me must follow me; and where I am, my servant also will be. My Father will honour the one who serves me.'

Psalm 34.1–8   Isaiah 42.5–12   2 Corinthians 4.5–10

Psalm 97.1–6,10–12   Micah 7.14–20   Matthew 28.16–20

SAINT BARNABAS
Red

11 June

COLLECT

Merciful Father, giver of all gifts,
you poured your Spirit upon your servant Barnabas:
Help us, by his example,
to be generous in our judgments
and unselfish in our service;
through Jesus Christ our Lord.   **Amen.**

PSALM 145.8–15 *or* 112

OLD TESTAMENT   *Job 29.11–16*

Job said,
'Whoever heard me spoke well of me,
and those who saw me commended me,
because I rescued the poor who cried for help,
and the fatherless who had none to assist him.
The man who was dying blessed me;
I made the widow's heart sing.
I put on righteousness as my clothing;

justice was my robe and my turban.
I was eyes to the blind and feet to the lame.
I was a father to the needy;
I took up the case of the stranger.'

EPISTLE *Acts 11.19–30*

Now those who had been scattered by the persecution in connection with Stephen travelled as far as Phoenicia, Cyprus and Antioch, telling the message only to Jews. Some of them, however, men from Cyprus and Cyrene, went to Antioch and began to speak to Greeks also, telling them the good news about the Lord Jesus. The Lord's hand was with them, and a great number of people believed and turned to the Lord.

News of this reached the ears of the church at Jerusalem, and they sent Barnabas to Antioch. When he arrived and saw the evidence of the grace of God, he was glad and encouraged them all to remain true to the Lord with all their hearts. He was a good man, full of the Holy Spirit and faith, and a great number of people were brought to the Lord.

Then Barnabas went to Tarsus to look for Saul, and when he found him, he brought him to Antioch. So for a whole year Barnabas and Saul met with the church and taught great numbers of people. The disciples were first called Christians at Antioch.

During this time some prophets came down from Jerusalem to Antioch. One of them, named Agabus, stood up and through the Spirit predicted that a severe famine would spread over the entire Roman world. (This happened during the reign of Claudius.) The disciples, each according to his ability, decided to provide help for the brothers living in Judea. This they did, sending their gift to the elders by Barnabas and Saul.

GOSPEL *John 15.12–17*

Jesus said, 'My command is this: Love each other as I have loved you. Greater love has no one than this, that one lay down his life for his friends. You are my friends if you do what I command. I no longer call you servants, because a servant does not know his master's business. Instead, I have called you friends, for everything that I learned from my

Father I have made known to you. You did not choose me,
but I chose you to go and bear fruit – fruit that will last. Then
the Father will give you whatever you ask in my name. This
is my command: Love each other.'

Psalm 101   Ecclesiastes 12.9–14 *or* Tobit 4.5–11   Acts 4.32–37

Psalm 15   Isaiah 45.5–12   Acts 9.26–31

THE BIRTH OF SAINT JOHN THE BAPTIST   *White*
24 June

COLLECT

Almighty God,
in your providence your servant John the Baptist
was wonderfully born,
and you sent him to prepare the way of your Son
by preaching repentance for the forgiveness of sins:
May we repent according to his preaching,
and after his example
constantly speak the truth, boldly rebuke vice,
and patiently suffer for the truth's sake;
through Jesus Christ our Lord.   **Amen.**

PSALM 80.1–7 *or* 119.161–168

OLD TESTAMENT   *Isaiah 40.1–11*

Comfort, comfort my people, says your God.
Speak tenderly to Jerusalem,
and proclaim to her
that her hard service has been completed,
that her sin has been paid for,
that she has received from the LORD's hand
double for all her sins.

A voice of one calling:
'In the desert prepare
the way for the LORD;
make straight in the wilderness
a highway for our God.
Every valley shall be raised up,

every mountain and hill made low;
the rough ground shall become level,
the rugged places a plain.
And the glory of the LORD will be revealed,
and all mankind together will see it.
For the mouth of the LORD has spoken.'

A voice says, 'Cry out.'
And I said, 'What shall I cry?'
'All men are like grass,
and all their glory is like the flowers of the field.
The grass withers and the flowers fall,
because the breath of the LORD blows on them.
Surely the people are grass.
The grass withers and the flowers fall,
but the word of our God stands for ever.'
You who bring good tidings to Zion,
go up on a high mountain.
You who bring good tidings to Jerusalem,
lift up your voice with a shout,
lift it up, do not be afraid;
say to the towns of Judah,
'Here is your God!'
See, the Sovereign LORD comes with power,
and his arm rules for him.
See, his reward is with him,
and his recompense accompanies him.
He tends his flock like a shepherd:
he gathers the lambs in his arms
and carries them close to his heart;
he gently leads those that have young.

EPISTLE *Acts 13.16–26*

Standing up, Paul motioned with his hand and said:
'Men of Israel and you Gentiles who worship God, listen
to me! The God of the people of Israel chose our fathers and
made the people prosper during their stay in Egypt. With
mighty power he led them out of that country and endured
their conduct forty years in the desert. He overthrew seven
nations in Canaan and gave their land to his people as their
inheritance. All this took about four hundred and fifty years.

'After this, God gave them judges until the time of Samuel
the prophet. Then the people asked for a king, and he gave

them Saul son of Kish, of the tribe of Benjamin, who ruled forty years. After removing Saul, he made David their king. He testified concerning him: "I have found David son of Jesse a man after my own heart; he will do everything I want him to do." From this man's descendants God has brought to Israel the Saviour Jesus, as he promised. Before the coming of Jesus, John preached repentance and baptism to all the people of Israel. As John was completing his work, he said: "Who do you think I am? I am not that one. No, but he is coming after me, whose sandals I am not worthy to untie."

'Brothers, children of Abraham, and you God-fearing Gentiles, it is to us that this message of salvation has been sent.'

GOSPEL *Luke 1.57–66,80 (57–80)*

When it was time for Elizabeth to have her baby, she gave birth to a son. Her neighbours and relatives heard that the Lord had shown her great mercy, and they shared her joy.

On the eighth day they came to circumcise the child, and they were going to name him after his father Zechariah, but his mother spoke up and said, 'No! He is to be called John.'

They said to her, 'There is no one among your relatives who has that name.'

Then they made signs to his father, to find out what he would like to name the child. He asked for a writing tablet, and to everyone's astonishment he wrote, 'His name is John.' Immediately his mouth was opened and his tongue was loosed, and he began to speak, praising God. The neighbours were all filled with awe, and throughout the hill country of Judea people were talking about all these things. Everyone who heard this wondered about it, asking, 'What then is this child going to be?' For the Lord's hand was with him.

And the child grew and became strong in spirit; and he lived in the desert until he appeared publicly to Israel.

Psalm 50   Judges 13   Matthew 11.2–19

Psalm 116   Malachi 4   Luke 3.1–20

SAINT PETER
29 June

COLLECT

Almighty God,
by your Son Jesus Christ
you gave your apostle Peter many excellent gifts,
and commanded him to feed your flock:
Make all bishops and pastors diligent to preach your word,
and your people to hear and follow it,
that they may receive the crown of everlasting glory;
through Jesus Christ our Lord.   **Amen.**

PSALM 125 *or* 18.33–37 (PB 32–36)

OLD TESTAMENT   *Ezekiel 3.4–11*

The Lord said to me: 'Son of man, go now to the house of
Israel and speak my words to them. You are not being sent
to a people of obscure speech and difficult language, but to
the house of Israel – not to many peoples of obscure speech
and difficult language, whose words you cannot understand. Surely if I had sent you to them, they would have
listened to you. But the house of Israel is not willing to listen
to you because they are not willing to listen to me, for the
whole house of Israel is hardened and obstinate. But I will
make you as unyielding and hardened as they are. I will
make your forehead like the hardest stone, harder than flint.
Do not be afraid of them or terrified by them, though they
are a rebellious house.'

And he said to me, 'Son of man, listen carefully and take
to heart all the words I speak to you. Go now to your
countrymen in exile and speak to them. Say to them, "This is
what the Sovereign LORD says," whether they listen or fail to
listen.'

EPISTLE   *1 Peter 2.19–25*

It is commendable if a man bears up under pain of unjust
suffering because he is conscious of God. But how is it to
your credit if you receive a beating for doing wrong and
endure it? But if you suffer for doing good and you endure it,
this is commendable before God. To this you were called,

because Christ suffered for you, leaving you an example, that you should follow in his steps.

'He committed no sin,
and no deceit was found in his mouth.'

When they hurled their insults at him, he did not retaliate; when he suffered, he made no threats. Instead, he entrusted himself to him who judges justly. He himself bore our sins in his body on the tree, so that we might die to sins and live for righteousness; by his wounds you have been healed. For you were like sheep going astray, but now you have returned to the Shepherd and Overseer of your souls.

GOSPEL   *Matthew 16.13–20*

When Jesus came to the region of Caesarea Philippi, he asked his disciples, 'Who do people say the Son of Man is?' They replied, 'Some say John the Baptist; others say Elijah; and still others, Jeremiah or one of the prophets.'

'But what about you?' he asked. 'Who do you say I am?'

Simon Peter answered, 'You are the Christ, the Son of the living God.'

Jesus replied, 'Blessed are you, Simon son of Jonah, for this was not revealed to you by man, but by my Father in heaven. And I tell you that you are Peter, and on this rock I will build my church, and the gates of Hades will not overcome it. I will give you the keys of the kingdom of heaven; whatever you bind on earth will be bound in heaven, and whatever you loose on earth will be loosed in heaven.' Then he warned his disciples not to tell anyone that he was the Christ.

Psalm 71   Ezekiel 2.1–7   Acts 9.32–43

Psalm 145   Ezekiel 34.11–16   John 21.15–22

SAINT THOMAS

3 July

COLLECT

Almighty and eternal God,
your apostle Thomas
doubted the resurrection of your Son
till word and sight convinced him:
Grant that, though we have not seen,
we may believe,
and so share in the fulness of Christ's blessing,
who lives and reigns with you and the Holy Spirit,
one God, now and for ever.   **Amen.**

PSALM 139.1–11

OLD TESTAMENT   *Genesis 12.1–4*

The LORD said to Abram, 'Leave your country, your people and your father's household and go to the land I will show you.

'I will make you into a great nation
and I will bless you;
I will make your name great,
and you will be a blessing.
I will bless those who bless you,
and whoever curses you I will curse;
and all peoples on earth
will be blessed through you.'

So Abram left, as the LORD had told him; and Lot went with him. Abram was seventy-five years old when he set out from Haran.

EPISTLE   *Hebrews 10.35 – 11.1*

So do not throw away your confidence; it will be richly rewarded. You need to persevere so that when you have done the will of God, you will receive what he has promised. For in just a very little while,

'He who is coming will come and will not delay.
But my righteous one will live by faith.

And if he shrinks back,
I will not be pleased with him.'

But we are not of those who shrink back and are destroyed,
but of those who believe and are saved.

Now faith is being sure of what we hope for and certain of
what we do not see.

GOSPEL *John 20.24–29*

Thomas (called Didymus) one of the Twelve, was not with
the disciples when Jesus came. When the other disciples told
him that they had seen the Lord, he declared, 'Unless I see
the nail marks in his hands and put my finger where the
nails were, and put my hand into his side, I will not believe
it.'

A week later his disciples were in the house again, and
Thomas was with them. Though the doors were locked,
Jesus came and stood among them, and said, 'Peace be with
you!' Then he said to Thomas, 'Put your finger here; see my
hands. Reach out your hand and put it into my side. Stop
doubting and believe.'

Thomas answered, 'My Lord and my God!'

Then Jesus told him, 'Because you have seen me, you have
believed; blessed are those who have not seen and yet have
believed.'

Psalm 34   Job 42.1–6   1 Peter 1.3–9

Psalm 92   2 Samuel 15.17–21   John 11.1–16

SAINT MARY MAGDALENE   *White*
22 July

COLLECT

Almighty God,
your blessed Son brought healing to Mary Magdalene,
and called her to be a witness
of his resurrection:
Forgive us and heal us by your grace,
that we may serve you
in the power of his risen life,
who is alive and reigns with you and the Holy Spirit,
one God, now and for ever.   **Amen.**

PSALM 30.1–5

OLD TESTAMENT *Zephaniah 3.14–20*

Sing, O Daughter of Zion;
shout aloud, O Israel!
Be glad and rejoice with all your heart,
O Daughter of Jerusalem!
The LORD has taken away your punishment,
he has turned back your enemy.

The LORD, the King of Israel, is with you;
never again will you fear any harm.
On that day they will say to Jerusalem.
'Do not fear, O Zion;
do not let your hands hang limp.
The LORD your God is with you,
he is mighty to save.
He will take great delight in you,
he will quiet you with his love,
he will rejoice over you with singing.'

'The sorrows for the appointed feasts
I will remove from you;
they are a burden and a reproach to you.
At that time I will deal
with all who oppressed you;
I will rescue the lame
and gather those who have been scattered.
I will give them praise and honour
in every land where they were put to shame.
At that time I will gather you;
at that time I will bring you home.
I will give you honour and praise
among all the peoples of the earth
when I restore your fortunes
before your very eyes,'
says the LORD.

EPISTLE *2 Corinthians 5.14–17*

Christ's love compels us, because we are convinced that one
died for all, and therefore all died. And he died for all, that
those who live should no longer live for themselves but for
him who died for them and was raised again.

So from now on we regard no one from a worldly point of view. Though we once regarded Christ in this way, we do so no longer. Therefore, if anyone is in Christ, he is a new creation; the old has gone, the new has come!

GOSPEL   *John 20.11–18*

Mary of Magdala stood outside the tomb crying. As she wept, she bent over to look into the tomb and saw two angels in white, seated where Jesus' body had been, one at the head and the other at the foot.

They asked her, 'Woman, why are you crying?'

'They have taken my Lord away,' she said, 'and I do not know where they have put him.' At this, she turned around and saw Jesus standing there, but she did not realize that it was Jesus.

'Woman,' he said, 'why are you crying? Who is it you are looking for?'

Thinking he was the gardener, she said, 'Sir, if you have carried him away, tell me where you have put him, and I will get him.'

Jesus said to her, 'Mary.'

She turned towards him and cried out in Aramaic, 'Rabboni!' (which means Teacher).

Jesus said, 'Do not hold on to me, for I have not yet returned to the Father. Go instead to my brothers and tell them, "I am returning to my Father and your Father, to my God and your God." '

Mary of Magdala went to the disciples with the news: 'I have seen the Lord!' And she told them that he had said these things to her.

Psalm 32   1 Samuel 16.14–23   Luke 8.1–3

Psalm 63   Hosea 14   Mark 15.40 – 16.8

SAINT JAMES
25 July

COLLECT

Merciful God,
your Son Jesus Christ called your apostle James,
who obeyed without delay
and left his father and all that he had:
Make us ready to forsake all,
and to follow your holy commandments;
through Jesus Christ our Lord.   **Amen.**

PSALM 15 or 75.6–11 (PB 7–12)

OLD TESTAMENT *Jeremiah 45*

This is what Jeremiah the prophet told Baruch son of Neriah in the fourth year of Jehoiakim son of Josiah king of Judah, after Baruch had written on a scroll the words Jeremiah was then dictating: 'This is what the Lord, the God of Israel, says to you, Baruch: You said, "Woe to me! The Lord has added sorrow to my pain; I am worn out with groaning and find no rest." '

The Lord said, 'Say this to him: "This is what the Lord says: I will overthrow what I have built and uproot what I have planted, throughout the land. Should you then seek great things for yourself? Seek them not. For I will bring disaster on all people, declares the Lord, but wherever you go I will let you escape with your life." '

EPISTLE *Acts 11.27 – 12.2*

Some prophets came down from Jerusalem to Antioch. One of them, named Agabus, stood up and through the Spirit predicted that a severe famine would spread over the entire Roman world. (This happened during the reign of Claudius.) The disciples, each according to his ability, decided to provide help for the brothers living in Judea. This they did, sending their gift to the elders by Barnabas and Saul.

It was about this time that King Herod arrested some who belonged to the church, intending to persecute them. He had James, the brother of John, put to death with the sword.

GOSPEL *Mark 10.35–45*

James and John, the sons of Zebedee, came to Jesus. 'Teacher,' they said, 'We want you to do for us whatever we ask.'

'What do you want me to do for you?' he asked.

They replied, 'Let one of us sit at your right and the other at your left in your glory.'

'You do not know what you are asking,' Jesus said. 'Can you drink the cup I drink or be baptized with the baptism I am baptized with?'

'We can,' they answered.

Jesus said to them, 'You will drink the cup I drink and be baptized with the baptism I am baptized with, but to sit at my right or left is not for me to grant. These places belong to those for whom they have been prepared.'

When the ten heard about this, they became indignant with James and John. Jesus called them together and said, 'You know that those who are regarded as rulers of the Gentiles lord it over them, and their high officials exercise authority over them. Not so with you. Instead, whoever wants to become great among you must be your servant, and whoever wants to be first must be slave of all. For even the Son of Man did not come to be served, but to serve, and to give his life as a ransom for many.'

Psalm 29   2 Kings 1.9–15   Luke 9.46–56

Psalm 94   Jeremiah 26.1–16   Mark 1.14–20

THE TRANSFIGURATION OF OUR LORD   *White*
6 August

COLLECT

Almighty God,
your Son Jesus Christ was transfigured
before chosen witnesses on the mountain,
and spoke of the exodus
he would accomplish at Jerusalem:
May we your servants see his glory,
and receive strength to bear our cross;
through Jesus Christ our Lord.   **Amen.**

PSALM 84

OLD TESTAMENT *Exodus 34.29–35*

When Moses came down from Mount Sinai with the two tablets of the Testimony in his hands, he was not aware that his face was radiant, and they were afraid to come near him. But Moses called to them; so Aaron and all the leaders of the community came back to him, and he spoke to them. Afterwards all the Israelites came near him, and he gave them all the commands the LORD had given him on Mount Sinai.

When Moses finished speaking to them, he put a veil over his face. But whenever he entered the LORD's presence to speak with him, he removed the veil until he came out. And when he came out and told the Israelites what he had been commanded, they saw that his face was radiant. Then Moses would put the veil back over his face until he went in to speak with the LORD.

EPISTLE *2 Corinthians 3.4–18*

Such confidence as this is ours through Christ before God. Not that we are competent to claim anything for ourselves, but our competence comes from God. He has made us competent as ministers of a new covenant – not of the letter but of the Spirit; for the letter kills, but the Spirit gives life.

Now if the ministry that brought death, which was engraved in letters on stone, came with glory, so that the Israelites could not look steadily at the face of Moses because of its glory, fading though it was, will not the ministry of the Spirit be even more glorious? If the ministry that condemns men is glorious, how much more glorious is the ministry that brings righteousness! For what was glorious has no glory now in comparison with the surpassing glory. And if what was fading away came with glory, how much greater is the glory of that which lasts!

Therefore, since we have such a hope, we are very bold. We are not like Moses, who would put a veil over his face to keep the Israelites from gazing at it while the radiance was fading away. But their minds were made dull, for to this day the same veil remains when the old covenant is read. It has not been removed, because only in Christ is it taken away. Even to this day when Moses is read, a veil covers their hearts. But whenever anyone turns to the Lord, the veil is taken away. Now the Lord is the Spirit, and where the Spirit of the Lord is, there is freedom. And we, who with unveiled faces all reflect the Lord's glory, are being transformed into his likeness with ever-increasing glory, which comes from the Lord, who is the Spirit.

GOSPEL *Luke 9.28–36*

Jesus took Peter, John and James with him and went up on to a mountain to pray. As he was praying, the appearance of his face changed, and his clothes became as bright as a flash of lightning. Two men, Moses and Elijah, appeared in glorious splendour, talking with Jesus. They spoke about his departure, which he was about to bring to fulfilment at Jerusalem. Peter and his companions were very sleepy, but when they became fully awake, they saw his glory and the two men standing with him. As the men were leaving Jesus, Peter said to him, 'Master, it is good for us to be here. Let us put up three shelters – one for you, one for Moses and one for Elijah.' (He did not know what he was saying.)

While he was speaking, a cloud appeared and enveloped them, and they were afraid as they entered the cloud. A voice came from the cloud, saying, 'This is my Son, whom I have chosen; listen to him.' When the voice had spoken, they found that Jesus was alone. The disciples kept this to themselves, and told no one at that time what they had seen.

Psalm 27   1 Kings 19.1–16 *or* Ecclesiasticus 48.1–10   2 Peter 1.12–19

Psalm 72   Exodus 24.12–18   1 John 3.1–3

SAINT BARTHOLOMEW   *Red*

24 August

COLLECT

Almighty God,
you gave to your apostle Bartholomew
grace truly to believe and to preach your word:
Grant that your Church
may love that word which he believed
and may faithfully preach and receive the same;
through Jesus Christ our Lord.   **Amen.**

PSALM 116.11–18 (PB 11–16) *or* 97

OLD TESTAMENT   *Isaiah 61.4–9*

They will rebuild the ancient ruins
and restore the places long devastated;
they will renew the ruined cities
that have been devastated for generations.
Aliens will shepherd your flocks;
foreigners will work your fields and vineyards.
And you will be called priests of the LORD,
you will be named ministers of our God.
You will feed on the wealth of nations,
and in their riches you will boast.
Instead of their shame
my people will receive a double portion,
and instead of disgrace
they will rejoice in their inheritance;
and so they will inherit a double portion in their land,
and everlasting joy will be theirs.

'For I, the LORD, love justice;
I hate robbery and iniquity.
In my faithfulness I will reward them
and make an everlasting covenant with them.
Their descendants will be known among the nations
and their offspring among the peoples.
All who see them will acknowledge
that they are a people the LORD has blessed.'

EPISTLE *Acts 5.12–16*

The apostles performed many miraculous signs and wonders among the people. And all the believers used to meet together in Solomon's Colonnade. No one else dared join them, even though they were highly regarded by the people. Nevertheless, more and more men and women believed in the Lord and were added to their number. As a result, people brought the sick into the streets and laid them on beds and mats so that at least Peter's shadow might fall on some of them as he passed by. Crowds gathered also from the towns around Jerusalem bringing their sick and those tormented by evil spirits, and all of them were healed.

GOSPEL *Luke 22.24–30*

A dispute arose among the disciples as to which of them was considered to be greatest. Jesus said to them, 'The kings of the Gentiles lord it over them; and those who exercise authority over them call themselves Benefactors. But you are not to be like that. Instead, the greatest among you should be like the youngest, and the one who rules like the one who serves. For who is greater, the one who is at the table or the one who serves? Is it not the one who is at the table? But I am among you as one who serves. You are those who have stood by me in my trials. And I confer on you a kingdom, just as my Father conferred one on me, so that you may eat and drink at my table in my kingdom and sit on thrones, judging the twelve tribes of Israel.'

Psalm 86   Isaiah 43.8–13   Matthew 10.1–15

Psalm 15   Deuteronomy 18.15–19   Matthew 10.16–22

THE BIRTH OF THE BLESSED VIRGIN MARY *White*

8 September

COLLECT

Almighty God
you chose the Blessed Virgin Mary
to be the mother of your only Son:
Grant that we who are redeemed by his blood
may share with her
in the glory of your eternal kingdom;
through Jesus Christ our Lord,
who lives and reigns with you and the Holy Spirit
one God, now and for ever. **Amen.**

PSALM 45.10–17 (PB 11–18) *or* MAGNIFICAT

OLD TESTAMENT *Micah 5.2–4*

'But you, Bethlehem Ephrathah,
though you are small among the clans of Judah,
out of you will come for me
one who will be ruler over Israel,
whose origins are from of old,
from ancient times.'

Therefore Israel will be abandoned
until the time when she who is in labour gives birth
and the rest of his brothers return
to join the Israelites.

He will stand and shepherd his flock
in the strength of the LORD,
in the majesty of the name of the LORD his God.
And they will live securely, for then his greatness
will reach to the ends of the earth.

EPISTLE *Revelation 21.1–7*

I, John, saw a new heaven and a new earth, for the first
heaven and the first earth had passed away, and there was
no longer any sea. I saw the Holy City, the new Jerusalem,
coming down out of heaven from God, prepared as a bride
beautifully dressed for her husband. And I heard a loud
voice from the throne saying, 'Now the dwelling of God is

with men, and he will live with them. They will be his people, and God himself will be with them and be their God. He will wipe every tear from their eyes. There will be no more death or mourning or crying or pain, for the old order of things has passed away.'

He who was seated on the throne said, 'I am making everything new!' Then he said, 'Write this down, for these words are trustworthy and true.'

He said to me: 'It is done. I am the Alpha and the Omega, the Beginning and the End. To him who is thirsty I will give to drink without cost from the spring of the water of life. He who overcomes will inherit all this, and I will be his God and he will be my son.'

GOSPEL *Luke 1.39–49*

Mary got ready and hurried to a town in the hill country of Judah, where she entered Zechariah's home and greeted Elizabeth. When Elizabeth heard Mary's greeting, the baby leaped in her womb, and Elizabeth was filled with the Holy Spirit. In a loud voice she exclaimed: 'Blessed are you among women, and blessed is the child you will bear! But why am I so favoured, that the mother of my Lord should come to me? As soon as the sound of your greeting reached my ears, the baby in my womb leaped for joy. Blessed is she who has believed that what the Lord has said to her will be accomplished!'

And Mary said:

'My soul praises the Lord
and my spirit rejoices in God my Saviour,
for he has been mindful of the humble state of his servant.
From now on all generations will call me blessed,
for the Mighty One has done great things for me –
holy is his name.'

or
Luke 2.1–19

In those days Caesar Augustus issued a decree that a census should be taken of the entire Roman world. (This was the first census that took place while Quirinius was governor of Syria.) And everyone went to his own town to register.

So Joseph also went up from the town of Nazareth in

Galilee to Judea, to Bethlehem the town of David, because he belonged to the house and line of David. He went there to register with Mary, who was pledged to be married to him and was expecting a child. While they were there, the time came for the baby to be born, and she gave birth to her firstborn, a son. She wrapped him in strips of cloth and placed him in a manger, because there was no room for them in the inn.

And there were shepherds living out in the fields near by, keeping watch over their flocks at night. An angel of the Lord appeared to them, and they were terrified. But the angel said to them, 'Do not be afraid. I bring you good news of great joy that will be for all the people. Today in the town of David a Saviour has been born to you; he is Christ the Lord. This will be a sign to you: You will find a baby wrapped in strips of cloth and lying in a manger.'

Suddenly a great company of the heavenly host appeared with the angel, praising God and saying,

'Glory to God in the highest,
and on earth peace to men
on whom his favour rests.'

When the angels had left them and gone into heaven, the shepherds said to one another, 'Let us go to Bethlehem and see this thing that has happened, which the Lord has told us about.'

So they hurried off and found Mary and Joseph, and the baby, who was lying in the manger. When they had seen him, they spread the word concerning what had been told them about this child, and all who heard it were amazed at what the shepherds said to them. But Mary treasured up all these things and pondered them in her heart.

Psalm 72   Isaiah 61.10 – 62.3   John 2.1–12

Psalm 98;138   Proverbs 8.22–31   John 19.23–27

SAINT MATTHEW

Red

21 September

COLLECT

Almighty God,
you called Matthew the tax-collector
to be an apostle and evangelist:
Give us grace
to forsake all covetousness and love of riches,
that we may follow the Lord Jesus Christ;
who lives and reigns with you and the Holy Spirit,
one God, now and for ever.   **Amen.**

PSALM 119.65–72 *or* 119.89–96

OLD TESTAMENT   *Proverbs 3.9–18*

Honour the LORD with your wealth,
with the firstfruits of all your crops;
then your barns will be filled to overflowing,
and your vats will brim over with new wine.

My son, do not despise the LORD's discipline
and do not resent his rebuke,
because the LORD disciplines those he loves,
as a father the son he delights in.

Blessed is the man who finds wisdom,
the man who gains understanding,
for she is more profitable than silver
and yields better returns than gold.
She is more precious than rubies;
nothing you desire can compare with her.
Long life is in her right hand;
in her left hand are riches and honour.
Her ways are pleasant ways,
and all her paths are peace.
She is a tree of life to those who embrace her;
those who lay hold of her will be blessed.

EPISTLE   *2 Corinthians 4.1–6*

Since through God's mercy we have this ministry, we do not
lose heart. Rather, we have renounced secret and shameful

ways; we do not use deception, nor do we distort the word of God. On the contrary, by setting forth the truth plainly we commend ourselves to every man's conscience in the sight of God. And even if our gospel is veiled, it is veiled to those who are perishing. The god of this age has blinded the minds of unbelievers, so that they cannot see the light of the gospel of the glory of Christ, who is the image of God. For we do not preach ourselves, but Jesus Christ as Lord, and ourselves as your servants for Jesus' sake. For God, who said, 'Let light shine out of darkness', made his light shine in our hearts to give us the light of the knowledge of the glory of God in the face of Jesus Christ.

GOSPEL *Matthew 9.9–13*

Jesus saw a man named Matthew sitting at the tax collector's booth. 'Follow me,' he told him, and Matthew got up and followed him.

While Jesus was having dinner at Matthew's house, many tax collectors and 'sinners' came and ate with him and his disciples. When the Pharisees saw this, they asked his disciples, 'Why does your teacher eat with tax collectors and "sinners"?'

On hearing this, Jesus said, 'It is not the healthy who need a doctor, but the sick. But go and learn what this means: "I desire mercy, not sacrifice." For I have not come to call the righteous, but sinners.'

Psalm 25   Ecclesiastes 5.4–12   Matthew 19.16–30
Psalm 34   1 Chronicles 29.9–18   1 Timothy 6.6–19

SAINT MICHAEL AND ALL ANGELS   *White*

29 September

COLLECT

Eternal Lord God,
you ordained and constituted the service
of angels and men in a wonderful order:
Grant that as your holy angels
always serve you in heaven,
so by your appointment
they may help and defend us on earth;
through Jesus Christ our Lord.   **Amen.**

PSALM 103.17–22 *or* 91.5–12

OLD TESTAMENT *2 Kings 6.8–17*

The king of Aram was at war with Israel. After conferring with his officers, he said, 'I will set up my camp in such a place.'

The man of God sent word to the king of Israel: 'Beware of passing that place, because the Arameans are going down there.' So the king of Israel checked on the place indicated by the man of God. Time and again Elisha warned the king, so that he was on his guard in such places.

This enraged the king of Aram. He summoned his officers and demanded of them, 'Will you not tell me which of us is on the side of the king of Israel?'

'None of us, my lord the king,' said one of his officers, 'but Elisha, the prophet who is in Israel, tells the king of Israel the very words you speak in your bedroom.'

'Go, find out where he is,' the king ordered, 'so that I can send men and capture him.' The report came back: 'He is in Dothan.' Then he sent horses and chariots and a strong force there. They went by night and surrounded the city.

When the servant of the man of God got up and went out early the next morning, an army with horses and chariots had surrounded the city. 'Oh, my lord, what shall we do?'' the servant asked.

'Do not be afraid,' the prophet answered. 'Those who are with us are more than those who are with them.'

And Elisha prayed, 'O LORD, open his eyes so that he may see.' Then the LORD opened the servant's eyes, and he looked and saw the hills full of horses and chariots of fire all around Elisha.

EPISTLE *Revelation 12.7–12*

There was war in heaven. Michael and his angels fought against the dragon, and the dragon and his angels fought back. But he was not strong enough, and they lost their place in heaven. The great dragon was hurled down – that ancient serpent called the devil or Satan, who leads the whole world astray. He was hurled to the earth, and his angels with him.

Then I heard a loud voice in heaven say:

'Now have come the salvation and the power and the
    kingdom of our God,

and the authority of his Christ.
For the accuser of our brothers,
who accuses them before our God day and night,
has been hurled down.
They overcame him by the blood of the Lamb
and by the word of their testimony;
they did not love their lives so much
as to shrink from death.
Therefore rejoice, you heavens
and you who dwell in them!
But woe to the earth and the sea,
because the devil has gone down to you!
He is filled with fury,
because he knows that his time is short.'

GOSPEL *Matthew 18.1–6, 10*

The disciples came to Jesus and asked, 'Who is the greatest in the kingdom of heaven?'

He called a little child and had him stand among them. And he said: 'I tell you the truth, unless you change and become like little children, you will never enter the kingdom of heaven. Therefore, whoever humbles himself like this child is the greatest in the kingdom of heaven. And whoever welcomes a little child like this in my name welcomes me.

'But if anyone causes one of these little ones who believe in me to sin, it would be better for him to have a large millstone hung around his neck and to be drowned in the depths of the sea.

'See that you do not look down on one of these little ones. For I tell you that their angels in heaven always see the face of my Father in heaven.'

Psalm 148   Daniel 10.4–21   Revelation 5

Psalm 91   Genesis 28.10–17   John 1.43–51

SAINT LUKE

18 October

Red

COLLECT

Almighty God,
you called Luke the physician
whose praise is in the gospel,
to be an evangelist
and physician of the soul:
Give your Church, by the grace of the Spirit,
and through the medicine of the Gospel,
the same love and power to heal;
through Jesus Christ our Lord. **Amen.**

PSALM 147.1–6 *or* 22.23–29 (PB 22–28)

OLD TESTAMENT *Isaiah 35.3–6*

Strengthen the feeble hands,
steady the knees that give way;
say to those with fearful hearts,
'Be strong, do not fear;
your God will come,
he will come with vengeance;
with divine retribution
he will come to save you.'
Then will the eyes of the blind be opened
and the ears of the deaf unstopped.
Then will the lame leap like a deer,
and the tongue of the dumb shout for joy.
Water will gush forth in the wilderness
and streams in the desert.

EPISTLE *Acts 16.6–12a*

Paul and his companions travelled throughout the region of
Phrygia and Galatia, having been kept by the Holy Spirit
from preaching the word in the province of Asia. When they
came to the border of Mysia, they tried to enter Bithynia, but
the Spirit of Jesus would not allow them to. So they passed
by Mysia and went down to Troas. During the night Paul
had a vision of a man of Macedonia standing and begging
him, 'Come over to Macedonia and help us.' After Paul had

691

seen the vision, we got ready at once to leave for Macedonia, concluding that God had called us to preach the gospel to them.

From Troas we put out to sea and sailed straight for Samothrace, and the next day on to Neapolis. From there we travelled to Philippi, a Roman colony and the leading city of that district of Macedonia.

or

2 Timothy 4.5–13

Keep your head in all situations, endure hardship, do the work of an evangelist, discharge all the duties of your ministry.

For I am already being poured out like a drink offering, and the time has come for my departure. I have fought the good fight, I have finished the race, I have kept the faith. Now there is in store for me the crown of righteousness, which the Lord, the righteous Judge, will award to me on that day – and not only to me, but also to all who have longed for his appearing.

Do your best to come to me quickly, for Demas, because he loved this world, has deserted me and has gone to Thessalonica. Crescens has gone to Galatia, and Titus to Dalmatia. Only Luke is with me. Get Mark and bring him with you, because he is helpful to me in my ministry. I sent Tychicus to Ephesus. When you come, bring the cloak that I left with Carpus at Troas, and my scrolls, especially the parchments.

GOSPEL   *Luke 10.1–9*

The Lord appointed seventy-two others and sent them two by two ahead of him to every town and place where he was about to go. He told them, 'The harvest is plentiful, but the workers are few. Ask the Lord of the harvest, therefore, to send out workers into his harvest field. Go! I am sending you out like lambs among wolves. Do not take a purse or bag or sandals; and do not greet anyone on the road.

'When you enter a house, first say, "Peace to this house." If a man of peace is there, your peace will rest on him; if not, it will return to you. Stay in that house, eating and drinking whatever they give you, for the worker deserves his wages.

Do not move round from house to house.

'When you enter a town and are welcomed, eat what is set before you. Heal the sick who are there and tell them, "The kingdom of God is near you." '

Psalm 103   Isaiah 55   2 Timothy 3.10–17

Psalm 19   Isaiah 61.1–6 *or* Ecclesiasticus 38.1–14   Colossians 4.7–18

SAINT SIMON AND SAINT JUDE   *Red*
28 October

COLLECT

Almighty God,
you have built your Church
upon the foundation of apostles and prophets
with Jesus Christ himself as the chief corner-stone:
So join us together in unity of spirit by their doctrine,
that we may be made a holy temple acceptable to you;
through Jesus Christ our Lord.   **Amen.**

PSALM 15 *or* 116.11–18 (PB 11–16)

OLD TESTAMENT   *Isaiah 28.9–16*

The priests and prophets of Ephraim complain,
'Who is it he is trying to teach?
To whom is he explaining his message?
To children weaned from their milk,
to those just taken from the breast?
For it is:
Do and do, do and do,
rule on rule, rule on rule;
a little here, a little there.'

Very well then, with foreign lips and strange tongues
God will speak to this people,
to whom he said,
'This is the resting-place, let the weary rest';
and, 'This is the place of repose' –
but they would not listen.
So then, the word of the LORD to them will become:
Do and do, do and do,

693

rule on rule, rule on rule;
a little here, a little there —
so that they will go and fall backwards,
be injured and snared and captured.
Therefore hear the word of the LORD, you scoffers
who rule this people in Jerusalem.
You boast, 'We have entered into a covenant with death,
with the grave we have made an agreement.
When an overwhelming scourge sweeps by,
it cannot touch us,
for we have made a lie our refuge
and falsehood our hiding-place.'

So this is what the Sovereign LORD says:

'See, I lay a stone in Zion, a tested stone,
a precious cornerstone for a sure foundation;
the one who trusts will never be dismayed.'

EPISTLE   *Ephesians 2.13–22*

Now in Christ Jesus you who once were far away have been
brought near through the blood of Christ.

For he himself is our peace, who has made the two one
and has destroyed the barrier, the dividing wall of hostility,
by abolishing in his flesh the law with its commandments
and regulations. His purpose was to create in himself one
new man out of the two, thus making peace, and in this one
body to reconcile both of them to God through the cross, by
which he put to death their hostility. He came and preached
peace to you who were far away and peace to those who
were near. For through him we both have access to the
Father by one Spirit.

Consequently, you are no longer foreigners and aliens,
but fellow-citizens with God's people and members of God's
household, built on the foundation of the apostles and
prophets, with Christ Jesus himself as the chief cornerstone.
In him the whole building is joined together and rises to
become a holy temple in the Lord. And in him you too are
being built together to become a dwelling in which God lives
by his Spirit.

GOSPEL *John 14.15–26*

Jesus said, 'If you love me, you will obey what I command. And I will ask the Father, and he will give you another Counsellor to be with you for ever – the Spirit of truth. The world cannot accept him, because it neither sees him nor knows him. But you know him, for he lives with you and will be in you. I will not leave you as orphans; I will come to you. Before long, the world will not see me any more, but you will see me. Because I live, you also will live. On that day you will realize that I am in my Father, and you are in me, and I am in you. Whoever has my commands and obeys them, he is the one who loves me. He who loves me will be loved by my Father, and I too will love him and show myself to him.'

Then Judas (not Judas Iscariot) said, 'But, Lord, why do you intend to show yourself to us and not to the world?'

Jesus replied, 'If anyone loves me, he will obey my teaching. My Father will love him, and we will come to him and make our home with him. He who does not love me will not obey my teaching. These words you hear are not my own; they belong to the Father who sent me.

'All this I have spoken while still with you. But the Counsellor, the Holy Spirit, whom the Father will send in my name, will teach you all things and will remind you of everything I have said to you.'

Psalm 124;125;126   Isaiah 45.18–25 *or* Wisdom 5.1–16
Revelation 21.9–14

Psalm 119.1–16   Jeremiah 3.11–18 *or* 1 Maccabees 2.42–66
Luke 6.12–23

ALL SAINTS

1 November

COLLECT

Almighty God,
you have knit together your elect
in one communion and fellowship
in the mystical body of your Son:
Give us grace to follow your blessed saints
in all virtuous and godly living,
that we may come to those unspeakable joys
which you have prepared for those who truly love you;
through Jesus Christ our Lord. **Amen.**

PSALM 145.8–13

OLD TESTAMENT *Jeremiah 31.31–34*

'The time is coming,' declares the LORD,
'when I will make a new covenant
with the house of Israel
and with the house of Judah.
It will not be like the covenant
I made with their forefathers
when I took them by the hand
to lead them out of Egypt,
because they broke my covenant,
though I was a husband to them,'
declares the LORD.

'This is the covenant that I will make with the house of Israel
after that time,' declares the LORD.
'I will put my law in their minds
and write it on their hearts.
I will be their God,
and they will be my people.
No longer will a man teach his neighbour,
or a man his brother, saying, "Know the LORD,"
because they will all know me,
from the least of them to the greatest,'
declares the LORD.

'For I will forgive their wickedness
and will remember their sins no more.'

or

2 Esdras 2.42–48

I, Ezra, saw on Mount Zion a great multitude, which I could not number, and they all were praising the Lord with songs. In their midst was a young man of great stature, taller than any of the others, and on the head of each of them he placed a crown, but he was more exalted than they. And I was held spellbound. Then I asked an angel, 'Who are these, my Lord?' He answered and said to me, 'These are they who have put off mortal clothing and have put on the immortal, and they have confessed the name of God; now they are being crowned, and receive palms.' Then I said to the angel, 'Who is that young man who places crowns on them and puts palms in their hands?' He answered and said to me, 'He is the Son of God, whom they confessed in the world.' So I began to praise those who had stood valiantly for the name of the Lord. Then the angel said to me, 'Go, tell my people how great and many are the wonders of the Lord God which you have seen.'

EPISTLE   *Revelation 7.2–4 and 9–17*

Then I, John, saw another angel coming up from the east, having the seal of the living God. He called out in a loud voice to the four angels who had been given power to harm the land and the sea: 'Do not harm the land or the sea or the trees until we put a seal on the foreheads of the servants of our God.' Then I heard the numbers of those who were sealed: one hundred and forty-four thousand from all the tribes of Israel.

After this I looked and there before me was a great multitude that no one could count, from every nation, tribe, people and language, standing before the throne and in front of the Lamb. They were wearing white robes and were holding palm branches in their hands. And they cried out in a loud voice:

'Salvation belongs to our God,
who sits on the throne,
and to the Lamb.'

All the angels were standing around the throne and around the elders and the four living creatures. They fell down on their faces before the throne and worshipped God, saying:

'Amen!
Praise and glory
and wisdom and thanks and honour
and power and strength
be to our God for ever and ever.
Amen!'

Then one of the elders asked me, 'These in white robes –
who are they, and where did they come from?'

I answered, 'Sir, you know.'

And he said, 'These are they who have come out of the
great tribulation; they have washed their robes and made
them white in the blood of the Lamb. Therefore,

'They are before the throne of God
and serve him day and night in his temple;
and he who sits on the throne
will spread his tent over them.
Never again will they hunger;
never again will they thirst.
The sun will not beat upon them,
nor any scorching heat.
For the Lamb at the centre of the throne will be their
    shepherd;
he will lead them to springs of living water.
And God will wipe away every tear from their eyes.'

or

Hebrews 12.18–24

You have not come to a mountain that can be touched and
that is burning with fire; to darkness, gloom and storm; to a
trumpet blast or to such a voice speaking words, so that
those who heard it begged that no further word be spoken to
them, because they could not bear what was commanded: 'If
even an animal touches the mountain, it must be stoned.'
The sight was so terrifying that Moses said, 'I am trembling
with fear.'

But you have come to Mount Zion, to the heavenly Jerusalem, the city of the living God. You have come to
thousands upon thousands of angels in joyful assembly, to
the church of the first-born, whose names are written in

heaven. You have come to God, the judge of all men, to the spirits of righteous men made perfect, to Jesus the mediator of a new covenant, and to the sprinkled blood that speaks a better word than the blood of Abel.

GOSPEL   Matthew 5.1–12

When Jesus saw the crowds, he went up on a mountainside and sat down. His disciples came to him, and he began to teach them, saying:

'Blessed are the poor in spirit,
for theirs is the kingdom of heaven.
Blessed are those who mourn,
for they will be comforted.
Blessed are the meek,
for they will inherit the earth.
Blessed are those who hunger and thirst for righteousness,
for they will be filled.
Blessed are the merciful,
for they will be shown mercy.
Blessed are the pure in heart,
for they will see God.
Blessed are the peacemakers,
for they will be called sons of God.
Blessed are those who are persecuted because of
    righteousness,
for theirs is the kingdom of heaven.

'Blessed are you when people insult you, persecute you and falsely say all kinds of evil against you because of me. Rejoice and be glad, because great is your reward in heaven, for in the same way they persecuted the prophets who were before you.'

or

Luke 6.20–23

Looking at his disciples, Jesus said:

'Blessed are you who are poor,
for yours is the kingdom of God.
Blessed are you who hunger now,
for you will be satisfied.
Blessed are you who weep now,

for you will laugh.
Blessed are you when men hate you,
when they exclude you and insult you
and reject your name as evil,
because of the Son of Man.

'Rejoice in that day and leap for joy, because great is your reward in heaven. For that is how their fathers treated the prophets.'

Psalm 97;149.1–5   Isaiah 65.17–25 *or* Ecclesiasticus 44.1–15
Luke 9.18–27

Psalm 111;112   Isaiah 40.27–31 *or* Wisdom 3.1–9   Hebrews 11.32 – 12.2

SAINT ANDREW   *Red*

30 November

COLLECT

Almighty God,
you gave such grace to your apostle Andrew
that he readily obeyed the call of your Son,
and brought his brother Simon to Jesus:
Call us by your holy Word,
and give us grace to follow you without delay,
and to work for the coming of your kingdom;
through Jesus Christ our Lord.   **Amen.**

PSALM 92.1–5 *or* 87

OLD TESTAMENT   *Zechariah 8.20–23*

This is what the LORD Almighty says: 'Many peoples and the inhabitants of many cities will yet come, and the inhabitants of one city will go to another and say, "Let us go at once to entreat the LORD and seek the LORD Almighty. I myself am going." And many peoples and powerful nations will come to Jerusalem to seek the LORD Almighty and to entreat him.'

This is what the LORD Almighty says: 'In those days ten men from all languages and nations will take firm hold of one Jew by the edge of his robe and say, "Let us go with you, because we have heard that God is with you." '

EPISTLE   *Romans 10.12–18*

There is no difference between Jew and Gentile – the same Lord is Lord of all and richly blesses all who call on him, for, 'Everyone who calls on the name of the Lord will be saved.'

How, then, can they call on the one they have not believed in? And how can they believe in the one of whom they have not heard? And how can they hear without someone preaching to them? And how can they preach unless they are sent? As it is written, 'How beautiful are the feet of those who bring good news!'

But not all the Israelites accepted the good news. For Isaiah says, 'Lord, who has believed our message?' Consequently, faith comes from hearing the message, and the message is heard through the word of Christ. But I ask, Did they not hear? Of course they did:

'Their voice has gone out into all the earth,
their words to the ends of the world.'

GOSPEL   *Matthew 4.12–20*

When Jesus heard that John had been put in prison, he returned to Galilee. Leaving Nazareth, he went and lived in Capernaum, which was by the lake in the area of Zebulun and Naphtali – to fulfil what was said through the prophet Isaiah:

'Land of Zebulun and land of Naphtali,
the way to the sea, along the Jordan,
Galilee of the Gentiles –
the people living in darkness have seen a great light;
on those living in the land of the shadow of death
a light has dawned.'

From that time on Jesus began to preach, 'Repent, for the kingdom of heaven is near.'

As Jesus was walking beside the Sea of Galilee, he saw two brothers, Simon called Peter and his brother Andrew. They were casting a net into the lake, for they were fishermen. 'Come, follow me,' Jesus said, 'and I will make you fishers of men.' At once they left their nets and followed him.

Psalm 47;48   Isaiah 49.1–9a   1 Corinthians 1.18–31

Psalm 67;96   Ezekiel 47.1–12   John 1.35–42

701

SAINT STEPHEN

26 December

COLLECT

Heavenly Father,
you gave your faithful martyr Stephen
grace to pray for those who stoned him:
Grant that in all our sufferings for the truth
we may follow his example of forgiveness;
and see the glory of your Son,
Jesus Christ our Lord.   **Amen.**

PSALM 119.17–24 *or* 119.161–168

OLD TESTAMENT *2 Chronicles 24.20–22*

The Spirit of God came upon Zechariah son of Jehoiada the priest. He stood before the people and said, 'This is what God says: "Why do you disobey the LORD's commands? You will not prosper. Because you have forsaken the LORD, he has forsaken you." '

But they plotted against him, and by order of the king they stoned him to death in the courtyard of the LORD's temple. King Joash did not remember the kindness Zechariah's father Jehoiada had shown him but killed his son, who said as he lay dying, 'May the LORD see this and call you to account.'

EPISTLE *Acts 7.54–60*

When they heard Stephen's speech, they were furious and gnashed their teeth at him. But Stephen, full of the Holy Spirit, looked up to heaven and saw the glory of God, and Jesus standing at the right hand of God. 'Look,' he said, 'I see heaven open and the Son of Man standing at the right hand of God.'

At this they covered their ears and, yelling at the top of their voices, they all rushed at him, dragged him out of the city and began to stone him. Meanwhile, the witnesses laid their clothes at the feet of a young man named Saul.

While they were stoning him, Stephen prayed, 'Lord Jesus, receive my spirit.' Then he fell on his knees and cried out, 'Lord, do not hold this sin against them.' When he had said this, he fell asleep.

GOSPEL *Matthew 23.34–39*

Jesus said, 'I am sending you prophets and wise men and teachers. Some of them you will kill and crucify; others you will flog in your synagogues and pursue from town to town. And so upon you will come all the righteous blood that has been shed on earth, from the blood of righteous Abel to the blood of Zechariah son of Berakiah, whom you murdered between the temple and the altar. I tell you the truth, all this will come upon this generation.

'O Jerusalem, Jerusalem, you who kill the prophets and stone those sent to you, how often I have longed to gather your children together, as a hen gathers her chicks under her wings, but you were not willing. Look, your house is left to you desolate. For I tell you, you will not see me again until you say, "Blessed is he who comes in the name of the Lord." '

Psalm 13;46   Exodus 18.13–26   Acts 6

Psalm 57;86   Genesis 4.1–10   John 15.20 – 16.4a

SAINT JOHN THE EVANGELIST   *White*
27 December

COLLECT

Merciful Father,
your Son came to be the light of the world:
Enlighten your Church with the doctrine
of your apostle and evangelist Saint John,
that we may live in the light of your truth,
and attain the light of everlasting life;
through Jesus Christ our Lord.   **Amen.**

PSALM 117 *or* 92.12–15

OLD TESTAMENT *Exodus 33.12–23*

Moses said to the LORD, 'You have been telling me, "Lead these people," but you have not let me know whom you will send with me. You have said, "I know you by name and you have found favour with me." If I have found favour in your eyes, teach me your ways so I may know you and continue to find favour with you. Remember that this nation is your people.'

The LORD replied, 'My Presence will go with you, and I will give you rest.'

Then Moses said to him, 'If your Presence does not go with us, do not send us up from here. How will anyone know that you are pleased with me and with your people unless you go with us? What else will distinguish me and your people from all the other people on the face of the earth?'

And the LORD said to Moses, 'I will do the very thing you have asked, because I am pleased with you and I know you by name.'

Then Moses said, 'Now show me your glory.'

And the LORD said, 'I will cause all my goodness to pass in front of you, and I will proclaim my name, the LORD, in your presence. I will have mercy on whom I will have mercy, and I will have compassion on whom I will have compassion. But,' he said, 'you cannot see my face, for no one may see me and live.'

Then the LORD said, 'There is a place near me where you may stand on a rock. When my glory passes by, I will put you in a cleft in the rock and cover you with my hand until I have passed by. Then I will remove my hand and you will see my back; but my face must not be seen.'

EPISTLE   *1 John 2.1–11*

My dear children, I write this to you so that you will not sin. But if anybody does sin, we have one who speaks to the Father in our defence – Jesus Christ, the Righteous One. He is the atoning sacrifice for our sins, and not only for ours but also for the sins of the whole world.

We know that we have come to know him if we obey his commands. The man who says, 'I know him,' but does not do what he commands is a liar, and the truth is not in him. But if anyone obeys his word, God's love is truly made complete in him. This is how we know we are in him: Whoever claims to live in him must walk as Jesus did.

Dear friends, I am not writing you a new command but an old one, which you have had since the beginning. This old command is the message you have heard. Yet I am writing you a new command, its truth is seen in him and you, because the darkness is passing and the true light is already shining.

Anyone who claims to be in the light but hates his brother is still in the darkness. Whoever loves his brother lives in the light, and there is nothing in him to make him stumble. But whoever hates his brother is in the darkness and walks around in the darkness; he does not know where he is going, because the darkness has blinded him.

GOSPEL *John 21.20–25*

Peter turned and saw that the disciple whom Jesus loved was following them. (This was the one who had leaned back against Jesus at the supper and had said, 'Lord, who is going to betray you?') When Peter saw him, he asked, 'Lord, what about him?' Jesus answered, 'If I want him to remain alive until I return, what is that to you? You must follow me.' Because of this, the rumour spread among the brothers that this disciple would not die. But Jesus did not say that he would not die; he only said, 'If I want him to remain alive until I return, what is that to you?'

This is the disciple who testifies to these things and who wrote them down. We know that his testimony is true.

Jesus did many other things as well. If every one of them were written down, I suppose that even the whole world would not have room for the books that would be written.

Psalm 97   Exodus 33.7–11a   1 John 5.1–12

Psalm 21   Isaiah 6.1–8   John 13.21–35

THE HOLY INNOCENTS   *Red*

28 December

COLLECT

Heavenly Father,
whose children suffered at the hands of Herod
though they had done no wrong:
Help us to defend all your children
from cruelty and oppression;
in the name of Jesus Christ who suffered for us,
but is alive and reigns with you and the Holy Spirit,
one God, now and for ever.   **Amen.**

PSALM 123 *or* 131

OLD TESTAMENT   *Jeremiah 31.15–17*

This is what the LORD says:

'A voice is heard in Ramah,
mourning and great weeping,
Rachel weeping for her children
and refusing to be comforted,
because her children are no more.'

This is what the LORD says:

'Restrain your voice from weeping
and your eyes from tears,
for your work will be rewarded,'
declares the LORD.
'They will return from the land of the enemy.
So there is hope for your future,'
declares the LORD.
'Your children will return to their own land.'

EPISTLE   *1 Corinthians 1.26–29*

Brothers, think of what you were when you were called. Not
many of you were wise by human standards; not many were
influential; not many were of noble birth. But God chose the
foolish things of the world to shame the wise; God chose the
weak things of the world to shame the strong. He chose the
lowly things of this world and the despised things – and the

things that are not – to nullify the things that are, so that no one may boast before him.

GOSPEL *Matthew 2.13–18*

After the Magi had gone, an angel of the Lord appeared to Joseph in a dream. 'Get up,' he said, 'Take the child and his mother and escape to Egypt. Stay there until I tell you, for Herod is going to search for the child to kill him.'

So he got up, took the child and his mother during the night and left for Egypt, where he stayed until the death of Herod. And so was fulfilled what the Lord had said through the prophet: 'Out of Egypt I called my son.'

When Herod realized that he had been outwitted by the Magi, he was furious, and he gave orders to kill all the boys in Bethlehem and its vicinity who were two years old and under, in accordance with the time he had learned from the Magi. Then what was said through the prophet Jeremiah was fulfilled:

'A voice is heard in Ramah,
weeping and great mourning,
Rachel weeping for her children
and refusing to be comforted,
because they are no more.'

Psalm 36   Genesis 37.13–20 *or* Baruch 4.21–27   1 Peter 4.12–19

Psalm 124;128   Isaiah 49.14–25   Matthew 18.1–10

TABLE OF READINGS FOR MORNING AND EVENING PRAYER

on Weekdays which are not Saints' Days, Holy Days or Seasons

---

1. MORNING PRAYER IN YEAR 1
   The readings from the left hand column are used.

   MORNING PRAYER IN YEAR 2
   The readings from the right hand column are used.

2. EVENING PRAYER IN YEAR 1
   The readings from the right hand column are used.

   EVENING PRAYER IN YEAR 2
   The readings from the left hand column are used.

3. When it is desired to have only one reading the Old Testament reading is omitted.

   When it is desired to have three readings the appropriate reading may be taken from the other column.

4. THE PSALMS may be read consecutively as set out.

5. On certain days the psalms and readings are appointed to be used always at Morning Prayer and Evening Prayer. These are indicated by a note in the lectionary.

9th BEFORE CHRISTMAS

Monday

Ps. 1; 2	Ps. 3; 4
Dan. 1	Prov. 1. 1–19
Matt. 1. 18–25	or Ecclus. 1. 1–10
	Rev. 1.

Tuesday

Ps. 5; 6	Ps. 7
Dan. 2. 1–24	Prov. 1. 20–33
Matt. 2. 1–12	or Ecclus. 1. 11–30
	Rev. 2. 1–11

Wednesday

Ps. 8; 9	Ps. 10
Dan 2. 25–49	Prov. 2
Matt. 2. 13–23	or Ecclus. 2
	Rev. 2. 12–29

Thursday

Ps. 11; 12	Ps. 13; 14
Dan. 3. 1–18	Prov. 3. 1–26
Matt. 3	or Ecclus. 4. 11–28
	Rev. 3. 1–13

Friday

Ps. 15; 16	Ps. 17
Dan. 3. 19–30	Prov. 3. 27 – 4. 19
Matt. 1–11	or Ecclus. 6. 14–31
	Rev. 3. 14–22

Saturday

Ps. 18. 1–32	Ps. 18. 33–52
Dan. 4. 1–18	Prov. 6. 1–19
Matt. 4. 12–22	or Ecclus. 7. 27–36
	Rev. 4

8th BEFORE CHRISTMAS

Monday

Ps. 19	Ps. 20; 21
Dan. 4. 19–37	Prov. 8. 1–21
Matt. 4. 23 – 5. 12	or Ecclus. 10. 6–8, 12–24
	Rev. 5

Tuesday

Ps. 22	Ps. 23; 24
Dan. 5. 1–12	Prov. 8. 22–36
Matt. 5. 13–20	or Ecclus. 14. 20–15. 10
	Rev. 6

Wednesday
Ps. 25
Dan. 5. 13–30
Matt. 5. 21–26

Ps. 26; 27
Prov. 9
  or Ecclus. 15. 11–20
Rev. 7

Thursday
Ps. 28; 29
Dan. 6
Matt. 5. 27–37

Ps. 30
Prov. 10. 1–13
  or Ecclus. 17. 1–24
Rev. 8

Friday
Ps. 31
Dan. 7. 1–14
Matt. 5. 38–48

Ps. 32
Prov. 11. 1–12
  or Ecclus. 22. 6–22
Rev. 9. 1–12

Saturday
Ps. 33
Dan 7. 15–28
Matt. 6. 1–18

Ps. 34
Prov. 12. 10–28
  or Ecclus. 22. 27 – 23. 15
Rev. 9. 13–21

7th BEFORE CHRISTMAS

Monday
Ps. 35
Dan. 9. 1–3, 20–27
Matt. 6. 19–34

Ps. 36
Prov. 14. 31–15. 17
  or Ecclus. 24. 1 – 22
Rev. 10

Tuesday
Ps. 37. 1–22
Dan. 10. 1–11. 1
Matt. 7. 1–12

Ps. 37. 23–41
Prov. 15. 18–33
  or Ecclus. 24. 23–34
Rev. 11. 1–13

Wednesday
Ps. 38
Dan. 12.
Matt. 7. 13–29

Ps. 39
Prov. 18. 10–24
  or Ecclus. 38. 1–14
Rev. 11. 14–19

Thursday
Ps. 40
Hosea 1. 1 – 2. 1
Matt. 8. 1–13

Ps. 41
Prov. 20. 1–22
  or Ecclus. 38. 24–34
Rev. 12.

Friday
Ps. 42; 43
Hosea 2. 2–17
Matt. 8. 14–22

Ps. 44
Prov. 22. 1–16
  or Ecclus. 39. 1–11
Rev. 13. 1–10

Saturday
Ps. 45; 46
Hosea 2. 18 – 3. 5
Matt. 8. 23–34

Ps. 47; 48
Prov. 24. 23–34
  or Ecclus. 39. 13–35
Rev. 13. 11–18.

6th BEFORE CHRISTMAS

Monday
Ps. 49
Hosea 4. 1–14
Matt. 9. 1–13

Ps. 50
Prov 25. 1–14
  or Ecclus. 42. 15–25
Rev. 14. 1–13

Tuesday
Ps. 51
Hosea 4. 15 – 5.7
Matt. 9. 14–26

Ps. 52; 53
Prov. 25. 15–28
  or Ecclus. 43. 1–12
Rev. 14. 14–20

Wednesday
Ps. 54; 55
Hosea 5. 8 – 6.6
Matt. 9. 27–38

Ps. 56; 57
Prov. 26. 12–28
  or Ecclus. 43. 13–33
Rev. 15

Thursday
Ps. (58); 59
Hosea 8
Matt. 10. 1–15

Ps. 60; 61
Prov. 27. 1–22
  or Ecclus. 50. 1–24
Rev. 16. 1–11

Friday
Ps. 62; 63
Hosea 9. 1–9
Matt. 10. 16–33

Ps. 64; 65
Prov. 30. 1–9
  or Ecclus. 51. 1–12
Rev. 16. 12–21

Saturday
Ps. 66; 67
Hosea 9. 10–17
Matt. 10. 34 – 11.1

Ps. 68
Prov. 31. 10–31
  or Ecclus. 51. 13–30
Rev. 17

5th BEFORE CHRISTMAS

Monday
Ps. 69
Hosea 10. 1–8
Matt. 11. 2–19

Ps. 70; 71
Isa. 40. 1-11
Rev. 18

Tuesday
Ps. 72
Hosea 10. 9–15
Matt. 11. 20–30

Ps. 73
Isa. 40. 12–26
Rev. 19

Wednesday
Ps. 74
Hosea 11. 1–11
Matt. 12. 1–21

Ps. 75; 76
Isa. 40. 27 – 41. 7
Rev. 20

Thursday
Ps. 77
Hosea 11. 12 – 12. 14
Matt. 12. 22–37

Ps. 78. 1–38
Isa. 41. 8–20
Rev. 21. 1–8

Friday
Ps. 78. 39–70
Hosea 13. 1–14
Matt. 12. 38–50

Ps. 79
Isa. 41. 21–29
Rev. 21. 9–21

Saturday
Ps. 80
Hosea 14
Matt. 13. 1–17

Ps. 81
Isa. 42. 1–9
Rev. 21. 22 – 22. 5

4th BEFORE CHRISTMAS   ADVENT 1

Monday
Ps. 82; 83
Isa. 1. 21–31 (or 1–31)
Matt. 13. 18–33

Ps. 84; 85
Isa. 42. 10–17
Rev. 22. 6–21

Tuesday
Ps. 86
Isa. 2. 1–11 (or 1–22)
Matt. 13. 34–43

Ps. 87; 88
Isa. 42. 18–25
1 Thess. 1

Wednesday
Ps. 89. 1–38
Isa. 3. 1–13
Matt. 13. 44–58

Ps. 89. 39–53
Isa. 43. 1–13
1 Thess. 2. 1–12

Thursday
Ps. 90
Isa. 4. 2 – 5. 7
Matt. 14. 1–12

Ps. 91
Isa. 43. 14–28
1 Thess. 2. 13–20

713

Friday
Ps. 92; 93
Isa. 5. 8–24
Matt. 14. 13–36

Ps. 94
Isa. 44. 1–8
1 Thess. 3

Saturday
Ps. 95; 96
Isa. 5. 25–30
Matt. 15. 1–20

Ps. 97; 98
Isa. 44. 9–23
1 Thess. 4. 1–12

3rd BEFORE CHRISTMAS   ADVENT 2

Monday
Ps. 99; 100; 101
Isa. 6
Matt. 15. 21–28

Ps. 102
Isa. 44. 24–28
1 Thess. 4. 13 – 5. 11

Tuesday
Ps. 103
Isa. 7. 1–17
Matt. 15. 29–39

Ps. 104
Isa. 45. 1–13
1 Thess. 5. 12–28

Wednesday
Ps. 105. 1–22
Isa. 8. 16 – 9. 7
Matt. 16. 1–12

Ps. 105. 23–45
Isa. 45. 15–25
2 Thess. 1

Thursday
Ps. 106. 1–24
Isa. 9. 8 – 10.4
Matt. 16. 13–28

Ps. 106. 25–50
Isa. 46
2 Thess. 2

Friday
Ps. 107. 1–22
Isa. 10. 5–19
Matt. 17. 1–13

Ps. 107. 23–43
Isa. 47
2 Thess. 3

Saturday
Ps. 108; (109); 110
Isa. 10. 20–32
Matt. 17. 14–21

Ps. 111; 112; 113
Isa. 48. 1–11
Jude

2nd BEFORE CHRISTMAS   ADVENT 3

Monday
Ps. 114; 115
Isa. 10. 33 – 11. 9
Col. 1. 1–14

Ps. 116; 117
Isa. 48. 12–22
Luke 20. 9–18

Tuesday
Ps. 118
Isa. 11. 10 – 12. 6
Col. 1. 15–29

Ps. 119. 1–24
Isa. 50. 4–10
Luke 20. 19–26

714

Wednesday
Ps. 119. 25–40
Isa. 13. 1–13
Col. 2. 1–15

Ps. 119. 41–56
Isa. 51. 1–8
Luke 20. 27–44

Thursday
Ps. 119. 57–72
Isa. 14. 3–20
Col. 2. 16 – 3. 11

Ps. 119. 73–88
Isa. 51. 9–16
Luke 21. 5–19

Friday
Ps. 119. 89–104
Isa. 21. 1–12
Col. 3. 12 – 4. 1

Ps. 119. 105–128
Isa. 51. 17–23
Luke 21. 20–28

Saturday
Ps. 119. 129–152
Isa. 22. 1–14
Col. 4. 2–18

Ps. 119. 153–176
Isa. 52. 1–12
Luke 21. 29–36

WEEK BEFORE CHRISTMAS   ADVENT 4

Monday
Ps. 120; 121
Isa. 24
2 John

Ps. 122; 123
Isa. 52. 13 – 53. 12
John 1. 19–37

Tuesday
Ps. 124; 125
Isa. 25. 1–9
3 John

Ps. 126; 127
Isa. 54
John 3. 22–36

Wednesday
Ps. 128; 129
Isa. 26. 1–13
Phil. 4. 4–9

Ps. 130; 131
Isa. 55
John 5. 30–47

Thursday
Ps. 132
Isa. 28. 1–13
Titus 3. 4–7

Ps. 133; 134
Isa. 56. 1–8
John 7. 37–44

Friday
Ps. 135
Isa. 28. 14–29
Philemon

Ps. 136
Isa. 57. 15–21
John 16. 29–17. 5

24 December

Note: The readings for Christmas Eve (below, and see pp. 362 ff.) take precedence of the weekday readings above, but if Christmas Eve falls on a Sunday, the readings are as provided for Advent 4.

24 December
Morning Prayer only
Ps. 137; 138
Isa. 58
Rom. 1. 1–7

Evening Prayer only
Ps. 85.
Isa. 32. 1–8
John 13. 1–17

WEEKDAYS BETWEEN CHRISTMAS AND THE EPIPHANY

29 December
Ps. 139
Isa. 29. 1–14
2 Cor. 8. 1–9

Ps. 140; 141
Isa. 59. 1–15a
John 12. 20–33

30 December
Ps. 142; 143
Isa. 29. 15–24
Eph. 3. 14–21

Ps. 144
Isa. 59. 15 – 60. 21
John 12. 34–50

31 December
Morning Prayer only
Ps. 145
Isa. 38. 1–20
1 John 5. 13–21

Evening Prayer only
Ps. 90
Deut. 10. 12 – 11. 1
Luke 21. 25–36

2 January
Ps. 146
Isa. 30. 1–18
Matt. 17. 22–27

Ps.147
Isa. 61
1 Cor. 1

3 January
Ps. 149; 150
Isa. 30. 19–33
Matt. 18. 1–20

Ps. 1;2;3
Isa. 62
1 Cor. 3

4 January
Ps. 4; 5; 6
Isa. 31
Matt. 18. 21–35

Ps. 7
Isa. 63
1 Cor. 4

5 January
Morning Prayer only
Ps. 9
Isa. 33. 1–16
Matt. 19. 1–15

Evening Prayer only
Ps. 98; 113
Isa. 41. 8–20
   or Baruch 4. 36 – 5. 9
Eph. 1. 3–14

WEEKDAYS BETWEEN THE EPIPHANY AND EPIPHANY 1

7 January
Ps. 10
Isa. 15
Matt. 19. 16–30

Ps. 11; 12
Isa. 60. 1–12
1 Cor. 5

8 January
Ps. 13; 14
Isa. 16
Matt. 20. 1–16

Ps. 15; 16
Isa. 60. 13–22
1 Cor. 6. 1–11

9 January
Ps. 17
Isa. 17
Matt. 20. 17–34

Ps. 18. 1–32
Isa. 64.
1 Cor. 6. 12–20

10 January
Ps. 18. 33–52
Isa. 18
Matt. 21. 1–17

Ps. 19
Isa. 65. 1–16
1 Cor. 7. 1–24

11 January
Ps. 20; 21
Isa. 19. 1–15
Matt. 21. 18–32

Ps. 22
Isa. 66. 1–9
1 Cor. 7. 25–40

12 January
Ps. 23; 24
Isa. 19. 16–25
Matt. 21. 33–46

Ps. 25
Isa. 66. 10–24
1 Cor. 8

EPIPHANY 1

Monday
Ps. 26; 27
Ezek. 1. 1–14
Matt. 22. 1–14

Ps. 28; 29
Jonah 1
1 Cor. 9. 1–14

Tuesday
Ps. 30
Ezek. 1. 15 – 2. 2
Matt. 22. 15–33

Ps. 31
Jonah 2
1 Cor. 9. 15–27

Wednesday
Ps. 32
Ezek. 2. 3 – 3. 11
Matt. 22. 34–46

Ps. 33
Jonah 3 and 4
1 Cor. 10. 1–13

Thursday
Ps. 34
Ezek. 3. 12–27
Matt. 23. 1–15

Ps. 35
Joel 1. 1–14
1 Cor. 10. 14 – 11. 1

Friday
Ps. 36
Ezek. 8. 1–18
Matt 23. 16–28

Ps. 37. 1–22
Joel 1. 15–20
1 Cor. 11. 2–22

Saturday
Ps. 37. 23–41
Ezek. 10. 1–19
Matt. 23. 29–39

Ps. 38
Joel 2. 1–17
1 Cor. 11. 23–34

EPIPHANY 2

Monday
Ps. 39
Ezek. 11. 14–25
Matt. 24. 1–14

Ps. 40
Joel 2. 18–27
1 Cor. 12. 1–11

Tuesday
Ps. 41
Ezek. 12. 17–28
Matt. 24. 15–28

Ps. 42; 43
Joel 2. 28–32
1 Cor. 12. 12–31

Wednesday
Ps. 44
Ezek. 13. 1–16
Matt. 24. 29–35

Ps. 45; 46
Joel 3. 1–3, 9–21
1 Cor. 13

Thursday
Ps. 47; 48
Ezek. 14. 1–11
Matt. 24. 36–51

Ps. 49
Lev. 1
  or 1 Macc. 1. 1–19
1 Cor. 14. 1–12

Friday
Ps. 50
Ezek. 14. 12–23
Matt. 25. 1–13

Ps. 51
Lev. 2
  or 1 Macc. 1. 20–40
1 Cor. 14. 13–25

Saturday
Ps. 52; 53
Ezek. 18. 1–20
Matt. 25. 14–30

Ps. 54; 55
Lev. 3
  or 1 Macc. 1. 41–64
1 Cor. 14. 26–40

EPIPHANY 3

Monday
Ps. 56; 57
Ezek. 20. 1–20
Matt. 25. 31–46

Ps. (58); 59
Lev. 4. 27–35
  or 1 Macc. 2. 1–28
1 Cor. 15. 1–11

Tuesday
Ps. 60; 61
Ezek. 24. 15–27
Matt. 26. 1–13

Ps. 62; 63
Lev. 5. 1–13
  or 1 Macc. 2. 29–48
1 Cor. 15. 12–19

Wednesday
Ps. 64; 65
Ezek. 28. 1–10
Matt. 26. 14–29

Ps. 66; 67
Lev. 8
  or 1 Macc. 2. 49–70
1 Cor. 15. 20–34

Thursday
Ps. 68
Ezek. 28. 11–19
Matt. 26. 30–46

Ps. 69
Lev. 9.
  or 1 Macc. 3. 1–26
1 Cor. 15. 35–49

Friday
Ps. 70; 71
Ezek. 33. 1–20
Matt. 26. 47–56

Ps. 72
Lev. 17
  or 1 Macc. 3. 27–41
1 Cor. 15. 50–58

Saturday
Ps. 73
Ezek. 33. 21–33
Matt. 26. 57–75

Ps. 74
Lev. 18. 1–6, 19–30
  or 1. Macc. 3. 42–60
1 Cor. 16

EPIPHANY 4

Monday
Ps. 75; 76
Ezek. 34. 1–16
Matt. 27. 1–10

Ps. 77
Lev. 19. 1–18
  or 1 Macc. 4. 1–25
Phil. 1. 1–11

Tuesday
Ps. 78. 1–38
Ezek. 34. 17–31
Matt. 27. 11–26

Ps. 78. 39–70
Lev. 19. 23–37
  or 1 Macc. 4. 26–35
Phil. 1. 12–30

Wednesday
Ps. 79
Ezek. 36. 1–15
Matt. 27. 27–44

Ps. 80
Lev. 23. 1–22
  or 1 Macc. 4. 36–61
Phil. 2. 1–18

Thursday

Ps. 81
Ezek. 36. 16–36
Matt. 27. 45–56

Ps. 82; 83
Lev. 23. 23–44
  or 1 Macc. 6. 1–17
Phil. 2. 19–30

Friday

Ps. 84; 85
Ezek. 37. 1–14
Matt. 27. 57–66

Ps. 86
Lev. 24. 1–9
  or 1 Macc. 6. 18–47
Phil. 3. 1– 4. 1

Saturday

Ps. 87; 88
Ezek. 37. 15–28
Matt. 28

Ps. 89. 1–38
Lev. 25. 1–24
  or 1 Macc. 7. 1–20
Phil. 4. 2–23

EPIPHANY 5

Monday

Ps. 89. 39–53
Ezek. 38. 14–23
Rev. 1. 12–20

Ps. 90
Esther 1
  or 1 Macc. 7. 21–50
1 Pet. 1. 1–12

Tuesday

Ps. 91
Ezek. 39. 21–29
Rev. 2. 1–11

Ps. 92.; 93
Esther 2. 5–11, 15–23
  or 1 Macc. 9. 1–22
1 Pet. 1. 13–25

Wednesday

Ps. 94
Ezek. 40. 1–4
Rev. 2. 12–29

Ps. 95; 96
Esther 3
  or 1 Macc. 13. 41–53; 14. 4–15
1 Pet. 2. 1–10

Thursday

Ps. 97; 98
Ezek. 43. 1–9
Rev. 3. 1–6

Ps. 99; 100; 101
Esther 4
  or 2 Macc. 6. 12–31
1 Pet. 2. 11–25

Friday

Ps. 102
Ezek. 44. 4–8
Rev. 3. 7–13

Ps. 103
Esther 5
  or 2 Macc. 7. 1–19
1 Pet. 3. 1–12

Saturday
Ps. 104
Ezek. 47. 1–12
Rev. 3. 14–22

Ps. 105. 1–22
Esther 6 and 7
   or 2 Macc. 7. 20–41
1 Pet. 3. 13–22

EPIPHANY 6

Monday
Ps. 105. 23–45
Exod. 16. 9–15
John 6. 25–35

Ps. 106. 1–24
Num. 9. 1–14
   or Baruch 1. 15 – 2. 10
1 Pet. 4

Tuesday
Ps. 106. 25–50
Isa. 60. 13–20
John 8. 12–19

Ps. 107. 1–22
Num. 16. 1–19
   or Baruch 2. 11–35
1 Pet. 5

Wednesday
Ps. 107. 23–43
Ezek. 34. 1–16
John 10. 7–16

Ps. 108; (109)
Num. 16. 20–35
   or Baruch 3. 1–8
2 Pet. 1. 1–15

Thursday
Ps. 110; 111
Dan. 12. 1–4
John 11. 17–27

Ps. 112; 113
Num. 16. 36–50
   or Baruch 3. 9–37
2 Pet. 1. 16–2. 3

Friday
Ps. 114
Prov. 8. 1–21
John 14. 1–6

Ps. 115
Num. 17. 1–11
   or Baruch 4. 21–30
2 Pet. 2. 4–22

Saturday
Ps. 116; 117
Isa. 5. 1–7
John 15. 1–8

Ps. 118
Num. 33. 50 – 34. 15
   or Baruch 4. 36 – 5. 9
2 Pet. 3

9th BEFORE EASTER   SEPTUAGESIMA

Monday
Ps. 1; 2; 3
Gen. 1. 1 – 2. 3
2 Cor. 1. 1–14

Ps. 4; 5; 6
Jer.1
John 1. 1–18

Tuesday
Ps. 7
Gen. 2. 4–25
2 Cor. 1. 15 – 2. 4

Ps. 8; 9
Jer. 2. 1–13
John 1. 19–34

Wednesday
Ps. 10
Gen. 3
2 Cor. 2. 5–17

Ps. 11; 12
Jer. 2. 14–32
John 1. 35–51

Thursday
Ps. 13; 14
Gen. 4. 1–16
2 Cor. 3

Ps. 15; 16
Jer. 3. 6–18
John 2. 1–12

Friday
Ps. 17
Gen. 6. 11 – 7. 10
2 Cor.4

Ps. 18. 1–32
Jer. 4. 1–14
John 2. 13–25

Saturday
Ps. 18. 33–52
Gen. 7. 11–8. 14
2 Cor. 5

Ps. 19
Jer. 4. 19–31
John 3. 1–15

8th BEFORE EASTER   SEXAGESIMA

Monday
Ps. 20; 21
Gen. 8. 15 – 9. 17
2 Cor. 6. 1–13

Ps. 22
Jer. 5. 1–19
John 3. 16–21

Tuesday
Ps. 23; 24
Gen. 11. 1–9
2 Cor. 6. 14 – 7. 1

Ps. 25
Jer. 5. 20–31
John 3. 22–36

Wednesday
Ps. 26; 27
Gen. 11. 27 – 12. 9
2 Cor. 7. 2–16

Ps. 28; 29
Jer. 6. 9–21
John 4. 1–26

Thursday
Ps. 30
Gen. 13. 2–18
2 Cor. 8. 1–15

Ps. 31
Jer. 6. 22–30
John 4. 27–42

Friday
Ps. 32
Gen.14
2 Cor. 8. 16 – 9. 5

Ps. 33
Jer. 7. 1–20
John 4. 43–54

Saturday

Ps. 34	Ps. 35
Gen. 16	Jer. 7. 21–34
2 Cor. 9. 6–15	John 5. 1–18

7th BEFORE EASTER   QUINQUAGESIMA

Monday

Ps. 36	Ps. 37. 1–22
Gen. 17. 1–22	Jer. 8. 18 – 9. 3
2 Cor. 10	John 5. 19–29

Tuesday

Ps. 37. 23–41	Ps. 39
Gen. 18	Jer. 9. 12–24
2 Cor. 11. 1–15	John 5. 30–47

For Ash Wednesday see pp. 417 ff.

Thursday

Ps. 40	Ps. 41
Gen. 19. 1–3, 12–29	Jer. 10. 1–16
2 Cor. 11. 16–21	John 6. 1–15

Friday

Ps. 42; 43	Ps. 44
Gen. 21. 1–21	Jer. 10. 17–24
2 Cor. 12	John 6. 16–29

Saturday

Ps. 45; 46	Ps. 47; 48
Gen. 22. 1–19	Jer. 11. 1–17
2 Cor. 13	John 6. 30–40

6th BEFORE EASTER   LENT 1

Monday

Ps. 49	Ps. 50
Gen. 23	Jer. 12. 1–6
Gal. 1	John 6. 41–51

Tuesday

Ps. 51	Ps. 52; 53
Gen. 24. 1–28	Jer. 13. 20–27
Gal. 2. 1–10	John 6. 52–59

Wednesday

Ps. 54; 55	Ps. 56; 57
Gen. 24. 29–67	Jer. 15. 10–21
Gal. 2. 11–21	John 6. 60–71

Thursday

Ps. (58); 59	Ps. 60; 61
Gen. 25. 7–11, 19–34	Jer. 17. 5–18
Gal. 3. 1–14	John 7. 1–13

Friday
Ps. 62; 63
Gen. 27. 1–40
Gal. 3. 15–29

Ps. 64; 65
Jer. 18. 1–12
John 7. 14–24

Saturday
Ps. 66; 67
Gen. 27. 41 – 28. 22
Gal. 4. 1–20

Ps. 68
Jer. 18. 13–23
John 7. 25–36

5th BEFORE EASTER   LENT 2

Monday
Ps. 69
Gen. 29. 1–30
Gal. 4. 21 – 5. 1

Ps. 70; 71
Jer. 19. 1–13
John 7. 37–52

Tuesday
Ps. 72
Gen. 31. 1–9, 14–21
Gal. 5. 2–26

Ps. 73
Jer. 19. 14 – 20.6
John 7. 53 – 8. 11

Wednesday
Ps. 74
Gen. 32. 3–30
Gal. 6

Ps. 75; 76
Jer 20. 7–18
John 8. 12–20

Thursday
Ps. 77
Gen. 35
Heb. 1

Ps. 78. 1–38
Jer. 21. 1–10
John 8. 21–30

Friday
Ps. 78. 39–70
Gen. 37
Heb. 2. 1–9

Ps. 79
Jer. 22. 1–5, 13–19
John 8. 31–47

Saturday
Ps. 80
Gen. 39
Heb. 2. 10–18

Ps. 81
Jer. 22. 20–30
John 8. 48–59

4th BEFORE EASTER   LENT 3

Monday
Ps. 82; 83
Gen. 40
Heb. 3

Ps. 84; 85
Jer 23. 1–15
John 9. 1–12

Tuesday
Ps. 86
Gen. 41. 1–40
Heb. 4. 1–13

Ps. 87; 88
Jer. 23. 16–29
John 9. 13–23

Wednesday
Ps. 89. 1–38
Gen. 41. 41–57
Heb. 4. 14 – 5. 14

Ps. 89. 39–53
Jer. 24
John 9. 24–41

Thursday
Ps. 90
Gen. 42
Heb. 6

Ps. 91
Jer. 25. 1–14
John 10. 1–10

Friday
Ps. 92; 93
Gen 43
Heb. 7. 1–10

Ps. 94
Jer. 26. 1–9
John 10. 11–21

Saturday
Ps. 95; 96
Gen. 44
Heb. 7. 11–28

Ps. 97; 98
Jer. 26. 10–24
John 10. 22–42

3rd BEFORE EASTER   LENT 4

Monday
Ps. 99; 100; 101
Gen. 45
Heb. 8

Ps. 102
Jer. 28
John 11. 1–16

Tuesday
Ps. 103
Gen. 46. 1–7, 28–34
Heb. 9. 1–14

Ps. 104
Jer. 29. 1–14
John 11. 17–27

Wednesday
Ps. 105. 1–22
Gen. 47. 1–27
Heb. 9. 15–28

Ps. 105. 23–45
Jer. 30. 1–11
John 11. 28–37

Thursday
Ps. 106. 1–24
Gen. 47. 28 – 48. 22
Heb. 10. 1–18

Ps. 106. 25–50
Jer. 30. 21–22
John 11. 38–44

Friday
Ps. 107. 1–22
Gen. 49. 1–32
Heb. 10. 19–39

Ps. 107. 23–43
Jer. 31. 1–14
John 11. 45–57

Saturday
Ps. 108; (109); 110
Gen. 49. 33 – 50. 26
Heb. 11. 1–12

Ps. 111; 112; 113
Jer. 31. 15–22
John 12. 1–11

2nd BEFORE EASTER   LENT 5

Monday
Ps. 114; 115
Exod. 1. 1–14, 22 – 2. 10
Heb. 11. 13–22

Ps. 116; 117
Jer. 31. 35–40
John 12. 12–19

Tuesday
Ps. 118
Exod. 2. 11 – 3. 12
Heb. 11. 23–31

Ps. 119; 1–24
Jer. 32. 1–15
John 12. 36b–50 (or 20–50)

Wednesday
Ps. 119. 25–40
Exod. 4. 1–23
Heb. 11. 32–40

Ps. 119. 41–56
Jer. 33. 1–13
John 13. 1–11

Thursday
Ps. 119. 57–72
Exod. 4. 27 – 6. 1
Heb 12. 1–13

Ps. 119. 73–88
Jer. 33. 14–26
John 13. 12–20

Friday
Ps. 119. 89–104
Exod. 7. 8–24
Heb. 12. 14–29

Ps. 119. 105–128
Jer. 36. 1–18
John 13. 21–30

Saturday
Ps. 119. 129–152
Exod. 10
Heb. 13

Ps. 119. 153–176
Jer. 36. 19–32
John 13. 31–38

For Holy Week see pp. 450 ff; for Easter Week see pp. 487 ff.

EASTER 1

Monday
Ps. 140
Exod. 15. 22–27
John 20. 1–10

Ps. 141
Ruth 1
1 Tim. 1. 1–17

Tuesday
Ps. 142; 143
Exod. 16
John 20. 11–23

Ps. 144
Ruth 2
1 Tim. 1. 18 – 2. 15

Wednesday
Ps. 145
Exod. 17
John 20. 24–31

Ps. 146; 147
Ruth 3
1 Tim. 3

Thursday
Ps. 148
Exod. 18. 1–12
John 21. 1–14

Ps. 149; 150
Ruth 4
1 Tim. 4

Friday
Ps. 1; 2
Exod. 18. 13–27
John 21. 15–19

Ps. 3; 4
Deut. 1. 3–18
1 Tim. 5. 1–16

Saturday
Ps. 5; 6
Exod. 19
John 21. 20–25

Ps. 7
Deut. 2. 1–25
1 Tim. 5. 17–25

EASTER 2

Monday
Ps. 8; 9
Exod. 20. 1–21
Luke 1. 1–25

Ps. 10
Deut. 2. 26 – 3. 5
1 Tim. 6. 1–10

Tuesday
Ps. 11; 12
Exod. 22. 30 – 23. 17
Luke 1. 26–38

Ps. 13; 14
Deut. 4. 1–13
1 Tim. 6. 11–21

Wednesday
Ps. 15; 16
Exod. 24
Luke 1. 39–56

Ps. 17
Deut. 4. 14–31
2 Tim. 1. 1–14

Thursday
Ps. 18. 1–32
Exod. 25. 1–22
Luke 1. 57–66

Ps. 18. 33–52
Deut. 4. 32–40
2 Tim. 1. 15 – 2. 13

Friday
Ps. 19
Exod. 28. 1–4; 29. 1–9
Luke 1. 67–80

Ps. 20; 21
Deut. 6
2 Tim. 2. 14–26

Saturday
Ps. 22
Exod. 29. 38 – 30. 16
Luke 2. 1–20

Ps. 23; 24
Deut. 8
2 Tim. 3

EASTER 3

Monday
Ps. 25
Exod. 32. 1–14
Luke 2. 21–32

Ps. 26; 27
Deut. 9. 1–21
2 Tim. 4

Tuesday
Ps. 28; 29
Exod. 32. 15–35
Luke 2. 33–40

Ps. 30
Deut. 10. 12–22
Titus 1

Wednesday
Ps. 31
Exod. 33
Luke 2. 41–52

Ps. 32
Deut. 11. 18–32
Titus 2

Thursday
Ps. 33
Exod. 34. 1–10, 27–35
Luke 3. 1–14

Ps. 34
Deut. 12. 1–14
Titus 3

Friday
Ps. 35
Exod. 35. 20 – 36. 7
Luke 3. 15–23

Ps. 36
Deut. 15. 1–18
1 Pet. 1. 1–12

Saturday
Ps. 37. 1–22
Exod. 40. 17–38
Luke 4. 1–13

Ps. 37. 23–41
Deut. 16. 1–20
1 Pet. 1. 13–25

EASTER 4

Monday
Ps. 38
Lev. 6. 8–30
Luke 4. 14–30

Ps. 39
Deut. 17. 8–20
1 Pet. 2. 1–10

Tuesday
Ps. 40
Lev. 19. 1–18, 30–37
Luke 4. 31–44

Ps. 41
Deut. 18. 9–22
1 Pet. 2. 11–25

Wednesday
Ps. 42; 43
Lev. 25. 1–24
Luke 5. 1–11

Ps. 44
Deut. 19
1 Pet. 3. 1–12

Thursday
Ps. 45; 46
Num. 9. 15–23
Luke 5. 12–26

Ps. 47; 48
Deut. 21. 22 – 22. 8
1 Pet. 3. 13–22

Friday
Ps. 49
Num. 12
Luke 5. 27–39

Ps. 50
Deut. 24. 5–22
1 Pet. 4

Saturday
Ps. 51   Ps. 52; 53
Num. 13.1–3, 17–33   Deut. 26
Luke 6. 1–11   1 Pet. 5

EASTER 5

For Rogation Days and Ascension Day see pp. 526 ff.

Friday
Ps. 64; 65   Ps. 66; 67
Num. 14. 1–25   Deut. 28. 58–68
Luke 6. 12–26   2 Pet. 1. 1–15

Saturday
Ps. 68   Ps. 69
Num. 20. 1–13   Deut. 30
Luke 6. 27–38   2 Pet. 1. 16–2. 3

SUNDAY AFTER ASCENSION

Monday
Ps. 70; 71   Ps. 72
Num. 21. 4–9   Deut. 31. 1–13
Luke 6. 39–49   2 Pet. 2. 4–22

Tuesday
Ps. 73   Ps. 74
Num. 22. 2–35   Deut. 31. 14–29
Luke 7. 1–10   2 Pet. 3

Wednesday
Ps. 75; 76   Ps. 77
Num 22. 36 – 23. 12   Deut. 31. 30 – 32. 14
Luke 7. 11–23   1 John 1.1 – 2.6

Thursday
Ps. 78. 1–38   Ps. 78. 39–70
Num. 23. 13–30   Deut. 32. 15–47
Luke 7. 24–35   1 John 2. 7–17

Friday
Ps. 79   Ps. 80
Num. 24   Deut. 33
Luke 7. 36–50   1 John 2. 18–29

Saturday
Morning Prayer only   *Evening Prayer only*
Ps. 81   Ps. 48; 145
Deut. 32.48–52 and 34   Deut. 16. 9–15
Luke 8. 1–15   John 7. 37–39

PENTECOST WHITSUNDAY

Monday
Ps. 82; 83
Ezek. 11. 14–20
1 Cor. 2

Ps. 84; 85
1 Sam. 10. 1–10
Matt. 3. 13–17

Tuesday
Ps. 86
Ezek. 36. 22–28
1 Cor. 3

Ps. 87; 88
1 Kings 19. 1–18
Matt. 9. 35 – 10. 20

Wednesday
Ps. 89. 1–38
Isa. 55. 6–11
1 Cor. 12. 1–13

Ps. 89. 39–53
Micah. 3. 1–8
Matt. 11. 25–30

Thursday
Ps. 90
Isa. 32. 9–20
1 Cor. 12. 27 – 13. 13

Ps. 91
Exod. 35. 30 – 36. 1
Matt. 12. 22–32

Friday
Ps. 92; 93
Num. 11. 16, 17, 24–29
Gal. 5. 13–26

Ps. 94
Jer. 31. 31–34
Matt. 18. 15–20

Saturday
Ps. 95; 96
Num. 27. 15–23
Eph. 6. 10–20

Ps. 97; 98
Isa. 44. 1–5
John 17. 17–26

TRINITY SUNDAY PENTECOST 1

Monday
Ps. 99; 100; 101
Josh. 1. 1–11
Luke 8. 16–25

Ps. 102
2 Chron. 1. 1–13
  or Wisdom 1
1 John 3

Tuesday
Ps. 103
Josh. 2
Luke 8. 26–39

Ps. 104
2 Chron. 2. 1–16
  or Wisdom 2
1 John 4

Wednesday
Ps. 105. 1–22
Josh. 3
Luke 8. 40–56

Ps. 105. 23–45
2 Chron. 5
  or Wisdom 3. 1–9
1 John 5. 1–12

Thursday
Ps. 106. 1–24
Josh. 4.1 – 5.1
Luke 9.1–9

Ps. 106. 25–50
2 Chron. 6. 1–21
  or Wisdom 4. 7–20
1 John 5. 13–21

Friday
Ps. 107. 1–22
Josh. 5. 13 – 6. 20
Luke 9. 10–17

Ps. 107. 23–43
2 Chron. 6. 22–42
  or Wisdom 5. 1–16
James 1. 1–11

Saturday
Ps. 108; (109); 110
Josh. 7. 1–15
Luke 9. 18–27

Ps. 111; 112; 113
2 Chron. 7
  or Wisdom 6. 1–21
James 1. 12–27

PENTECOST 2   TRINITY 1

Monday
Ps. 114; 115
Josh. 7. 16–26
Luke 9. 28–36

Ps. 116; 117
2 Chron. 12
  or Wisdom 7. 15 – 8. 4
James 2. 1–13

Tuesday
Ps. 118
Josh. 8. 10–29
Luke 9. 37–50

Ps. 119. 1–24
2 Chron. 13.1 – 14.1
  or Wisdom 8. 5–18
James 2. 14–26

Wednesday
Ps. 119. 25–40
Josh. 9. 3–27
Luke 9. 51–62

Ps. 119. 41–56
2 Chron. 14. 2–15
  or Wisdom 8. 21–9. 18
James 3

Thursday
Ps. 119. 57–72
Josh. 24. 1–28
Luke 10. 1–16

Ps. 119. 73–88
2 Chron. 17. 1–12
  or Wisdom 10. 15 – 11. 10
James 4. 1–12

Friday
Ps. 119. 89–104
Judges 2. 6–23
Luke 10. 17–24

Ps. 119. 105–128
2 Chron. 34. 1–18
  or Wisdom 11. 21 – 12. 2
James 4. 13 – 5. 6

Saturday
Ps. 119. 129–152
Judges 4
Luke 10. 25–37

Ps. 119. 153–176
2 Chron. 34. 15–33
  or Wisdom 12. 12–21
James 5. 7–20

PENTECOST 3   TRINITY 2

Monday

Ps. 120; 121	Ps. 122; 123
Judges 5	Jer. 37
Luke 10. 38–42	Rom. 1. 1–7

Tuesday

Ps. 124; 125	Ps. 126; 127
Judges 6. 1, 11–40	Jer. 38. 1–13
Luke 11. 1–13	Rom. 1. 8–17

Wednesday

Ps. 128; 129	Ps. 130; 131
Judges 7	Jer. 38. 14–28
Luke 11. 14–28	Rom. 1. 18–32

Thursday

Ps. 132	Ps. 133; 134
Judges 9. 1–21	Jer. 39
Luke 11. 29–36	Rom. 2. 1–16

Friday

Ps. 135	Ps. 136
Judges 9. 22–57	Jer. 40
Luke 11. 37–44	Rom. 2. 17–27

Saturday

Ps. 137; 138	Ps. 139
Judges 11. 1–6, 29–40	Jer. 41
Luke 11. 45–54	Rom. 3. 1–20

PENTECOST 4   TRINITY 3

Monday

Ps. 140	Ps. 141
Judges 13	Jer. 42
Luke 12. 1–12	Rom 3. 21–31

Tuesday

Ps. 142	Ps. 143
Judges 14	Jer. 43
Luke 12. 13–21	Rom. 4. 1–12

Wednesday

Ps. 144	Ps. 145
Judges 15	Jer. 44. 1–14
Luke 12. 22–31	Rom. 4. 13–25

Thursday

Ps. 146; 147	Ps. 148
Judges 16. 1–22	Jer. 44. 15–30
Luke 12. 32–40	Rom. 5. 1–11

Friday
Ps. 149; 150
Judges 16. 23–31
Luke 12. 41–48

Ps. 1; 2
2 Chron. 36. 11–21
Rom. 5. 12–21

Saturday
Ps. 3; 4
Judges 18. 1–20, 27–31
Luke 12. 49–59

Ps. 5; 6
Ezra 1
Rom. 6. 1–14

PENTECOST 5   TRINITY 4

Monday
Ps. 7
1 Sam. 1. 1–20
Luke 13. 1–9

Ps. 8; 9
Ezra 3
Rom. 6. 15–23

Tuesday
Ps. 10
1 Sam. 1. 21 – 2. 11
Luke 13. 10–21

Ps. 11; 12
Ezra 4. 1–5
Rom. 7. 1–6

Wednesday
Ps. 13; 14
1 Sam. 3. 1–19
Luke 13. 22–35

Ps. 15; 16
Ezra 4. 7–24
Rom. 7. 7–25

Thursday
Ps. 17
1 Sam. 4. 1–18
Luke 14. 1–11

Ps. 18. 1–32
Ezra 5
Rom. 8. 1–11

Friday
Ps. 18. 33–52
1 Sam. 5
Luke 14. 12–24

Ps. 19
Ezra 6
Rom. 8. 12–17

Saturday
Ps. 20; 21
1 Sam. 6. 1–16
Luke 14. 25–35

Ps. 22
Ezra 7
Rom. 8. 18–30

PENTECOST 6   TRINITY 5

Monday
Ps. 23; 24
1 Sam. 8
Luke 15. 1–10

Ps. 25
Ezra 8. 15–36
Rom. 8. 31–39

Tuesday
Ps. 26; 27
1 Sam. 9. 1–14
Luke 16. 1–18

Ps. 28; 29
Ezra 9
Rom. 9. 1–13

Wednesday
Ps. 30
1 Sam. 9. 15 – 10. 1
Luke 16. 19–31

Ps. 31
Ezra 10. 1–19
Rom. 9. 14–29

Thursday
Ps. 32
1 Sam. 10. 1–16
Luke 17. 1–10

Ps. 33
Neh. 1
Rom. 9. 30 – 10. 10

Friday
Ps. 34
1 Sam. 10. 17–27
Luke 17. 11–19

Ps. 35
Neh. 2
Rom. 10. 11–21

Saturday
Ps. 36
1 Sam. 11
Luke 17. 20–37

Ps. 37. 1–22
Neh. 4
Rom. 11. 1–12

PENTECOST 7   TRINITY 6

Monday
Ps. 37. 23–41
1 Sam. 12
Luke 18. 1–14

Ps. 38
Neh. 5
Rom. 11. 13–24

Tuesday
Ps. 39
1 Sam. 13
Luke 18. 15–30

Ps. 40
Neh. 6. 1–16
Rom. 11. 25–36

Wednesday
Ps. 41
1 Sam. 14. 1–15
Luke 18. 31–43

Ps. 42; 43
Neh. 8. 1–12
Rom. 12. 1–8

Thursday
Ps. 44
1 Sam. 14. 24–46
Luke 19. 1–10

Ps. 45; 46
Neh. 8. 13–18
Rom. 12. 9–21

Friday
Ps. 47; 48
1 Sam. 15. 1–23
Luke 19. 11–27

Ps. 49
Neh. 9. 1–23
Rom. 13

Saturday
Ps. 50
1 Sam. 16
Luke 19. 28–40

Ps. 51
Neh. 9. 24–38
Rom. 14. 1–12

PENTECOST 8   TRINITY 7

Monday
Ps. 52; 53
1 Sam. 17. 1–25
Luke 19. 41 – 20. 8

Ps. 54; 55
Neh. 13. 1–14
Rom. 14. 13–23

Tuesday
Ps. 56; 57
1 Sam. 17. 26–50
Luke 20. 9–26

Ps. (58); 59
Neh. 13. 15–31
Rom. 15. 1–13

Wednesday
Ps. 60; 61
1 Sam. 17. 55 – 18. 16
Luke 20. 27–40

Ps. 62; 63
Haggai 1. 1 – 2.9
Rom. 15. 14–21

Thursday
Ps. 64; 65
1 Sam. 19. 1–18
Luke 20. 41 – 21. 4

Ps. 66; 67
Haggai 2. 10–23
Rom. 15. 22–33

Friday
Ps. 68
1 Sam. 20. 1–17
Luke 21. 5–19

Ps. 69
Zech. 1. 1–17
Rom. 16. 1–16

Saturday
Ps. 70; 71
1 Sam. 20. 18–42
Luke 21. 20–38

Ps. 72
Zech. 1. 18 – 2. 13
Rom. 16. 17–27

PENTECOST 9   TRINITY 8

Monday
Ps. 73
1 Sam. 21. 1 – 22. 5
Luke 22. 1–13

Ps. 74
Zech. 3 and 4
Eph. 1. 1–14

Tuesday
Ps. 75; 76
1 Sam 22. 6–23
Luke 22. 14–23

Ps. 77
Zech. 6. 9–15
Eph. 1. 15–23

Wednesday
Ps. 78. 1–38
1 Sam. 23
Luke 22. 24–34

Ps. 78. 39–70
Zech. 7
Eph. 2. 1–10

Thursday
Ps. 79
1 Sam. 26
Luke 22. 35–46

Ps. 80
Zech. 8. 1–8
Eph. 2. 11–22

Friday
Ps. 81
1 Sam. 28. 3–25
Luke 22. 47–62

Ps.82; 83
Zech. 8. 9–23
Eph. 3. 1–13

Saturday
Ps. 84; 85
1 Sam. 31
Luke 22. 63 – 23. 5

Ps. 86
Job.1
Eph. 3. 14–21

PENTECOST 10   TRINITY 9

Monday
Ps. 87; 88
2 Sam. 1
Luke 23. 6–25

Ps. 89. 1–38
Job 2
Eph. 4. 1–16

Tuesday
Ps. 89. 39–53
2 Sam. 2
Luke 23. 26–43

Ps. 90
Job 3
Eph. 4. 17–32

Wednesday
Ps. 91
2 Sam. 5. 1–10, 17–25
Luke 23. 44–56a

Ps. 92; 93
Job 4
Eph. 5. 1–14

Thursday
Ps. 94
2 Sam. 6. 1–19
Luke 23. 56b–24. 12

Ps. 95; 96
Job 5
Eph. 5. 15–33

Friday
Ps. 97; 98
2 Sam 7. 1–17
Luke 24. 13–35

Ps. 99; 100; 101
Job 6
Eph. 6. 1–9

Saturday
Ps. 102
2 Sam. 7. 18–29
Luke 24. 36–53

Ps. 103
Job 7
Eph. 6. 10–24

PENTECOST 11   TRINITY 10

Monday
Ps. 104
2 Sam. 9
Acts 1. 1–14

Ps. 105. 1–22
Job 8
Mark 1. 1–13

Tuesday
Ps. 105. 23–45
2 Sam. 11
Acts 1. 15–26

Ps. 106. 1–24
Job 9
Mark 1. 14–28

Wednesday
Ps. 106. 25–50
2 Sam. 12. 1–25
Acts 2. 1–13

Ps. 107. 1–22
Job 10
Mark 1. 29–45

Thursday
Ps. 107. 23–43
2 Sam. 15. 1–12
Acts 2. 14–36

Ps. 108; (109)
Job 11
Mark 2. 1–12

Friday
Ps. 110; 111
2 Sam. 15. 13–37
Acts 2. 37–47

Ps. 112; 113
Job 12
Mark 2. 13–22

Saturday
Ps. 114
2 Sam. 16. 1–14
Acts 3. 1–10

Ps. 115
Job 13
Mark 2. 23 – 3. 6

PENTECOST 12   TRINITY 11

Monday
Ps. 116; 117
2 Sam. 17. 1–23
Acts 3. 11 – 4.4

Ps. 118
Job 14
Mark 3. 7–19a

Tuesday
Ps. 119. 1–24
2 Sam. 18. 1–18
Acts 4. 5–22

Ps. 119. 25–40
Job 15. 1–16
Mark 3. 19b–35

Wednesday
Ps. 119. 41–56
2 Sam. 18. 19 – 19. 8a
Acts 4. 23–31

Ps. 119. 57–72
Job 16. 1 – 17 .2
Mark 4. 1–20

Thursday
Ps. 119. 73–88
2 Sam. 19. 8b–23
Acts 4. 32 – 5. 11

Ps. 119. 89–104
Job 17. 3–16
Mark 4. 21–34

Friday
Ps. 119. 105–128
2 Sam. 19. 24–43
Acts 5. 12–26

Ps. 119. 129–152
Job 18
Mark 4. 35–41

Saturday
Ps. 119. 153–176
2 Sam. 23. 1–7
Acts 5. 27–42

Ps. 120; 121
Job 19
Mark 5. 1–20

PENTECOST 13   TRINITY 12

Monday

Ps. 122; 123	Ps. 124; 125
2 Sam. 23. 8–39	Job 21
Acts 6	Mark 5. 21–34

Tuesday

Ps. 126; 127	Ps. 128; 129
2 Sam. 24	Job 22
Acts 7. 1–16	Mark 5. 35–43

Wednesday

Ps. 130; 131	Ps. 132
1 Kings 1. 1–31	Job 23
Acts 7. 17–36	Mark 6. 1–13

Thursday

Ps. 133; 134	Ps. 135
1 Kings 1. 32–53	Job 24
Acts 7. 37–53	Mark 6. 14–29

Friday

Ps. 136	Ps. 137: 138
1 Kings 2. 1–12	Job 25 and 26
Acts 7. 54 – 8. 3	Mark 6. 30–44

Saturday

Ps. 139	Ps. 140; 141
1 Kings 3	Job 27
Acts 8. 4–25	Mark 6. 45–56

PENTECOST 14   TRINITY 13

Monday

Ps. 142; 143	Ps. 144
1 Kings 4. 29 – 5. 12	Job 28
Acts 8. 26–40	Mark 7. 1–13

Tuesday

Ps. 145	Ps. 146; 147
1 Kings 6. 1–22	Job 29. 1 – 30. 1
Acts 9. 1–19a	Mark 7. 14–23

Wednesday

Ps. 148	Ps. 149; 150
1 Kings 8. 1–30	Job 31. 13–40
Acts 9. 19b–31	Mark 7. 24–37

Thursday

Ps. 1; 2; 3	Ps. 4; 5; 6
1 Kings 10. 1–25	Job 32
Acts 9. 32–43	Mark 8. 1–10

Friday
Ps. 7
1 Kings 11. 1–13
Acts 10. 1–16

Ps. 8; 9
Job 33
Mark 8. 11–21

Saturday
Ps. 10
1 Kings 11. 26–43
Acts 10. 17–33

Ps. 11; 12
Job 38. 1–21
Mark 8. 22–26

PENTECOST 15   TRINITY 14

Monday
Ps. 13; 14
1 Kings 12. 1–24
Acts 10. 34–48

Ps. 15; 16
Job 38. 22–41
Mark 8. 27 – 9. 1

Tuesday
Ps. 17
1 Kings 12. 25–33
Acts 11. 1–18

Ps. 18. 1–32
Job 39
Mark 9. 2–13

Wednesday
Ps. 18. 33–52
1 Kings 13. 1–10
Acts 11. 19–30

Ps. 19
Job 40
Mark 9. 14–29

Thursday
Ps. 20; 21
1 Kings 13. 11–34
Acts 12. 1–11

Ps. 22
Job 41
Mark 9. 30–37

Friday
Ps. 23; 24
1 Kings 17
Acts 12. 12–25

Ps. 25
Job 42
Mark 9. 38–50

Saturday
Ps. 26; 27
1 Kings 18. 1–20
Acts 13. 1–12

Ps. 28; 29
Amos 1
Mark 10. 1–16

PENTECOST 16   TRINITY 15

Monday
Ps. 30
1 Kings 18. 21–46
Acts 13. 13–41

Ps. 31
Amos 2
Mark 10. 17–31

Tuesday
Ps. 32
1 Kings 19
Acts 13. 42 – 14. 7

Ps. 33
Amos 3
Mark 10. 32–34

Wednesday

Ps. 34   Ps. 35
1 Kings 20. 1–22   Amos 4
Acts 14. 8–28   Mark 10. 35–45

Thursday

Ps. 36   Ps. 37. 1–22
1 Kings 20. 23–43   Amos 5. 1–17
Acts 15. 1–21   Mark 10. 46–52

Friday

Ps. 37. 23–41   Ps. 38
1 Kings 21   Amos 5. 18–27
Acts 15. 22–35   Mark 11. 1–11

Saturday

Ps. 39   Ps. 40
1 Kings 22. 1–28   Amos 6
Acts 15. 36 – 16. 5   Mark 11. 12–26

PENTECOST 17   TRINITY 16

Monday

Ps. 41   Ps. 42; 43
1 Kings 22. 29–40   Amos 7
Acts 16. 6–24   Mark 11. 27–33

Tuesday

Ps. 44   Ps. 45; 46
2 Kings 2. 1–15   Amos 8
Acts 16. 25–40   Mark 12. 1–12

Wednesday

Ps. 47; 48   Ps. 49
2 Kings 3. 4–24   Amos 9
Acts 17. 1–15   Mark 12. 13–27

Thursday

Ps. 50   Ps. 51
2 Kings 4. 1–37   Micah 1
Acts 17. 16–34   Mark 12. 28–34

Friday

Ps. 52; 53   Ps. 54; 55
2 Kings 5   Micah 2
Acts 18. 1–21   Mark 12. 35–44

Saturday

Ps. 56; 57   Ps. (58); 59
2 Kings 6. 8–23   Micah 3
Acts 18. 22 – 19. 7   Mark 13. 1–13

PENTECOST 18   TRINITY 17

The Last Week after Pentecost takes precedence.

Monday
Ps. 60; 61
2 Kings 6. 24 – 7. 2
Acts 19. 8–20

Ps. 62; 63
Micah 4. 1 – 5. 1
Mark 13. 14–27

Tuesday
Ps. 64; 65
2 Kings 7. 3–20
Acts 19. 21–41

Ps. 66; 67
Micah 5. 2–15
Mark 13. 28–37

Wednesday
Ps. 68
2 Kings 9. 1–13
Acts 20. 1–16

Ps. 69
Micah 6
Mark 14. 1–11

Thursday
Ps. 70; 71
2 Kings 9. 14–37
Acts 20. 17–38

Ps. 72
Micah 7. 1–7
Mark 14. 12–25

Friday
Ps. 73
2 Kings 10. 18–28
Acts 21. 1–16

Ps. 74
Micah 7. 8–20
Mark 14. 26–42

Saturday
Ps. 75; 76
2 Kings 11. 21 – 12. 21
Acts 21. 17–36

Ps. 77
Nahum 1
Mark 14. 43–52

PENTECOST 19   TRINITY 18

The Last Week after Pentecost takes precedence.

Monday
Ps. 78. 1–38
2 Kings 17. 1–23
Acts 21. 37 – 22. 21

Ps. 78. 39–70
Nahum 2
Mark 14. 53–65

Tuesday
Ps. 79
2 Kings 17. 24–41
Acts 22. 22 – 23. 11

Ps. 80
Nahum 3
Mark 14. 66–72

Wednesday
Ps. 81
2 Kings 18. 1–12
Acts 23. 12–35

Ps. 82; 83
Hab. 1
Mark 15. 1–15

Thursday

Ps. 84; 85   Ps. 86
2 Kings 18. 13–37   Hab. 2
Acts 24. 1–23   Mark 15. 16–32

Friday

Ps. 87; 88   Ps. 89. 1–38
2 Kings 19. 1–19   Hab. 3. 2–19
Acts 24. 24 – 25. 12   Mark 15. 33–47

Saturday

Ps. 89. 39–53   Ps. 90
2 Kings 19. 20–37   Zeph. 1
Acts 25. 13–27   Mark 16

PENTECOST 20   TRINITY 19

The Last Week after Pentecost takes precedence.

Monday

Ps. 91   Ps. 92; 93
2 Kings 20   Zeph. 2
Acts 26. 1–23   Luke 10. 25–37

Tuesday

Ps. 94   Ps. 95; 96
2 Kings 22   Zeph. 3
Acts 26. 24–32   Luke 12. 13–21

Wednesday

Ps. 97   Ps. 98
2 Kings 23. 1–20   Mal. 1
Acts 27. 1–26   Luke 14. 16–24

Thursday

Ps. 99.; 100; 101   Ps. 102
2 Kings 23. 21 – 24. 7   Mal. 2. 1–16
Acts 27. 27–44   Luke 15. 11–32

Friday

Ps. 103   Ps. 104
2 Kings 24. 8 – 25. 12   Mal. 2. 17–3. 12
Acts 28. 1–16   Luke 16. 19–31

Saturday

Ps. 105. 1–22   Ps. 105. 23–45
2 Kings 25. 22–30   Mal. 3. 13 – 4. 6
Acts 28. 17–31   Luke 18. 9–14

PENTECOST 21   TRINITY 20

The Last Week after Pentecost takes precedence.

Monday
Ps. 106. 1–24	Ps. 106. 25–50
Song of Solomon 1. 9 – 2. 7	Exod. 30. 1–10
1 Tim. 1. 1–17	Luke 1. 5–23

Tuesday
Ps. 107. 1–22	Ps. 107. 23–43
Song of Sol. 2. 8–17	Lev. 11. 1–8, 44–47
1 Tim. 1. 18 – 2. 15	Acts 10. 9–16

Wednesday
Ps. 108; (109)	Ps. 110; 111
Song of Sol. 3	Lev. 12. 6, 7a, 8
1 Tim. 3	Luke 2. 21–32

Thursday
Ps. 112; 113	Ps. 114
Song of Sol. 5. 2 – 6. 3	Lev. 13. 1–3, 45, 46
1 Tim. 4	Luke 5. 12–14

Friday
Ps. 115	Ps. 116; 117
Song of Sol. 7. 10 – 8. 4	Lev. 14. 1–9
1 Tim. 5	Luke 17. 11–19

Saturday
Ps. 118	Ps. 119. 1–24
Song of Sol. 8. 5–7	Num 6. 1–5, 21–27
1 Tim. 6	Acts 21. 17–30

PENTECOST 22   TRINITY 21

The Last Week after Pentecost takes precedence.

Monday
Ps. 119. 25–40	Ps. 119. 41–56
Num. 9. 1–14	Exod. 16. 9–15
or Baruch 1. 15–2. 10	or Wisdom 1
2 Tim. 1. 1–14	John 6. 25–35

Tuesday
Ps. 119. 57–72	Ps. 119. 73–88
Num. 16. 1–19	Isa. 60. 13–20
or Baruch 2. 11–35	or Wisdom 2
2 Tim. 1. 15 – 2. 13	John 8. 12–19

Wednesday
Ps. 119. 89–104	Ps. 119. 105–128
Num. 16. 20–35	Ezek. 34. 1–16
or Baruch 3. 1–8	or Wisdom 5. 1–16
2 Tim. 2. 14 – 26	John 10. 7–16

Thursday

Ps. 119. 129–152	Ps. 119. 153–176
Num. 16. 36–50	Dan. 12. 1–4
or Baruch 3. 9–37	or Wisdom 6. 1–21
2 Tim. 3	John 11. 17–27

Friday

Ps. 120; 121	Ps. 122;123
Num. 17. 1–11	Prov. 8. 1–21
or Baruch 4. 21–30	or Wisdom 7. 15 – 8. 4
2 Tim. 4. 1–8	John 14. 1–6

Saturday

Ps. 124; 125	Ps. 126; 127
Num. 33. 50 – 34. 15	Isaiah 5. 1–7
or Baruch 4. 36–5. 9	or Wisdom 8. 21–9. 18
2 Tim. 4. 9–22	John 15. 1–8

LAST WEEK AFTER PENTECOST AND TRINITY

The Last Week after Pentecost takes precedence of Pentecost 18–21.

Old Testament readings are not interchangeable.

Monday

Ps. 128; 129	Ps. 130; 131
Eccles. 1	Eccles. 2. 1–23
Phil. 1. 1–11	Luke 17. 20–37

Tuesday

Ps. 132	Ps. 133; 134
Eccles. 3. 1–15	Eccles. 3. 16 – 4. 16
Phil. 1. 12–30	Luke 18. 1–17

Wednesday

Ps. 135	Ps. 136
Eccles. 5	Eccles. 6
Phil. 2. 1–18	Luke 18. 18–30

Thursday

Ps. 137; 138	Ps. 139
Eccles. 7	Eccles. 8
Phil. 2. 19–30	Luke 18. 35–43

Friday

Ps. 140; 141	Ps. 142; 143
Eccles. 9	Eccles. 11. 1–8
Phil. 3. 1 – 4. 1	Luke 19. 1–10

Saturday

Ps. 144	Ps. 145
Eccles. 11.9 – 12.14	Obadiah
Phil 4. 2–23	Luke 19. 11–27

COLLECTS AND READINGS

for Special Occasions

1 Collects and Readings are provided for the Holy Communion on special occasions, subject to the advice and pastoral guidance of the Ordinary.

2 Psalms and Readings from this section may be used at Morning or Evening Prayer.

3 Collects from this section may be used as occasional prayers at the discretion of the minister.

1 Ember Days

2 Thanksgiving for Harvest

3 The Dedication Festival of a Church

4 Community and World Peace

5 The Unity of the Church

6 The Guidance of the Holy Spirit

7 The Spread of the Gospel

8 The Appointment of a Bishop or an Incumbent

9 A Particular Commemoration

10 Mothering Sunday

11 Remembrance Day

1 EMBER DAYS (or at other times)
THE MINISTRY OF THE CHURCH

For those to be ordained

Almighty God,
the giver of all good gifts,
by your Holy Spirit you have appointed
various orders of ministers in the Church:
Look with mercy and favour on your servants
now called to be bishops/priests/deacons
(especially . . . .)
Maintain them in truth and renew them in holiness,
that by word and good example
they may faithfully serve you
to the glory of your name
and the benefit of your Church;
through the merits of our Saviour Jesus Christ.   **Amen.**

For vocations

Almighty God,
you have entrusted to your Church
a share in the ministry of your Son
our great High Priest:
Inspire by your Holy Spirit
the hearts and minds of many
to offer themselves for the sacred ministry,
that strengthened by his power,
they may work for the increase of your kingdom
and set forward the eternal praise of your Holy Name;
through Jesus Christ our Lord   **Amen.**

For the ministry of all Christian people

Almighty and everlasting God,
by whose Spirit the whole body of the Church
is governed and sanctified:
Hear our prayers which we offer
for all members of your Church,
that in their vocation and ministry
they may serve you in holiness and truth
to the glory of your Name;
through our Lord and Saviour Jesus Christ.   **Amen.**

Psalms and readings may be chosen from:

PSALM   *122 or 84. 8–12*

OLD TESTAMENT   *Jeremiah 1. 4–10 or Numbers 11. 16–17. 24–29 or Numbers 27. 15–23*

EPISTLE   *1 Peter 4. 7–11 or Acts 20. 28–35 or 1 Corinthians 3. 3–11*

GOSPEL   *Luke 12. 35–43 or Luke 4. 16–21 or John 4. 31–38*

2 THANKSGIVING FOR HARVEST

Almighty and everlasting God,
you have given us the fruits of the earth in their season:
Teach us to remember
that we do not live by bread alone,
and grant us to feed on him
who is the true bread from heaven,
Jesus Christ our Lord,
to whom, with you and the Holy Spirit,
be all honour and glory for evermore. **Amen.**

Heavenly Father,
you visit the earth and bless it,
you crown the year with your goodness:
We bless you for the fruits of the earth
which you have given for our use,
and we pray you
to sow the seed of your word in our hearts,
that it may bear fruit in our lives,
until we are gathered into your heavenly kingdom;
through Jesus Christ our Lord. **Amen.**

Psalms and readings may be chosen from:

PSALM   *65; 67; 104. 21–30; 145; 147; 148; 150*

OLD TESTAMENT   *Genesis 1. 1–3, 24–31a; Deuteronomy 8. 1–10; Deuteronomy 26. 1–11; Deuteronomy 28. 1–14*

EPISTLE   *Acts 10. 10–16; Acts 14. 13–17; 2 Corinthians 9. 6–15; 1 Timothy 6. 6–10; Revelation 14. 14–18*

GOSPEL   *Matthew 6. 24–34; Matthew 13. 18–30; Luke 12. 16–31; John 4. 31–38; John 6. 27–35*

3 THE DEDICATION FESTIVAL OF A CHURCH

Almighty God,
to whose glory we celebrate
the dedication of this house of prayer:
We praise you for the many blessings
you have given to those who worship here,
and we pray that all who seek you in this place
may find you,
and, being filled with the Holy Spirit,
may become a living temple acceptable to you
through Jesus Christ our Lord.   **Amen.**

Psalms and readings may be chosen from:

PSALM   *84. 1–7; 122 (MP/EP: 24; 48; 103; 132)*

OLD TESTAMENT   *1 Kings 8. 22–30; (MP/EP: Genesis 28. 10–22; 1
Chronicles 29. 6–19)*

EPISTLE   *1 Peter 2. 1–10; (MP/EP: 1 Corinthians 3. 9–17; Revelation 21.
9–14, 22–27)*

GOSPEL   *Matthew 21. 12–16; (MP/EP: John 2. 13–22; Luke 19. 1–10)*

4 COMMUNITY AND WORLD PEACE

Almighty God,
from whom all thoughts of truth and peace proceed:
Kindle, we pray, in the hearts of all men
the true love of peace;
and guide with your pure and peaceable wisdom
those who take counsel for the nations of the earth;
that in tranquillity your kingdom may go forward,
till the earth is filled with the knowledge of your love;
through Jesus Christ our Lord.   **Amen.**

or

Almighty God,
whose will is to restore all things
in your beloved Son, the king of all:
Govern the hearts and minds of those in authority
and bring the families of the nations,
divided and rent asunder by the ravages of sin,
to be subject to his just and gentle rule;
who lives and reigns with you and the Holy Spirit,
one God, now and for ever.   **Amen.**

PSALM   72. 1–7 or 85. 8–13
OLD TESTAMENT   Micah 4. 1–5
EPISTLE   1 Timothy 2. 1–6
GOSPEL   Matthew 5. 43–48

5 THE UNITY OF THE CHURCH

Heavenly Father,
your Son our Lord Jesus Christ said to his apostles,
Peace I leave with you, my peace I give to you:
Regard not our sins but the faith of your Church,
and grant it that peace and unity
which is agreeable to your will;
through Jesus Christ our Lord.   **Amen.**

or

Almighty Father,
whose blessed Son before his passion
prayed for his disciples that they might be one,
as you and he are one:
Grant that your Church,
being bound together in love and obedience to you,
may be united in one body by the one Spirit,
that the world may believe in him whom you have sent,
your Son Jesus Christ our Lord;
who lives and reigns
with you, in the unity of the Holy Spirit,
one God, now and for ever.   **Amen.**

or

Heavenly Father,
you have called us in the body of your Son Jesus Christ
to continue his work of reconciliation
and to reveal you to mankind:
Forgive us the sins which tear us apart;
give us the courage to overcome our fears
and to seek that unity
in truth, holiness and love
which is your gift and your will;
through Jesus Christ our Lord.   **Amen.**

PSALM *133 or 122*

OLD TESTAMENT *Jeremiah 33. 6–9*

EPISTLE *Ephesians 4. 1–6*

GOSPEL *John 17. 11b–23*

6 THE GUIDANCE OF THE HOLY SPIRIT

Suitable at the opening of meetings of Synod or Vestry

Almighty God,
at all times you teach the hearts of your faithful people
by sending them the light of your Holy Spirit:
Guide us by the same Spirit
to have a right judgment in all things
and evermore to rejoice in his holy comfort;
through Jesus Christ our Saviour,
who lives and reigns with you and the Holy Spirit,
one God, now and for ever. **Amen.**

Psalms and readings may be chosen from:

PSALM *25. 1–10; 143. 8–10*

OLD TESTAMENT *Isaiah 30. 15–21; Wisdom 9. 13–17*

EPISTLE *1 Corinthians 12. 4–13; Philippians 2. 1–11*

GOSPEL *John 14. 23–26; John 16. 13–15*

7 THE SPREAD OF THE GOSPEL

Almighty God,
who called your Church to witness
that you were in Christ reconciling men to yourself:
Help us so to proclaim the good news of your love,
that all who hear it may be reconciled to you;
through him who died for us and rose again
and reigns with you and the Holy Spirit,
one God, now and for ever. **Amen.**

PSALM *97 or 100*

OLD TESTAMENT *Isaiah 49. 1–6*

EPISTLE *Ephesians 2. 13–22*

GOSPEL *Matthew 28. 16–20*

8 THE APPOINTMENT OF A BISHOP OR AN INCUMBENT

Almighty God,
the giver of all good gifts:
Guide with your heavenly wisdom
those who are to choose a pastor for this diocese/parish
(*or* for the diocese/parish of …)
that we/they may receive one who will speak your word,
and serve your people according to your will;
through Jesus Christ our Lord.   **Amen.**

Psalms and readings may be chosen from:

PSALM   *15; 25. 1–6*

OLD TESTAMENT   *Numbers 11. 16–17, 24–29; 1 Samuel 16. 1–13a*

EPISTLE   *Acts 1. 15–17, 20–26; Ephesians 4. 7–16*

GOSPEL   *John 4. 34–38; John 15. 9–17*

9 A PARTICULAR COMMEMORATION

Almighty God,
you have built up your Church
through the love and devotion of your saints in all ages:
We give thanks for your servant …
whom we commemorate today:
inspire us to follow his/her example
that we in our generation may rejoice with him/her
in the vision of your glory;
through Jesus Christ our Lord.   **Amen.**

Readings may be selected as appropriate from the provisions for
ALL SAINTS (page 696) or from the following:

PSALM   *32; 34. 1–10; 34. 11–18; 112; 119. 1–8*

OLD TESTAMENT   *Proverbs 8. 1–11; 31. 10–31; Malachi 2. 5–7; Ecclesiasticus 2. 1–6*

EPISTLE   *2 Corinthians 4. 11–18; Hebrews 13. 1–3; Ephesians 4. 22–32; 6. 11–18*

GOSPEL   *Matthew 19.16–21; 25.31–46; Mark 10.42–45; Luke 10.38–42*

10 MOTHERING SUNDAY

Psalms and readings may be chosen from:

PSALM   *27. 1–6; 34; 84; 87; 122; 139. 1–18*

OLD TESTAMENT   *1 Samuel 1. 20–28; Proverbs 4. 1–9; Proverbs 31. 10–31; Micah 4. 1–5*

EPISTLE   *Colossians 3. 12–17; 2 Timothy 1. 3–10; 1 Peter 2. 1–10*

GOSPEL   *Mark 10. 13–16; Luke 2. 41–52; John 19. 23–27*

or the provisions for Pentecost 14.

11 REMEMBRANCE DAY

Psalms and readings may be chosen from:

PSALM   *46; 47; 93; 126; 130*

OLD TESTAMENT   *Isaiah 2. 1–5; Isaiah 10. 33 – 11. 9; Ezekiel 37. 1–14*

EPISTLE   *Romans 8. 31–39; Revelation 21. 1–7*

GOSPEL   *Matthew 5. 1–12; John 15. 9–17*

AN ORDER
FOR THE BAPTISM
OF CHILDREN

AN ORDER FOR THE BAPTISM OF CHILDREN

1 The Minister of every Parish shall teach the people the meaning of Baptism and the responsibilities of those who bring children to be baptized.

2 When there are children to be baptized, the parents shall give due notice to the Minister of the Parish, who shall thereupon appoint the time for the Baptism.

3 Sponsors and godparents must be baptized Christians and persons of discreet age, and at least two shall be members of the Church of Ireland or of a Church in communion therewith (Canon 25.4). It is desirable that parents be sponsors for their own children.

4 It is desirable that members of the parish be present to support, by their faith and prayer, those who are to be baptized and received into the fellowship of the Church.

5 When this order of Baptism is used with one of the prescribed services in any church, the Minister may dispense with such parts of that service as the Ordinary shall permit.

6 The font should be so situated that Baptism may be administered in an orderly fashion.

7 The priest shall be assured that the child has not already been baptized.

THE INTRODUCTION

1   The priest says to the people

Holy Baptism is administered to infants on the understanding that they will be brought up in the fellowship of Christ's Church; that they will be taught the Christian faith; and that, when they have publicly confessed this faith, they will be confirmed by the bishop and admitted to the Holy Communion.

2   The priest says to the parents and godparents
  I ask therefore

Will you bring up *this child* as *a Christian* within the family of the Church?
We will.

Will you help *him* to be regular in public worship and in private prayer, by your teaching, by your example and by your prayers for *him*?
We will.

Will you encourage *him* to come in due course to Confirmation and Holy Communion?
We will.

3   Priest

The Lord be with you;
And also with you.

Let us pray.

Heavenly Father, who at the baptism of Jesus Christ in the river Jordan declared him to be your only-begotten Son; grant that by your Spirit *this infant* may be born again and made your *child* by adoption and grace, through the same Jesus Christ our Lord.   **Amen.**

THE MINISTRY OF THE WORD

4   Two of the following shall be read

Hear the words of the Epistle written by Saint Paul to the Romans, in the sixth chapter, at the third verse:

All of us who have been baptized into Christ Jesus were baptized into his death. We were buried therefore with him by baptism into death, so that as Christ was raised from the dead by the glory of the Father, we too might walk in newness of life. For if we have been united with him in a death like his, we shall certainly be united with him in a resurrection like his. For we know that Christ being raised from the dead will never die again; death no longer has dominion over him. The death he died he died to sin, once for all, but the life he lives he lives to God. So you also must consider yourselves dead to sin and alive to God in Christ Jesus.

5   or this

Hear the words of the Gospel written by Saint Matthew, in the twenty-eighth chapter, at the eighteenth verse:

Jesus came and said to them, 'All authority in heaven and on earth has been given to me. Go therefore and make disciples of all nations, baptizing them in the name of the Father and of the Son and of the Holy Spirit, teaching them to observe all that I have commanded you; and lo, I am with you always, to the close of the age'.

6   or this

Hear the words of the Gospel written by Saint Mark, in the tenth chapter, at the thirteenth verse:

They were bringing children to Jesus, that he might touch them; and the disciples rebuked them. But when Jesus saw it he was indignant, and said to them, 'Let the children come to me, do not hinder them; for to such belongs the kingdom of God. Truly, I say to you, whoever does not receive the kingdom of God like a child shall not enter it.' And he took them in his arms and blessed them, laying his hands upon them.

7   A sermon may follow.

THE MINISTRY OF THE SACRAMENT

THE DECISION

8 The priest says to the parents and godparents

Those who are brought to be baptized must affirm through their sponsors their allegiance to Christ and their rejection of all that is evil. Therefore I ask,

Do you turn to Christ?
I do.

Do you then renounce the Devil and all his works?
I do, by God's help.

Will you obey and serve Christ?
I will, by God's help.

AT THE FONT

9 Water shall now be poured into the font, if this has not already been done.

10 Then being at the font with the sponsors and the children to be baptized the priest shall say

We give you thanks, almighty Father, everlasting God, through your most dearly beloved Son, Jesus Christ our Lord;

Because by his death and resurrection you have broken the power of evil, and by your sending of the Spirit you have made us partakers of eternal life;

We ask you to bless this water, that *he* who is to be baptized in it may be born again in Christ; that being baptized into Christ's death *he* may receive forgiveness of sins, and that knowing the power of Christ's resurrection *he* may walk in newness of life;

And grant that being cleansed by the washing of regeneration and renewed by the Holy Spirit, *he* may so faithfully serve you in this world that finally with all your people *he* may inherit the kingdom of your glory;

Through the same your Son Jesus Christ our Lord, to whom with you and the Holy Spirit be all honour and glory for ever and ever. **Amen.**

THE BAPTISM

11   The priest says to the parents and godparents

You have brought *this child* to be baptized, and now standing in the presence of God and his Church, you must confess the Christian faith in which *he* is to be baptized.

Do you believe in God, the Father almighty,
   creator of heaven and earth?
I believe.

Do you believe in Jesus Christ, his only Son, our Lord,
   and that he was conceived by the power of the Holy Spirit
   and born of the Virgin Mary;
   that he suffered under Pontius Pilate,
   was crucified, died and was buried;
   that he descended to the dead,
   and on the third day rose again;
   that he ascended into heaven,
   and is seated at the right hand of the Father;
   and that he will come again
   to judge the living and the dead?
I believe.

Do you believe in the Holy Spirit,
   the holy catholic Church,
   the communion of saints,
   the forgiveness of sins,
   the resurrection of the body,
   and the life everlasting?
I believe.

12   The priest takes the child in his arms or by the hand and says to the parents and godparents

Name this child.

13   Then the priest shall pour water on the child saying

N. I baptize you in the Name of the Father and of the Son and of the Holy Spirit.   Amen.

THE PRAYERS

14 The priest makes the sign of the cross on the forehead of the child, saying

Now that you have entered upon the Christian life, I sign you with the sign of the cross, to show that you must not be ashamed to confess the faith of Christ crucified and manfully to fight under his banner against sin, the world and the devil; and so continue Christ's faithful soldier and servant to your life's end.

15 All say

God has adopted you by baptism into his Church.
We therefore receive you into the household of faith,
As _a member_ of the body of Christ,
As _the child_ of the same heavenly Father,
And as _an inheritor_ with us of the kingdom of God.

Our Father in heaven,
   hallowed be your name,
   your kingdom come,
   your will be done,
      on earth as in heaven.
Give us today our daily bread.
Forgive us our sins
   as we forgive those who sin against us.
Lead us not into temptation
   but deliver us from evil.

For the kingdom, the power, and the glory are yours
   now and for ever.   Amen.

_or_

Our Father, who art in heaven,
   hallowed be thy name,
   thy kingdom come,
   thy will be done,
      on earth as it is in heaven.
Give us this day our daily bread.
And forgive us our trespasses,
   as we forgive those who trespass against us.
And lead us not into temptation,
   but deliver us from evil.

**For thine is the kingdom,
the power and the glory,
for ever and ever. Amen.**

16 The following prayers are said

Father, we thank you that *this child* has now been born again of water and the Holy Spirit, and has become your own *child* by adoption, and *a member* of your Church.

Grant that *he* may grow in the faith in which *he* has been baptized;

Grant that *he himself* may profess it when *he* comes to be confirmed;

Grant that *he* may bear witness to it by a life of service to *his* fellow men;

And that all things belonging to the Spirit may live and grow in *him;* through Jesus Christ our Lord. **Amen.**

Almighty God, bless the home of *this child*, and give such grace and wisdom to all who have the care of *him*, that by their word and good example they may teach *him* to know and love you; through Jesus Christ our Lord. **Amen.**

17 Priest

May almighty God, the Father of our Lord Jesus Christ, who has given us new life by water and the Holy Spirit, and has forgiven us all our sins, guard us by his grace now and for evermore. **Amen.**

18 The names of those who have been baptized, with the other particulars required, shall be entered in the Parish Register of Baptisms immediately after the service.

19 The parents may make a thankoffering.

INDEX OF COLLECTS

AUTHORIZATION

The Services in the *Alternative Prayer Book 1984*, together with the Calendar, Rules to Order the Service, and Lectionary, are authorized for use in the Church of Ireland from 1 July 1984.

ACKNOWLEDGEMENTS

Texts are reproduced with the permission of the copyright owners, from:

New International Version of the Holy Bible, copyright © 1978 by International Bible Society (extracts from Old and New Testament). Certain verbal changes have been made at the beginning of some readings; and contracted forms of verb and pronoun have been spelt out in full: these changes have been made with the permission of the International Bible Society and the Committee for Bible Translation of the New International Version. The changes made for the purpose of the *Alternative Prayer Book 1984* in no way indicate any intention of the copyright owners to change the actual text of *New International Version*.

The Revised Standard Version of the Bible, *The Common Bible*, © copyright 1973 by the Division of Christian Education of the National Council of the Churches of Christ in the United States of America (extracts from the Apocrypha and some sentences).

The Psalms: a new translation for worship, (*The Liturgical Psalter*) © English text 1976, 1977 David L Frost, John A Emerton, Andrew A Macintosh, all rights reserved. © pointing 1976, 1977 and 1984 William Collins Sons & Co Ltd.

The texts of The Apostles' and the Nicene Creeds, Glory to God, Introductory dialogue to the Thanksgiving Prayer, Lamb of God, Benedictus, Te Deum, Magnificat, Nunc Dimittis, are copyright © 1970, 1971, 1975 International Consultation on English Texts (ICET).

The Lord's Prayer, modern form, is adapted from a version agreed by the International Consultation on English Texts.

Collect of Pentecost 11, the Weekday Intercessions and Thanksgivings, and the canticle, Saviour of the World, are reproduced from *The Daily Office Revised*, by permission of SPCK on behalf of the Joint Liturgical Group of Churches in Great Britain.

Collect of Advent 4 is adapted from no. 556 in Frank Colquhoun, *Parish Prayers* (author unknown) by permission of Hodder & Stoughton Ltd; collects of Epiphany 5 and 7 before Easter are adapted from the Book of Common Prayer: reprinted from *The Daily Office Revised* by permission of SPCK on behalf of the Joint Liturgical Group.

Tables of Psalms and Readings for Morning and Evening Prayer and Holy Communion are © and are reproduced from *The Alternative Service Book 1980* with permission of the Central Board of Finance of the Church of England.

Various prayers and collects from *The Alternative Service Book 1980* are © Central Board of Finance of the Church of England and are reproduced with permission.

The canticle Song of Christ's Glory, and the collect of 8 September are reproduced by permission of the Church of the Province of Southern Africa (Anglican).

The prayers Father, we thank you; Father, we offer; and An Alternative Thanksgiving are reproduced from *An Australian Prayer Book 1978* © The Church of England in Australia Trust Corporation.